The Classic Western American

RAILROAD ROUTES

The Classic Western American

RAILROAD ROUTES

Bruce Clement Cooper
CONSULTANT EDITOR

CHARTWELL
BOOKS, INC.

Detail from "Westward the Star of Empire Takes its Way–Near Council Bluffs, Iowa" by Andrew Melrose, 1867 (E. William Judson Collection).

This edition published in 2010 by
CHARTWELL BOOKS, INC.
A division of BOOK SALES, INC.
276 Fifth Avenue Suite 206
New York, New York 10001
USA

Copyright © 2010 individual authors (see pages 8 and 9)
Concept, design, and layout © 2010 Bookcraft Ltd

Copyright under International, Pan American, and Universal Copyright Conventions. All rights reserved.
No part of this book may be reproduced or transmitted in any form or by any means, electronic or mechanical, including photocopying, recording, or by any information storage-and-retrieval system, without written permission from the copyright holder. Brief passages (not to exceed 1,000 words) may be quoted for reviews.

All images included in this volume are in the public domain, with the exception of those credited in individual captions.
Most of the images come from books, brochures, maps and postcards forming part of Bookcraft Ltd's 'Times Past Archive' (see www.memoriesoftimespast.com);
of the remainder many come from The Cooper Collection of U.S. Railroad History (see www.cprr.org).
Every effort has been made to ensure the accuracy of the information presented in this book, and every reasonable effort has been made to trace copyright holders.
The publisher will not assume liability for damages caused by inaccuracies in the data, or for any copyright inadvertantly breached, and makes no warranty whatsoever expressed or implied.
The publisher welcomes comments and corrections from readers, which will be incorporated in future editions.

The endpaper maps are reproduced from *Library Atlas of the World, Containing Colored Maps of Every Country and Civil Division upon the Face of the Globe*,
published by Rand McNally, Chicago and New York, in 1912

ISBN-10 0-7858-2573-8
ISBN-13 978-0-7858-2573-9

Project manager John Button
Design manager Lucy Guenot

Set in Stone Serif (text), Grant Antique and Orbit Antique (display), and designed by Bookcraft Ltd, Stroud, Gloucestershire, United Kingdom

1 2 3 4 5 12 11 10 09 08

Printed in Malaysia by Imago

"American Progress" by John Gast, *c*.1872. This famous painting is an allegorical representation of the principle of "manifest destiny." The female figure of Columbia, intended as a personification of the United States, leads civilization westward, stringing telegraph wire. She holds a book to signify the importance of education, and is followed by the railways. In the path of "progress" native peoples and animals flee.

CONTENTS

THE OVERLAND ROUTE

THE SOUTHERN PACIFIC "SUNSET ROUTE"

THE NORTHERN PACIFIC ROUTE

THE SANTA FE ROUTE

THE DENVER AND RIO GRANDE ROUTE

Detail from "Through to the Pacific," a Currier and Ives print (right).

Image from *The Railroad Picture Book*, McLaughlin Bros. Inc, New York, 1903 (below).

THE SHASTA ROUTE AND COAST LINE

THE CANADIAN PACIFIC

THE CONTRIBUTORS

Meredith MacArdle, Editorial Director for this project, is an editor and writer who has worked on several books on American history. She has researched extensively into the development of railroads in both the US and Canada.

Bruce Clement Cooper, Consultant Editor for the project, is an author, historian, avid railroad collector, and the great-great-grandson of Lewis M. Clement, the Central Pacific's chief assistant engineer from 1862 to 1881. Among his books is *Riding the Transcontinental Rails: Overland Travel on the Pacific Railroad 1865–1881*, and his family's massive illustrated website on the Central Pacific line (www.cprr.org) is considered to be the most complete resource on American railroad history on the web. In this volume, Bruce Cooper has also written:

Foreword
The Overland Route–Introduction
The Overland Route–Features

Elisabeth Bailey grew up in the train town of Galesburg, Illinois, which was, at that time, the only city in the United States to be serviced by Amtrak and Santa Fe at separate stations. A writer and editor living in the UNESCO world heritage village of Lunenburg, Nova Scotia, she rides the rails at every opportunity. Elisabeth Bailey's contributions to this volume are:

The Canadian Pacific–Introduction
The Canadian Pacific–Features

Nick Kingsley is Industry Editor of *Railway Gazette International*, the market-leading international trade journal for the rail industry. Nick studied at the Institute of Railway Studies at the National Railway Museum in York as part of his degree at the University of York. For this volume, Nick Kingsley has contributed:

Museums and Places to Visit

Maury Klein is a retired history professor who has written fifteen books on American history, including *Unfinished Business: The Railroad in American Life*, *Union Pacific: The Birth, 1862–1893*, and *Union Pacific: The Rebirth 1894–1969*. In this volume, Maury Klein has written:

The Sunset Route–Introduction
The Sunset Route–Features

John Lubetkin is the award-winning author of fiction and non-fiction books including *Jay Cooke's Gamble: The Northern Pacific Railroad, The Sioux, and the Panic of 1873*. He was on the Board of Directors of the Northern Pacific Railway Historic Association for six years. John Lubetkin has written:

The Northern Pacific–Introduction
The Northern Pacific–The Northwest
The Northern Pacific–From the East
The Northern Pacific–Bismarck to the West
The Railroad Act of 1862
The Railroad Act of 1864
Jay Cooke and Frederick Billings Biographies

Image from *The Railway that Glue Built*, Frederick A. Stokes Co., New York, 1908.

WILLIAM D. MIDDLETON served a long career as a US Naval Officer, followed by an assignment as the Chief Facilities Officer for the University of Virginia. He has also written close to a thousand articles on railroads and engineering, and is the author of more than twenty books, including *Encyclopedia of North American Railroads*, for which he was one of the editors and a writer. For this volume, William Middleton has written:

Shasta and Coast Routes–Introduction

Shasta and Coast Routes–Features

PAUL MROCZKA has been a professional writer for more than 25 years, and has created articles, video and film scripts, and books on a vast array of subjects, ranging from sports and gaming to economic and industrial history. The social and economic history of late nineteenth-century USA is his speciality. Paul Mroczka has written:

Main Introduction

What Time is that Train?

Railway Robberies

NANCY SHOCKEY has worked for several Chicago-based railroads as an analyst and in corporate planning. Now a freelance writer, she spends her time riding steam trains, chasing the ghost railroads of Colorado, and searching out just one more piece of dining car china. For this volume, Nancy Shockey has written:

The Northern Pacific–Crossing the Missouri

The Northern Pacific–Stampede Pass

BRIAN SOLOMON is a lecturer and writer on both contemporary and historical railroad subjects. His many books include *North American Railroad Bridges*, *Working on the Railroad*, *Railroad Photography*, and *Railway Masterpieces*. He is also known for his distinctive railroad photography. In this volume, Brian Solomon has written:

Santa Fe Route–Introduction

Santa Fe Route–Features

Denver and Rio Grande Route–Introduction

Denver and Rio Grande Route–Features

Locomotives

Railroad Equipment and Rolling Stock

Dining car on the Union Pacific, *c.*1906.

PUBLIC SCHOOL
THROUGH LINE
NEW YORK

FOREWORD

Bruce Clement Cooper

An 1863 portrait photograph of Lewis M. Clement by the Bradley & Rulofson Gallery, San Francisco.

The necessity that now exists for constructing lines of railroad and telegraphic communication between the Atlantic and Pacific coasts of this continent is no longer a question for argument; it is conceded by every one. In order to maintain our present position on the Pacific, we must have some more speedy and direct means of intercourse than is at present afforded by the route through the possessions of a foreign power.

Report of the Select Committee
on the Pacific Railroad and Telegraph, 1856

The early history of railroads in the United States mirrored that of the young nation itself. As the country's population and economy grew, so too did the many new "ribbons of iron" that began to crisscross its ever expanding landscape. The railroads provided the many new lines of communication necessary to support the transformation of the United States from a one time eighteenth-century confederation of former British colonies nestled along the Atlantic seaboard to a twentieth-century continent-wide industrial giant. However, the American West was so vast that it was daunting, and until the second half of the nineteenth century was still considered by most to be all but unconquerable.

A key figure in overcoming these challenges was Lewis M. Clement who, as the Central Pacific Railroad's Chief Assistant Engineer and Superintendent of Track from 1862 to 1881, had primary charge of locating, designing, and supervising the construction of the road's most difficult grade over California's daunting Sierra Nevada. In 1887 he told the US Pacific Railway Commission of the challenges and great obstacles–both physical and financial–which had to be overcome to build the CPRR:

Not only was it "impossible" to construct a railroad across the Sierras via Donner Pass, but owing to the great depth of snow, some years reaching an aggregate fall of nearly fifty feet, it would be impracticable to operate, and if built must be closed to traffic in the winter months, which would have been the case had not the road been protected at great cost by snowsheds.

Against these utterances from men of railroad experience the company had to battle in financial circles, forcing them to show that they were not attempting an impossibility, though always realizing the great difficulties.

California had no means for manufacturing for railroads. Only fourteen years prior to the beginning of the construction of this railroad was any considerable emigration directed to this coast, either by wagon, requiring as many months as now days from the Missouri River, by sailing vessels via Cape Horn, a long and tedious voyage of months, or by steamship. It was a country new, and only known as a mining region.

The completion of the "Pacific Railroad" (later known as the "Overland Route") in 1869 opened the way for other western routes in the decades that followed including the SP's "Sunset" and "Shasta" lines, the Santa Fe route, the Northern Pacific, the Denver and Rio Grande Western, and the Canadian Pacific, all of which are explored in depth in the following pages.

"The Pacific Railroad is the bond of iron which is to hold our glorious country in one eternal union," Lewis Clement observed when the line opened in 1869.

How right he was.

"Across the Continent," a Currier and Ives print.

INTRODUCTION

The development and evolution of the transcontinental railroad in America can be traced to England, with the invention of the steam engine, the creation of the first steam-driven locomotives, and the advent of the Industrial Revolution. In 1804 in Cornwall, England, Richard Trevithick is credited with creating the first steam-driven train when he used an engine designed by British inventor James Watt to pull multiple cars of iron ore. Eventually, the crude device was placed on a track. At that time in the US, other nations still controlled much of the landmass that would eventually become the 48 contiguous states of the United States of America.

The Louisiana Purchase had been completed just one year prior to Trevithick's steam-driven locomotive. But before Americans could fully exploit this developing mode of transportation, various events would need to transpire that would create a nation that reached from the Atlantic to the Pacific Oceans. Four wars would be fought–the War of 1812 (1812–15), the Texas War of Independence (1835–6), the Mexican War (1846–8), and the Civil War (1861–5). Each conflict helped make the concept of the United States of America a reality.

"The America of Manifest Destiny," a concept popularized by New York journalist John L. Sullivan, and that heard and followed the call of "Go West, young man!" by *New York Tribune* editor and political activist Horace Greeley, possessed a motherlode of potential. The railroad would eventually allow for the exploitation and utilization of that potential. In the process, fortunes were made and lost, livelihoods fostered, communities created, and lives transformed–and sometimes destroyed.

In the mid-nineteenth century, the Conestoga Wagon, Concord Stage, and Pony Express were all instrumental in settling the American frontier. Prior to the completion of America's first transcontinental railroad, traversing the continent often took six months or more. With the East and West coasts being joined by a ribbon of iron rails, that same journey was reduced to as little as a week.

Thirty-one years before Central Pacific Railroad President Leland Stanford drove the "Last Spike" at Promontory Summit, Utah Territory, on May 10, 1869, connecting the eastern and western lines of the nation's first transcontinental rail service, John Plumbe, Jr., who presented a proposal for a national route, was granted $2,000 by the Congress of the United States to survey a possible rail line from Milwaukee to Sinipee, Wisconsin. In 1839, he created a map of what he called a National Railroad, which would stretch all the way to

Views from Nelson's 1869 *Guide to the Union Pacific Railway.*

DEPARTURE FROM OMAHA

CROSSING THE PRAIRIES

ONE THOUSAND MILE TREE WEST FROM OMAHA.

the Pacific Ocean. However, his plan did not garner support and it died.

In 1845, Asa Whitney, a New York dry goods merchant active in the China trade, developed various proposals with the final one entitled "Railroad from Lake Michigan to the Pacific: Memorial of Asa Whitney, of New York City, Relative to the Construction of a Railroad from Michigan to the Pacific Ocean," which US Senator Zadock Pratt (D–NY) presented to his colleagues in the 28th Congress. Whitney's ideas were born of feasibility research that he conducted with a group of experts. Prior to developing his proposal the businessman, using his own funds, traveled along part of the suggested route, evaluating its potential. He created numerous propositions, pamphlets, and detailed maps, and enlisted the support of various politicians and businessmen. But Whitney was unable to assuage many of Congress's questions and doubts.

American westward expansion idealized in Emanuel Leutze's 1861 painting "Westward the Course of Empire Takes its Way." Its title comes from a 1726 poem by Bishop Berkeley, expressing the widely-held belief, known as "manifest destiny," that civilization moved steadily westward across the continent.

The project was seen as being too vast and overwhelming, the topography was thought by many to be at times insurmountable, and the massive amount of funding necessary to see such a route completed was a huge concern. There were also regional disputes regarding whether the track should cross the northern, central, or southern part of the country.

Theodore Dehone Judah (1826–63), who as a young civil engineer had overseen the construction of railroad trestles and bridges in New York and New England, created California's first rail line in 1852, the 22-mile Sacramento Valley Railroad. Once established in California, the incurably optimistic Bridgeport, Connecticut, native became convinced that it was possible to build a railway from the Pacific to join the existing railroad networks in the East. He spent much of the decade trying to convince others of the project's viability, and became so obsessed with the idea that people started calling him "Crazy Judah." The biggest question regarding the rail line concerned the ability to construct tracks across the imposing mountains.

An 1862 portrait of CPRR chief engineer Theodore D. Judah, by the noted San Francisco photographer Carleton E. Watkins (left).

In 1860, Judah used his experience as an engineer and surveyor to determine if the Sierra Nevada Mountains could be surmounted by iron rails and traversed by steam locomotives. Journeying out on his own with notebook in hand, Judah rode on horseback through the mountain range along a string of ridges that led to the summit, charting a route by which the Sierra Nevadas could be crossed. That done, Judah then set out to make his dream a reality.

ECONOMIC INSPIRATION, EXPLOITATION, AND INNOVATION

Judah found four merchants in Sacramento, California who would listen to him—dry goods dealer Charles Crocker, hardware store owners Mark Hopkins and Collis P. Huntington, and grocer Leland Stanford. The "Big Four," as they soon came to be known, were attracted by the commercial potential in building a transcontinental rail line.

The first two presidential candidates of the newly founded Republican Party, of which all four were members, were US Army Topographical Engineer and trans-Mississippi explorer Colonel John C. Frémont in 1856, and former Illinois Central Railroad lawyer Abraham Lincoln in 1860. Both men had made the building of a railroad across the continent west of the Mississippi River a part of their respective political platforms.

A $1000-dollar thirty-year Pacific Railroad Bond issued by the City and County of San Francisco in 1865. These bonds, though "authorized" by referendum in 1863, were highly controversial, and were not issued until two years later.

UNITED STATES OF AMERICA.

Pacific Rail Road Bond.

CITY & COUNTY of SAN FRANCISCO.

No 93.

PAYABLE MAY FIRST A.D. 1895.

The City & County of San Francisco in the State of California will pay to The Western Pacific Rail Road Company or to the holder hereof the sum of ONE THOUSAND DOLL? thirty years from the date hereof with interest thereon at the rate of SEVEN per cent per annum payable semi-annually on the First days of May and November of each year upon interest coupons hereto attached, both principal and interest payable at the City and County of San Francisco, in United States Gold Coin Dollar for Dollar. This Bond is transferable by delivery and binds the City and County of San Francisco to the payment of the principal and interest as herein expressed. This Bond is issued under and in pursuance of an Act of the Legislature of the State of California entitled "An act to authorize the Board of Supervisors of the City and County of San Francisco to take and subscribe One Million Dollars to the Capital Stock of the Western Pacific Rail Road Company and the Central Pacific Rail Road Company of California, and to provide for the payment of the same and other matters relating thereto" Approved April 22nd A.D. 1863, and the vote of the people of the City and County of San Francisco in favor of said subscription at an election held in pursuance of the provisions of said Act. The principal and interest named in this Bond are secured by, and payable out of the Special Funds created therefor by said Act, and known as the "Pacific Rail Road Interest Tax" and the "Pacific Rail Road Loan Fund."

The Laws and Ordinance by virtue whereof this Bond is issued, are indorsed hereon by reciting their titles, and made a part hereof.

In Testimony Whereof, and in accordance with the Act aforesaid and also of the order of said Board of Supervisors, the President of the Board of Supervisors, and the Auditor and Treasurer of the City & County of San Francisco, and ex officio ... have signed their names to this Bond, the County Clerk of the City & County aforesaid has countersigned the same, and the Board of Supervisors have caused the seal of said City & County to be affixed hereto, this First day of May A.D. One thousand eight hundred and sixty five.

STATE OF CALIFORNIA.

As the California gold rush got underway in 1850, the Congress awarded Frémont the first charter to build a railroad from St. Louis to Kansas City and then on to the Pacific. While that project never came to fruition, Frémont made the building of a transcontinental line a priority during his unsuccessful presidential run six years later as the Republican Party's first national candidate.

As a young railroad lawyer, Lincoln had represented a number of companies in various court cases, and in 1857 had spent time at Council Bluffs, Iowa, conducting research for a case in which his client, the Mississippi and Missouri Railroad (M&M), was involved. Dr. Thomas C. Durant, whose Union Pacific Railroad would one day be awarded the right to build the eastern section of the Pacific Railroad, had founded the M&M in 1854.

The future president of the United States spent two hours with local banker, freight forwarder, and civil engineer Grenville M. Dodge, who had surveyed part of the Mississippi and Missouri line, and after the Civil War would become chief engineer of the Union Pacific. Lincoln and Dodge talked about the viability of making Council Bluffs, which is located directly across the Missouri River from Omaha, Nebraska, the eastern terminus for the first railroad that would stretch west across the United States to the Pacific. After becoming president, Lincoln, who had won the Republican nomination on the third ballot when the delegation from Iowa changed its vote to him, selected that Iowa city as the spot where the Pacific Railroad would begin.

No "vision" is born in a vacuum, of course, and that was certainly the case for those who envisioned a rail line uniting East and West. America was naturally poised for that next step as the lands from the Missouri River to the Pacific Coast offered an area of potential robust richness and vast variety. It seemed to simply be waiting for the energies that would be generated by a mass emigration of settlers looking to stake their claims to a new life. A railway that could move people and goods en masse would outmatch previous forms of transport–the stagecoach, a wagon train, or a ship taking the dangerous route around Cape Horn–and would deliver the awe-inspiring and mind-boggling commercial potential of approximately 1.6 million square miles.

Breaking ground for the first transcontinental railroad at Sacramento, January 8, 1863; artist's study for the Southern Pacific Railroad Depot at Sacramento (from The Chris Graves Collection, Newcastle, California).

The Big Four realized that, although the risks were high for such a project, the opportunities were also monumental. In 1859, the Articles of Association of the Central Pacific Railroad Association were created and approved at the Pacific Railroad Convention. The Central Pacific Railroad Company of California (CPRR) was organized in Sacramento two years later on April 30, 1861, and formally incorporated on June 28 of that year. Judah was appointed chief engineer and lobbyist for the Central Pacific, and he promptly went about supervising the survey of potential routes across the Sierra Nevadas, developing finely detailed maps, devising more specific plans for the route, and advancing the project with government officials and legislators in California and Washington, D.C.

For Judah, 1861–2 was a watershed period. Starting in mid-winter 1861 and working through July 1862, he and his friend Dr. Daniel Strong, a druggist from the western slope Sierra Nevada town of Dutch Flat, led groups of surveyors and workers in plotting various routes through the rugged mountain range, investigating five different possible paths. The passage that they mapped across the Sierra Nevada via Donner Summit proved to be the one that would finally accommodate America's initial transcontinental route across California.

Judah also traveled to Washington, D.C., later in 1862 as official agent for the Central Pacific. It was not the first time that he lobbied Congress and the president, attempting to gain their favor in granting the Central Pacific the right to construct the western portion of the Pacific Railroad route, but it was his most successful effort. The resulting Pacific Railroad Act of 1862 authorized the Central Pacific to build east from the Pacific, provided the right-of-way along with massive land grants, and authorized the issuing of government bonds to help finance its construction. Completely ignoring the Native American inhabitants, the government considered its vast western territories to be "empty," and knew they would not fill up with Americans until easy transport was provided. Giving away empty land in order that the transport would be built seemed a fair and sensible exchange.

Upon receiving authorization to build the railway, Judah said to the Big Four, "We have drawn the Elephant. Now let us see if we can harness him." But before the CPRR could qualify for assistance, in the form of six-percent annual interest US Government bonds that had to be repaid at maturity after thirty years, the company was required to first string together forty miles of track on its own.

The route from the East was to be built by the Union Pacific, which was incorporated on July 1, 1862. The primary force behind the Union Pacific was Dr. Durant, whose tenure as VP of the Union Pacific would be mired in controversy and scandal. The Union Pacific started its trek west at Council Bluffs/Omaha, laying its first rails in July, 1865, and reaching the symbolic boundary between the "moist east and arid west" at the 100th meridian some 247 miles west of that point in October, 1866. The race was on to construct the first major rail passage route across North America, and saw the two companies lay close to 1,800 miles of track before the "Last Spike" was driven at Promontory Summit, Utah.

THE COST OF DOING BUSINESS

The Union Pacific and Central Pacific were to be issued the government bonds upon completing each forty-mile portion of tracked "first class railroad" at rates calibrated according to the difficulty of the terrain they were negotiating. The railroads were granted bonds at $16,000 per mile of track constructed on a relatively level grade, $32,000 per mile in the high plains, and $48,000 per mile (limited to a total of 300 miles) in the mountains. Additionally, Congress granted each railroad a right-of-way 400 feet wide, as well as 6,400 acres of land per mile of track divided into five segments along both sides of the track. In 1864 this was increased to 12,800 acres per mile divided into ten sections.

A tracklaying team in the Platte Valley (top right).

Snowsheds in the Sierra Nevada, *Harper's Magazine*, February 1872 (below).

Congress required that the Pacific Railroad be completed by July 1, 1876, that curves be drawn on a radius of at least 400 feet, and that no grade be greater than 2.2 percent, which equaled 116 feet per mile. Separate construction companies were to be created, providing more opportunities for investors. Although the companies building the railroad were supposed to be completely independent from the carriers, this was not the case with either road.

The Central Pacific secured loans from financial institutions and, as did the Union Pacific, also greatly benefited from the land grants and access to US government bonds that had been authorized by the Congress. Although the visionary Judah had been the true original moving force behind the creation of the Central Pacific, and through his later work in Washington, D.C., had ensured that it received the imprimatur and support of the Congress, during the spring and summer of 1863 the always single-minded chief engineer became increasingly disenchanted with the attitudes and business practices of the Big Four. Among other things Judah became convinced that Stanford *et al.* were countenancing substandard construction practices on the Central Pacific while also secretly diverting funds needed to build the railroad to improving and operating the Dutch Flat and Donner Lake Wagon Road Company which they also owned.

These disputes came to a head in September, leading Judah to break with the Big Four and leave California for the East Coast to raise funds to buy out their interests in the company and take over the Central Pacific himself. However, he contracted yellow fever during the trip while crossing the Isthmus of Panama, and the 37-year-old "father" of the CPRR died on November 2, 1863, just a week after he arrived in New York City. In what would prove to be Judah's last official act he designated his chief assistant, Samuel S. Montague, as "Resident Engineer" to assume charge of that department until he could return to take over the company. With his death, however, Montague was formally appointed Judah's successor as chief engineer, and Lewis M. Clement was named his chief assistant engineer.

On the other side of the country, Durant, who had proposed that the eastern terminus be built at Council Bluffs, Iowa/Omaha, Nebraska, was manipulating the prices of railroad stocks by instigating rumors regarding which lines would be directly joined to the Union Pacific. He first indicated that his M&M would be connected to the line. As M&M stock went up, Durant bought stock in the Cedar Rapids and Missouri Railroad (CR&M), whose stock was then depressed following a period of financial hardship. After accumulating a vast number of shares in CR&M, he indicated that it would be connected to the Union Pacific. CR&M stock went up and Durant sold at a profit. M&M stock went down and he bought it up, selling it later for a profit.

Durant was able to engage in questionable activities because he kept out of the spotlight by accepting the office of vice president of the Union Pacific and ensuring that men of "high moral character" served as the president of the company. This allowed him to devise a scheme whereby he could skirt the regulation prohibiting each partner in the railroad from owning more than ten percent of the stock. With the Union Pacific having difficulty selling shares, the vice president convinced others to buy stock with his own money, putting their names on the certificates. This scheme allowed Durant to own and control approximately 50 percent of the company's shares.

OPTIMISM, OPPORTUNITY, AND OPPRESSION

With the end of the Civil War, America focused on two specific challenges at hand—the reconstruction of the South, and further development of the lands west of the Mississippi River.

The Central Pacific faced demands in terms of securing supplies and labor. For the West, many of the building materials, which were easily accessed by the Union Pacific because of its proximity to already established eastern railroad routes, had to be sent via ship around Cape Horn. Of course, one reason the transcontinental route was being built was to make the process of shipping materials much easier.

The Big Four also faced labor shortages. This massive, complex undertaking needed the labor of tens of thousands of workers, but with the population centers in the US being primarily east of the Rocky Mountains, laborers had to be shipped in, and all too often once the men arrived they left the railroad in search of gold. To deal with the dilemma, Crocker decided that the descendents of those who built the Great Wall of China would make the perfect labor force.

A test group of Chinese laborers was hired, although many skeptics thought that these workers would be too small and fragile to handle the physically demanding tasks at hand. They performed admirably, however, and Crocker sent recruiters to the "Celestial Kingdom" (as China was often called) to enlist a work force that eventually numbered over 12,000 migrant workers who were quickly dubbed "Celestials." Often resented by their Caucasian colleagues, they lived separately from their counterparts and worked in groups of thirty, digging tunnels, reinforcing ledges, and drilling holes for black powder charges. The work was hard and dangerous, but the "Celestials" excelled at it.

In their heyday, the western railroads never referred to their foreign workers or passengers who had arrived from other lands to settle in the West as "immigrants." Instead, they were always "emigrants," and the special trains that carried settlers to their new homes were called "emigrant" trains.

On the other side of the Sierra Nevada Mountains, the Union Pacific also had a tough time securing workers during the Civil War years. Once the war was over, the workforce was composed of former Union and Confederate soldiers, as well as emigrants primarily from Ireland and Scandinavia. The workers lived in dormitory cars while their counterparts on the western end of the track congregated, ate, and slept in transient camps.

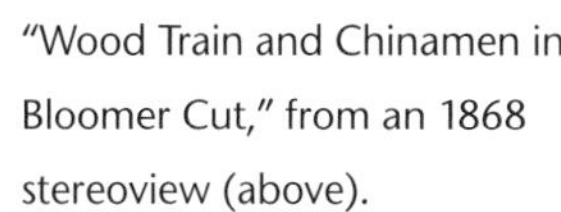

"Wood Train and Chinamen in Bloomer Cut," from an 1868 stereoview (above).

"Chinese laborers at work," *Harper's Weekly*, December 7, 1867 (below).

"A Snow Drift on the Pacific Railroad," a hand-colored wood block engraving from *Harper's Weekly*, March 19, 1870.

For the Central Pacific, the mountains were especially daunting, with a major concern being that winter snows would make it all but impossible for the railroad to run for weeks at a time. In the winter of 1866–7, for instance, there were 44 snowstorms leaving level accumulations of over fifteen feet and some drifts up to sixty feet deep as the railroad was being built. Supply trains were delayed, and construction was halted until 5,000 laborers cleared the snow. At one point an entire camp was lost in an avalanche, and was only found again when the spring thaw cleared the area. Construction moved slowly until the workers scaled and cleared the mountains, but once out of the Sierra Nevada Mountains the pace quickened.

The Union Pacific had easy going at first as track was constructed on the nearly level grade of the Platte River Valley. As the Sierras in California did for the CPRR, the Rocky Mountains posed a major challenge for the Union Pacific with winter snows, and extreme heat and summer dust storms plagued the workers on the treeless prairies.

Another major problem for the Union Pacific came from attacks by the Sioux and Cheyenne tribes, who rightly saw the railroad as a threat to their existence. While they rarely attacked wagon trains because those people were passing through on their way to California, the railroads left permanent structures and settlements that obstructed migration patterns, consumed natural resources, and impeded the free movement of the tribes. Additionally, hunters came and began shooting buffalo for sport and for their hides. Attacks by Native Americans were focused on the destruction of railroad property and creating fear in potential settlers, as the Sioux and Cheyenne attempted to preserve their way of life.

Ironically, a Native American war party was partly responsible for Grenville Dodge finding the much-needed pass through the Rocky Mountains. When Dodge and his surveying party were pursued by Native warriors, the railroad workers found refuge in what would become known as Sherman Pass. The serendipitous discovery of this pass would eventually provide the Union Pacific a relatively easy route to the desert regions east of Salt Lake City, then the only major community between Omaha and Sacramento.

For the Central Pacific, Native Americans were less of a problem, since the railroad company awarded passes to chiefs to ride in coaches and allowed braves to ride freight cars for free. Additionally, tribes west of the Rockies, such as the Payutes and Shoshoni, were not as aggressive as the Sioux and Cheyenne. The "Iron Horse" would eventually win the day, however, and Native American tribes would be relegated to reservations.

With the Civil War over, American industry was churning out iron, mechanical parts, and textiles, while farmers were utilizing the richness of the continent's soil. Mills were offering droves of emigrants jobs, and the public a wealth of commercially produced goods. There were opportunities galore. As the railroad neared completion, its untapped potential seemed boundless, and generated optimism throughout the country.

THE WORK AT HAND

Each mile of track was located, graded, and built according to standards set by the Congress of the United States on March 3, 1863. The standards, which were adopted after the Union Pacific first broke ground, were not always followed due to the fact that both companies were racing to lay as much track as possible in an attempt to win the lion's share of the government bonds authorized by the Congress.

Workers had to first establish the grade, which was elevated two feet in order to facilitate drainage. It was required that the roadbed be no less than fourteen feet wide and that excavation cuts be a minimum of twenty feet wide. Ballast used to securely support the track was to be at least two feet deep and composed of materials found locally.

Ties (or "sleepers") could be made of various types of wood, with oak being preferred. Cottonwood, which was used when other more durable woods were not available, was treated with zinc chloride in a process called "burnettizing" in order to extend its longevity. Ties could either be 6 inches × 6 inches × 8 feet or 6 inches × 8 inches × 8 feet, and were often manufactured locally. American-made sticks of iron "pear" rail that ranged from 28 to 30 feet in length and weighed 55 to 65 pounds per yard were spiked to the ties, although these were all eventually replaced by steel "T" rail which was much stronger and more durable.

Various types of iron coupling were used to join one rail to another. The first type was a slip-on clip known as a "rail chair," which had a lip that folded around and embraced the bottom edge of the rail. Another type of iron strip used to bind rails together was known as a fishplate, fishbar, or fish joint. These devices measured 20 inches × 2 inches × ⅝ of an inch, and had four evenly distributed holes through which a ¾-inch bolt could be placed and then secured by an oval collar. The bolts were fastened on the outside of the rail through oval holes which allowed for expansion. Either flat- or round-headed spikes were used to secure the rails to the ties. Made out of iron, they were 9/16 of an inch square and measured 5½ inches in length.

The amount of track laid in one day varied depending on the difficulty of the terrain, the weather, and the number of track gangs available. Crocker of the Central Pacific placed a $10,000 wager with Durant of the Union Pacific that his Central Pacific crew could lay ten miles of track in one workday. The gang surpassed the ten-mile goal by 54 feet and Crocker won his bet.

As the two companies moved towards their goal, they brought along their armies of workers including laborers, graders, track gangs, civil engineers, bridge builders, carpenters, blacksmiths, explosive specialists, loggers, telegraph workers, cooks and more. On both sides of the line, gambling parlors, saloons, and prostitutes

Camp Victory, Utah Territory, April 28, 1869. Eight Irishmen and an army of muscular Chinese laid more than ten miles of rail in one day to win a bet. Seen standing on the flatcar are CPRR construction superintendent James Harvey Strobridge (left) and track foreman Horace Hamilton Minkler (right).

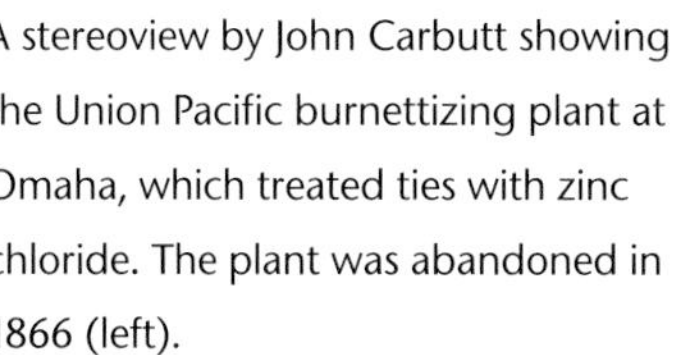

A stereoview by John Carbutt showing the Union Pacific burnettizing plant at Omaha, which treated ties with zinc chloride. The plant was abandoned in 1866 (left).

accompanied the work crews. Sunday was the designated day off and a time for letting loose in these temporary, mobile settlements, with many hard-partying folks being injured or even killed.

Although the ultimate goal was to join the Union Pacific and Central Pacific, the two companies competed mightily to lay the most track. In 1869, it got to the point where they passed each other in Utah by many unnecessary miles. Along with this wasteful construction, there were problems with sabotage. Men from each company raided their competitor's camps and destroyed their work. Finally, Congress decided to subvert the unproductive behavior of the companies and designated Promontory Summit, Utah Territory, as the meeting place of the two lines. It would become the site of one of the biggest events in America's industrial and commercial history.

PROMONTORY SUMMIT, UTAH, 1869

Although the Congress had given the Union Pacific and Central Pacific until the nation's centenary in 1876 to complete the project, neither company dawdled once the Civil War ended in April 1865. Driven by profits and the desire to capture as many government bonds as possible, both made massive efforts to lay track as quickly as possible.

Because the Union Pacific did not have to tackle the awesome challenge of building the difficult Sierra grade in California, it laid down more track than the CPRR with a total of 1,087 miles. The route started at Council Bluffs, crossed the Missouri River to Omaha and then traversed Nebraska (which was then known as Elkhorn) through a series of towns to Sidney, Nebraska. The line then went through the Colorado Territory, Wyoming Territory, and into the Utah Territory, connecting with the Central Pacific at Promontory Summit.

The Central Pacific, which laid 690 miles of track, began its journey in Sacramento, California, and then made its way across the Sierra Nevada Mountains to Nevada. Among the towns that grew up along its grade were Illinoistown (now called Colfax) and Truckee in California, and Reno, Battle Mountain, and Wells in Nevada, before it crossed into Utah where it joined with the Union Pacific.

Lewis Clement (right) and Jacob Blickenderfer (left) inspecting the CPRR grade at Argenta, Nevada, on March 1, 1869 (above).

Once the two lines connected, the Central Pacific extended its line west, first to Alameda and Oakland on San Francisco Bay by acquiring the Western Pacific. The Union Pacific completed its physical connection to the railroads of the east in 1871 with the construction and opening of its Missouri River Bridge between Council Bluffs and Omaha, thus eliminating the need for a ferry service to carry its trains across the river.

The ceremony joining the CPRR and the UPRR took place at Promontory Summit on May 10, 1869. Real-time news of the event was to be instantly transmitted across the continent by means of a telegraph wire fixed to the silver hammer used to drive the final spike—each hammer stroke was translated as a telegraph click that was sent from there to telegraph stations throughout the nation.

Durant arrived from the east via engine No. 119 and Stanford rode his train from the west pulled by the *Jupiter*. Stanford brought the ceremonial "Last Spike" made of California gold, which was engraved with the names of the Central Pacific's Board of Directors, while the tie into which it was driven was cut from California laurel and wrapped with silver bands. Stanford drove the first hammer stroke and missed, hitting the rail. Durant went second and also dinged the rail. The engineers of the respective railways, Montague of the Central Pacific and Dodge of the Union Pacific, drove in the spike and with that the message "DONE" was tapped out by a Union Pacific telegrapher and sent across the country.

"Meeting of Engines; Laying the Last Rail, Promontory." Detail of a stereograph by Charles R. Savage, taken at Promontory Summit, Utah, May 10, 1869 (opposite).

Detail from an A. A. Hart stereoview of the Central Pacific's 4–6–0 William Mason-built locomotive *Sen. John Conness* (CPRR No. 6), seen in early 1865 on a temporary turntable at the west end of the almost-finished trestle at Newcastle, California, 31 miles east of Sacramento.

After both engines were uncoupled from their trains, each locomotive traveled across the area where the final spike had been driven. A group picture was taken, speeches were delivered, and a band played. The dignitaries of both railroads then made their way to Stanford's private railcar for a celebratory dinner.

America's first transcontinental railroad, a venture of which many had dreamed and which many had dismissed as being an impossible and impractical undertaking, was about to transform the nation.

THE BIG IMPACT

With both sides of the continent united, the more heavily populated and industrialized East could now access the western regions with relative ease. The vast spaces of the West were now opened up for white settlement, agriculture, industrialization, and development. In its early years, the US was an agricultural nation, with small-scale, localized businesses, but the railroads were the model for modern, national, corporate entities. They were not only the important customers themselves for products such as lumber, steel, and copper, but they also transformed the industrial nature of the country, permitting nationwide businesses to flourish and encouraging the growth of urban industrialized centers.

In time, railroads even influenced population shifts as millions of emigrants found security in western regions, and a new age of mass transportation, communication, and commercialization began to take shape in the late-nineteenth through the early-twentieth centuries.

At that time American railroad maps displayed a complex system of interconnecting lines that looked like one octopus lying upon another, and then yet another octopus joining the pile. The result was a system that enabled the nation and its inhabitants to travel, communicate, and grow in ways that had been heretofore unrealized. The American railroads were responsible for creating opportunities for farmers, tradesmen, communications workers, entrepreneurs, entertainers, salesmen, manufacturers, laborers and many more. Additionally, the first transcontinental railroad allowed for the development and expansion of the other great long-haul railroads of the West that followed.

THE DEVELOPMENT OF THE CLASSIC WESTERN ROUTES

In the United States, the expansion of the railway system was prodigious. In 1830, there were 23 miles of track in operation in the nation. During the Civil War, approximately 36,000 miles of tracks, mostly in the North and South, were available for travel and shipping purposes. When the railroads united at Promontory Summit in 1869, America had almost 47,000 miles of track, and just five years later a total of 72,385 miles of iron rails crisscrossed the nation. Rail trackage in the United States reached its peak in 1916 at 254,036 miles. The first transcontinental line was just the beginning.

Although there were a few local rail lines in the West prior to the completion of the first transcontinental, major rail routes did not develop until after the last spike was driven at Promontory Summit to complete the Overland Route. Just a few major lines would redefine North America's developing West and play significant parts in transforming the Pacific Coast, and as these classic western routes were established, they encouraged the growth and development of agriculture, business, education, entertainment, and other areas.

The Northern Pacific Railroad was chartered in 1864 by Congress as the nation's second transcontinental railroad, and was built to serve the area between western Lake Superior at Duluth, Minnesota and Puget Sound. Plagued by questionable NP management and unanticipated Indian hostility, Jay Cooke's partners panicked, thereby triggering the Panic of 1873 and the temporary bankruptcy of the Northern Pacific. By the decade's end construction had resumed, although the 1883 transcontinental completion of the NP was a month behind that of the Southern Pacific Railroad. By the early 1890s, transcontinental competition from both the Great Northern (in the US) and the Canadian Pacific permanently weakened the NP.

A typical network map, showing the reach of the Northern Pacific system in 1900.

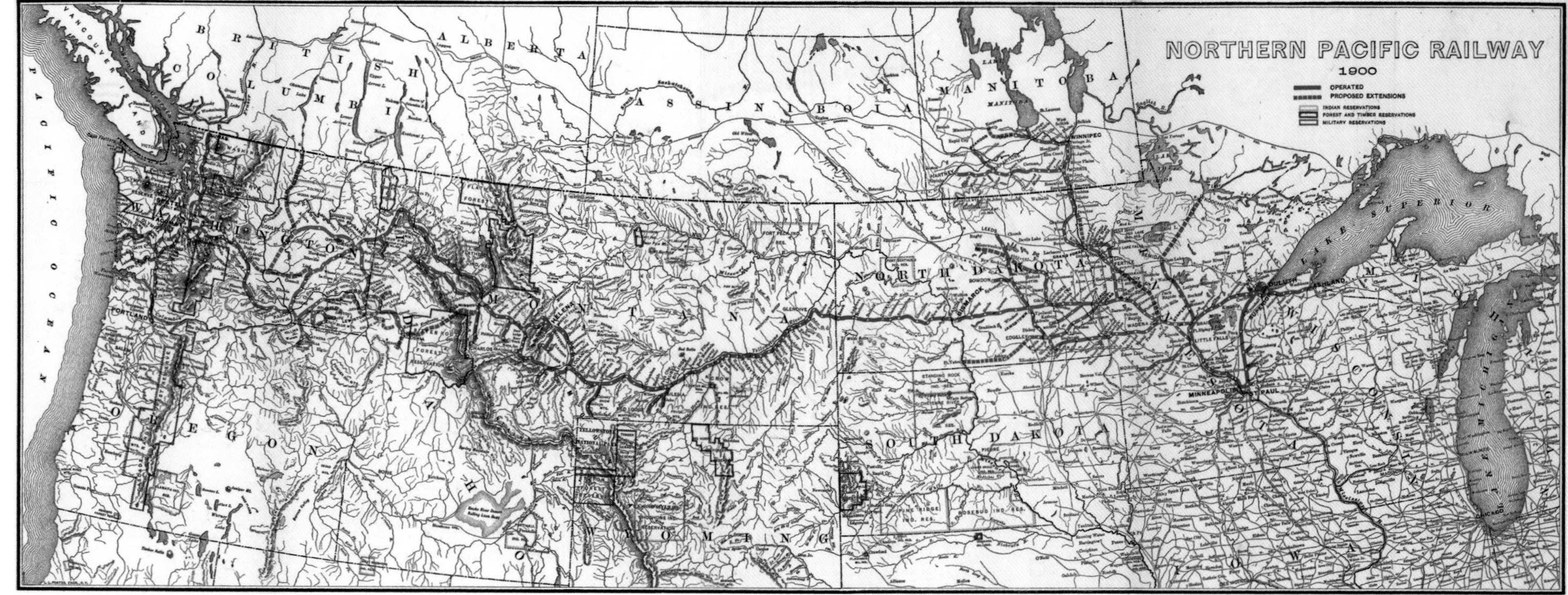

Four Great Routes for Transcontinental Travel
Sunset Route—By Southern Pacific steamships from New York or by rail to New Orleans; thence via Houston, San Antonio, and El Paso to San Diego (Carriso Gorge), Los Angeles and San Francisco. Apache Trail Highway enroute.
Golden State Route—The direct line, Chicago to Los Angeles, San Diego (Carriso Gorge), and Santa Barbara, via Kansas City and El Paso. Apache Trail Highway enroute.
Overland Route—(Lake Tahoe Line)—Shortest route across mid-continent, Chicago to San Francisco, via Ogden, crossing Great Salt Lake by rail and over the scenic Sierra Nevada.
Shasta Route—Pacific Northwest to California, via Portland, Crater Lake and Mt. Shasta, for travelers from the East over northern lines. Choice of two scenic lines, Cascade and Siskiyou, through Oregon.
Southern Pacific Lines
Only Southern Pacific Offers this Choice · Go One Way, Return Another
NON-TRANSFERABLE TICKET
GOOD FOR ONE CONTINUOUS PASSAGE
Pullman Company

A 1930 Southern Pacific ticket (above left), 1940s SP ticket envelope with route map, and 1921 Pullman Company "sleeper car" ticket (above right).

The second transcontinental line to start running, the Southern Pacific, was technically completed in 1881 when it linked with the Santa Fe Railroad at Deming, New Mexico. As its name suggests, this route was established across the southern states, from New Orleans to Los Angeles and San Francisco, and in 1883 it became called the "Sunset Route" when it created its own through route. A highlight of the line was the Pecos Viaduct built in 1892 across the Pecos River, which was at that time the tallest bridge in the US and the third tallest in the world at 321 feet, although later on the bridge was reinforced and another inch or so were added.

The Southern Pacific Railroad was one of the most expansive rail companies in the country, operating four major long-haul passenger routes, including those that ran north and south along the nation's Pacific Coast. The Shasta Route, which was completed in 1887, went from San Francisco–Sacramento to Portland and Seattle. Finished in 1901, the Coast Line connected Los Angeles and San Francisco via Santa Barbara, and was one of the Southern Pacific's most famous routes.

From the extreme North to the middle of the continent and below in the South, the Northern Pacific, Overland Route, and Southern Pacific were settling the West. Two other western rail lines would become legendary—the Santa Fe, and the Denver and Rio Grande. The route of the Santa Fe went from Kansas City, Kansas (eventually from Chicago), to Los Angeles, California, and was part of the Atchison, Topeka and Santa Fe Railway system established by Cyrus K. Holliday in 1860 with the intention of constructing a rail line from Topeka, Kansas, to Santa Fe, New Mexico. The route reached the Pacific Coast in 1881 by connecting with the Southern Pacific in Deming, New Mexico, but although the Santa Fe was responsible for helping to settle the state of Kansas and make Kansas City a major US city, ironically the line never did travel through its primary namesake, Santa Fe.

The summit of Pike's Peak, from *Rocky Mountain Views*, published by the Inter-State Company in Denver in 1906 (right).

The Royal Gorge on the Denver and Rio Grande Route, from *Rocky Mountain Views* (left).

The major connector between Salt Lake City, Utah, and Denver, Colorado, was the Denver and Rio Grande Western Railroad, generally referred to as the Rio Grande. Of all major rail lines in the West, it climbed the highest, rising to over 10,240 feet as it scaled Colorado's Tennessee Pass, crossing the Continental Divide at Marshall Pass (10,858 feet), and reaching nearly to the 14,109-foot summit of Pikes Peak. The Rio Grande's Royal Gorge Route passed through Gunnison, Colorado, on its way to spectacular views that included Black Canyon along the Gunnison River and the Curecanti Needle, a striking natural rock formation rising more than 700 feet from the ground. The Denver and Rio Grande was distinctive because, of the major Western railroads, it was the only one that ran on narrow gauge track, which was about a foot narrower than rails adhering to the standard gauge.

Canada realized its initial transcontinental route when the Canadian Pacific's last spike was driven at Craigellachie, British Columbia, on November 7, 1885. This line from Calgary, Alberta, to Vancouver, British Columbia became that nation's classic western route. The road crossed the Rockies, making for spectacular views and enabling easy transport of passengers and freight to the Pacific Coast of Canada, and traveled through Kicking Horse Pass, an ultra-steep grade that was responsible for many runaway train accidents until the line completed the construction of its Spiral Tunnels in 1909. These tunnels lessened the severity of the grade, making the passage through Kicking Horse Pass much safer. Soon after other major lines were built, including the Canadian Northern, which stretched across Canada to many isolated areas.

These great western routes were the most important rail lines in the West. They opened the way for commerce, population growth, and the exploitation of natural resources. Although the East had enjoyed the convenience of rail travel for more than thirty years prior to the completion of the initial transcontinental and had access to what was then called the Middle West, growth and development in the western territories and states were truncated until the railroads opened up the region. North America had never before experienced such a massive infusion of energy, optimism, and opportunity that was engendered by the era of the Iron Horse and the classic railroad routes of the West.

A postcard book of 22 views of the Denver & Rio Grande, published by Van Noy Interstate Company, Denver, in 1909 (left).

THE PACIFIC RAILROAD ACT OF 1862

Thirty Seventh
Congress of the United States,
At the Second Session
BEGUN AND HELD AT THE CITY OF WASHINGTON
in the District of Columbia
on Monday the second day of December one thousand eight hundred and sixty one
AN ACT To aid in the construction of a railroad and telegraph line from the Missouri river to the Pacific ocean, and to secure to the government the use of the same for postal, military, and other purposes:

The Pacific Railroad Act of 1862 (12 Statutes at Large 489) is arguably one of the most significant pieces of legislation in American history. Signed by President Abraham Lincoln on July 1, 1862, it established the mechanism for the nation's first transcontinental railroad system linking the nation's East and West. The act did not set up a government entity to build the railroad, but rather left the effort entirely in private hands, with all the positives and negatives inherent with business leadership. The Act created one of the two railroads building along the route, the Union Pacific Railroad building west from Council Bluffs, Iowa/Omaha, Nebraska, and authorized it to meet with the tracks of the Central Pacific Railroad which would be constructed east from Sacramento, California. Both received essentially similar government benefits, including significant land grants and access to US Government Bonds to help finance the project.

PASSAGE

After being blocked for almost a decade by resistance from the Southern states, which feared a "northern" route via Chicago and through Nebraska, in 1862 the railroad legislation still faced significant opposition and questions in the House of Representatives. The crux of the debate was not the road's necessity, but rather was centered on "incentives," i.e., how much money and land was enough to attract private capital without giving away too much. One decision, for example, eliminated all mineral rights, which were considered too much of a give-away. The fact that the debate occurred during a period of exceptionally heavy Civil War fighting (McClellan's Peninsula campaign and Grant's Shiloh) during which the North's resources were under heavy strain also colored deliberations. Ultimately, however, transcontinental interests prevailed as the wartime mood of Congress, President Lincoln (who had frequently represented railroad interests in his legal practice), and the American public were unanimous in wanting to link the East with California and Nevada. Not only did the West have a population rapidly approaching half a million, but the gold and silver there was also of great appeal. On May 6, the House passed the bill 79 to 49, the Senate voted 35 to 5 on June 20, and the Act was signed by the President on July 1.

THE ACT'S PROVISIONS

Officially entitled "An Act to aid in the construction of a railroad and telegraph line from the Missouri river to the Pacific ocean, and to secure to the government the use of the same for postal, military, and other purposes," the complex legislation incorporated and named the Union Pacific Railroad, then gave it and the Central Pacific various incentives. Land grants for commerce dated back to the first canal grant in 1827, while the first railroad land grant was made to the Illinois Central in 1850. The Act also set aside additional land for railroad infrastructure such as sidings, depots, repair shops, yards, etc., and extinguished all Indian titles where the tracks crossed their land.

Each company was promised access to six percent, thirty-year US first mortgage bonds for completed, certified track, and was supported by the promise of government traffic over the line including mail and military personnel and supplies. Among other provisions were technical issues such as track width, which was chosen by Lincoln as 4 feet 8½ inches, the "standard" or English gauge.

AFTERMATH

Both companies broke ground in 1863 (the CPRR in January, the UPRR in December), but despite the government's seeming largesse, the financial incentives, in part due to wartime conditions and shortages, proved inadequate to attract ample private capital, thus limiting progress for the first couple of years. In order to improve the situation and attract capital, the Congress passed the Pacific Railroad Act of 1864 which substantively modified the original 1862 legislation.

THE PACIFIC RAILROAD ACT OF 1864

The Pacific Railroad Act of 1864 created the Northern Pacific Railroad as well as adding significant land and financial modifications to the 1862 Act. These land, dollar, and other incentives were to materially assist the Union Pacific and the Central Pacific railroads in selling their bonds.

UNION AND CENTRAL PACIFIC RAILROADS

Key inducements and changes from the 1862 legislation included doubling the land grants from ten to twenty square miles (12,800 acres) per mile of completed track, and permitting mineral rights to flow to the railroads. This was an exceptionally valuable "sweetener," since mineral rights had been denied in the 1862 Act. The railroads were also allowed to sell their own first mortgage bonds, with the government essentially taking a second mortgage position. This was coupled with permission to sell two-thirds of the bonds after grading (not the laying of track) in twenty-mile increments.

To show its ostensible evenhandedness, Congress modestly reduced each railroad's right-of-way from 400 feet to 200 feet, although, as in the earlier legislation, additional land was set aside for railroad operations such as switching yards, repair facilities, depots, and the like. The overwhelmingly favorable nature of the legislation was facilitated by a variety of lobbying practices illegal today, including (but far from limited to) the distribution of a quarter of a million dollars of Union Pacific stock to influential Congressmen.

THE NORTHERN PACIFIC

The second major part of the 1864 Act established the Northern Pacific Railroad. The concept of a geographically northern transcontinental route, crossing the country's northern tier of states and territories, had never been seriously considered by Congress given the area's limited population, lack of minerals, and the limitations of the day's railroad construction technology. This, when combined with the lack of financial and political support, had left the idea dormant in Washington. The situation worsened when the route's leading proponent, General Isaac I. Stevens, who in 1853 had been in charge of the party of US Army Topographical Engineers that had originally surveyed the route, was killed in the Battle of Chantilly in 1862.

Stevens had been dead less than a month when the first of many massive gold strikes was made in Idaho and Montana. Additionally, a Lake Superior to Puget Sound route found a champion in Josiah Perham, who asserted his ability to raise money for a "People's Pacific Railway," called the Northern Pacific, by selling low denomination bonds to the public. Most members of Congress were indifferent or thought the railroad would fail, and adamantly refused funding, soon inserting a provision that "no money should be drawn from the treasury of the United States to aid in the construction of the Northern Pacific." In addition to regional support, the Northern Pacific also had the backing of the cantankerous, exceptionally powerful Vermont-born chairman of both the House Ways and Means Committee and the House Select Railroad Committee, Thaddeus Stevens (R–PA). Working with Vermont's Northern Pacific lobbyist Thomas H. Canfield, he tacked the Northern Pacific onto the Union and Central Pacific's efforts and then guided the combined legislation through Congress.

To compensate for not including financial grants, Congress increased the size of the Northern Pacific's land grants to 12,800 acres per mile in states and 25,600 in territories. Most estimates put the Northern Pacific's total grant in the fifty million acre range, but the number is uncertain as the exact route was not chosen for years and overlapped other railroad land grants. The technical provisions of the Act (e.g., track gauge) were generally the same or similar to the 1862 legislation. Under Stevens' guidance, the legislation passed the House, 74 to 50, on May 31. The Senate acted on June 27, taking the bill from committee and passing it "without division" that same day, and President Lincoln signed the bill on July 2, 1864.

A FEW HINTS TO OVERLAND TRAVELERS

FROM *THE ILLUSTRATED RAILROAD GUIDE OF THE UNION AND CENTRAL PACIFIC RAILROADS*
PUBLISHED BY ADAMS PUBLISHING CO., CHICAGO, OMAHA AND SAN FRANCISCO, 1879

No matter how thoroughly he is "coached" and generally advised, everybody who makes the transcontinental journey is quite ready at the end of it to supplement all that has been said before with fresh ideas of his own; and, notwithstanding the fact that before starting he avails himself of the counsel of a most experienced friend, he invariably discovers many little things that ought to be arranged by intending travelers which have never been mentioned to him, and which, according to his mind, are essential to full enjoyment and comfort. The few hints that we have to offer are, therefore, presented—not with any air of infallibility, but simply as personal suggestions which may or may not be followed with advantage, though the writer's private belief is that no one will do amiss in giving ear to them.

The fare from New York, Boston, or Philadelphia, is about $137, and the cost of the sleeping-car, which is almost indispensable, must be added, although some tourists have sufficiently vigorous constitutions to endure the journey without more repose than they can get in the ordinary first or second class car. The sleeping-car fare for one berth is five dollars to Chicago; two dollars and fifty cents from Chicago to Omaha by the Rock Island, and three dollars by either the Chicago, Burlington & Quincy or the Northwestern route; eight dollars from Omaha to Ogden, and six dollars from Ogden to San Francisco, making a total of twenty-two dollars. A section is double and a drawing-room about quadruple these rates, the drawing-room having accommodations for four persons, and affording privacy and great luxury to its inmates. If four persons are traveling together they should by all means secure a drawing-room, by which they will realize the perfection that railway locomotion has attained in America.

The Pullman cars go no farther west than Ogden, but the Central Pacific road runs commodious sleeping-cars of its own to and from that point. In order to secure good locations, the lower middle berths being preferable, it is advisable to request them by telegraph in advance, especially as passengers cannot obtain a through sleeping-car ticket from New York to San Francisco, and must rebook themselves at Chicago, Omaha, and Ogden. All baggage also is rechecked at Ogden; and, speaking about baggage, we urge everybody to take as little of it as possible, for the reason that it is always an

The illustrations in this section are colored versions of engravings from Charles Nordhoff's 1874 classic *California: A Book for Travellers and Settlers*.

impediment, and also because anything in excess of one hundred pounds costs about twenty cents per pound extra from Omaha to the Pacific coast. Crossing the continent some time ago, our sympathies were enlisted by an English lady, who was vernacularly "stuck" to the amount of sixty dollars by extra baggage, which might have been left behind; and we beg to remind the reader that in pleasure-traveling as well as armies mobility is a most excellent thing.

It always seems to us that the young men one meets in the Pacific Railways who carry a small hand-bag are the happiest creatures on the train; and unquestionably the unhappiest are those who, encumbered by such unwieldy equipments as Saratoga trunks contain, are frequently compelled to lighten their pocket-books in settling accounts with the baggage-master. At the same time it is wise to carry wraps and overcoats; for if you leave Omaha with the thermometer at 90 degrees on Monday, it is quite possible that, even in July, the air becomes chilly as you rise above the billows of the Plains and pause under the shadow of the Rocky Mountains at Cheyenne on Tuesday. In summer the common linen or alpaca "duster" is indispensable, the dust of the Plains, especially between Elko and Humboldt, being ruinous and dense. A pair of Lisle-thread or cotton gloves add much to one's comfort, and also give one the incomparable satisfaction of having clean hands.

In regard to the commissaire, the train stops three times a day for meals, which are usually plain but good, and in some instances they are excellent. It is a novel and interesting experience to alight at sun-down on the platform of a little station in the wilderness with no projection between the sky and the land as far as one can see, and to be ushered into a clean and substantially furnished apartment, with tables handsomely set for supper, the attendants being ruddy-faced, neat, modest girls, and the silver-ware and crystal-ware and linen being irreproachable. The inevitable hurry takes away from the enjoyment, but the food is ample.

Old travelers over the Pacific Railways are in the habit of providing themselves with lunch-baskets, which may be obtained and filled at either end of the route. There is much comfort and security in a lunch-basket. You may not be disposed to sit down at the regular table for meals; perhaps you are tired of the recurrent menu, or have not an appetite; and then the wicker repository, which, if it has been filled with discretion, must surely contain many good things, is a consolation and a delight. The porter will adjust a small table in your section of the car, and forthwith you spread your napkin and contentedly sit down to so simple a lunch as a biscuit and a glass of sherry (let us hope that the sherry is genuine), or something more elaborate, in the way of sardines, boned-turkey, and a bottle of Extra Dry.

You have full possession of the car, probably, and can smile as you think of the haste and clatter that are going on in the dining-room of the depot. In winter the lunch-basket is to the overland traveler what the life-preserver is to the traveler on a dangerous ocean. It is not safe to go without it, and it is all the better if it includes a spirit-lamp; for accidents arising from snow and bad weather often disturb the culinary arrangements of the best-managed eating-houses. Both wicker-baskets and their "furniture" may be purchased reasonably at Oakland, Sacramento, and Omaha. The invariable price for the table d'hote at the stations is one dollar, but there are lunch-counters at which ten cents is charged for a cup of coffee or tea, and twenty-five cents for a cut from a cold joint.

Many side-trips, which will not only break the monotony of the continuous journey, but also afford views of interesting life and scenery, may be made by those who have time and money to spare. The hunter will do well to try the sport in the neighborhood of Evanston, and the lover of the picturesque and the scientist, especially the geologist or paleontologist, should by all means spend a few days at Green River. The tavern expenses will not be more than two or three dollars a day, and riding-horses, guides, and vehicles, may be hired at fair prices. Alighting at Cheyenne, you should take the Colorado Central Railway as far as Denver, calling at the many interesting points on the line and ascending Gray's or James's Peak if the weather is favorable.

A good idea of what a wonderful state Colorado is with its mountains, cañons, and mines, can be obtained at an expenditure of fifty dollars. Above all things, do not omit a run from Ogden down to Salt Lake City. The trains from the East arrive at the former station about 6 p.m., and connect with trains on the Utah Central road, which run by the borders of the lake to the city, the time being about two hours, and the fare three dollars. Returning to Ogden, the tourist leaves Salt Lake City at about four o'clock in the afternoon, and connects at six o'clock with the overland train. The side-trip to Virginia City and its mines require more time and money, and at the time of writing there is no direct connection at Reno.

CONNECTIONS OF THE UNION AND CENTRAL PACIFIC RAILWAYS

The extraordinary rapidity with which railways are projected, built, and extended west of the Missouri River, makes a table of the branch connections of the main line imperfect very soon after preparation. Not many months ago the writer was at Fort Garland, Southern Colorado, which was then over eighty miles from any railway, and it seemed to be the loneliest of outposts. It was a three days' ride from the nearest town, and only received a mail twice a week. A narrow-gauge road has since linked it with Eastern and Western civilization, and it is now surrounded by a growing city the same way places that at present seem very remote may soon be in steam communication with the principal lines of transcontinental travel; for, work that in older countries would take years to complete, is done in the great protoplastic West in months.

WHAT TIME IS THAT TRAIN?

A major complication affecting mid-nineteenth-century scheduled train travel was the fact that local time in each community was established locally, which made it exceedingly complicated for the railroads to schedule trains and for travelers to follow timetables. The railroads finally solved this problem for themselves in 1883, when they agreed as an industry to establish "Standard Railway Time" to schedule and manage all rail operations in the United States. The public at large, however, was slow to adopt this "radical" new system, and today's now universally accepted Standard Time Zones based on those first determined by the railroads—Eastern, Central, Mountain, and Pacific—were not finally established nationally until the adoption by Congress of the Standard Time Act on March 19, 1918.

William H. Armstrong, the US Commissioner of Railroads, gave the following account of the new time system in his Report to the Secretary of the Interior for 1883:

> *Under the present system each railway is operated independently on the local time of some principal point or points on said road, but this plan was found to be highly objectionable, owing to the fact that some fifty standards, intersecting and interlacing each other, were in use throughout the country. By the plan which has been adopted this number will be reduced to four, the difference in time being one hour between each, viz, the 75th, 90th, 105th, and 120th degrees of longitude west from Greenwich. The adoption of these standards will not cause a difference of more than thirty minutes from the local time at any point which is now used as a standard.*
>
> *The new arrangement goes into effect November 18, 1883, and all changes of time are to occur at the termini of roads, or at the ends of divisions. The seventy-fifth meridian being almost precisely the central meridian for the system of roads now using standards based upon the time of the Eastern cities, and the ninetieth meridian being equally central for roads now running by the time of Western cities, the time of these meridians has been adopted for the territory which includes 90 percent of the whole railway system of the country. Nearly all of the larger cities have abolished local time and adopted that of the nearest standard meridian in use by the railways.*

Thus what people began to call "railroad time" in 1883 became synonymous in 1918 with officially being "on time."

RAILWAY ROBBERIES

"A Train Robbery," a wood engraving from *Harper's Weekly*, January 16, 1892.

In America, the railroads of the West were often easy prey for robbers. Isolated stretches of track, payroll and gold coin shipments, and inadequate security precautions made western railways especially tantalizing to bandits.

Train robberies have been romanticized by Hollywood, which has often focused on the daring exploits and adventurous nature of icons such as Jesse James, Butch Cassidy and the Sundance Kid, and the Dalton Gang. But the truth is that the typical film scenario of a bunch of bandits riding alongside a passenger train, boarding it, and then strong-arming railway personnel is more fiction than fact.

Train robbers employed two common methods—boarding the train while it was at a station and then waiting for the right time to surprise railroad workers, or derailing the train. The first moving train robbery, where bandits held up a train while it was in transit, occurred in Indiana in 1866 when the Reno Gang stole over $10,000 from an Ohio and Mississippi train. Their success inspired many more to engage in this practice.

The first such robbery in the West took place at Verdi, Nevada, in the early morning of November 5, 1870, when eight armed bandits led by a Sunday school superintendent named John Chapman held up the Central Pacific Railroad's eastbound *Overland Express* just as it left the station. Some $41,600 in gold coin belonging to Wells, Fargo & Co. was taken from a strongbox in the train's express car, but after a two-state chase the robbers were caught. Ironically, the second such train robbery in the West took place just twenty hours later when the very same train was held up again near the Utah border!

Train robberies peaked in the early 1870s, with express cars, which carried baggage and freight and often included a safe for cash, coin, and other valuables, being the primary targets. The famous outlaw Jesse James robbed trains outside of Council Bluffs, Iowa, while Butch Cassidy with the Sundance Kid and the gang known as the Wild Bunch were especially active in Wyoming.

What is called the Last Great Train Robbery of the West occurred in Oregon on the Southern Pacific's Shasta Line on October 11, 1923.

$15,900.00 REWARD

IN GOLD

Train Hold-up and Murder

MAIL CAR AFTER HOLDUP.
Where the postal clerk was cremated.

Case No. 57883-D

$15,900.00 Reward in Gold!

$15,900.00 REWARD!

UNITED STATES
Post Office Department

Read this Story of a Terrible Crime

Train Hold-up and Murder

OF

Three Trainmen and a Mail Clerk in the Siskiyou Mountains of Oregon.

This will interest you, and $15,900.00 in Gold will be paid for information leading to the arrest and conviction of the guilty men.

All law abiding citizens, especially peace officers, dentists, opticians, barbers, loggers, jewelers and seamen, please read carefully and retain for future reference.

Communicate information to—

C. RIDDIFORD,
Post Office Inspector in Charge,
Spokane, Washington.

D. O'CONNELL,
Chief Special Agent,
Southern Pacific Company
San Francisco, Calif.

$15,900.00 Reward in Gold!

Prison photographs of Ray, Roy, and Hugh d'Autremont.

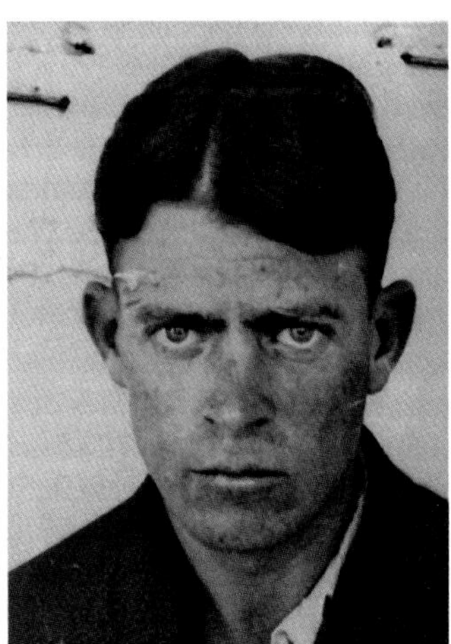

Twenty-three-year-old twins Roy and Ray d'Autremont and their younger brother Hugh heard rumors that the train called the *Gold Special* would be hauling a half-million dollars in gold, and decided to board the train in Tunnel 13 when it was crawling up the steep mountain grade. Roy and Hugh successfully jumped the train, forced the engineer to stop, and helped Ray, who had been waiting at the other end of the tunnel with a load of dynamite, to blow up the express car. The blast was so massive it killed the clerk inside, but with the car on fire and smoke impairing their vision, the robbers were unable to locate any valuables. Instead they killed three more railway men as they made their escape.

Despite a massive manhunt the three bandits managed to remain free until 1927, when they were finally caught and sentenced to life in prison.

Although train robberies carried a certain celebrity cachet and piqued prurient interests, they destroyed lives, cost the railroads money, vandalized passengers' pockets, and taxed resources. The tide turned in favor of the railroads in the 1880s, when companies reinforced express cars, incorporated larger, stronger safes, and hired trained armed guards. The heyday of the train robber lasted less than two decades.

A posse of Pinkerton detectives, UP agents and trackers, taken in June 1900 after the second big Union Pacific robbery by Butch Cassidy and his "Wild Bunch" (below).

TWO RAILROAD PIONEERS

JAY COOKE

Jay Cooke (1821–1905), known as the "Financier of the Civil War," had a significant impact on the westward expansion of the US by agreeing to finance the Northern Pacific Railroad that pushed the frontier 400 miles west to the Missouri River (Bismarck) between 1870 and 1873. The railroad also created Yellowstone National Park, caused the decision to build the Canadian Pacific Railroad, set off a surge in emigration to western Minnesota and eastern Dakota, reignited the Great Sioux War, and resulted in the rehabilitation of George Armstrong Custer, and on September 18, 1873 the collapse of Cooke's banking house directly triggered the Panic of 1873.

Cooke was born in Sandusky, Ohio, where in 1826 his classic "frontier entrepreneur" father, Eleutheros, was granted one of the nation's first railroad charters (Mad River & Lake Erie Railroad), and in 1831 was elected to Congress as a member of the short lived "Anti-Jacksonian Party." As a teenager, Cooke worked in St. Louis while also acquiring a lifetime interest in the Northwest. Offered a job in the Philadelphia banking house of E. W. Clarke & Co., Cooke proved to be so brilliant that he was made a partner and received one-eighth interest in the company gratis on his twenty-first birthday. In 1861 the then wealthy forty-year-old banker started his own firm, Jay Cooke & Co., and was soon taking the lead role in selling Pennsylvania war bonds. By mid-1865 he had sold over $1.6 billion in war bonds for the Union which represented approximately 27 percent of all money raised to pay the war's cost. His scrupulous honesty made him a hero to the public and the military alike.

By war's end Cooke was the nation's leading banker, having made a fortune using inside information against anti-government speculators including J. P. Morgan. Cooke's life was fraught with contradictions, however. While he was active in the abolitionist movement, at one point hiding one of John Brown's sons after Harper's Ferry, he refused to let African-American soldiers ride his trolley cars in Washington during the war. A man of deep and sincere religious conviction, Cooke nevertheless was second to none in bribing Congressmen. His philanthropic activities were legendary, but he also designed his own massive marble summer home located on Gibraltar Island in Lake Erie called "The Castle," which was briefly the country's largest and most opulent mansion. Cooke was a generous manager and his banking house was based on a meritocracy system, but he unilaterally made all final decisions of importance.

Cooke anticipated becoming President Grant's Secretary of the Treasury in 1869, but was bypassed in favor of a less idiosyncratic personality, George S. Boutwell. Cooke, who had been making large Minnesota railroad and land investments, then jumped at the chance to finance the Northern Pacific, believing that there was a Higher Reason for the opportunity, one that he had rejected two years earlier. In all, he raised just over $20 million for the railroad, but his initiatives were thwarted by the Franco–Prussian War that halted Scandinavian emigration, Canadian and British interests who feared western Canada's going the way of Texas and California, Congressional allies of the Central Pacific and Union Pacific railroads, and Northern Pacific mismanagement and corruption. By late 1870, Cooke was being increasingly drawn into the railroad's daily affairs. As president, J. Gregory Smith's management became increasingly illogical and complaints about his honesty and management system increased, so Cooke found himself taking an active role in the railroad to the detriment of his banking house.

Convinced of Smith's dishonesty, Cooke forced his resignation in 1872, but then had no operational replacement for months. Meanwhile Cooke's younger banking partners, angry at his inability to develop new business as well as the time he was spending on Northern Pacific matters, became increasingly concerned about the company's future. Making matters worse, publicity concerning Indian attacks on the railroad's surveyors meant that bond sales dried up. By mid-1873, both his banking house and the Northern Pacific were all but out of cash; Cooke's New York partners then rebelled, literally shutting the doors to his Wall Street office.

Cooke lived in retirement after 1873, seemingly content after emerging from bankruptcy with a few million dollars: "I have been to the top of the tower and do not wish to do so again."

FREDERICK BILLINGS

Frederick Billings (1823–90) was a Vermont native, lawyer, and businessman who played a major role in the development of the Northern Pacific Railroad and its emigration policies, and for whom the Montana city is named. After graduating from the University of Vermont at age twenty, he practiced law, but caught up by gold rush fever, he was in California by early 1849, becoming one of the state's leading and wealthiest attorneys. Billings played an active role in keeping California in the Union, but in 1864 returned to Vermont. A longtime friend of Northern Pacific president J. Gregory Smith, Billings purchased a one-twelfth interest in the railroad in 1869 and joined its board of directors the following March.

A major goal of the Northern Pacific was to attract emigrants from northern Europe through the sale of Federally-certified lands, and in 1870 the Northern Pacific's board selected Billings to chair its Land Committee. Billings was soon quarreling with Smith and his backers, and was given little support to survey and get title to land paralleling completed track, an estimated 2.9 million acres in Minnesota. Working closely with Jay Cooke, Billings also undertook a massive effort to attract emigrants (over a million dollars was spent), but was stymied by European politics when the 1870 Franco–Prussian War forced Scandinavian countries to temporarily prohibit emigration to the United States.

Following the Northern Pacific's 1873 bankruptcy, Billings played a key role in keeping the railroad solvent. That the Northern Pacific would even survive was in doubt, for it had financial obligations to more than 11,000 bondholders, to say nothing of outside creditors and political forces wanting its termination. These issues were not fully resolved until mid-1875, leaving the railroad existent but without a penny of credit. Given these problems and his unquestioned ability, that same year Billings was chosen to be chairman of the Northern Pacific's executive committee.

With operational economies and increasing land sales, construction was renewed in 1876. Primary efforts were on the west coast to reach western Cascade coal deposits forty miles from Tacoma, and in turn other spurs were initiated in Minnesota and Dakota. In 1878 Billings put together a $2 million bond package for track between Bismarck and the Yellowstone at Glendive Creek, construction beginning the next spring, and in May 1879 he assumed the Northern Pacific presidency upon Charles B. Wright's resignation for health reasons. Highly respected, Billings was soon closeted with Anthony J. Drexel and J. P. Morgan to finance the railroad's completion, resulting in a $40 million first mortgage bond issue dated January 1, 1881.

Because of Billings' reputation and Wall Street support, the western part of the Northern Pacific's route was suddenly seen as a competitive threat by the president of the Oregon Railway and Navigation Co., Henry Villard. In a series of complex legal and financial moves, including the famous "blind pool" with which he purchased Northern Pacific stock, Villard seized control of the Northern Pacific in June 1881, forcing Billings to resign. To everyone's surprise, Billings and Villard soon became friends and entered into an effective working relationship, Villard appointing him chairman of the Northern Pacific's executive committee that September, and asking him to make one of the major speeches at the final spike ceremonies two years later. With Villard's 1884 resignation, Billings had the opportunity to become president again, but declined for reasons of health and devoted the last years of his life to philanthropy, travel, and family affairs.

THE BOOK THAT GATHERS NO DUST

Nothing better reflects the reach of the nation's once-extensive railway network than a single bulky periodical, *The Official Guide of the Railways and Steam Navigation Lines of the United States, Porto Rico, Canada, Mexico and Cuba.* At one time it was the world's biggest monthly publication—more than sixteen hundred pages of train schedules and related information. The first issue appeared in June 1868 in New York City, and the last *Official Guide* was published as late as 1995. It has been described as "the book that gathers no dust," because for years it enjoyed heavy use in every railroad station across the United States. It is no coincidence that the widely acclaimed "inventor" of standard time (see page 31) was William F. Allen, who became editor of the *Official Guide* in 1873.

Month after month for more than a century, the publication's pages faithfully chronicled the expansion, consolidation, and contraction of the North American railway network. For any given minute the *Official Guide* showed where every scheduled passenger train in North America was supposed to be.

For several of the routes in this volume, we have reproduced facsimile pages from the August 1906 edition, with detailed information about main line and connecting services, and the facilities offered en route.

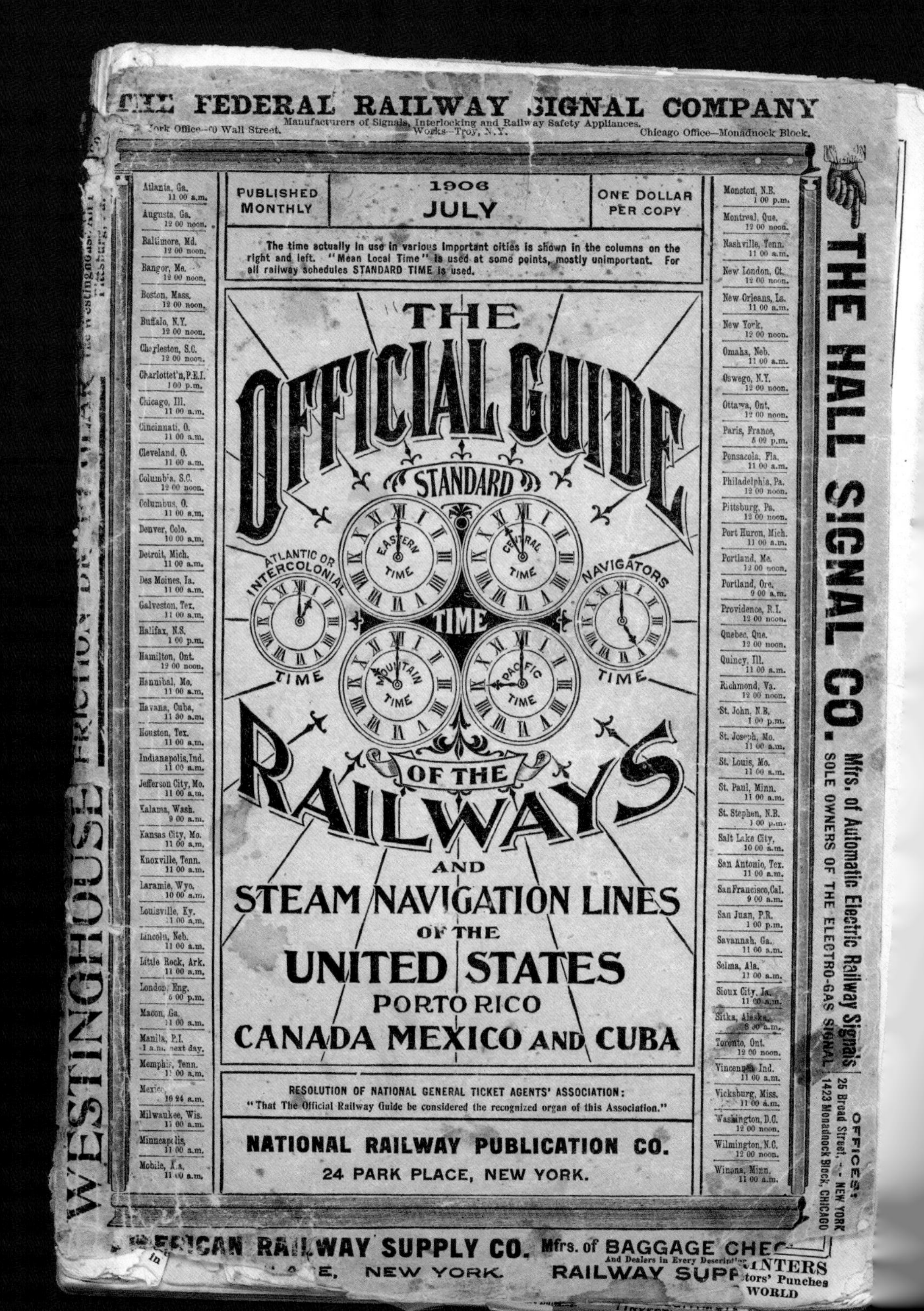

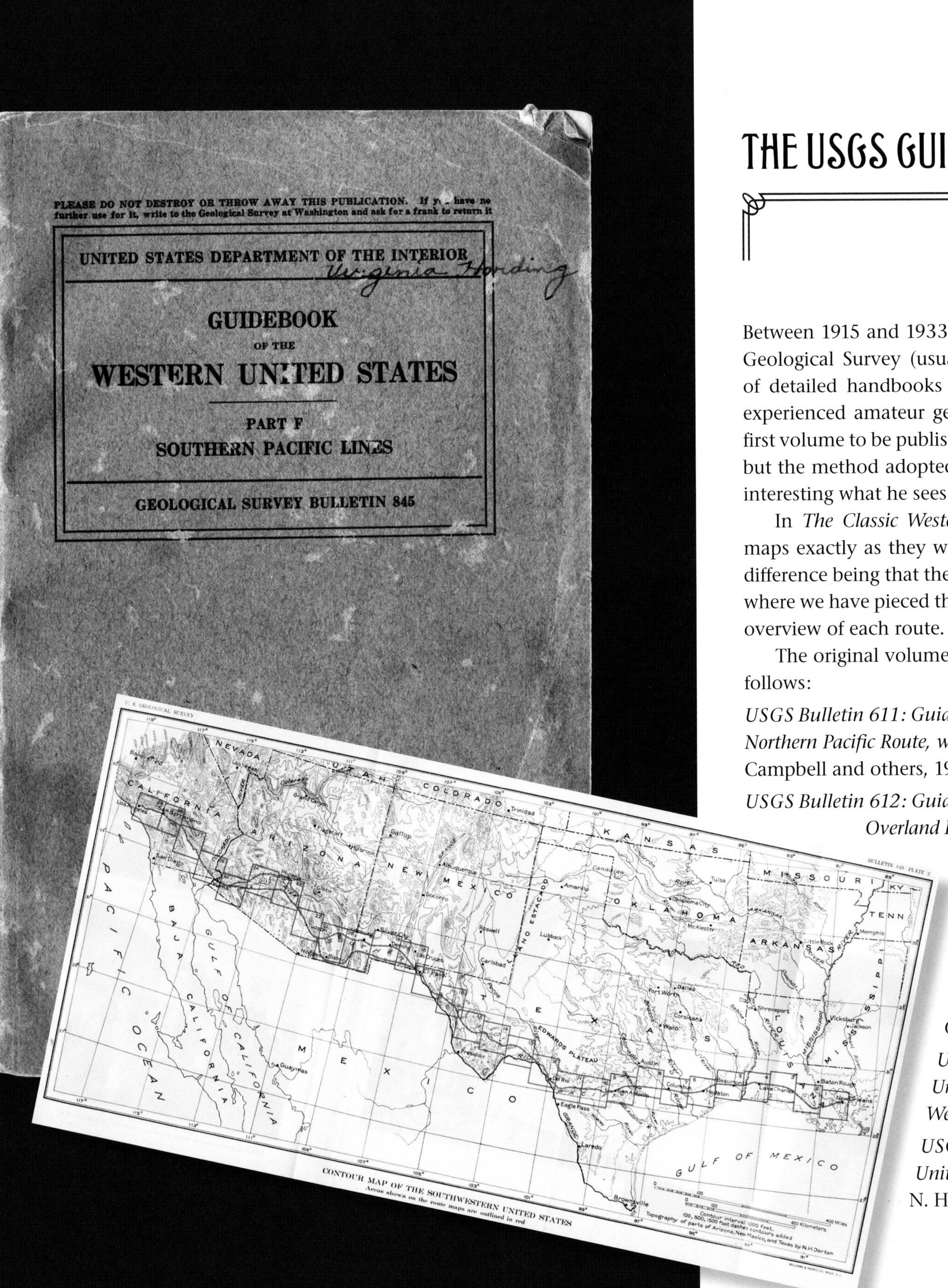

THE USGS GUIDEBOOKS

Between 1915 and 1933 the United States Department of the Interior Geological Survey (usually referred to as USGS) produced a series of detailed handbooks for railroad travelers, many of whom were experienced amateur geologists. As George Otis Smith wrote in the first volume to be published, "These books are educational in purpose, but the method adopted is to entertain the traveler by making more interesting what he sees from the car window."

In *The Classic Western Railroad Routes* we have reproduced the maps exactly as they were printed in the original volumes, the only difference being that they were originally included as foldout sections where we have pieced them together jigsaw-wise to present a seamless overview of each route.

The original volumes from which the maps are reproduced are as follows:

USGS Bulletin 611: Guidebook of the Western United States; Part A: The Northern Pacific Route, with a side trip to Yellowstone Park, by Marius R. Campbell and others, 1915.

USGS Bulletin 612: Guidebook of the Western United States; Part B: The Overland Route, by Willis T. Lee, Ralph W. Stone, Hoyt S. Gale and others, 1915.

USGS Bulletin 613: Guidebook of the Western United States; Part C: The Santa Fe Route, by N. H. Darton and others, 1915.

USGS Bulletin 614: Guidebook of the Western United States; Part D: The Shasta Route and Coast Line, by J. S. Diller and others, 1915.

USGS Bulletin 707: Guidebook of the Western United States; Part E: The Denver & Rio Grande Western Route, by Marius R. Campbell, 1922.

USGS Bulletin 845: Guidebook of the Western United States; Part F: Southern Pacific Lines, by N. H. Darton, 1933.

THE OVERLAND ROUTE

UNION PACIFIC/CENTRAL PACIFIC, OMAHA TO SAN FRANCISCO

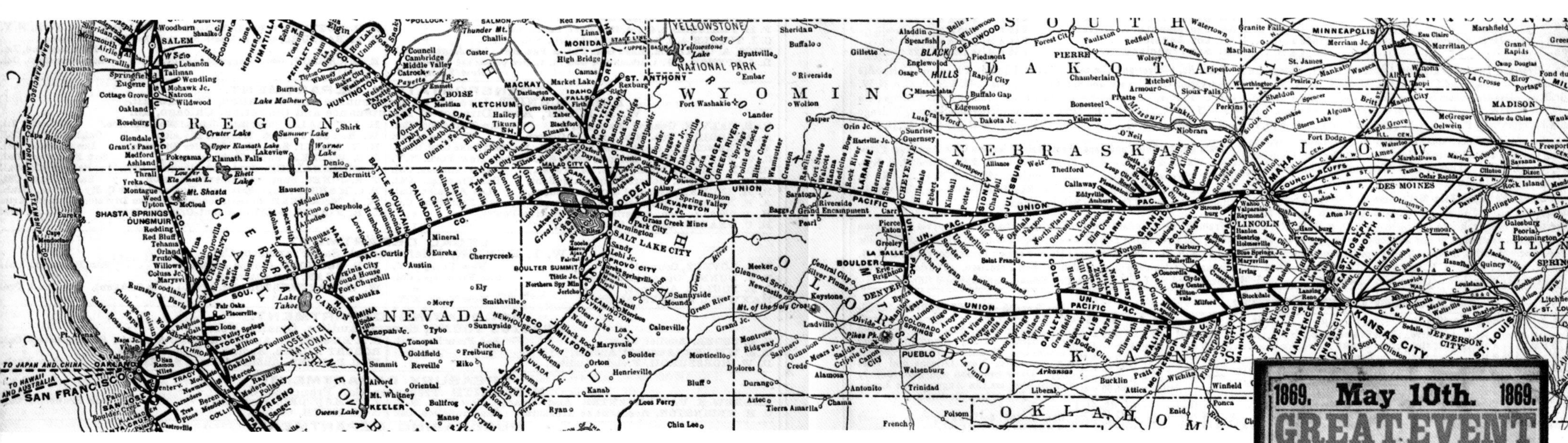

"Dot, Dot, Dot … D–O–N–E."

This simple message, sent out in the spring of 1869 over a plain copper telegraph wire from an otherwise barren desert plateau high in the Utah Territory, was greeted throughout the still relatively young continental nation of which it was a part by the pealing of church bells, firing of cannons, great fireworks displays, flowery congratulatory speeches, and dancing in the streets. The joyful news that this single word carried told the country that it finally had a transcontinental railroad.

Since the first spade of muddy, rain-soaked earth of the monumental new "Pacific Railroad" (as it was then popularly known) had been turned in Sacramento, California, six years and four months earlier on January 8, 1863 (not to mention another four decades of "dreaming, scheming, talking, and toiling" before that), the dispatch of this simple combination of eleven "dots" and "dashes" of American Morse (or "railroad") code had been eagerly anticipated by the American people in much the same way that their great-great-grandchildren would await the words "That's one small step for a man; one giant leap for mankind" spoken by another American almost exactly a century later from a far more desolate and remote "desert" some quarter of a million miles distant from the first.

In just a few fleeting seconds, each of these two succinct messages told both America and the world of the successful accomplishment of what would arguably prove to be the country's greatest and most significant engineering achievements of the nineteenth and twentieth centuries respectively. The first message was tapped out from Promontory Summit, Utah Territory, by Union Pacific telegrapher W. N. Skilling in the early afternoon of May 10, 1869, announcing that the rails of the Central Pacific Railroad of California built east from Sacramento, and of the Union Pacific Railroad built west from Omaha, had been successfully joined with the driving of a "Last Spike" to form what would eventually come to be known as the "Overland"

1869. May 10th. 1869.
GREAT EVENT
Rail Road from the Atlantic to the Pacific
GRAND OPENING OF THE
Union Pacific
RAIL ROAD,
PLATTE VALLEY ROUTE.
PASSENGER TRAINS LEAVE
OMAHA
ON THE ARRIVAL OF TRAINS FROM THE EAST.
THROUGH TO SAN FRANCISCO
In less than Four Days, avoiding the Dangers of the Sea!
Travelers for Pleasure, Health or Business
LUXURIOUS CARS & EATING HOUSES
ON THE UNION PACIFIC RAIL ROAD.
PULLMAN'S PALACE SLEEPING CARS
GOLD, SILVER AND OTHER MINERS!
CHEYENNE for DENVER, CENTRAL CITY & SANTA FE
THROUGH TICKETS FOR SALE AT ALL PRINCIPAL RAILROAD OFFICES!
Be Sure they Read via Platte Valley or Omaha

Palisade Canyon, Nevada, *c.*1902.

"Big engineering" on the Central Pacific–Newcastle Trestle, Placer County, California (left); the Bloomer Cut in the western foothills of the Sierras between the California towns of Auburn and Newcastle (right).

route to California – the first complete rail link across the continental United States from the Atlantic to the Pacific.

The second message was uttered equally matter-of-factly on July 20, 1969 by Neil Armstrong from the "magnificent desolation" of the surface of the moon from where it was transmitted along with a faint television signal to be relayed around the world. More than half a billion people heard or watched the transmission as the then 38-year-old American astronaut and *Apollo 11* commander became the first man to ever set foot on the surface of a globe other than the earth's.

Just a dozen men–all Americans–would eventually leave their footprints on the lunar landscape between 1969 and 1972 when the Apollo project was halted after just six manned landings. After that memorable day in 1869, however, literally tens of millions of men, women, and children from every corner of this world would ride the rails of the Overland route across the plains, deserts, and mountains of the American West as they traveled between the nation's heartland and its "Golden Gate" to the Pacific. With the railway's completion, Lewis M. Clement, the Central Pacific's then 32-year-old Canadian-born chief assistant engineer and the man mainly responsible for the location and construction of the road's most challenging section of grade over California's rugged Sierra Nevada mountains, called the new route "the bond of iron which is to hold our glorious country in one eternal union." Veteran Union Pacific consulting engineer Silas Seymour agreed as he declared simply that there was "Nothing like it in the world."

THE GREAT ENTERPRISE

The physical and financial obstacles that had to be overcome in building the "Great Enterprise" had been almost universally considered to still be far beyond the capability of both the government and the private interests that took on the challenge of building the vast new railroad. But its

A Pullman dining car being laid for dinner, a hand-colored plate from Charles Nordhoff's 1874 classic *California: A Book for Travellers and Settlers*. The illustration shows how magnificently the Pullmans were appointed.

importance in physically binding together the two halves of the continually expanding young nation, and the potential rewards to the companies for doing so, were too compelling for either to ignore. The CPRR's Clement reflected on these dual imperatives almost two decades later in a statement he made in 1887 to the US Pacific Railway Commission. "At the beginning of the construction, the company, knowing the political and commercial necessities demanding the rapid completion of the railroad, determined that nothing which was in their power to prevent should for a single day arrest its progress," he told the Commission.

"With this determination in view all energies were bent, fully realizing the physical obstacles and financial difficulties to be overcome. The financial difficulties were not lessened by the opinions circulated to the effect that the obstacles were insurmountable; that the railroads then constructed in Europe were as bagatelles compared with the difficulties to be met in constructing the Central Pacific Railroad, and failure was clearly written on the rocky sides of the canyons and the bold granite walls of the Sierra Nevada mountains.

"Not only was it impossible to construct a railroad across the Sierras via Donner Pass, but owing to the great depth of snow, some years reaching an aggregate fall of nearly fifty feet, it would be impracticable to operate, and if built must be closed to traffic in the winter months, which would have been the case had not the road been protected at great cost by snowsheds.

"Against these utterances from men of railroad experience the company had to battle in financial circles, forcing them to show that they were not attempting an impossibility, though always realizing the great difficulties."

The Pacific Railroad Act of 1862 that was signed into law by President Abraham Lincoln on July 1, 1862 gave the Central Pacific and Union Pacific Railroad Companies until July 1, 1876—the eve of the nation's centennial—to complete the great project of physically connecting the Atlantic and Pacific by rail. However, despite those many seemingly "insurmountable obstacles and challenges" in their paths—not to mention three

more years of a bitter Civil War which had been raging since 1861—amazingly the two companies not only beat that deadline, but did so with more than seven years to spare!

The benefit to the nation of the opening of the "Pacific Railroad" between Council Bluffs/Omaha (where it connected to the existing eastern rail network) and San Francisco (via Sacramento) was immediate and profound as it finally made "rapid" (as little as a week) coast-to-coast overland travel both practical and affordable to the masses for the first time. Travelers could now avoid the previous necessity to devote anywhere from six weeks to up to six months to make such a trip, and could do so mostly without the exposure to such perils as disease, shipwreck, bandits, and the extremes of climate, which all such voyagers had previously faced in order to make the arduous passage by sailing ship around Cape Horn, 17,000 miles by sea, via ocean-going mail steamers and the Panama Railway, or overland by "prairie schooner" across the often hostile plains, harsh deserts, towering Rockies, and snowy Sierras. The railroad also opened up vast untapped lands in the West to settlement and development.

California souvenir playing cards c.1900, showing a snowplow and Cape Horn (above left).

Omaha (top right) and the Truckee River, c.1910 (bottom right).

The *Overland Limited* entering the yards of Oakland Station, 1903.

"The railroad was a catalyst, an exciter, a pump primer which speeded up the process of settlement and escalated the West's income from agriculture, trade and industry," observed the noted Utah historian, Professor Leonard Arrington, on the occasion of the Overland Route's centenary in 1969. "Completion of the first transcontinental line set in motion a chain reaction of developments which culminated in advanced economics of such great cities as Los Angeles, San Francisco, Salt Lake City, Denver, Phoenix, and Omaha. But the railroad was more. It was a medium of cultural interchange and excitement. Trains brought visitors from Boston, New York, London, Berlin, and Tokyo to observe the 'New America.' They were impressed and wrote books—tons of them. While the railroad helped to build the western economy, it also helped to create the 'myth' of the West—a myth that has been preserved in thousands of novels, movies, and television serials. The West of immigration and the West of reality were both products of the joining of the rails at Promontory, Utah, on May 10, 1869."

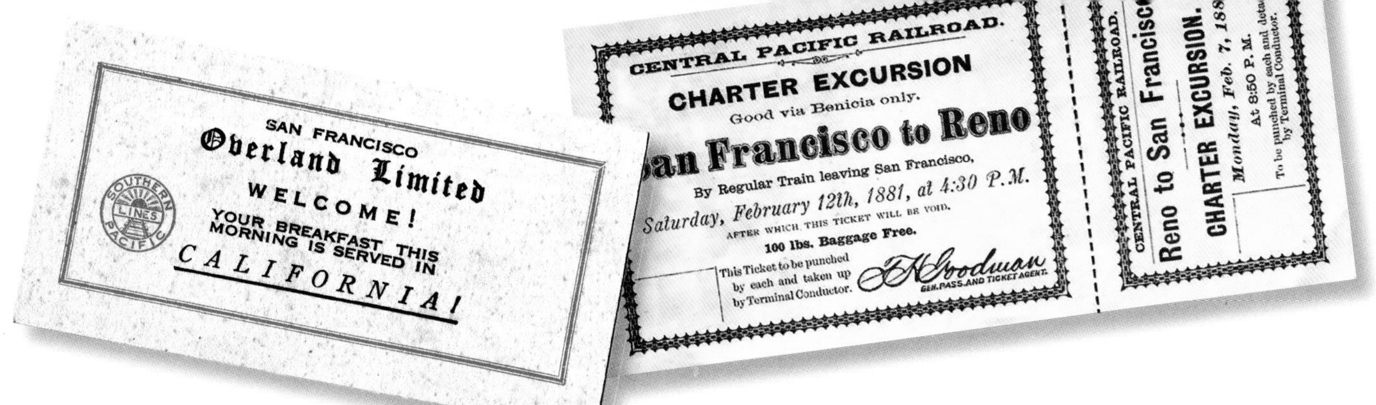

OVERLAND RAIL TRAVEL BY EMIGRANT CAR

Although a vast improvement over earlier methods, most transcontinental rail travel in the 1870s and 1880s was nonetheless often still fraught with unexpected challenges, delays, and hardships, especially for those who made the journey to seek their fortunes as they ventured beyond the Mississippi and Missouri Rivers on the early "emigrant" trains of the Union and Central Pacific.

Famed Scottish novelist Robert Louis Stevenson, who made such a "steerage" journey between Omaha and San Francisco in 1879, noted that the cars "destined for emigrants on the Union Pacific are only remarkable for their extreme plainness, nothing but wood entering in any part into their constitution, and for the usual inefficacy of the lamps, which often went out and shed but a dying glimmer even while they burned. The benches are too short for anything but a young child. Where there is scarce elbowroom for two to sit, there will not be space enough for one to lie."

Emigrant trains usually crawled along at just twenty miles an hour or less, and often spent an hour or more periodically sitting on remote sidings to allow higher priority traffic to pass on the otherwise single track line. At seven and a half days, the scheduled time for a trip from Omaha to San Francisco on an emigrant train was a full three days longer than for the express service, and even this was approximate at best. Stops for food were haphazard and often far too brief for a comfortable meal. Coaches were often broiling hot in summer and freezing in winter, during which emigrant trains also suffered frequent delays owing to snowdrifts, track closures, and breakdowns.

"Haste is not the foible of an emigrant train," observed Stevenson of his seemingly endless journey. "It gets through on sufferance, running the gauntlet among its more considerable brethren; should there be a block, it is unhesitatingly sacrificed; and they cannot, in consequence, predict the length of the passage within a day or so. Civility is the main comfort that you miss. Equality, though conceived very largely in America, does not extend so low down as to an emigrant. Thus in all other trains, a warning cry of 'All aboard!' recalls the passengers to take their seats; but as soon as I was alone with emigrants, and from the Transfer all the way to San Francisco, I found this ceremony was pretermitted; the train stole from the station without note of warning, and you had to keep an eye upon it even while you ate. The annoyance is considerable, and the disrespect both wanton and petty."

Still, travel by such a train for emigrants was far superior, cheaper, and easier than any earlier alternative, and over the decades after the route opened it helped to both quickly populate the West, and to enrich the country by providing the first real artery of transportation for the exchange of goods as well as people in both directions.

OVERLAND RAIL TRAVEL BY PALACE CAR

Those who could afford rail travel on one of the "more considerable brethren" referred to by Stevenson did so in style, riding in "Pullman Palace Cars" on the Union Pacific and "Silver Palace Cars" on the Central Pacific, taking their meals on board in beautifully-appointed dining cars. Charles Nordhoff, a noted American travel writer and onetime managing editor of the *New York Evening Post*, wrote of the unexpected luxury he found on such a trip in his popular 1874 treatise *California: A Book for Travellers and Settlers.*

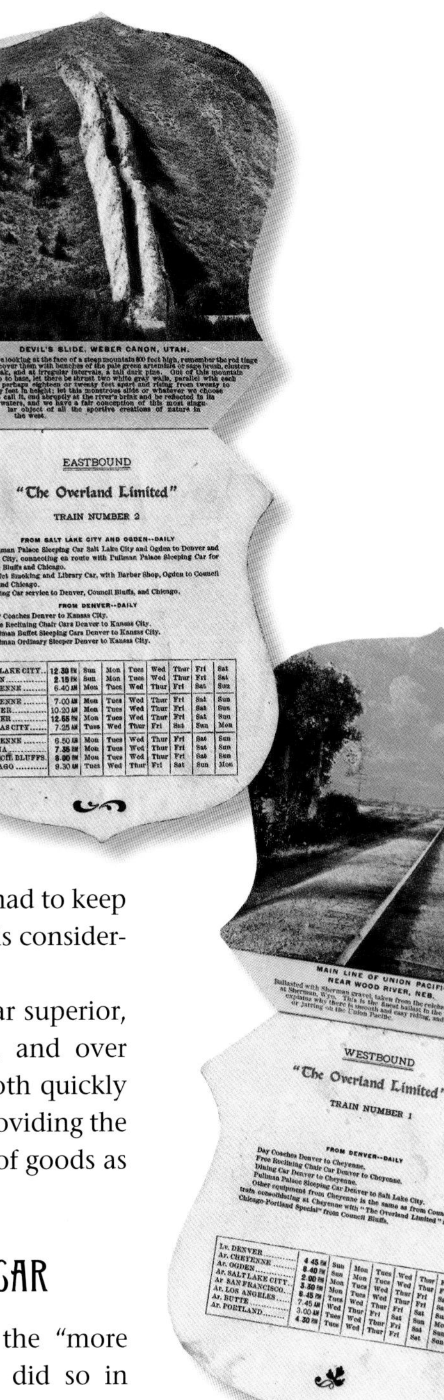

Ephemera from the Overland Route—tickets and pocket timetables.

Train emerging from a snowshed on the Ogden Route (above).

Pullman Palace drawing room and sleeping car (below).

"The superiority of the American sleeping cars is in their cleanliness, the perfection of their heating and ventilating contrivances, and the presence of everything which can make a car convenient to live in," he noted. "There is nothing like them in Europe, and all European travelers in this country have been surprised and delighted with them.

"The Pullman hotel car is one of the most ingenious as well as one of the most convenient of all modern arrangements for travel. It can seat forty persons at the tables; it contains not only a kitchen–which is a marvel of compactness, having a sink, with hot and cold water faucets, and every 'modern convenience'–but a wine closet, a china closet, a linen closet, and provision lockers so spacious as to contain supplies for thirty people all the way from Chicago to the Pacific if necessary."

The route's first scheduled "extra fare" service began after its completion with the establishment in October, 1869, of a weekly "Special Palace Car Express" leaving Omaha every Tuesday morning and arriving in San Francisco on Friday, with the return service departing California on Monday morning for a Thursday arrival in Omaha. The fare for the four-day passage was $168.00 including double berth in a sleeping car, or the equivalent of almost $2,800 today.

This premium service was soon abandoned, however, as being both uneconomical and because the speeds necessary to maintain an 81-hour schedule of the unusually weighty train equipment left "roadmasters complaining that the regular scheduling of these fast, heavy trains were reducing tracks and right of way to a condition where they would soon be inoperable." The original line was built using iron "pear" rail which was much softer and less durable than the heavier steel track that would eventually replace it, so wear was of considerable concern.

THE OVERLAND ROUTE

The name "Overland" was not formally adopted for any part of the Omaha to San Francisco route until almost two decades after it opened, when the Union Pacific inaugurated service of its *Overland Flyer* on November 13, 1887 between Omaha and Ogden, Utah, where passengers and through cars were transferred to the Southern Pacific which had acquired the CPRR's operations on that line in 1885 under a 99-year lease. The UP changed its designation to the *Overland Limited* on November 17, 1895, and service continued as a daily train under that name in one form or another for almost seven decades. For the first dozen years that the SP met the UP's "Overland" trains, however, it dubbed its service "The Ogden Gateway Route" with its connecting westbound trains operating as the *Pacific Express* and eastbound trains as the *Atlantic Express*, before finally adopting the name the *Overland Limited* in 1899 for its portion of the run as well.

The original 1,911 miles of the route from Omaha to San Francisco traversed some of the most desolate–as well as some of the most picturesque–lands of the western two-thirds of the North American continent. While the trip originally took the early "emigrant" trains a full week or more to complete, by the 1920s and 1930s the all-Pullman extra fare *Overland Limited* trains covered the route in just two days, largely as a result of upgrades and technical improvements to the route's infrastructure, locomotives, and rolling stock.

Over the years, both the SP's and UP's roads were completely double tracked, the rickety and often precariously high temporary wooden trestles were either filled in or replaced with steel structures, and many of the more challenging segments along their grades were realigned or shortened to improve both the comfort and efficiency of transcontinental overland travel. Among the most important of these improvements to the original grade was a completely new 102.9-mile stretch built right after the turn of the century just west of Ogden, Utah known as "The Lucin Cutoff," which included a

The *Overland Limited* at Floriston, California, *c.*1902.

spectacular twelve-mile-long trestle originally built on wooden pilings across the Great Salt Lake. This new section of the line cut 43.8 miles off the trip, eliminated 3,919 degrees of curvature, and removed 1,515 feet of gradient from the route, which thus decreased the steepest SP grade in Utah from 90 feet per mile to a far more manageable 21.

Except for double tracking and other similar system-wide upgrades in basic infrastructure, however, many other sections of the original grade proved to have been so skillfully located by the original surveyors and engineers who laid them out in the 1860s that they remain virtually unchanged even today. Key among these is the original grade over the Sierra Nevada between Colfax, California, and Reno, Nevada, as it was first located a century and a half ago by the CPRR's original chief engineer, T. D. Judah, and his two key assistants, S. S. Montague and L. M. Clement. After Judah's death in 1863, Montague and Clement also supervised the entire CPRR route's construction efforts as chief engineer and chief assistant engineer respectively.

There have been some changes along their original grade in the Sierras, of course, such as the removal of many of the original wooden snowsheds (or their replacement by nonflammable concrete ones), and the eventual abandonment in 1993 of the 6.7-mile section of the Track No. 1 crossing of the summit through Donner Pass between Norden and Eder, which includes the original 1,659-foot long Summit Tunnel (No. 6). Traffic was sent instead over the easier-to-maintain Track No. 2 and through the 10,322-foot-long tunnel called "The Big Hole" (No. 41) which had been driven under Mount Judah just a mile south of the pass when that portion of the line was double tracked in 1925. Aside from those modifications, however, the rest of the "Sierra Grade" remains virtually unchanged, and thus still looks much the same way to train passengers as it did when this part of the line first opened in 1868.

THE DEMISE OF THE OVERLAND LIMITED

As intercity passenger rail travel began to decline after the Second World War and into the 1950s with the growth of the airline industry and development of the Interstate Highway System, the Overland Route gradually lost its luster and service declined. After almost seven decades of continuous operation, the *Overland Limited* officially came to an end as a daily train on July 16, 1962, when the Interstate Commerce Commission approved termination of the service. While the train continued to run until Labor Day (with some additional holiday runs from Christmas to the New Year), the name "Overland" did not appear in the schedules of the UP or SP again after its last run on January 2, 1963. The only daily passenger train service between Omaha (now via Denver and Salt Lake City) and San Francisco today is provided by the *California Zephyr* operated by the US government-owned National Railroad Passenger Corporation (Amtrak), which took over all long-haul intercity passenger train service in the United States in May, 1971.

PROMONTORY

Meeting of East and West

Promontory Trestle, one of the last hurdles in the race to complete the Overland Route.

Although it was clear by late 1868 that the Union Pacific's grade would reach Ogden ahead of its western rival, the CPRR's Leland Stanford understood well the strategic importance of the line west of Ogden between Blue Creek and Monument Point. If this line could be graded, occupied, and defended in time, the Central Pacific might yet gain the leverage they needed to extend into Ogden, or certainly to halt the Union Pacific's progress westwards. Both companies thus sent in their crews to attack this last stretch of difficult terrain, with the Central Pacific contracting additional Mormon laborers to step up the pace, and the Union Pacific belatedly relocating gangs from Humboldt Wells, Nevada, in response.

Stanford's plan eventually succeeded, and by the year's end much of this line had been surveyed and graded under the determined direction and supervision of CPRR resident engineer Lewis M. Clement before the Union Pacific crews had even begun to move west of Ogden. Spurred on by their rival's progress, however, and in an apparent attempt to interfere with the work of the Central Pacific crews already in progress, Union Pacific surveyors hurriedly ran lines from Ogden to Bear River, crisscrossing those already marked out by Clement's crews. The federal government objected to the needless extra work, so a compromise was finally arrived at between the two companies which, when ratified by Congress on April 10, 1869, granted both lines access to the Great Basin with a common terminus established at Ogden. Although the Union

The final race by the Central Pacific and Union Pacific toward each other took place in the barren deserts and treacherous mountains of the Utah Territory, where it culminated with the meeting of the two roads at a rugged mountain pass through the Promontory Mountains, just north of the Great Salt Lake and some 53 rail miles northwest of the Great Basin city of Ogden. While the CP's approach from the west to the 4,943-foot summit of this pass, rising some 731 feet above the level of the lake, was deceptively gradual as the grade sloped its way to the crest over sixteen relatively gentle miles, the UP's eastern grade was far more challenging as it covered topography almost twice as steep.

Thomas Hill's famous painting, "The Last Spike," and two photographs of the actual event by A. J. Russell.

CENTRAL PACIFIC

RAILROAD.

COMMENCING MAY 17, 1869, EXpress Trains will run daily as follows:

EASTWARD.	Miles.	Time.
Leave Sacramento	—	6:39 A. M.
" Colfax	54	9:50 A. M
" Truckee	120	2:10 P. M.
" Reno	154	4:20 P. M.
" Wadsworth	189	6:30 P. M.
" Winnemucca	324	1:45 A. M.
" Carlin	445	8:30 A. M.
" Elko	468	10:00 A. M.
" Toano	559	3:15 P. M.
Arrive at Promontory	690	11:05 P. M.

WESTWARD.	Miles.	Time.
Leave Promontory	—	6:15 P. M.
" Toano	131	3:00 A. M.
" Elko	222	8:25 A. M
" Carlin	245	9:35 A. M.
" Winnemucca	366	4:10 P. M.
" Wadsworth	501	12:05 A. M.
" Reno	536	2:10 A. M.
" Truckee	570	4:20 A. M.
" Colfax	636	9:50 A. M.
Arrive at Sacramento	690	1:20 P. M.

FARE.

	Coin
Sacramento to Terminus	$50 0

Children not over twelve (12) years of age half fare; under five (5) years of age, free 100 pounds baggage (per passenger) free.

Two Trains daily (Sundays excepted) between Sacramento and Marysville, without any change of cars:

Leave Sacramento at 6:30 A. M. and 2 P. M.
Arrive at Marysville at 9:30 A. M. and 5:30 P. M
Leave Marysville at 5:30 A. M. and 10:10 A. M.
Arrive at Sacramento at 9:45 A. M. and 1:20 P. M.

For tickets and other information, apply at the Company's offices in Sacramento.

CHAS. CROCKER,
General Superintendent.
T. H. GOODMAN,
Gen'l. Passenger Agent.

The following are the present rates of fare via UNION PACIFIC and connecting Roads:

Promontory to—	Currency.
Omaha	$81 50
St. Louis	101 50
Chicago	103 50
Cincinnati	114 85
Niagara Falls	118 90
New York	123 50
Boston	126 50

(Rates are subject to change.)

May 17, 1869. 265d&sw tf

An 1869 view of "Promontory City," the temporary town established by the CPRR to help fulfil all its workers' "needs" (above).

A May, 1869, display advertisement from the Salt Lake *Daily Telegraph* for the CPRR's newly opened through service to Promontory, and a handbill promoting the meal service for train travelers at Promontory's "Golden Spike Hotel."

A hand-colored full-page engraving of the "Last Spike" ceremony from *Harper's Weekly* (opposite).

Pacific continued to build its line west from Ogden to the summit, it agreed to sell the 53-mile segment of the grade to the Central Pacific once the rails of the two lines were joined a month later.

On May 10, 1869, government and railway officials joined hundreds of tired but jubilant construction workers from both railroads for a ceremonial linking of the two lines' tracks at the otherwise barren summit pass located some 27 miles north of the tip of Promontory Point. Amidst great noise and commotion, Union Pacific locomotive No. 119 and Central Pacific's No. 60 (called *Jupiter*) were drawn up "pilot-to-pilot," so that little more than the span of a final tie made of polished California laurel separated the two steam engines. "The crowd pushed upon the workmen so closely that less than twenty persons saw the affair entirely," wrote newspaperman John H. Beadle in the *Utah Daily Reporter* of the chaotic scene.

Central Pacific president Leland Stanford and Union Pacific vice president Thomas Durant were to perform the ceremonial coupling, but seemingly nervous and awkward among the true "iron men" of the railroad, both men bungled the symbolic driving of the last spike. To the crowd's loud amusement, each missed the spike entirely, leaving it to their more "hands on" colleagues, construction superintendents James Strobridge of the CP and Sam Reed of the UP, to complete the job. The importance of the occasion was not lost on its many spectators as one of the United States' first nationwide, even global, media events, and it remains so significant even today that the US state quarter issued in 2007 commemorating Utah's 1896 admission to the Union depicts the last spike ceremony as "Crossroads of the West" on the reverse ("tails") side of the coin.

In spite of the formidable costs in coin and labor of building the grade over Promontory Summit, ironically use of the route was relatively short-lived. As early as 1902 the Southern Pacific Railroad (which had leased the Central Pacific's portion of the "Overland Route" in 1885) decided to replace it with "The Lucin Cutoff" across the Great Salt Lake, which cut 43 miles off the overall route when it opened in 1904. Redundant and disused, the rails over Promontory Summit were finally taken up as salvage in 1942 for use in the war effort, thus bringing this chapter of the story of the great Overland Route to a conclusion.

LUCIN CUTOFF

Conquering the Great Salt Lake

The famed Lucin Cutoff west of Ogden, Utah, was one of a number of the key improvements made to the Overland Route under the direction of the Southern Pacific's legendary chief engineer, William Hood, during the tenure of Edward Henry Harriman who was president of the SP from 1901 until his death in 1909. Designed as a bypass for the original convoluted 1869 grade around the north end of the Great Salt Lake through Promontory Summit with its difficult curvatures and gradients, the 102-mile-long cutoff included an innovative twelve-mile raised causeway that crossed the deep salt flats and waters of the lake and shortened the original length of the section of the route between Ogden and Lucin by 43.8 miles.

The possibility of a cutoff running across the Great Salt Lake had been toyed with by the Central Pacific as early as the 1860s when soundings were taken of the lake, but without sufficient experience to interpret the results the company was unable to accurately resolve where the bottom of the lake was or its relative stability. At the time the CP was also unable to determine the effect of salt on the construction materials, and another unknown factor was the impact of storm conditions and wind-driven waves on the causeway. The lake route was thus thought to constitute too forbidding a challenge during the line's original construction, forcing the Central Pacific to opt for the less desirable land route to its north. As technology advanced, by the turn of the century the SP revisited the original CPRR surveys—then more than thirty years old—which, along with William Hood's newer 1899 engineering study, led Harriman to shut his ears to the protestations of the rival Salt Lake City lobby and take on the challenge of building a railroad across the lake.

The wooden trestle built across the water between 1902 and 1904 was an engineering wonder of its time. In bridge-and-fill work it was the most ambitious engineering and construction project yet attempted, with over 23 miles of trestle built in the lake's waters (much of it used just for the construction) employing over 28,000 piles, each around 120 feet long. The project was to require the sweat and toil of 3,000 men working as a veritable private army of laborers, carpenters, mechanics, and engineers. Living in boarding houses raised on piles beyond the reach of the waves, these men worked in ten-hour shifts for seven days a week. Liquor was banned, and any packages addressed to the workmen were opened and searched to ensure that the prohibition was enforced. There was no entertainment other than music for those that could play, or books for the few who could read. Only the men with wives and children had the benefit of society with folk who were not at work on the railroad.

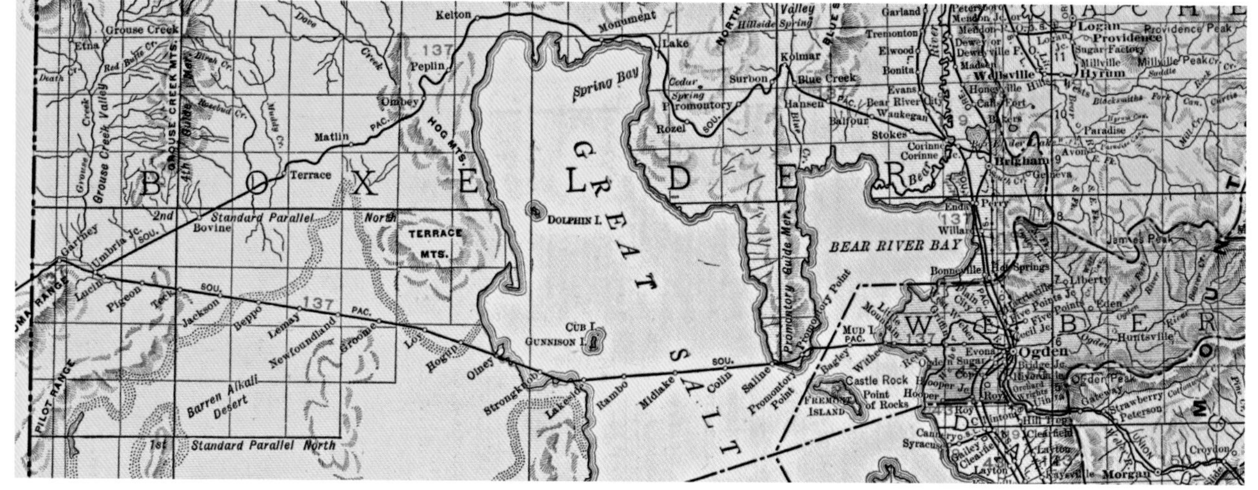

Great Salt Lake map from *The Library Atlas of the World*, 1912.

In the early days of the Cutoff it was common practice for the train to stop at the Salt Lake saltbeds for passengers to marvel at their country's equivalent of the Dead Sea, from *The Great Salt Lake Country*, published by The Williamson-Haffner Engraving Co., Denver, in 1906.

"The Great Lucien (sic) Cutoff,"
from *The Great Salt Lake Country*.

The Lucin Cutoff quickly became a favorite icon of illustrators and designers—trains running into the sunset promise of the Far West. Back cover and illustrations from *The Overland Route to the Road of a Thousand Wonders*, published by the Passenger Departments of the Union Pacific and Southern Pacific Railroads in 1908.

Progress was slow, though the procession of cars loaded up with rock from the quarries came steadily, hauled in by locomotives night and day like an endless caravan. Thousands of tons of rock were dumped off the end of the track into the apparently bottomless chasm beneath the oily surface of the lake. There were repeated episodes of sinking or "settling," most notoriously in Bear River Bay and a spot in the western arm of the lake called Rambo, when the weight of the fill broke its way through successive layers of crust and gradually found the true bottom surface. Records showed hundreds of occurrences of such settling of up to eight feet at a time continuing even well after the first freight trains had begun their to'ing and fro'ing across the tracks.

With the lake all but tamed, a permanent trestle was constructed to replace the temporary framework built for the construction phase. The last wood piles of a forest of timber were driven into the bed and, atop heavy redwood planking, three inches of asphalt roofing and a further fourteen inches of gravel ballast were laid, making it ready for opening at last.

On Thanksgiving Day, 1903, Harriman led a party of sixty railway company executives and eastern railroad leaders out across the track in fifteen luxury private cars brought in especially for the occasion. It was a moment of triumph for the ambitious railroad financier, and the benefits were immediately seen when freight trains began to use the Cutoff on March 6, 1904, to be joined by passenger trains six months later on September 18. The old road had reached its limits while the capacity of the new was increased out of all recognition. Formerly it had taken three locomotives from 30 to 36 hours to move 950 tons of freight. Across The Lucin Cutoff a single engine could haul almost two and a half times the load in less than nine hours.

LUCIN CUT-OFF, GREAT

LAKE TAHOE

"The Lake of The Sky"

The narrow gauge branch line from Truckee, California, to the waterfront at Lake Tahoe was the brainchild of Duane L. Bliss, an early prospector from the days of the Gold Rush of 1849. Turned entrepreneur and then banker, Bliss had a remarkable talent for anticipating the phases of development through which virgin country must pass to build a sustainable local economy. Bliss anticipated first the growing demand for and subsequent decline of the timberlands as they were needed as a resource for the burgeoning mines of the Comstock Lode, and then later he predicted the potential of the lakefront as a popular vacation spot for wealthy San Francisco residents. With that in mind he shrewdly developed his railroads to keep with the pace of change.

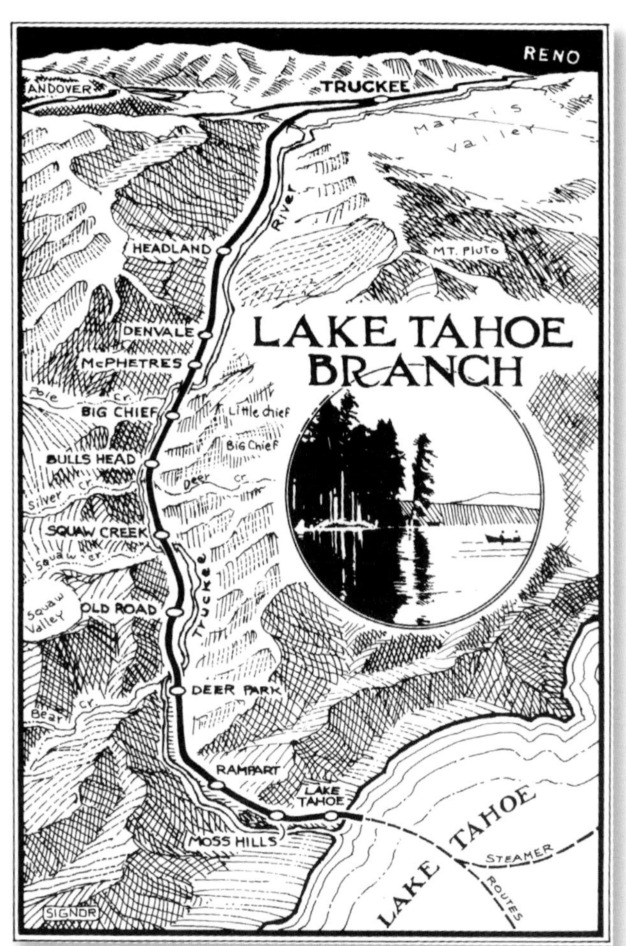

Cashing in on the mining boom centered on exploiting the rich ore deposits of the Comstock Lode, Bliss's love affair with Tahoe began with the purchase of extensive timberlands on the lake's eastern shores. Under the direction of the Carson-Tahoe Lumber & Fluming Company (in which Bliss was a partner) and backed by business associates at the Bank of California, in 1871 Bliss was able to obtain the right-of-way and credit to build an 8.75-mile-long connection between the sawmills of Glenbrook and the flume, or chute, at Spooner Summit, from where the lumber could be floated down valley to Carson. This short railroad featured numerous trestles and a short tunnel near the summit, and its construction was to provide important experience for the considerably more ambitious line that was to follow.

Albert Bierstadt's 1869 painting of "The Sierras from Lake Tahoe" shows an untouched, idyllic landscape, yet clearly daunting to the railroad builder.

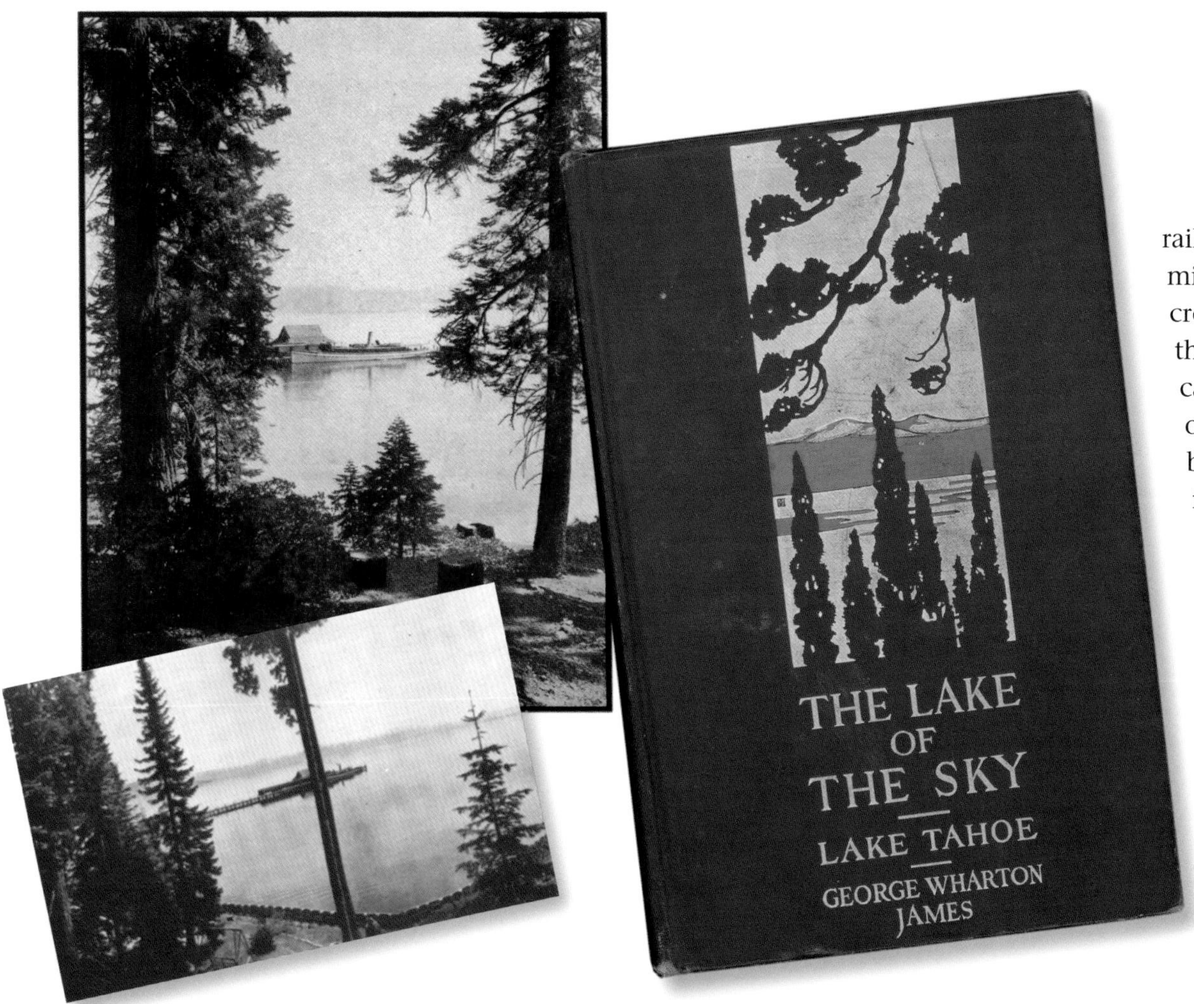

railroad began in 1898. To keep curvature to a minimum, the line was engineered to criss-cross the river over a succession of bridges, thus affording the traveler startling views of the canyon and the wild, helter-skelter crashing of logs "shooting the chutes" into the waters beneath. Rails, locomotives, passenger and freight cars, and all maintenance facilities were torn up and transported bodily across the Lake from Glenbrook.

Bliss had envisaged, and now executed to perfection, the development not only of a branch line, but also of a resort that would be second to none for luxury and style. Commissioning his son's architectural firm in San Francisco, he set about building a hotel, the Tahoe Tavern, and a pier from whence the railway would rendezvous with steam vessels that would tour the lake for the benefit of the visitors. Hotel guests were delivered in a grand and breath-taking downhill sweep via a special branch line to the very front door of their stylish accommodation. Here they enjoyed the finest hospitality that money could buy.

When the railroad arrived, Lake Tahoe was already a favored tourist destination. The station at Lake Tahoe was built on the jetty from which the lake steamer departed each morning (above).

Lake Tahoe, from *Land of Living Color*, published by J. B. Scofield, San Francisco, 1915

After barely a decade of successful operation, the slopes of the eastern shore of the lake were denuded of trees by the late 1880s while the mines began to be exhausted of their ore. That being the case, Bliss perceived that it was time to set in motion plans for the formation of the Lake Tahoe Railway & Transportation Company with a view to opening up the northwestern shore to tourists coming over the pass from San Francisco.

Construction on the fifteen-mile route up the Truckee River valley to the junction with the Southern Pacific Company

Vacationers soon came in droves—on three trains daily through June, July, and August—though the world they entered was exclusive despite its popularity. From the moment travelers exchanged their cars at Truckee for the handsome narrow gauge coaches of the Tahoe Line, they entered a world that Duane L. Bliss had built for them. It was a far-sighted vision, and one that was to make him a very wealthy man.

DONNER PASS

"The Hill"—King of Grades

The original line of the summit route is clearly seen in this aerial view courtesy of Google Earth (right).

Even as the nascent Central Pacific Railroad Company of California was being organized between November, 1860, and the spring of 1861, to many the notion of building a railroad across the mighty Sierra Nevada still seemed to be little more than a pipedream at best. Not only did Theodore "Crazy" Judah's proposed route still exist only on paper, most potential investors doubted both Judah's business acumen and the ultimate feasibility of his plan, which would require his proposed railroad to be built over the 7,000-foot heights of the Donner Pass in California; to span multiple deep ravines and gorges; engineer and bore numerous tunnels through the hardest of granites; and cope with winter snowfalls, avalanches, and up to sixty-foot drifts along the steep, mountainous grade before it plunged down the Truckee River Canyon to the Nevada border.

Meandering leisurely by train up the western face of the range today through its fabled tunnels, remaining snowsheds, and along the curves and ridges above the Sierra's distinctive deep and narrow canyons, it is hard to imagine what the first crews setting to work on the line must have made of the challenge that lay before them. Judah's planned route sought to conquer the same infamously cruel mountain country that during the winter of 1846–7 had claimed the lives through starvation and exposure of 26 early pioneers who were members of the notoriously ill-fated George Donner party that was emigrating from Illinois to California.

At Cape Horn, the famous scenic mountain promontory just east of Colfax, California (then called Illinoistown), overlooking the gorge of the north fork of the American River, the CPRR began its assault on the Sierra in earnest. Here gangs of Chinese laborers, while being precariously supported from above by ropes as they worked, used hand drills and black powder to carve a narrow shelf out of the steep cliff's red sedimentary rock some 1,300 feet above the river.

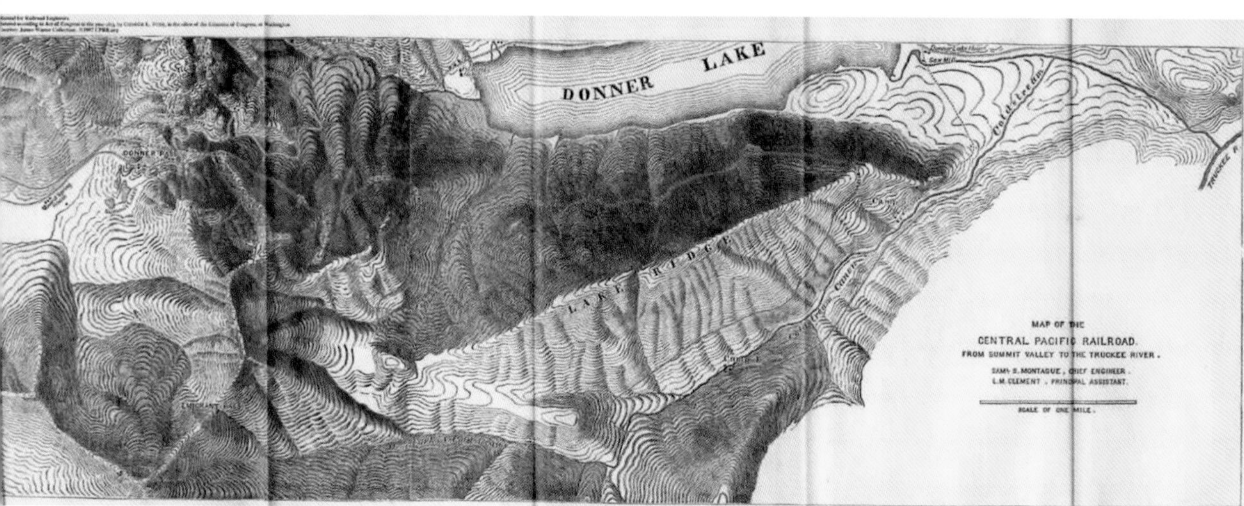

The Donner Summit—a map from *The Railroad Constructor*, May 1873, showing the route of the line and the tunnels (below).

Albert Bierstadt's 1873 "Donner Lake from the Summit" clearly shows railroad construction in progress (left), Fine Arts Museum of San Francisco.
Construction of the railroad was a popular theme with stereograph publishers (below).

J. H. Becker, Snow Sheds on the Central Pacific in the Sierra Nevada Mountains, *c.*1872, Thomas Gilcrease Institute of American Art and History, Tulsa.

Another Bierstadt painting of 1873, capturing the majesty of sunrise over Donner Lake (above), New York Historical Society.

One of the many thousands of Chinese laborers who built the summit line (right).

I am a railroad worker.
The hot sun shining on my body.
The cold wind blowing at my face.
My body is shaking because of hunger.
The railroad has no ending.
The road is uneven.
The wage is low.
I am losing tears like losing blood.
I feel like crying.
I am losing energy.
But no one knows.

Anon, Chinese, c.*1867*

From there the Sierra grade proceeded another 46 rail miles east to Donner Summit before descending to Truckee and along the Truckee River to the California–Nevada border. By May 1868, however, construction workers had successfully driven sixteen tunnels through the tough Sierra granite that was believed at the outset to be impenetrable.

Over two historically harsh winters (1865–7), thousands of mostly Chinese and, to a far lesser degree, Irish and other European emigrant workers, battled their way through granite, snow, and ice. Laboring in the bitter cold to master the use of explosives without precedent to guide them, they then cleared the blasted rock with their bare hands. Working seemingly endless shifts, they toiled day and night in subfreezing temperatures that often dropped below 15 degrees Fahrenheit. The most challenging and difficult of the works on the entire Sierra grade was Tunnel No. 6 (the "Summit Tunnel"), which CPRR locating engineer Lewis Clement had laid out just 400 feet north of Donner Pass. At 1,659 feet in length, it was the CPRR's longest bore and at its greatest depth carried the grade 124 feet below the surface of the tough granite.

To help hasten this essential tunnel's completion, Clement had a shaft sunk more than a hundred feet from above near the middle of the tunnel's path to permit work being done simultaneously on four "headings" instead of just the two from the east and west portals. To expedite progress even more, the powerful explosive nitroglycerine was introduced in place of black powder early in 1867. Because of its inherent instability it had to be made on the spot, but its use increased the average progress of excavation from 1.18 feet per day to 1.82 feet–an improvement of 54 percent. When the last of the headings was finally "holed through" on August 28, 1867, Clement's engineering proved so accurate that all four bores matched each other in alignment and grade to within an inch.

The Summit Tunnel was finally opened to rail traffic on June 18, 1868, and remained in continuous daily operation for the next 125 years until the 6.7-mile section of Track No. 1 over the summit between Shed 41 at Norden and the crossovers in Shed 47 a mile east of the old flyover at Eder was abandoned in 1993. With this closure, all summit traffic now follows Track No. 2 through the 10,322-foot-long Tunnel No. 41 ("The Big Hole") running under nearby Mt. Judah, which opened in 1925 when the summit crossing was first double tracked. The longer tunnel is much easier to keep open during the harsh winter months, shortens the route by 1.29 miles, and lowers the summit crossing by 132.7 feet. Abandoning the original Summit Tunnel route, however, reverted this short section of the grade back to being single track, thus complicating bidirectional traffic management.

C. P. R. R.

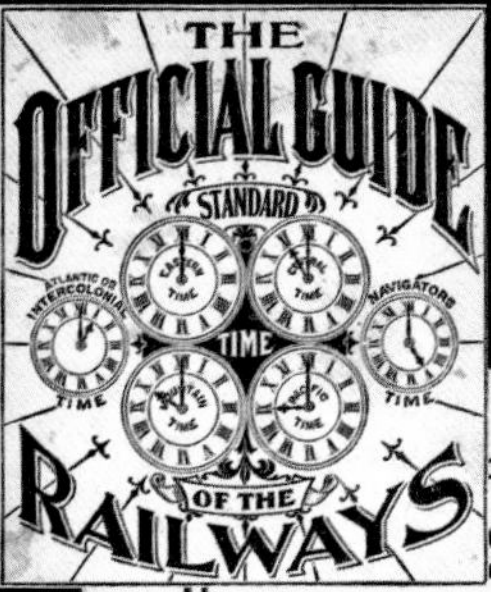

UNION PACIFIC OVERLAND ROUTE TIMETABLES, 1906

N PACIFIC, "THE OVERLAND ROUTE"

AND CONNECTING LINES.

WESTBOUND.

No. 1—THE OVERLAND LIMITED—Electric Lighted.

Station	Time							
Lve. **Council Bluffs**	9 00 A M	Sun.	Mon.	Tues	Wed.	Thu.	Fri.	Sat.
Lve. **Omaha**	9 40 A M	"	"	"	"	"	"	"
Arr.. **Ogden**	4 00 P M	Mon.	Tues	Wed.	Thu.	Fri.	Sat.	Sun.
Arr.. **Salt Lake**	6 15 P M	"	"	"	"	"	"	"
Arr.. **Butte**	2 45 A M	Tues	Wed.	Thu.	Fri.	Sat.	Sun.	Mon.
Arr.. **Portland**	5 00 P M	"	"	"	"	"	"	"
Arr.. **Spokane**	7 30 P M	"	"	"	"	"	"	"
Arr.. **San Francisco**	5 48 P M	"	"	"	"	"	"	"
Arr.. **Los Angeles**	8 55 A M	Wed.	Thu.	Fri.	Sat.	Sun.	Mon.	Tues

No. 101—THE OVERLAND LIMITED.

Station	Time							
Lve. **Kansas City**	6 20 P M	Sun.	Mon.	Tues	Wed.	Thu.	Fri.	Sat.
Lve. **Leavenworth**	4 15 P M	"	"	"		"	"	"
Lve. **Denver**	6 10 P M	Mon.	Tues	Wed.	Thu.	Fri.	Sat.	Sun.
Arr.. **Ogden**	4 00 P M	Tues	Wed.	Thu.	Fri.	Sat.	Sun.	Mon.
Arr.. **Salt Lake**	5 15 P M	"	"	"	"	"	"	"
Arr.. **Portland**	5 00 P M	Wed.	Thu.	Fri.	Sat.	Sun.	Mon.	Tues
Arr.. **Spokane**	7 30 P M	"	"	"	"	"	"	"
Arr.. **San Francisco**	5 48 P M	"	"	"	"	"	"	"
Arr.. **Los Angeles**	8 55 A M	Thu.	Fri.	Sat.	Sun.	Mon.	Tues	Wed.

No. 3—THE CHINA AND JAPAN FAST MAIL.

Station	Time							
Lve. **Council Bluffs**	3 20 P M	Sun.	Mon.	Tues	Wed.	Thu.	Fri.	Sat.
Lve. **Omaha**	4 15 P M	"	"	"	"	"	"	"
Arr. **Denver**	7 50 A M	Mon.	Tues	Wed.	Thu.	Fri.	Sat.	Sun.
Arr.. **Ogden**	3 45 A M	Tues	Wed.	Thu.	Fri.	Sat.	Sun.	Mon.
Arr.. **Salt Lake**	5 15 A M	"	"	"	"	"	"	"
Arr.. **Portland**	7 15 A M	Wed.	Thu.	Fri.	Sat.	Sun.	Mon.	Tues
Arr.. **San Francisco**	12 48 Noon	"	"	"	"	"	"	"
Arr.. **Los Angeles**	7 05 A M	Thu.	Fri.	Sat.	Sun.	Mon.	Tues	Wed.

No. 103—THE CHINA AND JAPAN FAST MAIL.

Station	Time							
Lve. **Kansas City**	10 05 A M	Sun.	Mon.	Tues	Wed.	Thu.	Fri.	Sat.
Lve. **Leavenworth**	9 20 A M	"	"	"		"	"	"
Arr.. **Portland**	7 15 A M	Wed.	Thu.	Fri.	Sat.	Sun.	Mon.	Tues

No. 5—THE CHICAGO-PORTLAND SPECIAL.

Station	Time							
Lve. **Council Bluffs**	3 25 P M	Sun.	Mon.	Tues	Wed.	Thu.	Fri.	Sat.
Lve. **Omaha**	4 25 P M	"	"	"	"	"	"	"
Arr.. **Butte**	4 15 P M	Tues	Wed.	Thu.	Fri.	Sat.	Sun.	Mon.
Arr.. **Portland**	5 15 P M	Wed.	Thu.	Fri.	Sat.	Sun.	Mon.	Tues

No. 7—THE LOS ANGELES LIMITED—Electric Lighted.

Station	Time							
Lve. **Council Bluffs**	11 00 A M	Sun.	Mon.	Tues	Wed.	Thu.	Fri.	Sat.
Lve. **Omaha**	11 30 A M	"	"	"	"	"	"	"
Arr.. **Ogden**	2 45 P M	Mon.	Tues	Wed.	Thu.	Fri.	Sat.	Sun.
Arr.. **Salt Lake**	4 25 P M	"	"	"	"	"	"	"
Arr.. **Los Angeles**	5 15 P M	Tues	Wed.	Thu.	Fri.	Sat.	Sun.	Mon.

No. 11—THE COLORADO SPECIAL.

Station	Time							
Lve. **Council Bluffs**	7 15 A M	Sun.	Mon.	Tues	Wed.	Thu.	Fri.	Sat.
Lve. **Omaha**	7 45 A M	"	"	"	"	"	"	"
Arr.. **Denver**	9 30 P M	"	"	"	"	"	"	"

EASTBOUND.

No. 2—THE OVERLAND LIMITED—Electric Lighted.

Station	Time							
Lve. **Los Angeles**	5 00 P M	Sun.	Mon.	Tues	Wed.	Thu.	Fri.	Sat.
Lve. **San Francisco**	11 00 A M	Mon.	Tues	Wed.	Thu.	Fri.	Sat.	Sun.
Lve. **Portland**	9 30 A M	"	"	"	"	"	"	"
Lve. **Salt Lake**	1 30 P M	Tues	Wed.	Thu.	Fri.	Sat.	Sun.	Mon.
Lve. **Ogden**	3 00 P M	"	"	"	"	"	"	"
Arr.. **Denver**	10 50 A M	Wed.	Thu.	Fri.	Sat.	Sun.	Mon.	Tues
Arr.. **Kansas City**	8 50 A M	Thu.	Fri.	Sat.	Sun.	Mon.	Tues	Wed.
Arr.. **Leavenworth**	11 55 A M	"	"	"		"	"	"
Arr.. **Omaha**	8 18 P M	Wed.	Thu.	Fri.	Sat.	Sun.	Mon.	Tues
Arr.. **Council Bluffs**	8 53 P M	"	"	"	"	"	"	"

No. 104—THE ATLANTIC EXPRESS.

Station	Time							
Lve. **Los Angeles**	3 50 P M	Sun.	Mon.	Tues	Wed.	Thu.	Fri.	Sat.
Lve. **San Francisco**	9 00 A M	Mon.	Tues	Wed.	Thu.	Fri.	Sat.	Sun.
Lve. **Salt Lake**	6 05 P M	Tues	Wed.	Thu.	Fri.	Sat.	Sun.	Mon.
Lve. **Ogden**	7 30 P M	"	"	"	"	"	"	"
Arr.. **Denver**	6 00 P M	Wed.	Thu.	Fri.	Sat.	Sun.	Mon.	Tues
Arr.. **Kansas City**	5 00 P M	Thu.	Fri.	Sat.	Sun.	Mon.	Tues	Wed.
Arr.. **Leavenworth**	5 35 P M	"	"	"		"	"	"

No. 4—THE ATLANTIC EXPRESS.

Station	Time							
Lve. **Los Angeles**	3 50 P M	Sun.	Mon.	Tues	Wed.	Thu.	Fri.	Sat.
Lve. **San Francisco**	9 00 A M	Mon.	Tues	Wed.	Thu.	Fri.	Sat.	Sun.
Lve. **Salt Lake**	6 05 P M	Tues	Wed.	Thu.	Fri.	Sat.	Sun.	Mon.
Lve. **Ogden**	7 30 P M	"	"	"	"	"	"	"
Arr.. **Omaha**	9 30 A M	Thu.	Fri.	Sat.	Sun.	Mon.	Tues	Wed.
Arr.. **Council Bluffs**	10 05 A M	"	"	"	"	"	"	"

No. 6—THE PORTLAND-CHICAGO SPECIAL.

Station	Time							
Lve. **Portland**	8 15 P M	Sun.	Mon.	Tues	Wed.	Thu.	Fri.	Sat.
Lve. **Spokane**	4 30 P M	"	"	"	"	"	"	"
Lve. **Butte**	5 00 P M	Mon.	Tues	Wed.	Thu.	Fri.	Sat.	Sun.
Arr.. **Denver**	10 50 A M	Wed.	Thu.	Fri.	Sat.	Sun.	Mon.	Tues
Arr.. **Kansas City**	8 50 A M	Thu.	Fri.	Sat.	Sun.	Mon.	Tues	Wed.
Arr.. **Leavenworth**	11 55 A M	"	"	"		"	"	"
Arr.. **Omaha**	5 10 P M	Wed.	Thu.	Fri.	Sat.	Sun.	Mon.	Tues
Arr.. **Council Bluffs**	6 05 P M	"	"	"	"	"	"	"

No. 6—THE CHINA AND JAPAN FAST MAIL.

Station	Time							
Lve. **San Francisco**	6 00 P M	Sun.	Mon.	Tues	Wed.	Thu.	Fri.	Sat.
Lve. **Salt Lake**	7 10 A M	Tues	Wed.	Thu.	Fri.	Sat.	Sun.	Mon.
Lve. **Ogden**	8 20 A M	"	"	"	"	"	"	"
Arr.. **Denver**	10 50 A M	Wed.	Thu.	Fri.	Sat.	Sun.	Mon.	Tues
Arr.. **Kansas City**	8 50 A M	Thu.	Fri.	Sat.	Sun.	Mon.	Tues	Wed.
Arr.. **Leavenworth**	11 55 A M	"	"	"		"	"	"
Arr.. **Omaha**	5 10 P M	Wed.	Thu.	Fri.	Sat.	Sun.	Mon.	Tues
Arr.. **Council Bluffs**	6 05 P M	"	"	"	"	"	"	"

No. 8—THE LOS ANGELES LIMITED—Electric Lighted.

Station	Time							
Lve. **Los Angeles**	2 45 P M	Sun.	Mon.	Tues	Wed.	Thu.	Fri.	Sat.
Lve. **Salt Lake**	5 55 P M	Mon.	Tues	Wed.	Thu.	Fri.	Sat.	Sun.
Lve. **Ogden**	7 00 P M	"	"	"	"	"	"	"
Arr.. **Omaha**	10 45 P M	Tues	Wed.	Thu.	Fri.	Sat.	Sun.	Mon.
Arr.. **Council Bluffs**	11 15 P M	"	"	"	"	"	"	"

THROUGH CAR SERVICE.

WESTBOUND.

TRAIN No. 1—THE OVERLAND LIMITED.—Electric Lighted.

From Council Bluffs and Omaha—(*Daily.*)—Through Composite Observation Car Chicago and Council Bluffs to San Francisco, and Pullman Drawing-room and Private Compartment Sleeping Cars Chicago and Council Bluffs to San Francisco, via C. & N. W. and C. M. & St. P., U. P. and S. P., connecting at Port Costa or Oakland Pier with Pullman Sleepers for Los Angeles, and at Oakland with Buffet Sleeping Cars and Tourist Sleeping Cars for Santa Barbara and Los Angeles, via Coast Line. Pullman Drawing-room and Private Compartment Sleeping Car Chicago and Council Bluffs to Portland, via C. & N. W., U. P., O. S. L. and O. R. & N. Co. Dining Car service Chicago and Council Bluffs to San Francisco and Portland.

From Kansas City and Denver—(*Daily.*)—Day Coaches Kansas City to Denver and Cheyenne. Free Reclining Chair Car Kansas City to Denver and Denver to Cheyenne. Pullman Drawing-room Sleeping Car Kansas City to Denver and Salt Lake City. Pullman Tourist Sleeping Car Kansas City to Portland (No. 1 from Cheyenne), via U. P., O. S. L. and O. R. & N. Co. Dining Car Kansas City to Topeka and Denver to Cheyenne.

From Leavenworth—(*Daily, except Sunday.*)—Day Coaches to Lawrence, with the same equipment from Lawrence as from Kansas City.

TRAIN No. 3—CHINA AND JAPAN FAST MAIL.

(*Called The Colorado Express east of Denver.*)

From Council Bluffs and Omaha—(*Daily.*)—Pullman Drawing-room Sleeping Car Chicago to San Francisco, via C. & N. W. and C. M. & St. P., U. P. and S. P. (No. 5 Omaha to Cheyenne), Chicago to Denver, via C. & N. W., C. M. & St. P. and U. P., and Council Bluffs and Omaha to Cheyenne. Pullman Tourist Sleeping Cars Chicago to San Francisco, via C. & N. W. and C. M. & St. P., U. P. and S. P. (No. 5 Omaha to Cheyenne). Personally conducted Tourist Cars (from Council Bluffs) Thursday and Friday, from Chicago to Los Angeles, via C. & N. W., U. P., D. & R. G. and S. P., and Wednesday and Friday (from Council Bluffs) Chicago to Los Angeles, via C. & N. W., U. P. and S. P. (No. 5 Omaha to Cheyenne). Free Reclining Chair Car Chicago to Denver, via C. & N. W., C. M. & St. P. and U. P. Day Coach Council Bluffs and Omaha to Ogden. Dining Car Service Chicago to San Francisco.

From Kansas City and Denver—(*Daily.*)—Pullman Drawing-room Sleeping Car Kansas City to Denver and Salt Lake City. Free Reclining Chair Car Kansas City to Denver and Salt Lake City. Dining Car service Kansas City to Ellis. Day Coaches Kansas City to Denver and Cheyenne, and Kansas City to Salina. Pullman Tourist Sleeping Car St. Louis, Kansas City and Denver to Los Angeles, via Wabash, U. P., O. S. L. and Salt Lake Route (No. 3 Cheyenne to Ogden).

From Leavenworth—(*Daily, except Sunday.*)—Day Coaches Leavenworth to Lawrence, with same equipment from Lawrence as from Kansas City.

TRAIN No. 5—THE CALIFORNIA AND OGDEN EXPRESS.

(*Called The Chicago-Portland Special Green River to Portland.*)

From Council Bluffs and Omaha—(*Daily.*)—Pullman Drawing-room Sleeping Cars Chicago to San Francisco, via C. & N. W. and C. M. & St. P., U. P. and S. P. (No. 3 from Cheyenne). Omaha to Portland,

Continued on following page.

UNION PACIFIC, "THE OVERLAND ROUTE"

AND CONNECTING LINES.

THROUGH CAR SERVICE.—WESTBOUND—Continued.

via U. P., O. S. L. and O. R. & N. Co. Pullman Tourist Sleeping Cars Chicago to San Francisco, via C. & N. W., and C. M. & St. P., U. P. and and S. P. (No. 3 from Cheyenne). Chicago to Portland, via C. & N. W., U. P., O. S. L. and O. R. & N. Co. Personally Conducted Tourist Cars Wednesday and Friday from Council Bluffs, Chicago to Los Angeles, via C. & N. W., U. P. and S. P. (No. 3 from Cheyenne) and Wednesday from Omaha, Chicago to Portland, via C. & N. W., U. P., O. S. L. and O. R. & N. Co. Free Reclining Chair Car Chicago to Portland, via C. & N. W., U. P., O. S. L. and O. R. & N. Co. Day Coach Omaha to Ogden. Dining Car service Chicago to Cheyenne and Green River to Portland.

TRAIN No. 7—THE LOS ANGELES LIMITED—Electric Lighted.

From Council Bluffs and Omaha—Composite Observation Car, Pullman Drawing-room and Private Compartment Sleeping Cars, Pullman Tourist Sleeping Car Chicago, Council Bluffs and Omaha to Salt Lake City and Los Angeles, via C. & N. W., U. P. and S. P. L. A. & S. L. R.Rs. Dining Car Service en route.

TRAIN No. 11—THE COLORADO SPECIAL.

From Council Bluffs and Omaha—(*Daily.*)—Pullman Drawing-room Sleeping Cars, Free Reclining Chair Car and Buffet, Smoking and Library Car Chicago and Council Bluffs to Denver, via C. & N. W. and U. P. Pullman Drawing-room Sleeping Car and Free Reclining Chair Car Chicago to Denver, via C. M. & St. P. and U. P. Dining Car Chicago to Denver.

EASTBOUND.

TRAIN No. 2—THE OVERLAND LIMITED.—Electric Lighted.

From San Francisco—(*Daily.*)—Composite Observation Car, Double Pullman Drawing-room and Private Compartment Sleepers and Dining Car service to San Francisco and Chicago, via S. P., U. P., C. & N. W. and C. M. & St. P. Rys. Connections made en route with Pullman Palace Sleeper to Denver and Kansas City. Connects at Ogden with Pullman Drawing-room Sleeping Car Salt Lake City to Denver. Pullman Buffet Sleeping Car from Los Angeles makes connection with No. 2, "The Overland Limited" at Port Costa.

From Cheyenne and Denver—(*Daily.*)—Pullman Drawing-room Sleeping Car Salt Lake City to Denver and Kansas City. Pullman Tourist Sleeping Car Los Angeles to Denver, Kansas City and St. Louis (No. 6 Ogden to Cheyenne). Free Reclining Chair Car Ogden to Denver and Kansas City (No. 6 Ogden to Cheyenne). Day Coach Cheyenne to Denver and Kansas City. Dining Car Cheyenne to Denver and Topeka to Kansas City.

From Portland—(*Daily.*)—Pullman Drawing-room and Private Compartment Sleeping Car Portland to Council Bluffs and Chicago, via O. R. & N. Co., O. S. L., U. P. and C. & N. W. Rys. Pullman Tourist Sleeping Cars Portland to Kansas City, via O. R. & N. Co., O. S. L. and U. P. (No. 4 from Ogden). Chair Cars Portland to Ogden (connecting at Ogden with No. 4). Dining Car Service. Connects at Green River with through equipment from San Francisco and Salt Lake City for Denver, Kansas City, Omaha and Chicago.

TRAIN No. 4—THE ATLANTIC EXPRESS.

First and second-class business from Portland, Spokane and points intermediate to Ogden, on The Overland Limited, is carried in Tourist Sleeper and Chair Cars east of Ogden on this train.

From San Francisco—Personally Conducted Pullman Tourist Sleeper every Tuesday and Thursday from Los Angeles to Omaha, Council Bluffs and Chicago, via S. P., U. P. and C. & N. W. (No. 12 North Platte to Omaha).

From Salt Lake City and Ogden—(*Daily.*)—Free Reclining Chair Car Salt Lake City to Denver and Kansas City. Pullman Drawing-room Sleeping Car Salt Lake City to Denver and Kansas City and Cheyenne to Omaha. Pullman Tourist Sleeping Car Portland to Kansas City, via O. R. & N. Co., O. S. L. and U. P. (No. 2 Portland to Ogden). Dining Car Grand Island to Omaha and Council Bluffs.

From Cheyenne and Denver—(*Daily*).—Pullman Drawing-room Sleeping Car Salt Lake City to Denver and Kansas City. Pullman Tourist Sleeping Car Portland to Denver and Kansas City (No. 2 Portland to Ogden). Free Reclining Chair Cars Salt Lake City to Denver and Kansas City. Day Coaches Cheyenne to Denver and Kansas City. Dining Car Ellis to Kansas City. Connecting at Sacramento with Pullman Buffet Sleeping Car Los Angeles to Lathrop and Sacramento, and at Ogden with Pullman Palace Sleeping Car from San Francisco to Ogden, and Day Coaches San Francisco to Ogden.

TRAIN No. 12—THE CHICAGO SPECIAL.

From Denver—(*Daily.*)—Pullman Drawing-room Sleeping Cars, Free Reclining Chair Car and Buffet, Smoking and Library Car to Council Bluffs and Chicago, via U. P. and C. & N. W. Rys. Pullman Drawing-room Sleeping Car, Cafe Observation Car and Free Reclining Chair Car Denver to Chicago, via U. P. and C. M. & St. P. Personally Conducted Tourist Cars from Los Angeles Tuesdays and Thursdays on No. 4 are attached to No. 12 at North Platte on Saturdays and Mondays. Dining Car Denver to North Platte.

TRAIN No. 6—THE PORTLAND-CHICAGO SPECIAL.

From Portland—(*Daily.*)—Pullman Drawing-room Sleeping Car Portland to Omaha and Council Bluffs, via O. R. & N. Co., O. S. L. and U. P. Rys. Free Reclining Chair Car Portland to Council Bluffs and Chicago. Pullman Tourist Sleeping Car Portland to Omaha, Council Bluffs and Chicago (No. 10 Green River to Cheyenne). Pullman Tourist Sleeping Car for Omaha, Council Bluffs and Chicago, via O. R. & N. Co., O. S. L., U. P. and C. & N. W. Rys. Personally conducted every Tuesday from Portland (No. 10 Green River to Cheyenne).

From Butte—(*Daily.*)—Free Reclining Chair Cars, Dining Car and Palace Sleeping Cars, Butte to Pocatello, with same equipment as from Portland. Connects at Green River with through equipment from San Francisco and Ogden on No. 6 with which this train is consolidated.

TRAIN No. 6—THE CHINA AND JAPAN FAST MAIL.

From San Francisco—(*Daily.*)—Through Pullman Drawing-room Sleeping Car San Francisco to Council Bluffs and Chicago, via S. P., U. P., C. & N. W. and C. M. & St. P. Rys. (No. 10 Green River to Cheyenne). Pullman Tourist Sleeping Cars San Francisco to Council Bluffs and Chicago, via S. P., U. P., C. & N. W. and C. M. & St. P. Rys. (No. 10 Green River to Cheyenne). Dining Car service San Francisco to Omaha and Council Bluffs, connecting en route at Ogden with Day Coach Ogden to Omaha and Council Bluffs. Pullman Tourist Sleeping Car Los Angeles to Kansas City and St. Louis, via Salt Lake Route, O. S. L., U. P. and Wabash R.R. (On No. 102 Cheyenne to Kansas City), and Los Angeles (Thursday only) to Salt Lake City, Omaha, St. Paul and Minneapolis, via S. P. L. A. & S. L., O. S. L., U. P., C. & N.W. and C. St. P. M. & O. (No. 10 Green River to Omaha.)

From Denver—(*Daily.*)—Pullman Drawing-room Sleepers and Free Reclining Chair Cars Denver to Council Bluffs and Chicago, via Julesburg, U. P. and C. & N. W. and C. M. & St. P. Personally Conducted Tourist Car (Saturday and Sunday from Denver) Los Angeles to Chicago, via S. P., R. G. W., D. & R. G., U. P. and C. & N. W. Dining Car North Platte to Omaha. (Equipment of No. 6 from Denver is attached to No. 10 Julesburg to Omaha.)

TRAIN No. 8—THE LOS ANGELES LIMITED—Electric Lighted.

From Los Angeles and Salt Lake City—(*Daily*).—Pullman Drawing-room Sleeping Cars, Composite Observation Car, Pullman Tourist Sleeping Car and Dining Car Los Angeles and Salt Lake City to Omaha, Council Bluffs and Chicago, via S. P. L. A. & S. L., U. P. and C. & N. W. R.Rs., connecting at Cheyenne with through equipment for Denver and Kansas City.

TRAIN No. 10—THE FAST MAIL.—(*Daily.*)

Mail Cars and Baggage Cars Ogden to Omaha and Council Bluffs. Pullman Tourist Sleeping Car Portland to Omaha and Chicago, via O. R. & N., O. S. L., U. P. and C. & N. W. (No. 6 from Cheyenne), and San Francisco to Omaha and Chicago, via S. P., U. P. and C. & N. W. and C. M. & St. P. (No. 6 from Cheyenne). Pullman Tourist Sleeping Car Los Angeles (Thursday only) to Omaha and Minneapolis, via S. P. L. A. & S. L., U. P. and C. St. P. M. & O. Through equipment from Denver to Omaha (No. 6 Denver to Julesburg). Dining Car North Platte to Omaha.

LIST OF PASSENGER AND FREIGHT AGENTS—Continued.

Pittsburgh, Pa.—708-9 Park Building—
G. G. Herring, General Agent.
Sam'l A. Myers, Traveling Passenger Agent.
W. A. Golden, Traveling Passenger Agent
C. C. Phillips, Contracting Freight Agent.
J. E. Corfield, Traveling Freight Agent.

Portland, Ore.—
A.L. Craig, Gen. Pas. Agt., O. R.R. & N. Co.
C. W. Stinger, City Ticket Agent, 3d and Washington Streets.

Pueblo, Colo.—216 North Main Street—
L. M. Tudor, Commercial Agent.

St. Joseph, Mo.—Board of Trade Building—
S. M. Adsit, G. F. & P. A. St. J. & G. I. Ry.
Jo. Hansen, Ticket Agent, Union Station.

St. Louis, Mo.—903 Olive St. (Century Bldg)—
L. E. Townsley, General Agent.
E. R. Tuttle, Traveling Passenger Agent.
C. M. Rollings, Traveling Pas. Agent.

St. Louis, Mo.—*Continued.*
Arnold S. Borglum, Contracting Fht. Agt.
Geo. Carroll, Traveling Freight Agent.
D. Asbury, Traveling Freight Agent.

St. Paul, Minn.—376 Robert Street—
H. F. Carter, Traveling Passenger Agent.

Sacramento, Cal.—1007 Second Street—
James Warrack, Freight and Passenger Agt.
Albert J. Watts, Agent Passenger Dept.

Salt Lake City, Utah—
D. E. Burley, Gen. Pas. Agt. O. S. L. R.R.
D. R. Gray, Gen. Agent, 201 Main Street.

San Francisco, Cal.—1704 Fillmore Street—
S. F. Booth, Gen. Agent Passenger Dept.
T. R. Tilley, City Passenger Agent.
H. M. MacGregor, Traveling Pas. Agent.
P. B. Norton, Traveling Passenger Agent.

San Francisco, Cal.—1704 Fillmore St.—*Con'd*
C. Clifford, General Agent Freight Dept.
Samuel F. Hilton, Traveling Freight Agent.

San Jose, Cal.—7 West Santa Clara St.—
R. S. Ruble, Traveling Passenger Agent.
Leander M. Cheshire, Contracting Fht. Agt.

Seattle, Wash.—608 First Avenue—
E. E. Ellis, Gen. Agent, O. R.R. & N. Co.

Spokane, Wash.—430 Riverside Avenue—
Geo. J. Mohler, General Agent, O. R.R. & N. Co.

Tacoma, Wash.—1108 Pacific Avenue—
Robert Lee, Agent, O. R.R. & N. Co.

Toronto, Ont.—14 Janes Building—
J. O. Goodsell, Traveling Passenger Agent.

Yokohama, Japan—4 Water Street—
T. D. McKay, General Passenger Agent, San Francisco Overland Route.

UNION PACIFIC, "THE OVERLAND ROUTE"

AND CONNECTING LINES.

CONDENSED SCHEDULE OF THROUGH TRAINS.

Colorado Special. No. 11	The Chic.-Portland Special. No. 5	China & Japan Fast Mail. No. 3	Los Angeles Limited. No. 7	Overland Limited. No. 1	June 17, 1906.	Overland Limited. No. 2	Atlantic Express. No. 4	Chic.Spl. No. 12 Atl. Exp. No. 4	China & Japan Fast Mail. No. 6	Fast Mail. No. 10	Los Angeles Limited. No. 8
*7 00 PM	*11 00 PM	*11 00 PM	*10 05 PM	*8 02 PM	lv. Chicago..(C.&N.W.) ar.	9 00 AM		8 50 PM	7 30 AM	7 30 AM	11 55 AM
7 10 AM	3 25 PM	3 25 PM	10 52 AM	8 50 AM	ar. Council Bluffs.. " lv.	8 58 PM		8 20 AM	6 10 PM	6 10 PM	11 22 AM
7 30 AM	3 45 PM	3 45 PM	11 15 AM	9 15 AM	ar. Omaha........ " lv.	8 38 PM		8 00 AM	5 50 PM	5 50 PM	11 00 PM
*6 05 PM	*10 25 PM	10 25 PM		8 00 PM	lv. Chicago..(C.M.&St.P.) ar.	9 25 AM		9 55 PM	8 35 AM		
7 10 AM	2 45 PM	2 45 PM		8 55 AM	ar. Council Bluffs.. " lv.	8 45 PM		8 20 AM	6 10 PM		
7 35 AM	3 10 PM	3 10 PM		9 20 AM	ar. Omaha........ " lv.	8 20 PM		7 55 AM	5 45 PM		
	*11 30 PM	*11 30 PM		6 00 PM	lv. Chicago..(C. Gt. W.) ar.					8 15 AM	
	3 30 PM	3 30 PM		9 00 AM	ar. Omaha........ " lv.					*5 40 PM	
6 00 PM	2 55 AM	2 55 AM		6 00 PM	lv. Chicago........(I. C.) ar.			9 50 PM	7 30 AM		
7 30 AM	3 55 PM	3 55 PM		7 30 AM	ar. Omaha........ " lv.			8 00 AM	6 00 PM		
				8 00 PM	lv. St. Louis.(Wab. R.R.) ar.				7 15 AM		
				8 40 AM	ar. Omaha........ " lv.				*6 30 PM		
				2 05 PM	lv. St. Louis..(Mo. Pac.) ar.	4 50 PM	7 10 AM				
	See Note ⊙.	See Note ⊙.		6 30 AM	ar. Omaha........ " lv.	11 15 PM	9 00 AM				
				8 30 PM	lv. Minneapolis (C.St.P.M.&O.) ar.	8 05 AM		8 10 PM	8 05 AM		
				9 05 PM	lv. St. Paul....... " ar.	7 30 AM		7 40 PM	7 30 AM		
		12 10 Noon		6 00 AM	lv. Sioux City (C.&N.W.) ar.	11 10 PM		10 55 AM	11 10 PM		
		3 25 PM		9 10 AM	ar. Council Bluffs.. " lv.	8 43 PM		8 10 AM	8 43 PM		
		3 45 PM		9 35 AM	ar. Omaha........ " lv.	8 28 PM		7 50 AM	8 28 PM		
				8 00 PM	lv. St. Paul....(Ill. Cent.) ar.			7 30 PM	8 25 AM		
				8 35 PM	lv. Minneapolis..... " ar.			6 50 PM	7 50 AM		
				8 05 AM	ar. Omaha........ " lv.			†7 25 AM	7 50 PM		
*8 00 PM				*8 00 PM	lv. Minneapolis (C.Gt.W.) ar.	8 00 AM		7 15 PM	8 00 AM		
8 35 PM				8 35 PM	lv. St. Paul....... " ar.	7 20 AM		6 42 PM	7 20 AM		
7 10 AM				7 10 AM	ar. Omaha........ " lv.	8 30 PM		7 45 AM	8 30 PM		
*7 15 AM	*3 25 PM	*3 20 PM	*11 00 AM	*9 00 AM	lv. Council Bluffs (U.P.) ar.	8 53 PM	10 05 AM	8 15 AM	6 05 PM	3 55 PM	11 15 PM
7 45 AM	4 25 PM	4 15 PM	11 30 AM	9 40 AM	lv. Omaha........ " ar.	8 18 PM	9 30 AM	7 44 AM	5 10 PM	3 30 PM	10 45 PM
10 06 AM	7 30 PM	6 55 PM	1 47 PM	12 10 Noon	ar. Columbus....... " lv.	5 53 PM	6 00 AM	5 25 AM	2 25 PM	12 55 Noon	8 38 PM
		8 30 PM			lv. Minneapolis (C.St.P.M.&O.) ar.	8 10 PM	8 15 AM		8 10 PM		
		9 05 PM			lv. St. Paul....... " ar.	7 40 PM	7 45 AM		7 40 PM		
		8 00 AM			lv. Sioux City..... " ar.	9 20 AM	3 55 PM		9 20 AM		
		12 45 Noon			ar. Columbus.....(U. P.) lv.	7 10 PM	†7 15 AM		7 10 PM		
10 06 AM	7 30 PM	6 55 PM	1 47 PM	12 10 Noon	lv. Columbus....... " ar.	5 53 PM	6 00 AM	5 25 AM	2 25 PM	12 55 Noon	8 38 PM
11 30 AM	10 00 PM	8 45 PM	3 15 PM	1 50 PM	ar. Grand Island..... " lv.	4 25 PM	3 45 AM	3 58 AM	12 35 Noon	11 00 AM	7 05 PM
		*10 15 AM		*8 10 PM	lv. St. Joseph.(St.J.&G.I.) ar.	7 30 AM	4 35 PM	4 35 PM	7 30 AM		
		8 20 PM		6 45 AM	ar. Grand Island..... " lv.	*9 15 PM	*7 00 AM	*7 00 AM	*9 15 PM		
11 35 AM	10 10 PM	8 55 PM	3 20 PM	1 55 PM	lv. Grand Island..(U.P.) ar.	4 20 PM	3 35 AM	3 53 AM	12 25 Noon	10 50 AM	7 00 PM
3 05 PM	3 05 AM	12 45 Night	6 35 PM	5 20 PM	ar. North Platte..... " lv.	1 08 PM	11 00 PM	12 45 Night	8 50 AM	7 35 AM	3 47 PM
2 10 PM	2 10 AM	12 01 Night	5 40 PM	4 25 PM	lv. North Platte..... " ar.	12 03 Noon	9 50 PM	11 35 PM	7 40 AM	6 25 AM	2 44 PM
4 10 PM	4 52 AM	2 20 AM	7 40 PM	6 30 PM	ar. Julesburg....... " lv.	10 23 AM	7 15 PM	9 45 PM	5 40 AM	4 25 AM	— —
9 30 PM		7 50 AM			ar. Denver......... " lv.			*4 35 PM	*10 20 PM	*10 20 PM	
	4 52 AM	2 35 AM	7 40 PM	6 30 PM	lv. Julesburg....... " ar.	10 23 AM	7 15 PM	7 15 PM	5 40 AM	4 12 AM	— —
	10 20 AM	8 30 AM	11 50 PM	11 10 PM	ar. Cheyenne....... " lv.	7 03 AM	2 40 PM	2 40 PM	1 40 AM	12 35 Night	9 46 AM
	10 10 PM	10 10 PM		*9 00 AM	lv. St. Louis..(Mo. Pac.) ar.	6 01 PM	7 10 AM	7 10 AM	6 01 PM		
	7 10 AM	7 10 AM		5 15 PM	ar. Kansas City..... " lv.	*10 10 AM	*9 15 PM	*9 15 PM	*10 10 AM		
	*10 15 PM	*10 15 PM		*9 00 AM	lv. St. Louis.(Wab.R.R.) ar.	6 10 PM	6 50 AM	6 50 AM	6 10 PM		
	7 10 AM	7 10 AM		5 15 PM	ar. Kansas City..... " lv.	*10 20 AM	*9 00 PM	*9 00 PM	*10 20 AM		
	8 25 PM	8 25 PM		4 30 PM	lv. Memphis.(Frisco Sys.) ar.	11 10 AM	8 00 PM	8 00 PM	11 10 AM		
	9 40 AM	9 40 AM		5 30 PM	ar. Kansas City..... " lv.	10 45 AM	6 30 PM	6 30 PM	10 45 AM		
	11 28 PM	11 28 PM		9 06 AM	lv. St. Louis..(C. & A.) ar.	5 50 PM	6 59 AM	6 59 AM	5 50 PM		
	7 30 AM	7 30 AM		5 10 PM	ar. Kansas City..... " lv.	10 00 AM	9 15 PM	9 15 PM	10 00 AM		
	*6 00 PM	*6 00 PM			lv. Chicago......... " ar.		8 20 AM	8 20 AM			
	8 00 AM	8 00 AM			ar. Kansas City..... " lv.		*8 20 PM	*8 20 PM			
	*10 05 AM	*10 05 AM	*6 20 PM	*6 20 PM	lv. Kansas City..(U.P.) ar.	8 50 AM	5 00 PM	5 00 PM	8 50 AM		5 00 PM
	11 08 AM	11 08 AM	7 16 PM	7 16 PM	ar. Lawrence........ " lv.	7 50 AM	*3 55 PM	*3 55 PM	7 50 AM		*3 55 PM
	†9 20 AM	†9 20 AM	†4 15 PM	†4 15 PM	lv. Leavenworth.... " ar.	†11 55 AM	†5 40 PM	†5 40 PM	†11 55 AM		†5 40 PM
	11 08 AM	11 08 AM	*7 16 PM	*7 16 PM	lv. Lawrence........ " ar.	7 50 AM	3 55 PM	3 55 PM	7 50 AM		3 55 PM
	11 50 AM	11 50 AM	7 55 PM	7 55 PM	lv. Topeka.......... " lv.	7 05 AM	3 10 PM	3 10 PM	7 05 AM		3 10 PM
	7 55 PM	7 55 PM	2 25 AM	2 25 AM	ar. Ellis............ " lv.	12 45 Night	7 55 AM	7 55 AM	12 45 Night		7 55 AM
	7 05 PM	7 05 PM	1 30 AM	1 30 AM	lv. Ellis............ " ar.	11 40 PM	6 45 AM	6 45 AM	11 40 PM		6 45 AM
	6 30 AM	6 30 AM	11 35 AM	11 35 AM	ar. Denver.......... " lv.	1 30 PM	*7 40 PM	7 40 PM	1 30 PM		7 40 PM
	7 00 AM	7 00 AM	6 10 PM	6 10 PM	lv. Denver.......... " ar.	10 50 AM	6 00 PM	6 00 PM	10 50 AM		6 00 PM
	10 55 AM	10 45 AM	12 01 Night	11 20 PM	lv. Cheyenne....... " ar.	6 52 AM	2 20 PM	2 20 PM	1 30 AM	12 20 Night	9 36 AM
	10 30 PM	9 20 PM	8 55 AM	9 50 AM	ar. Green River..... " lv.	9 20 PM	3 10 AM	3 10 AM	2 55 PM	*2 45 PM	12 30 Night
	11 30 PM	10 27 PM	9 55 AM	11 05 AM	ar. Granger......... " lv.	8 13 PM	2 00 AM	2 00 AM	1 42 PM		11 40 PM
		3 45 AM	2 50 PM	4 00 PM	ar. Ogden........... " lv.	*3 00 PM	*7 30 PM	*7 30 PM	*8 20 AM		*7 00 PM
		5 15 AM	4 25 PM	5 15 PM	ar. Salt Lake City (O.S.L.) lv.	*1 30 PM	*6 05 PM	*6 05 PM	*7 10 AM		*5 55 PM
			5 15 PM	8 00 AM	ar. Los Angeles (S.P.L.A.&S.L.) lv.				*8 00 PM		*2 45 PM
		4 30 AM		4 20 PM	lv. Ogden..........(S.P.Co.) ar.	2 30 PM	6 10 PM	6 10 PM	7 10 AM		
		7 55 AM		2 15 PM	lv. Sacramento (Pac. time.) " lv.	2 20 PM	12 50 Noon	12 50 Noon	11 35 PM		
		12 48 Noon		5 48 PM	ar. San Francisco " " lv.	11 00 AM	9 00 AM	9 00 AM	6 00 PM		
		7 05 AM		8 55 AM	ar. Los Angeles " " lv.	c5 00 PM			11 30 PM		
					ar. Los Angeles " (Coast L.) " lv.	3 50 PM	8 30 AM	8 30 AM			
	10 35 PM	10 35 PM		&10 20 AM	lv. Green River.....(U. P.) ar.	8 55 PM			2 25 PM		
	11 35 PM	11 35 PM		11 20 AM	lv. Granger.....(O.S.L.) ar.	8 00 PM			1 30 PM		
	6 10 AM	6 10 AM		5 30 PM	ar. Pocatello....... " lv.	12 40 Noon	12 50 Noon	12 50 Noon	5 00 AM		
	4 15 PM	4 15 PM		2 45 AM	ar. Butte........... " lv.	2 45 AM	2 45 AM	2 45 AM	5 00 PM		
	11 10 PM	11 10 PM			ar. Helena....(G. N. Ry.) lv.	6 55 PM	6 55 PM	6 55 PM	8 35 AM		
	11 35 PM	11 35 PM		11 20 AM	lv. Granger....(O. S. L.) ar.	8 00 PM			1 30 PM		
	5 00 PM	5 00 PM		3 40 AM	ar. Huntington. ... " lv.	2 25 AM			2 00 PM		
	4 15 PM	4 15 PM		2 55 AM	lv. Huntington.(O.R.R.&N.Co.) ar.	1 10 AM			12 40 Noon		
	9 35 AM	9 35 AM		7 30 PM	ar. Spokane........ " lv.	7 25 AM			4 30 PM		
	7 15 AM	7 15 AM		5 25 PM	ar. Portland........ " lv.	*9 30 AM			*8 15 PM		

Central time. — Mt. time. — Central time. — Mount. time. — Mount. time. — Pac. time.

⊙ Train No. 3 is known as the Colorado Express east of Denver, and California Express west of there. Train No. 5 is known as the California and Oregon Express east of Green River, and Chicago-Portland Special west of there.

* Daily; † daily, except Sunday; a the Chicago-Portland Special; c the Overland Limited.

UNION PACIFIC, "THE OVERLAND ROUTE"

AND CONNECTING LINES.

UNION PACIFIC RAILROAD CO. Line Council Bluffs to Denver.

Colo. Exp. 3	Colo. Spec'l 11	Miles.	June 10, 1906.	Elev.	Chic. Spec'l 12	Fast Mail 10
P M	A M	....	LVE.] Cent. time. [ARR.	....	A M	P M
*3 20	*7 15	....	+.Council Bluffs ♁	980	8 15	3 55
3 35	7 30	....	arr...+Omaha ♁..lve.	1031	8 00	3 40
4 15	7 45	0	lve.....Omaha.....arr.	1031	7 44	3 30
4 25	....	4	...South Omaha ♁	1104	— —	3 18
— —	— —	29	.....Elkhorn......♁	1161	— —	— —
— —	— —	35	.......Valley......♁	1137	— —	— —
5 38	9 00	46	+.....Fremont.....♁	1192	6 25	2 02
h	— —	76	+.....Schuyler.....♁	1346	— —	1 22
6 55	10 06	91	+....Columbus....♁	1442	5 25	12 55
8 00	— —	132	+...Central City...♁	1697	— —	11 42
8 45	11 30	154	arr..+Grand Island .lve.	1860	3 58	11 00
8 55	11 35	154	lve...Grand Island...arr.	1860	3 53	10 50
— —	— —	177	.......Shelton......♁	2016	— —	— —
10 02	12 40	196	+.....Kearney.....♁	2146	2 55	9 50
— —	— —	211	.....Elm Creek.....♁	2262	— —	— —
11 00	h	231	+....Lexington.....♁	2385	— —	8 55
11 40	— —	256	....Gothenburg....♁	2557	— —	— —
12 45	3 05	....	ar. Central time. lv.		12 45	7 35
		291	+North Platte ♁	2796		
12 01	2 10	....	lv. Mountain time. ar.		11 35	6 25
— —	— —	310	....Sutherland.....		— —	5 56
— —	— —	322	.......Paxton........	3050	— —	5 38
1 28	— —	342	.....Ogallala.......	3207	— —	— —
2 20	4 10	372	arr...Julesburg ♁ lve.	3456	9 45	4 25
2 25	4 15	372	lve...Julesburg...arr.	3456	9 40	4 10
3 10	— —	402	.......Crook........	3695	— —	3 10
3 31	— —	418	.......Iliff.........	3820	— —	2 40
3 55	— —	430	+.....Sterling.....♁	3920	8 15	2 20
4 15	5 57	442	......Merino.......♁	4021	— —	1 53
4 39	6 27	459	......Snyder.......♁	4160	7 27	1 25
4 55	6 47	471	+...Fort Morgan...♁	4263	7 10	1 05
5 24	— —	490	......Orchard......♁	4391	6 37	12 32
5 51	— —	507	......Hardin........	4513	— —	12 01
6 20	8 10	523	arr...La Salle ♁..lve.	4663	5 45	11 35
7 50	9 30	569	arr...+Denver ♁	5170	*4 35	*10 20
A M	P M		[ARRIVE] [LEAVE		P M	P M

NORFOLK BRANCH.—Columbus to Norfolk.

Connection to and from Columbus.

29	77	Mls	June 10, 1906.	Elev.	30	78
P M	A M		(Central time.)		Noon	P M
*7 30	†7 15	0	lve.+Columbus ♁ arr.	1442	12 45	7 10
7 48	7 50	9	.......Oconee.....♁	1480	12 24	6 10
8 02	8 25	15	....Platte Center...♁	1538	12 13	5 45
8 30	9 25	26	+....Humphrey.....♁	1533	11 53	4 45
8 53	10 30	35	+.....Madison......♁	1574	11 33	4 00
9 10	11 13	45	....Warnerville.....	1590	11 13	3 20
9 30	12 10	50	arr..+Norfolk ♁..lve.	1514	*11 00	†3 00
P M	Noon		(C. St. P. M. & O. Ry.)		A M	P M
	3 55	126	.....Sioux City....♁	1107	†8 00	....
	P M		ARRIVE] [LEAVE		A M	....

ALBION BRANCH.—Columbus to Albion.

Connection to and from Columbus.

33	81	Mls	June 10, 1906.	Elev.	34	82
P M	A M		(Central time.)		Noon	P M
†2 25	†7 00	0	lve...Columbus ♁ arr.	1442	12 55	8 15
2 45	7 30	9	.......Oconee.....♁	1480	12 35	7 48
2 55	7 50	13	.......Munroe......♁	1518	12 25	7 00
3 20	8 20	20	........Genoa......♁	1573	12 10	6 30
3 36	8 45	26	......Woodville.....♁	1636	11 47	5 35
3 44	9 15	31	.....St. Edward.....♁	1656	11 38	5 25
3 56	9 45	36	........Boone......♁	1692	11 26	5 00
4 10	10 45	43	+......Albion......♁	1747	†11 10	†4 40
P M	A M		ARRIVE] [LEAVE		A M	P M

CEDAR RAPIDS BRANCH.—Genoa to Spalding.

31	79	Mls	June 10, 1906.	Elev.	32	80
P M	A M		(Central time.)		A M	P M
†3 17	†8 30	0	lve......Genoa ♁...arr.	1573	11 59	5 30
3 50	9 30	14	+.....Fullerton.....♁	1623	11 32	4 40
4 11	10 00	23	......Belgrade......♁	1700	11 09	4 11
4 28	10 52	30	+...Cedar Rapids...♁	1775	10 52	3 20
5 00	12 30	44	......Spalding......♁		†10 20	†2 00
P M	Noon		ARRIVE] [LEAVE		A M	P M

KEARNEY BRANCH.—Kearney to Callaway.

93	95	Mls	June 10, 1906.	Mls	94	96
P M	A M		(Central time.)		A M	P M
†3 35	†5 00	0	lve..Kearney ♁..arr.	65.5	9 45	3 00
3 51	5 20	5.5	..Glenwood Park.....	60.0	9 27	2 30
4 05	5 45	10.1	......Riverdale.....♁	55.4	9 15	2 10
4 25	6 15	16.8	......Amherst.......♁	48.7	8 58	1 45
4 43	6 30	22.8	.....Watertown......	42.8	8 43	1 20
4 55	6 45	26.3	........Miller.......♁	39.2	8 33	1 05
5 12	7 20	32.5	........Sumner......♁	33.0	8 15	12 38
5 36	7 53	40.4	.....Eddyville......♁	25.1	7 53	12 10
5 53	8 15	45.9	........Lomax.......	19.6	7 37	11 54
6 12	8 53	52.1	........Oconto.......♁	13.4	7 21	11 35
6 33	9 15	59.1	.........Lodi.........	6.4	7 01	11 15
6 55	10 00	65.5	.....Callaway.....♁		†6 45	†11 00
P M	A M		ARRIVE] [LEAVE		A M	A M

UNION PACIFIC RAILROAD CO.—Line Council Bluffs and Omaha to Ogden.

North Platte Local. 13	Los Ang. Lim. 7	Cal. & Ore. Exp. 5	China & Jap. Mail. 3	Over-land Lim. 1	Colo-rado Spl. 11	Miles.	June 10, 1906.	Atl. Exp. 4	Over-land Lim. 2	Fast Mail 10	China & Jap. Mail. 6	Chi-cago Spl. 12	Los Ang. Lim. 8	North Platte Local. 14
A M	A M	P M	P M	A M	A M	...	LVE.] Cent. time. [ARR.	A M	P M	P M	P M	A M	P M	P M
*7 25	*11 00	*3 25	*3 20	*9 00	*7 15	...	+.Council Bluffs. ♁	10 05	8 53	3 55	6 05	8 15	11 15	5 25
7 40	11 15	3 40	3 35	9 15	7 30	...	ar..+Omaha ♁.lv.	9 50	8 38	3 40	5 50	8 00	11 00	5 10
8 10	11 30	4 25	4 15	9 40	7 45	0	lv....Omaha...ar.	9 30	8 18	3 30	5 10	7 44	10 45	4 50
8 25	— —	4 35	4 25	— —	— —	4	.South Omaha ♁	9 15	— —	3 18	4 55	— —	— —	4 35
8 38	— —	— —	— —	— —	— —	10	......Gilmore...♁	9 00	— —	— —	— —	— —	— —	4 20
8 48	— —	— —	— —	— —	— —	15	.....Papillion...♁	8 48	— —	— —	— —	— —	— —	4 12
9 00	— —	— —	— —	— —	— —	20	......Millard....♁	8 20	— —	— —	— —	— —	— —	4 00
9 15	— —	— —	— —	— —	— —	29	......Elkhorn...♁	8 04	— —	— —	— —	— —	— —	3 45
9 22	— —	— —	— —	— —	— —	31	.....Waterloo...♁	7 59	— —	— —	— —	— —	— —	3 38
9 32	— —	5 26	— —	— —	— —	35	......Valley.....♁	7 52	— —	— —	— —	— —	— —	3 30
9 42	— —	— —	— —	— —	— —	41	......Mercer......	— —	— —	— —	— —	— —	— —	3 15
9 58	12 40	5 50	5 38	10 56	9 00	46	+..Fremont..♁	7 30	7 08	2 02	3 35	6 25	9 37	3 05
10 10	— —	— —	— —	— —	— —	53	.......Ames.....♁	7 14	— —	— —	— —	— —	— —	2 45
10 28	— —	6 20	— —	— —	— —	61	+..North Bend..♁	6 58	— —	— —	— —	— —	— —	2 32
10 42	— —	6 35	— —	— —	— —	68	......Rogers....♁	6 45	— —	— —	— —	— —	— —	2 20
10 58	— —	6 52	h —	— —	— —	76	+...Schuyler...♁	6 32	— —	1 22	m —	— —	— —	2 10
11 13	— —	— —	— —	— —	— —	84	......Benton....♁	6 15	— —	— —	— —	— —	— —	1 55
11 28	1 47	7 30	6 55	12 10	10 03	91	+..Columbus..♁	6 00	5 53	12 55	2 25	5 25	8 38	1 43
11 41	— —	— —	— —	— —	— —	99	......Duncan......	5 40	— —	— —	— —	— —	— —	1 17
11 57	— —	8 12	— —	— —	— —	109	....Silver Creek..♁	5 20	— —	— —	— —	— —	— —	12 58
— —	— —	— —	— —	— —	— —	115	......Havens......	— —	— —	— —	— —	— —	— —	— —
12 30	— —	8 36	— —	— —	— —	121	......Clarks....♁	5 00	— —	— —	— —	— —	— —	12 30
— —	— —	— —	— —	— —	— —	126	.....Thummel.....	— —	— —	— —	— —	— —	— —	— —
12 55	— —	9 05	8 00	— —	— —	132	+ Central City ♁	4 30	— —	11 42	— —	— —	— —	12 05
— —	— —	— —	— —	— —	— —	135	.....Paddock.....	— —	— —	— —	— —	— —	— —	11 57
1 15	— —	9 25	— —	— —	— —	142	.....Chapman...♁	4 05	— —	— —	— —	— —	— —	11 49
1 25	— —	— —	— —	— —	— —	148	.....Lockwood..♁	— —	— —	— —	— —	— —	— —	11 41
‖1 40	3 15	10 00	8 45	1 50	11 30	154	ar.+Grand Island lv.	3 45	4 25	11 00	12 35	3 58	7 05	11 30
2 05	3 20	10 10	8 55	1 55	11 35	154	lv. Grand Island ♁ ar.	3 35	4 20	10 50	12 25	3 53	7 00	11 20
2 17	— —	— —	— —	— —	— —	161	.......Alda.....♁	— —	— —	— —	— —	— —	— —	11 02
2 31	— —	10 42	— —	— —	— —	169	....Wood River.♁	3 06	— —	— —	— —	— —	— —	10 50
2 47	— —	10 59	— —	— —	— —	177	......Shelton....♁	2 50	— —	— —	— —	— —	— —	10 35
3 00	— —	11 11	— —	— —	— —	183	......Gibbon....♁	2 38	— —	— —	— —	— —	— —	10 25
3 12	— —	— —	— —	— —	— —	191	.......Buda.....♁	— —	— —	— —	— —	— —	— —	10 08
3 25	g —	11 42	10 02	d —	12 40	196	+...Kearney...♁	2 10	m —	9 50	11 08	2 55	m —	9 50
3 41	— —	— —	— —	— —	— —	205	......Odessa......	— —	— —	— —	— —	— —	— —	9 20
3 51	— —	12 10	— —	— —	— —	211	....Elm Creek...♁	1 45	— —	— —	— —	— —	— —	9 07
4 10	— —	12 28	— —	— —	— —	220	.....Overton....♁	1 34	— —	— —	— —	— —	— —	8 50
4 30	g —	12 55	11 00	d —	h —	231	+...Lexington...♁	1 18	m —	8 55	10 15	— —	m —	8 35
5 05	— —	1 24	— —	— —	— —	245	......Cozad.....♁	12 42	— —	— —	— —	— —	— —	8 13
5 14	— —	— —	— —	— —	— —	250	...Willow Island.♁	12 30	— —	— —	— —	— —	— —	8 05
5 25	— —	1 50	11 40	— —	— —	256	....Gothenburg .♁	12 20	— —	— —	— —	— —	— —	7 55
5 44	— —	2 18	— —	— —	— —	268	...Brady Island.♁	11 55	— —	— —	— —	— —	— —	7 35
5 58	— —	2 35	— —	— —	— —	277	.....Maxwell...♁	11 33	— —	— —	— —	— —	— —	7 20
6 25	6 35	3 05	12 45	5 20	3 05	...	ar..Central time..lv.	11 00	1 08	7 35	8 50	12 45	3 47	*7 00
P M	.....	.....	.....	.....	.....	291	+.North Platte.♁	.....	.....	.....	.....	.....	.....	A M
.....	5 40	2 10	12 01	4 25	2 10	...	lv..Mount.time..ar.	9 50	12 03	6 25	7 40	11 35	2 44	
.....	— —	2 34	— —	— —	— —	304	.....Hershey...♁	9 29	— —	6 05	— —	— —	— —	.....
.....	— —	2 46	— —	— —	— —	310	....Sutherland..♁	9 17	— —	5 56	— —	— —	— —	.....
.....	— —	3 10	— —	— —	— —	322	......Paxton....♁	8 56	— —	5 38	— —	— —	— —	.....
.....	— —	3 52	1 28	— —	— —	342	.....Ogalalla...♁	8 15	— —	— —	6 24	— —	— —	.....
.....	— —	4 25	— —	— —	— —	361	....Big Springs..♁	7 42	— —	4 43	— —	— —	— —	.....
.....	7 40	4 52	2 20	6 30	4 10	372	ar..Julesburg..lv.	7 15	10 23	4 25	5 40	*9 45	— —	.....
.....	7 40	4 52	2 35	6 30	P M	372	lv.Julesburg ♁ ar.	7 15	10 23	4 12	5 40	P M	— —	.....
.....	— —	— —	3 09	— —		387	.....Chappell...♁	6 36	— —	— —	— —		— —	.....
.....	— —	— —	3 37	— —	.....	396	....Lodge Pole..♁	6 18	— —	— —	— —	.....	— —	.....
.....	8 50	6 25	4 25	7 45	.....	414	ar....Sidney....lv.	5 50	9 23	3 10	4 25	.....	12 04	.....
.....	8 55	6 30	4 30	7 50	.....	414	lv....Sidney ♁..ar.	‖5 30	9 18	3 05	4 20	.....	12 01	.....
.....	— —	a —	4 50	— —	.....	422	.....Brownson.....	5 14	— —	— —	— —	.....	— —	.....
.....	— —	a —	5 19	— —	.....	433	.......Potter.....♁	4 56	— —	— —	— —	.....	— —	.....
.....	— —	7 49	6 02	— —	.....	451	......Kimball....♁	4 27	— —	— —	3 24	.....	— —	.....
.....	— —	a —	— —	— —	.....	463	.....Bushnell....♁	4 09	— —	— —	— —	.....	— —	.....
.....	— —	8 42	6 58	— —	.....	473	....Pine Bluffs..♁	3 53	— —	— —	— —	.....	— —	.....
.....	— —	a —	7 22	— —	.....	484	......Egbert.....♁	3 33	— —	— —	— —	.....	— —	.....
.....	— —	a —	7 52	— —	.....	496	.....Hillsdale...♁	3 13	— —	— —	— —	.....	— —	.....
.....	— —	a —	8 02	— —	.....	502	.....Durham......	3 02	— —	— —	— —	.....	— —	.....
.....	— —	a —	8 14	— —	.....	508	......Archer.....♁	2 54	— —	— —	— —	.....	— —	.....
.....	11 50	10 20	8 30	11 10	.....	516	ar+Cheyenne.lv.	2 40	7 03	12 35	1 40	.....	9 46	.....
.....	12 01	10 55	10 45	11 20	.....	516	lv..Cheyenne ♁ ar.	2 20	6 52	12 20	1 30	.....	9 36	.....
.....	— —	11 52	— —	— —	.....	535	..Granite Canon ♁	1 44	— —	— —	— —	.....	— —	.....
.....	— —	12 16	— —	— —	.....	543	......Buford....♁	1 29	— —	— —	— —	.....	— —	.....
.....	— —	12 28	— —	— —	.....	547	.....Sherman ...♁	1 20	— —	— —	— —	.....	— —	.....
.....	— —	12 42	— —	— —	.....	555	.....Hermosa....♁	1 03	— —	— —	— —	.....	— —	.....
.....	1 50	‖1 15	1 00	1 30	.....	573	ar..+Laramie..lv.	12 20	5 00	10 30	11 20	.....	8 06	.....
.....	1 55	1 35	1 10	1 33	.....	573	lv....Laramie ♁ ar.	‖11 59	4 55	10 25	11 15	.....	8 03	.....
.....	— —	2 22	— —	— —	.....	601	.....Lookout....♁	11 09	— —	— —	— —	.....	— —	.....
.....	— —	2 42	— —	— —	.....	612	...Rock River.♁	10 42	— —	— —	— —	.....	— —	.....
.....	— —	3 15	— —	— —	.....	630	...Medicine Bow.♁	9 56	— —	— —	9 07	.....	— —	.....
.....	— —	3 24	— —	— —	.....	634	.......Allen.....♁	9 48	— —	— —	— —	.....	— —	.....
.....	— —	4 02	3 32	— —	.....	650	......Hanna.....♁	9 18	— —	8 11	8 30	.....	— —	.....
.....	— —	4 20	— —	— —	.....	659	.......Dana.....♁	9 02	— —	— —	— —	.....	— —	.....
.....	— —	4 55	— —	— —	.....	675	....Fort Steele..♁	8 25	— —	— —	7 38	.....	— —	.....
.....	5 10	‖5 30	4 45	5 00	.....	690	ar.+Rawlins ♁ lv.	8 00	1 35	7 05	7 15	.....	4 43	.....
.....	5 15	5 50	4 50	5 15	.....	690	lv...Rawlins..ar.	‖7 40	1 30	‖6 45	7 10	.....	4 40	.....
.....	— —	6 59	— —	— —	.....	719	......Creston....♁	6 36	— —	— —	— —	.....	— —	.....
.....	— —	7 27	6 32	— —	.....	731	....Wamsutter..♁	6 05	— —	5 35	5 57	.....	— —	.....
.....	— —	8 32	— —	— —	.....	764	...Bitter Creek.♁	5 10	— —	— —	— —	.....	— —	.....
.....	— —	9 06	— —	— —	.....	784	..Point of Rocks ♁	4 30	— —	— —	4 18	.....	— —	.....
.....	8 34	9 50	8 50	9 26	11	809	+.Rock Springs.♁	3 45	9 50	3 14	3 28	16	1 01	12
.....	8 55	10 30	9 20	9 50	A M	824	ar..Green River..lv.	3 10	9 20	2 45	2 55	P M	12 30	P M
.....	9 00	10 35	9 30	10 10	*10 20	824	lv..Green River ♁ ar.	3 00	9 10	2 35	2 35	2 25	12 25	8 55
.....	9 55	11 30	10 27	11 05	11 15	854	.....Granger...♁	*2 00	*8 13	*1 40	*1 40	*1 30	*11 30	*8 03
	A M	P M	P M	A M	A M	...	ARRIVE] [LEAVE	A M	P M	P M	P M	P M	P M	P M

STANDARD OF TIME—East of North Platte, *Central time.* East of Sparks, Nev., and Huntington, *Mountain time.* West of Sparks, Nev., and Huntington, *Pacific time.*

* Daily; † daily, except Sunday; *a* stops to leave from east of Julesburg; *d* stops to take for points west of Green River; *g* stops to take for Ogden and points south; *h* stops to take Colorado passengers only; *m* stops to take for Omaha and east. ‖ Meals. + Coupon stations; ♁ Telegraph stations.

Time from 1 00 p.m. to 12 59 night, *bold-faced type.*

SAFETY CAR HEATING & LIGHTING CO.
160 BROADWAY, NEW YORK.
PINTSCH GAS
Steam Heat: Straight Port Steam Coupling

Grand Island
Bird's-eye view, *c.*1910
Schimmer Lake, 1906

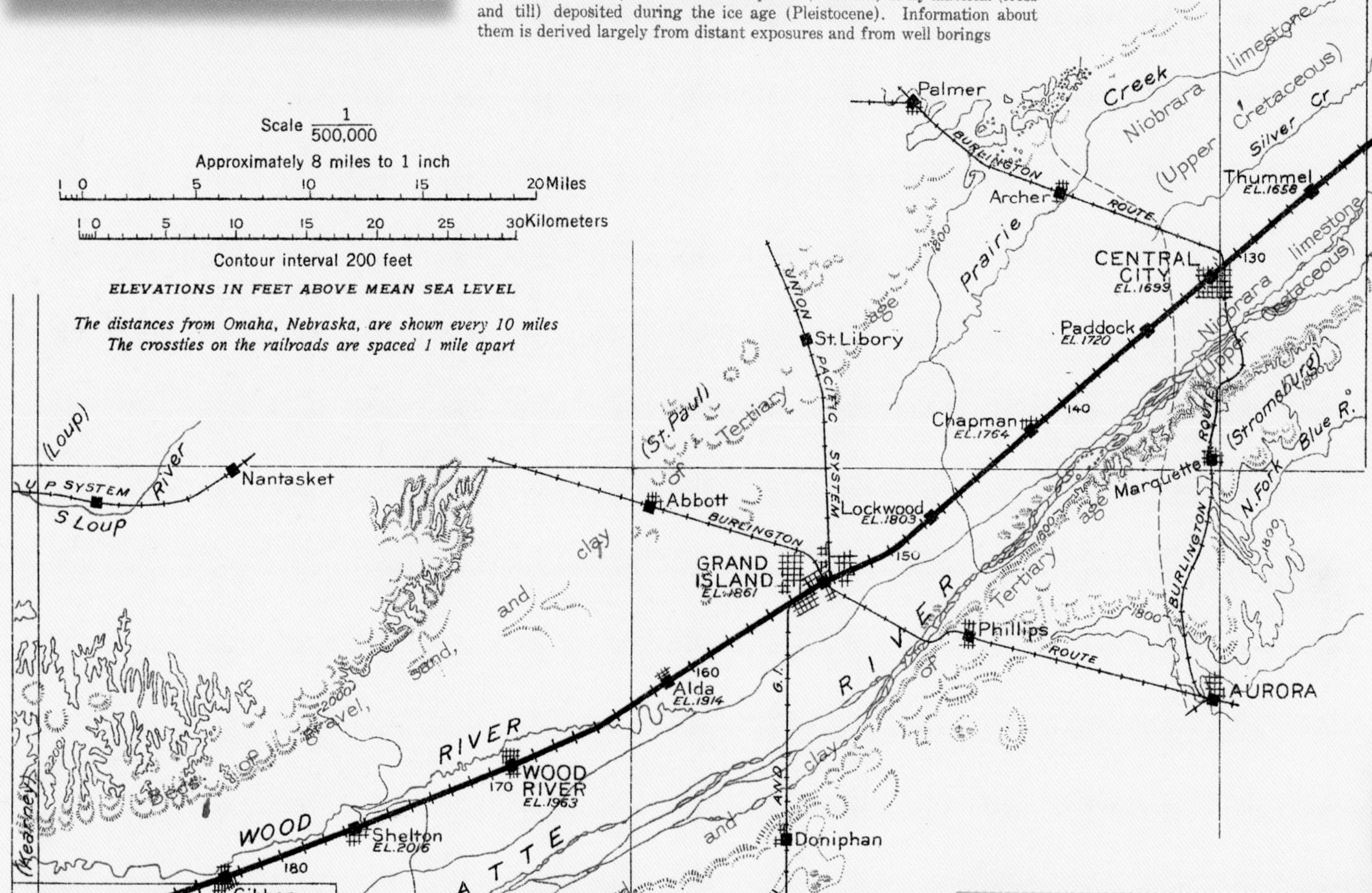

EXPLANATION

The rock formations indicated on this map can not be seen from the train. They are covered by recent stream deposits (alluvium) or by material (loess and till) deposited during the ice age (Pleistocene). Information about them is derived largely from distant exposures and from well borings

Scale $\frac{1}{500,000}$

Approximately 8 miles to 1 inch

Contour interval 200 feet

ELEVATIONS IN FEET ABOVE MEAN SEA LEVEL

The distances from Omaha, Nebraska, are shown every 10 miles
The crossties on the railroads are spaced 1 mile apart

Columbus
Town Gate, 1920
New Loup River Bridge, 1920s

Central City
G Street, late 1920s

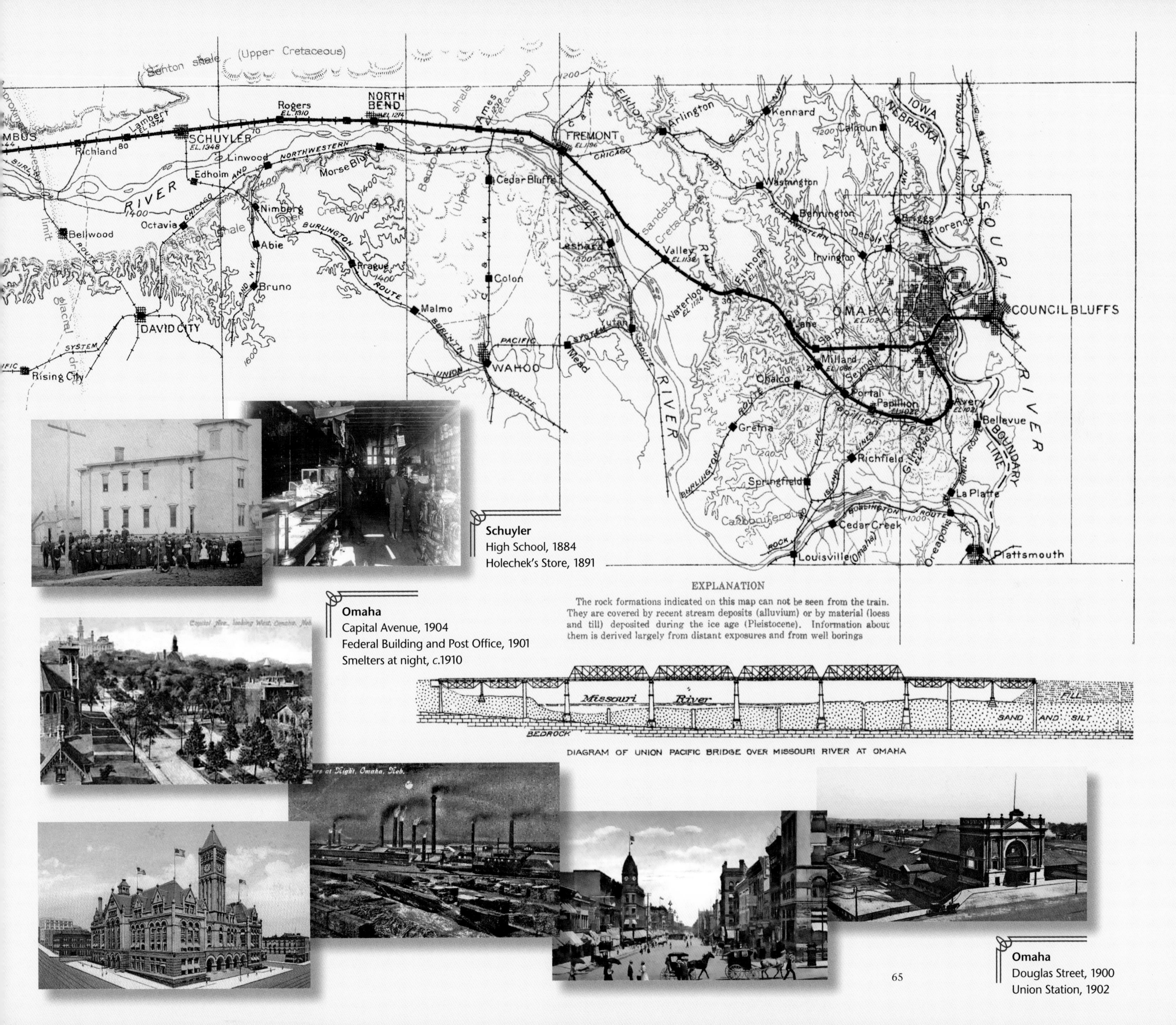

Schuyler
High School, 1884
Holechek's Store, 1891

Omaha
Capital Avenue, 1904
Federal Building and Post Office, 1901
Smelters at night, *c.*1910

Omaha
Douglas Street, 1900
Union Station, 1902

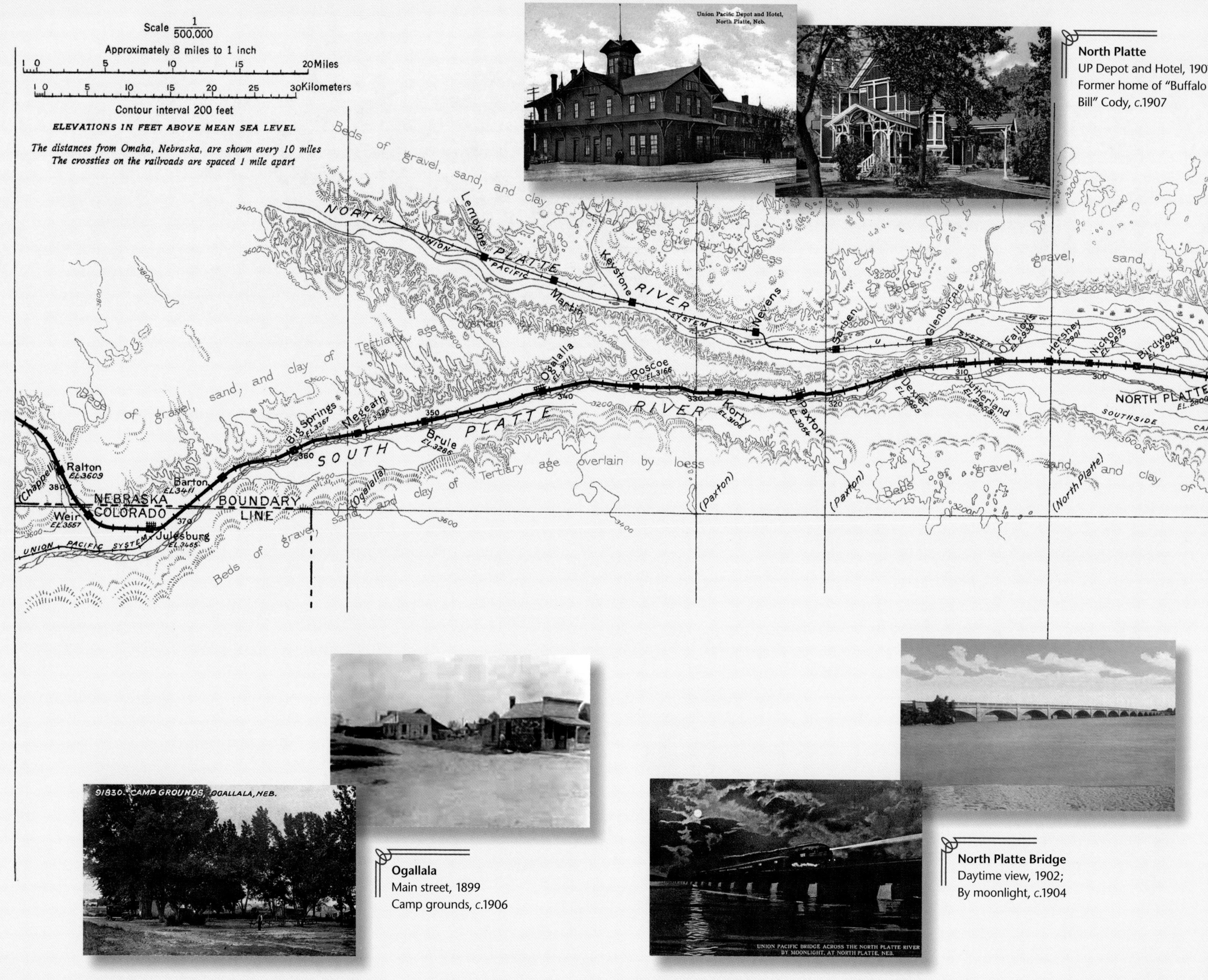

North Platte
UP Depot and Hotel, 1901
Former home of "Buffalo Bill" Cody, *c.*1907

Ogallala
Main street, 1899
Camp grounds, *c.*1906

North Platte Bridge
Daytime view, 1902;
By moonlight, *c.*1904

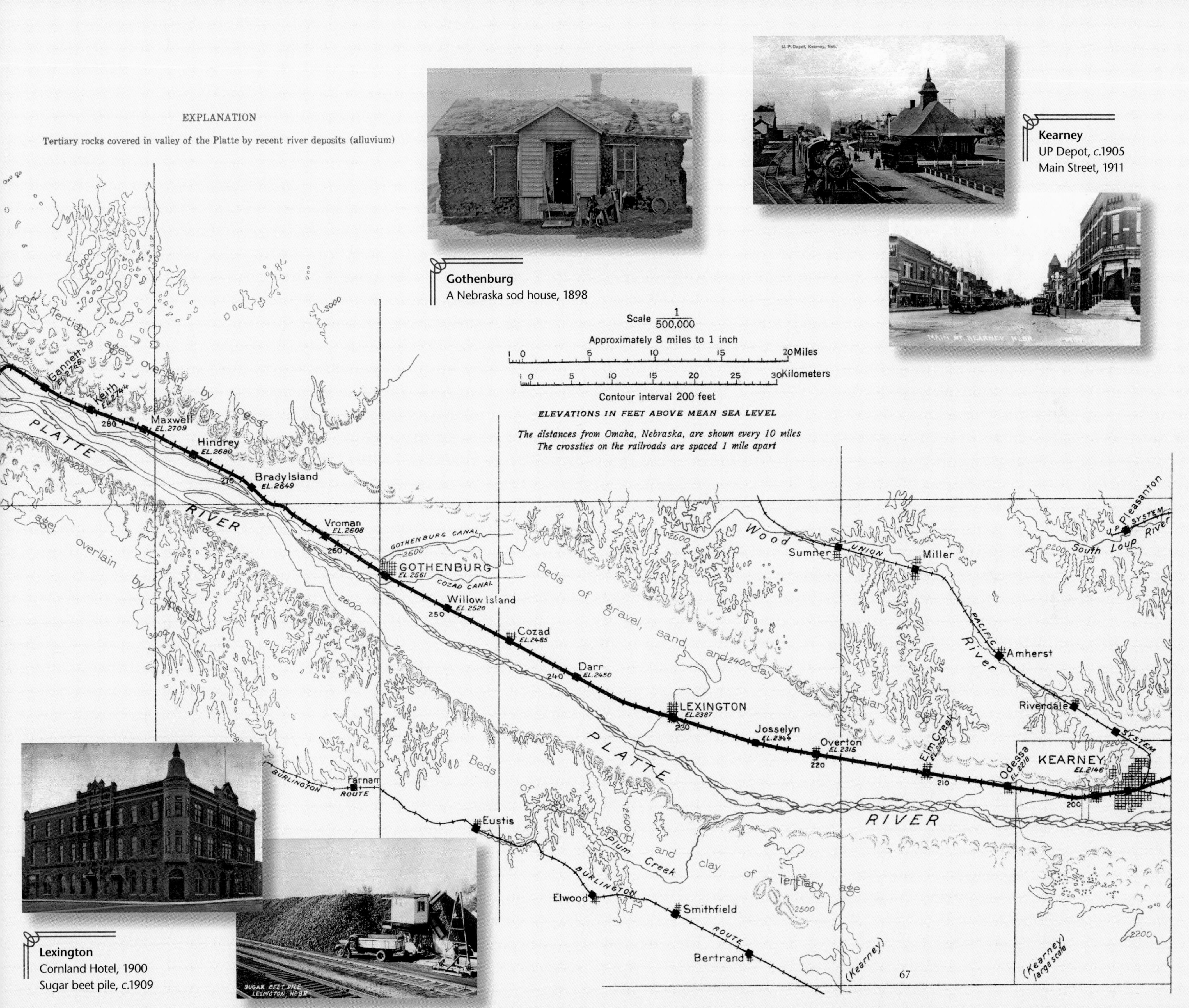

Gothenburg
A Nebraska sod house, 1898

Kearney
UP Depot, *c.*1905
Main Street, 1911

Lexington
Cornland Hotel, 1900
Sugar beet pile, *c.*1909

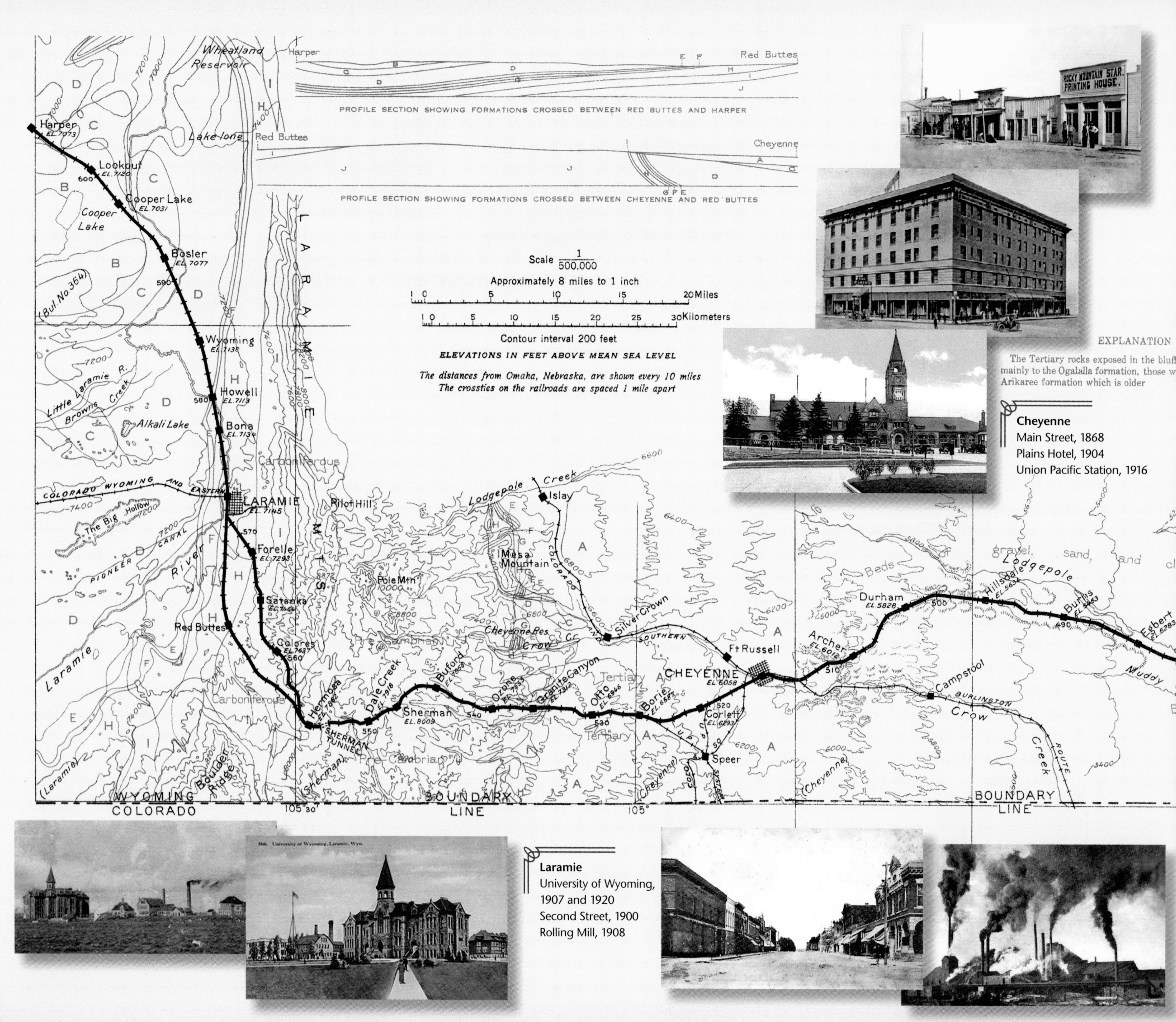

Cheyenne
Main Street, 1868
Plains Hotel, 1904
Union Pacific Station, 1916

Laramie
University of Wyoming, 1907 and 1920
Second Street, 1900
Rolling Mill, 1908

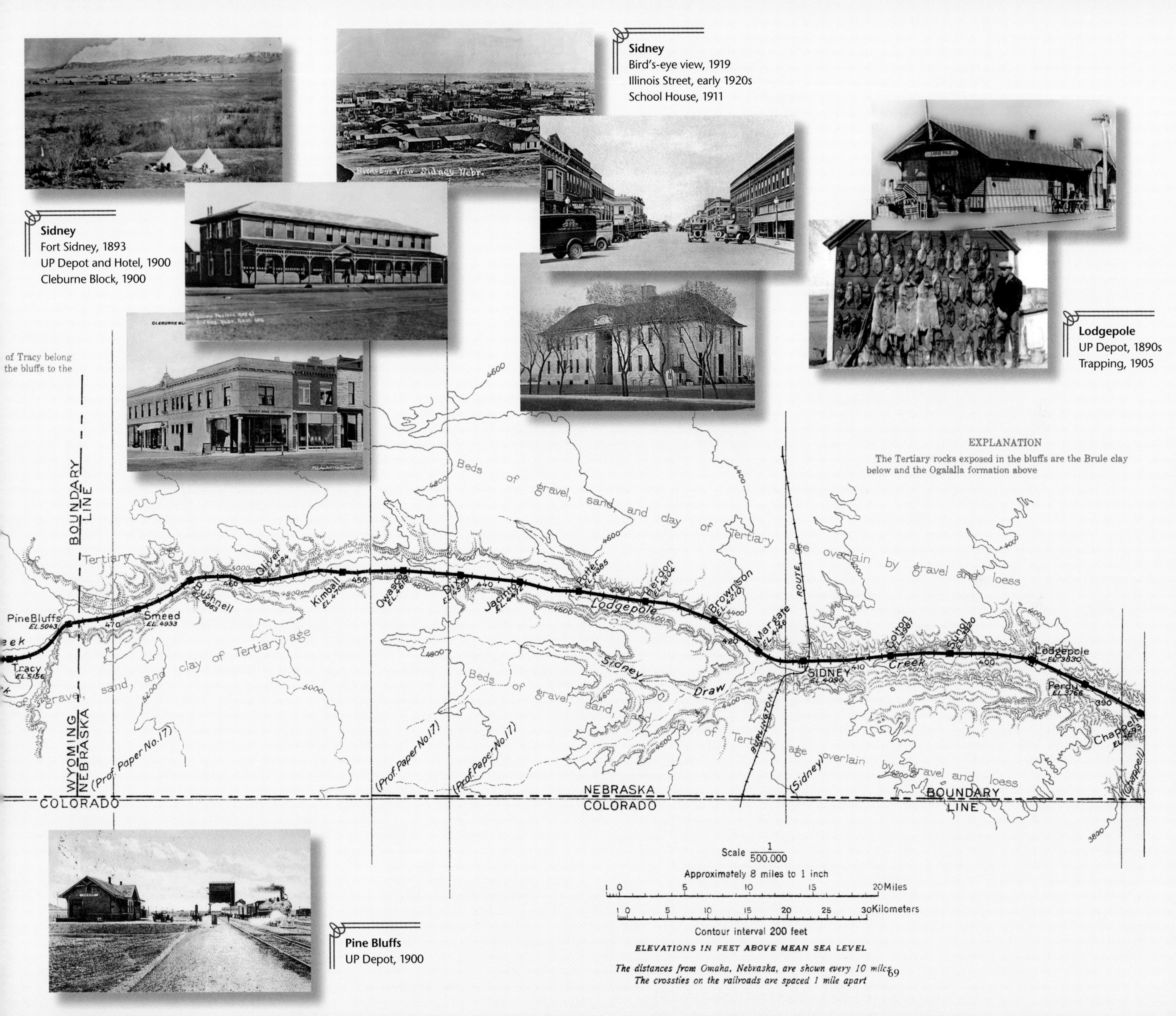

Sidney
Bird's-eye view, 1919
Illinois Street, early 1920s
School House, 1911

Sidney
Fort Sidney, 1893
UP Depot and Hotel, 1900
Cleburne Block, 1900

Lodgepole
UP Depot, 1890s
Trapping, 1905

Pine Bluffs
UP Depot, 1900

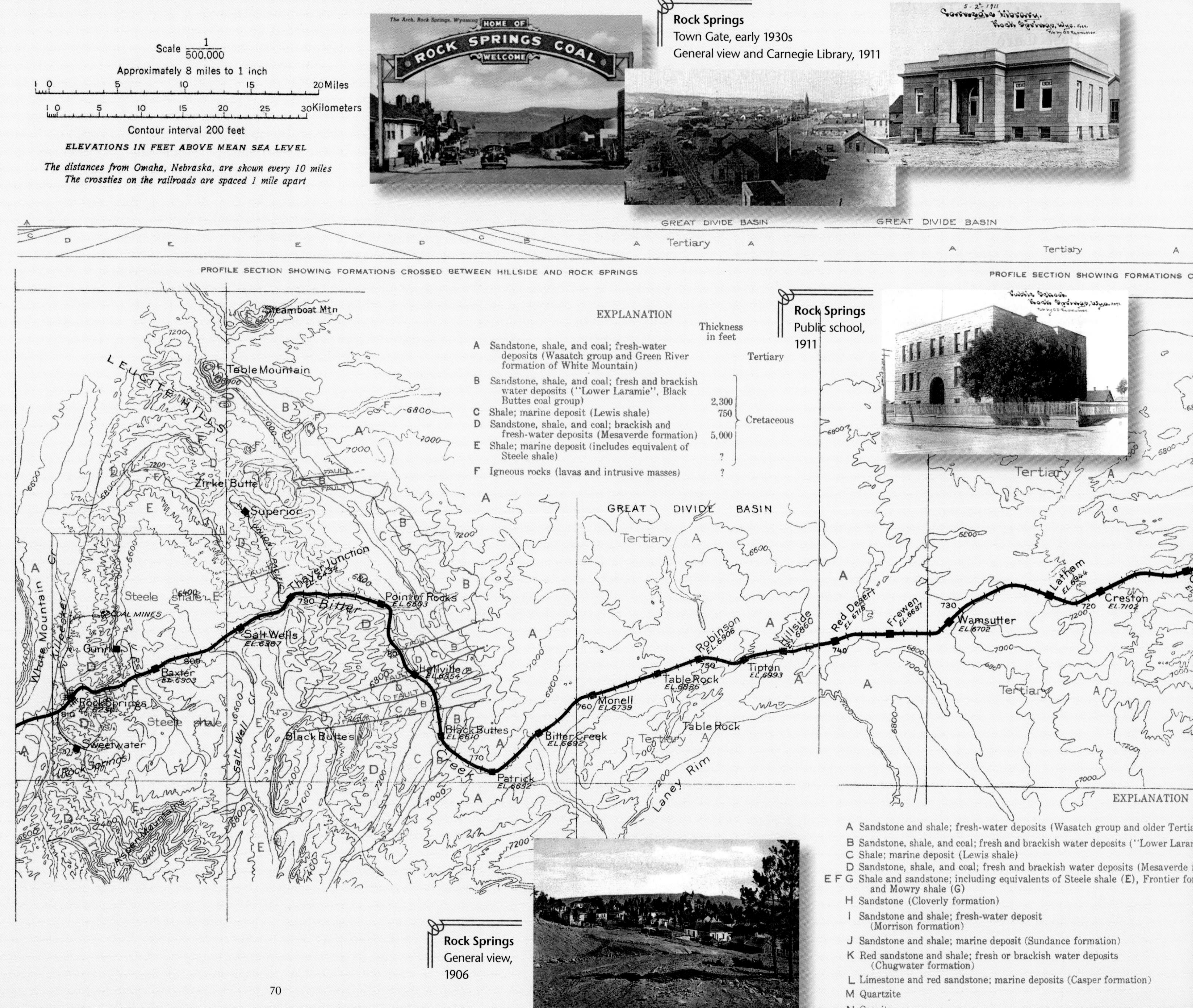

Scale 1/500,000
Approximately 8 miles to 1 inch
Miles
Kilometers
Contour interval 200 feet
ELEVATIONS IN FEET ABOVE MEAN SEA LEVEL
The distances from Omaha, Nebraska, are shown every 10 miles
The crossties on the railroads are spaced 1 mile apart
The Arch, Rock Springs, Wyoming
HOME OF
ROCK SPRINGS COAL
WELCOME
GREAT DIVIDE BASIN
Tertiary
PROFILE SECTION SHOWING FORMATIONS CROSSED BETWEEN HILLSIDE AND ROCK SPRINGS
PROFILE SECTION SHOWING FORMATIONS CR
EXPLANATION
Thickness in feet
A Sandstone, shale, and coal; fresh-water deposits (Wasatch group and Green River formation of White Mountain) Tertiary
B Sandstone, shale, and coal; fresh and brackish water deposits ("Lower Laramie", Black Buttes coal group) 2,300
C Shale; marine deposit (Lewis shale) 750
D Sandstone, shale, and coal; brackish and fresh-water deposits (Mesaverde formation) 5,000
E Shale; marine deposit (includes equivalent of Steele shale) ?
Cretaceous
F Igneous rocks (lavas and intrusive masses) ?
Steamboat Mtn
Table Mountain
LEUCITE HILLS
Zirkel Butte
Superior
Thayer Junction
Point of Rocks
Bitter Creek
Salt Wells
Gunn
Baxter
Rock Springs
Sweetwater
Steele shale
COAL MINES
White Mountain
Black Buttes
Hallville
Patrick
Bitter Creek
Monell
Table Rock
Tipton
Robinson
Hillside
Red Desert
Frewen
Wamsutter
Latham
Creston
Laney Rim
Salt Well Cr
Aspen Mountain
GREAT DIVIDE BASIN
EXPLANATION
A Sandstone and shale; fresh-water deposits (Wasatch group and older Tertia
B Sandstone, shale, and coal; fresh and brackish water deposits ("Lower Laram
C Shale; marine deposit (Lewis shale)
D Sandstone, shale, and coal; fresh and brackish water deposits (Mesaverde f
E F G Shale and sandstone; including equivalents of Steele shale (E), Frontier for and Mowry shale (G)
H Sandstone (Cloverly formation)
I Sandstone and shale; fresh-water deposit (Morrison formation)
J Sandstone and shale; marine deposit (Sundance formation)
K Red sandstone and shale; fresh or brackish water deposits (Chugwater formation)
L Limestone and red sandstone; marine deposits (Casper formation)
M Quartzite
N Granite

Rock Springs
Town Gate, early 1930s
General view and Carnegie Library, 1911

Rock Springs
Public school, 1911

Rock Springs
General view, 1906

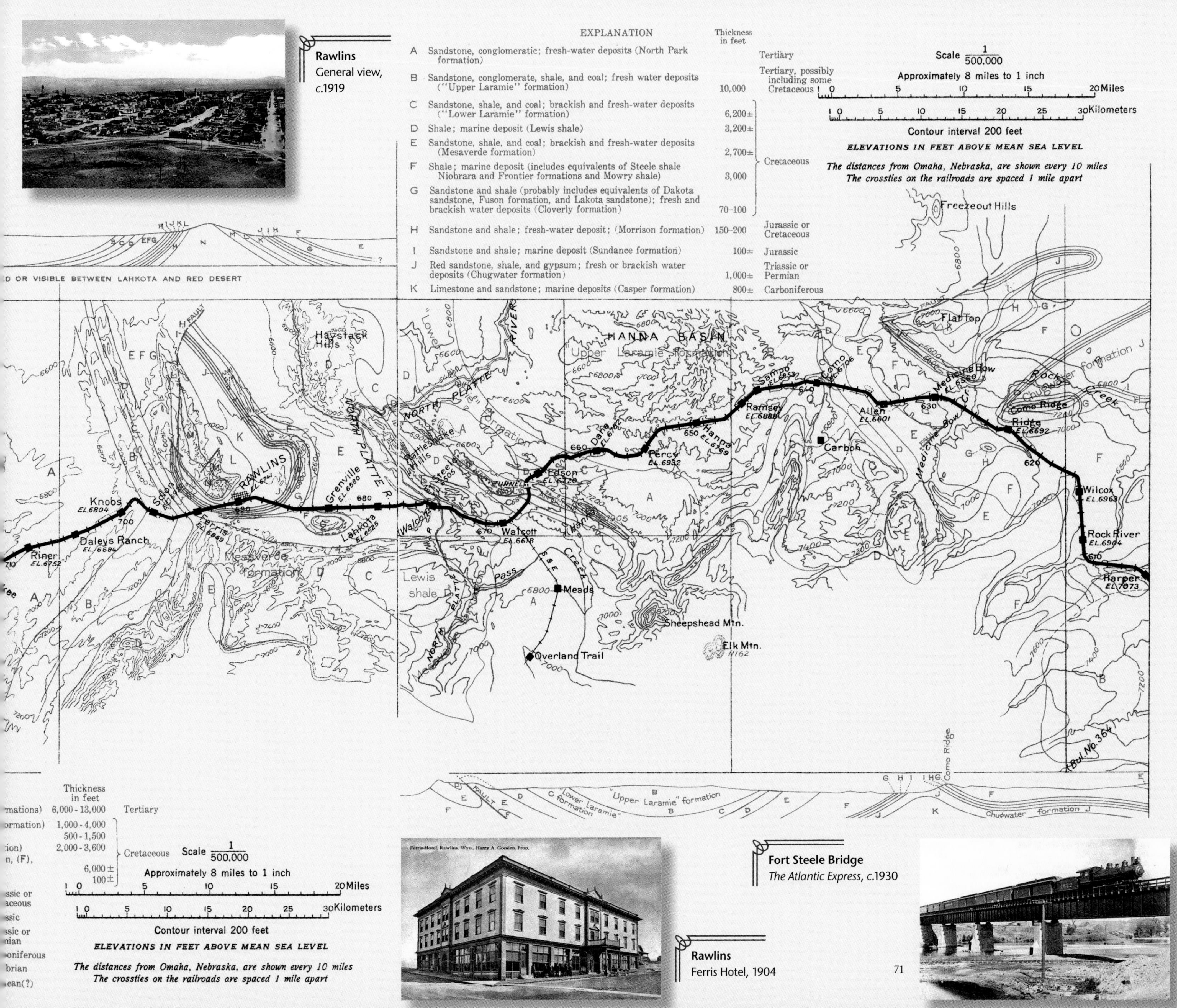
EXPLANATION
Thickness in feet
A Sandstone, conglomeratic; fresh-water deposits (North Park formation) — Tertiary
B Sandstone, conglomerate, shale, and coal; fresh water deposits ("Upper Laramie" formation) — 10,000 — Tertiary, possibly including some Cretaceous
C Sandstone, shale, and coal; brackish and fresh-water deposits ("Lower Laramie" formation) — 6,200±
D Shale; marine deposit (Lewis shale) — 3,200±
E Sandstone, shale, and coal; brackish and fresh-water deposits (Mesaverde formation) — 2,700±
F Shale; marine deposit (includes equivalents of Steele shale Niobrara and Frontier formations and Mowry shale) — 3,000
G Sandstone and shale (probably includes equivalents of Dakota sandstone, Fuson formation, and Lakota sandstone); fresh and brackish water deposits (Cloverly formation) — 70-100
Cretaceous
H Sandstone and shale; fresh-water deposit; (Morrison formation) — 150-200 — Jurassic or Cretaceous
I Sandstone and shale; marine deposit (Sundance formation) — 100± — Jurassic
J Red sandstone, shale, and gypsum; fresh or brackish water deposits (Chugwater formation) — 1,000± — Triassic or Permian
K Limestone and sandstone; marine deposits (Casper formation) — 800± — Carboniferous
Scale 1/500,000
Approximately 8 miles to 1 inch
0 5 10 15 20 Miles
0 5 10 15 20 25 30 Kilometers
Contour interval 200 feet
ELEVATIONS IN FEET ABOVE MEAN SEA LEVEL
The distances from Omaha, Nebraska, are shown every 10 miles
The crossties on the railroads are spaced 1 mile apart
D OR VISIBLE BETWEEN LAHKOTA AND RED DESERT
Freezeout Hills
Haystack Hills
HANNA BASIN
Upper Laramie formation
NORTH PLATTE RIVER
Lower Laramie formation
Flat Top
Chugwater formation
Como Ridge
Rock Creek
Medicine Bow
Sampo
Como
Ramsey
Allen
Ridge
Hanna
Dana
Percy
Carbon
Edson
Rattlesnake Hills
Steele
TUNNEL
Walcott
RAWLINS
Solon
Knobs
Daleys Ranch
Riner
Ferris
Grenville
Lahkota
Wilcox
Rock River
Harper
Mesaverde formation
Lewis shale
Pass Creek
Meads
Sheepshead Mtn.
Elk Mtn.
Overland Trail
Medicine Bow Cr.
(Bul. No. 364)
"Upper Laramie" formation
"Lower Laramie" formation
FAULT
Chugwater formation
Thickness in feet
6,000-13,000 — Tertiary
1,000-4,000
500-1,500
2,000-3,600 — Cretaceous
6,000±
100±
Scale 1/500,000
Approximately 8 miles to 1 inch
0 5 10 15 20 Miles
0 5 10 15 20 25 30 Kilometers
Contour interval 200 feet
ELEVATIONS IN FEET ABOVE MEAN SEA LEVEL
The distances from Omaha, Nebraska, are shown every 10 miles
The crossties on the railroads are spaced 1 mile apart
Ferris Hotel, Rawlins, Wyo., Harry A. Gonden, Prop.

Rawlins
General view, c.1919

Rawlins
Ferris Hotel, 1904

Fort Steele Bridge
The Atlantic Express, c.1930

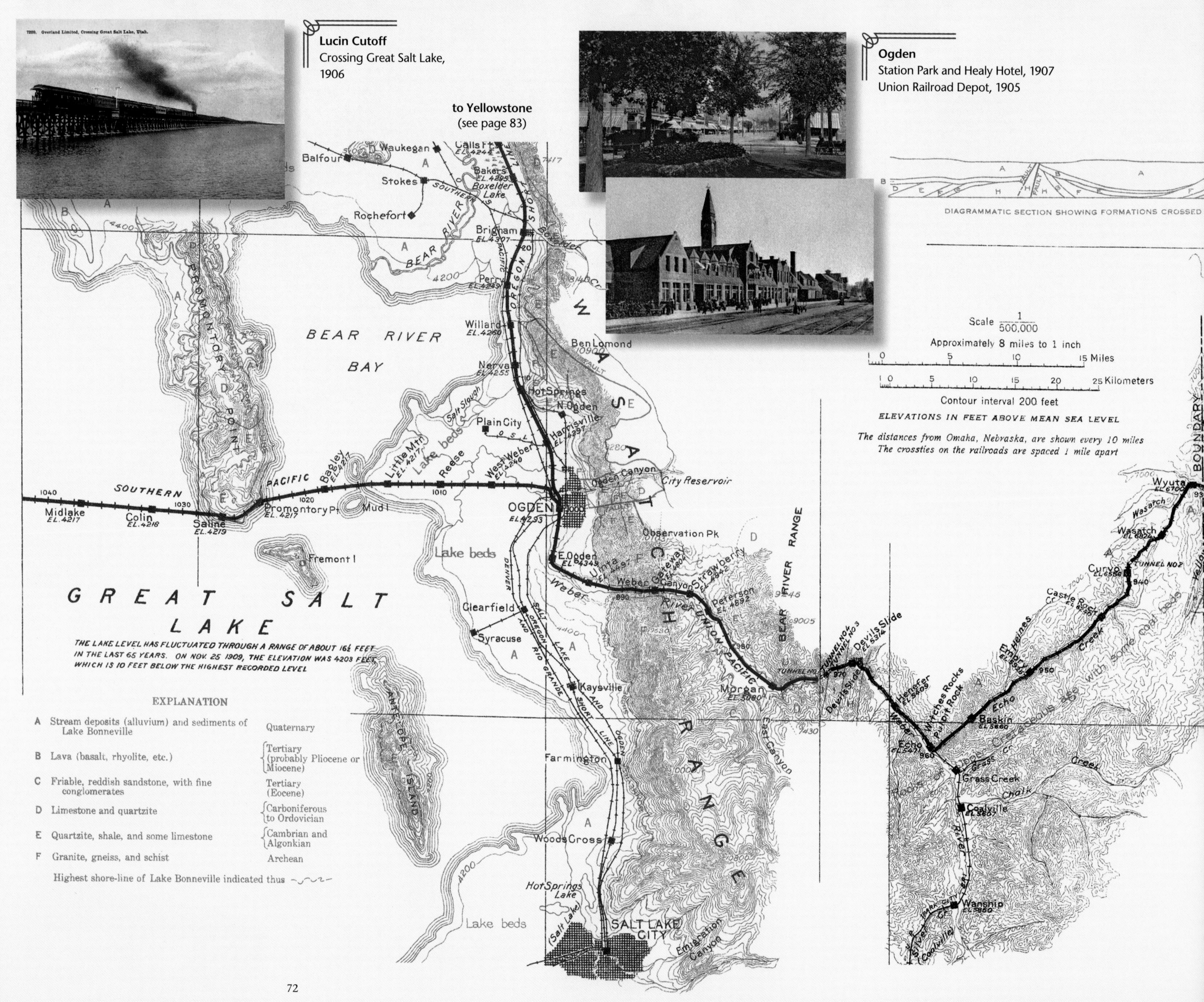

Lucin Cutoff
Crossing Great Salt Lake, 1906

to Yellowstone
(see page 83)

Ogden
Station Park and Healy Hotel, 1907
Union Railroad Depot, 1905

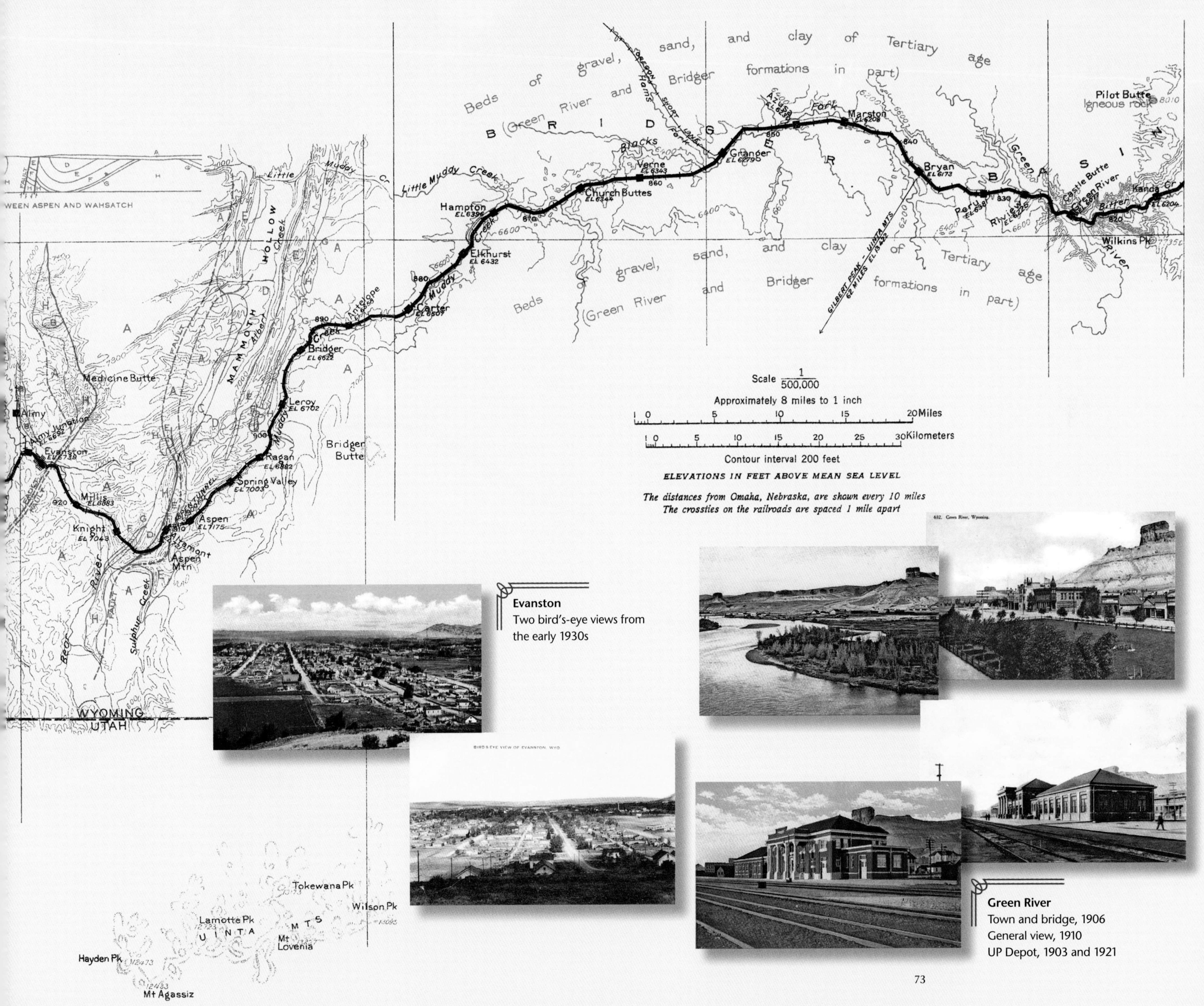

Evanston
Two bird's-eye views from the early 1930s

Green River
Town and bridge, 1906
General view, 1910
UP Depot, 1903 and 1921

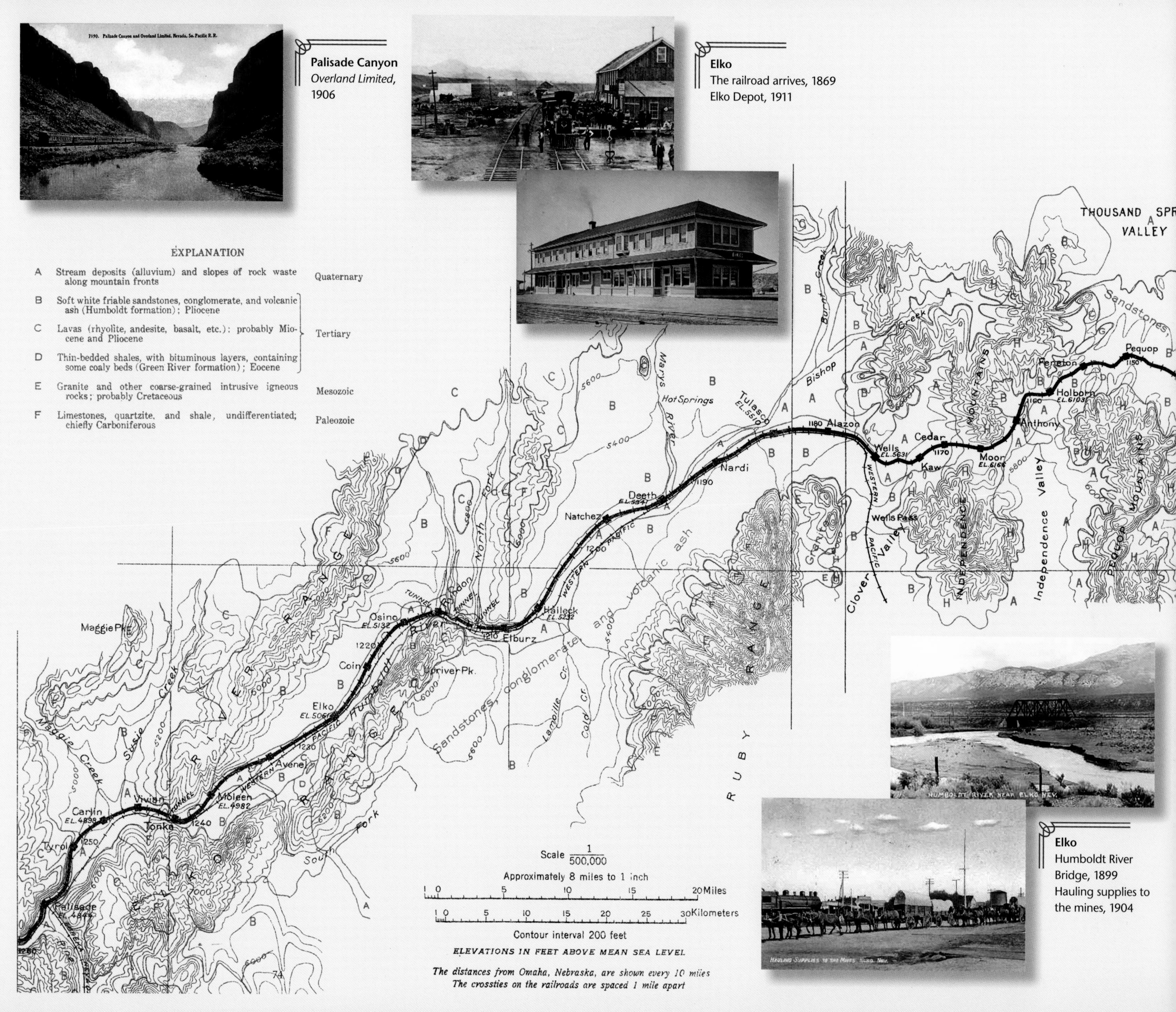

7190. Palisade Canyon and Overland Limited, Nevada, So. Pacific R.R.
EXPLANATION
A Stream deposits (alluvium) and slopes of rock waste along mountain fronts — Quaternary
B Soft white friable sandstones, conglomerate, and volcanic ash (Humboldt formation); Pliocene
C Lavas (rhyolite, andesite, basalt, etc.); probably Miocene and Pliocene — Tertiary
D Thin-bedded shales, with bituminous layers, containing some coaly beds (Green River formation); Eocene
E Granite and other coarse-grained intrusive igneous rocks; probably Cretaceous — Mesozoic
F Limestones, quartzite, and shale, undifferentiated; chiefly Carboniferous — Paleozoic
THOUSAND SPR
VALLEY
Pequop
Peneton
Holborn EL.6103
Anthony
Moor EL.6166
Cedar
Kaw
Wells EL.5631
Alazon
Tulasco EL.5510
Bishop
Burnt Creek
Hot Springs
Marys River
Nardi
Deeth EL.5341
Natchez
Wells Pass
Clover Valley
Independence Valley
INDEPENDENCE MOUNTAINS
PEQUOP MOUNTAINS
RUBY RANGE
Halleck EL.5232
Elburz
Osino EL.5132
Upriver Pk.
Coin
Elko EL.5061
Humboldt River
North Fork
Lamoille Cr.
Cold Cr.
Sandstones, conglomerate, and volcanic ash
Maggie Pk.
Maggie Creek
Susie Creek
Avenel
Moleen EL.4982
Vivian
Carlin EL.4898
Tonka
Tyrol
Palisade EL.4844
South Fork
WESTERN PACIFIC
TUNNEL
Scale 1/500,000
Approximately 8 miles to 1 inch
0 5 10 15 20 Miles
0 5 10 15 20 25 30 Kilometers
Contour interval 200 feet
ELEVATIONS IN FEET ABOVE MEAN SEA LEVEL
The distances from Omaha, Nebraska, are shown every 10 miles
The crossties on the railroads are spaced 1 mile apart
HUMBOLDT RIVER NEAR ELKO NEV.
HAULING SUPPLIES TO THE MINES, ELKO, NEV.

Palisade Canyon
Overland Limited, 1906

Elko
The railroad arrives, 1869
Elko Depot, 1911

Elko
Humboldt River Bridge, 1899
Hauling supplies to the mines, 1904

Scale $\frac{1}{500,000}$

Approximately 8 miles to 1 inch

0 5 10 15 20 Miles

0 5 10 15 20 25 30 Kilometers

Contour interval 200 feet

ELEVATIONS IN FEET ABOVE MEAN SEA LEVEL

The distances from Omaha, Nebraska, are shown every 10 miles
The crossties on the railroads are spaced 1 mile apart

GREAT SALT LAKE DESERT

Scale $\frac{1}{500,000}$

Approximately 8 miles to 1 inch

0 5 10 15 20 Miles

0 5 10 15 20 25 30 Kilometers

Contour interval 200 feet

ELEVATIONS IN FEET ABOVE MEAN SEA LEVEL

The distances from Omaha, Nebraska, are shown every 10 miles
The crossties on the railroads are spaced 1 mile apart

Lucin
A Pullman car taking on water, 1906

Lucin Cutoff
Postcards from 1906, showing a train on the trestle and Midlake Station
Two 1903 photographs showing the building of the trestle

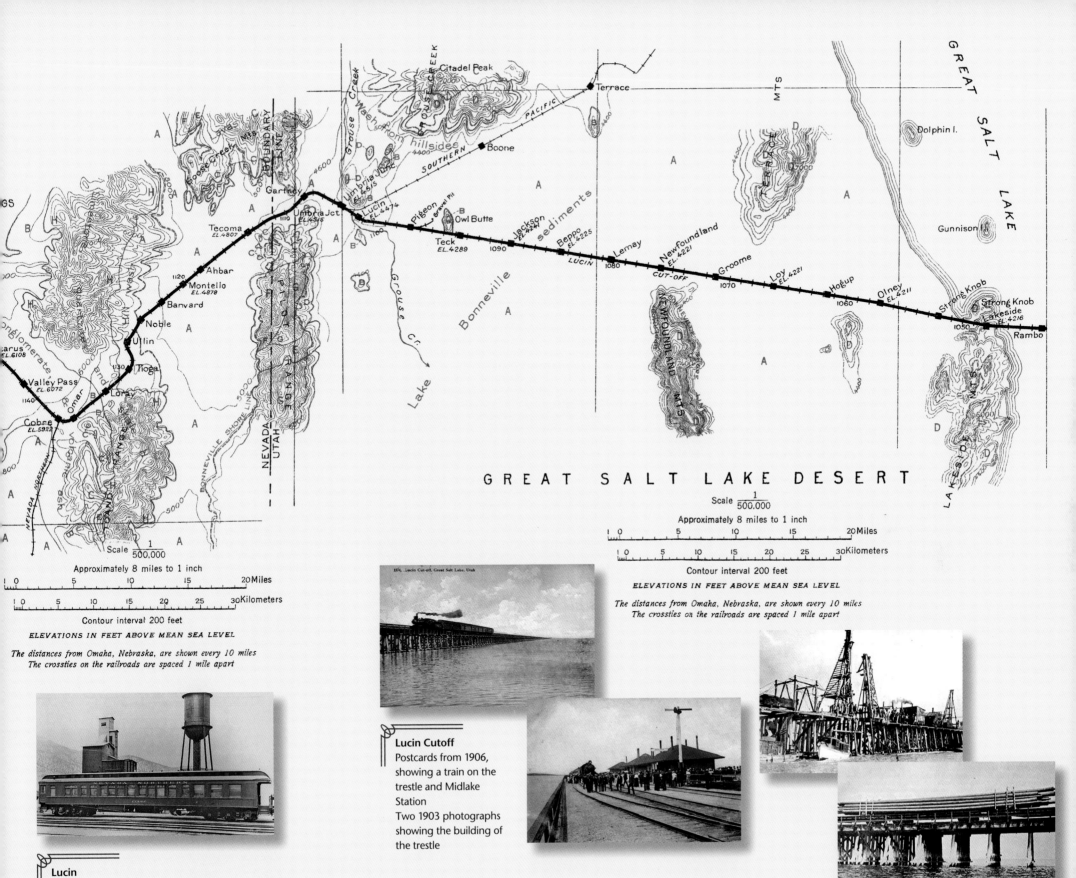

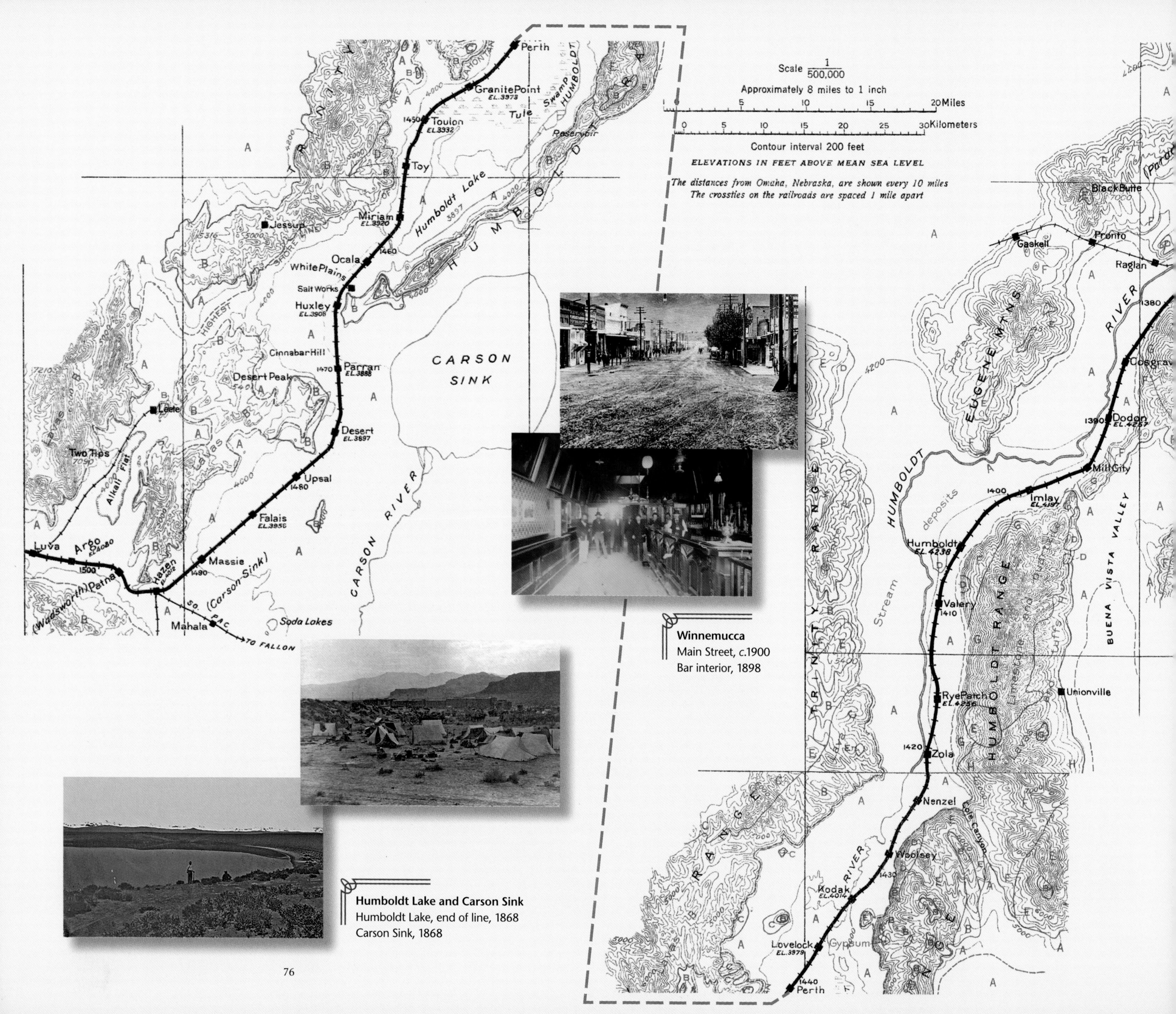

Winnemucca
Main Street, *c.*1900
Bar interior, 1898

Humboldt Lake and Carson Sink
Humboldt Lake, end of line, 1868
Carson Sink, 1868

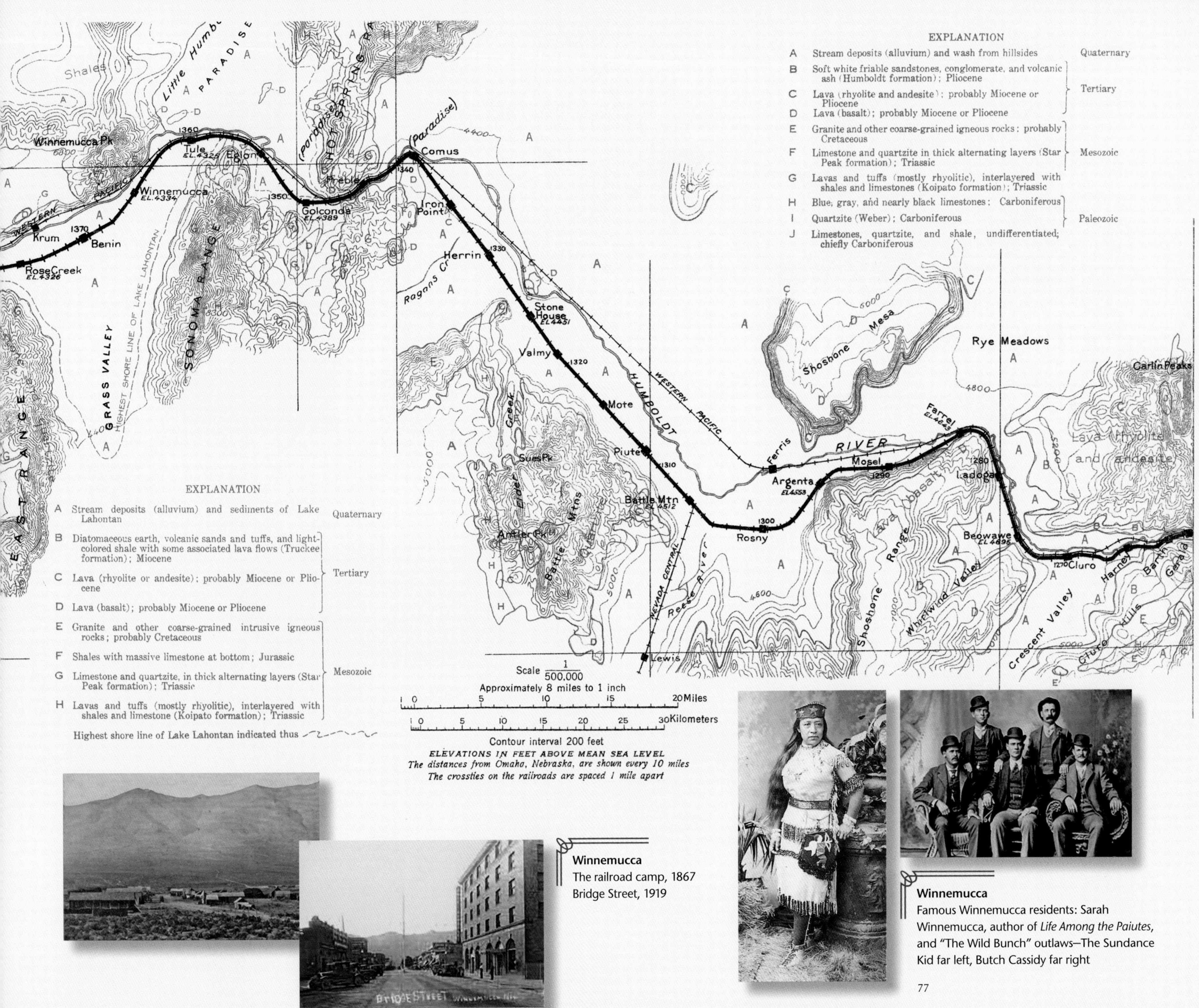
EXPLANATION
A Stream deposits (alluvium) and wash from hillsides — Quaternary
B Soft white friable sandstones, conglomerate, and volcanic ash (Humboldt formation); Pliocene
C Lava (rhyolite and andesite); probably Miocene or Pliocene
D Lava (basalt); probably Miocene or Pliocene — Tertiary
E Granite and other coarse-grained igneous rocks; probably Cretaceous
F Limestone and quartzite in thick alternating layers (Star Peak formation); Triassic
G Lavas and tuffs (mostly rhyolitic), interlayered with shales and limestones (Koipato formation); Triassic — Mesozoic
H Blue, gray, and nearly black limestones; Carboniferous
I Quartzite (Weber); Carboniferous
J Limestones, quartzite, and shale, undifferentiated; chiefly Carboniferous — Paleozoic
EXPLANATION
A Stream deposits (alluvium) and sediments of Lake Lahontan — Quaternary
B Diatomaceous earth, volcanic sands and tuffs, and light-colored shale with some associated lava flows (Truckee formation); Miocene
C Lava (rhyolite or andesite); probably Miocene or Pliocene
D Lava (basalt); probably Miocene or Pliocene — Tertiary
E Granite and other coarse-grained intrusive igneous rocks; probably Cretaceous
F Shales with massive limestone at bottom; Jurassic
G Limestone and quartzite, in thick alternating layers (Star Peak formation); Triassic
H Lavas and tuffs (mostly rhyolitic), interlayered with shales and limestone (Koipato formation); Triassic — Mesozoic
Highest shore line of Lake Lahontan indicated thus
Scale 1/500,000
Approximately 8 miles to 1 inch
0 5 10 15 20 Miles
0 5 10 15 20 25 30 Kilometers
Contour interval 200 feet
ELEVATIONS IN FEET ABOVE MEAN SEA LEVEL
The distances from Omaha, Nebraska, are shown every 10 miles
The crossties on the railroads are spaced 1 mile apart
Winnemucca Pk
Rose Creek
Krum
Benin
Winnemucca EL.4334
Tule EL.4325
Eglon
Golconda EL.4389
Preble
Comus
Iron Point
Herrin
Stone House EL.4431
Valmy
Mote
Piute
Battle Mtn EL.4512
Rosny
Argenta EL.4553
Ferris
Mosel
Farrel EL.4643
Ladoga
Beowawe EL.4695
Cluro
Harney
Barth
Gerald
Lewis
Paradise
Little Humboldt
Hot Springs Range
Sonoma Range
Grass Valley
Highest shore line of Lake Lahontan
East Range
Ragans Cr
Humboldt River
Western Pacific
Nevada Central
Reese River
Shoshone Mesa
Rye Meadows
Carlin Peaks
Lava (rhyolite and andesite)
Sues Pk
Antler Pk
Elder Creek
Battle Mtns
Lava (basalt)
Shoshone Range
Whirlwind Valley
Crescent Valley
Cluro Hills
Bridge Street Winnemucca Nev.

Winnemucca
The railroad camp, 1867
Bridge Street, 1919

Winnemucca
Famous Winnemucca residents: Sarah Winnemucca, author of *Life Among the Paiutes*, and "The Wild Bunch" outlaws—The Sundance Kid far left, Butch Cassidy far right

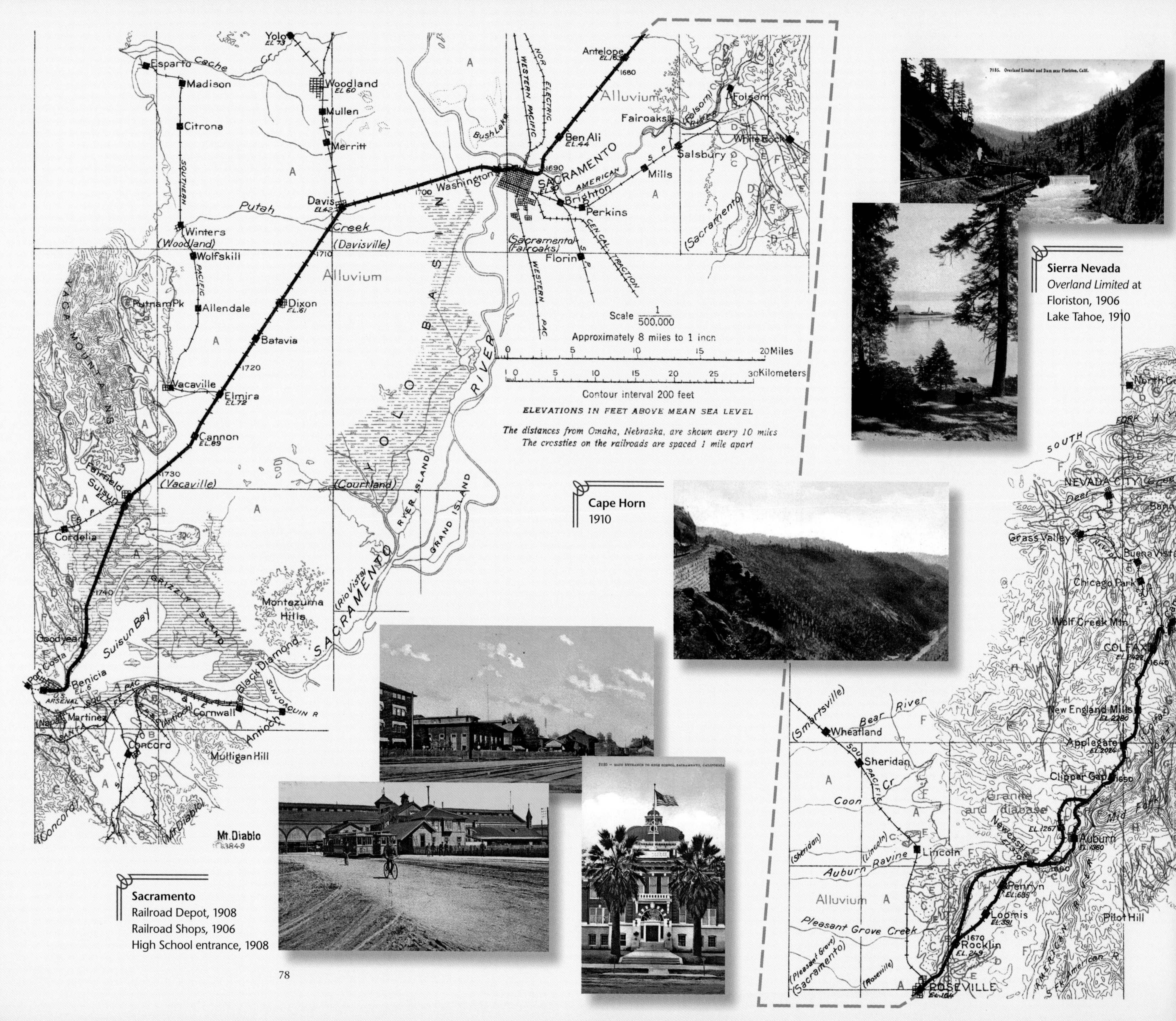

Sierra Nevada
Overland Limited at Floriston, 1906
Lake Tahoe, 1910

Cape Horn
1910

Sacramento
Railroad Depot, 1908
Railroad Shops, 1906
High School entrance, 1908

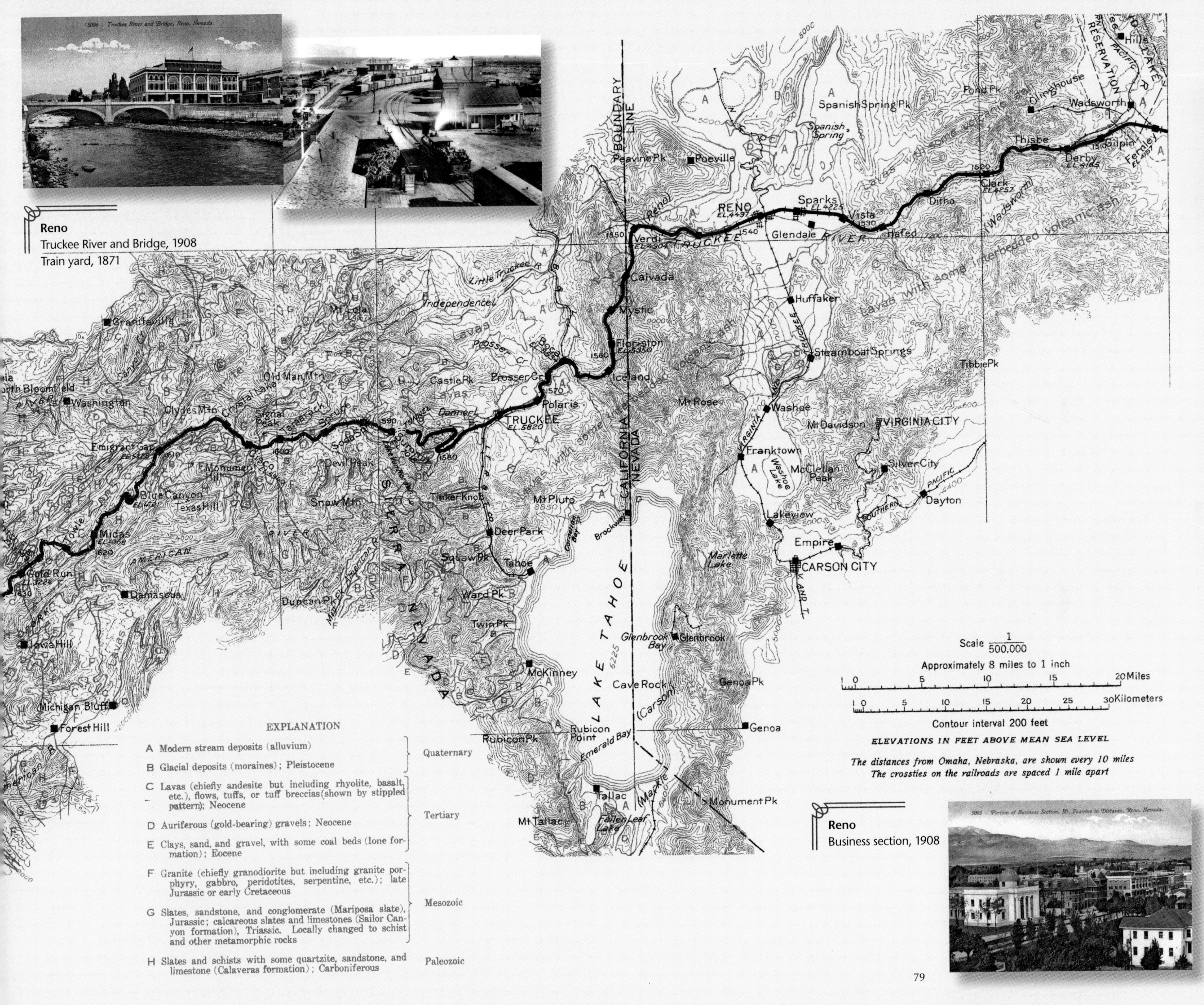
5006 – Truckee River and Bridge, Reno, Nevada.
5003 – Portion of Business Section, Mt. Peavine in Distance, Reno, Nevada.
EXPLANATION
A Modern stream deposits (alluvium)
B Glacial deposits (moraines); Pleistocene
Quaternary
C Lavas (chiefly andesite but including rhyolite, basalt, etc.), flows, tuffs, or tuff breccias (shown by stippled pattern); Neocene
D Auriferous (gold-bearing) gravels; Neocene
E Clays, sand, and gravel, with some coal beds (Ione formation); Eocene
Tertiary
F Granite (chiefly granodiorite but including granite porphyry, gabbro, peridotites, serpentine, etc.); late Jurassic or early Cretaceous
G Slates, sandstone, and conglomerate (Mariposa slate), Jurassic; calcareous slates and limestones (Sailor Canyon formation), Triassic. Locally changed to schist and other metamorphic rocks
Mesozoic
H Slates and schists with some quartzite, sandstone, and limestone (Calaveras formation); Carboniferous
Paleozoic
Scale 1/500,000
Approximately 8 miles to 1 inch
0 5 10 15 20 Miles
0 5 10 15 20 25 30 Kilometers
Contour interval 200 feet
ELEVATIONS IN FEET ABOVE MEAN SEA LEVEL
The distances from Omaha, Nebraska, are shown every 10 miles
The crossties on the railroads are spaced 1 mile apart
BOUNDARY LINE
CALIFORNIA
NEVADA
LAKE TAHOE
SIERRA NEVADA
RENO
TRUCKEE
CARSON CITY
VIRGINIA CITY

Reno
Truckee River and Bridge, 1908
Train yard, 1871

Reno
Business section, 1908

San Francisco
Souvenir book published by Cardinell-Vincent, *c.*1912
Market Street, "The Great White Way"
City and Bay from Fairmont Hotel
St. Francis Hotel and Union Square
Market and Outpost Streets
Esplanade and Beach Boulevard

Benicia
Train ferry, 1905

EXPLANATION

A	Stream deposits (alluvium), sand dunes, and beach sands	Quaternary
B	Fresh-water gravels, sands, and clays (Santa Clara formation, early Quaternary and Pliocene); marine clay, sandstone, and conglomerate (Merced formation, Pliocene); and stratfied light-colored pumice (Pinole tuff, Pliocene)	Quaternary and Tertiary
C	Light-colored soft sandstone and chalky bituminous shale (San Pablo formation and Monterey group); Miocene	Tertiary
D	Hard sandstone above (Tejon formation); chiefly conglomerate with sandstone; some shale and thin limestone (Martinez formation) below; Eocene	
E	Lava flows (basalt and rhyolite)	
F	Massive yellowish sandstone with conglomerate member below (Chico formation, Upper Cretaceous), underlain by calcareous and arenaceous shale (Knoxville formation, Lower Cretaceous)	Mesozoic
G	Chiefly intrusive rocks (basalt, diabase, gabbro, peridotite, pyroxenite, serpentine); Jurassic (?)	
H	Sandstones with subordinate shales, locally alternating with varicolored radiolarian cherts and some limestone; local schists due to metamorphism on contact of igneous rocks (Franciscan group); Jurassic (?)	
I	Granite (quartz diorite)	Pre-Jurassic (?)

Scale $\frac{1}{500.000}$

Approximately 8 miles to 1 inch

0 5 10 15 20 Miles

0 5 10 15 20 25 30 Kilometers

Contour interval 200 feet

ELEVATIONS IN FEET ABOVE MEAN SEA LEVEL

The distances from Omaha, Nebraska, are shown every 10 miles
The crossties on the railroads are spaced 1 mile apart

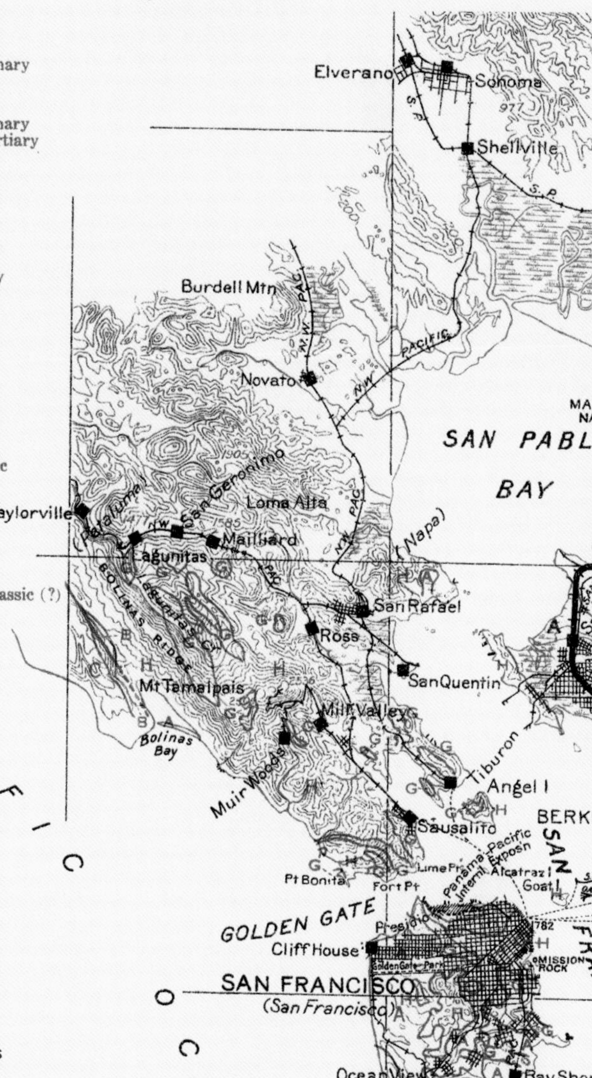

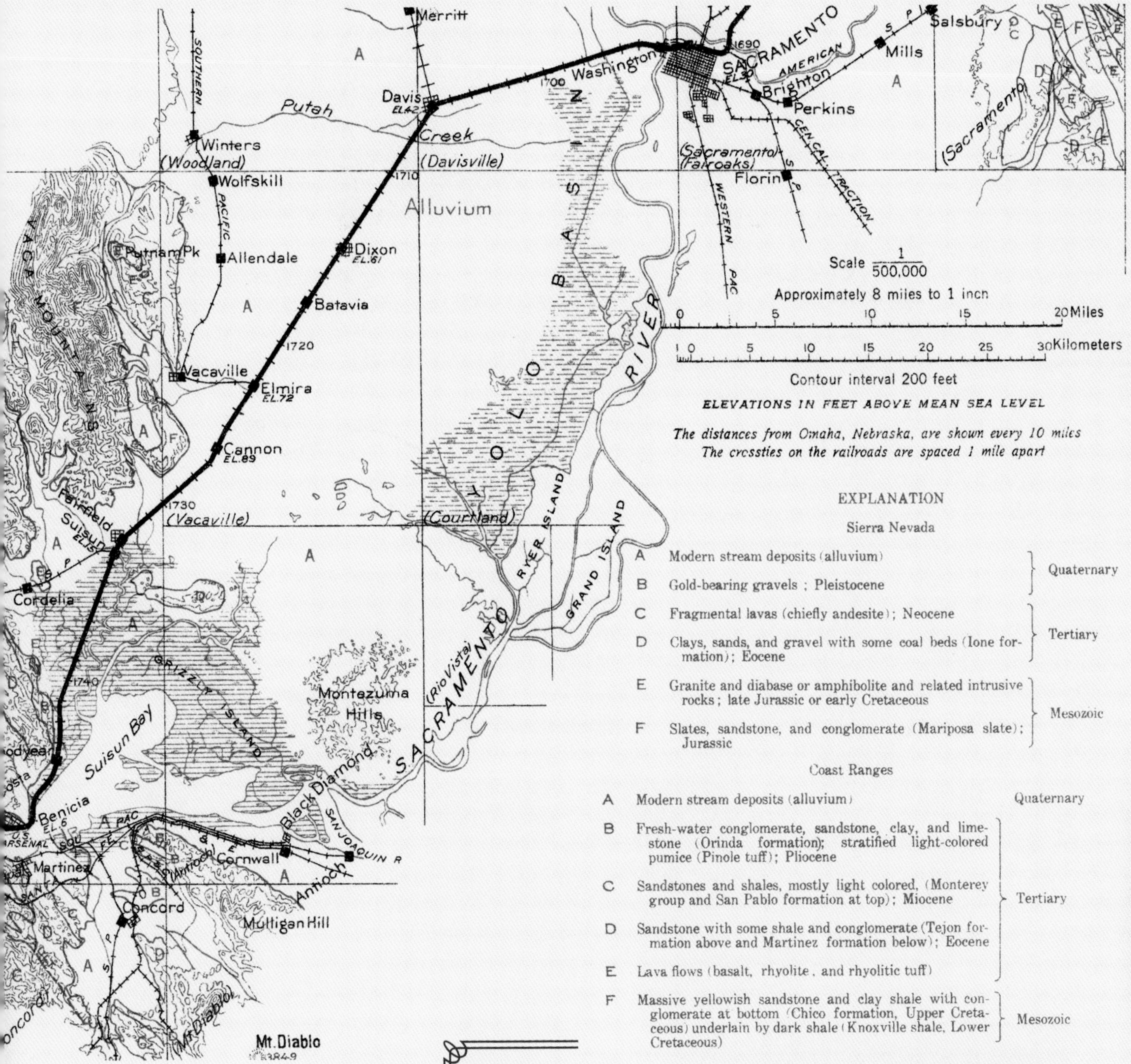

Merritt
SACRAMENTO
Salsbury
Mills
AMERICAN
Brighton
Perkins
Washington
Davis
Putah
Creek
(Davisville)
Winters
(Woodland)
Wolfskill
SOUTHERN PACIFIC
Alluvium
(Sacramento)
(Fairoaks)
Florin
CEN. CAL. TRACTION
WESTERN PAC
Putnam Pk
Allendale
Dixon
Batavia
VACA MOUNTAINS
Vacaville
Elmira
Cannon
(Vacaville)
Fairfield
Suisun
Cordelia
YOLO BASIN
RIVER
(Courtland)
RYER ISLAND
GRAND ISLAND
(Rio Vista)
SACRAMENTO
GRIZZLY ISLAND
Montezuma Hills
Suisun Bay
Benicia
Black Diamond
SAN JOAQUIN R
Cornwall
Antioch
Martinez
Concord
Mulligan Hill
Mt.Diablo
Scale 1/500,000
Approximately 8 miles to 1 inch
0 5 10 15 20 Miles
0 5 10 15 20 25 30 Kilometers
Contour interval 200 feet
ELEVATIONS IN FEET ABOVE MEAN SEA LEVEL
The distances from Omaha, Nebraska, are shown every 10 miles
The crossties on the railroads are spaced 1 mile apart
EXPLANATION
Sierra Nevada
A Modern stream deposits (alluvium) — Quaternary
B Gold-bearing gravels ; Pleistocene — Quaternary
C Fragmental lavas (chiefly andesite); Neocene — Tertiary
D Clays, sands, and gravel with some coal beds (Ione formation); Eocene — Tertiary
E Granite and diabase or amphibolite and related intrusive rocks; late Jurassic or early Cretaceous — Mesozoic
F Slates, sandstone, and conglomerate (Mariposa slate); Jurassic — Mesozoic
Coast Ranges
A Modern stream deposits (alluvium) — Quaternary
B Fresh-water conglomerate, sandstone, clay, and limestone (Orinda formation); stratified light-colored pumice (Pinole tuff); Pliocene — Tertiary
C Sandstones and shales, mostly light colored, (Monterey group and San Pablo formation at top); Miocene — Tertiary
D Sandstone with some shale and conglomerate (Tejon formation above and Martinez formation below); Eocene — Tertiary
E Lava flows (basalt, rhyolite, and rhyolitic tuff) — Tertiary
F Massive yellowish sandstone and clay shale with conglomerate at bottom (Chico formation, Upper Cretaceous) underlain by dark shale (Knoxville shale, Lower Cretaceous) — Mesozoic

San Leandro
L.Chabot
San Lorenzo
Haywards
Eden
Halvern

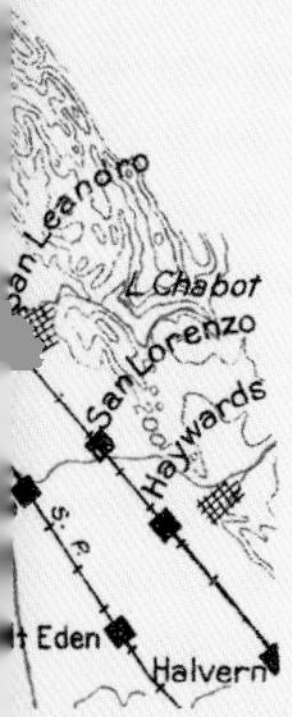

Sacramento
SP Depot, 1908
State Capitol, 1910
High School entrance, 1908
SP Bridge, 1914

604 – SOUTHERN PACIFIC DRAWBRIDGE OVER SACRAMENTO RIVER, SACRAMENTO, CALIFORNIA.

74 – Southern Pacific R. R. Bridge at Sacramento, California.

Berkeley
Bird's-eye view, 1899
SP Station, 1904

1666 - Southern Pacific Station, Berkeley, California.

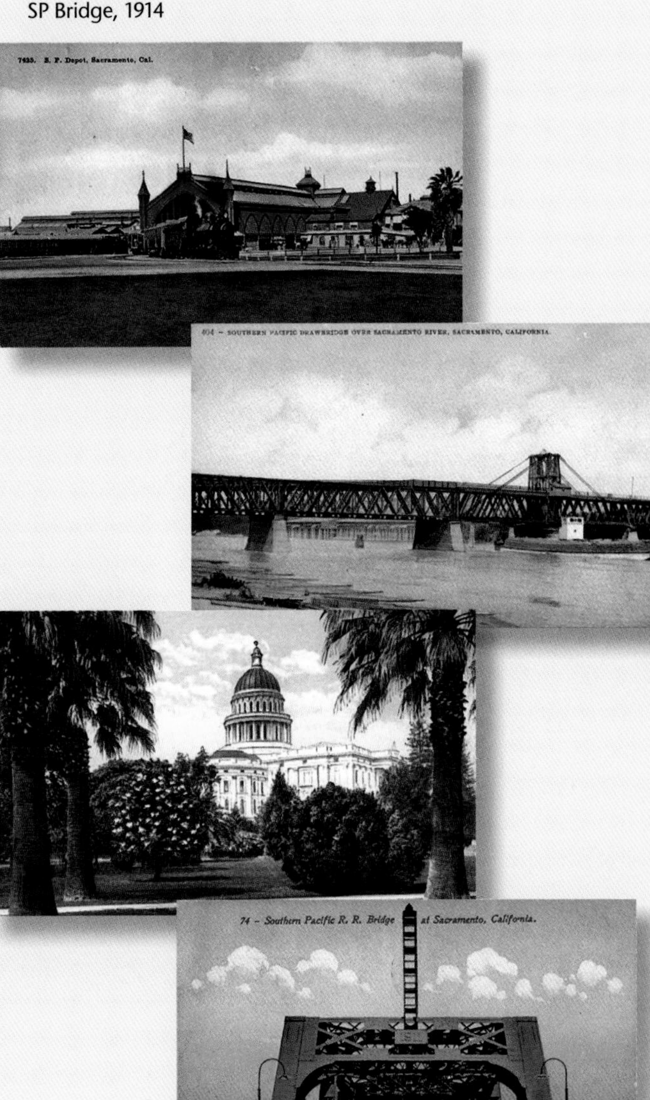

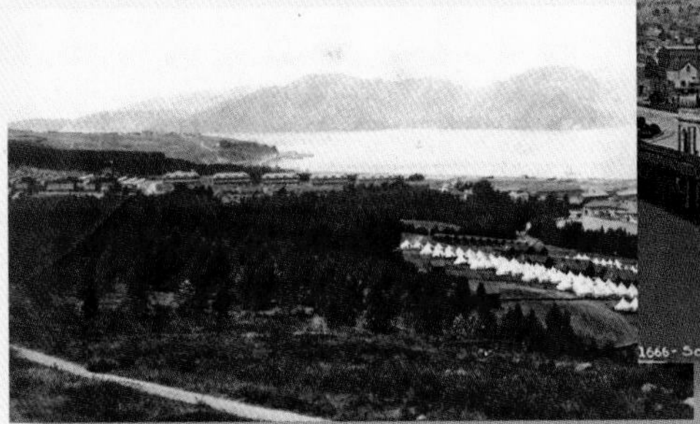

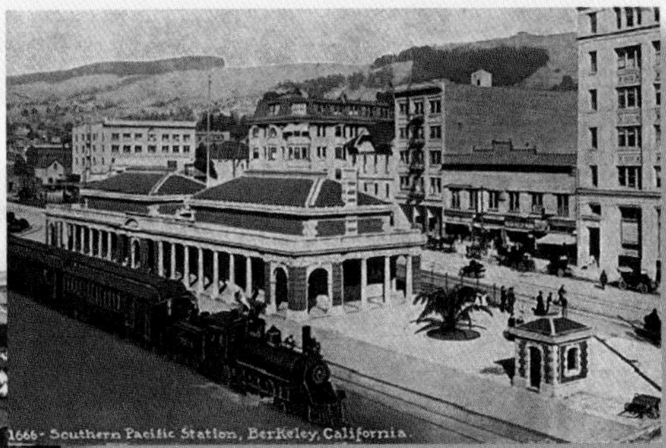

THE YELLOWSTONE PARK ROUTE

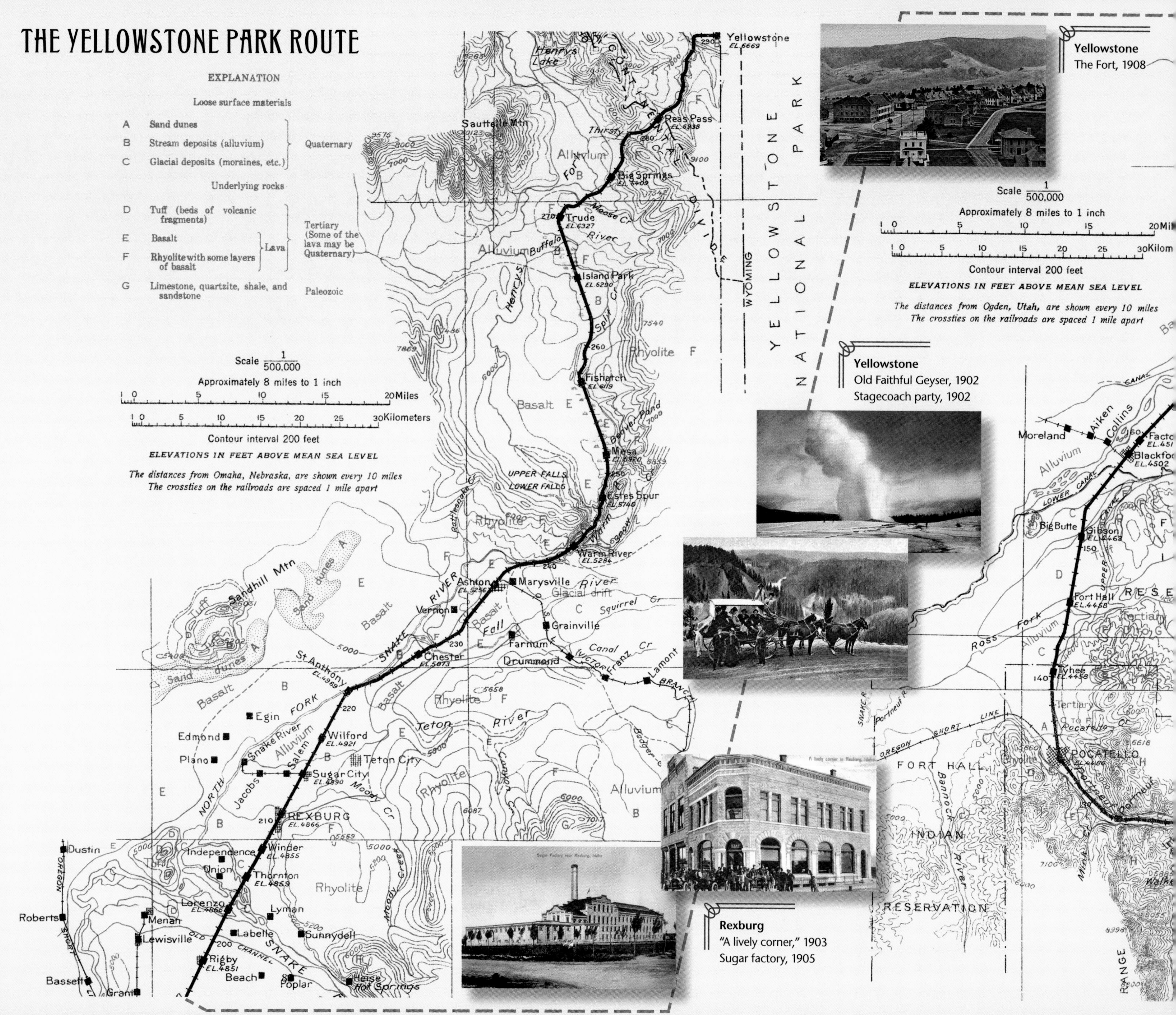

Yellowstone
The Fort, 1908

Yellowstone
Old Faithful Geyser, 1902
Stagecoach party, 1902

Rexburg
"A lively corner," 1903
Sugar factory, 1905

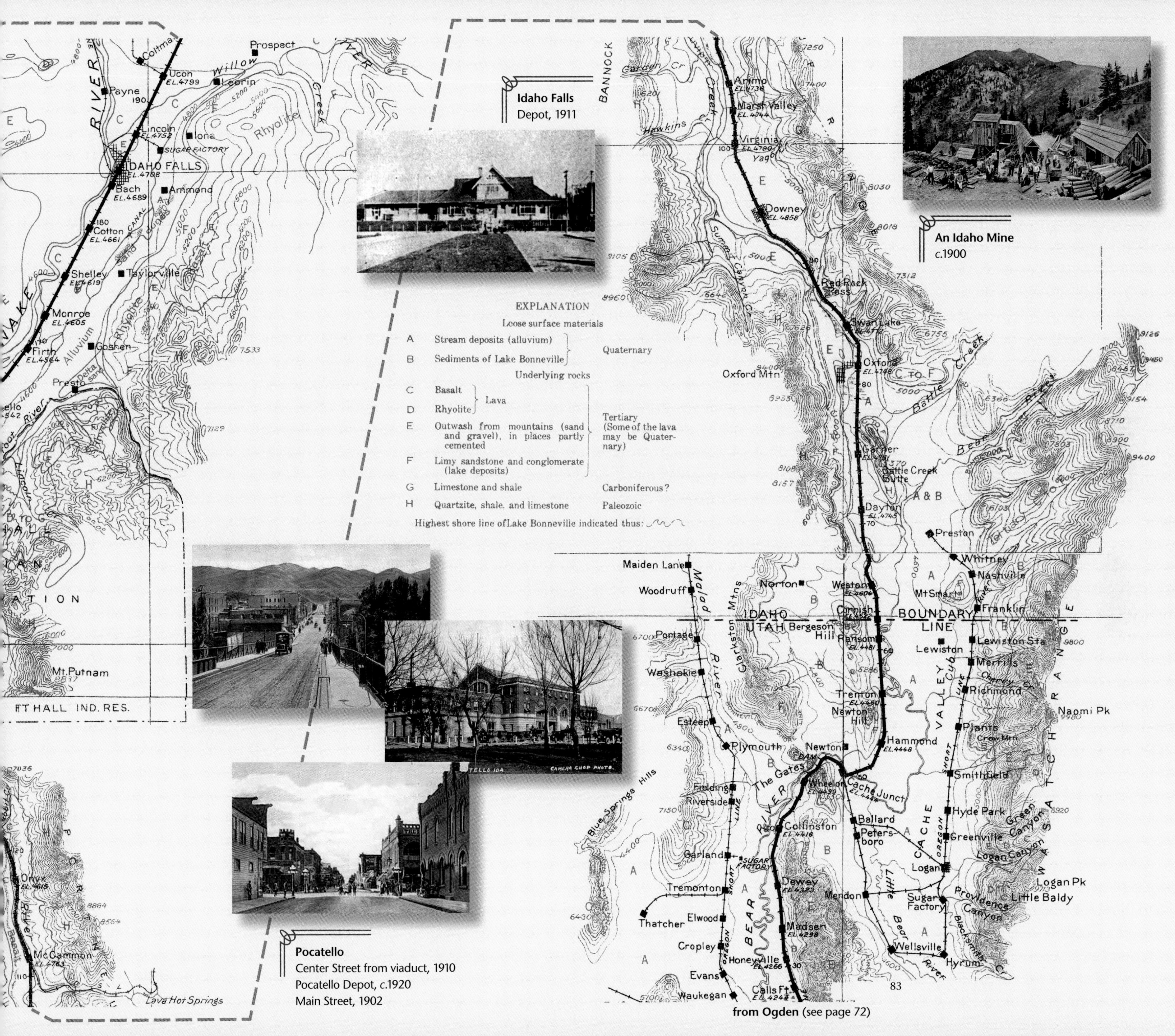

Idaho Falls
Depot, 1911

An Idaho Mine
*c.*1900

Pocatello
Center Street from viaduct, 1910
Pocatello Depot, *c.*1920
Main Street, 1902

from Ogden (see page 72)

THE SOUTHERN PACIFIC "SUNSET ROUTE"

NEW ORLEANS TO LOS ANGELES

The Sunset Route arose as an offshoot of the grandest American construction project of the nineteenth century, the transcontinental railroad. The term itself is misleading. So vast was the continent that no railroad was ever built from the Atlantic to the Pacific Coast—in the United States a "transcontinental railroad" was one that reached from the Missouri River to the Pacific Coast. Even so, the construction of a railroad across the Great Plains, several mountain ranges, and long stretches of desert became a daunting and spectacular achievement.

During the mid-1850s a survey ordered by Congress produced five feasible routes for a transcontinental road—the Northern route (between the 47th and 48th parallels), the Overland route (41st–42nd parallels), the Buffalo Trail (38th–39th parallels), the 35th parallel, and the Southern route (32nd parallel). The first transcontinental line, built from opposite directions by the Central Pacific and Union Pacific railroads, followed the Overland route and opened in 1869. Its success spurred interest in constructing roads along the other routes, and the builders of the Central Pacific, known as the "Big Four," turned their attention to warding off competitors by securing a stranglehold on most of the railroads in California. From their ambitious plans to seize the southern route for themselves emerged one of the most important and scenic rail routes in the United States, stretching from the San Francisco Bay area to New Orleans.

The most determined and talented member of the Big Four, Collis P. Huntington (1821–1900), drove the campaign to capture the southern route. The severe weather and high elevations along the Overland route convinced him that ultimately the Southern route would prove more feasible even though at the time it crossed sparsely-inhabited territory. During the 1860s and 1870s Huntington and his partners bought up as many rival California roads as they could. One such road, the Southern Pacific, had been chartered in 1865 to build the western end of a southern transcontinental line from San Jose to the Colorado River at Yuma,

Collis P. Huntington (above).

A classic Southern Pacific image on the cover of a 1909 booklet (left).

Moonlight on the Salton Sea, from *The Sunset Route from El Paso to Los Angeles*, published by the Van Noy-Interstate Company c.1906 (far left).

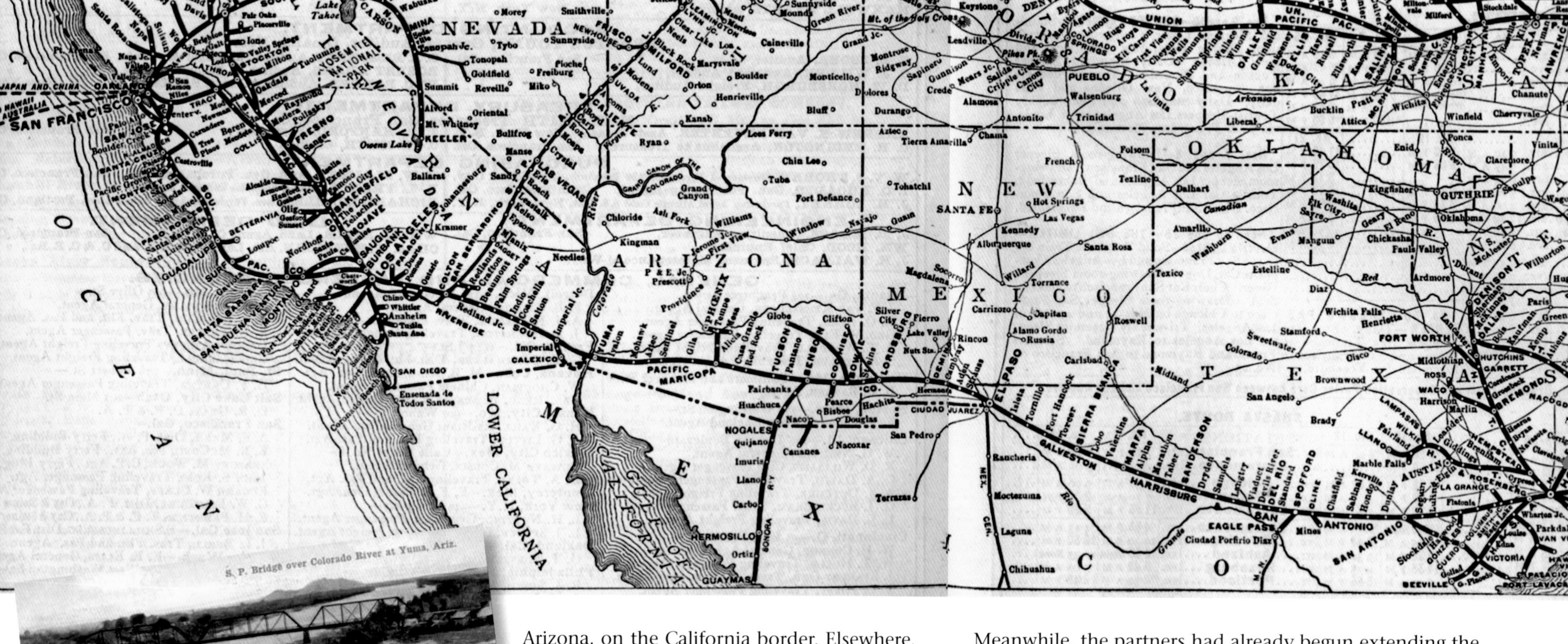

Yuma Bridge carrying the Southern Pacific over the Colorado River.

Arizona, on the California border. Elsewhere, the Atlantic & Pacific (A&P), had a subsidy to build westward from Missouri toward Yuma.

Huntington got into the game by acquiring the as yet unbuilt Southern Pacific in 1868. With it came not only a state charter, but also a federal franchise and land grants. The challenge was a daunting one because of the rugged terrain that had to be crossed.

Beginning in 1869, the Big Four extended the Central Pacific southward into the San Joaquin Valley through Fresno until it reached Goshen in 1872. From there the Southern Pacific laid track southward until it reached Bakersfield in 1874. Ahead lay the rugged Tehachapi Mountains, which took two more years and some extraordinary engineering feats to conquer. The combined Central Pacific–Southern Pacific line reached Los Angeles in September 1876. Although not yet a large city, it later emerged as the first major destination on what became known as the Sunset Route.

Meanwhile, the partners had already begun extending the Southern Pacific eastward from Los Angeles across the San Gabriel and San Bernardino valleys toward Yuma. A new threat had arisen in the form of the Texas & Pacific Railroad and its guiding hand, Tom Scott, who waged a relentless campaign in Washington to get a subsidy for building to the Pacific Coast. Huntington saw the urgency of pushing his road across the Colorado Desert and past the Salton Sink to Yuma, one of only two available crossings of the Colorado River. His access to the bridging site included a piece of the Fort Yuma Military Reservation, which required permission from the Secretary of War. Huntington got approval to lay temporary tracks pending a final decision, and promptly erected a permanent bridge over the Colorado River and track across the reservation. In the autumn of 1877 the first Southern Pacific train rolled into Yuma, where later it crossed the Colorado River over a substantial truss bridge.

Ahead lay a long stretch of desert across Arizona to the small outpost town of El Paso on the Texas border. Huntington finally

'Map of the Southern Pacific Company,' from the 1906 edition of *The Official Guide of the Railways*.

browbeat his reluctant partners into going along with his plan. In 1879, under charters procured from the states of Arizona and New Mexico, the Southern Pacific pushed further eastward. While his crews battled the stifling heat and lack of water, Huntington waged a political fight in Washington and a business fight with Jay Gould (1836–92), the most brilliant and unorthodox businessman of the era. Broke and broken in spirit by his failure to get a government subsidy, Scott sold the Texas & Pacific to Gould, who was piecing together a formidable rail empire of his own. Another potential rival appeared in the form of the Atchison, Topeka & Santa Fe, which agreed in the fall of 1879 with the St. Louis & San Francisco (Frisco) to control the moribund A&P and construct a transcontinental line from Albuquerque, New Mexico into California.

The A&P drove toward Needles, California, the only other suitable place for crossing the Colorado River. Huntington had no intention of letting the A&P into California, but he was overextended by his many enterprises, and he had Gould to reckon with. Their struggle was a clash of titans, a classic collision between the lion and the fox. The two roads marched relentlessly toward each other, threatening to parallel one another for ninety miles through a region that had no business to offer either of them. Gould increased the pressure by joining the syndicate to extend the A&P westward. However, the Southern Pacific reached El Paso in May 1881, ahead of Gould.

Both antagonists were practical men who recognized that they were stretched thin and facing an adversary who would not back down. Accordingly, on Thanksgiving Day in 1881 they signed an historic agreement to share the disputed ninety miles of track east of El Paso, to divide earnings, and to build no competing lines. Although Huntington never trusted Gould, he was practical enough to see the need for some sort of accommodation between them and, to the surprise of many observers, the agreement remained intact with only four amendments until 1927. Two months after coming to terms, Huntington and Gould joined forces to buy a half interest in the Frisco, which owned a half interest in the A&P, and thereby stifled that threat. While Gould continued to fashion his own southwestern rail system, Huntington turned to completing his line through Texas and Louisiana to New Orleans.

As early as 1878, Huntington had begun investing in the Galveston, Harrisburg & San Antonio (GH&SA), a Texas road that was building westward from the harbor between Galveston and Houston. A year earlier the road had reached San Antonio; Huntington was intent on pushing construction through the rugged country between El Paso and San Antonio. He laid tracks east from El Paso to seize the only pass from the city. Beginning in June and July 1881, the track crews took nearly eleven months to complete the 126 miles to Sanderson, Texas. Their opposite numbers, building westward from San Antonio, reached Del Rio, Texas, in June 1882. Beyond it lay the canyon of the Rio Grande River, tall limestone cliffs rising precipitously from the water's edge. For several miles to Devil's River the crews had to blast the rock for footings, a slow and costly process along one of the most picturesque sections of the road.

Once past this obstacle, the crews encountered the Pecos River. To cross it required two tunnels, one on each side of the river, as well as a bridge. Finally, on January 12, 1883,

The cover of the Southern Pacific's 1892 timetable for the Sunset Route.

A classic Southern Pacific scene as the *Sunset Limited* crosses Arizona against a summer sunset in 1905 in a painting by T. K. S. Brewster.

at a point near the west bank tunnel, the rails were joined, completing the line to Houston.

While construction through west Texas was underway, Huntington took steps to fill the gap from Houston to New Orleans. The situation in that region was complex, with a particularly ambitious project planned by steamer-line operator Charles Morgan, who aimed to create a unified rail–steamer network that tied the southwest Gulf to the Mississippi Valley, northern Latin America, and both the Atlantic and Pacific coasts.

It was an audacious plan, but Morgan died in 1878 at the age of 83 before his larger vision had gone very far. For five years the officers of his Morgan Louisiana & Texas Railroad & Steamship Company worked to lay track and consolidate companies under Morgan's original plan. By 1882, however, the strategic situation in the southwest Gulf was complicated by Huntington and Gould's projects. Several smaller roads were put together to form a complete line between Houston and New Orleans, and Huntington began investing in some of these roads in 1881. Gould also invested in Morgan roads that gave him access to New Orleans from the northwest. By March 1882 the Morgan system provided both men with entry into the city, and with the Texas segment of the line nearing completion, the Southern Pacific bought control of the Morgan system on February 1, 1883.

Four days later the first trains to run between San Francisco and New Orleans departed those cities, carrying with them the first passengers to traverse the entirety of the Sunset Route. To shorten the line, Huntington, in 1892, agreed to erect a new bridge over the Pecos River at a point dominated by a 300-foot deep gorge. The towering new structure gave passengers a heart-stopping experience as well as breathtaking views of the scenery.

For most Americans during the era before the automobile, the West and Southwest remained a distant, exotic land filled with wonders, myths, and characters made larger than life by exaggerated accounts of their exploits. It remained a place known more from dime novels than actual experience. Those who ventured there to live or visit were overwhelmed by its sheer size. According to one story, a traveler on the *Sunset Limited* asked the porter of his sleeping car one morning where they were. "In Texas," came the reply. The next morning he asked the same question and received the same answer. "No place can be that big," he muttered. On the third morning he asked again and got the same answer: "We're in Texas, sir!" The passenger eyed the porter suspiciously and growled, "You are a God damned liar!"

But he was not. Even the best passenger trains of the era might go far, but they didn't go fast. For ordinary passengers the journey across the Sunset Route was as exhausting as the scenery was exhilarating. Wooden passenger cars carried them over rough, uneven roadbeds that made coach seats even more uncomfortable. Ventilation was poor, and temperatures veered from the stifling heat of the desert to the chill of the mountains. Unsavory meals had to be gulped down hastily at

San Bernardino Range, Banning, from *The Sunset Route from El Paso to Los Angeles.*

food stops. Even after dining cars made their appearance in the mid-1880s, many passengers could not afford them.

The tourist trade that would later characterize California and the Southwest had yet to develop, and the country through which travelers passed was long on rugged beauty and short on people. The region between San Antonio and El Paso, for example, had only 19,170 inhabitants spread over 43,726 square miles, prompting one SP official to say that the territory "had more square miles to the man and more square men to the mile" than any other section in the world.

From 1883 to 1894 a single passenger train ran each way on the Sunset Route. In 1894 the Southern Pacific inaugurated service on a new luxury train, the *Sunset Limited*, which soon took its place among the storied named trains of the golden era of passenger travel. When it made its debut, ironically at a time when the nation was deep into a depression, it offered people of means a far more enjoyable—and expensive—way to cross the West's enormous distances. The *Sunset Limited* ran a 75-hour schedule both ways between San Francisco and New Orleans in what passed for luxurious splendor in railway cars. The cars were specially ordered from Pullman, bore the train's name, and were used only on it. They included sleeping cars, combination sleepers with drawing rooms en suite, a stunning diner named the "Epicure," and a lounge car. The meals served were no less deluxe, made with fresh food from the region and served in an opulent setting. The vestibules were tightly locked, making passage from one car to another easy.

The *Sunset Limited* connoted for passengers a comfortable journey through an alien landscape beneath a perpetual sun. In 1897–8 it was rerouted to the newly opened Coast Line between San Francisco and Los Angeles, then returned to its normal route on a weekly schedule in 1911. That same year it was equipped with all-steel cars.

In 1913 the *Sunset Limited* became even more elegant, boasting a variety of new amenities. Its equipment consisted of one six-compartment drawing-room observation sleeping car, two twelve-section drawing room standard Pullman sleeping cars, the dining car, and a dynamo, mail, and baggage car. Electricity had come to the train in the form of a telephone connection, stock quotations and news items received by telegraph, and electric lamps in each berth. A library housed magazines and the latest novels; there were writing desks with stationery, and any letter or telegram could be dispatched at the next stop. Meals were described as "equal to that of the highest-class cafes." The porter asked passengers what time they wished to eat breakfast and summoned them at that hour.

After various refits and changes in route, in January 1942 the *Sunset Limited* ran only from Los Angeles to New Orleans, yet it continued as the Southern Pacific's premier train. In 1950 it was dieselized, and the SP invested $15 million to buy five sets of cars, 78 in all. In an age of dwindling passenger traffic the *Sunset Limited* was the last passenger train traveling the Sunset Route when Amtrak took over most passenger service in 1971.

Huntington had, in 1884, swept the Southern Pacific, Central Pacific, and all the Big Four's other railroad holdings west of the Mississippi River into a holding company called the Southern Pacific Company. After Huntington's death in 1900, the Southern Pacific stock in his estate was acquired by E. H. Harriman (1848–1909), the most brilliant railroad man of the era, who had brought the Union Pacific back from bankruptcy to become one of the nation's leading railroads. Harriman proceeded to combine the two Pacific roads into one great system, and spent lavishly to upgrade the Southern Pacific to his superior standards. The two systems were run as one until 1912, when the Supreme Court in a federal antitrust suit ordered them split apart. The Southern Pacific system was independent once again, and remained so until 1995, when the Union Pacific acquired it in a merger.

Indian Head Mountain, Arizona, from *The Sunset Route from El Paso to Los Angeles*.

IMPERIAL VALLEY AND THE SALTON SINK

Bridge over Salton Sea–S. P. R. R.
California--Arizona Route

A 1906 postcard of a Southern Pacific train crossing the Salton Sea viaduct (above).

A photograph from about 1900 (right) of the flimsy wooden structure holding the Colorado River waters from the nine-foot drop into the California Development Company's main drain. It was this structure that collapsed in the disastrous flood of 1905 (California Historical Society).

Population along the Sunset Route increased steadily, if unevenly, between 1890 and 1920. One area in particular underwent rapid growth that was nearly obliterated by a disaster. For centuries the southeastern corner of California had been an arid desert created by an ancient change in course of the capricious Colorado River. The shift created an inland salt lake as large as the Great Salt Lake in Utah. Over the centuries this sea evaporated into a depression known as the Salton Sink, 100 miles long, 35 miles wide, and 1,000 feet deep at its lowest point. The process also created a huge alluvial plain ranging from 80 feet above to 280 feet below sea level in a desert region where temperatures climbed as high as 120 degrees. The Sink supported only a few salt mines, while the soil and climate of the plain were ideal for farming but lacked a water supply.

In 1901 a development company provided water by cutting an irrigation channel into the Colorado River. Settlers poured into the region, which received the idyllic name of Imperial Valley, until the population reached 10,000 by 1905. The Sunset Route crossed the eastern rim of Salton Sink and built a branch into the burgeoning valley. When growth outran the water supply, the developers unwisely decided to open two new cuts and, although the turbulent Colorado carried an estimated sixty million tons of silt past Yuma every year, they spent nothing on dredging, sluicing, or settling basins.

Then disaster struck. Two floods in February 1905 surged through the openings, widened the irrigation channels and overflowed onto the plains. The alarmed developers appealed to Harriman, who had no interest in their company but ended up taking charge of it and the fight to halt the raging Colorado. By June 1905 the waters lapped at the rail line skirting Salton and poured into the Sink, flooding out the salt works. Then the connecting Gila River unleashed a furious flood that sent the Colorado's discharge soaring from 12,000 to 115,000 cubic feet per second.

In effect the river had changed course and was seeking out its ancient basin, threatening to destroy the entire Imperial Valley and its irrigation system. Ironically, the Valley faced two possible fates: It would either be drowned in water or perish from loss of its water supply. Harriman poured large

RAILROAD TO RETREAT.

Salton Sea Again Compels Southern Pacific to Move Its Main Line.

LOS ANGELES, Cal., July 3.—Because of the rising of Salton Sea, the Southern Pacific Railroad Company will move its main line in that vicinity for the fifth time. The waters are now approaching the track, and it may be necessary to build the new line within sixty days. Four times within the past year the company has been compelled to retreat. The water is pouring into the sink through the canal intake from the Colorado River, and the sea is rising more than two inches daily.

A cutting from the *New York Times* for July 1906 (above).

In late 1906 and early 1907 thousands of Southern Pacific workers battled for 42 days to close the breach in the banks of the Colorado River (right) (Richard J. Orsi collection).

sums into the effort to divert the river back to its own bed, but the Colorado remained at near record levels through 1906. By June the runaway river had widened the cut to half a mile and spread across an area nearly ten miles wide before splitting into streams heading toward the Salton Sea, which rose at the incredible rate of seven inches a day over a 400-square-mile area. As the region's loose soil washed out, it created a series of rapids, then cascades and waterfalls 80 feet deep and 1,000 feet wide. Five times that summer the Southern Pacific had to move its tracks to higher ground.

Never one to back down from a challenge, Harriman threw more resources into stopping the river. For three weeks two divisions of the Southern Pacific were virtually shut down to feed equipment and supplies to the workmen. Finally, in February 1907 the river was pushed back behind a rock dam and a double row of levees nearly twenty miles long. At a cost of $3.1 million Harriman saved the Imperial Valley from extinction; by 1917 it was fast becoming a garden spot of the West with a population of 40,000. The Salton did not evaporate but remained an inland lake; both it and the Valley became two more prime attractions along the Sunset Route.

A postcard of *c.*1902 featuring cotton production in the Imperial Valley.

THE PECOS RIVER VIADUCT

Crossing in Thin Air

Three postcard views of the Pecos High Bridge, dating from between 1906 and 1915.

The Pecos River, winding snake-like into Lake Amistad, was the major obstacle in constructing the Texas portion of the Sunset Route. The first crossing in 1882 used a simple iron truss bridge at the bottom of the canyon where the Pecos and Rio Grande rivers met. It proved expensive to construct and costly to maintain, for the steep grades and series of curves leading into and out of the canyon limited the size and weight of trains and were prone to falling rocks. In 1890 Major James Converse, the Southern Pacific's general superintendent and chief engineer, conceived a plan for crossing the Pecos on a high viaduct that would eliminate eleven miles of steep, curving grades.

Work on the new bridge began in February 1891. All the supporting piers and footings were grounded in bedrock. Seven of the key footings had copings cut from Texas pink granite and hauled two hundred miles, while the piers were made from concrete and local limestone cut from the canyon bottom and floated into place. By November 1891 the piers and footings were in place, and construction started on the iron and steel towers and spans. Since no heavy locomotive cranes then existed, the engineers devised an apparatus called a "traveler" to lower the heavy iron beams into place. This strange-looking device had an overhanging arm 124.6 feet in length counterbalanced by a 57-foot wheelbase clamped to a completed section of the bridge.

Beginning on the east side of the canyon, the traveler gingerly lowered sections of bridgework until the midpoint was reached. It then returned to the east rim, was dismantled, loaded onto a rail car, and hauled via the original bridge across the river to the west canyon rim. There it was reassembled and proceeded to lay bridgework toward the already completed structure. Using a work crew of 67 people, this remarkable bridge took only 103 days to build at a cost of $250,108. It was 2,180 feet long, towered 321 feet above the water, and featured a combined cantilever and 185-foot section of suspended lattice over the river. The ironwork alone weighed 1,820 tons.

Laden with company dignitaries, the first train rolled across the bridge on March 31, 1892, and ever since travelers have enjoyed heart-stopping views from it. For years it ranked as the highest bridge in the United States and third highest in the world. In 1910 and again in 1929 the viaduct, as it is known, was substantially reinforced to increase capacity for longer and heavier trains.

206 Pecos High Bridge

EL PASO

Town of Six Nations

El Paso has been a continental crossroads since the sixteenth century. It lies at the far western tip of Texas where New Mexico and the Mexican state of Chihuahua meet in the rugged desert climate around the slopes of Mount Franklin on the Rio Grande River, the border between the United States and Mexico. Over the years this remote but strategic location has been ruled by six nations: Spain, the Tigua Indians, the Republic of Mexico, the Republic of Texas, the Confederate States of America, and the United States.

Until the twentieth century El Paso remained a frontier town. Fort Bliss was established there in 1848 to guard the border and protect settlers and travelers heading for California. In 1877 the region endured its own little civil war, the Salt War of San Elizario, which had more to do with clashes between Texans and Mexicans than with salt. Four years later the town underwent the beginning of a profound change with the arrival of the first railroad. By 1882 three major lines, the Southern Pacific, the Texas & Pacific, and the Atchison, Topeka & Santa Fe, converged on El Paso, transforming the sleepy village of a few hundred inhabitants into a wide-open boomtown that became the county seat in 1883 and boasted a population of 10,000 by 1890.

The surge of prosperity around the railroads turned El Paso into a lawless haven of saloons, gambling dives, dance-halls, and whorehouses. For a time it was known as "Sin City" and the "Six Shooter Capital," where a small police force led by rotating city marshals offered the only protection against outlaws and gunslingers. The marshals had to be tougher and more vicious than the men they tried to subdue, and several lost their lives in the attempt. Not until the 1890s did reform-minded citizens work to curb the town's thriving vice industry. Only then did the town grow into a city, its population swelling from 15,906 in 1900 to 77,560 in 1925.

By 1905 six railroads had reached El Paso, all with separate depots until the splendid Union Depot Passenger Station, designed by the noted architectural firm of Daniel H. Burnham, opened that year as a central station in the city. It was the first passenger depot constructed for international railway traffic, since one of the railroads was the Nacional de México. Although the gunslingers had vanished by then, El Paso remained an important crossroads for travelers and commerce alike.

Rio Grande Bridge and Great Customs Smelter, El Paso, Texas, from *The Sunset Route from El Paso to Los Angeles*, published by the Van Noy-Interstate Company *c.*1906.

International Bridge, El Paso, from *The Sunset Route from El Paso to Los Angeles*.

YUMA

The Sunniest Place on Earth

According to the *Guinness Book of Records*, Yuma enjoys the distinction of being the sunniest place on Earth, basking in sunshine 90 percent of daylight hours. Situated on bluffs overlooking the Colorado River, it lies three miles west of the Colorado's convergence with the Gila River on the California border just north of Mexico, and Yuma did in fact belong to Mexico until the Gadsden Purchase of 1854 made it part of the United States. Between 1850 and 1870 it served as a gateway to California, with a steamboat landing to supply mines and military outposts. The discovery of gold deposits along the rivers in 1858 touched off a gold rush that made Yuma the receiving point for steamboats bearing goods, equipment, and people to the deposits. When the Southern Pacific bridged the Colorado River in 1870 as part of its Sunset Route, Yuma became a rail stop as well, as its charming depot attests.

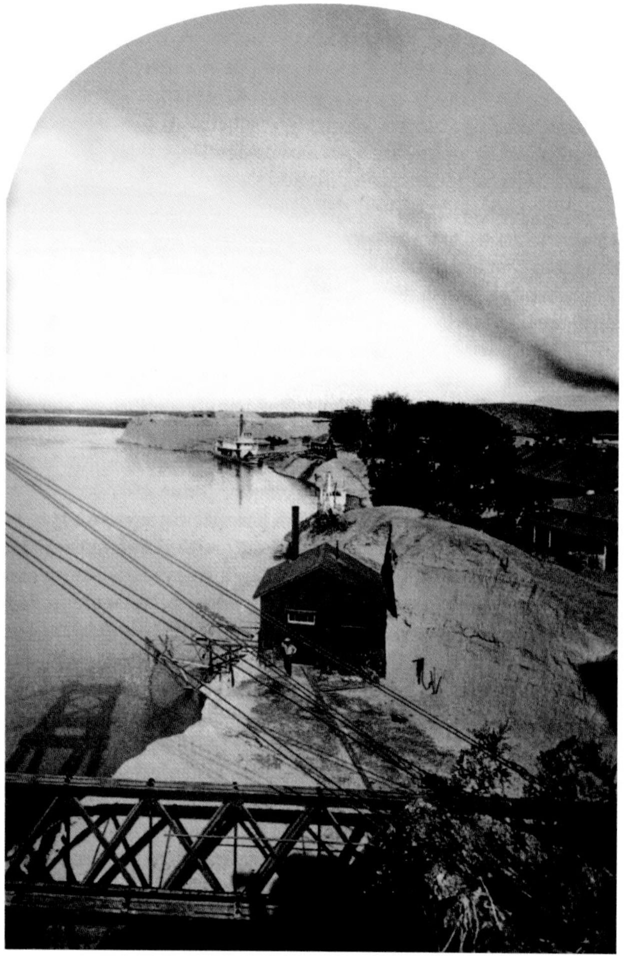

Largely because of its remote location, Yuma was destined to remain an outpost and then a stop on the Southern Pacific. It never grew into a large city. In 1880 it boasted a population of only 1,200; by 1920 it had grown only to 4,237. The town gained the territorial prison in 1876 but lost its military fort seven years later. Even its gold rush was temporary, the mines giving out in the 1880s, and in 1909 the prison was moved elsewhere, leaving Yuma as primarily an agricultural town surrounded by spectacular scenery. Silt and minerals from the two powerful rivers that border Yuma to the north and west turned Yuma Valley into rich, fertile ground for farming. Jagged mountain ranges surround the town—the Gila Mountains to the east, the Picacho and Chimney peaks of California to the northwest, and the rugged peaks of Mexico 26 miles to the southwest.

Despite its arid desert climate, Yuma has always been a creature of its rivers. Completion of the Laguna Dam in 1909 diverted water from the Colorado River for irrigation on a grand scale similar to that of the Imperial Valley, turning 109,000 acres of desert into farmland. The Yuma Mesa, a vast area of sandy loam soil stretching from the Colorado River southward into Mexico and the Gulf of California, became one of the nation's most productive regions thanks to its long and frost-free growing season.

Coal-fired steam-powered pumping station on the Colorado River, photographed by Carleton E. Watkins, the Southern Pacific Railroad photographer, *c.*1880.

Southern Pacific Depot, Yuma, Arizona, from *The Sunset Route from El Paso to Los Angeles*.

THE TEHACHAPI LOOP

The Railroad Turns on Itself

Surveying and building a railroad with the primitive technologies of the nineteenth century was tough enough, but it became even more grueling in mountain country. Engineers on horseback searched desperately for passes through the rugged countryside. Where possible they followed rivers through the mountains; otherwise they had to carve a line through the barriers of rock. The challenge always was to find the straightest line with the lowest grade.

In constructing its route from Oakland to Los Angeles, the Southern Pacific ran headlong into a mountain barrier consisting of the northeastern arm of the Tehachapi Mountains and the southernmost part of the Sierra Nevada Mountains. On the north side of the barrier lay the lush San Joaquin Valley; on the south side sprawled the harsh, forbidding landscape of the Mojave Desert. The point where the two mountain ranges met came to be known as Tehachapi Pass, named after a nearby village. It had an elevation of 3,793 feet. The task of conquering the pass fell to William Hood, the Southern Pacific's brilliant engineer, who concluded that the line had no choice but to go through it.

But how? The approaches to the pass were rugged and unforgiving, filled with gorges and narrow shelves. Any line that looked even remotely straight was out of the question. The route would have to snake around the obstacles from the base of the mountains to the pass, sixteen miles away. Part of the line followed the Tehachapi Creek until the terrain forced it to curve around an elevation. At that point Hood came up with an inspired if daring design idea. To raise the grade gradually around a particularly tough obstacle he conceived a loop that circled a cone-shaped hill and swung back over and above itself. From this concept emerged what has been called one of the seven wonders of the railroad world—the Tehachapi Loop.

Construction of the line and the loop became a monumental task. It involved laying down 28 miles of track through mostly solid and decomposed granite using the most basic of tools. In 1874 engineer J. B. Harris, the chief of construction, threw a force of three thousand Chinese laborers into the project. Using picks and shovels, loading their debris on horse-drawn carts, fighting their way through the rock with blasting powder, his diligent workers hacked and clawed their way slowly forward. The line required eighteen tunnels and ten bridges, along with numerous water towers to feed the thirsty steam locomotives climbing the pass. In designing the loop Hood resorted to surveying his line from the summit downward instead of the usual method of starting at the bottom. His final version averaged only a 2.2 percent grade for its entire 28-mile length.

Remarkably, the crews managed to complete the road in 1876, only two years after beginning the work. Once in place, the loop hastened the completion of the crucial link between Oakland and Los Angeles, and, apart from its own intrinsic value, the new line enabled the construction of the Sunset Route from Los Angeles south to New Orleans.

Writing in 1877, only a year after the road through the loop opened, a traveler extolled the "great variety of scenery and climate ... You roll across the vast level wheat fields of the great San Joaquin Valley ... until you enter the Mojave Desert, arid, bald, and bare; yet with a strange beauty of its own ... The fame of the 'Loup' has become world-wide. I know of nothing like it."

From the air the loop resembled a helix, while on the ground it offered observers the fascinating spectacle of a long

The Tehachapi Loop, photographed by an unknown photographer in the mid-1890s. Calling it "just a common sense plan," Southern Pacific's chief engineer William Hood shrugged off efforts to name the loop in his honor.

train passing over itself, and since its opening the loop has remained a favorite subject for rail photographers and fans. In 1952 a major earthquake shook southern California, destroying four tunnels along one 11-mile stretch of the loop and severely damaging four others. By constructing a giant shoofly or temporary track 640 feet long and bringing in massive earth-moving machinery, the Southern Pacific managed to restore the line to service in only 25 days. Some observers considered this a feat comparable to the building of the original line.

To the great pleasure of rail enthusiasts, the Tehachapi Loop still serves both the Union Pacific Railroad, which acquired the Southern Pacific in 1996, and the Burlington Northern Santa Fe, which has trackage rights over it. Until recently 34 to 36 trains ran across it every day. While the Union Pacific has been engaged in double-tracking the Sunset Route, the loop remains a single track through forbidding terrain—heavily traveled but not expandable. In the age of diesels that can haul much longer trains through the use of distributed power, the spectacle of them winding around the loop like a mechanical snake provides an even more impressive sight. In October 1998 the site was commemorated as a National Historic Civil Engineering Landmark.

The Tehachapi Loop today, courtesy of Google Earth.

Train No. 17, *The Los Angeles Express*, poses at the summit of the Loop in the early 1880s (far right).

THE MUSSEL SLOUGH AFFAIR

Tragedy Turns to Myth

The clash at Mussel Slough in California on May 11, 1880, involved squatters occupying Southern Pacific land and company agents sent to evict them under a court order. An illegal squatter militia, The Settlers' Grand League, confronted the federal marshal and Southern Pacific land agents trying to serve the first order. Tempers flared, a shot was fired, and a brief gun battle broke out. When the smoke cleared, five squatters and two land agents lay dead or dying. From this tragic encounter evolved a myth that endured for decades.

Public sentiment rallied around the settlers, who portrayed themselves as simple farmers about to lose their land to the powerful and greedy railroad. Growing anti-corporate sentiment in California and elsewhere helped elevate them to martyrs. In 1901 novelist Frank Norris immortalized their cause in his popular novel *The Octopus*, which ignored historical facts to portray the event as one in which righteous farmers found themselves caught helplessly in the coils of the railroad and its politically powerful owners whose duplicity knew no bounds. In this widely accepted version the settlers were lured onto Southern Pacific lands, developed them into farms, and were then ousted when the railroad refused to give them title or demanded exorbitant prices for their improved acres.

The historical facts could hardly have been more different. Most of the "settlers" were in fact squatters who had no intention of paying for the land. Many asserted claims on land they did not occupy, some put forward multiple claims on hundreds or even thousands of acres, and others were merchants who lived in nearby towns. The Southern Pacific was forced to act by the demands of genuine settlers who had actually paid the railroad for land, only to find their tract occupied by squatters. At first the Southern Pacific tried to compromise with the squatters, who only grew more defiant, then finally the company resorted to the courts to force eviction.

The courts at every level upheld the Southern Pacific's claim, but the squatters kept coming. Although hundreds of them hurried to accept a generous offer from the Southern Pacific after the Mussel Slough affair, the conflict dragged on well into the early twentieth century as efforts to evict the squatters sometimes lasted years or even decades. The myth of the Southern Pacific as the "Octopus" endured even longer, still lingering today in the popular imagination.

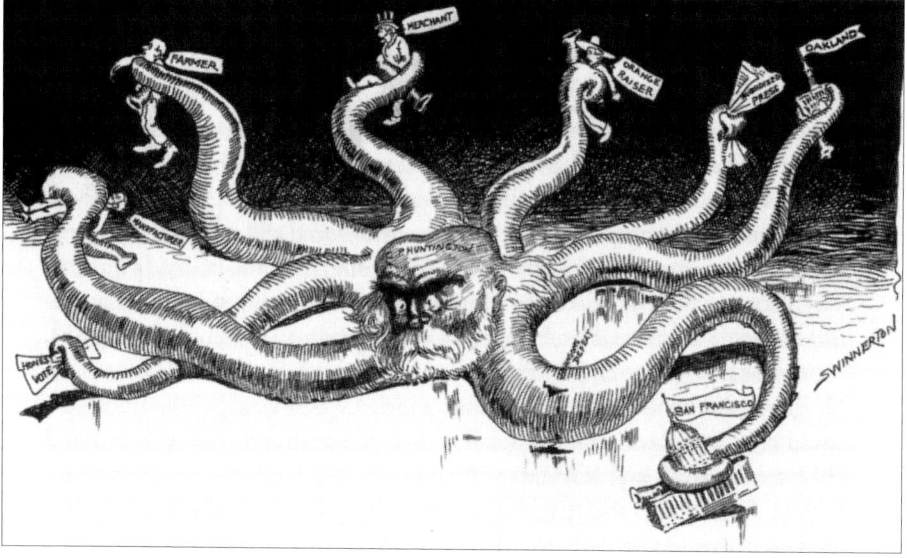

The Octopus, a cartoon by Jimmy Swinnerton which appeared in the *San Fransisco Examiner* on December 14, 1896 (right).

Impending Retribution, a cartoon by Edward Keller, from *The Wasp*, October 7, 1882 (far right).

ANTI MONOPOLY
MUSSEL SLOUGH VICTIMS
NOB HILL
PUBLIC OPINION
KELLER

EVANGEL

The Teaching Train Comes to Town

Contrary to what its many enemies charged, the Southern Pacific did not seek to crush the life out of farmers. Instead it worked hard to promote settlement and agriculture in the territory it traversed because more farmers raising better crops meant more business for the railroad. From its earliest days the Southern Pacific conducted research, promoted scientific agriculture, and partnered with the University of California's College of Agriculture. The railroad collected and disseminated agricultural data, published papers and bulletins, and provided weather data from its numerous weather stations. Between 1908 and 1912 it also joined with the College to sponsor a farm demonstration train that toured the rural areas of California. Later called the "Evangel Train," it attracted large crowds everywhere it stopped.

The Southern Pacific Depot at Yuma, Arizona, in 1900, with the irrigated demonstration garden showing how new crops could be grown in the region.

In every town farmers and their families flocked to greet the special train that was adorned with blue and gold banners. Local dignitaries stepped forward, often with the accompaniment of a school band, to welcome the railroad and university officials, after which a formal lecture program commenced. Experts imparted their wisdom from flatcar beds, the station platform, and sometimes a nearby church or lodge. When they were done, the crowd flocked into the exhibit cars to view everything from displays of crop pests, insecticides, and new seed varieties to model farm kitchens and practical demonstrations of farm techniques. The train stayed several hours or sometimes overnight, then moved on down the line.

The Evangel Train also journeyed beyond California to the other states in Southern Pacific territory, and by May 1909 it had covered nearly every farming district from Oregon to the Imperial Valley. As the program gained momentum and aroused enthusiasm, invited guests such as farm journal editors, local dignitaries, and regional farm experts joined the train. The university's president, Benjamin Ide Wheeler, found the experience so fulfilling that he became a regular participant.

During its final and most successful season, 1911–12, the train traveled more than 4,000 miles, made 238 stops, and attracted some 102,000 visitors. The cost of this promotional work was $30,000 a year, and gave both the railroad and the university a much more positive image. The program ended in part because it had been so successful. The interest it aroused could be better served in other ways, and the train had become a drain on both the railroad's finances and the schedules of its lecturers. Although later trains made brief revival tours, none of them captured the freshness and excitement of the original Evangel Train.

A Southern Pacific agricultural demonstration train at Erath, Louisiana, October 15, 1910, taken by the SP's official photographer, Edward Kemp. The twelve-day tour was sponsored by the railroad and Louisiana State University. It began on October 3, visited forty cities and towns, and ended at Erath. Erath school children sang "America" and "twice as many people … [were] present as the town has population," according to the *New Orleans Picayune*, which sent a reporter with the train. Erath was "demonstration-train 'mad' for the time being," he wrote. Eight professors were on hand to instruct about sugar cane, corn, rice, dairy, meat cattle, and hogs.

THE PACIFIC FRUIT EXPRESS

Fresh Food for Faraway Tables

The first special fast fruit train left Sacramento on the Southern Pacific on June 24, 1886.

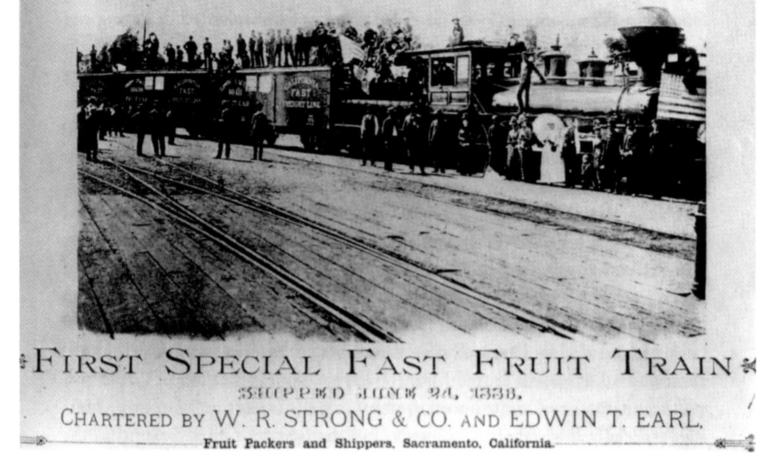

For centuries fresh fruit and vegetables were delicacies people could obtain only in season from their own or nearby gardens. California and other West Coast states produced a cornucopia of perishables, but had no way to get them to distant markets. After completion of the transcontinental railroad in 1869, attempts were made to move them first by boxcar and then by specially ventilated cars, but both failed miserably, and early attempts to refrigerate cars with ice also failed because the technology was too crude.

The rise of large-scale meatpacking helped expedite the development of better refrigeration techniques. Early versions utilized boxcars insulated with sawdust and cooled by bunkers filled with ice, which required ice plants along the road to replenish the supply. In June 1886 the Southern Pacific ran the first of what became known as fast fruit trains, with entire consists made up of perishables. However, their movement in mass quantities remained out of reach until after 1900.

In 1906 the Southern Pacific and Union Pacific, then both under the command of E. H. Harriman, formed a joint company called Pacific Fruit Express (PFE) for the specific task of hauling perishables from the burgeoning fields of the Far West. For starters Harriman ordered 6,600 new refrigerator cars (called "reefers") for PFE, with 30,000-pound capacity and bunkers that held 11,500 pounds of ice. In a remarkably short time PFE turned into a cash cow for its owners, so great was the demand for fresh fruit and vegetables across the continent. In 1907 PFE carried 48,900 carloads of perishables;

A selection of the many thousands of "giant produce" postcards on sale in California between 1900 and the 1920s.

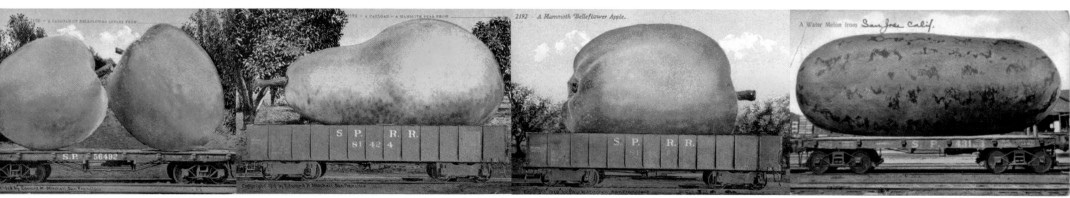

Front cover of the *Texas Rice Book*, published by the Southern Pacific in 1893 to promote rice production and consumption in Texas and Lousiana.

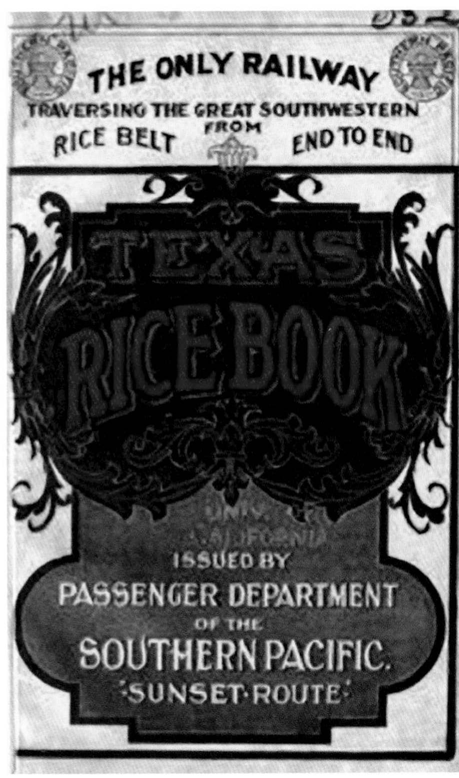

by 1921 it owned 19,200 cars that hauled 170,000 loads. "In the summertime," boasted a Union Pacific officer, "... we'd have one fruit train after another coming to us from the SP."

At first ice was harvested from lakes and stored at five facilities along the road. So rapidly did the business grow that in 1907 the Southern Pacific acquired all the ice-making and icing facilities of the important Armour Lines in California, and in 1908 the company built the first part of what became a huge ice-making and car-icing facility in Roseville, California, northeast of Sacramento. Other artificial ice-making plants sprang up across the line to feed the swelling number of reefers.

These dogged efforts to improve transportation galvanized the production and marketing of perishables even as it revolutionized American eating habits. Fresh fruit and vegetables became staples instead of seasonal treats.

SOUTHERN PACIFIC.

SUNSET ROUTE.

All Sunset Route Passenger trains now arrive and depart from UNION STATION, Howard Avenue and Rampart Street, New Orleans, in the heart of the City.

CONDENSED SCHEDULE OF THROUGH PULLMAN STANDARD SLEEPING CAR SERVICE.

NEW ORLEANS, SAN ANTONIO, SAN FRANCISCO.

No. 9	No. 7	November 12, 1905.	No. 8	No. 10
		(M. L. & T.)		
*11 55 A M	*9 00 P M	lve. **New Orleans** (C. T.) arr.	8 35 A M	6 45 P M
8 48 P M	6 38 A M	arr. **Orange**...(T. & N. O.) lve.	10 45 P M	9 43 A M
9 30 P M	7 25 A M	lve. **Beaumont** » arr.	9 57 P M	9 00 A M
12 05 Night	10 15 A M	arr. **Houston**.. » lve.	7 20 P M	6 30 A M
12 30 Night	10 35 A M	lve. Houston.(G. H. & S. A.) arr.	7 00 P M	6 00 A M
1 35 A M	11 52 A M	lve. **Rosenberg** » lve.	5 43 P M	4 30 A M
6 30 A M	8 00 P M	arr. San Antonio. » lve.	*11 40 A M	10 30 P M
9 00 A M		lve. San Antonio. » arr.		8 00 P M
8 00 A M		arr. **El Paso**... » lve.		8 00 P M
		(Pacific time.)		
7 45 A M		lve. **El Paso**.(G. H. & S. A.) arr.		5 00 P M
7 55 A M		lve. Rio Grande..(So. Pac.) arr.		4 50 P M
5 25 P M		lve. **Benson**... » lve.		7 57 A M
7 30 P M		lve. **Tucson**.... » lve.		5 40 A M
10 00 P M		lve. **Maricopa**. » lve.		2 42 A M
3 50 P M		lve. Los Angeles. » lve.		12 10 Noon
9 10 A M		arr. San Francisco » lve.		*5 45 P M

GALVESTON AND SAN ANTONIO.

No. 9		No. 10
*7 05 P M	lve. **Galveston**...(G. H. & S. A. Ry.) arr.	8 35 A M
8 50 P M	arr. **Houston** » lve.	6 58 A M
12 30 Night	lve. **Houston** » arr.	6 00 A M
1 35 A M	lve. **Rosenberg** » lve.	4 30 A M
6 30 A M	arr. **San Antonio** » lve.	*10 30 P M

GALVESTON AND NEW ORLEANS.

No. 8		No. 7
*5 00 P M	lve. **Galveston**........(G. H. & S. A.) arr.	12 10 Noon
6 55 P M	arr. **Houston** » lve.	10 30 A M
7 20 P M	lve. **Houston**........(T. & N. O.) arr.	10 15 A M
8 35 A M	arr. **New Orleans**......(M. L. & T.) lve.	*9 00 P M

Pullman Standard Sleeper daily, Galveston and Fort Worth, via Houston and H. & T. C., also Galveston and St. Louis, via Houston, H. & T. C. and M. K. & T.

For Map, see pages 666-667.

SONORA RAILWAY.

J. A. NAUGLE, Assistant General Manager, Guaymas, Mex.
W. G. SHERLOCK, Assistant Auditor, »
L. M. De La HOZ, Jr., General Attorney, »
C. C. ROSS, Asst. Gen. Freight and Passenger Agent, »
W. C. BUDGE, Trainmaster, Guaymas, Mex.
W. S. PRATT, Acting Resident Engineer, »
R. A. JOHNSON, Master Mechanic, »

4	6	No. 2	Mls.	March 1, 1906.	No. 1	5	3
				(Southern Pacific)			
		*3 25 P M		lve...+**Tucson** ♁..arr.	10 05 A M		
		4 05 »		Vail ♁	9 25 »		
		4 29 »		Pantano ♁	9 04 »		
		‖5 20 »		arr...+**Benson** ♁..lve.	8 15 »		
		5 50 »		lve.....**Benson**....arr.	‖7 50 »		
		6 02 »		St. Davids	7 37 »		
		6 26 »		**Fairbanks** ♁	7 13 »		
		6 49 »		Huachuca ♁	6 49 »		
		7 28 »		Sonoita	6 09 »		
		7 49 »		Crittenden	5 46 »		
		7 55 »		Patagonia ♁	5 38 »		
		8 33 »		Calabasas	4 56 »		
		8 55 P M		arr....**Nogales** ♁..lve.	*4 35 A M		
	A M			(Sonora Ry.)		P M	
	†8 00	*11 00 P M	0	lve....**Nogales**....arr.	3 30 A M	6 30	
	8 35	11 20 »	6	Encina	3 10 »	5 55	
	9 00	11 40 P M	12	Agua Zarca	2 47 »	5 10	
	9 40	12 05 Night	21	Cibuta	2 21 »	4 25	
	9 57	12 16 »	26	Casita	2 09 »	4 05	
	10 15	12 28 »	30	Quijano ♁	1 56 »	3 45	
	10 40	12 45 »	36	Cumeral	1 37 »	3 12	
	10 48	12 51 Night	39	Cerro Blanco	1 30 »	3 00	
	11 25	1 10 A M	42	Imuris ♁	1 20 A M	2 40	
	11 47	1 24 »	47	Pierson	12 57 Night	1 50	
	11 57	1 31 »	49	San Ignacio	12 50 »	1 35	
	12 55	1 45 »	54	Magdalena ♁	12 34 »	1 15	
	1 13	1 54 »	58	Lorenzo	12 25 »	12 40	
	2 45	2 15 »	65	Santa Ana ♁	12 05 Night	12 10	
	3 10	2 28 »	70	Gutierrez	11 52 P M	10 52	
	3 50	2 50 »	80	Llano ♁	11 29 »	10 15	
	4 50	3 25 »	95	Puerto	10 54 »	9 15	
	5 30	3 43 »	103	Querobabi ♁	10 36 »	8 35	
	6 00	3 56 »	109	Camou	10 22 »	8 05	
	6 40	4 13 »	127	Poza ♁	10 04 »	7 25	
A M	7 30	4 40 »	130	arr.....**Carbo** ♁...lve.	9 35 »	†6 30	P M
†7 00	P M	4 50 »	130	lve.....**Carbo**....arr.	9 26 »	A M	8 00
7 35		5 11 »	139	Selva	9 04 »		7 23
8 15		5 37 »	151	Pesqueira ♁	8 57 »		6 15
8 50		5 54 »	160	Zamora	8 19 »		5 40
9 00		6 00 »	162	Alamito	8 13 »		5 27
9 10		6 06 »	166	Gandara	8 07 »		5 16
11 50		6 50 »	172	**Union**	7 49 »		4 35
11 53		6 52 »	173	Rio Sonora	7 20 »		3 22
12 30		7 09 »	181	Willard	7 02 »		2 49
12 55		7 23 »	188	Vega	6 48 »		2 22
2 10		‖8 00 »	196	Torres ♁	‖6 30 »		1 50
2 45		8 21 »	206	Lujan	5 48 »		12 19
3 01		8 31 »	210	Escalante	5 38 »		11 59
3 20		8 43 »	215	Moreno	5 24 »		11 30
3 55		8 59 »	222	Tapia	5 07 »		10 55
4 45		9 17 »	231	Ortiz ♁	4 45 »		10 15
5 08		9 27 »	234	Anita	4 35 »		9 59
5 18		9 40 »	240	Santa Rosa	4 22 »		9 40
5 38		9 54 »	245	Maytorena ♁	4 08 »		9 08
5 55		10 01 »	248	Tres Jitos	4 00 »		8 52
6 10		10 09 »	252	Batamotal ♁	3 52 »		8 35
6 25		10 14 »	255	Empalme ♁	3 46 »		8 20
6 38		10 17 »	256	Pleamar	3 43 »		8 15
6 45		10 20 »	258	Batuecas	3 40 »		8 10
7 00		10 30 A M	260	**Guaymas** ♁	*3 30 P M		†8 00
P M				ARRIVE] [LEAVE			A M

HERMOSILLO BRANCH.

104	102	Ms.	November 19, 1905.	101	103
P M	A M		LEAVE] [ARRIVE	A M	P M
*7 22	*6 23	0	**Union**	6 50	7 49
7 32	6 33	2.5	**Hermosillo** ♁	*6 43	*7 42
P M	A M		ARRIVE] [LEAVE	A M	P M

CONDENSED SCHEDULE.

TUCSON AND GUAYMAS.

Through Pullman Sleeping Car.

*3 25 P M	lve. **Tucson**........(So. Pac.) arr.	10 05 A M
5 50 P M	lve. **Benson** » arr.	7 50 A M
8 55 P M	arr. **Nogales** » lve.	4 35 A M
11 00 P M	lve. **Nogales**....(Sonora Ry.) arr.	3 30 A M
4 40 A M	arr. **Carbo** » lve.	9 36 P M
10 30 A M	arr. **Guaymas** » lve.	*3 30 P M

SAN FRANCISCO AND GUAYMAS.

5 45 P M	lve. **San Francisco** (So. Pac.) arr.	9 10 A M
7 10 A M	lve. **Santa Barbara**. » arr.	8 00 P M
12 10 Noon	lve. **Los Angeles** » arr.	12 55 Noon
2 43 P M	lve. **Colton** » arr.	10 32 A M
9 30 P M	lve. **Yuma** » arr.	3 35 A M
2 42 A M	lve. **Maricopa** » arr.	10 00 P M
3 25 P M	lve. **Tucson** » arr.	10 05 A M
5 20 P M	arr. **Benson** » lve.	8 15 A M
5 50 P M	lve. **Benson** » arr.	7 50 A M
8 55 P M	arr. **Nogales** » lve.	4 35 A M
11 00 P M	lve. **Nogales**....(Sonora Ry.) arr.	3 30 A M
4 40 A M	arr. **Carbo** » lve.	9 36 P M
10 30 A M	arr. **Guaymas** » lve.	3 30 P M

NEW ORLEANS AND GUAYMAS.

11 55 A M	lve. **New Orleans** (M. L. & T.) arr.	6 45 P M
8 48 P M	lve. **Orange**.....(T. & N. O.) arr.	9 43 A M
9 30 P M	lve. **Beaumont** » arr.	9 00 A M
12 05 Night	arr. **Houston** » lve.	6 30 A M
12 30 Night	lve. **Houston**..(G. H. & S. A.) arr.	6 00 A M
1 35 A M	lve. **Rosenberg** » lve.	4 30 A M
6 30 A M	arr. **San Antonio** » lve.	10 30 P M
9 00 A M	lve. **San Antonio** » arr.	8 00 P M
8 00 A M	arr. **El Paso** » lve.	8 00 P M
9 45 A M	lve. **El Paso**........(So. Pac.) arr.	7 00 P M
10 56 A M	lve. **Deming** » lve.	2 15 P M
12 49 Noon	lve. **Lordsburg** » lve.	12 24 Noon
5 25 P M	arr. **Benson** » lve.	7 57 A M
5 50 P M	lve. **Benson** » arr.	7 50 A M
8 55 P M	arr. **Nogales** » lve.	4 35 A M
11 00 P M	lve. **Nogales**....(Sonora Ry.) arr.	3 30 A M
4 40 A M	arr. **Carbo** » lve.	9 36 P M
10 30 A M	arr. **Guaymas** » lve.	3 30 P M

* Daily.
† Daily, except Sunday.
‖ Meals.
\+ Coupon stations.
♁ Telegraph stations.

SOUTHERN PACIFIC.

SUNSET ROUTE.

All Sunset Route Passenger trains now arrive and depart from UNION STATION, Howard Avenue and Rampart Street, New Orleans, in the heart of the City.

CONDENSED SCHEDULE OF THROUGH SUNSET EXCURSION SLEEPING CAR SERVICE.

ST. LOUIS-SAN FRANCISCO, VIA SAN ANTONIO.

Westbound.		(Central time.)	Eastbound.	
Tue	8 32 P M	lve. **St. Louis**...(M. K. & T.) arr.	7 54 A M	Mon
Thu	9 00 A M	lve. **San Antonio**..(G.H.&S.A.) arr.	8 00 P M	Sat.
Fri.	8 00 A M	arr. **El Paso** » lve.	8 00 P M	Fri.
		(Pacific time.)		
Fri.	7 45 A M	lve. **El Paso** arr.	5 00 P M	Fri.
Sat.	12 55 Noon	arr. **Los Angeles** lve.	12 10 Noon	Thu
Sun.	7 08 P M	arr. **San Francisco**...(S. P.) lve.	10 20 A M	Wed
		(Via San Joaquin Valley Line.)		

ST. LOUIS-LOS ANGELES, VIA TEXAS & PACIFIC-IRON MOUNTAIN.

Westbound.				Eastbound.		
Tue	Sat	8 30 A M	lve **St. Louis**........(I. M.) arr.	7 30 P M	Sat	Tue
Tue	Sat	9 15 A M	lve. **Memphis** » arr.	2 40 P M	Sat	Tue
Tue	Sat	7 25 P M	lve. **Little Rock** » arr.	8 10 A M	Sat	Tue
Tue	Sat	12 01 Night	lve. **Texarkana**......(T. & P.) arr.	3 40 A M	Sat	Tue
Wed	Sun	7 50 A M	lve. **Dallas** » arr.	7 10 P M	Fri	Mon
Wed	Sun	9 45 A M	lve. **Fort Worth** » arr.	5 30 P M	Fri	Mon
Thu	Mon	8 45 A M	arr. **El Paso** » lve.	7 50 P M	Thu	Sun
Fri	Tue	5 30 A M	arr. **Phoenix**........(S. P.) lve.	7 30 P M	Wed	Sat
Fri	Tue	12 55 Noon	arr. **Los Angeles** » lve.	12 10 Noon	Wed	Sat

NEW ORLEANS-SAN FRANCISCO.

Westbound.		(Central time.)	Eastbound.	
Mon	11 55 A M	lve. **New Orleans**..(M. L. & T.) arr.	6 45 P M	Wed
Mon	12 05 Night	arr. **Houston**...(T. & N. O.) lve.	6 30 A M	Wed
Mon	12 30 Night	lve. **Houston**..(G. H. & S. A.) arr.	6 00 A M	Wed
Tue	6 30 A M	arr. **San Antonio** » lve.	10 30 P M	Tue
Tue	9 00 A M	lve. **San Antonio** » arr.	8 00 P M	Tue
Wed	8 00 A M	arr. **El Paso** » lve.	8 00 P M	Mon
		(Pacific time.)		
Wed	7 45 A M	lve. **El Paso** arr.	5 00 P M	Mon
Thu	12 55 Noon	arr. **Los Angeles** lve.	12 10 Noon	Sun
Fri	9 10 A M	arr. **San Francisco**..(S. P.) lve.	5 45 P M	Sat

CHICAGO-LOS ANGELES, VIA C. R. I. & P. AND EL PASO.

Westbound.			(Daily Service.)	Eastbound.		
	Tue	8 30 A M	lve. **Chicago**....(C. R. I. & P.) arr.	10 35 P M	Thu	
Daily.	Tue	11 00 P M	lve. **Kansas City** » arr.	6 50 A M	Thu	Daily.
	Wed	1 05 A M	lve. **Topeka** » arr.	4 50 A M	Thu	
	Wed	10 00 P M	lve. **Santa Rosa** » arr.	4 25 A M	Wed	
	Thu	8 00 A M	arr. **El Paso** » lve.	6 35 P M	Tue	
	Thu	7 10 P M	arr. **Tucson**........(S. P.) lve.	5 40 A M	Tue	
	Fri.	12 55 Noon	arr. **Los Angeles** » lve.	12 10 Noon	Mon	

WASHINGTON, D.C.-SAN FRANCISCO, VIA NEW ORLEANS.

Westbound.					Eastbound.			
Fri.	Wed	Mon	7 30 P M	lv. Washington (E.T.)(S.Ry.) ar.	11 05 A M	Sun.	Tue	Thu
Sat.	Thu	Tue	4 30 P M	ar. **Atlanta** » lv.	2 00 P M	Sat.	Mon	Wed
Sat.	Thu	Tue	4 20 P M	lv. Atlanta (C.T.)(A.&W.P.) ar.	11 40 A M	Sat.	Mon	Wed
Sun.	Fri.	Wed	7 15 A M	ar. **New Orleans** (L. & N.) lv.	8 15 P M	Fri.	Sun.	Tue
»	»	»	11 55 A M	lv. New Orleans..(M.L.&T.) ar.	6 45 P M	»	»	»
»	»	»	12 30 Night	lv. **Houston** (G.H.&S.A.) lv.	6 30 A M	»	»	»
Mon	Sat.	Thu	9 00 A M	lv. San Antonio... » lv.	10 30 P M	Thu	Sat.	Mon
Tue	Sun.	Fri.	8 00 A M	ar. **El Paso** » lv.	8 00 P M	Wed	Fri.	Sun.
Tue	Sun.	Fri.	7 45 A M	lv. El Paso (P.T.)(G.H.&S.A.) ar.	5 00 P M	Wed	Fri.	Sun.
Wed	Mon	Sat.	12 55 Noon	ar. Los Angeles...(S.P.) lv.	12 10 N'n	Tue	Thu	Sat.
Thu	Tue	Sun.	9 10 A M	ar. San Francisco. » lv.	5 45 P M	Mon	Wed	Fri.

CINCINNATI-SAN FRANCISCO VIA NEW ORLEANS.

Westbound.			Eastbound.	
Tue.	6 00 P M	lve. **Cincinnati** (B. & O. S. W.) arr.	9 15 P M	Sun.
»	9 40 P M	lve. **Louisville**...(Ill. Cent.) lve.	5 45 P M	»
Wed	9 05 A M	lve. **Memphis** » lve.	6 45 A M	»
»	8 15 P M	arr. **New Orleans** » lve.	7 10 P M	Sat.
Thu	11 55 A M	lve. **New Orleans** (M. L. & T.) arr.	6 45 P M	»
»	12 30 Night	lve. **Houston**....(G. H. & S. A.) lve.	6 30 A M	»
Fri.	9 00 A M	lve. **San Antonio** » lve.	10 30 P M	Fri.
Sat.	7 45 A M	lve. **El Paso** » lve.	8 00 P M	Thu
Sun.	12 55 Noon	lve. **Los Angeles**..(S. P. Co.) lve.	12 10 Noon	Wed
Mon	9 10 A M	arr. **San Francisco**. » lve.	5 45 P M	Tue.

CHICAGO-SAN FRANCISCO, VIA ILLINOIS CENTRAL AND NEW ORLEANS.

Westbound.		(Central time.)	Eastbound.	
Friday.	9 40 A M	lve. **Chicago**.......(I. C. R. R.) arr.	9 30 P M	Tuesday.
»	11 20 P M	lve. **Memphis** » arr.	6 25 A M	»
Saturday	10 35 A M	arr. **New Orleans** » lve.	7 10 P M	Monday.
»	11 55 A M	lve. **New Orleans**...(M. L. & T.) arr.	6 45 P M	»
»	12 30 Night	lve. **Houston**...(G. H. & S. A.) lve.	6 30 A M	»
Sunday.	9 00 A M	lve. **San Antonio** » lve.	10 30 P M	Sunday.
Monday.	8 00 A M	arr. **El Paso** » lve.	8 00 P M	Saturday
		(Pacific time.)		
Monday.	7 45 A M	lve. **El Paso**...(G. H. & S. A.) arr.	5 00 P M	Saturday
Tuesday.	12 55 Noon	arr. **Los Angeles**... (S. P.) lve.	12 10 Noon	Friday.
Wed'day.	9 10 A M	arr. **San Francisco**. » lve.	5 45 P M	Thursday.

The Through Excursion Sleeping Cars running between Washington, Chicago, Cincinnati, New Orleans, St. Louis and San Francisco are the finest and best equipped Sleeping Cars operated by the Pullman Company. First or second-class tickets are accepted for passage. A uniformed porter is always in attendance, and a **"Sunset Excursion Agent"** accompanies each car through for the purpose of looking after the comfort of passengers; ladies and children traveling alone are guaranteed the utmost protection under his care.

THE BERTH RATES IN THESE SLEEPERS ARE HALF THE RATES CHARGED IN STANDARD SLEEPERS!

SAFETY CAR HEATING & LIGHTING CO. 160 BROADWAY, NEW YORK. | Pintsch Gas Steam Heat | Used on most of the Prominent Railways in Europe and the United States.

SOUTHERN PACIFIC.

SAN FRANCISCO, LOS ANGELES AND NEW ORLEANS—SUNSET ROUTE.

6	50	84	26	8	Mls	April 1, 1906.	7	25	49	31	83	3
Sunset Express.	The Coaster.	Via Mendota								Via Niles. / The Coaster.		Sunset Express.
P M	P M	A M	P M	A M		LEAVE] [ARRIVE	A M	P M	A M	Noon	P M	Noon
*6 00	*3 20	*8 20	*5 00	*10 20	0	+ San Francisco ♁	7 08	8 48	10 08	4 08	4 48	12 48
6 34	3 49	8 47	5 28	10 48	5	...Oakland Pier. ♁	6 36	8 20	11 42	3 42	4 15	12 18
6 41	3 53	8 53	5 35	10 54	7	+ Oakland (16th St.) ♁	6 30	8 14	11 34		4 08	12 12
7 30	4 45	9 37	6 20	11 45	32	....Port Costa.. ♁	5 40	7 25	10 49		3 24	11 30
a	4 53	9 45	—	11 54	36	....Martinez.... ♁	5 28	—	10 38		3 15	—
—	5 35	10 20	—	a	55	....Antioch.... ♁	4 48	—	9 59		2 43	—
a	5 58	10 45	—	12 53	68	.....Byron..... ♁	4 23	—	9 33		2 23	—
8 55	6 25	11 20	7 35	1 20	83	arr. + Tracy ♁ lve.	3 55	6 02	9 03	1 10	2 00	*10 07
P M		11 35	7 40		83	lve. + Tracy ♁ arr.				12 40		A M
		1 27	9 13		141	...Los Banos.. ♁				10 47		
		2 35	10 15		176	....Mendota.... ♁				9 50		
		3 05	—		194	.....Collis..... ♁				9 08		
		P M	11 05		209	ar. + Fresno ♁ lv.				*8 40		
	6 50	11 35		1 30	83	lve. + Tracy ♁ arr.	3 50	5 35	8 42	A M	11 45	
	7 15	11 58		1 52	94	+ ...Lathrop.... ♁	3 30	5 35	8 22		1 25	
	7 52	12 30		2 42	114	+ ...Modesto.... ♁	2 42	—	7 44		12 47	
	8 32	1 06		3 08	137	....Livingston.... ♁	1 56	—	7 03			
	9 00	1 30		3 35	152	+ ....Merced.... ♁	1 30	—	6 40		11 51	
	9 23	1 56		4 45	168	.....Minturn..... ♁	12 56	—	6 12		11 27	
	8 44	2 10		5 07	178	....Berenda.... ♁	12 40	—	5 57		11 15	
	9 56	2 24		5 25	185	+ ....Madera.... ♁	12 27	—	5 45		11 03	11
12	10 14	—		5 49	197	....Herndon.... ♁	12 07	—	5 25		—	P M
*8 40	10 30	3 05	11 09	6 20	207	+ ....Fresno.... ♁	11 50	2 40	*5 10		10 35	7 12
8 51	P M	3 13	—	6 31	212	.....Malaga..... ♁	11 21	—	A M		10 18	6 59
9 01		3 21	—	6 43	216	.....Fowler..... ♁	11 09				10 07	6 43
9 12		3 30	—	6 57	222	+ ....Selma..... ♁	10 56				9 55	6 33
9 22		3 39	—	7 09	227	....Kingsburg.... ♁	10 44				9 44	6 20
9 33		3 51	—	7 19	232	.....Traver..... ♁	10 32				9 33	6 08
10 00		4 05	—	7 37	241	..Goshen Junc ♁	10 15				9 19	*5 50
10 40		4 54		8 00	248	arr.. Visalia ..lve.	*9 50				*7 45	*5 15
10 45				8 03	254	arr.. Hanford.lve.	*8 20				*8 20	*5 10
A M		4 23	12 20	7 59	251	+ ....Tulare.... ♁	9 45	1 17			9 00	P M
		4 42	—	8 20	262	.....Tipton..... ♁	9 25	—			8 42	
		4 54	—	8 32	268	.....Pixley..... ♁	9 14	—			8 32	
		5 15	—	8 55	282	.....Delano..... ♁	8 49	—			8 13	
		5 34	—	9 18	294	.....Famosa.... ♁	8 31	—			7 57	
		5 52	—	—	307	.....Jewetta.... ♁	8 07	—			—	
		6 05	2 07	10 12	314	+ .Bakersfield ♁	7 55	11 40			*7 30	
	P M			10 45	329	.....Bena..... ♁	7 25				A M	
				11 10	336	.....Caliente.... ♁	6 46					
				12 25	350	.....Keene..... ♁	6 05					
				12 55	355	.....Marcel..... ♁	5 50					
				1 30	362	....Tehachapi.. ♁	5 30					
				1 55	372	.....Cameron.... ♁	5 05					
		5 13		2 35	382	+ ....Mojave.... ♁	4 20	8 42				
				3 02	396	....Rosamond.... ♁	3 29					
				3 33	407	....Lancaster.... ♁	3 00	7 57				
				3 55	415	....Palmdale.... ♁	2 50					
				4 25	422	.....Vincent.... ♁	2 35					
				4 46	430	.....Ravenna.... ♁	2 07					
				5 13	440	......Lang...... ♁	1 49					
				5 49	457	....Saugus.... ♁	12 56	6 15				
		7 35	8 55	7 05	484	ar. Los Angeles ♁ lv.	*11 30	*5 00				
10	22	20							19	21		9
P M	A M	A M	A M	A M		(Via Coast Division.)	P M	P M	P M	A M		A M
*5 45	*8 30	*8 00				lv. San Francisco ar.			9 30	11 45		9 10
7 30	9 55	9 25			50	....San Jose.... ♁			8 05	10 15		7 40
9 10	11 13	10 38			99	.....Pajaro..... ♁			6 42	8 33		5 45
9 32	11 27	10 55			110	..Castroville ♁			6 22	8 13		5 24
9 55	11 50	—			118	.....Salinas.... ♁			—	8 00		5 10
1 02	2 54	1 38			216	....Paso Robles....			3 36	4 58		2 06
2 50	4 25	3 05	98	96	253	.San Luis Ob spo ♁		97	2 15	3 35	99	12 40
7 00	8 10	6 14	P M	A M	371	ar. Santa Barbara ♁ lv.		P M	11 15	12 10	P M	8 10
7 10	8 15	6 19	*3 05	*7 30	371	lv. Santa Barbara ..ar.		11 40	11 05	11 55	7 10	8 00
		All Parlor Cars.	3 31	7 56	383	...Carpinteria.. ♁		11 08			6 38	
8 05	9 03		4 00	8 30	400	.San Buena Ventura ♁		10 28		11 06	5 55	6 45
8 16	—		4 14	8 42	405	.....Montalvo.... ♁		10 22			5 45	6 33
8 26	—				410	+ ....Oxnard.... ♁				10 45		6 20
9 26	—				430	.....Moorpark... ♁						5 39
10 42	—				466	.....Burbank..... ♁						4 21
			4 15	8 42	405	.....Montalvo.. ♁		10 20	All Parlor Cars.		5 43	
			4 37	9 10	416	+ .Santa Paula. ♁		9 48			5 18	
			4 59	9 32	426	.....Fillmore... ♁		9 32			4 59	
			6 15	10 35	450	.....Saugus.... ♁		8 35			3 53	
			6 19	10 41	453	.....Newhall... ♁		8 24			3 45	
			6 42	11 04	461	.....Fernando... ♁		7 59			3 23	
10 44	— —	— —	7 01	11 25	472	.....Burbank.. ♁		7 30	— —	— —	2 59	4 21
11 20	11 45	9 30	7 35	12 01	482	+ Los Angeles..		*7 00	*8 00	*8 30	*2 30	*3 50
A M	P M	P M	P M	Noon		ARRIVE] [LEAVE		A M	A M	A M	P M	P M

10	44	18	Mls	March 1, 1906.	17	9	43	19
Sunset Exp.						Sunset Express.		
Noon	Noon	A M		LEAVE] [ARRIVE	A M	Noon	P M	A M
*12 10	*12 01	*9 00	482	+ Los Angeles ♁	9 45	12 55	4 15	4 35
12 34	12 25	9 22	488	..Dolgeville. ♁	9 22	12 32	3 50	4 15
		9 27	491	..San Gabriel.. ♁	9 16			4 07
		9 33	495	.....Monte..... ♁	9 08			3 58
			498	.....Bassett.... ♁	9 03			3 52
			506	.....Covina..... ♁				3 37
			512	....Lordsburg.. ♁				3 22
			516	.....Pomona... ♁				3 10
		9 44	502	.....Puente..... ♁	8 57			
		9 55	508	.....Lemon..... ♁	8 48			
1 31	1 15	10 13	515	+ ...Pomona.. ♁	8 36	11 27	3 05	3 10
			519	.....Narod..... ♁	8 29			
1 47		10 25	521	+ ...Ontario.... ♁	8 26	11 11		2 42
			526	...Cucamonga.. ♁	8 19			2 36
			535	..Bloomington.. ♁	8 05			2 17
2 25	2 05	10 57	540	arr + Colton ♁ lve.	7 57	10 34	2 25	2 10
2 48	2 48	11 15	547	arr. Riverside ♁ lve.	*7 30	*10 07		*1 30
2 57	2 57	12 44	544	ar. S. Bernardino ♁ lv.	*7 35	*10 05		*1 55
2 30	2 05	1 49	540	lve. Colton ♁ arr.	7 32	10 29	2 25	2 05
2 43	2 20	2 05	545	arr. Redlands Jn. ♁	7 38	10 17	2 10	1 55
3 00		2 15	548	ar. Redlands ♁ lv.	*7 28	*10 00		1 45
7 10		P M	552	arr. Crafton ♁ lve.	*7 15	A M		*1 30
3 14			554	.....El Casco.. ♁	A M	9 58		P M
3 41			563	....Beaumont.. ♁		9 42		
3 54			569	.....Banning.... ♁		9 21		
4 04			575	.....Cabazon.. ♁		9 02		
4 29			589	..Palm Springs ♁		8 40		
5 10	4 38		612	......Indio.... ♁		7 23	11 32	
6 02			632	.....Salton.... ♁		6 25		
6 20			648	.....Bertram.... ♁		6 08		
6 45			661	.....Volcano.... ♁		5 45		
7 05	6 08		666	Imperial Junc ♁		5 32	9 48	
7 48			683	.....Mammoth.. ♁		5 06		
8 13			697	......Glamis.... ♁		4 46		
8 48			715	......Ogilby.... ♁		4 18		
9 20	8 00		731	arr. + Yuma ...lve.		3 45	8 10	
9 30	8 05		731	lve... Yuma ♁ .arr.		3 35	8 02	
9 57			745	....Blaisdell.. ♁		2 58		
10 10			757	......Dome.... ♁		2 44		
10 37			768	.....Wellton.... ♁		2 22		
11 17			791	.....Mohawk.. ♁		1 29		
11 47			810	......Aztec.... ♁		12 51		
12 17			825	.....Sentinel.... ♁		12 17		
1 07	11 14		854	+ .....Gila.... ♁		11 32	4 42	
1 58			876	.....Estrella.... ♁		10 48		
2 42	12 36		896	+ ..Maricopa .. ♁		10 00	3 23	
3 22			917	..Casa Grande. ♁		9 17		
4 21			950	.....Red Rock.. ♁		8 23		
4 52		12	962	.....Rillito..... ♁	11	7 58		
5 25	2 55	P M	984	arr. + Tucson...lve.	7 28	7 30	7 10	
5 40	3 05	*3 25	984	lve. Tucson ♁ .arr.	10 05	7 00	1 00	
6 30		4 05	1002	......Vail...... ♁	9 25	6 33		
6 58		4 29	1011	.....Pantano.... ♁	9 04	6 13		
7 57	5 13	5 20	1031	+ ....Benson.... ♁	*8 15	5 25	11 17	
9 07		P M	1053	.....Dragoon.... ♁	A M	4 28		
9 23			1063	.....Cochise.... ♁		4 05		
9 42			1073	+ ...Willcox.... ♁		3 55		
10 34	7 24		1097	+ ....Bowie.... ♁		2 35	9 08	
11 01			1113	.....Simon..... ♁		2 00		
11 45			1123	.....Stein's.... ♁		1 29		
12 24	8 58		1147	+ ..Lordsburg.. ♁		12 49	7 43	
1 05			1167	......Separ..... ♁		12 07		
1 37			1187	......Gage..... ♁		11 30		
2 15	10 30		1207	+ ....Deming.... ♁		10 56	6 04	
2 57			1233	.....Cambray.. ♁		9 53		
3 23			1246	......Aden..... ♁		9 34		
4 03			1268	.....Lanark.... ♁		8 55		
4 23			1280	.....Strauss.... ♁		8 35		
4 50	12 40		1291	ar. Rio Grande.lv.		*7 55	*3 35	
P M	Noon			(Pacific time.)		A M	P M	
P M	P M			(Central time.)		A M	P M	
6 50	2 40		1291	lv. Rio Grande.ar.		9 55	5 35	
7 00	2 50		1294	arr. El Paso ♁ lve.		*9 45	*4 20	
8 00	P M		1294	lve.. El Paso..arr.		8 00	P M	
8 00			1918	..San Antonio..		9 00		
6 00			2127	....Houston....		12 30		
6 45			2489	..New Orleans..		*11 55		
P M				ARRIVE] [LEAVE		A M		

Burbank and Chatsworth Park—Leaves Burbank †7 52 a.m. for Kester, Reseda, Chatsworth Park and Chatsworth, arriving Oxnard (60 miles) 1 00 p.m. Returning, leaves Oxnard *11 00 a.m., Chatsworth †2 10 p.m., arriving Burbank 4 15 p.m.

Oil City Branch.—Leaves Bakersfield for Oil City (10 miles) *7 00 a.m. Leaves Oil City *3 30 p.m., arriving Bakersfield 4 45 p.m.

Bakersfield and Olig Line.—Leaves Bakersfield *7 00 a.m., arrives McKittrick (48 miles) 9 40 a.m., and Olig (49 miles) 10 00 a.m. Returning, leaves Olig *11 10 a.m., McKittrick *12 50 noon, arrives Bakersfield 4 20 p.m.

EXPLANATION OF SIGNS.

Trains marked * run daily; † daily, except Sunday.
a Stops to leave passengers.
‖ Meals. + Coupon stations; ♁ Telegraph stations.

For additional local train service between Los Angeles, Riverside, San Bernardino, etc., see page 672.

Exeter Branch.—Leaves Fresno, *6 20 p.m., arrives Exeter (51 miles), 8 06 p.m. Returning, leaves Exeter *6 43 a.m., arrives Fresno 8 30 a.m.

Pollasky Branch.—Leaves Fresno †9 35 a.m., arrives Pollasky (24 miles) 11 20 a.m. Returning, leaves Pollasky †11 30 a.m., arrives Fresno 1 30 p.m.

Valley Spring Branch.—Trains leave Valley Spring for Lodi (27 miles) and Woodbridge (29 miles) *10 00 a.m.; for Lodi ‡3 15, †3 30 p.m. Returning, leaves Woodbridge *1 05 p.m., arrives at Valley Spring 2 50 p.m. Leave Lodi †7 00, ‡8 30 a.m., arrive Valley Spring 9 30, 9 45 a.m.

SOUTHERN PACIFIC.

SAN JOSE, STOCKTON, SACRAMENTO, VIA NILES.

112	6	40	110	88	38	108	94	106	32	82	122	90	Ms	April 1, 1906.	39	81	87	109	91	83	3	105	31	107	37	95	85
P M	P M	P M	P M	P M	P M	P M	....	A M	A M	A M	....	....	....	LEAVE] [ARRIVE	A M	....	A M	A M	....	....	Noon	P M	P M	P M	P M	....	A M
‡9 00	*6 00	*6 20	†5 20	*4 40	*4 00	*3 40	....	*11 40	*8 40	*7 40	....	....	0	+ San Francisco. ♁	7 08	....	8 48	9 48	....	....	12 48	2 48	4 08	7 48	7 28	....	11 48
9 27	6 34	6 48	5 48	5 07	4 27	4 07	....	12 07	9 08	8 07	....	....	4	...Oakland Pier. ♁	6 42	....	8 12	9 14	....	....	12 18	2 20	3 42	7 22	7 02	....	11 12
9 35	Via Byron.	6 56	5 56	5 15	4 35	4 15	P M	12 15	9 16	8 16	....	A M	7	..Oakland (1st St.) ♁	6 33	....	8 04	9 06	A M	....	Via Byron.	2 12	3 32	7 14	6 53	P M	11 03
10 20		7 47	6 47	6 11	5 14	5 00	*2 47	1 05	10 05	8 58	....	†7 20	30	arr.... Niles ♁ ...lve.	5 47	....	7 12	8 22	10 05	....		1 20	2 45	*6 21	6 11	5 05	‡10 10
10 27		7 53	6 54	6 22	....	P M	2 57	P M	10 23	....	....	7 31	34	......Irvington......	5 38	....	6 47	8 15	9 54	....		1 03	....	P M	....	4 57	....
10 55		8 20	7 20	6 50	....		3 25		10 52	....	....	8 25	48	arr. + San Jose ♁ .lve.	*5 15	....	†6 15	*7 50	*9 25	....		*12 30	....		....	*4 30	....
P M		P M	50	6 29	— —	124	P M	8	10 32	— —	....	84	37	.......Sunol....... ♁	25	....	6 51	49	A M	....		7	2 23	....	5 54	121	9 51
P M	....	....	P M	6 55	5 47	P M		P M	11 02	9 27	A M	A M	48	......Livermore...... ♁	A M	A M	†6 30	A M	A M	P M		P M	2 03	125	5 32	P M	‡9 30
*1 12	9 00	....	*6 50	P M	6 35	*3 00	A M	*1 30	‖12 15	10 15	*8 00	*11 35	72	.......Tracy....... ♁	5 55	7 50	A M	8 42	8 50	1 45	10 00	3 50	‖1 10	A M	4 43	7 30	A M
1 53	9 21	....	7 10	....	6 52	3 35	*11 57	1 50	12 41	10 32	8 30	11 55	83	+ ....Lathrop.... ♁	*5 35	7 32	....	*8 22	8 30	*1 25	9 40	*3 30	12 24	11 50	4 17	7 10	....
2 13	9 42	....	P M	....	7 10	4 00	12 25	P M	1 05	10 50	8 50	A M	92	+ ....Stockton.... ♁	A M	7 16	....	A M	*8 05	P M	9 21	P M	12 05	*11 30	*4 00	— —	....
P M	10 07	....	....	....	7 35	4 32	Noon	....	1 32	A M	9 23		104	+ ......Lodi...... ♁	....	*6 55	....	....	A M	....	8 58		11 28	A M	P M	6 23	....
....	10 22	....	....	....	P M	4 51	....	....	1 50	....	9 38	134	113	.......Galt....... ♁	....	A M	....	....	....	....	8 45	133	11 10	....	....	6 08	....
....	— —	....	....	....	....	5 18	....	....	2 12	....	9 59	A M	124	......Elk Grove...... ♁	....	....	....	....	....	....	— —	P M	10 44	....	....	5 47	....
....	11 00	....	....	....	....	5 45	....	....	2 35	....	10 25	*9 25	134	......Brighton...... ♁	....	....	....	....	....	....	8 10	3 50	10 25	....	....	5 30	....
....	11 15	....	....	....	....	6 00	....	....	2 50	....	10 40	9 40	140	+ ..Sacramento.. ♁	....	....	....	....	....	....	*7 55	*3 35	*10 10	....	....	*5 15	....
....	P M	....	....	....	....	P M	....	....	P M	....	A M	A M	....	ARRIVE] [LEAVE	....	....	....	....	....	....	A M	P M	A M	....	....	P M	....

SAN FRANCISCO, MARTINEZ AND AVON.

60	144	8	46	84	142	Ms	April 1, 1906.	141	81	143	145	59
A M	P M	A M	A M	A M	A M	...	LEAVE] [ARRIVE	A M	A M	P M	P M	P M
‡7 40	*4 00	*10 20	*9 40	*8 20	†7 40	0	+ .San Francisco. ♁	9 28	10 28	6 08	6 48	6 08
8 07	4 28	10 48	10 05	8 47	8 07	5	...Oakland Pier. ♁	9 02	10 02	5 44	6 14	5 44
9 12	5 38	11 45	11 04	9 37	9 12	32	....Port Costa.. ♁	7 52	9 12	4 48	5 13	4 48
9 20	5 46	11 54	11 14	9 45	9 25	36	.....Martinez... ♁	7 39	9 03	4 22	*4 53	4 30
9 27	5 53	— —	A M	*b* —	9 40	39	......Avon...... ♁	*7 32	— —	†4 10	P M	‡4 20
A M	P M	1 30	....	‖11 35	A M	83	......Tracy......	A M	7 52	P M	....	P M
....	....	1 50	....	11 55	....	95	.....Lathrop.....	....	7 32	....	....	....
....	....	4 00	....	1 00	....	103	....Stockton....	....	*7 16	....	....	....
....	....	P M	....	P M	....	...	ARRIVE] [LEAVE	....	A M	....	....	....

‖ Meals. + Coupon stations; ♁ Telegraph stations.

Felton and Boulder Creek Line.—Lve. Santa Cruz for Felton and Boulder Creek (15 miles) †8 15, ‡9 30 a.m., †5 25, ‡6 30 p.m. Leave Felton for Boulder Creek ‡7 00, †8 38, ‡9 53 a.m., *12 01 noon, *2 05, *5 53 p.m. Returning, leave Boulder Creek for Santa Cruz †6 50, ‡8 10 a.m., *4 00, ‡5 10 p.m.; for Felton †6 50, ‡8 10, *11 30 a.m., *1 35, *4 00, ‡5 10 p.m.

New Almaden Branch.—Lvs. San Jose for New Almaden, via Hillsdale (13 miles), *e*10 05 a.m. Returning, lvs. New Almaden *e*11 45 a.m.

COAST DIVISION.—SAN JOSE, MONTEREY, SANTA BARBARA LINE.

56	50	10	46	30	28	36	34	22	20	24	32	Ms	March 1, 1906.	31	35	37	9	29	27	45	23	49	19	21	55
P M	P M	P M	P M	P M	P M	A M	A M	A M	A M	A M	A M	...	lv. San Francisco .ar.	A M	A M	A M	A M	A M	Noon	P M	P M	P M	P M	P M	P M
*k*11 35	*6 30	*5 45	*5 30	*3 30	*3 00	*10 30	*9 00	*8 30	*8 00	*7 00	*6 10	0	+ .*Third Street*.. ♁	6 36	7 55	8 36	9 10	10 35	12 15	1 20	4 30	6 30	9 30	11 45	9 15
— —	6 40	— —	*s* —	3 40	— —	— —	9 10	— —	— —	7 10	6 20	3	..*Valencia Street*. ♁	6 26	7 45	— —	— —	— —	— —	1 09	— —	6 19	— —	— —	9 05
12 06	7 03	— —	*s* —	4 05	— —	— —	9 32	— —	— —	— —	6 45	13	.So. San Francisco ♁	5 57	7 19	— —	— —	— —	— —	12 39	— —	5 54	— —	— —	8 42
12 18	7 20	— —	6 12	4 21	— —	11 18	9 50	— —	— —	7 41	7 09	21	....San Mateo.. ♁	5 38	7 01	7 53	— —	9 52	11 32	12 19	3 47	5 28	— —	*d* —	8 20
12 38	7 45	— —	6 36	4 46	— —	11 45	10 16	— —	— —	8 04	7 40	34	+ ..Palo Alto... ♁	5 00	6 35	7 27	— —	9 31	11 08	11 52	3 26	4 55	— —	*d* —	7 50
12 58	8 14	— —	7 00	5 14	4 12	12 15	10 42	— —	— —	8 25	8 10	47	..Santa Clara.. ♁	4 35	6 10	7 05	— —	9 11	— —	11 25	3 06	4 26	— —	— —	7 21
1 03	8 20	7 30	7 05	5 25	4 25	12 20	10 50	9 55	9 25	8 35	8 15	50	+ ...San Jose.... ♁	*4 30	†6 05	*7 00	7 40	9 05	10 45	*11 20	3 00	*4 18	8 05	10 15	‡7 15
A M	P M	— —	P M	5 35	— —	Noon	A M	— —	— —	8 50	A M	55	....Hillsdale.....	A M	A M	A M	— —	8 50	— —	A M	2 37	P M	— —	— —	P M
....	102	8 29	110	6 22	5 14	P M	106	10 41	— —	9 46	....	80	......Gilroy .... ♁	101	103	....	6 22	*7 45	9 46	P M	1 45	111	— —	9 12	105
For additional trains to San Jose, see Santa Cruz Line.	A M	9 10	P M	P M	5 46	*1 05	Noon	11 13	10 38	10 25	....	99	+ ....Pajaro.... ♁	A M	A M	....	5 45	A M	9 00	5 35	1 05	P M	6 42	8 33	P M
	‡8 45	9 32	*8 15	*6 25	6 10	1 25	*12 35	11 27	10 55	10 45	....	110	ar. Castroville ♁ lv.	10 40	11 10	....	5 24	....	8 45	5 15	12 30	9 25	6 22	*8 13	5 55
	9 21	10 07	8 55	6 57	6 43	1 58	1 08	12 10	....	11 35	....	125	+ ..Monterey .. ♁	10 08	10 33	....	....	....	8 03	4 40	11 55	8 45	5 35	7 25	5 20
	9 30	10 15	9 05	7 05	6 55	2 05	1 15	12 20	....	11 45	....	127	ar + Pacific Grove ♁ lv.	*10 00	*10 25	....	....	....	*7 55	*4 30	*11 45	*8 35	*5 25	*7 15	‡5 10
	A M	9 32	P M	P M	6 22	P M	P M	11 27	10 55	10 45	....	110	lv. Castroville .ar.	A M	A M	....	5 24	....	8 30	P M	12 25	P M	6 22	8 13	P M
	....	9 55	....	....	6 45	....	....	11 50	— —	11 05	....	118	+ ....Salinas.......	....	....	....	5 10	....	*8 15	....	*12 10		— —	8 00	....
	....	10 39	....	....	P M	....	....	12 36	....	A M	....	144	.......Soledad.... ♁	....	....	....	4 15	....	A M	....	Noon	....	— —	7 10	....
	....	1 02	....	....	....	....	....	2 54	1 38	....	....	217	....Paso Robles....	....	....	....	2 06	....	....	....	....	....	3 36	4 58	....
	....	1 53	....	....	....	....	....	3 35	— —	....	....	236	..Santa Margarita ♁	....	....	....	1 25	....	....	....	....	....	— —	4 20	....
	....	2 50	....	....	....	....	....	4 25	3 05	....	....	253	+ San Luis Obispo ♁	....	....	....	12 40	....	....	....	....	1 25	2 15	3 35	....
	....	3 38	....	....	....	....	....	5 13	— —	....	....	277	.... Guadalupe... ♁	....	....	....	11 33	....	....	....	....	P M	— —	2 44	....
	....	4 36	....	....	....	....	....	6 02	— —	....	....	304	.........Surf....... ♁	....	....	....	10 35	....	....	....	....	5 50	— —	2 00	....
	....	5 05	....	....	....	....	....	6 30	....	....	....	313	....Lompoc.... ♁	....	....	....	....	....	....	....	....	*5 25	....	*1 25	....
	....	7 00	....	....	....	....	....	8 10	6 14	....	....	372	ar. + Santa Barbara ♁ lv.	....	....	....	*8 10	....	....	....	....	P M	11 15	*12 10	....
	....	11 20	....	....	....	....	....	11 45	9 30	....	....	482	+ .Los Angeles. ♁	....	....	....	*3 50	....	....	....	....	....	*8 00	*8 30	....
	....	A M	....	....	....	....	....	P M	P M	....	....	...	ARRIVE] [LEAVE	....	....	....	P M	....	....	....	....	....	A M	A M	....

Almaden Line.—Leaves San Jose for New Almaden, via Campbell (14 miles), *4 45 p.m. Ret'g, leaves New Almaden for San Jose *7 00 a.m.
Centerville Line.—Leave Newark for Centerville (3 miles) *9 50 a.m., *4 25, *5 45 p.m. Returning, leave Centerville for Newark †6 50, ‡8 55 a.m., *3 35, *5 15 p.m.

Additional Trains—Leaves San Francisco *2 15 p.m., arrives San Jose 4 00 p.m. Leave San Francisco †6 15, *8 00, ‡11 35 p.m., arrive Palo Alto 7 25, 9 15 p.m., 12 38 night. Returning, leaves San Jose *8 10 a.m., arrives San Francisco 9 50 a.m. Leave Palo Alto †5 30, *8 50 a.m., †7 50 p.m., arrive San Francisco 6 46, 10 15 a.m., 9 15 p.m. **Equipment.—Nos. 9 and 10**—Diner, Standard and Tourist Sleepers and Chair Cars San Francisco and Los Angeles. **Nos. 21 and 22**—Diner and Chair Cars San Francisco, Del Monte and Los Angeles. **Nos. 19 and 20**—Solid Parlor Car trains, with Diner, San Francisco and Los Angeles.

SANTA CRUZ LINE, VIA PAJARO.

90	88	86	84	24	82	M	March 1, 1906.	81	33	85	23	87	89
P M	P M	P M	A M	A M	A M	..	LEAVE] [ARRIVE	A M	A M	A M	Noon	P M	P M
*9 15	*6 50	*5 55	*11 25	*10 40	*9 00	0	+ .. Pajaro .. ♁	8 50	10 15	11 05	12 55	6 35	8 15
9 20	6 55	6 00	11 30	10 45	9 05	2	+ Watsonville ♁	8 44	10 08	10 59	12 49	6 30	8 10
9 33	7 07	6 18	11 48	11 02	9 15	7	.... Ellicott	8 33	9 55	10 48	12 38	6 18	7 58
9 56	7 31	6 41	12 15	11 26	9 33	16	.....Capitola.. ♁	8 10	9 33	10 25	12 15	5 55	7 31
10 10	7 45	6 55	12 30	11 40	9 45	21	+ .Santa Cruz. ♁	*7 55	*9 15	*10 10	*12 01	*5 40	*7 15
P M	P M	P M	Noon	A M	A M	..	ARRIVE] [LEAVE	A M	A M	A M	Noon	P M	P M

TRES PINOS BRANCH.

248	30	252	250	246	M	March 1, 1906.	29	245	247	251	249
P M	P M	P M	P M	A M	..	LEAVE] [ARRIVE	A M	P M	P M	P M	P M
‡1 45	*6 22	*5 25	†1 45	*10 50	0	.....Gilroy ... ♁	7 50	1 30	5 05	9 00	8 55
2 15	6 55	5 57	2 50	— —	14	.... Hollister .. ♁	7 20	1 00	4 35	8 00	8 25
2 35	7 15	6 20	3 20	11 50	20	.. Tres Pinos ♁	*7 00	*12 40	*4 15	†7 15	‡8 05
P M	P M	P M	P M	A M	..	ARRIVE] [LEAVE	A M	Noon	P M	P M	P M

COAST DIVISION.—(Narrow Gauge).—SAN JOSE, BIG TREES, SANTA CRUZ.

508	44	42	506	504	38	502	Ms	March 1, 1906.	505	39	503	47	501	51	507	509
A M	P M	P M	P M	P M	A M	A M	...	LEAVE] [ARRIVE	A M	A M	A M	P M	P M	P M	A M	P M
‡7 45	†5 00	*4 30	*4 15	†2 15	*11 30	*8 15	0	+ San Francisco ♁	8 55	9 00	10 55	5 40	5 55	7 40	10 55	9 16
8 03			4 33	2 33		8 33	3	.. Alameda Mole ♁	8 25		10 25		5 25		10 25	8 48
8 45	⊡	⊡	5 24	3 18	⊡	9 24	20	...... Mt. Eden .... ♁	7 40	⊡	9 41	⊡	4 35	⊡	9 41	8 01
9 00			5 43	3 37		9 46	29	...... Newark .... ♁	7 20		9 22		4 14		9 22	7 39
9 26	6 31	5 59	6 14	4 12	1 15	10 18	44	....Santa Clara.. ♁	6 52	7 30	8 47	3 55	3 43	5 55	8 47	7 11
9 33	6 40	6 05	6 22	4 23	1 20	10 30	46	+ ....San Jose.... ♁	6 45	7 21	8 40	*3 50	3 35	*5 50	8 40	7 05
9 42	6 51	P M	6 33	4 33	P M	10 42	51	...... Campbell .... ♁	6 35	7 10	8 26	P M	3 18	P M	8 26	6 55
9 53	7 05	.....	6 45	4 44	.....	10 53	55	+ ...Los Gatos... ♁	†6 25	†7 00	8 15	.....	3 05	.....	‡8 15	6 45
10 20	P M	.....	P M	5 12	.....	11 13	66	.... Wright ..... ♁	A M	A M	7 54	.....	2 41	.....	A M	6 24
11 02	.....	.....	.....	5 53	.....	11 55	74	.......Felton..... ♁	.....	.....	7 13	.....	1 59	.....	.....	5 40
11 04	.....	.....	.....	5 55	.....	11 57	75	.... Big Trees......	.....	.....	7 11	.....	1 56	.....	.....	5 38
11 25	.....	.....	.....	6 15	.....	12 20	80	+ .. Santa Cruz .. ♁	.....	.....	†6 50	.....	*1 35	.....	.....	‡5 15
A M	.....	.....	.....	P M	.....	Noon	...	ARRIVE] [LEAVE	.....	.....	A M	.....	P M	.....	.....	P M

Trains marked * run daily.
† Daily, except Sunday.
‡ Daily, except Saturday.
‡ Sunday only.
b Stops to take passengers.
d Stops to leave passengers from east of San Jose.
e Tuesday and Friday.
k Saturday only.
s Stops Sundays.
⊡ Via Santa Barbara Line.

"SUNSET ROUTE" MILE-BY-MILE

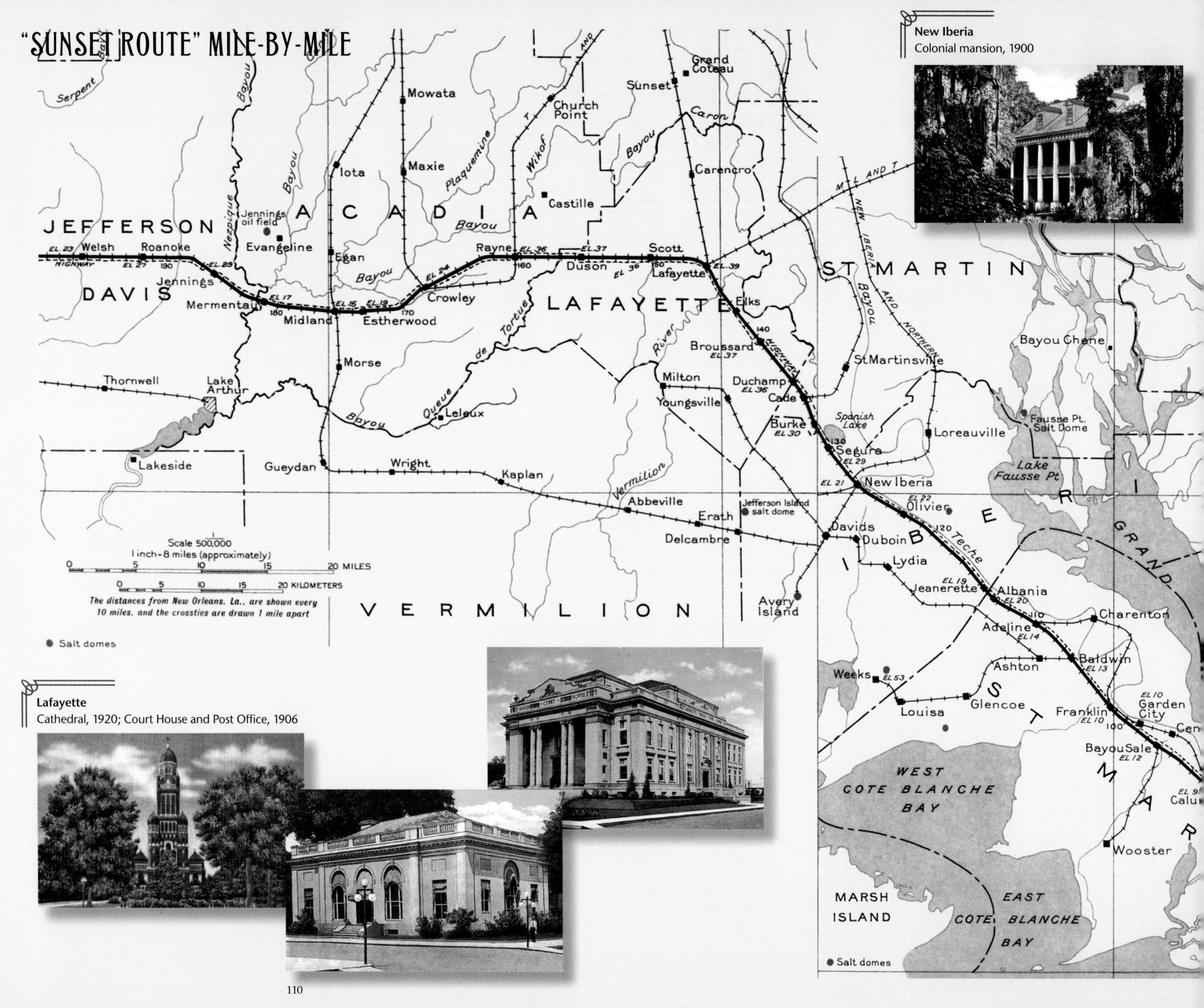

New Iberia
Colonial mansion, 1900

Lafayette
Cathedral, 1920; Court House and Post Office, 1906

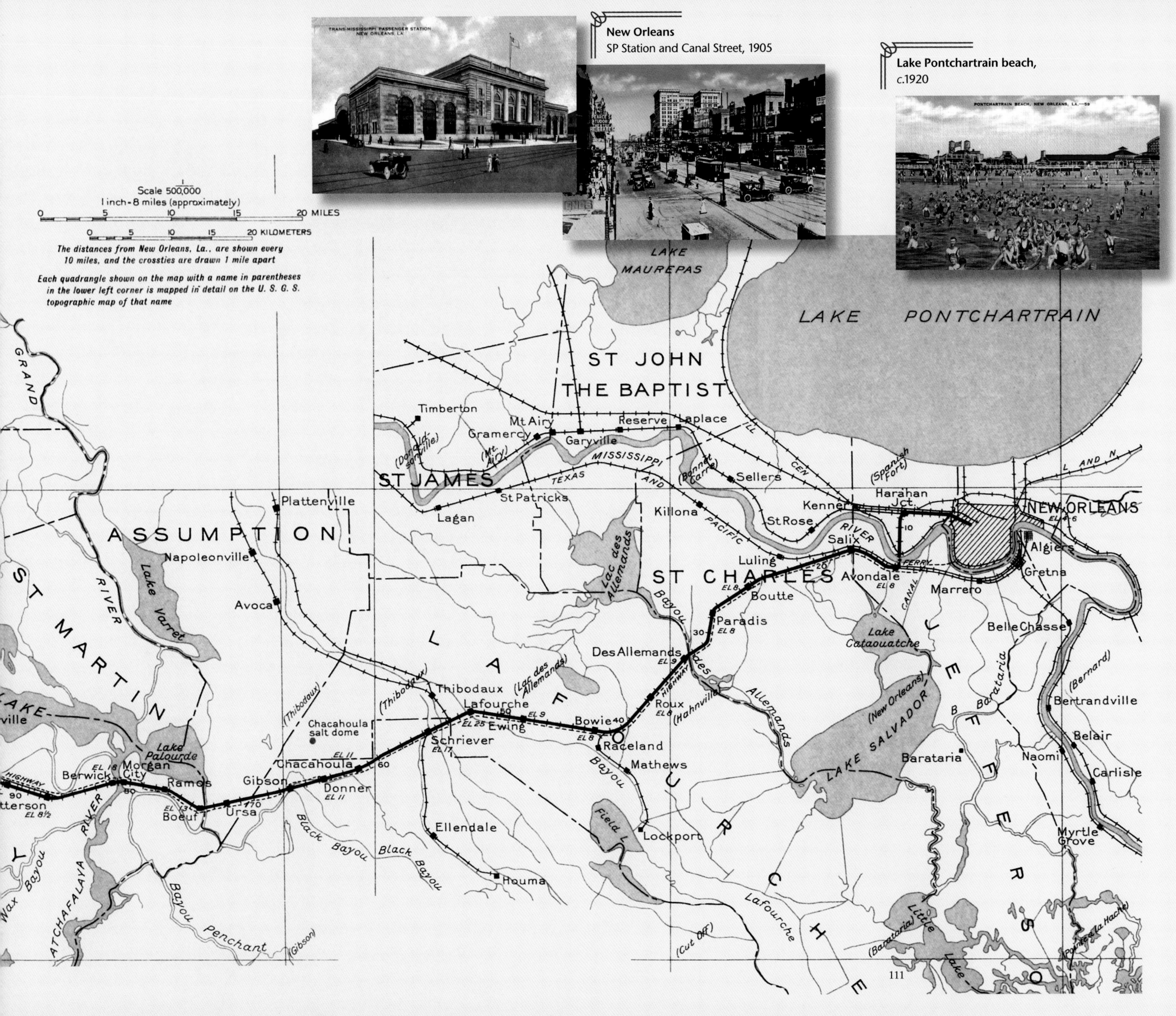

New Orleans
SP Station and Canal Street, 1905

Lake Pontchartrain beach, *c.*1920

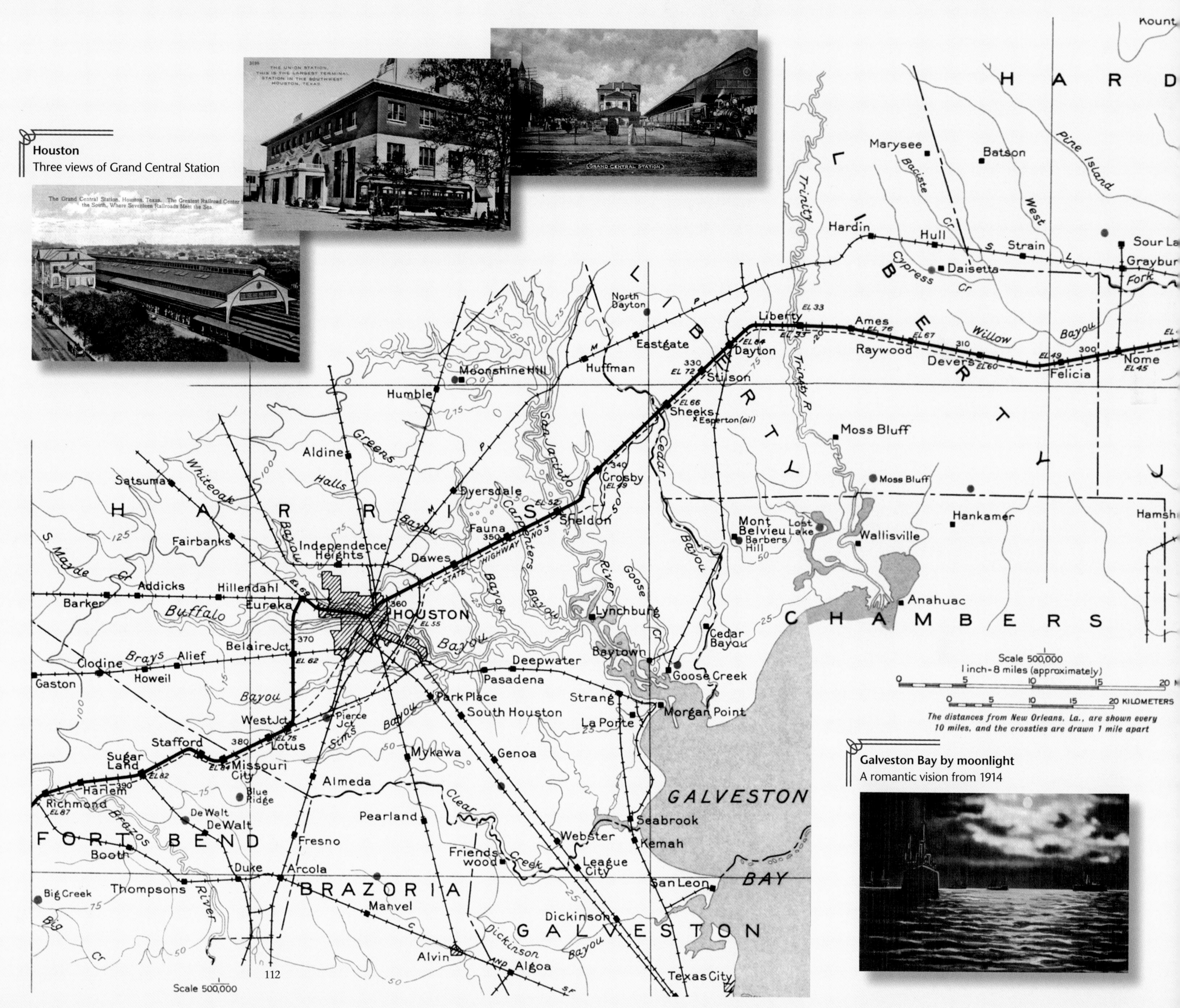

Houston
Three views of Grand Central Station

Galveston Bay by moonlight
A romantic vision from 1914

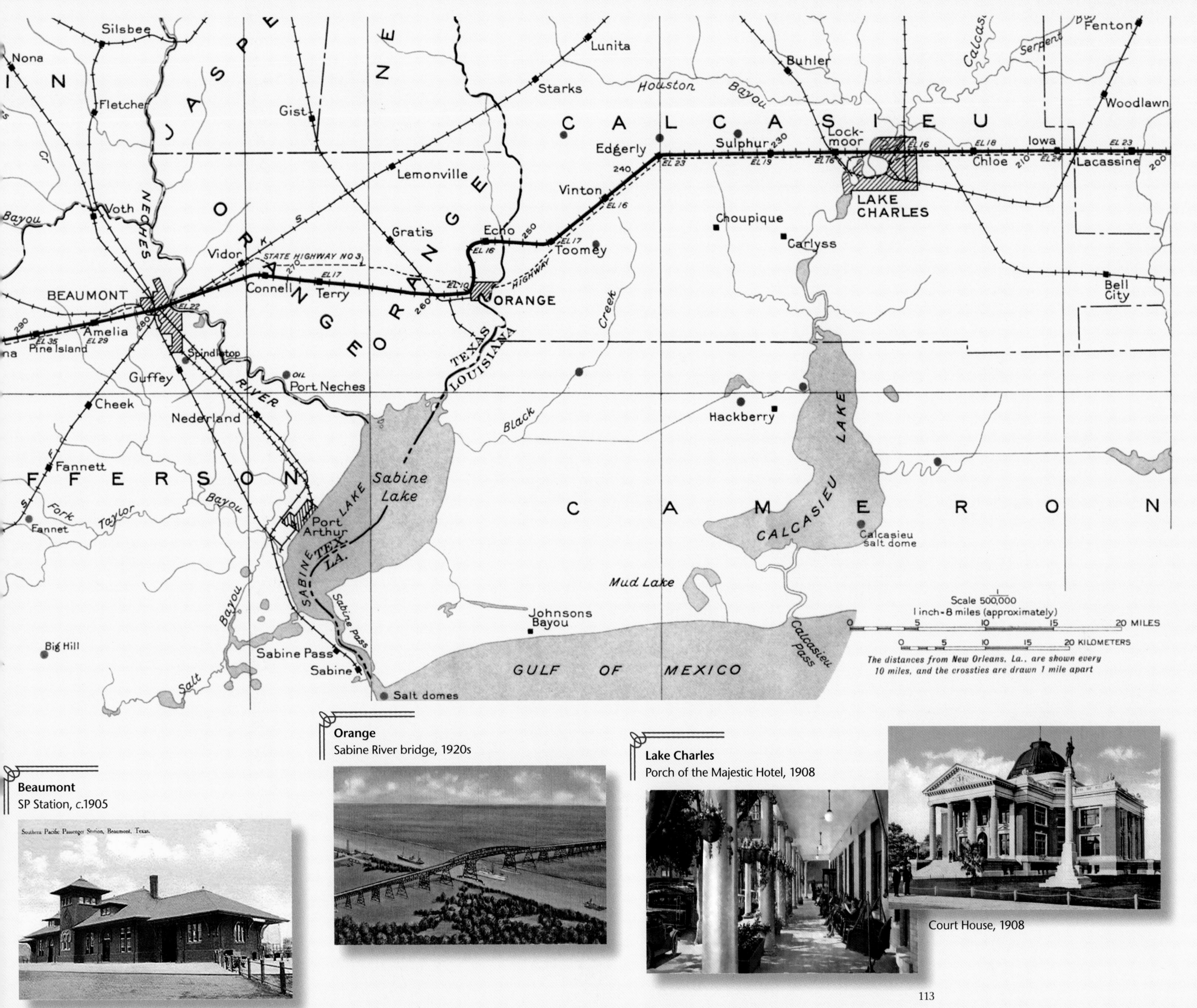

Beaumont
SP Station, *c.*1905

Orange
Sabine River bridge, 1920s

Lake Charles
Porch of the Majestic Hotel, 1908

Court House, 1908

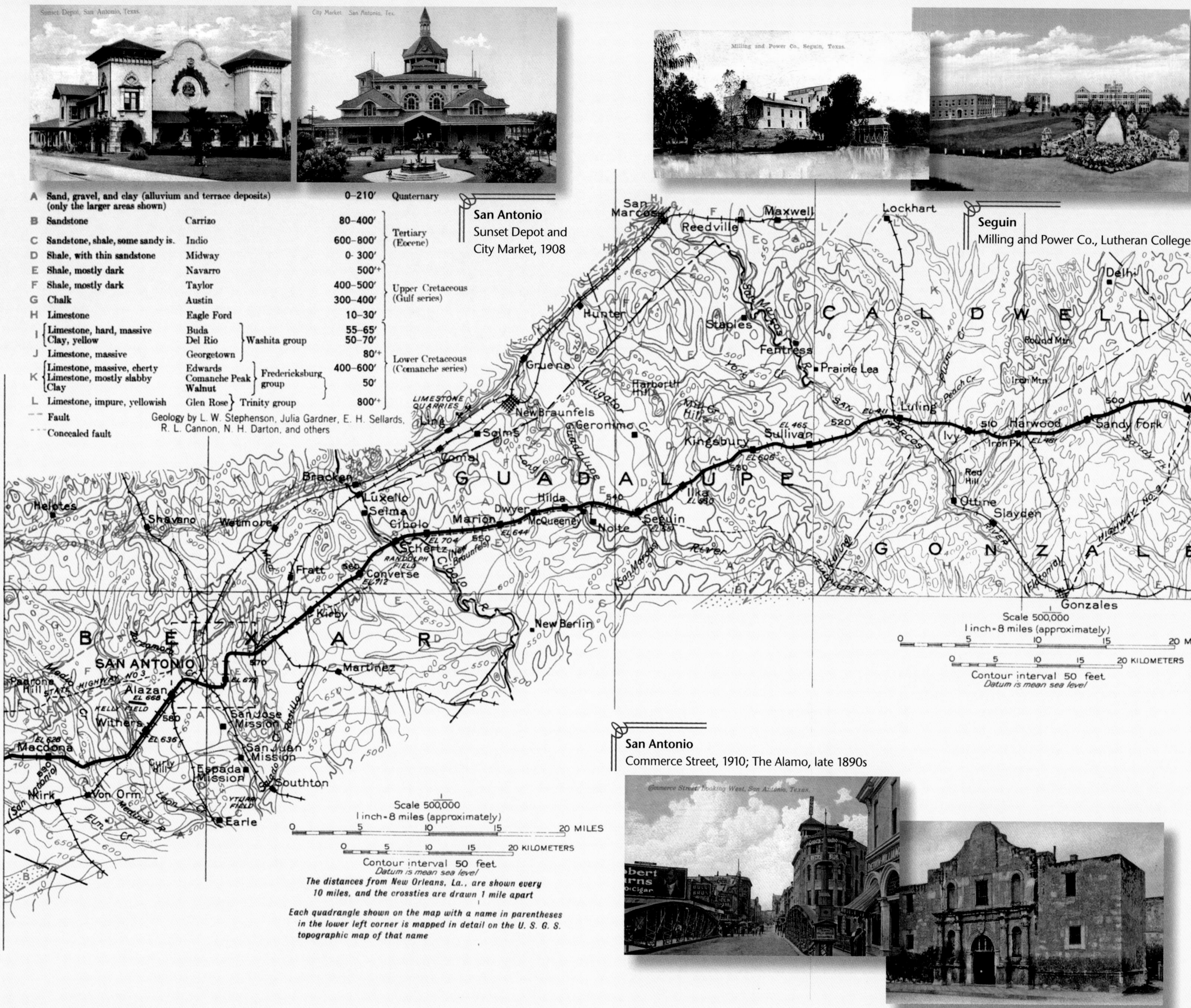

Sunset Depot, San Antonio, Texas.
City Market. San Antonio, Tex.
Milling and Power Co., Seguin, Texas.
A Sand, gravel, and clay (alluvium and terrace deposits) (only the larger areas shown) 0–210′ Quaternary
B Sandstone Carrizo 80–400′
C Sandstone, shale, some sandy is. Indio 600–800′
D Shale, with thin sandstone Midway 0–300′ Tertiary (Eocene)
E Shale, mostly dark Navarro 500′+
F Shale, mostly dark Taylor 400–500′
G Chalk Austin 300–400′ Upper Cretaceous (Gulf series)
H Limestone Eagle Ford 10–30′
I Limestone, hard, massive Buda 55–65′; Clay, yellow Del Rio 50–70′ Washita group
J Limestone, massive Georgetown 80′+
K Limestone, massive, cherty Edwards; Limestone, mostly slabby Comanche Peak; Clay Walnut; Fredericksburg group 400–600′; 50′ Lower Cretaceous (Comanche series)
L Limestone, impure, yellowish Glen Rose Trinity group 800′+
Fault
Concealed fault
Geology by L. W. Stephenson, Julia Gardner, E. H. Sellards, R. L. Cannon, N. H. Darton, and others
BEXAR
GUADALUPE
CALDWELL
GONZALES
SAN ANTONIO
New Braunfels
Seguin
San Marcos
Luling
Lockhart
Gonzales
Scale 1/500,000
1 inch = 8 miles (approximately)
0 5 10 15 20 MILES
0 5 10 15 20 KILOMETERS
Contour interval 50 feet
Datum is mean sea level
The distances from New Orleans, La., are shown every 10 miles, and the crossties are drawn 1 mile apart
Each quadrangle shown on the map with a name in parentheses in the lower left corner is mapped in detail on the U. S. G. S. topographic map of that name
Commerce Street, Looking West, San Antonio, Texas.

San Antonio
Sunset Depot and City Market, 1908

Seguin
Milling and Power Co., Lutheran College

San Antonio
Commerce Street, 1910; The Alamo, late 1890s

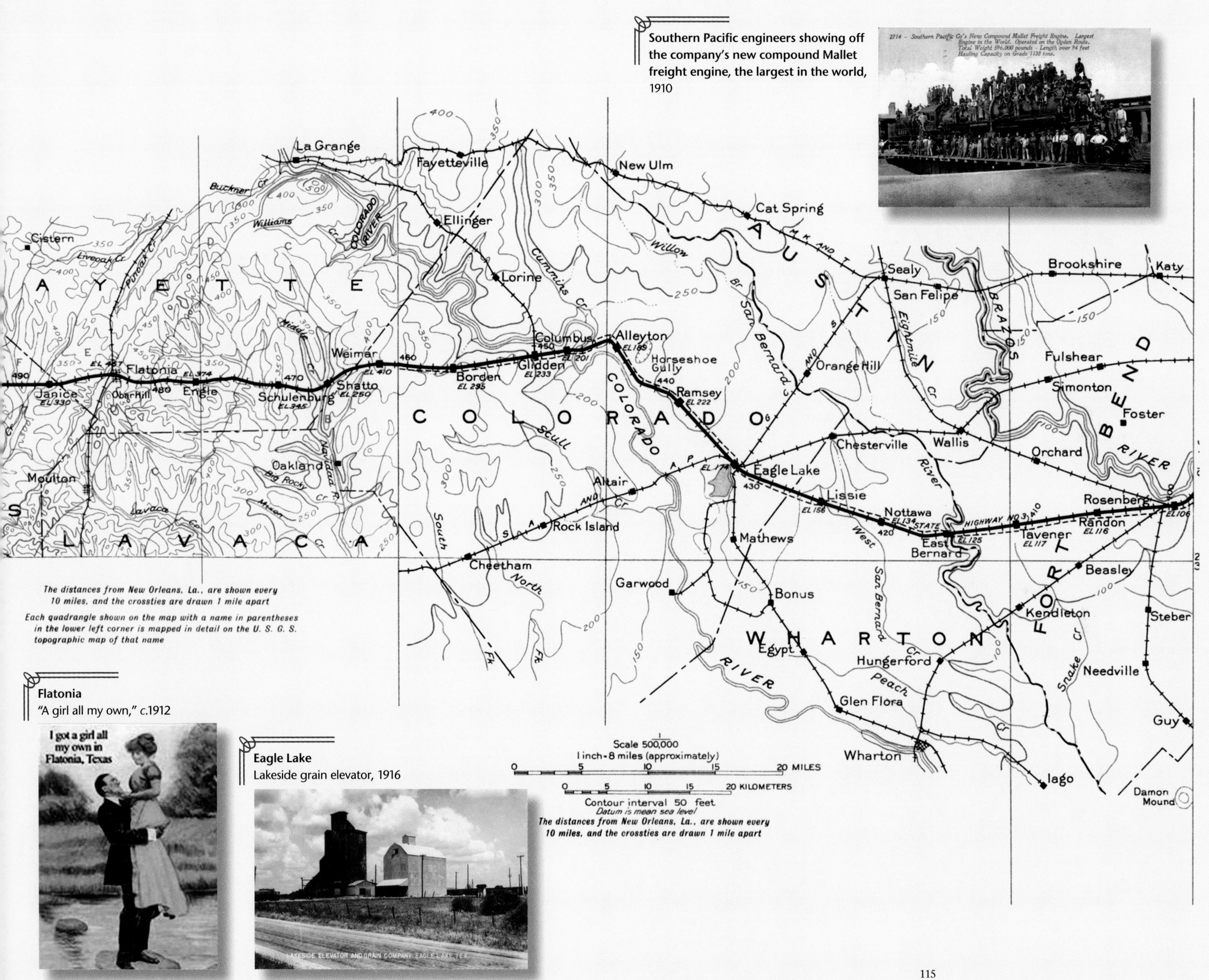

Southern Pacific engineers showing off the company's new compound Mallet freight engine, the largest in the world, 1910

Flatonia
"A girl all my own," *c.*1912

Eagle Lake
Lakeside grain elevator, 1916

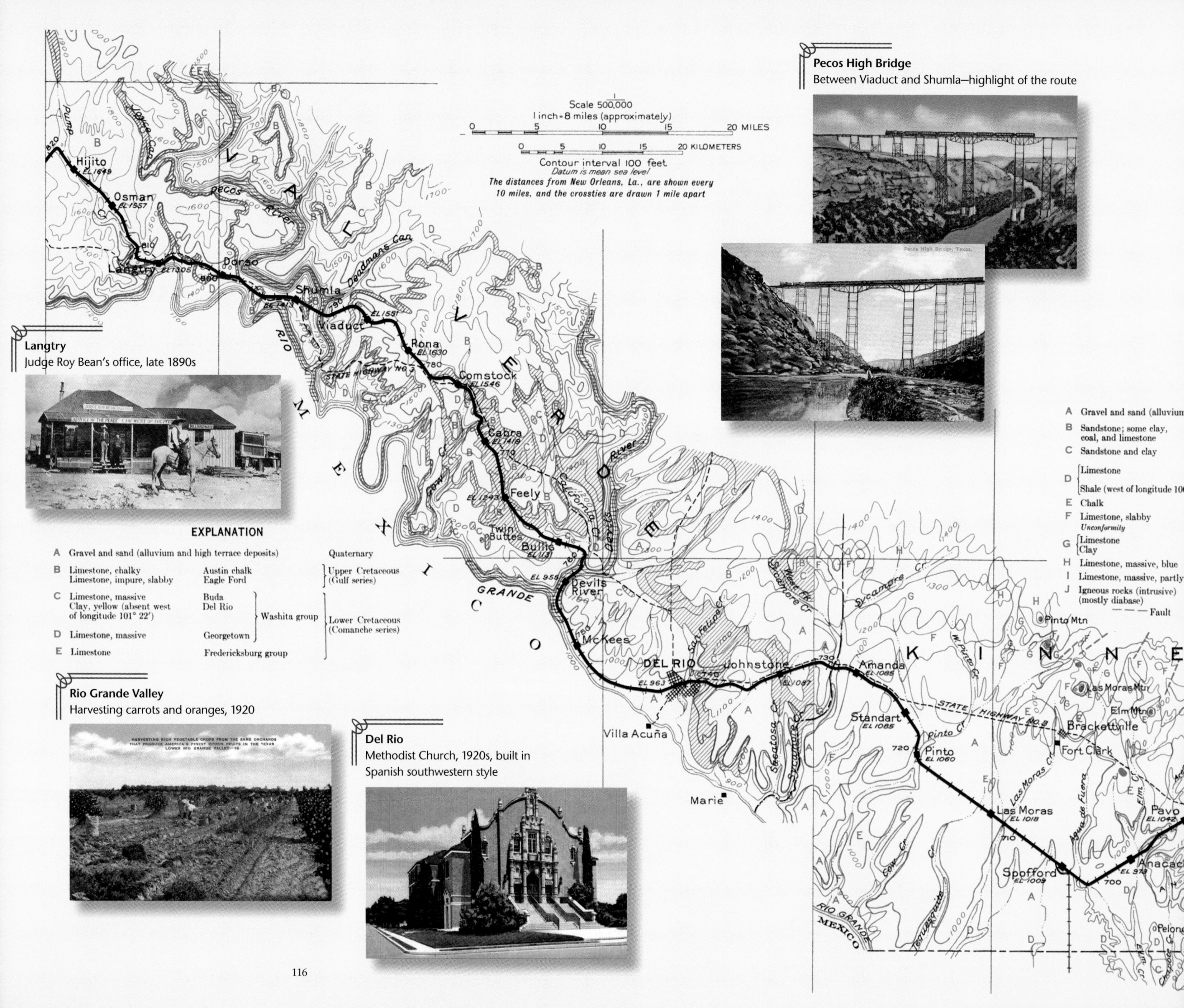

Pecos High Bridge
Between Viaduct and Shumla—highlight of the route

Langtry
Judge Roy Bean's office, late 1890s

Rio Grande Valley
Harvesting carrots and oranges, 1920

Del Rio
Methodist Church, 1920s, built in Spanish southwestern style

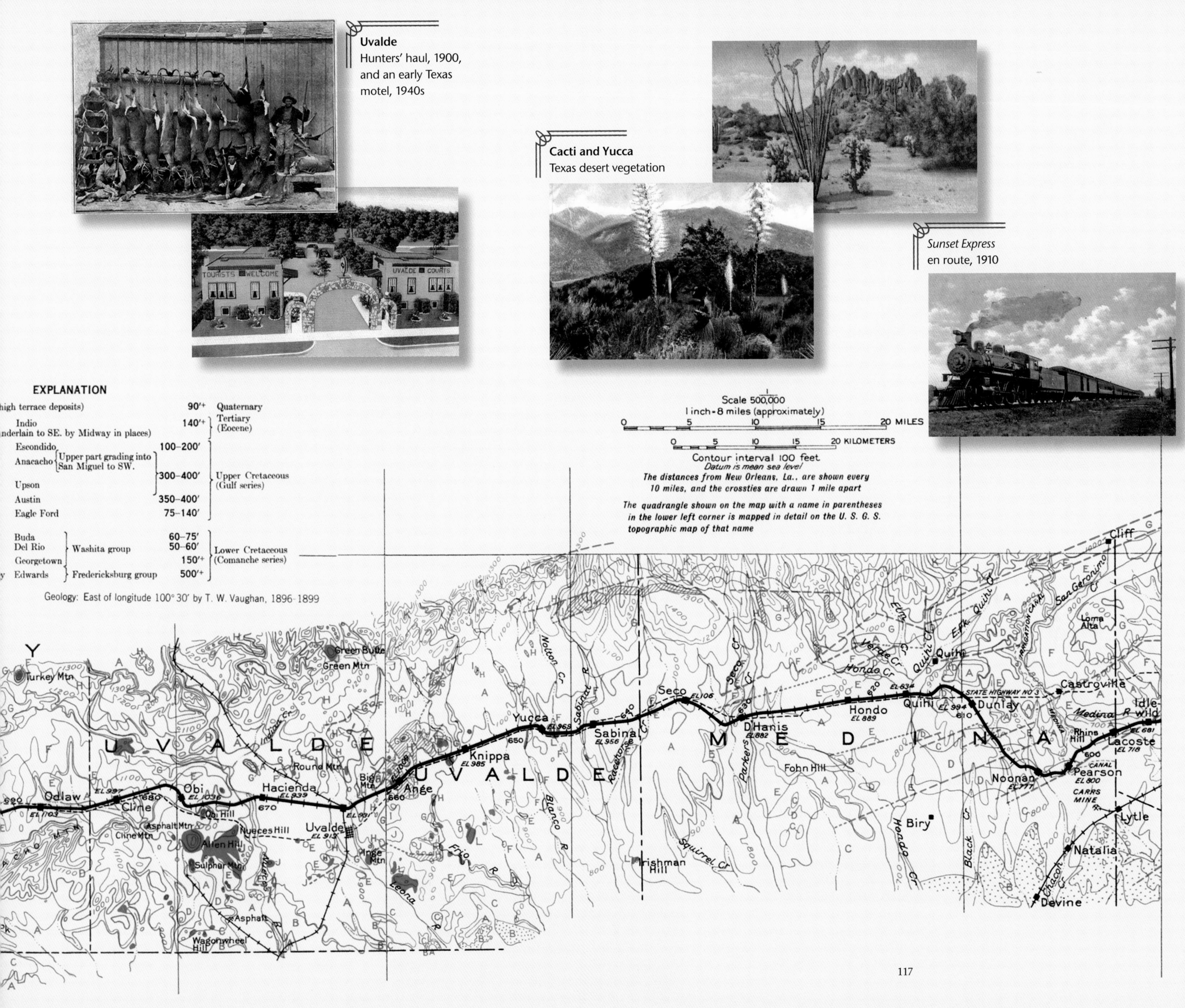

TOURISTS WELCOME
UVALDE COURTS
EXPLANATION
high terrace deposits) 90'+ Quaternary
Indio 140'+ Tertiary (Eocene)
nderlain to SE. by Midway in places)
Escondido 100–200'
Anacacho {Upper part grading into San Miguel to SW.
Upson 300–400' Upper Cretaceous (Gulf series)
Austin 350–400'
Eagle Ford 75–140'
Buda 60–75'
Del Rio } Washita group 50–60'
Georgetown 150'+ Lower Cretaceous (Comanche series)
Edwards } Fredericksburg group 500'+
Geology: East of longitude 100° 30' by T. W. Vaughan, 1896-1899
Scale 1/500,000
1 inch = 8 miles (approximately)
0 5 10 15 20 MILES
0 5 10 15 20 KILOMETERS
Contour interval 100 feet
Datum is mean sea level
The distances from New Orleans, La., are shown every 10 miles, and the crossties are drawn 1 mile apart
The quadrangle shown on the map with a name in parentheses in the lower left corner is mapped in detail on the U. S. G. S. topographic map of that name
UVALDE
MEDINA
Turkey Mtn
Green Butte
Green Mtn
Odlaw
Cline
Obi
Hacienda
Round Mtn
Big Mtn
Ange
Uvalde
Knippa
Yucca
Sabinal
Seco
D'Hanis
Hondo
Quihi
Dunlay
Castroville
Idlewild
Lacoste
Rhins Hill
Pearson
Noonan
Lytle
Natalia
Devine
Biry
Fohn Hill
Irishman Hill
Cliff
Loma Alta
Obi Hill
Asphalt Mtn
Cline Mtn
Allen Hill
Nueces Hill
Sulphur Mtn
Inge Mtn
Asphalt
Wagonwheel Hill
CARRS MINE
STATE HIGHWAY NO 3

Uvalde
Hunters' haul, 1900, and an early Texas motel, 1940s

Cacti and Yucca
Texas desert vegetation

Sunset Express
en route, 1910

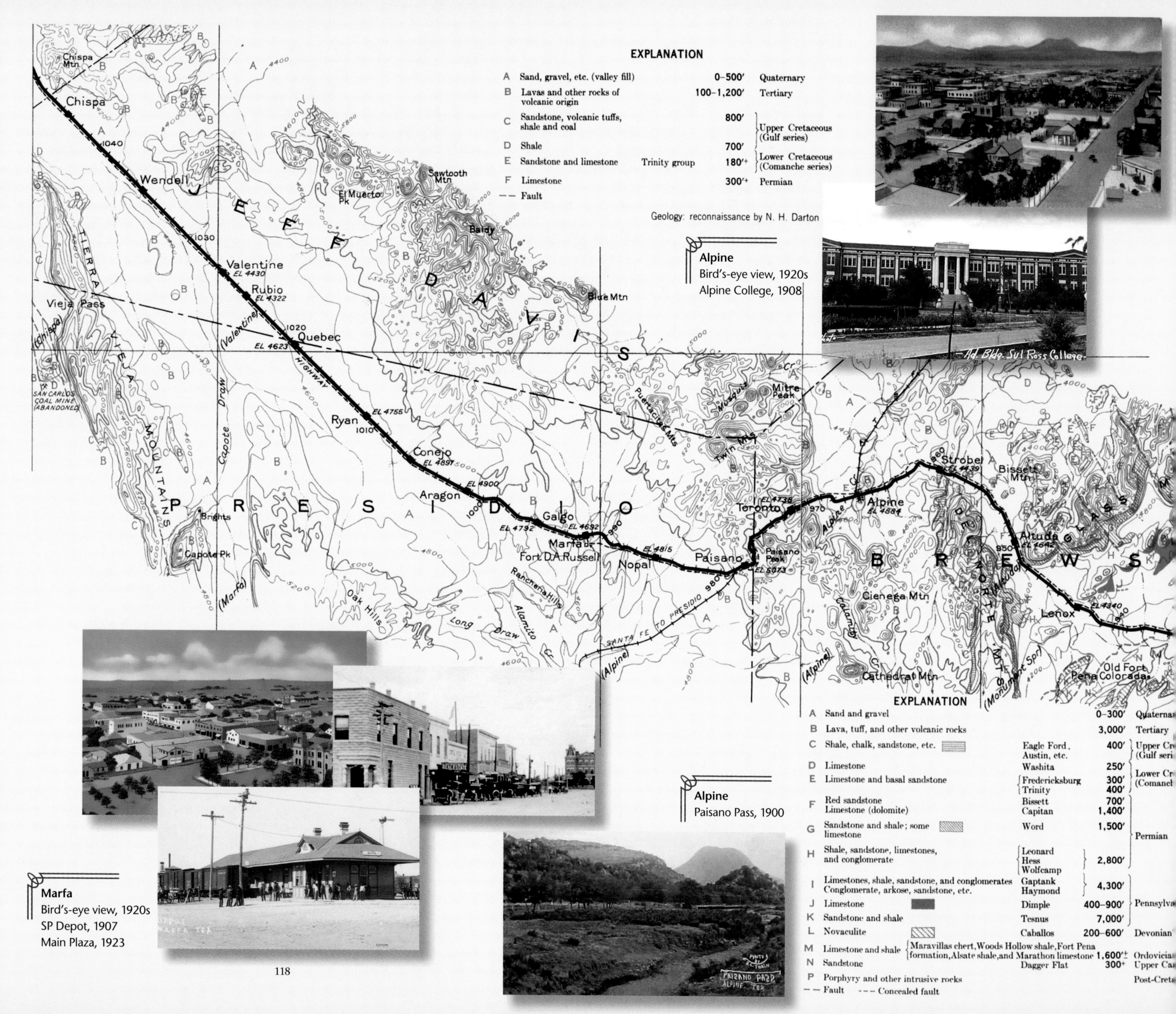
EXPLANATION
A Sand, gravel, etc. (valley fill) 0–500′ Quaternary
B Lavas and other rocks of volcanic origin 100–1,200′ Tertiary
C Sandstone, volcanic tuffs, shale and coal 800′
D Shale 700′ Upper Cretaceous (Gulf series)
E Sandstone and limestone Trinity group 180′+ Lower Cretaceous (Comanche series)
F Limestone 300′+ Permian
Fault
Geology: reconnaissance by N. H. Darton
Chispa Mtn
Chispa
Wendell
Valentine
EL 4430
Rubio
EL 4322
Quebec
EL 4623
Vieja Pass
San Carlos Coal Mine (Abandoned)
Tierra Vieja Mountains
Capote Draw
Highway
Ryan
EL 4755
Conejo
EL 4897
Aragon
EL 4900
Brights
Capote Pk
Galgo
EL 4732
EL 4692
Marfa
Fort D.A. Russell
EL 4815
Nopal
Paisano
Paisano Peak
EL 5073
Oak Hills
Ranchería Hills
Long Draw
Alamito Cr
Santa Fe to Presidio
Sawtooth Mtn
El Muerto Pk
Baldy
Blue Mtn
Puertacitas Mts
Musquiz Cr
Mitre Peak
Twin Mts
Toronto
EL 4738
Alpine
EL 4484
Strobel
EL 4439
Bissett Mtn
Altuda
EL 4642
Cienega Mtn
Calamity
Cathedral Mtn
Monument Spr
Old Fort Pena Colorada
Lenox
EL 4340
Jeff Davis
Presidio
Brewster
Del Norte Mts
Glass
EXPLANATION
A Sand and gravel 0–300′ Quaternary
B Lava, tuff, and other volcanic rocks 3,000′ Tertiary
C Shale, chalk, sandstone, etc. Eagle Ford, Austin, etc. 400′ Upper Cretaceous (Gulf series)
D Limestone Washita 250′
E Limestone and basal sandstone Fredericksburg 300′ Trinity 400′ Lower Cretaceous (Comanche series)
F Red sandstone Bissett 700′; Limestone (dolomite) Capitan 1,400′
G Sandstone and shale; some limestone Word 1,500′ Permian
H Shale, sandstone, limestones, and conglomerate Leonard Hess Wolfcamp 2,800′
I Limestones, shale, sandstone, and conglomerates Gaptank; Conglomerate, arkose, sandstone, etc. Haymond 4,300′
J Limestone Dimple 400–900′ Pennsylvanian
K Sandstone and shale Tesnus 7,000′
L Novaculite Caballos 200–600′ Devonian
M Limestone and shale Maravillas chert, Woods Hollow shale, Fort Pena formation, Alsate shale, and Marathon limestone 1,600′± Ordovician
N Sandstone Dagger Flat 300+ Upper Cambrian
P Porphyry and other intrusive rocks Post-Cretaceous
Fault
Concealed fault
Ad. Bldg. Sul Ross College
Depot Marfa Tex
Paisano Pass Alpine Tex

Alpine
Bird's-eye view, 1920s
Alpine College, 1908

Alpine
Paisano Pass, 1900

Marfa
Bird's-eye view, 1920s
SP Depot, 1907
Main Plaza, 1923

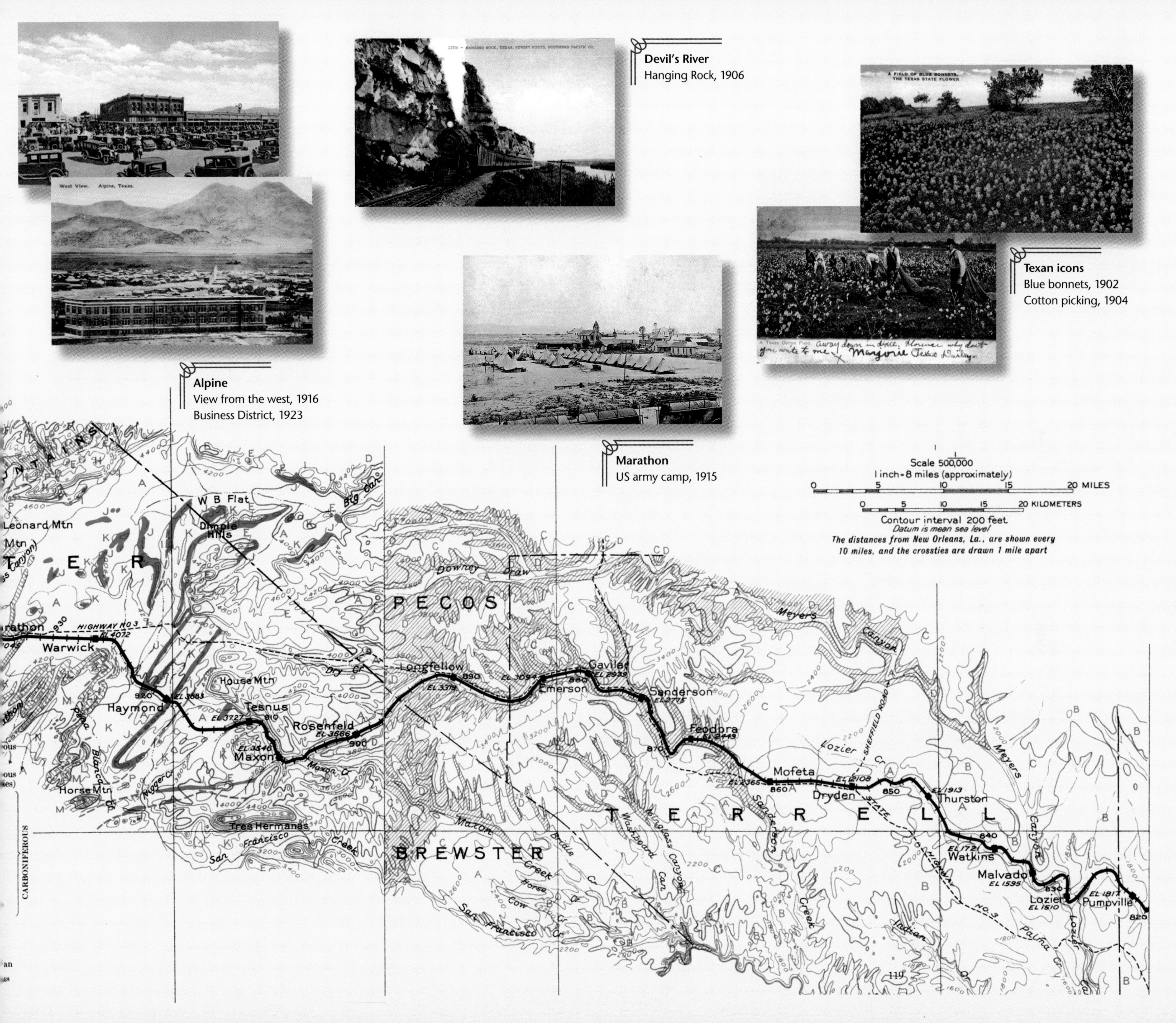

Devil's River
Hanging Rock, 1906

Texan icons
Blue bonnets, 1902
Cotton picking, 1904

Alpine
View from the west, 1916
Business District, 1923

Marathon
US army camp, 1915

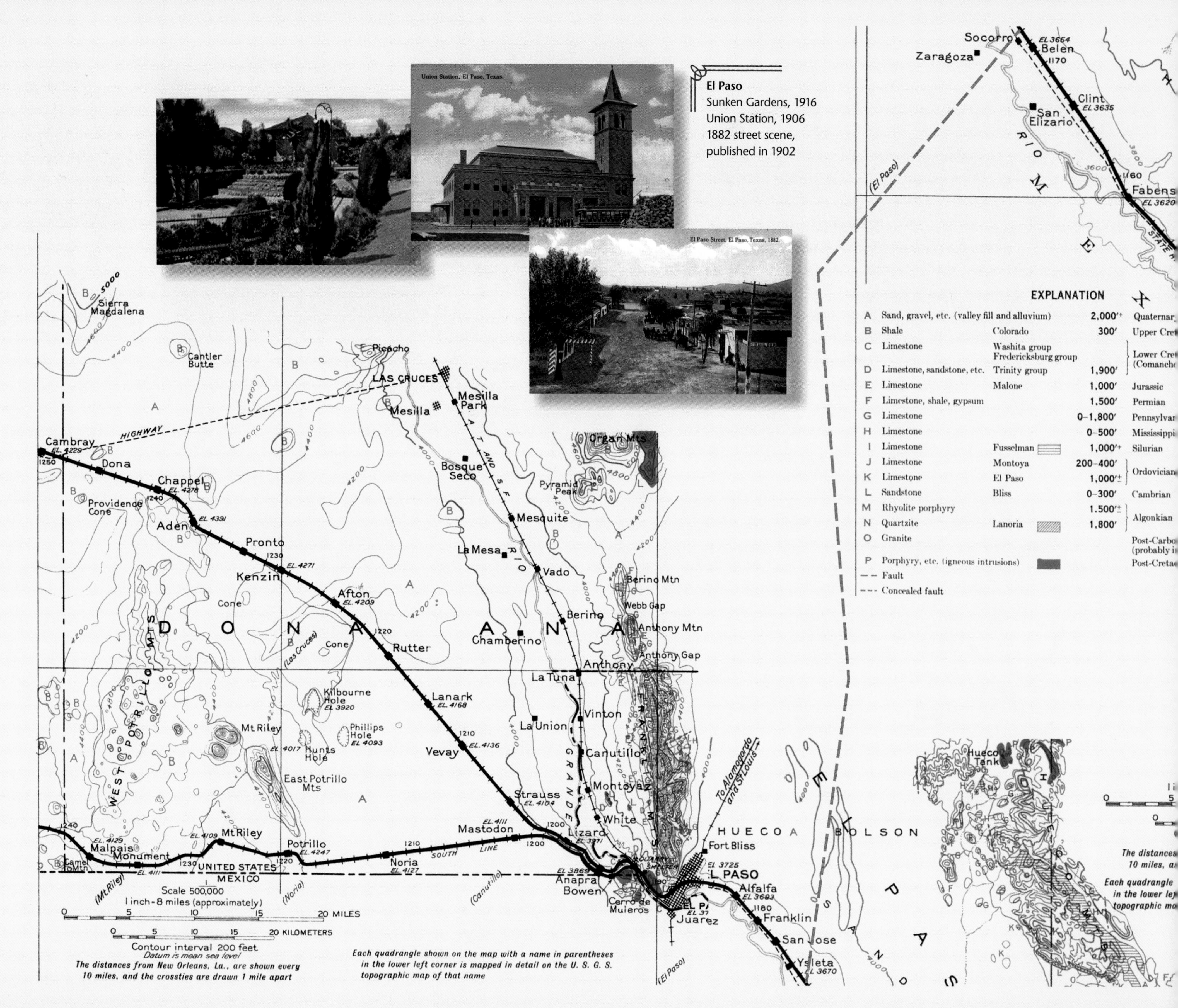
Union Station, El Paso, Texas.
El Paso Street, El Paso, Texas, 1882.
EXPLANATION
A Sand, gravel, etc. (valley fill and alluvium) 2,000'+ Quaternar
B Shale Colorado 300' Upper Cre
C Limestone Washita group Fredericksburg group Lower Cre (Comanch
D Limestone, sandstone, etc. Trinity group 1,900'
E Limestone Malone 1,000' Jurassic
F Limestone, shale, gypsum 1,500' Permian
G Limestone 0–1,800' Pennsylvar
H Limestone 0–500' Mississippi
I Limestone Fusselman 1,000'+ Silurian
J Limestone Montoya 200–400' Ordovician
K Limestone El Paso 1,000'±
L Sandstone Bliss 0–300' Cambrian
M Rhyolite porphyry 1,500'± Algonkian
N Quartzite Lanoria 1,800'
O Granite Post-Carbo (probably i
P Porphyry, etc. (igneous intrusions) Post-Creta
Fault
Concealed fault
Socorro
Zaragoza
Belen
Clint
San Elizario
Fabens
RIO GRANDE
Cambray
Dona
Chappel
Providence Cone
Aden
Pronto
Kenzin
Afton
Rutter
Lanark
Vevay
Strauss
Mastodon
Lizard
Sierra Magdalena
Cantler Butte
Picacho
LAS CRUCES
Mesilla
Mesilla Park
Bosque Seco
Mesquite
La Mesa
Vado
Berino
Chamberino
Anthony
La Tuna
Vinton
La Union
Canutillo
Montoya
White
Organ Mts
Pyramid Peak
Berino Mtn
Webb Gap
Anthony Mtn
Anthony Gap
FRANKLIN MTS
DONA ANA
WEST POTRILLO MTS
Kilbourne Hole
Phillips Hole
Hunts Hole
Mt Riley
East Potrillo Mts
Malpais
Monument
Potrillo
Noria
UNITED STATES
MEXICO
SOUTHERN PACIFIC LINES
HUECO BOLSON
EL PASO
Fort Bliss
Anapra
Bowen
Cerro de Muleros
Juarez
Alfalfa
Franklin
San Jose
Ysleta
Hueco Tank
HUECO MTS
To Alamogordo and St Louis
HIGHWAY
Scale 500,000
1 inch = 8 miles (approximately)
20 MILES
20 KILOMETERS
Contour interval 200 feet.
Datum is mean sea level
The distances from New Orleans, La., are shown every 10 miles, and the crossties are drawn 1 mile apart
Each quadrangle shown on the map with a name in parentheses in the lower left corner is mapped in detail on the U. S. G. S. topographic map of that name

El Paso
Sunken Gardens, 1916
Union Station, 1906
1882 street scene, published in 1902

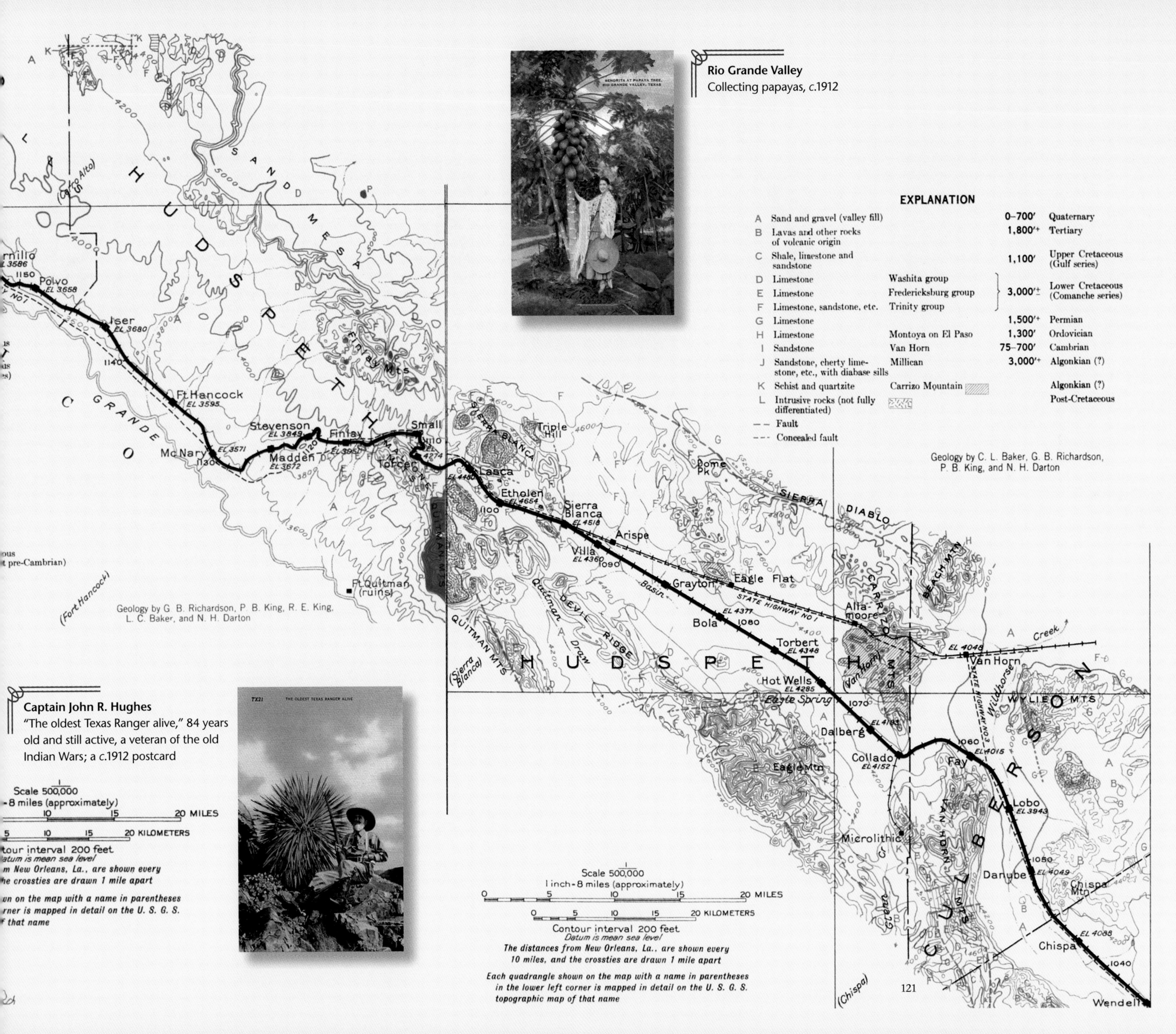
EXPLANATION
A Sand and gravel (valley fill) 0–700′ Quaternary
B Lavas and other rocks of volcanic origin 1,800′+ Tertiary
C Shale, limestone and sandstone 1,100′ Upper Cretaceous (Gulf series)
D Limestone Washita group
E Limestone Fredericksburg group
F Limestone, sandstone, etc. Trinity group
3,000′± Lower Cretaceous (Comanche series)
G Limestone 1,500′+ Permian
H Limestone Montoya on El Paso 1,300′ Ordovician
I Sandstone Van Horn 75–700′ Cambrian
J Sandstone, cherty limestone, etc., with diabase sills Millican 3,000′+ Algonkian (?)
K Schist and quartzite Carrizo Mountain Algonkian (?)
L Intrusive rocks (not fully differentiated) Post-Cretaceous
Fault
Concealed fault
Geology by C. L. Baker, G. B. Richardson, P. B. King, and N. H. Darton
Geology by G. B. Richardson, P. B. King, R. E. King, L. C. Baker, and N. H. Darton
HUDSPETH
CULBERSON
RIO GRANDE
SAND MESA
Finlay Mts
SIERRA BLANCA
QUITMAN MTS
SIERRA DIABLO
CARRIZO MTS
BEACH MTN
WYLIE MTS
VAN HORN MTS
DEVIL RIDGE
Eagle Mtn
Eagle Flat
Eagle Spring
Polvo EL 3658
Iser EL 3680
Ft Hancock EL 3595
McNary EL 3571
Stevenson EL 3849
Madden EL 3672
Finlay
Small
Torcer
Lasca
Etholen EL 4654
Sierra Blanca EL 4518
Arispe
Villa EL 4360
Grayton
Bola EL 4377
Torbert EL 4348
Hot Wells EL 4285
Dalberg EL 4193
Collado EL 4152
Alla-moore
Van Horn EL 4048
Fay EL 4015
Lobo EL 3943
Microlithic
Danube EL 4049
Chispa EL 4088
Chispa Mtn
Wendell
Triple Hill
Dome Pk
Ft Quitman (ruins)
STATE HIGHWAY NO 1
STATE HIGHWAY NO 3
Wildhorse Creek
Quitman Draw
Basin
(Fort Hancock)
(Sierra Blanca)
(Van Horn)
(Chispa)
(Cerro Alto)
Scale 1/500,000
1 inch-8 miles (approximately)
0 5 10 15 20 MILES
0 5 10 15 20 KILOMETERS
Contour interval 200 feet
Datum is mean sea level
The distances from New Orleans, La., are shown every 10 miles, and the crossties are drawn 1 mile apart
Each quadrangle shown on the map with a name in parentheses in the lower left corner is mapped in detail on the U. S. G. S. topographic map of that name
SEÑORITA AT PAPAYA TREE, RIO GRANDE VALLEY, TEXAS
TX21 THE OLDEST TEXAS RANGER ALIVE

Rio Grande Valley
Collecting papayas, *c.*1912

Captain John R. Hughes
"The oldest Texas Ranger alive," 84 years old and still active, a veteran of the old Indian Wars; a *c.*1912 postcard

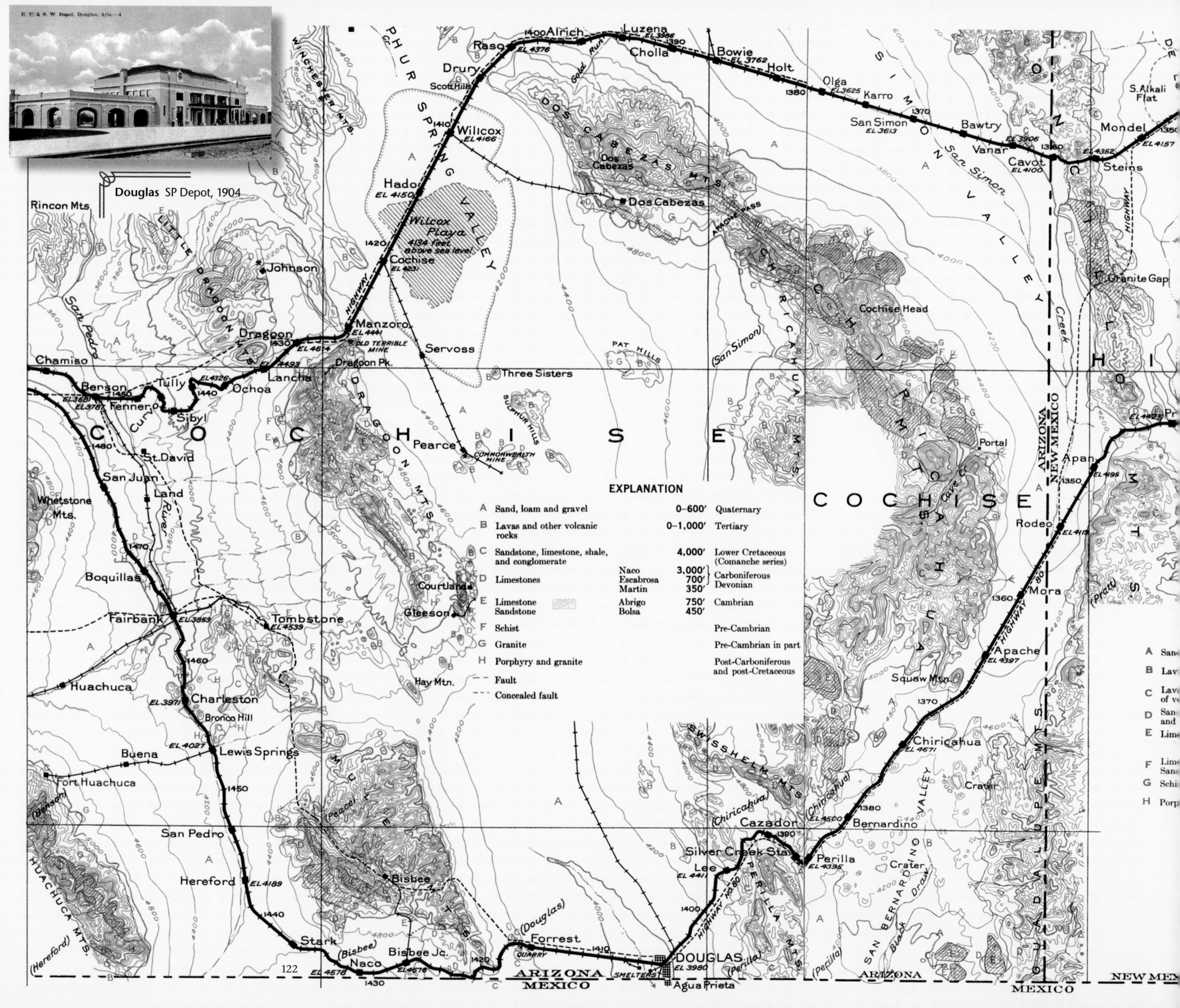

Douglas SP Depot, 1904

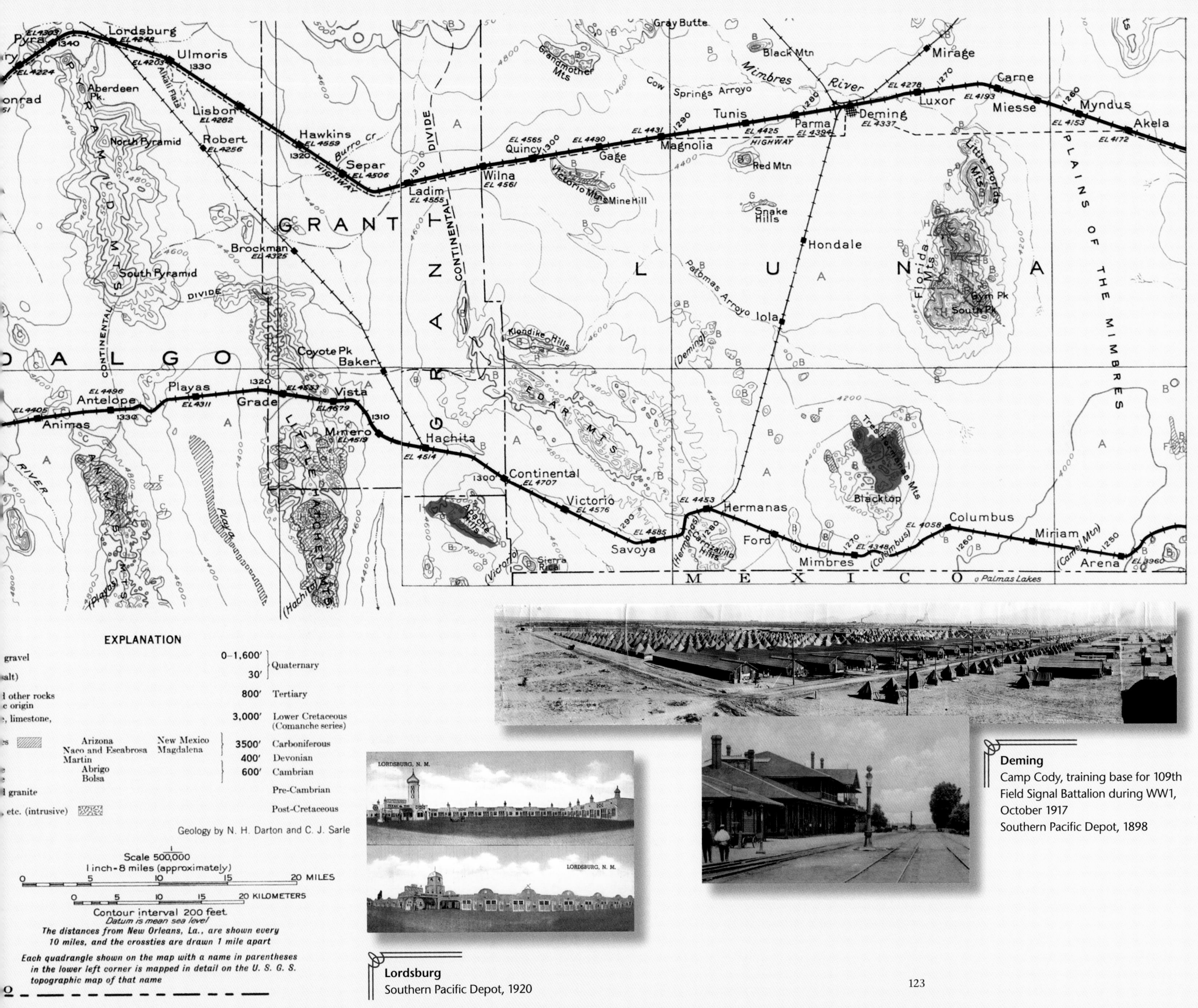

Deming
Camp Cody, training base for 109th Field Signal Battalion during WW1, October 1917
Southern Pacific Depot, 1898

Lordsburg
Southern Pacific Depot, 1920

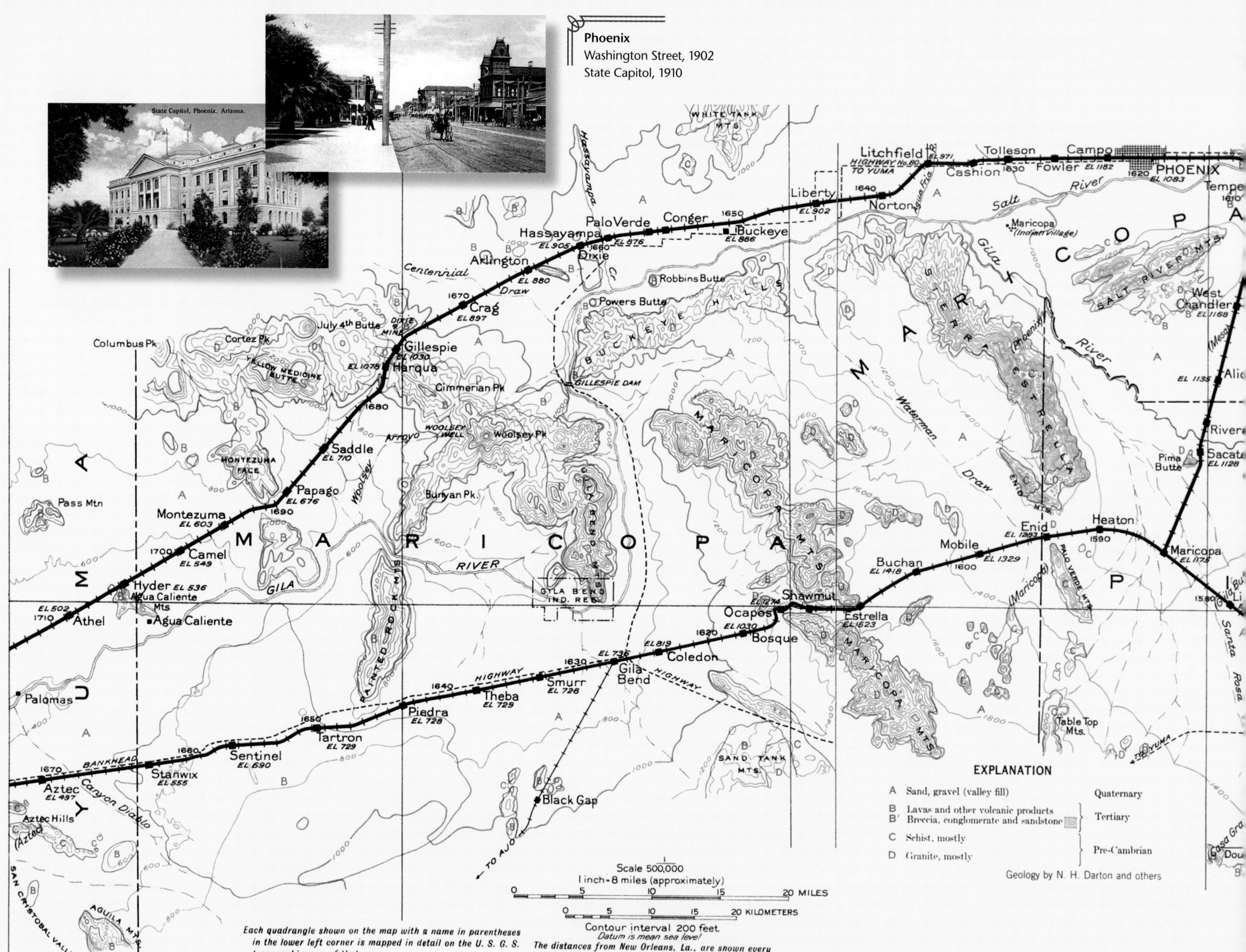
State Capitol, Phoenix, Arizona.
WHITE TANK MTS
Hassayampa
Litchfield
HIGHWAY No. 80 TO YUMA
Tolleson
Cashion
Campo
Fowler
PHOENIX
Tempe
Liberty
Norton
Agua Fria
Salt River
Maricopa (Indian Village)
Conger
Buckeye
Palo Verde
Hassayampa
Dixie
Arlington
Centennial Draw
Robbins Butte
Powers Butte
BUCKEYE HILLS
SIERRA ESTRELLA
SALT RIVER MTS
West Chandler
Gila River
Crag
July 4th Butte
DIXIE MINE
Gillespie
Harqua
Columbus Pk
Cortez Pk
YELLOW MEDICINE BUTTE
GILLESPIE DAM
Cimmerian Pk
Waterman Draw
WOOLSEY WELL
Woolsey Pk
Arroyo
Saddle
MONTEZUMA FACE
Papago
Woolsey
Bunyan Pk.
MARICOPA MTS
GILA BEND MTS
Pima Butte
Sacaton
Pass Mtn
Montezuma
Camel
MARICOPA
RIVER
GILA
Hyder
Agua Caliente Mts
Athel
Agua Caliente
PAINTED ROCK MTS
GILA BEND IND. RES.
Shawmut
Ocapes
Estrella
Buchan
Mobile
Enid
Heaton
Maricopa
PALO VERDE MTS
Bosque
Coledon
Gila Bend
HIGHWAY
Smurr
Theba
Piedra
Tartron
Sentinel
Stanwix
Aztec
BANKHEAD
Canyon Diablo
Aztec Hills
Palomas
Table Top Mts.
TO YUMA
SAND TANK MTS.
Black Gap
TO AJO
SAN CRISTOBAL VALLEY
AGUILA MTS
EXPLANATION
A Sand, gravel (valley fill) — Quaternary
B Lavas and other volcanic products — Tertiary
B′ Breccia, conglomerate and sandstone — Tertiary
C Schist, mostly — Pre-Cambrian
D Granite, mostly — Pre-Cambrian
Geology by N. H. Darton and others
Scale 1/500,000
1 inch = 8 miles (approximately)
0 5 10 15 20 MILES
0 5 10 15 20 KILOMETERS
Contour interval 200 feet.
Datum is mean sea level
Each quadrangle shown on the map with a name in parentheses in the lower left corner is mapped in detail on the U. S. G. S. topographic map of that name
The distances from New Orleans, La., are shown every 10 miles, and the crossties are drawn 1 mile apart

Phoenix
Washington Street, 1902
State Capitol, 1910

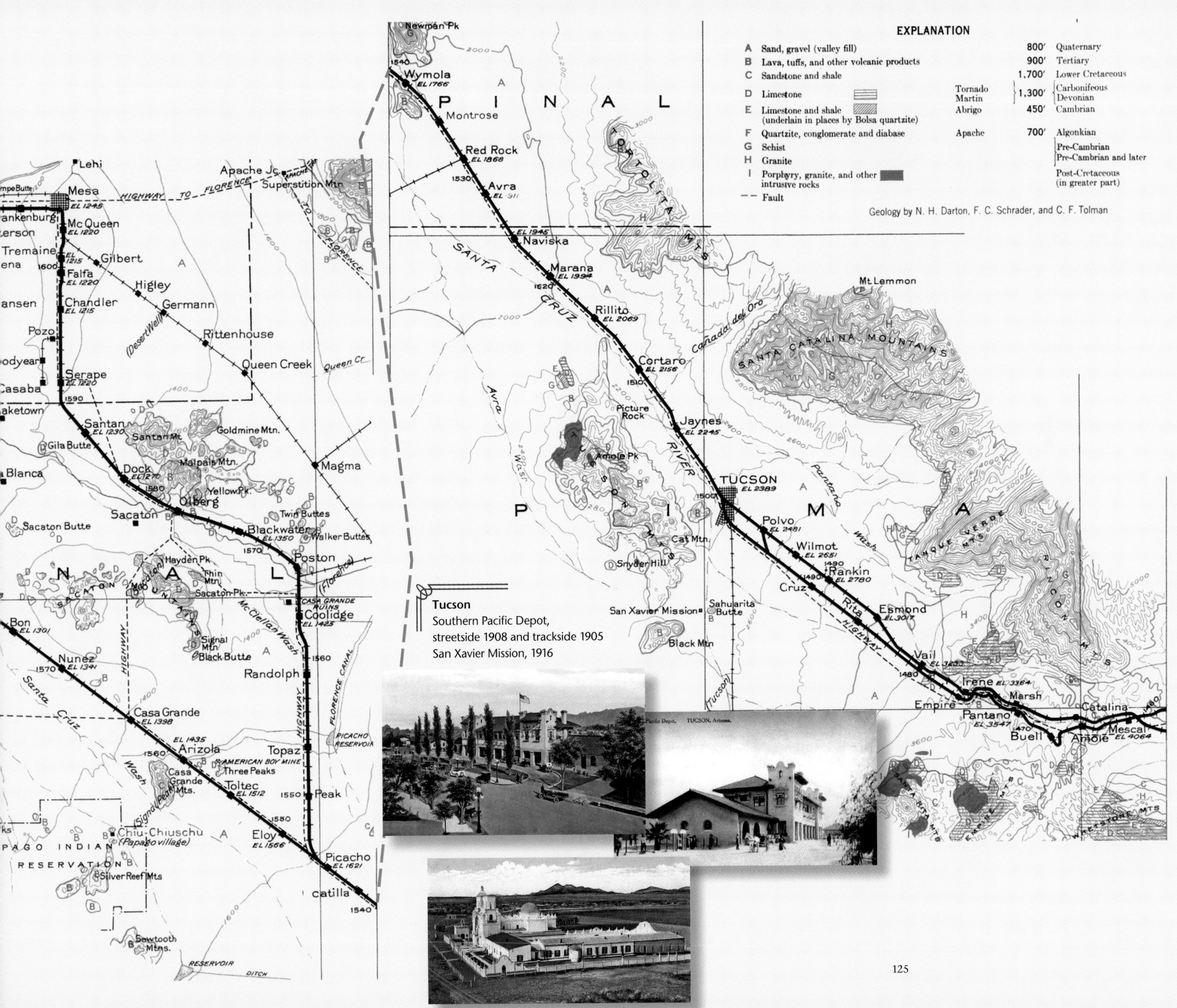

Tucson
Southern Pacific Depot, streetside 1908 and trackside 1905
San Xavier Mission, 1916

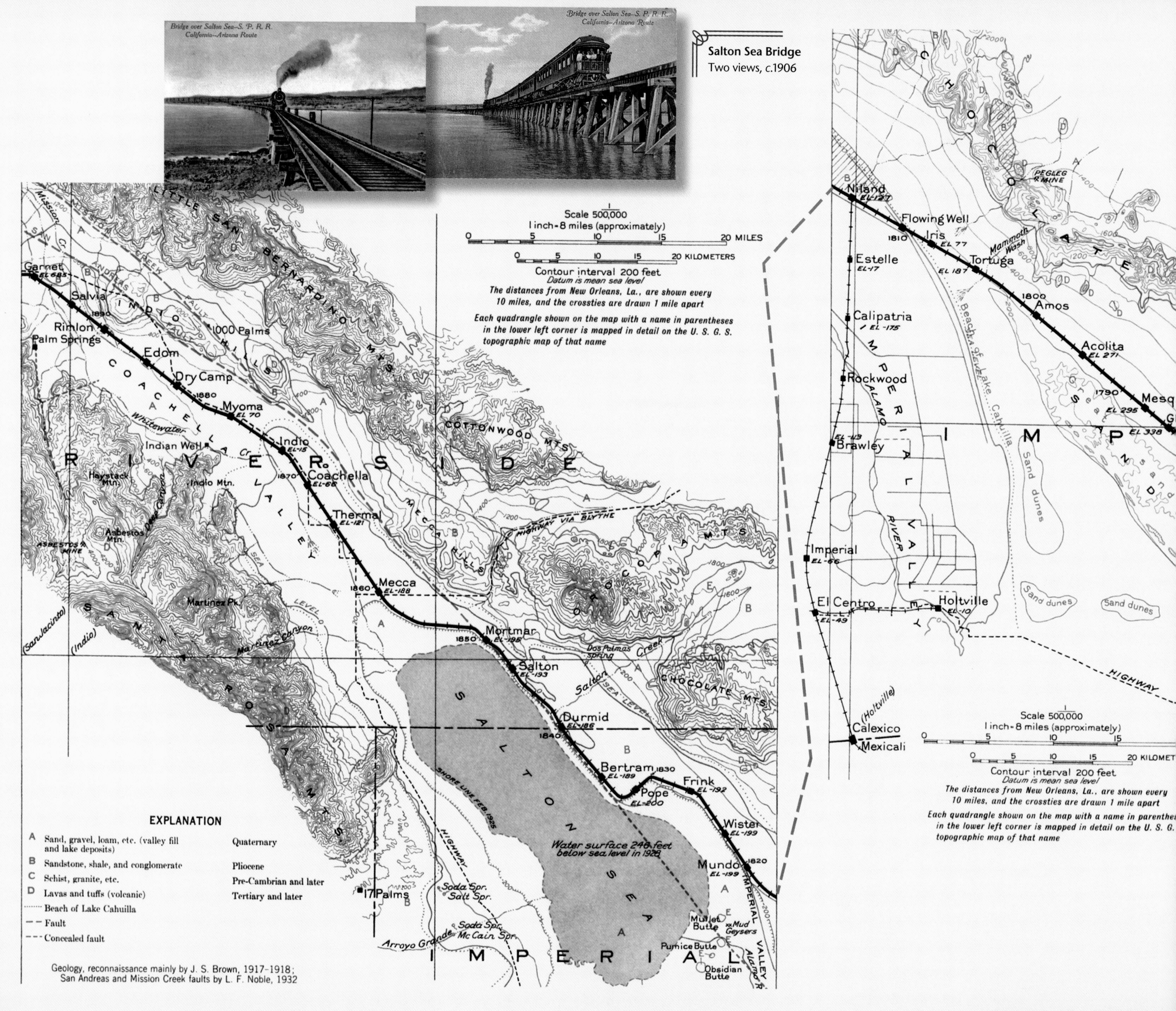
Bridge over Salton Sea–S. P. R. R.
California–Arizona Route
Bridge over Salton Sea–S. P. R. R.
California–Arizona Route
Scale 1/500,000
1 inch = 8 miles (approximately)
0 5 10 15 20 MILES
0 5 10 15 20 KILOMETERS
Contour interval 200 feet
Datum is mean sea level
The distances from New Orleans, La., are shown every 10 miles, and the crossties are drawn 1 mile apart
Each quadrangle shown on the map with a name in parentheses in the lower left corner is mapped in detail on the U. S. G. S. topographic map of that name
EXPLANATION
A Sand, gravel, loam, etc. (valley fill and lake deposits) Quaternary
B Sandstone, shale, and conglomerate Pliocene
C Schist, granite, etc. Pre-Cambrian and later
D Lavas and tuffs (volcanic) Tertiary and later
Beach of Lake Cahuilla
Fault
Concealed fault
Geology, reconnaissance mainly by J. S. Brown, 1917–1918; San Andreas and Mission Creek faults by L. F. Noble, 1932
RIVERSIDE
IMPERIAL
LITTLE SAN BERNARDINO MTS
COACHELLA VALLEY
COTTONWOOD MTS
CHOCOLATE MTS
SANTA ROSA MTS
SALTON SEA
Water surface 248 feet below sea level in 1928
IMPERIAL VALLEY
Garnet
Salvia
Rimlon
Palm Springs
Edom
Dry Camp
Myoma
Indio
Coachella
Thermal
Mecca
Mortmar
Salton
Durmid
Bertram
Pope
Frink
Wister
Mundo
Niland
Flowing Well
Iris
Tortuga
Amos
Acolita
Estelle
Calipatria
Rockwood
Brawley
Imperial
El Centro
Holtville
Calexico
Mexicali
Sand dunes
HIGHWAY

Salton Sea Bridge
Two views, c.1906

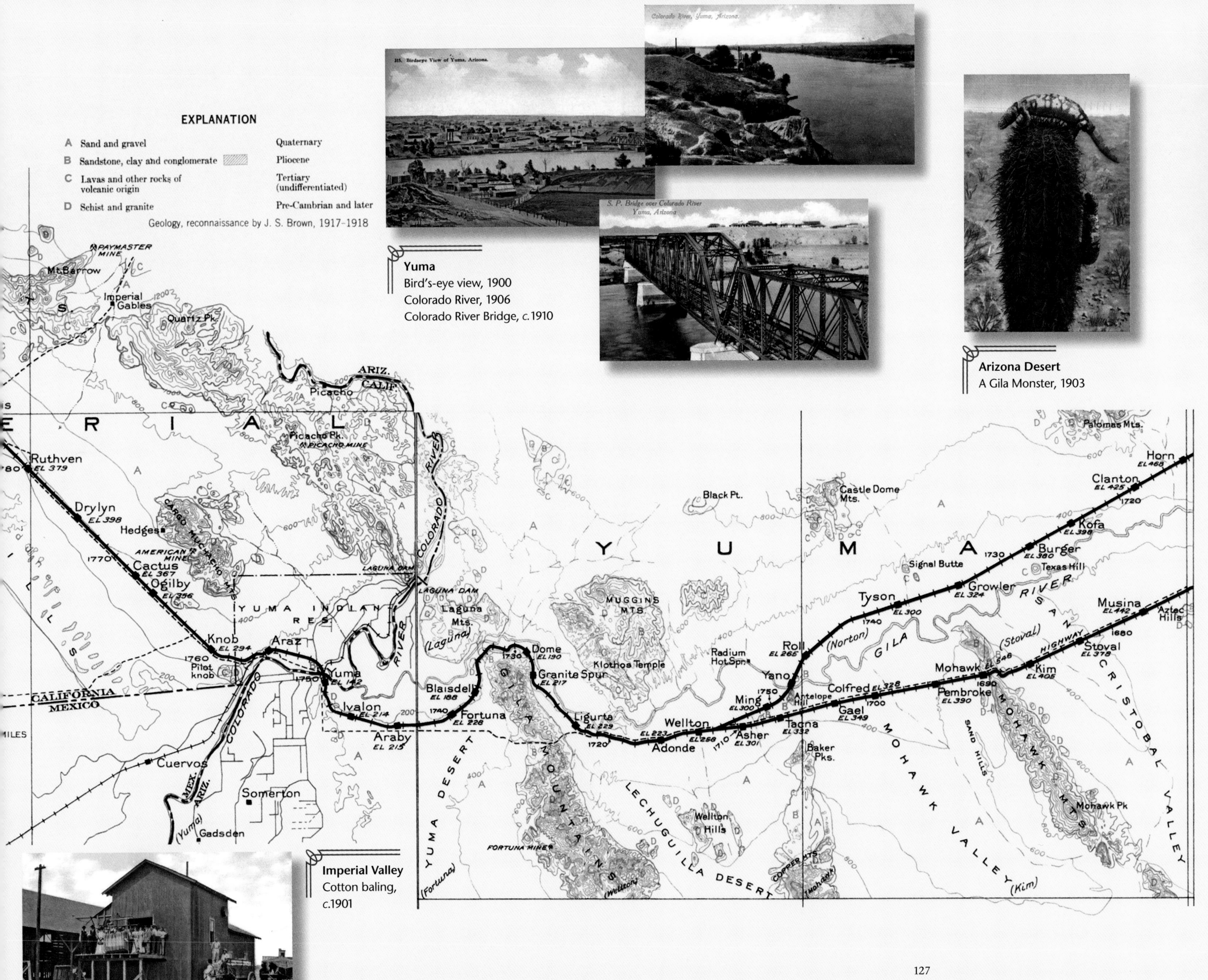

Yuma
Bird's-eye view, 1900
Colorado River, 1906
Colorado River Bridge, *c.*1910

Arizona Desert
A Gila Monster, 1903

Imperial Valley
Cotton baling, *c.*1901

1723 — A ROSE BORDERED SIDEWALK, PASADENA, CALIFORNIA.

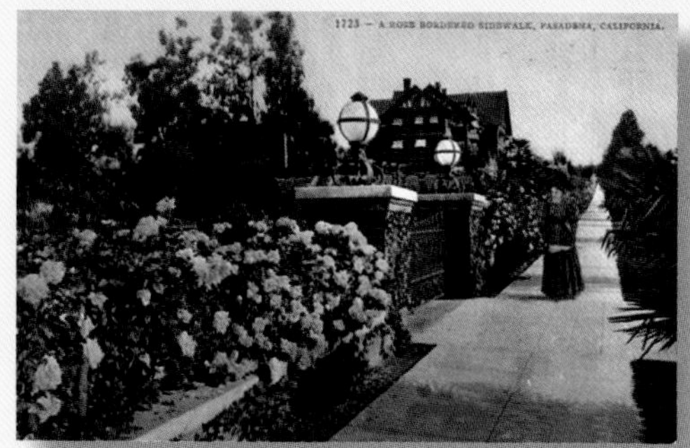

Pasadena
"A Rose-bordered Sidewalk," 1901

Los Angeles
Waiting room, SP Depot, 1905
Southern Pacific Depot, 1910

Waiting Room, S.P. Depot – Los Angeles, Cal.

Entrance to Southern Pacific Depot, Los Angeles, Cal.

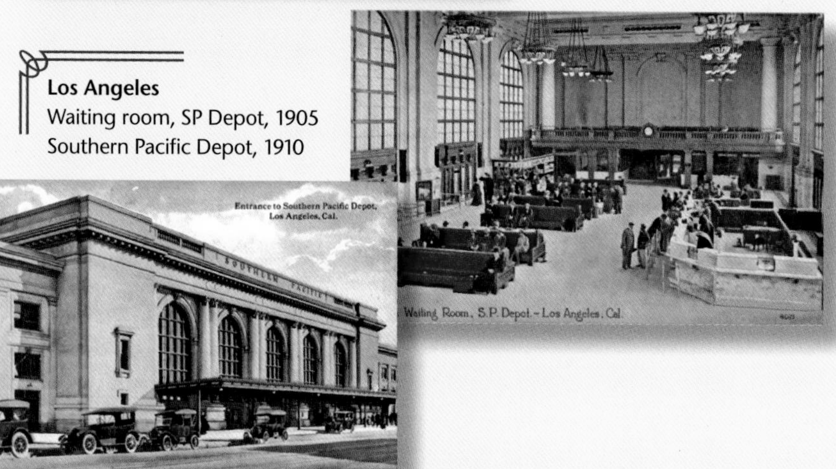

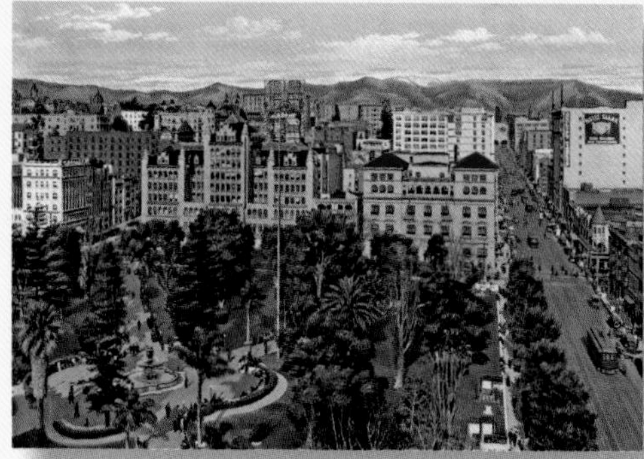

Los Angeles
Pershing Square, 1906

Pomona
"Old Baldy" from the Pomona Valley, 1906

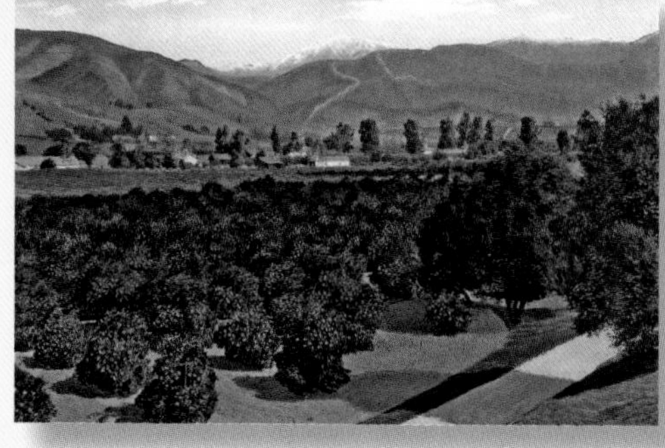

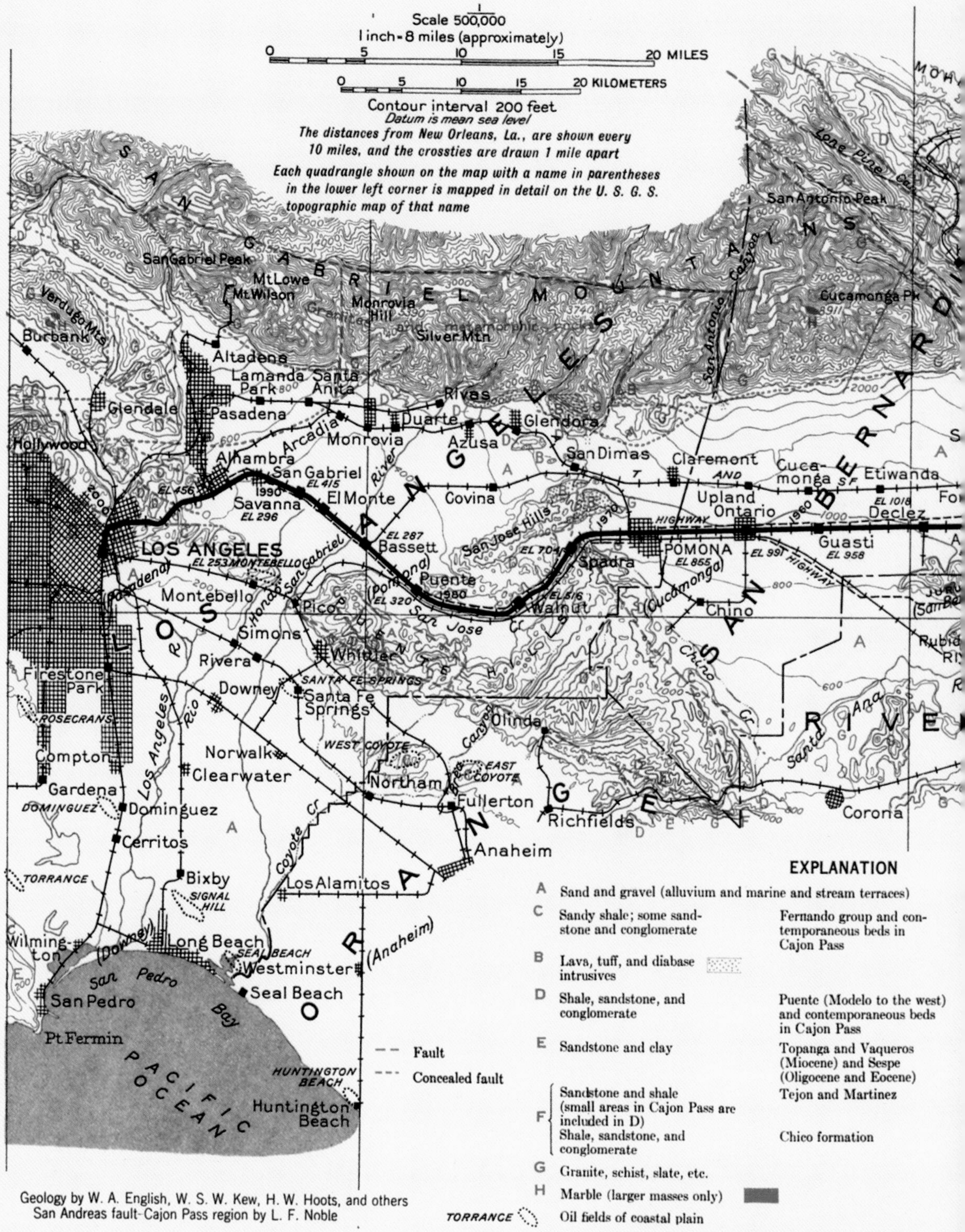

Scale 1/500,000
1 inch = 8 miles (approximately)
0 5 10 15 20 MILES
0 5 10 15 20 KILOMETERS
Contour interval 200 feet
Datum is mean sea level
The distances from New Orleans, La., are shown every 10 miles, and the crossties are drawn 1 mile apart
Each quadrangle shown on the map with a name in parentheses in the lower left corner is mapped in detail on the U. S. G. S. topographic map of that name
SAN GABRIEL MOUNTAINS
SAN BERNARDINO
LOS ANGELES
SAN ANA RIVER
ORANGE
PACIFIC OCEAN
San Gabriel Peak
Mt Lowe
Mt Wilson
Monrovia Hill
Silver Mtn
San Antonio Peak
Cucamonga Pk
Burbank
Altadena
Lamanda Park
Santa Anita
Glendale
Pasadena
Rivas
Duarte
Glendora
Hollywood
Monrovia
Azusa
San Dimas
Claremont
Cucamonga
Etiwanda
Alhambra
San Gabriel
El Monte
Covina
Upland
Ontario
Declez
Savanna
Bassett
Guasti
LOS ANGELES
Montebello
Puente
Spadra
POMONA
Walnut
Chino
Pico
Simons
Whittier
Rivera
Firestone Park
Downey
Santa Fe Springs
Olinda
Compton
Norwalk
Clearwater
Gardena
Dominguez
Northam
Fullerton
Richfields
Corona
Cerritos
Anaheim
Bixby
Los Alamitos
Long Beach
Westminster
San Pedro
Seal Beach
Pt. Fermin
San Pedro Bay
Huntington Beach
EXPLANATION
A Sand and gravel (alluvium and marine and stream terraces)
C Sandy shale; some sandstone and conglomerate — Fernando group and contemporaneous beds in Cajon Pass
B Lava, tuff, and diabase intrusives
D Shale, sandstone, and conglomerate — Puente (Modelo to the west) and contemporaneous beds in Cajon Pass
E Sandstone and clay — Topanga and Vaqueros (Miocene) and Sespe (Oligocene and Eocene)
F Sandstone and shale (small areas in Cajon Pass are included in D) — Tejon and Martinez
Shale, sandstone, and conglomerate — Chico formation
G Granite, schist, slate, etc.
H Marble (larger masses only)
TORRANCE Oil fields of coastal plain
Fault
Concealed fault
Geology by W. A. English, W. S. W. Kew, H. W. Hoots, and others
San Andreas fault-Cajon Pass region by L. F. Noble

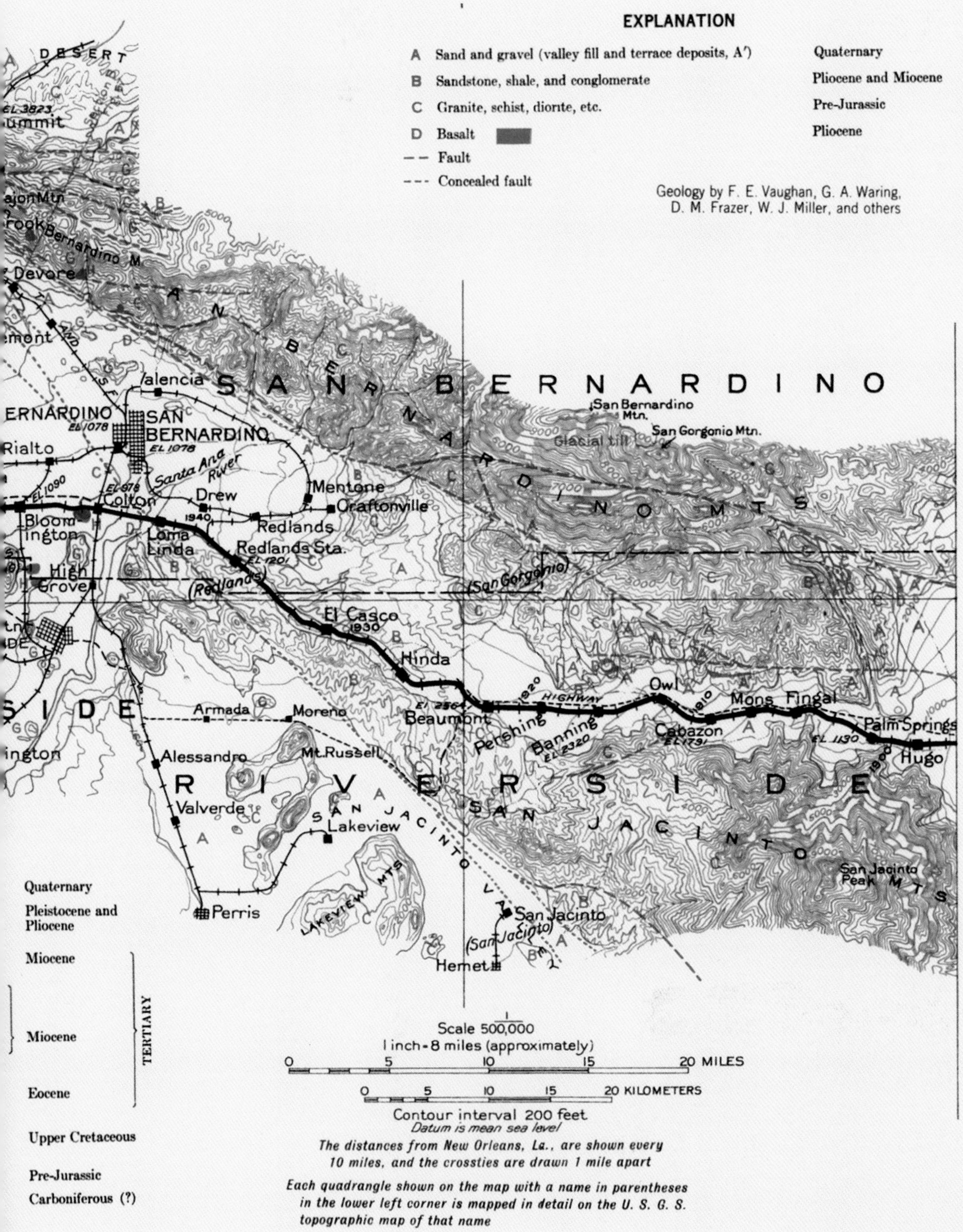

EXPLANATION
A Sand and gravel (valley fill and terrace deposits, A′) Quaternary
B Sandstone, shale, and conglomerate Pliocene and Miocene
C Granite, schist, diorite, etc. Pre-Jurassic
D Basalt Pliocene
Fault
Concealed fault
Geology by F. E. Vaughan, G. A. Waring, D. M. Frazer, W. J. Miller, and others
SAN BERNARDINO
SAN BERNARDINO MTS
San Bernardino Mtn.
San Gorgonio Mtn.
Glacial till
SAN BERNARDINO
EL 1078
Rialto
Colton
Santa Ana River
Drew
Mentone
Craftonville
Redlands
Redlands Sta.
Loma Linda
Bloomington
Highgrove
(Redlands)
(San Gorgonio)
El Casco
Hinda
Beaumont
Pershing
Banning
Owl
Cabazon
Mons
Fingal
Palm Springs
Hugo
HIGHWAY
Armada
Moreno
Alessandro
Mt. Russell
RIVERSIDE
Valverde
SAN JACINTO MTS
Lakeview
LAKEVIEW MTS
Perris
San Jacinto
(San Jacinto)
Hemet
San Jacinto Peak
Quaternary
Pleistocene and Pliocene
Miocene
Miocene
TERTIARY
Eocene
Upper Cretaceous
Pre-Jurassic
Carboniferous (?)
Scale 1/500,000
1 inch = 8 miles (approximately)
0 5 10 15 20 MILES
0 5 10 15 20 KILOMETERS
Contour interval 200 feet
Datum is mean sea level
The distances from New Orleans, La., are shown every 10 miles, and the crossties are drawn 1 mile apart
Each quadrangle shown on the map with a name in parentheses in the lower left corner is mapped in detail on the U. S. G. S. topographic map of that name

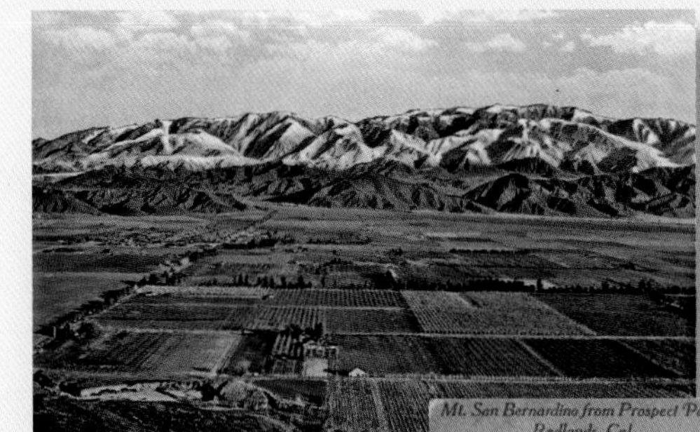

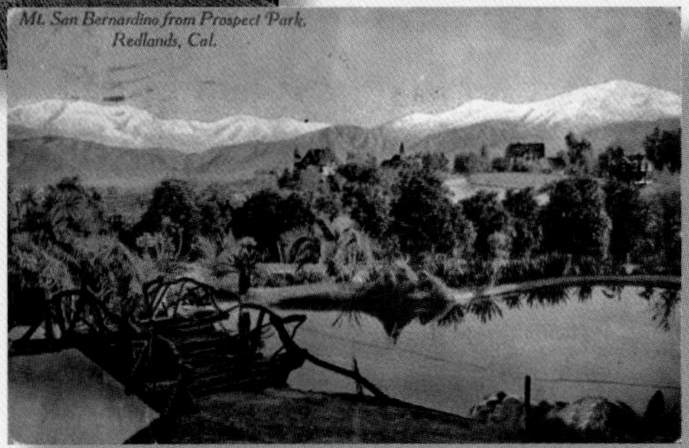

Mt. San Bernardino from Prospect Park, Redlands, Cal.

San Bernardino Range
The San Bernardino Range from Banning, 1906
Mount San Bernardino from Prospect Park, Redlands, 1901

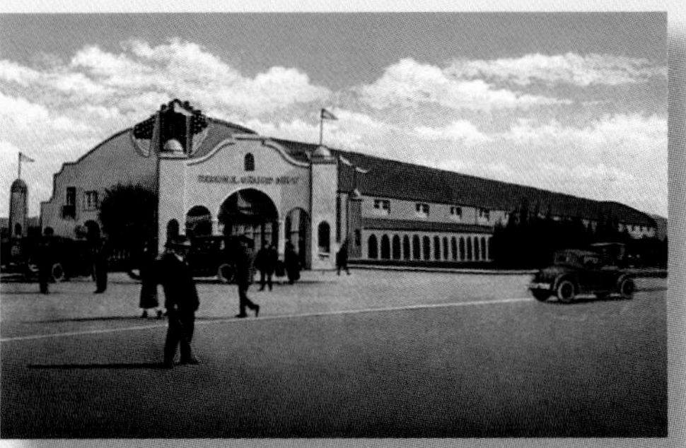

San Bernardino
SP Depot, *c.*1920

1218 A Home amid the Orange Groves of California
Barrage Residence at Redlands.

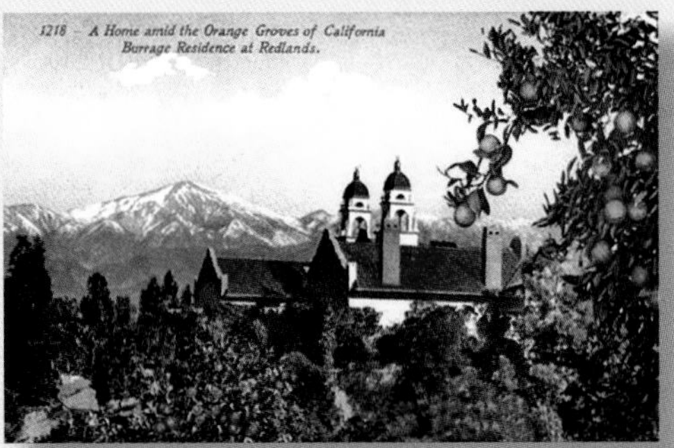

Redlands
Barrage Residence, 1916

THE NORTHERN PACIFIC ROUTE

ST. PAUL TO SEATTLE, WITH A SIDE TRIP TO YELLOWSTONE PARK

The Northern Pacific Railroad (NP), chartered in 1864 by Congress as the nation's second transcontinental railroad, was built to serve the area between western Lake Superior (Duluth, Minnesota) and Puget Sound at Tacoma, Washington.

Supported by banker and financier Jay Cooke (1821–1905), the road received its initial financing in 1870. Plagued by questionable management and unanticipated Indian hostility, Jay's partners panicked, triggering the Panic of 1873 and the NP's temporary bankruptcy. Under Frederick Billings (1823–90), it resumed transcontinental construction in 1879 from both east and west, but two years later (1881) a competitor, the Oregon Transportation Company led by Henry Villard (1835–1900), seized control of the Northern Pacific. Under Villard track from Duluth to Tacoma, via Portland, Oregon, was completed on September 9, 1883 at 2,168 miles.

However, the project was too hurried and the Northern Pacific again fell into desperate financial straits. While the railroad completed a major short cut to the Seattle–Tacoma area from the Columbia River (Pasco, Washington) by mid-1887, in the 1890s competition from the Great Northern system, which had a more direct route from Chicago to Puget Sound, permanently weakened the NP.

Historically Jay Cooke and the Northern Pacific played a key role in encouraging Scandinavian emigration, created Yellowstone Park, reignited Indian fighting, and was the competitive impetus for the Canadian Pacific.

The line's background began in 1840, when civil engineer Edwin F. Johnson (1803–72) published his first article concerning a transcontinental railroad to the Pacific based, of course, on the pre-Mexican War boundaries of the USA. The discovery of massive amounts of gold and silver (in California, Nevada, and then Colorado), suspect Mormon loyalty in Utah, and the advent of the Civil War, all worked in favor of a transcontinental road. The 1862 Pacific Railroad Act (signed on July 20), part of the nation's overall Civil War effort, created a road designed to cross the western US between Omaha, Nebraska and Sacramento, California. Construction was undertaken by the Central Pacific, building east from Sacramento, and the Union Pacific, coming west from Omaha. No 1862 provision was made for a more northerly route.

However Johnson, financially supported by the president of the Vermont Central Railroad, J. Gregory Smith (1818–91), had numerous political allies from the northern tier of states. One individual frozen out by the Union Pacific was Josiah Perham (1803–68), a well-known railroad promoter with an uneven business record. Needing to act quickly, Smith turned to Perham, who was only too happy to "lead" a northern Pacific railroad. As it transpired, the 1862 Act provided insufficient financial incentives for the Union Pacific and Central Pacific. At the same time, significant gold and silver strikes were being made in Idaho and Montana. As the UP and CP returned to Congress, hats in hands, Smith put together a

Jay Cooke (1821–1905), photographed c.1875.

Northern Pacific Depot, Seattle, from a postcard c.1905 (opposite).

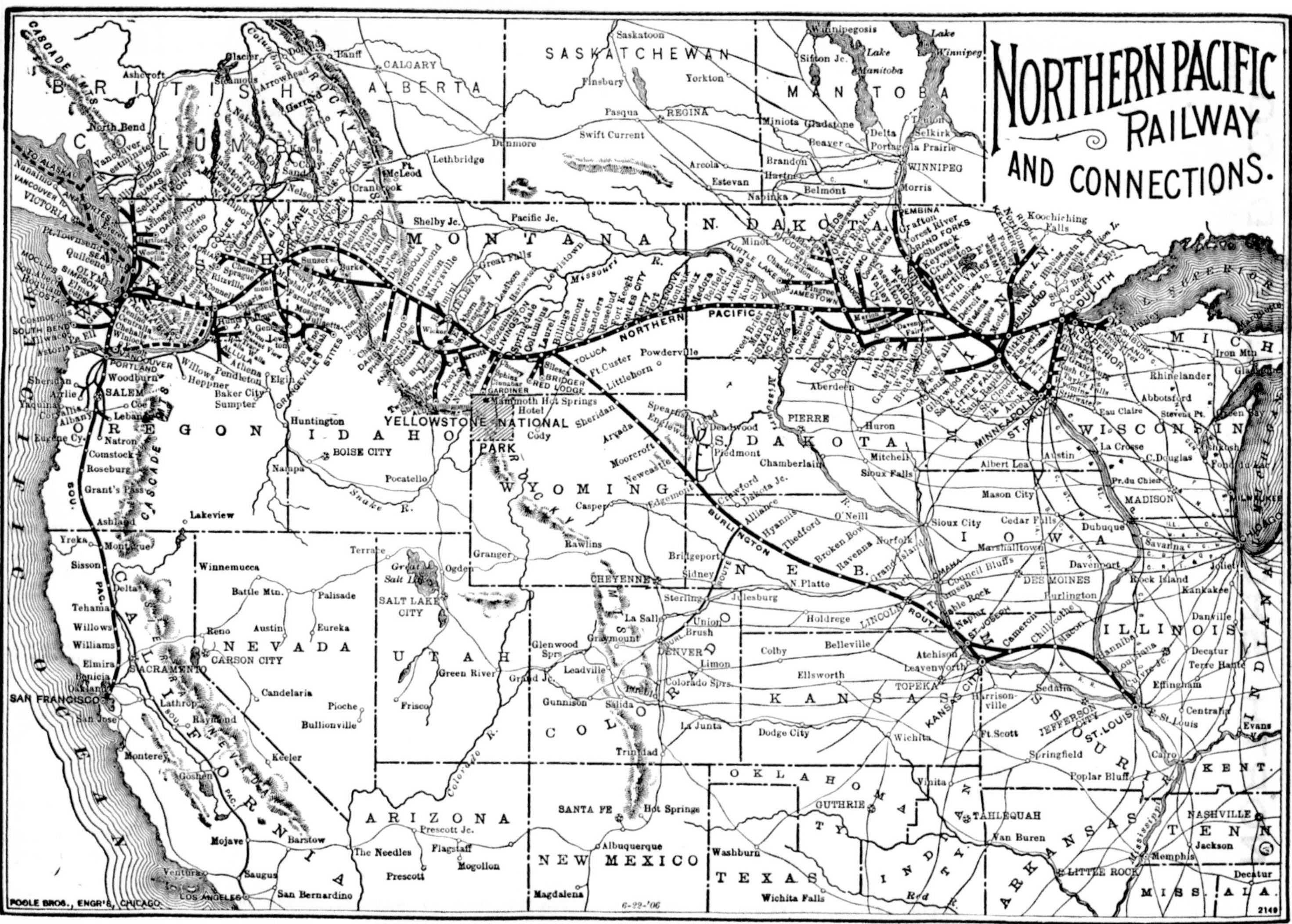

"Northern Pacific Railway and Connections" from the 1906 edition of *The Official Guide of the Railways.*

strong lobbying team that not only supported the two railroads, but also requested that a northern route be chartered. The House of Representatives passed the legislation (1864 Pacific Railroad Act) on May 31 by a 74 to 50 vote. The Senate then unanimously passed the bill, and the Northern Pacific was officially chartered on July 2.

THE INITIAL CONSTRUCTION OF THE LINE

The Congress gave the Northern Pacific a checkerboard land grant for every 25 miles of completed and government-certified track; 12,800 acres (twenty square miles) in states, 25,600 acres in territories. However, not a dollar in funding was provided, and few people expected that the money would be raised. Following a year of futility, Perham broke down and resigned, at which point Smith, his Vermont gubernatorial duties now ended, stepped in and seized control. Smith combined a long-time interest in a northern route, a strong work ethic, solid intelligence, and natural leadership. By 1870 his 900-mile Vermont Central, the nation's ninth largest system, had come to epitomize common business sense as he expanded it with small acquisitions and limited annual construction.

Despite Smith's ability to run the Vermont Central, he proved to be incompetent in delegating management planning, construction, operations, and traffic creation for the envisioned 2,100-mile Northern Pacific. Additionally, his record

indicates continual deficiencies in estimating and establishing new passenger and freight business, and also a lack of interest in the broad category of "sales." No promoter, he!

As the Northern Pacific's president, Smith brought together a nationally known board of directors including William G. Fargo (1818–81) of Wells Fargo fame and William B. Ogden (1805–77), president of the Chicago and Northwestern. However Smith could raise only a quarter of a million dollars, enough to begin surveying in eastern Minnesota in 1868 and to lobby Congress to renew the charter, but not nearly enough to begin construction.

If the Northern Pacific's future looked bleak in early 1869, newly elected President U. S. Grant's decision not to include Jay Cooke in his cabinet changed everything. Cooke's bank was America's largest, he kept scores of Congressmen on his payroll, built the largest mansion in the US, and was considered the country's second most powerful man. A man of deep faith, Cooke firmly believed that he was nothing less than "God's chosen instrument" to build the Northern Pacific.

The Northern Pacific under construction, probably in western Dakota, *c.*1878.

Cooke's concept was to finance the Northern Pacific from European and American bond sales, by selling the NP's land to settlers, and through the development of freight and passenger traffic between Lake Superior and Puget Sound. But he (and Smith) failed to anticipate that they would have to fight every step of the way—against the financial interests behind the Central Pacific Railroad/Union Pacific Railroad route from Omaha/Council Bluffs to San Francisco (completed in May 1869), and against the British government as well.

Before making a final decision, however, Cooke cautiously had a survey undertaken between Walla Walla, Washington, and the Yellowstone River (present-day Livingston, Montana) in mid-1869. On reading the optimistic report in late September, Cooke notified Smith of his intention to proceed. The papers were officially signed on January 1, 1870.

In just weeks Cooke raised $9 million. Ground was broken on February 15, 1870, twenty miles southwest of Duluth at Carlton Junction. Cooke also began steps to acquire two floundering adjacent roads, the Lake Superior and Mississippi (between St. Paul and Duluth) and the debt-ridden St. Paul and Pacific, whose unfinished track ran to central and western Minnesota.

A railroad construction crew at work, as illustrated on a stock certificate for the Wayne, Cincinnati & Louisville Railroad, *c.*1850.

Although given ample notice by Cooke, Smith did not select a Minnesota route until April. Every effort was made to bypass existing communities such as Superior, Wisconsin, and Crow Wing and Georgetown in Minnesota in order to maximize profits in land speculation. Smith's choice to lead the Lake Superior and Puget Sound Land Company was the dapper former horse-dealer Thomas A. Canfield (1822–97), who proceeded to override Northern Pacific engineers when it came to selecting river crossings, then infuriated everyone by designing communities with narrow, expensive lots that did not attract settlers.

Despite his new Northern Pacific duties, Smith continued to manage his own Vermont Central (which began suffering significant financial difficulties), working from his St. Albans, Vermont, offices and seldom visiting Minnesota. Until forced to resign thirty months later, Smith made scores of purchasing and contract-letting decisions that remain inexplicable other than in the context of benefiting Smith, the Vermont Central, or both.

BROAD STREETS WITH WALL STREET—VIEW OF THE SUB-TREASURY, JAY COOKE & CO.'S BANK,
PH OFFICE, FROM THE DREXEL BUILDING, ON FRIDAY, SEPT. 19TH.

The events of September 18, 1873, when crowds intent on withdrawing their money filled the streets around Cooke's office in Wall Street, New York, and police were called in to prevent rioting, from *Frank Leslie's Illustrated Weekly Newsletter*, October 11, 1873.

Weak management and graft caused immediate construction difficulties. Construction west of Carlton Junction (where the Northern Pacific met the St. Paul–Duluth track) was delayed until August 1870, where track soon entered 150 miles of wetlands. Roadbed through muck, sometimes thirty feet deep, was cheaply built and hastily filled, and settled during the 1870–1 winter. Worse, by October Smith was so far behind schedule that he ordered 3,000 laborers to continue throughout the winter, laying track over miles of ice and permafrost. After the 1871 spring thaw, large sections of the line proved inoperable or literally sank. One story that gained wide currency, perhaps apocryphal, tells of a locomotive sinking entirely out of sight. Crews from other projects were called in, construction fell further behind schedule, important sections of track were never built (including the St. Cloud to Brainerd spur), and by the end of 1871 the road had not reached the Red River.

By 1872 the Smith–Cooke feud had destroyed all vestiges of management cohesion. Shortly before his Vermont Central collapsed that year, Smith was forced from office, although Cooke did not think to have a replacement ready to step in. Nor did anyone until December. Despite the lack of obstacles between the Red and Missouri Rivers, it was June 1873 before the near-bankrupt Northern Pacific reached Bismarck in North Dakota, completing 454 miles of track from Duluth.

However, before its September 1873 bankruptcy the Northern Pacific did achieve a degree of self-sufficiency and no longer needed cash infusions to meet its operating costs. This was accomplished through land sales under Frederick Billings (Smith had unaccountably delayed doing this), from developing freight and passenger traffic, and with management economies put in place by the new president, the able George W. Cass (1810–88). In the third quarter of 1873 revenue exceeded expenditure for the first time.

Meanwhile Cooke's European bond sales failed. Cooke had supported a proposal that the US should annex western Canada and had given clandestine backing to Louis Riel's 1869–70 Rebellion in what is now Manitoba. In response the British and Canadian governments announced their

The Northern Pacific Depot in Tacoma, a color postcard *c.*1906.

own transcontinental railroad, the Canadian Pacific. The British government blocked Cooke's efforts to sell bonds in Great Britain, and worked through J. P. Morgan's banking house in Europe and the US to discredit and compete with Cooke. Besides the Franco–Prussian War's impact on reducing Scandinavian emigration, it also acted to dry up or temporarily freeze European banking houses, another significant blow to Cooke. Another disaster was the renewed fighting between Plains Native Americans and the US Army, largely caused by the NP's intrusion on native lands. Investors took fright, and Cooke was unable to sell the bonds and thereby raise money.

West Coast construction–a Congressional requirement–was always the Northern Pacific's poor sister, although not devoid of the corporate infighting, wasteful spending, and bad luck that similarly characterized its Minnesota–Dakota efforts. Despite these problems, 105 miles were operational between Tacoma and Kalama, Washington (thirty miles north of Portland on the Columbia River) by mid-January, 1874.

SURVIVAL AND EXPANSION

Somehow the Northern Pacific weathered the Panic of 1873, although it was forced to seek bankruptcy protection on September 19, 1873, and then financially limped along for years. Revenue after the Panic began was based on rail traffic from numerous sources. Bismarck became the Upper Missouri's premier steamboat port; land sales grew, Bonanza farms developed, and new settlement picked up (especially Scandinavian emigrants as the decade ended); Red River agricultural production rose dramatically; animal furs from across the American and Canadian northwest poured into Bismarck and Fargo; and the port of Duluth (wheat, lumber, and the discovery of huge iron ore ranges) grew in importance.

The Northern Pacific's financial problems caused predictable legal maneuvering, resulting in its being placed in receivership under Cass in April 1875. While Charles B. Wright (1822–98) assumed the presidency, the railroad's legal reorganization reflected Billings' efforts, with his actions putting the railroad on a firm financial footing. Thus, for the fiscal year of 1875, earnings ($619,000) significantly exceeded expenses ($446,000). Two years later, net earnings jumped to $560,000. This positive trend, which included selling hundreds of thousands of acres of land, was not sufficient to sustain transcontinental construction, although it did substantially reduce NP indebtedness and reinforce the company's viability in the minds of financiers.

In the spring of 1878, in a strategic boost to operational efficiency, the Brainerd to St. Cloud short cut opened, reducing travel time between Bismarck and St. Paul to 24 hours. The next year construction began on 205 miles of new grade from Bismarck to Glendive, Montana. Because there was no bridge over the Missouri, the Northern Pacific built on the river's frozen surface to transport more than a hundred miles' worth of construction materials before the spring thaw began. May 24, 1879 saw the installation of Frederick Billings, the Northern Pacific's largest shareholder, as president. As the nation's economy and confidence recovered, Billings also raised funds for some 140 miles of grade between Spokane Falls, Washington, and the junction of the Snake and Columbia Rivers. Soon another seventy miles were planned to Lake Pend Oreille.

Even as transcontinental construction continued, Northern Pacific engineers were examining a more direct route to Puget Sound, the one through the Stampede Pass east of Seattle that had been laid out in the summer of 1882. This route was built in 1886–7, saving 145 miles versus the Portland route.

As 1880 ended, the Northern Pacific momentum had been restored. A satisfactory 855 miles of the road were operational and 234 miles were in various phases of construction.

Henry Villard (1835–1900), photographed in 1885.

Oregon and Transcontinental stock owned by Henry Villard.

Land sales had netted $9 million (averaging $3.50 per acre), and tens of millions of acres were still in reserve. Best of all, financial arrangements had been made with financier J. P. Morgan (1837–1913), who led a $40 million syndicate. An agreement had also been reached with Henry Villard for the use of his track between Wallula Junction and Portland. Not since 1870 had the Northern Pacific's future looked so bright.

HENRY VILLARD

Villard, who immigrated to America from Germany at the age of eighteen, became a journalist, friend of Abraham Lincoln, and a war correspondent. He married well, and in 1874 began representing German financial interests in defaulted transportation companies. In 1875 Villard became president of both the Oregon and California Railroad Company and the Oregon Steamship Company (not to be confused with the Oregon Steam Navigation Company that was under Northern Pacific control), between them the controlling forces in Oregon and southern Washington transportation.

By the late 1870s, with the American economy rapidly recovering and his reputation high for having held off financier Jay Gould's takeover attempts, Villard turned his sights on upgrading his aging fleet and connecting his railroad system with the east via the Union Pacific. Villard moved quickly, but, under pressure from the Central Pacific, the Union Pacific backed out, leaving Villard with huge obligations in his newly named Oregon Railway and Navigation Company (OR&N) with no rail partner with track to the east.

Until Billings' financial successes in the late fall of 1880, Villard did not see the Northern Pacific as a significant factor in transcontinental traffic or the cause for competitive concern. However, as 1881 began, he suddenly found himself facing a larger, better financed, and well-operated competitor. Worse, in the eat-or-be-eaten world of cut-throat capitalism, Villard faced the definite prospect of all his companies being swallowed up.

Villard then reached a stunning conclusion—he had to directly acquire control of the Northern Pacific. However, he faced the problem that if he openly bid for the NP, the stock price would rise beyond his ability to purchase a controlling interest. Villard's answer was his audacious "blind pool" at a time when the Northern Pacific had some $19 million cash with which to fight. Virtually overnight, Villard raised $8 million from fifty investors without stating the purpose of their subscriptions. Based on the respect in which Villard was held, he not only was oversubscribed but also charged a hefty premium for participation.

Purchasing Northern Pacific stock on the open market, Villard soon acquired a controlling interest, although he did not announce what he had done until June 24, 1881, when he raised another $12 million for construction. The complexity of the hostile takeover quickly led to predictable lawsuits, but a compromise was reached leaving much of the NP's management and board in place, but with Villard elected as president on September 15, 1881.

If Villard's audacity had been shocking, what happened next was nothing short of a miracle. He and Billings discovered that they genuinely liked each other, the two working well together and quickly becoming an effective team.

COMPLETION AND FINANCIAL DISASTER

The story for the next two years was one of construction undertaken too rapidly as a "damn the expenses" attitude prevailed. In the West, a 208-mile line was completed in 1881 from Pasco (formerly Ainsworth) via Ritzville and Spokane Falls past the Idaho line to Algoma, just south of Sandpoint. The 43 miles from Algoma to the Montana state line were completed in 1882. Montana's 224 west-to-east miles at Gold Creek, including Missoula, were finished in late August 1883.

Coming from the east, the 298 miles from Bismarck to Miles City, via Mandan, Dickinson, and Glendive, were completed in 1881. The final 442 miles of Montana construction, Miles City to Gold Creek via Forsyth, Billings, Livingston, Bozeman, and Helena took place over a two-year period. The September 8, 1883 "last spike" activities—not a golden spike but rather the very first spike driven in 1870 (or so it was said)—took place along Gold Creek, 65 miles southeast of Missoula and just off today's Interstate 90 (exit 166).

Numerous physical obstacles had to be overcome by Northern Pacific personnel in Montana including, but certainly not limited to, the Bozeman Pass, Stampede Pass (1886–7), and Mullan Pass at the Continental Divide. Suffice to say, some of these and similar projects were sufficiently difficult and technically interesting to later become the subject of individual books. In Montana, with over six hundred miles of its grade paralleling the Yellowstone, Clark's Fork, Blackfoot, and Flathead rivers and streams (all of which flooded at various times), engineering requirements called for safe track beds above likely high-water marks. Hundred-foot-high wooden bridges and trestles (often crossing rapids) were built, tunnels were driven through high passes and along river beds, and cliffs and buttes situated at a river's edge were routinely blasted away.

Like many transcontinental railroads, significant labor problems were to plague construction efforts over the years. As reflected by period photographs, most railroad construction was still done "by hand" as power equipment (pile drivers and Otis steam shovels) was still in its infancy. In 1870–1 the NP banned liquor among its workforce, resulting in riots in temporary Minnesota labor camps. Periodic crackdowns on gambling and prostitution were, predictably, of no long-term impact; unpaid wages (a not infrequent problem) caused work stoppages, rioting, and property destruction; and relationships between lower-paid Chinese versus European workers versus management on the western end of construction is a subject avoided by the few writers of Northern Pacific history.

The completion of the Northern Pacific's transcontinental line at Gold Creek, Montana, September 8, 1883, photographed by F. Jay Haynes.

POST-1883

Villard's decision to press ahead with rapid construction came at a huge cost, both in short-term financing and long-term lost business opportunities. As the Northern Pacific floundered, James J. Hill (1838–1916) was putting together his Great Northern system, which under him became financially the stronger of the two systems, although in the decades following his death the two roads battled it out on fairly even terms.

At the turn of the century Hill, E. H. Harriman, and J. P. Morgan struggled to control the lines, consolidating the two as part of the Northern Securities Company. However, President Theodore Roosevelt declared the company a trust, a decision that was upheld by the Supreme Court in 1904. By 1970, with air and highway traffic expanding, railroads across the country were increasingly forced to merge and the Northern Pacific ceased operations, becoming a "fallen flag" and incorporated into today's Burlington Northern and Santa Fe system.

The front cover of a brochure published by the Northern Pacific in 1925 to celebrate the silver anniversary of the *North Coast Limited.*

THE NORTHWEST

A Bright Future

Bird's-eye view of Bozeman, and the Great Northern Depot at Spokane, postcards c.1910 (below).

Spokane River bridges, 1906 (far right).

When the Northern Pacific Railroad broke ground in 1870 at Carlton (Thomson Junction), Minnesota, twenty miles southwest of Duluth, few Americans lived between Duluth and Bozeman, Montana. The 250-mile route along the NP's future track until the Red River had limited settlement and trade, the non-native population likely not exceeding five thousand. Including soldiers, the population along the railroad's future 785 miles from the Red River to Bozeman was less than a thousand.

West of Bozeman the situation was different. The 1863 discovery of gold deposits in Montana led to an increase in the then territory's population (20,595 in 1870), although only a few dozen lived east of Bozeman and Fort Benton, a site on the Missouri River. West of Missoula, there were no significant emigrant settlements until Walla Walla in south-central Washington.

The largest northwest community was Portland, Oregon (35,000 in 1883), located strategically at the junction of the Willamette and Columbia Rivers but suffering from treacherous tidal waters. By 1870 it was clear that the Northwest's international trading future lay through calmer waters: Puget Sound and the Strait of Juan de Fuca.

WESTERN DEVELOPMENT

In 1883, with economic development occurring all along its line, the future looked bright for the Northern Pacific. As western construction began across the isthmus between Puget Sound and the Columbia, in August 1873 the NP finally selected New Tacoma over Seattle as its terminus. However the railroad's participation in the development of Oregon and Washington was modest.

The NP retained the route to Portland established by the Oregon Transportation Company that paralleled the Columbia from where the Snake River entered it at Wallula Junction. To reach Stampede Pass in 1887 the NP followed a northwestern route, thus forming a gigantic, wide "V" in Washington. The Yakima River from the west and the Snake River from the east enter the Columbia within ten miles of each other, creating a natural trading area. Pasco (originally named Ainsworth) on the eastern side of the Columbia became a major NP maintenance and repair facility, and the whole area grew into a transportation center and agricultural distribution hub.

Spokane Falls, as Spokane was known in 1883, is strategically located along nature's largest east–west highway in Washington. An Indian trading area, the falls were virtually unpopulated (1,600 people) when a Jay Cooke-sponsored scouting party passed by in 1869. The Northern Pacific became the first to lay track past the falls, and then took advantage of its land grants by selling parcels in the Palouse Country, an area extending from Spokane to the Snake River that promised exceptional grain and soybean production.

By 1915 almost a dozen railroads passed through Spokane carrying lumber, agricultural products, ores, and Far Eastern imports in addition to passenger traffic. Aided by adjacent gold strikes in Idaho, Spokane quickly became the largest city between Seattle–Tacoma and Minneapolis–St. Paul, a status it still enjoys.

FROM THE EAST

Scandinavians and Bonanzas

EASTERN MINNESOTA

When Jay Cooke visited Duluth in 1867 he found a tiny trading community dwarfed by adjacent Superior, Wisconsin, on eastern St. Louis Bay. Spurred by potential land speculation profits, the Northern Pacific chose the smaller Duluth as its terminal, spending $2 million and encouraging the population of the Minnesota town to grow to 12,000 in 1883. Over the following decades the NP took advantage of Minnesota's iron ore deposits, quarrying, western grain shipments, lumber, dairy products, and packed meats and fish, seeing Duluth–Superior rise to become not just the nation's largest freshwater cargo port, but by the early 1900s second only to New York in gross tonnage.

At the Mississippi River the Northern Pacific founded Brainerd in 1870. With 7,000 residents in 1883 (13,000 today), it became a railroad division boundary where the NP built a hotel, a medical center, emigration reception, and extensive maintenance facilities. Today the empty buildings with their broken windows have become a ghost town.

Few states experienced greater emigration from Scandinavia (Denmark, Sweden, and Norway) than Minnesota, and no organization made greater efforts to attract newcomers than the Northern Pacific. From 1870 to 1873 the NP spent $1 million in northern Europe promoting emigration, and by 1880 the number of new settlers dramatically increased. The 1890 census revealed that overall 36% of Minnesota's population was foreign-born.

Swedish settlers in front of a Chicago County farmhouse, *c.*1895 (top); Scandinavian American National Bank at 52–54 South Fourth Street, Minneapolis, postcard *c.*1916 (below).

NORTH DAKOTA AND THE VALLEY OF THE RED RIVER

The valley of the Red River of the North was once covered by a 700-mile-long, 200-feet-deep glacial lake. A thick, black subsoil remains, producing crops that legendarily grew twice as large as those from southern Minnesota. The river, which marks the border between Minnesota and North Dakota, is also a natural trade route to Canada.

Fargo–Moorhead was selected as the site of the river crossing for speculative reasons. While the logical crossing would have been ten miles north at the confluence of the Sheyenne where there was a trading post, Northern Pacific executives overrode engineering objections and chose today's location as they looked to profit again from their land speculations.

Moorhead (population 4,000 in 1883), named after Cooke's partner and NP Director William G. Moorhead, was christened on September 22, 1871. Almost from the first, however, neighboring Fargo (1883 population 10,000), which was named for NP board member William Fargo (*the* Fargo in Wells Fargo & Co), became dominant as the jumping-off point for North Dakota settlers, and remains today the state's agricultural and distribution hub.

Some of those settlers would have been heading for the large, specialized farms that were developed in the mid-1870s and known as Bonanza Farms. They had a short-lived history (the land became too valuable and the farms were split), but they nevertheless publicized North Dakota, attracted settlers, improved farming methods, and created new railroad traffic. By 1883 NP branch lines were rapidly sprouting with three already operational and hundreds of additional miles planned.

The Columbian on the summit of the Rocky Mountains, from *Lake Michigan to Puget Sound*.

BISMARCK TO THE WEST

Buffalos, Skulls, and Minerals

NORTH DAKOTA TO BILLINGS

Located 454 miles from Duluth, in what would become North Dakota in 1889, Bismarck was named for Otto von Bismarck, Prussia and Germany's "Iron Chancellor," in order to attract German investment. A railroad bridge built across the Missouri River in 1882 confirmed the city's long-term commercial importance, and a dozen steamships plied the river complementing the NP's operations. In 1883 Bismarck became the capital of the then Dakota Territory, the decision partially reflecting Northern Pacific influence.

Despite the railroad's construction of four hundred miles of track between Bismarck and Billings in Montana between 1879 and 1882, the area's economic development was limited. Miles City, MT, (population 2,500 in 1883) was the jumping-off point for buffalo hunters, although while the herds survived it was also common to shoot at them from the train.

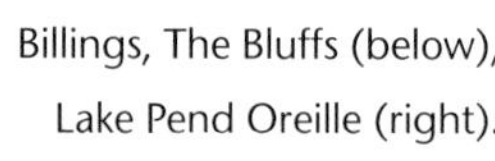

Billings, The Bluffs (below), Lake Pend Oreille (right).

BILLINGS TO LIVINGSTON

Billings (2,200 in 1883) is situated in one of the most gorgeous locations in the Yellowstone Valley. The dramatic 400-foot-high Rimrocks are immediately to the north, where legend states that in the 1800s a hunting party that had found its village destroyed by smallpox rode off the cliffs, giving the location the names "Skull Butte" and "Place of the Skulls." At Livingston passengers switched trains to reach the scenic Paradise Valley and Yellowstone Park (there is more information about the Park Line starting on page 144), and west-bound trains added a second locomotive to help make the twenty-mile climb across the Bozeman Pass, as freight trains still do today.

WESTERN MONTANA AND IDAHO

Bozeman (3,000 in 1883 and 28,000 today) is steeped in history, not least because it was near one of explorer William Clark's 1806 campsites. With rich soil, it became a successful farming center, while different types of riches—copper and gold respectively—made Butte and Helena two other important destinations in Montana. The NP and the Union Pacific appeared to have reached a "sphere of influence" agreement in the region as the NP initially stayed out of Butte and the UP out of Helena. Further mineral strikes meant that for a brief period Helena was America's richest city on a per capita basis until silver prices plummeted in 1893. For that reason, the NP found it politically necessary to serve Helena although the route to the city, which was reached in 1883, required crossing the Continental Divide over the difficult Mullan Pass fifteen miles to the west.

To the northwest at Missoula, a scenic crossroads of rivers and valleys, the NP created another division point, then ran north 35 miles to the Flathead and Clark's Fork. The more difficult Clark's Fork route out of Missoula became a branch road in the 1890s, not meeting the NP's main track. At picturesque Sandpoint, today a year-round tourist destination on the northern shore of Idaho's Lake Pend Oreille, the NP then cut southwest to complete its line at Spokane.

Flathead Lake looking southwards, from Vol. XII–Book I of *Explorations for a Route for a Pacific Railroad*, 1855.

CROSSING THE MISSOURI

The Million-Dollar Bridge

The completed Northern Pacific bridge across the Missouri River at Bismarck—the troublesome east pier is visible in foreground (top right)

The east pier being slid approximately 23 inches back into position, May 29, 1898 (bottom right)

Crossing the Missouri River proved to be a substantial challenge for the Northern Pacific. In 1871, the railroad started laying track east from Kalama, Washington and west from Duluth, Minnesota, keeping the work going throughout the harsh winter weather despite hardships and inevitable delays. In 1873, the line reached the Missouri River at Bismarck, North Dakota.

Unfortunately, the global economic depression and financial Panic of 1873 all but brought the Northern Pacific to its knees. The company's bonds were worthless, and payment to bondholders meant giving up much of the land it owned in North Dakota. The failure of Jay Cooke and Company brought the efforts to raise capital to a halt and the NP was forced to declare bankruptcy in 1875.

If the Northern Pacific was to survive, the railroad had to conquer and cross the Missouri River. As long as the road was cut into two parts by the river, the company could not be a long-term viable entity. The Northern Pacific continued to push on, however slowly, devising temporary solutions to the problem of not being able to bridge the river. In the summer, the NP used ferries to shift freight across the river. In the winter, beginning in the winter of 1877–8, track was annually laid over ice, thus permitting trains to operate for three or four months each winter. This feat attracted national attention.

These daring innovations kept freight inching forward. By mid-1879, however, the economy had slowly improved and Frederick Billings had become president of the NP. He was determined to push the construction project forward, but it would be ten long years before a bridge was completed.

In 1881, European investor Henry Villard bought control of the Northern Pacific, became the railroad's president, and hastened the building of the bridge. In October of that year the bridge was officially opened after a successful test of its strength involving eight locomotives moving out on the spans. The Missouri River Bridge cost an amazing amount of money for the time—$1 million dollars.

From the beginning the bridge had problems with shifting, and between 1882 and 1887 the massive east pier shifted an average of three inches a year. The engineering response was to move the pier itself to a larger and deeper foundation in 1898, but this did not prove to be a permanent solution for in 1902 the shifting problems returned. Despite its problems and all the necessary repairs, the bridge still stands today as a majestic example of engineering and perseverance.

The source of the Missouri, Three Forks, Montana, from *Lake Michigan to Puget Sound.*

The Northern Pacific bridge over the Missouri at Bismarck, North Dakota, from a postcard of *c.*1900. This shows the rebuilt bridge with round-topped trusses.

YELLOWSTONE PARK

The NP and the Great Sioux War

Title page of *Through Wonderland*, produced by the Northern Pacific *c.*1914; a postcard of a Northern Pacific train and the Gardiner Gateway, the entrance to Yellowstone Park (below).

A glimpse of Yellowstone River (right).

NATURAL WONDERS

Well before Philadelphia banker Jay Cooke signed papers on January 1, 1870 to finance the Northern Pacific Railroad, he was aware of credible rumors of an exceptional find of natural wonders located at the source of the Yellowstone River. He instantly recognized the tourist potential of the three hundred geysers, thousands of hot springs, boiling "pots" of mud, and more.

Cooke convinced Congress to finance an 1871 government survey of the region. This expedition's official report created an instant sensation, and Cooke's powerful lobbying machine went to work, persuading the 42nd Congress—a group of lawmakers considered amongst the most venal in US history—to pass legislation creating Yellowstone National Park on March 1, 1872, giving it 2,221,773 acres (some 3,468 square miles).

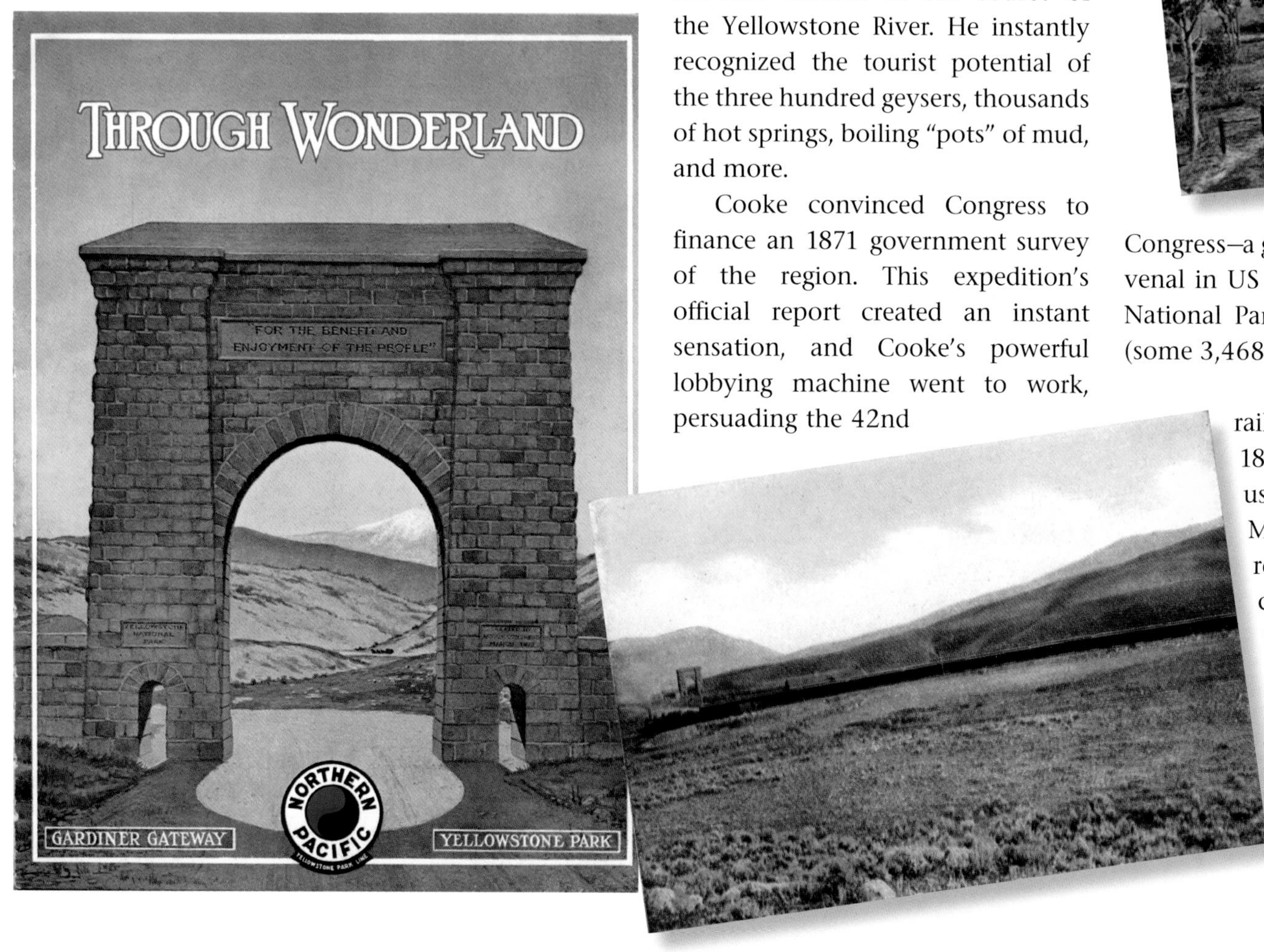

THROUGH WONDERLAND
FOR THE BENEFIT AND ENJOYMENT OF THE PEOPLE
NORTHERN PACIFIC
GARDINER GATEWAY
YELLOWSTONE PARK

Through a subsidiary, the Northern Pacific began railroad operations to the Park on September 22, 1883 from Livingston, Montana to Cinnabar, at first using stagecoaches for the final six miles to Gardiner, Montana in the north of the Park. An alternative route from Bozeman to West Yellowstone had been considered, but the one via Gardiner won on cost terms. The tracked grade and the Yellowstone National Park Hotel at Mammoth (Hot Springs) were completed in time for a visit by President Chester A. Arthur in 1883, during which rumors that a Mexican bandit was about to kidnap him caused a cavalry company from Fort Ellis to rush to his "rescue." The rail spur enabled many attending the 1883 "last spike" Gold

Creek ceremonies to visit the Park afterward, and for many years the NP was the means by which most visitors reached Yellowstone. The railroad proudly added "Yellowstone Park Line" to its logo.

An advertisement for Yellowstone Park, *c.*1913.

TREATY VIOLATIONS

Paralleling the government's Yellowstone Park activities, five surveying expeditions were undertaken during the summers of 1871, 1872 and 1873 by the NP and the US Army in the Yellowstone Valley, which was almost in the middle of the last great hunting grounds of the remaining northern Great Plains Indians such as the Lakota Sioux, Northern Cheyenne, and Arapaho. By choosing this route, the NP's surveys ended the fragile truce of the 1868 Fort Laramie Treaty between the US and the Plains Native Americans, and reignited the Great Sioux War. It also set the stage for the discovery of gold in the Black Hills and the 1876–7 military campaigns which helped send the Northern Pacific into bankruptcy and contributed to the Panic of 1873.

On October 4, 1871, a 500-strong survey party from Fort Rice on the Missouri River, some twenty miles south of present-day Bismarck, North Dakota, reached the Yellowstone and accomplished the major goal of finding a railroad route through the Badlands. That winter, however, the great militant Sioux leader, Sitting Bull, discovered the purpose of the expeditions and announced that the surveyors would be killed if they entered the Yellowstone Valley. By late July 1872 at least 2,000 warriors had gathered along the Powder River to defend their lands.

The NP's plan in 1872 was to complete its "line of survey" by sending parties from east and west to meet in Montana at the junction of the Powder and Yellowstone Rivers. The expeditions went ahead, leading to the first hostilities. Amongst the dead was Lieutenant Lewis Dent Adair, a first cousin of President U. S. Grant's wife, Julia Dent Grant. His death considerably embarrassed the Army and caused great anger in the Grant family, arguably hardening the President's attitude towards the Lakota.

To both overawe Sitting Bull and his Sioux, Cheyenne, and Arapaho allies, and to complete the Northern Pacific's engineering survey, in 1873 the Army fielded a force of 1,535 officers and men, including Lieutenant Colonel George A. Custer. A Scientific Corps and a group of newspaper correspondents also joined the column.

A front-page illustration featuring the exploits of Sitting Bull, from *Harpers Weekly*, December 8, 1877.

On August 4, Custer's ninety-strong scouting force barely escaped a hastily planned ambush by 200-plus Sioux and Cheyenne, then coped with a separate, small-scale ambush. Custer gave chase, and on August 11 Sitting Bull had some 350 mounted warriors swim the Yellowstone and attack Custer in a pincer movement. The piecemeal attack was defeated and, without further incident, the Northern Pacific's engineers completed their surveying, only to discover that the Panic of 1873 had begun.

Sitting Bull's opposition cost the Northern Pacific engineers an extra year to complete their work as well as ending Jay Cooke's ability to sell its stock. Custer's dramatic report of the fighting, coupled with stories from the 1873 survey's correspondents, made the public feel that the Northern Pacific was being built through a "war zone." This had a significant business impact as the negative publicity crippled Jay Cooke's efforts to sell NP bonds. The railroad had planned to construct track between Bismarck and the Yellowstone in 1874, but its bankruptcy halted construction at Bismarck.

AFTERMATH

No longer needed for "escort" duty, Custer was sent to explore the Black Hills with an unstated goal of seeing if rumors of gold deposits were true. The discovery of gold and the resulting "rush" was to further contract Sioux and Cheyenne hunting grounds.

As for Yellowstone Park, Gardiner might not have been the best choice for the NP. When visitor numbers rose, it was clear that the Old Faithful geyser to the west of the Park was the most popular attraction, and as competing trains began serving West Yellowstone from 1908, the NP's Gardiner route slowly forfeited its primacy.

The Land of Geysers, front cover of a Northern Pacific promotional booklet from 1915 (right).

A bird's-eye view of the park, from *Through Wonderland*, published by the Northern Pacific, *c.*1912 (far right).

Absaroka Range
Grand Cañon
Yellowstone Lake
Lower Fall
Upper Fall
Lake Colonial Hotel
Cañon Hotel
Thumb Lunch Station
Three Tetons and Shoshone Lake
Norris Geyser Basin
Upper Geyser Basin and Old Faithful Inn
Lower Geyser Basin and Fountain Hotel
Midway Geyser Basin
Firehole River
Madison River
Tower Fall
Mount Washburn
Dunraven Peak
Hedges Peak
Mount Everts
Yellowstone River
Gardiner River
Mammoth Hot Springs and Hotel
Obsidian Cliff
Golden Gate
Gardiner Station and Entrance Arch
Electric Peak

STAMPEDE PASS

Tunnel through the Cascades

For the Northern Pacific, the 1880s were years of economic rebuilding, competition, and construction. While the country was recovering from the Panic of 1873, the NP was recovering from bankruptcy it had declared in 1875.

At the same time, the cities of Seattle and Tacoma were competing with each other to become the northwestern terminus of the expanding transcontinental railroad system. As required by its charter, the Northern Pacific was intent upon completing a direct connection to the Puget Sound area. If the railroad failed to do this, the penalty was to be the forfeiture of millions of acres of land grants back to the federal government. Anxious to have this connection completed, the government gave the Northern Pacific an ultimatum and an extremely tight deadline.

The western entrance to the Cascade Tunnel, a postcard from 1908.

The first obstacle was finding a way through the steep and densely wooded western slope of the Cascade Mountain Range. It was not until the NP hired Virgil Bogue (1846–1916) in the early 1880s, a civil engineer with substantial experience building railroads in and through mountain ranges, that the company had an employee who was capable of locating a route and engineering a railway to reach the Sound. Bogue agreed to locate a way through the Cascades for the NP, but his initial efforts in 1880 proved futile.

Starting his search again in 1881, Bogue discovered a pass. While it wasn't ideal—a perfect pass would have a long and gentle slope—it was still possible to locate a portion of the railroad there. Construction began with several switchbacks on both the east and the west sides of the Cascades. The grade was substantial. Work crews carried in their supplies and equipment, setting up several work camps along the way.

At the same time as the crews were working on the switchbacks approaching Stampede Pass, other crews were preparing to complete the direct connection to Puget Sound. This would be a tunnel going under the pass through two miles of granite rock.

Construction on what was to become known as Stampede Tunnel began in February 1886 and was finished in late May 1888. It cost more than $1,000,000 and, unfortunately, the lives of 33 laborers as well. Construction was not easy on either the switchbacks or the tunnel as annual winter snowfalls of up to forty feet are not uncommon. Work was finished in time to beat the deadline, however, and the Northern Pacific, along with the population of the Seattle and Tacoma area celebrated, once again, the completion of a transcontinental link.

The Stampede Tunnel was expanded with another track (double tracked) between 1912 and 1915, thereby improving its ability and efficiency at handling cross-country traffic. But how did Stampede Pass and Tunnel get their unusual names? As one of the legends goes, a rather unpleasant foreman was assigned to the project, resulting in the work crews "stampeding" back to Seattle.

The West Slope of the Cascades, from *Lake Michigan to Puget Sound*.

Through Pacific Coast and California tickets are honored via Seattle.

Northern Pacific Railway

ARRANGEMENT OF THROUGH CAR SERVICE.

Train No. 1—WESTBOUND. THE NORTH COAST LIMITED, VIA BUTTE AND SEATTLE. Train No. 2—EASTBOUND.

Broad Vestibuled Electric Lighted, Steam Heated Train—St. Paul to Portland, via Butte, Spokane, Seattle and Tacoma—Daily.

Observation Library Car, with Barber and Bath, St. Paul and Minneapolis to Portland.

Pullman Sleeping Car St. Paul and Minneapolis to Portland.

Pullman Sleeping Car Seattle to Portland.

Pullman Sleeping Car Tacoma to Portland.

Pullman Tourist Sleeping Car St. Paul and Minneapolis to Portland.

Dining Car and First and Second-class Coaches St. Paul and Minneapolis to Portland.

Day	Daily.	STATIONS.	Daily.	Day
1st	10 15 A M	lve....St. Paul....arr.	2 20 P M	4th
"	10 45 A M	lve...Minneapolis..arr.	1 50 P M	"
"	8 30 A M	lve....Duluth.....arr.	6 25 P M	"
"	8 45 A M	lve....Superior....arr.	6 10 P M	"
"	5 25 P M	lve....Fargo......arr.	7 00 A M	"
2d	11 07 A M	arr....Billings....lve.	9 10 A M	3d
"	2 25 P M	arr...Livingston...lve.	6 15 A M	"
"	6 55 P M	arr....Helena.....lve.	12 01 Night	2d
"	7 30 P M	arr....Butte......lve.	12 50 Night	"
"	8 50 P M	arr...Anaconda....lve.	9 50 P M	"
"	11 15 P M	arr...Missoula....lve.	8 25 P M	"
3d	6 45 A M	arr....Spokane....lve.	10 50 A M	"
"	8 15 P M	arr....Tacoma.....lve.	7 25 P M	1st
"	8 15 P M	arr....Seattle.....lve.	9 30 P M	"
4th	7 00 A M	arr....Portland....lve.	2 00 P M	1st

Broad Vestibuled, Electric Lighted, Steam Heated Train—Portland to St. Paul, via Tacoma, Seattle, Spokane and Butte—Daily.

Observation Library Car, with Barber and Bath, Portland to Minneapolis and St. Paul.

Pullman Sleeping Car Portland to Minneapolis and St. Paul.

Pullman Sleeping Car Tacoma to Spokane.

Pullman Sleeping Car Butte to Minneapolis and St. Paul.

Pullman Sleeping Car Livingston to Minneapolis and St. Paul from Yellowstone Park.

Pullman Tourist Sleeping Car Portland to Minneapolis and St. Paul.

Dining Car, First and Second-class Coaches Portland to Minneapolis and St. Paul.

Train No. 3—WESTBOUND. PACIFIC AND TWIN CITY EXPRESS, VIA HELENA. Train No. 4—EASTBOUND.

Broad Vestibuled, Steam Heated Train—St. Paul to Portland, via Helena, Spokane and Tacoma—Daily.

Pullman Sleeping Car St. Paul and Minneapolis to Portland, via Helena. Pullman Sleeping Car St. Paul and Minneapolis to Butte. Pullman Sleeping Car St. Paul and Minneapolis to Winnipeg. Pullman Sleeping Car St. Paul and Minneapolis to Gardiner (Yellowstone Park). Pullman Sleeping Car Gardiner to Portland. Pullman Sleeping Car and Chair Car Helena to Seattle (from Kansas City), and Tourist Sleeping Car Helena to Seattle (from St. Louis), via C. B. & Q. Ry. and Billings. Pullman Sleeping Car Denver to Gardiner. Through Dining Car Service. Pullman Tourist Sleeping Car St. Paul and Minneapolis to Portland. Dining Car and First and Second-class Coaches St. Paul and Minneapolis to Winnipeg and Portland.

Day	Daily.	STATIONS.	Daily.	Day
1st	10 15 P M	lve....St. Paul....arr.	7 40 A M	5th
"	10 45 P M	lve...Minneapolis..arr.	7 05 A M	"
"	7 30 P M	lve....Duluth.....arr.	7 55 A M	"
"	7 45 P M	lve....Superior....arr.	7 40 A M	"
2d	2 00 P M	arr....Winnipeg....lve.		
"	6 00 A M	arr....Fargo......lve.	10 55 P M	4th
1st	9 01 P M	lve....St. Louis....arr.	6 50 P M	5th
2d	9 50 A M	lve...Kansas City...arr.	11 40 A M	"
"	8 30 P M	lve....Denver.....arr.		
3d	1 05 A M	arr....Billings....lve.	11 00 P M	3d
"	4 50 A M	arr...Livingston...lve.	7 40 P M	"
"	9 50 A M	arr....Helena.....lve.	2 25 P M	"
"	10 47 A M	arr....Butte......lve.	12 45 Noon	"
"	1 35 P M	arr...Anaconda....lve.	11 10 A M	"
"	9 50 P M	arr....Spokane....lve.	10 40 P M	2d
4th	1 15 P M	arr....Tacoma.....lve.	7 45 A M	"
"	1 15 P M	arr....Seattle.....lve.	7 45 A M	"
"	6 50 P M	arr....Portland....lve.	11 45 P M	1st

Broad Vestibuled Steam Heated Train—Portland to St. Paul, via Tacoma, Seattle, Spokane and Helena—Daily.

Pullman Sleeping Car Portland to Minneapolis and St. Paul.

Pullman Sleeping Car Portland to Seattle.

Pullman Sleeping Car Portland to Tacoma.

Pullman Sleeping Car Seattle to Helena.

Pullman Sleeping Car and Chair Car, Seattle to Helena (through to Kansas City), and Tourist Sleeping Car Seattle to Helena (through to St. Louis), via Billings and the C. B. & Q. Ry. Through Dining Car Service.

Pullman Tourist Sleeping Car Portland to Minneapolis and St. Paul.

Dining Car Seattle to Minneapolis and St. Paul.

First and Second-class Coaches Portland to Minneapolis and St. Paul.

Train No. 5—WESTBOUND. WESTERN AND EASTERN EXPRESS. Train No. 6—EASTBOUND.

Broad Vestibuled—St. Paul and Minneapolis to Seattle and Tacoma, via Butte and Spokane, with direct connections to and from Helena and to Portland.

Pullman Sleeping Cars St. Paul and Minneapolis to Tacoma, St. Paul and Minneapolis to Fargo, Duluth to Fargo and Billings to Seattle. Dining Car St. Paul and Minneapolis to Seattle and through service from St. Louis and Kansas City. Pullman Tourist Cars St. Paul and Minneapolis to Seattle and Billings to Seattle. Reclining Chair Car—Billings to Seattle. First and Second-class Coaches St. Paul and Minneapolis to Seattle. First-class Coach—St. Paul and Minneapolis to Jamestown and Leeds, N.D. NOTE.—Pullman and Tourist Sleeping Cars and Second-class Coach from Kansas City and Chair Car from St. Louis, via C. B. & Q. Ry., and Billings.

Day	Daily.	STATIONS.	Daily.	Day
1st	10 35 P M	lve....St. Paul....arr.	6 20 P M	4th
"	11 05 P M	lve...Minneapolis..arr.	5 50 P M	"
"	7 30 P M	lve....Duluth.....arr.	6 25 P M	"
"	7 45 P M	lve....Superior....arr.	6 10 P M	"
2d	7 40 A M	arr....Fargo......lve.	9 10 P M	"
1st	8 02 A M	lve....St. Louis....arr.	7 19 A M	5th
"	6 05 P M	lve...Kansas City...arr.	11 20 P M	4th
"	7 45 P M	lve....St. Joseph...arr.	8 55 P M	"
"	11 10 P M	lve....Omaha.....arr.	7 40 P M	"
		lve....Denver.....arr.	10 55 A M	"
3d	7 50 A M	lve....Billings....lve.	8 40 A M	3d
"	11 32 A M	arr...Livingston...lve.	5 10 A M	"
"	4 45 P M	arr....Butte......lve.	11 40 P M	2d
"	8 50 P M	arr...Anaconda....lve.	9 50 P M	"
4th	5 00 A M	arr....Spokane....lve.	12 25 P M	"
"	8 00 P M	arr....Seattle.....lve.	3 00 P M	1st
"	7 55 P M	arr....Tacoma.....lve.	3 00 P M	"
5th	9 05 P M	arr....Portland....lve.	3 50 P M	"

Broad Vestibuled—Tacoma and Seattle to Minneapolis and St. Paul, via Spokane and Butte, with direct connections from Portland and to and from Helena.

Pullman Sleeping Cars Tacoma to Minneapolis and St. Paul, Portland to Gardiner (Yellowstone Park) Seattle to Billings, Helena to Billings and Gardiner to Denver. Dining Car Seattle to Minneapolis and St. Paul and through service to Kansas City. Pullman Tourist Sleeping Cars Seattle to Minneapolis and St. Paul, and Seattle to Billings. Reclining Chair Cars Seattle to Billings. First and Second-class Coaches Seattle to Minneapolis and St. Paul, Northome and M. & I. points to Minneapolis and St. Paul. NOTE.—Pullman Sleeping Car and Reclining Chair Car for Kansas City and Tourist Sleeping Car for St. Louis, via Billings and C. B. & Q. Ry.

Train No. 7—WESTBOUND. MINNESOTA AND DAKOTA LOCAL. Train No. 8—EASTBOUND.

St. Paul, Minneapolis, Duluth and Superior to Brainerd M. & I. Points and Jamestown.

Dining Car St. Paul and Minneapolis to Fargo.

First and Second-class Coaches St. Paul and Minneapolis to Jamestown and St. Paul and Minneapolis to Northome.

Day	Daily.	STATIONS.	Daily.	Day
1st	8 20 A M	lve....St. Paul....arr.	7 25 A M	2d
"	8 50 A M	lve...Minneapolis..arr.	6 50 A M	"
"	8 30 A M	lve....Duluth.....arr.	7 55 A M	"
"	8 45 A M	lve....Superior....arr.	7 40 A M	"
"	3 28 P M	arr....Detroit.....lve.	11 55 P M	1st
		arr...Crookston...lve.	8 25 P M	"
		arr..Grand Forks..lve.	7 25 P M	"
		arr....Grafton....lve.	5 40 P M	"
		arr...Winnipeg....lve.	1 40 P M	"
1st	4 55 P M	arr...Moorhead....lve.	9 45 P M	1st
"	5 00 P M	arr....Fargo......lve.	9 40 P M	"
"	9 05 P M	arr...Jamestown....lve.	3 50 P M	"

Winnipeg, Leeds, N.D., and Jamestown to Minneapolis, St. Paul, Duluth and Superior—Daily

Pullman Sleeping Car Winnipeg to Minneapolis and St. Paul.

Pullman Sleeping Car Fargo to Minneapolis and St. Paul.

Pullman Sleeping Car Fargo to Duluth.

First and Second-class Coaches Winnipeg to Minneapolis and St. Paul, via Grand Forks and Crookston.

Through First and Second-class Coaches Leeds and Jamestown to Minneapolis and St. Paul.

Dining Car Pembina to Grand Forks.

Trains Nos. 13 and 14—"PUGET SOUND LIMITED"—Between Seattle and Portland—Parlor and Dining Cars—Daily.

"DULUTH SHORT LINE."

Daily. No. 106	Daily. No. 104	Ex. Sun. No. 102	STATIONS.	Ex. Sun. No. 101	Daily. No. 103	Daily. No. 105
10 30 P M	2 00 P M	8 15 A M	lve.......Minneapolis.......arr.	3 30 P M	7 00 P M	7 00 A M
11 10 P M	2 25 P M	8 55 A M	lve.........St. Paul.........arr.	2 50 P M	6 25 P M	6 20 A M
5 55 A M	6 35 P M	2 19 P M	arr.........Superior.........lve.	8 45 A M	2 19 P M	11 39 P M
6 30 A M	7 00 P M	2 19 P M	arr.........Duluth..........lve.	9 00 A M	1 55 P M	11 10 P M

Trains 101 and 102—Through Cafe Parlor Observation Car and Broad Vestibule First-class Coaches.
Trains 103 and 104—Electric Lighted, Steam Heated Observation Cafe and Parlor Cars. First-class Coach and Combination Baggage and Smoking Car.
Trains 105 and 106—Broad Vestibuled Sleeping Cars and First-class Coaches. Passengers may occupy Sleeping Cars at 9 00 p.m. and remain in them until 8 00 a.m.

YELLOWSTONE PARK ROUTE.

ST. PAUL, MINNEAPOLIS AND PACIFIC COAST LINE.

9	5	7	3	1	Mls	June 10, 1906.	2	4	8	6	10
P M	P M	A M	P M	A M	....	(Central time.)	P M	A M	A M	P M	A M
†6 30	*10 35	*8 20	*10 15	*10 15	0	lve....+St. Paul ♂...arr.	2 20	7 40	7 25	6 20	10 30
7 00	11 05	8 50	10 45	10 45	11	lve...Minneapolis ♂.arr.	1 50	7 05	6 50	5 50	10 00
7 42	11 50	9 33	- -	- -	29	+........Anoka........♂	- -	6 25	6 08	5 08	9 17
8 03	12 12	9 55	- -	- -	41	.........Elk River......♂	- -	- -	5 47	4 45	8 55
8 18	12 32	10 12	- -	- -	49	..........Big Lake......♂	- -	- -	5 30	4 28	8 37
8 32	12 45	10 23	- -	- -	57	...........Becker.......♂	- -	- -	5 17	4 13	8 22
8 43	12 58	10 35	- -	- -	64	.........Clear Lake.....♂	- -	- -	5 05	4 00	8 08
9 05	1 21	10 55	12 35	12 45	76	+......St. Cloud......♂	11 50	5 05	4 45	3 40	7 47
9 10	1 25	11 00	- -	- -	77	+....Sauk Rapids....♂	- -	- -	4 40	3 32	7 42
9 34	1 47	11 29	- -	- -	90	+..........Rices........♂	- -	- -	4 18	3 09	7 18
9 45	2 00	11 42	- -	- -	97	.........Royalton.......♂	- -	- -	4 05	2 58	7 06
10 05	2 20	12 15	1 23	1 35	108	+.....Little Falls.....♂	11 01	4 05	3 45	2 40	6 45
....	3 27	1 20	2 20	2 30	142	arr.....+Staples ♂...lve.	*10 12	2 55	2 30	1 30	....
†10 10	....	†12 15	....	†10 10	108	lve..+Little Falls....arr.	6 40	....	....	2 25	6 40
10 22	....	12 27	....	10 22	112	.......Belle Prairie.....♂	6 26	....	....	2 10	6 26
10 40	....	12 44	....	10 40	121	........Fort Ripley.....♂	6 10	....	....	1 54	6 10
10 59	....	1 03	....	10 59	130	........Crow Wing........	5 57	....	....	1 42	5 57
11 15	....	1 20	....	11 15	138	+.......Brainerd.......♂	†5 45	....	....	†1 30	†5 45
P M	....	P M	....	P M	....	ARRIVE] [LEAVE	A M	....	....	P M	A M
....	....	Noon	Night	Noon	....	LEAVE] [ARRIVE	P M	A M	....	P M	....
....	....	*12 20	*12 05	*12 20	138	+.......Brainerd........	2 25	3 55	....	2 25	....
....	....	12 43	12 31	12 43	142	..........Pillager.........	2 03	3 31	....	2 03	....
....	....	12 58	12 47	12 58	160	..........Motley........♂	1 48	3 17	....	1 48	....
....	....	1 10	1 00	1 10	167	arr.....+Staples.....lve.	*1 35	*3 05	....	*1 35	....
....	3 40	1 35	2 27	2 37	142	lve....+Staples.....arr.	10 05	2 45	2 15	1 10	....
....	3 53	1 47	- -	- -	149	..........Aldrich..........	- -	- -	1 59	12 56	....
....	4 01	1 55	- -	- -	153	+.......Verndale.......♂	- -	- -	1 50	12 48	....
....	4 15	2 08	- -	- -	159	+.......Wadena........♂	- -	2 10	1 35	12 35	....
....	4 25	2 18	- -	- -	164	..........Bluffton..........	- -	- -	1 24	12 26	....
....	4 41	2 33	- -	- -	172	.....New York Mills...♂	- -	- -	1 07	12 10	....
....	5 00	2 50	- -	- -	183	..........Perham.......♂	- -	- -	12 42	11 49	....
....	5 38	3 28	4 04	4 03	204	+.........Detroit.......♂	8 31	12 53	11 55	11 05	....
....	5 53	3 41	- -	- -	211	.........Audubon.......♂	- -	- -	11 37	10 51	....
....	6 04	3 51	- -	- -	217	.........Lake Park.....♂	- -	- -	11 25	10 41	....
....	6 20	4 05	4 47	- -	224	+..Winnipeg Junc...♂	- -	h -	11 05	10 24	....
....	6 37	4 20	- -	- -	231	.........Muskoda.......♂	- -	- -	10 24	10 06	....
....	6 53	4 36	5 15	- -	241	+.......Glyndon.......♂	- -	- -	10 06	9 49	....
....	7 14	4 55	5 35	- -	249	+.....Moorhead......♂	7 14	11 15	9 45	9 30	....
....	7 20	5 00	5 40	5 15	250	arr......+Fargo..♂..lve.	7 10	11 10	9 40	9 25	....
....	7 40	5 35	6 00	5 25	250	lve.......Fargo.......arr.	7 00	10 55	7 30	9 10	....
....	8 08	6 02	- -	- -	263	+.......Mapleton......♂	- -	10 25	6 54	8 40	....
....	8 25	6 19	6 39	- -	270	+.......Casselton......♂	6 17	10 10	6 38	8 25	....
....	8 39	6 34	- -	- -	277	+.....Wheatland.......♂	- -	- -	6 22	8 07	....
....	9 00	6 55	- -	- -	286	..........Buffalo.........♂	- -	- -	5 57	7 39	....
....	9 13	7 08	- -	- -	292	+......Tower City.......♂	- -	- -	5 47	7 22	....
....	9 26	7 20	- -	- -	298	..........Oriska..........♂	- -	- -	5 37	7 07	....
....	9 49	7 45	7 53	7 00	308	+......Valley City......♂	5 05	8 45	5 16	6 40	....
....	10 18	8 15	8 22	- -	319	+.......Sanborn........♂	- -	8 15	4 46	6 21	....
....	11 10	9 05	9 00	8 05	343	arr.+Jamestown..♀lve.	4 10	7 20	*3 50	*5 45	....
....	4 45	P M	....	....	451	arr.....+Leeds ♂....lve.	....	....	†10 15	....	....
....	11 45		- -	- -	350	..........Eldridge..........	- -	- -	A M	5 22	....
....	12 33		- -	- -	372	..........Medina........♂	- -	6 11		4 43	....
....	12 47		- -	- -	380	......Crystal Springs......	- -	- -	....	4 28	....
....	1 15		- -	- -	393	+........Dawson........♂	- -	5 28	....	4 03	....
....	1 35		- -	- -	401	..........Steele..........♂	- -	5 12	....	3 50	....
....	2 13		- -	- -	420	.........Sterling.........♂	- -	4 33	....	- -	....
....	2 27		- -	- -	426	........McKenzie.......♂	- -	4 20	....	- -	....
....	3 05		12 05	10 58	445	+......Bismarck.......♂	1 07	3 43	....	2 28	....
....	3 25		12 25	11 20	450	arr....+Mandan ♂...lve.	12 50	3 25	....	2 10	....
....	....		....	....	....	Mountain time — West — One hour earlier than Central time.	....	....	....	....	....
....	2 35		11 35	10 30	450	lve....+Mandan ♂...arr.	11 40	2 15	....	1 00	....
....	3 40		12 28	- -	479	........New Salem......♂	- -	1 21	....	11 55	....
....	3 57		- -	- -	484	...........Sims..........♂	- -	- -	....	11 32	....
....	4 35		1 19	- -	508	........Glenullen.......♂	- -	12 20	....	10 53	....
....	4 57		1 39	- -	521	..........Hebron........♂	- -	11 55	....	10 33	....
....	5 58		- -	- -	549	........Gladstone.......♂	- -	- -	....	9 40	....
....	6 35		3 00	1 40	560	+......Dickinson.......♂	8 05	10 37	....	9 20	....
....	7 20		- -	- -	580	.........Belfield........♂	- -	- -	....	8 32	....
....	7 57		4 11	- -	600	.........Medora.........♂	- -	9 03	....	7 37	....
....	8 41		- -	- -	616	......Sentinel Butte.....♂	- -	- -	....	7 10	....
....	9 30		5 19	- -	635	.........Wibaux.........♂	- -	7 52	....	6 35	....
....	10 45		6 25	5 00	666	+.......Glendive........♂	4 10	6 45	....	5 20	....
....	11 13		- -	- -	681	...........Hoyt..........♂	- -	- -	....	4 46	....
....	12 10		7 30	- -	705	...........Terry..........♂	- -	5 23	....	3 57	....
....	12 55		- -	- -	725	..........Shirley.........♂	- -	- -	....	3 18	....
....	1 39		8 36	7 03	745	+......Miles City.......♂	1 42	4 07	....	2 38	....
....	1 48		- -	- -	747	........Fort Keogh......♂	- -	- -	....	2 32	....
....	2 08		- -	- -	756	..........Horton..........	- -	- -	....	2 14	....
....	2 29		- -	- -	765	........Hathaway.......♂	- -	- -	....	1 56	....
....	2 58		9 33	- -	778	.........Rosebud........♂	- -	2 58	....	1 32	....
....	3 30		10 05	8 22	790	.........Forsythe........♂	12 26	2 32	....	1 05	....
....	4 54		- -	- -	833	........Big Horn........♂	- -	- -	....	11 30	....
....	5 10	.....	11 27	- -	839	..........Custer..........♂	- -	12 50	....	11 16	....
....	5 26	.....	- -	- -	847	...........Waco...........	- -	- -	....	11 01	....
....	5 55	43	- -	- -	863	......Pompey's Pillar...♂	- -	- -	44	10 34	....
....	6 33	Night	- -	- -	879	.........Huntley.........♂	- -	- -	P M	9 58	....
....	7 50	*12 10	1 15	11 17	892	+.......Billings........♂	9 20	11 10	10 30	9 30	....
....	8 15	12 37	- -	- -	907	..........Laurel..........♂	- -	- -	10 05	8 15	....
....	8 30	12 52	- -	- -	915	........Park City.......♂	- -	- -	9 51	8 00	....
....	9 05	1 30	- -	- -	932	+.......Columbus.......♂	- -	- -	9 18	7 28	....
....	9 31	1 58	- -	- -	949	........Reedpoint.......♂	- -	- -	8 46	6 55	....
....	9 58	2 27	- -	- -	962	.........Greycliff........♂	- -	- -	8 26	6 35	....
....	10 22	2 49	3 36	- -	973	+......Big Timber......♂	7 05	8 37	8 04	6 13	....
....	10 51	3 23	- -	- -	988	........Springdale.......♂	- -	- -	7 40	5 50	....
....	11 30	4 05	4 50	2 25	1007	arr.+Livingston..♂lve.	*6 15	*7 40	*7 10	*5 10	....
....	A M	A M	A M	P M	1061	arr...Yellowstone Park..lve.	A M	P M	P M	A M	....

* Daily; † daily, except Sunday; *h* stops to leave passengers from west of Fargo. + Coupon stations; ♂ Telegraph stations.

Standards.—East of Mandan, *Central time.* Between Mandan and Trout Creek, *Mountain time.* West of Trout Creek, *Pacific time.*

43	5	3	1	Mls	June 10, 1906.	2	4	6-8	44
A M	A M	A M	P M	....	(Mountain time.)	A M	P M	A M	P M
*4 15	*11 40	*5 00	*2 35	1007	lv.+Livingston...ar.	6 05	7 30	5 00	7 00
4 53	12 13	- -	- -	1019	..........Muir.........♂	- -	- -	4 29	- -
5 16	12 26	- -	- -	1024	.......Chestnut.......♂	- -	- -	4 15	6 14
5 39	12 45	6 16	3 40	1032	+.....Bozeman......♂	4 53	6 20	3 55	5 53
5 56	1 02	- -	- -	1042	+.....Belgrade......♂	- -	- -	3 29	5 25
6 14	1 20	- -	- -	1051	......Manhattan.....♂	- -	- -	3 04	5 01
6 26	1 30	7 02	4 15	1057	arr......Logan ♂...lve.	3 48	5 15	2 50	4 48
....	1 35	7 10	4 20	1057	lve......Logan ♂...arr.	3 43	3 50	2 45	....
....	- -	7 19	- -	1063	......Three Forks...♂	- -	3 36	- -	....
....	2 05	7 45	- -	1076	.....Sappington....♂	- -	3 13	2 02	....
....	2 40	8 27	- -	1095	+....Whitehall.....♂	2 35	2 40	1 25	....
....	- -	10 01	- -	1118	.......Homestake....♂	- -	1 27	- -	....
....	4 45	10 47	7 30	1128	arr....+Butte.......♂	12 50	12 45	11 40	....
....	5 45	1 35	8 50	1153	arr.+Anaconda ♂.lve.	*9 50	*11 10	*9 50	....
6 31	....	7 07	4 25	1057	lve......Logan.....arr.	2 15	5 10	....	4 43
7 16	....	- -	5 09	1077	+.....Lombard......♂	1 38	- -	....	3 58
8 02	....	8 27	5 44	1097	+.....Townsend.....♂	1 05	3 43	....	3 18
8 45	....	- -	6 11	1110	.........Winston......♂	12 40	- -	....	2 55
9 15	....	- -	6 42	1126	+.Prickly Pear Jn. ♂	12 09	- -	....	- -
9 30	P M	9 50	6 55	1130	arr...+Helena ♂...lve.	*12 01	2 25	P M	*2 15
A M	*4 10	10 10	P M	1130	lve.....Helena....arr.	Night	1 55	11 20	P M
	- -	- -	Via Butte Branch.	1139	..Clough Junction..	Via Butte Branch.	- -	- -	
	4 45	- -		1143	.........Austin........♂		1 18	10 44	
	5 20	11 15		1151	.......Blossburg......♂		1 00	10 25	
	5 38	11 32		1159	........Elliston........♂		12 32	10 00	
	5 58	- -		1168	..........Avon..........♂		12 09	9 40	
	6 20	12 07		1181	ar..+Garrison..♂.lv.		11 40	*9 10	
	*4 55	*9 50	*7 40	1232	lve....+Butte....arr.	12 40	2 50	11 30	
	6 30	12 12	9 15	1181	lve..+Garrison...arr.	10 37	11 35	9 0[illegible]	
	7 13	12 45	- -	1202	+ ...Drummond...♂	- -	10 50	8 08	
	7 38	1 03	- -	1214	......Bearmouth....♂	- -	10 25	7 38	
	8 20	1 38	- -	1237	........Clinton.......♂	- -	9 40	6 47	
	8 40	1 57	- -	1248	........Bonner........♂	- -	9 20	6 26	
	9 10	2 20	11 25	1255	+....Missoula.......♂	8 25	9 05	6 05	
	- -	- -	- -	1261	......De Smet.......♂	- -	- -	5 40	
	9 55	3 00	- -	1271	.........Evaro.........♂	- -	8 15	5 15	
	10 41	3 41	- -	1292	+.......Ravalli........♂	- -	7 15	4 10	
	10 55	- -	- -	1299	.........Dixon.........♂	- -	- -	3 55	
	11 52	4 45	- -	1332	.........Plains........♂	- -	6 05	2 56	
	12 15	- -	- -	1346	.........Eddy..........♂	- -	- -	2 27	
	12 35	5 30	2 40	1357	+ ..Thompson Falls..♂	- -	5 15	2 06	
	1 25	6 20	3 40	....	arr. *Mountain time* lve.	4 15	4 30	1 25	
	12 25	5 20	2 40	....	arr..*Pacific time*..lve.	3 15	3 30	12 25	
	.....	.....	.....	1380	....Trout Creek..♂	.....	.....	.....	
	1 30	6 30	3 45	....	lve. *Mountain time* arr.	4 10	4 25	1 20	
	12 30	5 30	2 45	....	lve..*Pacific time*..arr.	3 10	3 25	12 20	
	1 22	- -	- -	1405	..........Heron........♂	- -	- -	11 20	
	2 10	7 08	- -	1428	.........Hope.........♂	1 38	1 33	10 23	....
....	2 40	7 38	- -	1444	+....Sand Point....♂	1 07	1 02	9 47	16
....	4 05	8 57	- -	1486	+.Rathdrum, Idaho.♂	11 44	11 35	8 08	and
15-7	- -	- -	- -	1492	..Hauser Junction..	- -	- -	- -	14
P M	5 00	9 50	6 45	1513	arr..+Spokane.♂lve.	10 50	10 40	7 05	P M
*4 00	5 10	10 00	6 55	1513	lve....Spokane...arr.	10 40	10 30	6 55	3 40
- -	- -	- -	- -	1522	......Marshall.....♂	- -	- -	6 30	3 17
4 45	5 47	10 35	- -	1529	+.....Cheney......♂	- -	9 50	- -	3 00
5 30	6 37	11 22	- -	1554	+.....Sprague.....♂	- -	8 50	5 15	2 02
6 14	7 25	12 06	8 48	1577	+.....Ritzville.....♂	8 35	8 10	4 35	1 20
6 50	8 00	12 40	- -	1595	+........Lind........♂	- -	7 30	3 55	12 40
7 57	8 52	- -	- -	1623	........Connell......♂	- -	6 22	2 52	11 40
9 15	10 10	3 00	11 30	1658	+.......Pasco.......♂	5 55	5 23	1 30	10 20
9 25	10 20	3 10	- -	1661	......Kennewick....♂	- -	5 00	- -	10 00
10 12	11 05	- -	- -	1682	.........Kiona........♂	- -	4 22	- -	9 02
10 50	11 40	4 30	- -	1699	........Prosser.......♂	- -	3 50	- -	8 10
11 20	12 05	4 55	- -	1710	+......Mabton.......♂	- -	3 27	- -	7 45
12 05	12 45	5 37	- -	1729	......Toppenish....♂	- -	2 50	10 43	7 05
1 00	1 25	6 20	2 15	1748	+...North Yakima...♂	3 20	2 15	10 05	6 20
2 47	2 53	8 00	3 47	1785	+....Ellensburg.....♂	2 20	1 07	8 50	4 55
3 06	- -	- -	- -	1793	.........Thorp........♂	- -	12 45	- -	4 30
3 50	3 42	8 56	- -	1810	+.....Clealum.......♂	- -	12 10	7 47	3 50
4 18	4 05	9 25	- -	1823	.........Easton.......♂	- -	11 45	- -	3 25
4 42	- -	- -	- -	1831	.........Martin.......♂	- -	- -	- -	3 05
5 25	- -	- -	- -	1847	.........Lester........♂	- -	10 35	6 05	2 15
5 30	5 13	10 40	6 00	1849	......Hot Springs......	11 55	10 30	6 00	2 10
6 20	6 07	11 27	- -	1870	......Kanaskat......	- -	9 35	4 55	1 16
7 10	6 55	12 15	7 15	1890	arr....Auburn ♂..lve.	10 15	8 40	4 00	12 20
8 10	8 00	1 15	8 15	1913	arr..+Seattle..♂lve.	*9 30	*7 45	*3 00	*11 30
*6 30	*6 15	11 15	*6 15	1913	lve....Seattle...arr.	9 10	.....	.....	1 10
7 20	7 05	12 25	7 25	1890	lve....Auburn....arr.	- -	8 25	3 45	12 10
7 32	7 25	12 45	7 46	1897	........Sumner.......♂	- -	8 10	3 27	11 54
- -	- -	- -	- -	1899	........Meeker.......♂	- -	- -	- -	- -
8 00	7 55	1 15	8 15	1909	arr....Tacoma.♂ lve.	7 35	7 45	*3 00	*11 30
8 40	P M	11 15	10 20	....	lve....Seattle....arr.	9 10	7 05	4 15	10 55
10 15	.....	1 30	12 05	1909	lve.+Tacoma.....arr.	7 20	5 20	2 25	9 35
10 30	.....	- -	- -	1913	.....South Tacoma...♂	- -	5 00	2 10	- -
10 40	.....	- -	- -	1916	......Lakeview.....♂	- -	- -	- -	- -
11 44	.....	2 48	1 45	1947	.........Tenino.........	5 55	- -	12 59	- -
12 15	.....	3 10	2 10	1958	+.....Centralia.....♂	5 35	3 25	12 35	7 58
12 35	.....	3 20	2 25	1962	+.....Chehalis.....♂	5 23	3 15	12 13	7 45
2 03	.....	4 48	4 31	2002	.........Kelso.........	4 01	1 51	10 41	- -
2 30	.....	5 10	5 00	2012	........Kalama.......♂	3 40	1 30	10 20	- -
3 00	.....	5 40	5 30	2013	.........Goble........♂	3 10	1 00	9 50	5 40
4 30	.....	6 50	7 00	2053	+.....Portland.....♂	*2 00	*11 45	*8 30	*4 30
P M	.....	P M	A M	....	ARRIVE] [LEAVE	P M	P M	A M	P M

ELMA BRANCH.—Elma to Simpson (10 miles). No train service.

Additional Train—Leaves Seattle *4 30 p.m., Tacoma *5 50 p.m., arriving Portland 10 55 p.m.

STEAM HEAT The SAFETY systems are in use on over 150 railroads in the U. S. | SAFETY CAR HEATING & LIGHTING CO. NEW YORK. CHICAGO. ST. LOUIS.

Northern Pacific Railway.

Washburn Branch—Leaves Iron River for Washburn (34 miles) 6 05 p.m. Returning, leaves Washburn †7 15 a.m.

*Daily; †daily, except Sunday; ¶daily, except Monday; b Tuesday, Thursday and Saturday; g Monday, Wednesday and Friday.

+ Coupon stations. ♁ Telegraph stations.

LAKE SUPERIOR DIVISION.

No. 1	No. 11	No. 3-13	Mls	May 27, 1906.	No. 4-14	No. 2-12
*8 20 A M	....	*4 25 P M	0	lve...+Ashland..♁ arr.	11 00 A M	7 00 P M
9 15 "	....	5 19 "	28	+....Iron River......	9 56 "	5 59 "
10 37 "	....	6 36 "	63	+.....Superior.....♁	8 35 "	4 35 "
10 48 "	....	6 44 "	67	+Superior (Central Ave.)♁	8 25 "	4 25 "
11 15 A M	....	7 10 P M	76	arr....+Duluth♁...lve.	*8 00 A M	*4 00 P M
	*8 30 A M	*7 30 P M	0	lve....+Duluth.....arr.	7 55 A M	6 25 P M
	8 55 "	7 55 "	4	+.....Superior.....♁	7 30 "	6 00 "
	9 35 "	8 46 "	28	........Carlton......♁	6 50 "	5 20 "
	10 15 "	9 33 "	49	........Cromwell......♁	6 09 "	4 39 "
	11 28 A M	10 58 "	91	+.......Aitkin.......♁	4 48 "	3 21 "
	12 15 Noon	11 55 P M	119	arr. .+Brainerd♁..lve.	*4 05 A M	*2 30 P M
	5 15 P M	5 40 A M	257	arr.....+Fargo.......lve.	11 10 P M	7 10 A M
	8 05 P M	9 00 A M	349	arr..+Jamestown ..lve.	7 20 P M	4 10 A M
	6 55 P M	9 50 A M	1136	arr....+Helena.....lve.	2 25 P M	12 01 Night
	8 15 P M	1 15 P M	1915	arr....+Tacoma ....lve.	7 45 A M	7 35 P M
	8 15 P M	1 15 P M	1936	arr....+Seattle ....lve.	7 45 A M	9 10 P M
	7 00 A M	6 50 P M	2059	arr...+Portland....lve.	*11 45 P M	*2 00 P M

FARGO AND SOUTHWESTERN BRANCH.

109	105	Mls.	June 10, 1906.	108	110
A M	A M	....	LEAVE] [ARRIVE	P M	P M
†6 30	†8 30	0	+.......Fargo.......♁	7 05	5 00
6 46	8 42	4.2	........Cotters........	6 52	4 35
7 10	8 57	10.7	........Horace.......♁	6 35	4 00
7 30	9 09	16.2	........Warren........	6 22	3 30
7 45	9 15	19.4	+.....Davenport.....♁	6 15	3 10
8 30	9 36	29.2	........Leonard......♁	5 51	2 15
9 00	9 50	35.5	........Coburn........	5 36	1 40
10 12	10 02	41.7	+......Sheldon......♁	5 20	1 05
10 45	10 22	50.7	........Buttzville........	5 00	12 15
12 30	10 38	56.4	+.......Lisbon.......♁	4 42	11 45
1 23	11 14	68.9	........Englevale......♁	4 07	10 20
3 50	‖12 35	88.2	+....La Moure.....♁	3 20	9 05
4 08	1 05	98.2	........Berlin........	2 57	8 30
4 50	1 40	109.6	arr..+Edgeley♁.lve.	†2 30	†7 45
P M	b2 50	109.6	lve....Edgeley....arr.	11 15	A M
....	5 40	139.6	........Gackle........	8 30	....
....	6 40	150.7	arr...Streeter♁.lve.	g7 30	....

CASSELTON BRANCH.

No. 127	Ms.	June 10, 1906.	No. 128
....	....	LEAVE] [ARRIVE	....
†9 15 A M	0	....Casselton...♁	6 50 P M
9 52 "	12	......Embden.....♁	5 13 "
10 37 "	27	........Lucca......♁	4 28 "
11 15 "	41	.....Kathryn.....♁	3 48 "
11 50 A M	52	.....Litchville....♁	3 12 "
12 15 Noon	60	.......Marion.....♁	†2 50 P M
....	....	ARRIVE] [LEAVE	....

Boulder Br.—From Helena to Jefferson 20 mls., Boulder 37 mls. and Calvin 50 mls.

PHILIPSBURG BRANCH.

....	117	Mls	June 10, 1906.	118	....
....	P M	....	LEAVE] [ARRIVE	A M	....
....	†1 45	0	+.Drummond.♁	10 35	....
....	1 59	2.9	..New Chicago....	10 20	....
....	2 33	12.4	.......Stone.......	9 52	....
....	2 46	15.4	.......Flint.......	9 39	....
....	3 25	25.4	+.Philipsburg.♁	†9 10	....
....	P M	31.4	arr.. Rumsey ..lve.	A M	....

ROCKY FORK AND CLARK'S FORK BRS.

23	21	Mls	June 10, 1906.	24	22
A M	A M	....	LEAVE] [ARRIVE	P M	P M
b9 10	*10 30	0	.......Billings......♁	4 40	6 30
10 00	11 00	0	lve.....Laurel♁..arr.	3 45	5 55
10 30	11 12	7.5	........Mason........	3 20	5 38
10 45	11 25	9.6	.......Silesia......♁	3 10	5 35
1 05	....	28.8	arr.....Bridger♁..lve.	b2 00	....
P M	11 31	17.6	........Wilsey........	P M	5 11
....	12 02	28.4	........Selmes........	....	4 45
....	12 16	31.7	........Merritt........	....	4 35
....	1 00	44.0	+....Red Lodge.....♁	....	*4 00
....	P M	....	ARRIVE] [LEAVE	....	P M

MARYSVILLE BRANCH.

No. 111	Mls	June 10, 1906.	No. 112
†1 15 P M	0	lve....+Helena♁..arr.	5 30 P M
1 40 "	9.1	..Clough Junction..	5 00 "
1 57 "	15.5	........Cruse........	4 35 "
2 30 P M	21.5	arr..+Marysville♁.lve.	†4 15 P M

Roslyn Branch.—Leaves **Clealum**♁ †9 15 a.m., arriving Roslyn♁ (3 miles) 9 30 a.m. Lvs. Roslyn †11 30 a.m., arriving Clealum 11 45 a.m.

BUTTE BRANCH.

1	5	13	Ms	June 10, 1906.	14	6	2
P M	A M	P M	....	LEAVE] [ARRIVE	P M	P M	Night
*7 40	*4 55	*9 50	0	.......Butte.......♁	2 50	11 30	12 40
--	--	10 05	7	....Silver Bow.....♁	2 33	--	--
8 09	5 22	10 17	14	.......Durant.......	2 19	10 43	11 55
--	5 31	10 18	18	arr.....Stuart♁..lve.	2 10	10 27	--
--	5 31	10 18	18	lve.....Stuart.....arr.	2 10	10 27	--
--	5 42	10 37	25	....Warm Springs...♁	1 58	10 11	--
8 48	6 05	11 01	41	+....Deer Lodge....♁	1 32	9 35	11 03
9 10	6 25	11 25	52	+.....Garrison.....♁	*1 10	*9 10	*10 48
P M	P M	P M	....	ARRIVE] [LEAVE	P M	P M	P M

LITTLE FALLS AND DAKOTA BRANCH.

No. 105	Mls	June 10, 1906.	No. 106
†10 15 A M	....	lve.... St. Paul♁ .arr.	2 20 P M
†2 45 P M	0	lve.+Little Falls♁arr.	10 45 A M
3 06 "	8	........Flensburg........	10 25 "
3 21 "	16	........Swanville.......♁	10 10 "
3 42 "	25	.......Grey Eagle.....♁	9 49 "
3 50 "	28	........Birch Lake........	9 41 "
3 55 "	30	........Spaulding........	9 35 "
4 10 "	37	+...Sauk Center...♁	9 20 "
4 38 "	48	........Westport ......♁	8 53 "
4 48 "	53	........Villard ....♁	8 42 "
5 05 "	60	+.....Glenwood.....♁	8 25 "
5 26 "	68	+.....Starbuck ......♁	8 04 "
5 49 "	79	........Cyrus.........♁	7 41 "
6 15 P M	88	arr...+Morris. ♁ .lve.	†7 20 A M

JAMES RIVER AND OAKES BRANCHES.

No. 10	Mls	June 10, 1906.	No. 9
†10 00 A M	0	lv+.Jamestown. ♁ar.	6 00 P M
10 53 "	19	......Montpelier.....♁	4 58 "
11 33 "	33	........Dickey........♁	4 13 "
11 59 A M	41	.....Grand Rapids.....	3 45 "
12 25 Noon	49	arr...La Moure♁.lve.	3 20 "
12 25 Noon	49	lve...La Moure....arr.	3 20 "
12 43 Noon	54	....Oakes Junction....	3 05 "
1 30 P M	69	arr...+Oakes♁...lve.	†2 30 P M

DEVILS LAKE & SYKESTON BRANCHES.

165	135	Ms	June 10, 1906.	138	168
....	A M	....	(*Central time.*)	P M	....
....	†11 40	0	lv+.Jamestown. ♁ar.	3 35	....
....	12 16	13	........Buchanan........	2 58	....
....	1 10	35	........Melville.......♁	2 00	....
....	1 35	44	+....Carrington.....♁	1 35	....
....	2 19	60	+..New Rockford...♁	12 20	....
....	3 15	79	+......Oberon.......♁	11 30	....
....	3 46	90	+..Minnewaukan...♁	11 02	....
P M	4 45	108	arr....+Leeds♁...lve.	†10 15	Noon
†2 00	P M	44	lv..+Carrington♁.ar.	A M	12 35
2 37	....	57	........Sykeston.......♁	....	11 58
3 20	....	71	........Bowdon........♁	....	11 15
4 35	....	98	........Denhoff........♁	....	10 00
6 30	....	129	arr..Turtle Lake..lve.	....	†8 00

OBERON BRANCH.

No. 145	Mls	June 10, 1906.	No. 148
†3 30 P M	0	lve.....Oberon♁..arr.	9 45 A M
4 10 "	10	........Flora........	8 55 "
4 40 "	15	........Maddock.......♁	8 25 "
5 00 "	20	........Hesper........	7 40 "
5 15 "	24	........Pendennis........	7 20 "
5 30 P M	27	arr.....Rhodes♁..lve.	†7 00 A M

FORT SHERMAN BR.

7	25	Mls.	FORT SHERMAN BR.	8	26
P M	A M	....	LEAVE] [ARRIVE	A M	P M
*5 30	*9 15	0	...Cœur d'Alene...♁	8 45	3 55
5 55	9 40	9	......Post Falls......	8 20	3 30
6 07	9 52	14	........Hauser........	8 10	3 20
6 45	10 35	34	.......Spokane.....♁	*7 30	*2 40
P M	A M	....	ARRIVE] [LEAVE	A M	P M

Ruby Valley Branch.—Train leaves **Whitehall** †7 50 a.m., arriving Alder (46 miles) 11 00 a.m. Returning, leaves Alder †11 20 a.m., arriving Whitehall 2 25 p.m.

COOPERSTOWN BRANCH.

115	Ms.	June 10, 1906.	118
A M	....	LEAVE] [ARRIVE	P M
†10 30	0	+.......Sanborn.......♁	4 30
10 55	10	........Rogers........♁	3 59
11 16	18	........Dazey.........♁	3 36
11 39	27	........Hannaford......♁	3 10
12 05	37	+..Cooperstown...♁	2 42
12 29	46	........Jessie.........♁	2 20
12 43	51	........Binford.........♁	2 09
1 15	63	.......McHenry......♁	†1 40
P M	....	ARRIVE] [LEAVE	P M

MANITOBA DIVISION.

No. 7	Mls	June 10, 1906.	No. 8
*10 15 P M	....	lve...+St. Paul...arr.	7 25 A M
10 45 P M	....	lve.+Minneapolis..arr.	6 50 A M
*4 55 A M	....	lve.+Winnipeg Jn♁ arr.	10 40 P M
5 43 "	26	+.....Twin Valley...♁	9 49 "
6 22 "	46	+.......Fertile......♁	9 10 "
7 05 "	68	+.....Crookston....♁	8 25 "
8 10 "	96	+...Grand Forks...♁	7 25 "
8 42 "	112	........Meckinock........	6 50 "
9 48 "	144	........Grafton........	5 40 "
10 24 "	160	........Drayton........	5 02 "
11 22 "	189	+.......Pembina.......♁	4 02 "
11 45 A M	192	arr..+Emerson♁..lve.	*3 52 P M

CANADIAN NORTHERN RY.

A M	A M	Mls	June 3, 1906.	P M	P M
*11 45	*5 07	0	lve.+Emerson♁.arr.	*7 23	3 47
12 05	5 36	11	........Letellier........	7 02	3 30
12 23	5 54	20	...St. Jean Baptiste.♁	6 44	3 12
12 37	6 06	26	+.......Morris........♁	6 30	3 00
12 52	--	34	......Silver Plains......	--	2 46
1 09	--	45	......St. Agathe......	--	2 30
1 50	7 05	64	Portage Junction	5 30	1 50
2 00	7 15	67	+.....Winnipeg.....♁	*5 20	*1 40
P M	A M		ARRIVE] [LEAVE	P M	P M
....	†9 00	67	lve...Winnipeg...arr.	3 50	....
....	9 58	89	........Sanford........	2 58	....
....	11 20	119	........Carman........	1 45	....
....	12 20	139	........Leary's........	12 55	....
....	1 15	154	........Somerset........	12 15	....
....	3 15	194	........Belmont........	10 30	....
....	4 40	212	........Wawanesa........	8 55	....
....	†6 10	237	+.......Brandon........	†7 05	....
....	P M		ARRIVE] [LEAVE	A M	....

PORTAGE LA PRAIRIE BR.—C. N. RY.

....	1	Mls	June 3, 1906.	2	....
....	Noon	....	LEAVE] [ARRIVE	A M	....
....	*12 30	0	.......Winnipeg.......	11 20	....
....	12 30	3	...Portage Junc....	11 10	....
....	1 01	14	......Headingley......	10 47	....
....	1 41	36	........Eustache........	10 02	....
....	2 20	56	+.Portage La Prairie.♁	[illegible]	....
....	....	72	arr.......Delta♁..lve.	....	....
....	2 46	66	........Rignold........♁	8 53	....
....	3 06	75	........Beaver........♁	*8 34	....
....	P M	....	ARRIVE] [LEAVE	A M	....

VIA RED LAKE FALLS.

No. 155	Mls	June 3, 1906.	No. 156
†2 00 A M	....	lv. Winnipeg Junc ar.	1 00 A M
†6 30 A M	0	lve..+Fertile♁..arr.	7 05 P M
7 08 "	13	........Dugdale........	6 35 "
7 45 "	23	+..Red Lake Falls..♁	6 05 "
8 38 "	41	......South Euclid......	4 57 "
10 00 "	54	...Carthage Junction....	4 40 "
10 25 A M	60	arr.+Grand Forks lve.	†3 15 P M

Linton Branch.—Train leaves **McKenzie** g2 35 p.m., arrive Linton (45 m.) 5 35 p.m. Leaves Linton b8 00 a.m., arrives McKenzie 10 30 a.m.

FERGUS FALLS BRANCH.

No. 9	Mls	June 10, 1906.	No. 10
*8 20 A M	....	lve....St. Paul♁..arr.	*6 20 P M
*1 50 P M	0	lve..+Staples♁..arr.	*12 50 Noon
2 23 "	17	........Wadena........	12 15 Noon
2 48 "	27	......Deer Creek.......♁	11 48 A M
2 56 "	31	........Parkton........	11 38 "
3 05 "	35	........Henning.......♁	11 27 "
3 18 "	41	........Vining........♁	11 12 "
3 29 "	46	......Battle Lake......♁	10 57 "
3 54 "	58	......Underwood......♁	10 20 "
4 20 "	69	+..Fergus Falls...♁	9 50 "
4 35 "	75	........French........	9 35 "
5 15 "	94	+..Breckenridge..♁	8 55 "
5 20 "	95	arr..+Wahpeton..lve.	8 50 "
5 20 "	95	lve...Wahpeton...arr.	8 45 "
5 38 "	102	......Farmington.....♁	8 25 "
5 53 "	108	........Mooreton.......♁	8 12 "
6 08 "	115	........Barney........	7 57 "
6 25 "	126	........Wyndmere........	7 40 "
7 00 "	136	........Milnor.......♁	7 20 "
7 25 "	146	........Gwinner........	6 58 "
7 42 "	153	........Stirum........	6 23 "
8 00 "	160	........Crete........	6 05 "
8 20 P M	168	arr...+Oakes♁...lve.	*5 45 A M

PARK BRANCH.

101	103	Mls	June 10, 1906.	104	102
A M	A M	....	LEAVE] [ARRIVE	P M	P M
*10 15	*10 15	....	lve....St. Paul♁.arr.	7 40	6 20
*2 45	*8 00	0	lv..+Livingston♁.ar.	11 50	10 00
4 02	--	31	........Daileys........	11 58	8 38
4 27	--	42	........Sphinx........	11 38	8 03
5 15	10 15	54	+......Gardiner......♁	*10 45	*7 15
P M	A M	....	ARRIVE] [LEAVE	A M	P M

YELLOWSTONE PARK ROUTE.

TACOMA AND SEATTLE LINE.

12	14	2	10	8	104	4	Ms.	June 10, 1906.	11	7	27	105	9	13	109	1
P M	P M	P M	P M	P M	A M	A M	....	(*Pacific time.*)	A M	A M	A M	P M	P M	P M	P M	P M
*11 30	*9 40	*7 35	*7 10	*2 40	*10 55	*5 35	0	lv.+Tacoma♁ ar.	8 00	10 05	11 15	1 15	4 10	5 40	7 55	11 50
11 45	--	--	--	3 00	11 10	5 50	9	+.Puyallup.♁	7 40	9 46	10 55	12 55	3 50	--	7 35	11 27
11 54	--	--	7 34	3 10	11 20	6 00	12	....Sumner...♁	7 32	9 37	10 45	12 45	3 40	--	7 25	11 20
12 20	--	--	7 50	3 25	11 35	6 15	19	....Auburn..♁	7 20	9 23	--	12 25	3 25	--	7 05	11 08
12 33	--	8 31	8 01	3 37	11 47	6 27	24	......Kent....♁	7 00	9 11	10 17	11 49	3 12	--	6 45	10 57
1 10	10 55	9 10	8 40	4 15	12 25	7 05	41	+..Seattle...♁	*6 30	*8 40	*9 45	*11 15	*2 35	*4 30	*6 15	*10 20
A M	P M	P M	P M	P M	Noon	A M	....	ARRIVE] [LEAVE	A M	A M	A M	A M	P M	P M	P M	P M

Train lvs. Seattle *7 45 a.m., arr. Tacoma 9 20 a.m. Lvs. Tacoma *12 45 noon, arr. Seattle 2 15 p.m.

OLYMPIA AND GRAY'S HARBOR BRS.

9	27	Mls	June 10, 1906.	28	10
P M	A M	....	(*Mountain time.*)	Noon	P M
*4 20	*11 25	0	lve..+Tacoma♁.arr.	12 35	7 00
4 43	11 48	7	.......Lakeview.....♁	12 10	6 35
--	--	20	........Sherlock........	11 45	--
5 40	12 50	32	+.....Olympia.....♁	11 15	5 40
6 25	1 30	51	arr.......Gate♁...lve.	10 30	5 00
*5 45	*12 55	0	lve...Centralia...arr.	11 10	5 30
6 25	1 30	13	..........Gate..........	10 40	5 00
7 03	2 10	32	..........Elma..........	9 42	4 21
8 05	3 23	57	.......Hoquiam.......	*8 30	*3 20
P M	4 13	53	lve...Cosmopolis..arr.	7 42	P M
....	5 15	72	arr......Ocosta....lve.	*6 40	....
....	4 17	69	........Tulips........	6 34	....
....	4 41	77	........Onslow........	6 08	....
....	5 10	85	........Moclips........	*5 40	....
....	P M	....	ARRIVE] [LEAVE	A M	....

Additional Trains—Leave Tacoma *8 10 a.m., *6 30 p.m., arrive Olympia 9 25 a.m., 7 45 p.m. Leave Olympia *1 30, *10 00 p.m., arrive Tacoma 2 45, 11 15 p.m.

CŒUR D'ALENE LINE.

No. 141	Ms.	June 10, 1906.	No. 142
*7 40 A M	....	lve....Missoula....arr.	4 20 P M
8 00 "	0	lve....De Smet♁...arr.	4 00 "
8 20 "	11	........Frenchtown ....♁	3 28 "
10 15 "	58	.....Iron Mountain...♁	1 11 P M
10 50 "	74	........St. Regis......♁	12 12 Noon
11 55 A M	96	..........Saltese........♁	11 00 A M
1 35 P M	122	+........Mullan........♁	9 25 "
2 00 P M	128	arr...+Wallace♁..lve.	*9 00 A M

CLEARWATER SHORT LINE.

No. 111	Mls.	June 10, 1906.	No. 112
†1 50 P M	0	lve...+Lewiston♁..arr.	10 45 A M
2 35 "	14	..........Arrow..........	10 00 "
3 17 "	27	..........Lenore........♁	9 24 "
5 10 "	65	..........Kamiah........♁	7 35 "
5 35 "	71	..........Kooskia........♁	7 12 "
5 45 P M	74	arr.....+Stites.....lve.	†7 00 A M

BRANCH LINES FROM TACOMA.

No. 20	Mls	June 10, 1906.	No. 19
*6 00 P M	0	lve.......Tacoma♁.....arr.	11 30 A M
6 43 "	17	............Orting ....♁	10 47 "
6 49 "	21	...........Crocker...........	10 41 "
7 00 P M	25	.........South Prairie.......♁	10 33 A M
--	27	....Cascade Junction..♁	--
*7 15 P M	28	...........Burnett.........♁	10 05 A M
7 40 "	32	...........Wilkeson.........♁	9 45 "
7 55 "	34	+........Carbonado ....♁	9 30 "
8 25 P M	41	arr.........Fairfax.........lve.	†9 00 A M
--	27	....Cascade Junction...♁	--
7 20 P M	30	+.........Buckley..........♁	10 15 A M
7 47 P M	42	arr......+Palmer♁.....lve.	†9 52 A M

YACOLT BRANCH.

No. 409	Mls	June 10, 1906.	No. 410
†6 30 A M	0	lve.........Yacolt ....arr.	3 30 P M
8 00 "	13	.........Battle Ground.........	2 30 "
8 36 "	20	...........Glenwood...........	1 46 "
8 43 "	21	...........Barberton...........	1 41 "
8 53 "	23	.............Hidden.............	1 32 "
9 30 A M	31	arr....+Vancouver.....lve.	†1 00 P M

BURKE BRANCH

No. 164	No. 162	Mls	June 10, 1906.	No. 161	No. 163	....
*3 45 P M	†9 30 A M	0	lve...+Wallace♁..arr.	11 30 A M	6 00 P M	....
4 45 P M	10 30 A M	7	arr....+Burke♁...lve.	†10 45 A M	*5 00 P M	....

GREEN RIVER BRANCH.—Leaves **Kanaskat** *8 00 p.m., arriving Keriston (12.9 miles) 8 40 p.m. Leaves Keriston †8 25 a.m., arriving Kanaskat 9 25 a.m.

ORTING BRANCH.—**Orting** to Puyallup River (7.6 miles).

CROCKER BRANCH.—**Crocker** to Douty (5.1 miles).

RED BLUFF AND PONY BRANCHES.—Train leaves **Sappington** †9 15 a.m., arrives at Harrison (10 miles) 10 05 a.m., Norris (21 mes) 10 45 a.m. Returning, leaves Norris †11 15 a.m., arrives Sappington 1 40 p.m. Train leaves Harrison †11 50 a.m., arrives Pony (7 miles) 12 10 noon. Returning, leaves Pony †12 30 noon, arrives Harrison 12 50 noon.

RED MOUNTAIN BRANCH.—**Helena** to Rimini (16.8 miles).

STEAMSHIP LINES FROM SEATTLE, WASH.

....	Pas.	Pas.	Pas.	Mls	PORTS.	Mls	Pas.	Pas.	Pas.	....
....	P M	Night	A M	....	LEAVE] [ARRIVE	....	P M	A M	P M	....
....	‡10 00	g12 00	†9 00	0	........Seattle........	82	2 00	3 15	5 00	....
....	--	4 00	11 45	72	....Port Townsend....	38	9 30	11 30	--	....
....	5 30	--	--	106	.......Anacortes.......	....	--	--	9 30	....
....	7 00	--	--	125	.......Bellingham.......	....	--	--	†8 00	....
....	A M	2 00	3 00	110	........Victoria........	0	h5 30	†8 00	A M	....
....	....	P M	P M	....	ARRIVE] [LEAVE	....	P M	P M	....	....

SOUTH BEND BRANCH.

No. 37	Mls	June 10, 1906.	No. 38
*12 50 Noon	0	lve.+Centralia♁.arr.	9 45 A M
1 05 P M	4	lve.+Chehalis♁..arr.	9 30 "
1 24 "	10	..........Adna..........	9 19 "
1 39 "	15	..........Ceres..........	9 04 "
1 56 "	21	..........Dryad.......♁	8 46 "
2 15 "	27	..........Pe Ell.......♁	8 29 "
2 36 "	34	..........Pluvius..........	8 09 "
2 53 "	40	..........Frances.......♁	7 44 "
3 10 "	47	..........Holcomb..........	7 26 "
3 50 P M	62	arr. + South Bend♁.lve.	*6 50 A M

WASHINGTON CENTRAL BRANCH.

No. 13	Mls	June 10, 1906.	No. 14
*2 00 P M	....	lve....Spokane♁.arr.	11 15 A M
2 40 P M	0	lve.... Cheney♁..arr.	10 35 A M
3 10 "	10	+...Medical Lake...♁	10 10 "
3 50 "	27	.........Reardan.......♁	9 33 "
4 30 "	41	+......Davenport......♁	9 00 "
5 25 "	64	.........Creston.......♁	8 10 "
5 50 "	74	+.......Wilbur.......♁	7 48 "
6 25 "	88	+.......Almira.......♁	7 17 "
7 15 P M	106	arr.Coulee Jn..♁.lve.	6 37 A M
7 20 P M	108	arr.+Coulee City.lve.	*6 30 A M
†9 05 P M	127	arr.....Adrian....lve.	†5 10 A M

VANCOUVER BRANCH.

No. 407	Mls	June 10, 1906.	No. 408
*3 00 P M	0	lve....Kalama♁..arr.	9 50 A M
3 33 "	9.0	.... Woodland	9 17 "
3 56 "	14.9	.... Ridgefield	8 54 "
4 26 "	23.1	.... Felida	8 24 "
4 50 P M	28.5	arr..Vancouver..lve.	*8 00 A M

PORTLAND & SAN FRANCISCO LINE.

The Shasta All-Rail Route.

SOUTHERN PACIFIC CO. TO SAN FRANCISCO.

Pas.	Mail	Mls	STATIONS.	Mail	Pas.
A M	P M	....	LEAVE] [ARRIVE	A M	P M
*8 30	*8 45	0	.......Portland.......	7 25	5 55
8 35	8 50	0	... East Portland ...	7 20	5 50
9 22	9 32	15	.....Oregon City.....	6 41	5 04
10 00	--	28	........Aurora........	--	4 30
10 27	10 18	36	......Woodburn......	6 00	4 15
10 35	--	39	........Gervais........	--	4 01
11 13	10 56	53	........Salem	5 23	3 29
12 28	11 57	80	........Albany........	4 30	2 27
†4 00	.....	92	.......Lebanon.......	.....	†9 35
1 07	--	97	........Halsey........	--	1 44
1 27	--	106	.....Harrisburg.....	--	1 27
2 15	1 32	123	........Eugene........	2 51	12 42
4 51	4 06	181	........Oakland........	12 14	10 15
‖5 45	5 05	198	.......Roseburg.......	11 35	9 35
10 40	10 05	297	....Grant's Pass....	6 30	5 10
12 08	11 41	333	........Phœnix........	4 56	3 56
12 55	12 35	341	........Ashland........	4 40	3 40
6 06	6 23	434	........Sisson........	11 18	10 20
10 30	10 50	512	........Redding........	6 35	‖5 40
.....	3 00	630	......Marysville......	2 05	--
4 55	4 45	682	.....Sacramento.....	12 15	10 55
7 48	8 48	772	...San Francisco...	*8 20	*8 00
P M	A M	....	ARRIVE] [LEAVE	P M	A M

WEST SIDE.—(*Southern Pacific.*)

Exs.	Mail	Mls	December 20, 1905.	Mail	Exs.
P M	A M	....	LEAVE] [ARRIVE	P M	A M
*4 50	*7 30	0	.......Portland.......	5 50	8 25
6 04	8 44	21	.... Hillsboro	4 31	7 12
6 20	9 00	26	.....Forest Grove.....	4 16	6 57
7 21	10 00	50	.....McMinnville.....	3 10	5 59
7 30	10 10	76	.......Whiteson.......	3 00	*5 50
P M	11 45	97	.......Corvallis.......	*1 20	A M
.....	A M	....	ARRIVE] [LEAVE	P M	.....

Elkhorn Branch.—**Boulder** to Hot Springs (4 miles), Finn (9 miles), Queen Siding (16 miles) and Elkhorn (21 miles). Service discontinued.

BITTER ROOT BRANCH.

No. 137	Mls	June 10, 1906.	No. 138
*5 00 P M	0	lve..+Missoula♁..arr.	8 25 A M
5 11 "	4	.......Bitter Root.......	8 10 "
5 27 "	11	.........Lo Lo.........	7 55 "
5 47 "	20	........Florence.......♁	7 38 "
6 06 "	28	+.... Stevensville ....♁	7 20 "
6 24 "	35	+........Victor........♁	7 02 "
6 39 "	43	.... Woodside	6 45 "
6 43 "	46	.........Riverside.........	6 40 "
6 50 P M	47	+.....Hamilton.....♁	*6 35 A M
....	....	ARRIVE] [LEAVE	....

Sunnyside Branch.—Train leaves North Yakima *3 00 p.m., Sunnyside Junction (22 mls.) *4 00 p.m., arrives Sunnyside (34 mls.) 4 50 p.m. Returning, leaves Sunnyside *7 00 a.m., arrives North Yakima 8 45 a.m.

PALOUSE, FARMINGTON AND LEWISTON BRANCHES.

31	109	11	9	Mls	June 10, 1906.	10	12	110	32	....
P M	.....	P M	A M	....	(*Mountain time.*)	P M	A M	.....	A M	....
*5 00	.....	*11 30	*8 05	0	lve.+ Spokane♁ arr.	3 55	6 20	.....	11 30	....
5 25	.....	11 55	8 30	9	.......Marshall.....♁	3 35	5 50	.....	11 05	....
7 00	A M	1 40	10 02	46	+.... Oakesdale .....♁	2 10	4 30	A M	9 15	....
7 15	†9 30	1 55	10 18	52	arr..+Belmont♁.lve.	2 00	4 15	10 25	9 00	....
.....	9 55	.....	.....	57	ar..+ Farmington ♁.lv.	.....	.....	†10 00	.....	....
7 32	A M	2 20	10 35	58	+......Garfield......♁	1 43	3 55	A M	8 45	....
7 57		2 50	11 05	68	+.......Palouse.......♁	1 18	3 30		8 20	....
8 45	.....	3 55	11 55	84	arr..+Pullman♁..lve.	12 35	2 40	.....	*7 35	....
P M	17	.....	1 40	103	+....Uniontown.....♁	8 20	.....	18	A M	....
.....	A M	.....	2 10	113	arr.+Genesee♁..lve.	*7 45	.....	P M	.....	....
.....	†10 00	6 45	2 35	133	...........Arrow..........	10 00	11 45	2 35	.....	....
.....	10 15	--	2 45	136	..Lapwai Junction..	9 45	--	2 20	.....	....
.....	10 45	7 30	3 20	147	+.....Lewiston.....♁	*9 10	*11 00	†1 50	.....	....
.....	A M	A M	P M	....	ARRIVE] [LEAVE	A M	P M	P M	.....	....

LAPWAI BRANCH.—Leaves **Lapwai Junction** for Sweetwater †2 55 p.m., arrives Cul de Sac♁ (12 miles) 3 50 p.m. Leaves Cul de Sac †4 20 p.m., arrives Lapwai Junction 5 20 p.m.

*Daily; †daily, except Sunday; ‡daily, except Saturday; ¶daily, except Monday; g Monday, Wednesday and Friday; h Sunday, Tuesday and Thursday. ‖ Meals. + Coupon stations; ♁ Telegraph stations.

OCEAN STEAMSHIP CO., Ltd.,

—AND—

CHINA MUTUAL STEAM NAVIGATION CO., Ltd.,

FROM PUGET SOUND TO CHINA, JAPAN, AUSTRALIA, MANILA, SINGAPORE, PENANG, COLOMBO AND EUROPEAN PORTS.

Steamers leave Tacoma as follows: **Tydeus**, July 11th; **Stertor**, August 8th; **Cyclops**, September 5th; **Oanfa**, October 3d and every 28 days thereafter. These boats are operated in connection with the Northern Pacific Railway. For rates, etc., apply to any representative of the Northern Pacific Railway or to

DODWELL & CO., Ltd., Tacoma, Wash.

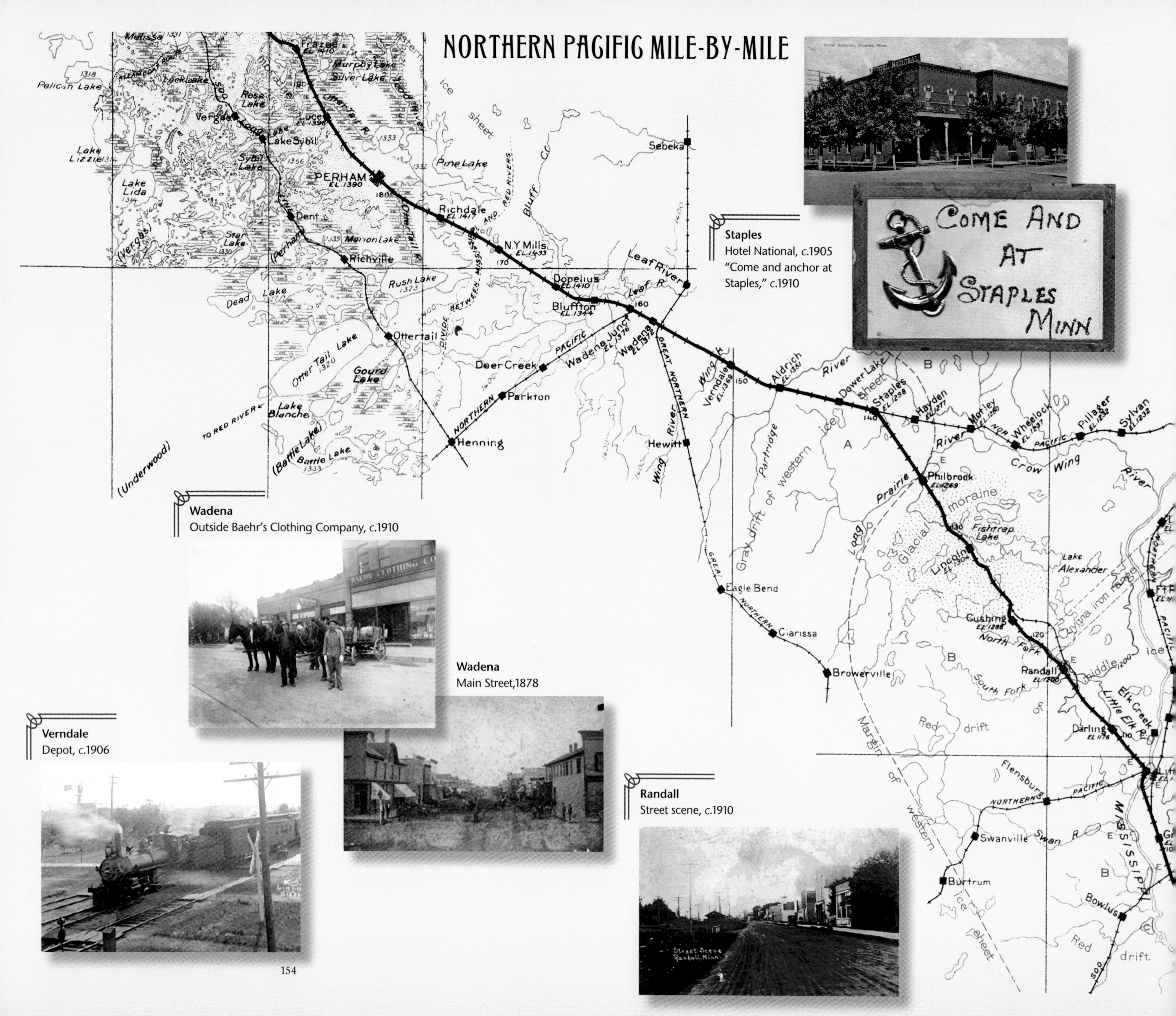

NORTHERN PACIFIC MILE-BY-MILE

Staples
Hotel National, *c.*1905
"Come and anchor at Staples," *c.*1910

Wadena
Outside Baehr's Clothing Company, *c.*1910

Wadena
Main Street, 1878

Verndale
Depot, *c.*1906

Randall
Street scene, *c.*1910

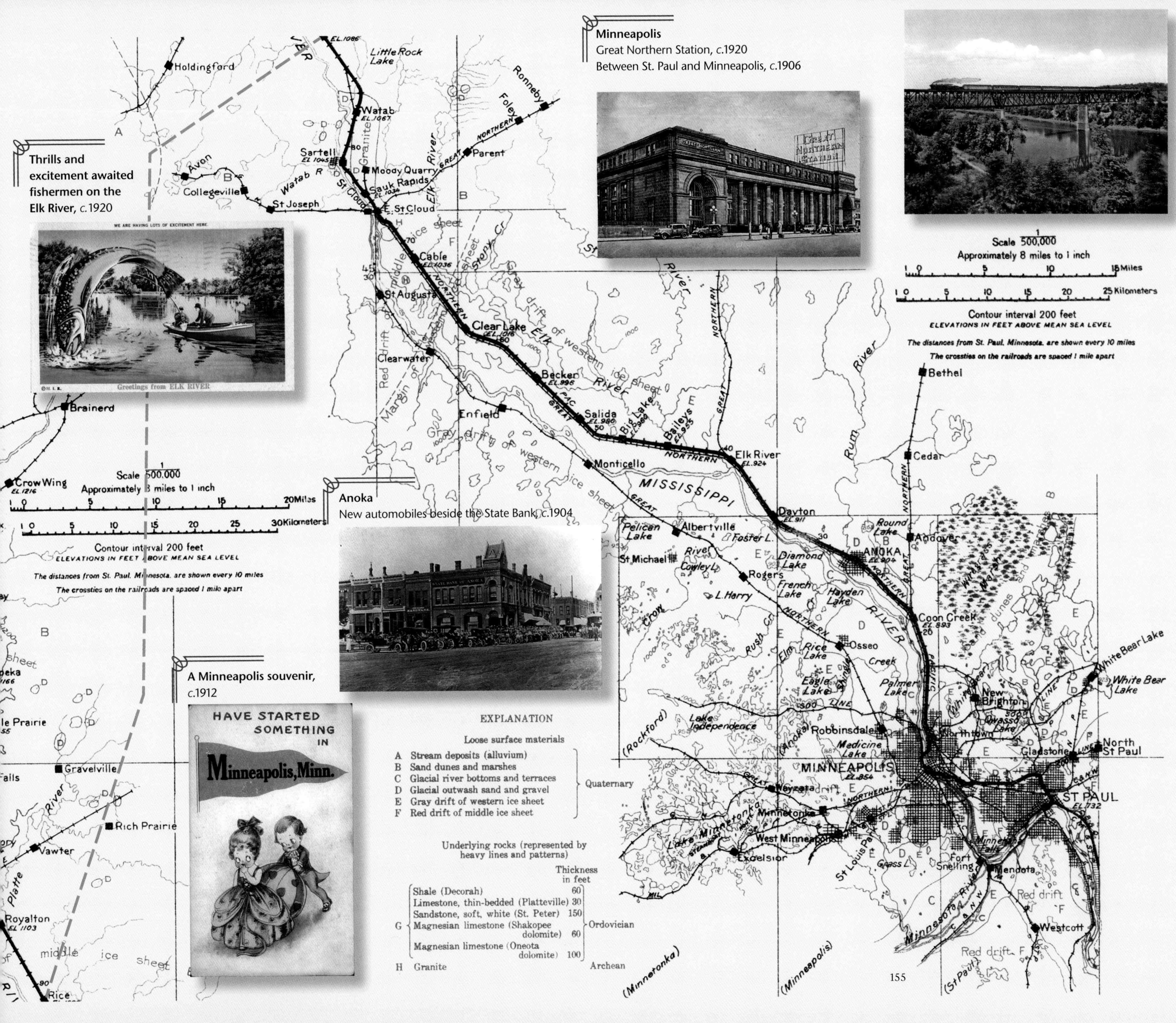

Thrills and excitement awaited fishermen on the Elk River, *c.*1920

Minneapolis
Great Northern Station, *c.*1920
Between St. Paul and Minneapolis, *c.*1906

Anoka
New automobiles beside the State Bank, *c.*1904

A Minneapolis souvenir, *c.*1912

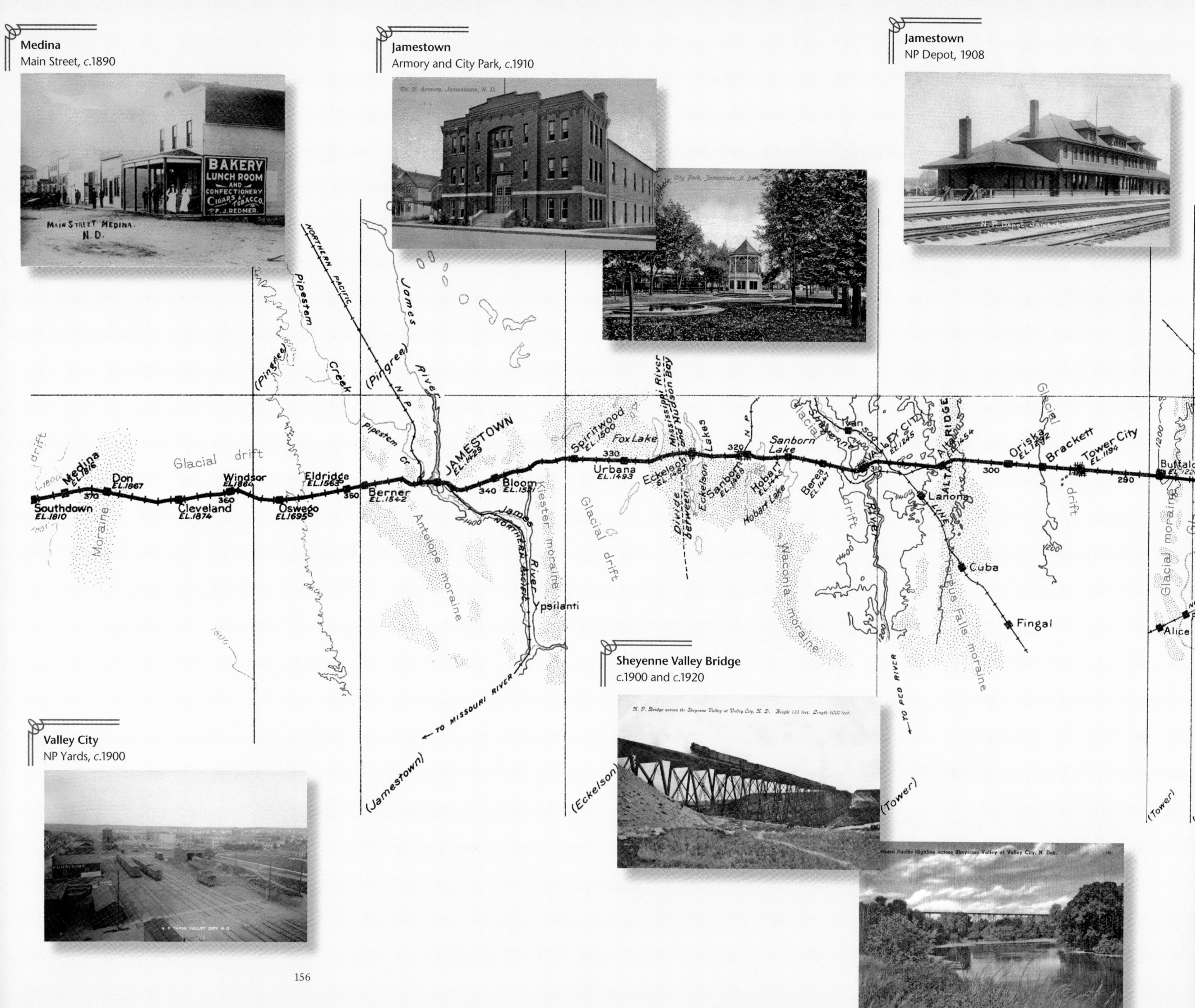

Medina
Main Street, *c.*1890

Jamestown
Armory and City Park, *c.*1910

Jamestown
NP Depot, 1908

Sheyenne Valley Bridge
*c.*1900 and *c.*1920

Valley City
NP Yards, *c.*1900

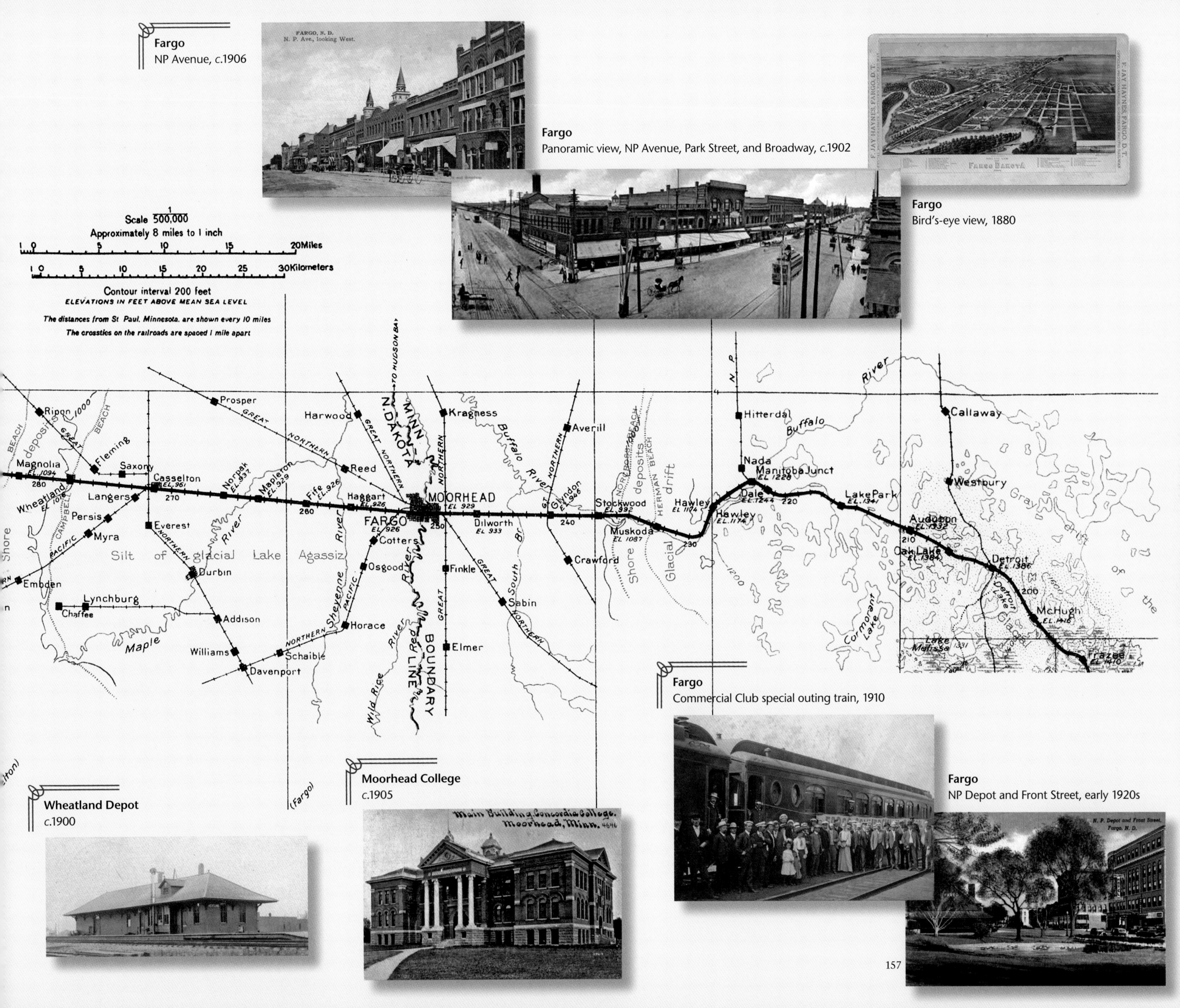

Fargo
NP Avenue, *c.*1906

Fargo
Panoramic view, NP Avenue, Park Street, and Broadway, *c.*1902

Fargo
Bird's-eye view, 1880

Fargo
Commercial Club special outing train, 1910

Fargo
NP Depot and Front Street, early 1920s

Moorhead College
*c.*1905

Wheatland Depot
*c.*1900

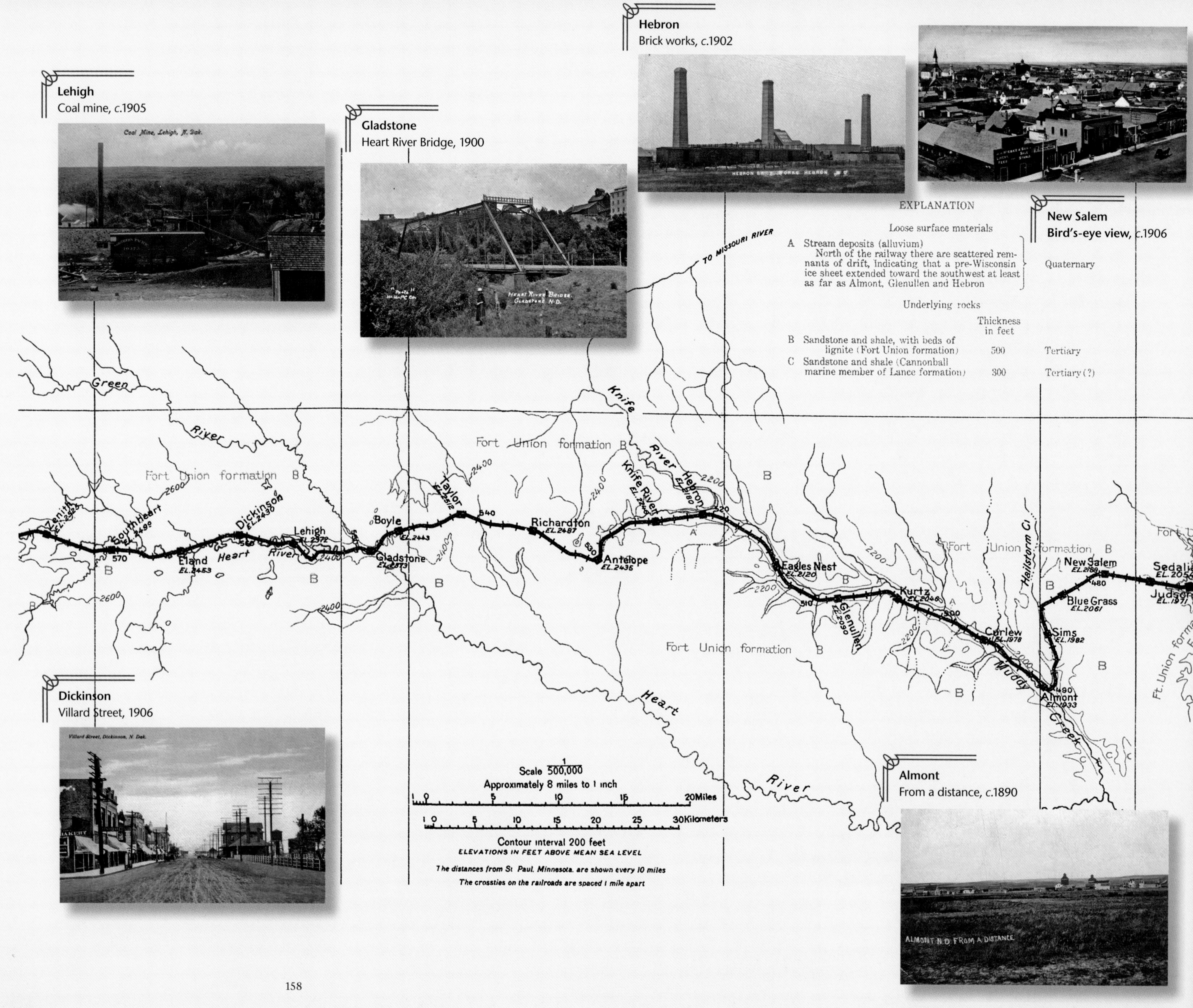

Lehigh
Coal mine, *c.*1905

Gladstone
Heart River Bridge, 1900

Hebron
Brick works, *c.*1902

New Salem
Bird's-eye view, *c.*1906

Dickinson
Villard Street, 1906

Almont
From a distance, *c.*1890

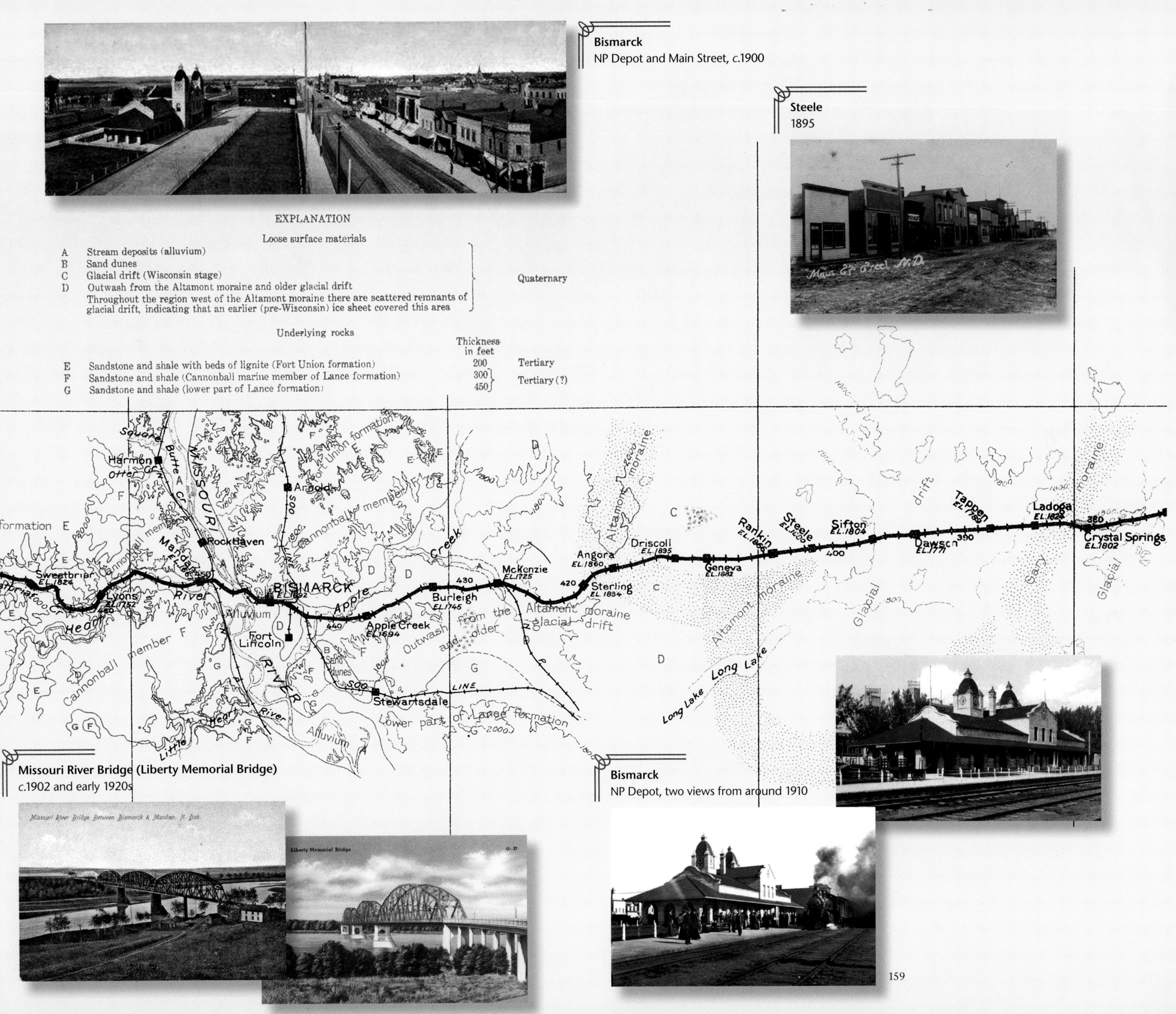

Bismarck
NP Depot and Main Street, *c.*1900

Steele
1895

Missouri River Bridge (Liberty Memorial Bridge)
*c.*1902 and early 1920s

Bismarck
NP Depot, two views from around 1910

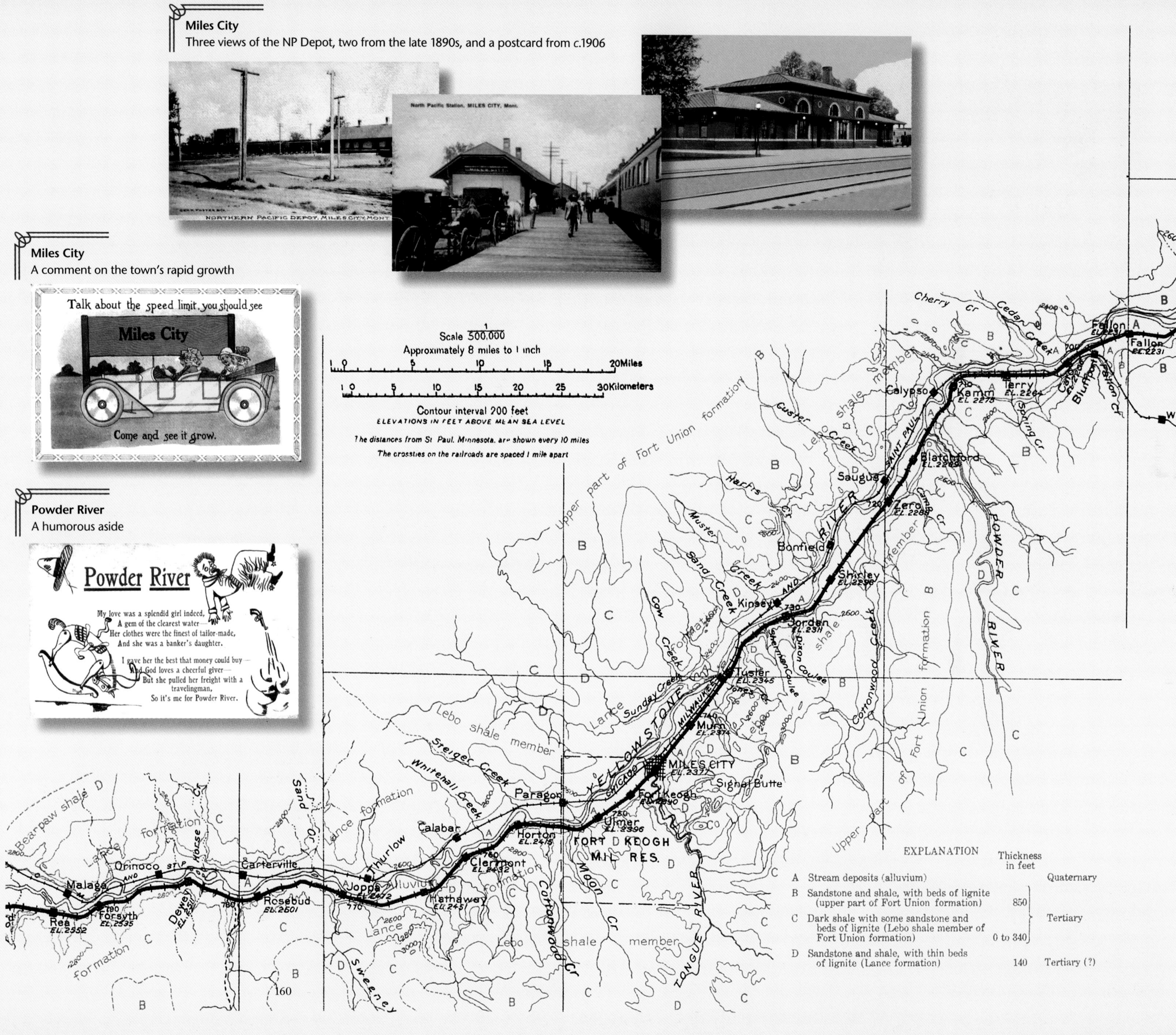
NORTHERN PACIFIC DEPOT, MILES CITY, MONT.
North Pacific Station, MILES CITY, Mont.
Talk about the speed limit, you should see
Miles City
Come and see it grow.
Powder River
My love was a splendid girl indeed,
A gem of the clearest water—
Her clothes were the finest of tailor-made,
And she was a banker's daughter.
I gave her the best that money could buy—
And God loves a cheerful giver—
But she pulled her freight with a
travelingman,
So it's me for Powder River.
Scale 1/500,000
Approximately 8 miles to 1 inch
20 Miles
30 Kilometers
Contour interval 200 feet
ELEVATIONS IN FEET ABOVE MEAN SEA LEVEL
The distances from St. Paul, Minnesota, are shown every 10 miles
The crossties on the railroads are spaced 1 mile apart
EXPLANATION
Thickness in feet
A Stream deposits (alluvium) Quaternary
B Sandstone and shale, with beds of lignite (upper part of Fort Union formation) 850
C Dark shale with some sandstone and beds of lignite (Lebo shale member of Fort Union formation) 0 to 340 Tertiary
D Sandstone and shale, with thin beds of lignite (Lance formation) 140 Tertiary (?)
MILES CITY
FORT KEOGH MIL. RES.
YELLOWSTONE RIVER
POWDER RIVER
TONGUE RIVER
Upper part of Fort Union formation
Lebo shale member
Lance formation
Fallon
Terry
Kamm
Calypso
Blatchford
Saugus
Zero
Bonfield
Shirley
Kinsey
Jordon
Tusler
Murn
Signal Butte
Fort Keogh
Ulmer
Paragon
Horton
Calabar
Thurlow
Clermont
Hathaway
Jopps
Carterville
Rosebud
Orinoco
Malaga
Forsyth
Rea
Dewey

Miles City
Three views of the NP Depot, two from the late 1890s, and a postcard from c.1906

Miles City
A comment on the town's rapid growth

Powder River
A humorous aside

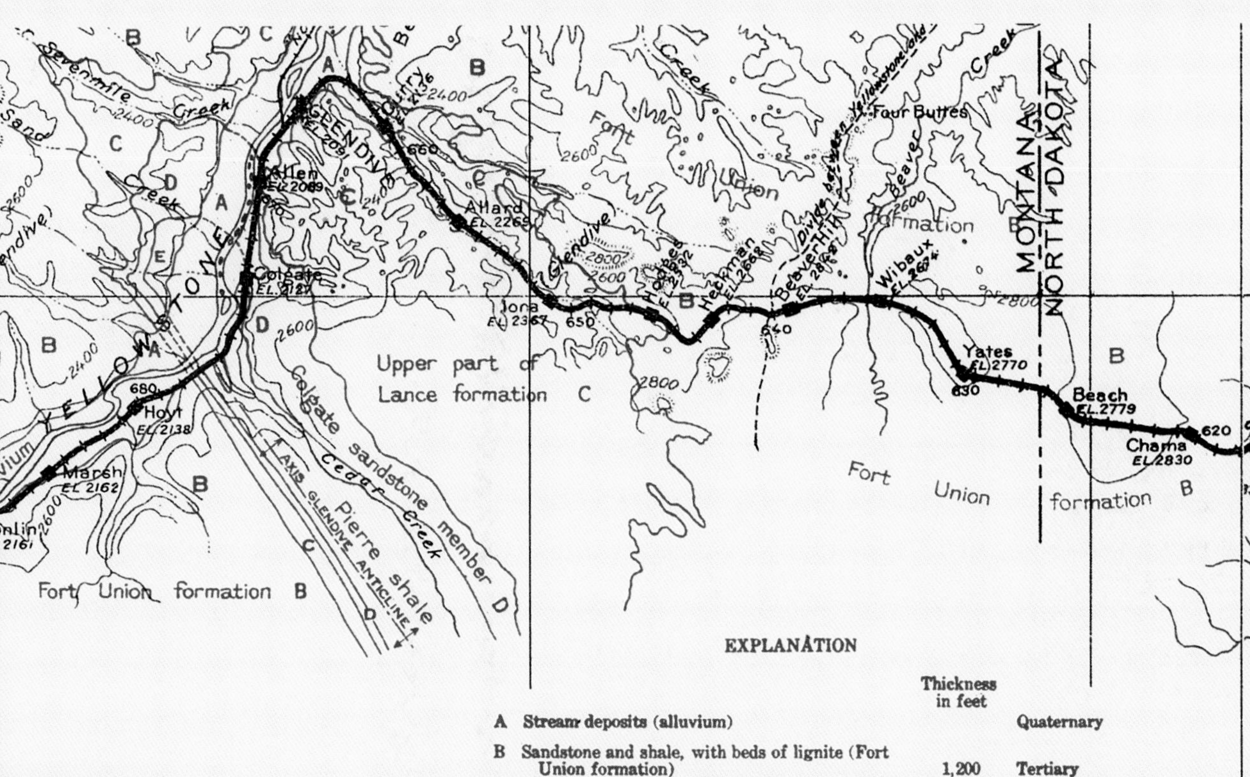

EXPLANATION

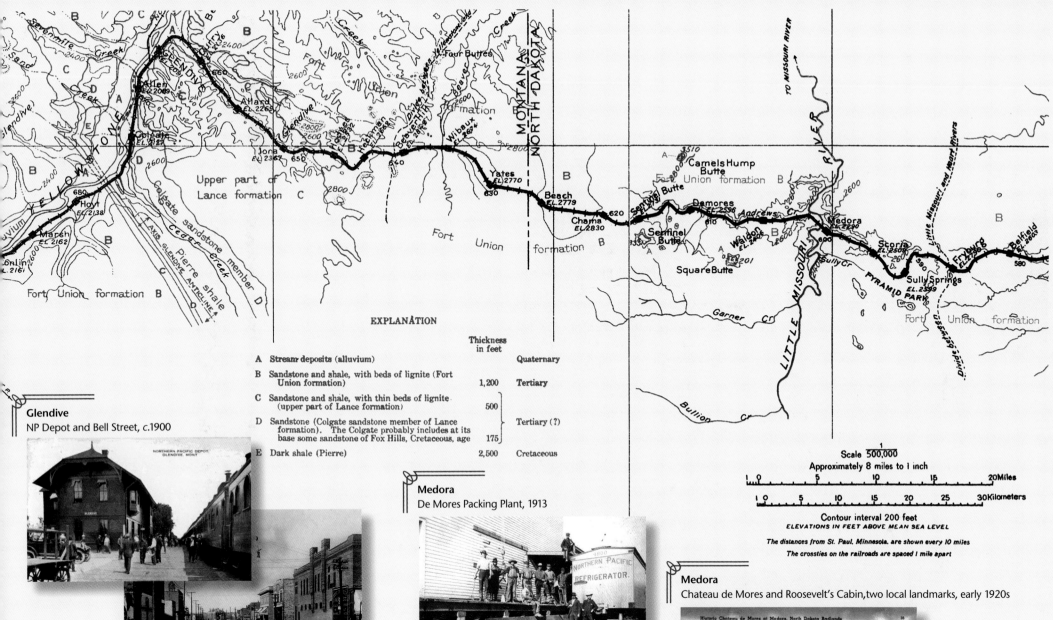

		Thickness in feet	
A	Stream deposits (alluvium)		Quaternary
B	Sandstone and shale, with beds of lignite (Fort Union formation)	1,200	Tertiary
C	Sandstone and shale, with thin beds of lignite (upper part of Lance formation)	500	Tertiary (?)
D	Sandstone (Colgate sandstone member of Lance formation). The Colgate probably includes at its base some sandstone of Fox Hills, Cretaceous, age	175	
E	Dark shale (Pierre)	2,500	Cretaceous

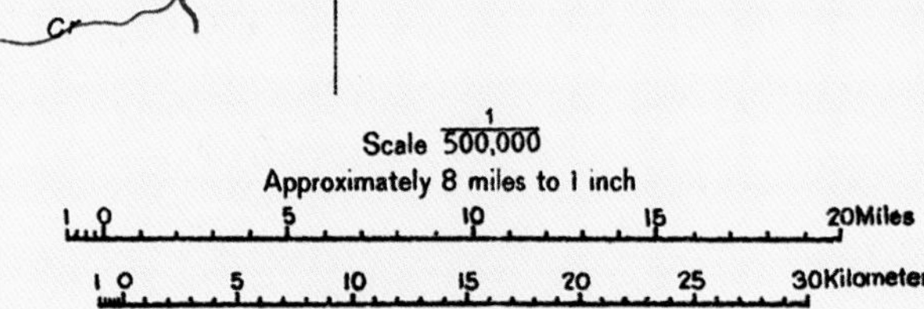

Contour interval 200 feet

ELEVATIONS IN FEET ABOVE MEAN SEA LEVEL

The distances from St. Paul, Minnesota, are shown every 10 miles

The crossties on the railroads are spaced 1 mile apart

Glendive
NP Depot and Bell Street, *c.*1900

Medora
De Mores Packing Plant, 1913

Medora
Chateau de Mores and Roosevelt's Cabin,two local landmarks, early 1920s

ROOSEVELT'S CABIN ON RANCH NEAR MEDORA, NORTH DAKOTA
WHERE HE LIVED FROM 1883 TO 1886

Glendive
The wreck of August 11, 1908, when a fireman was killed in a head-on smash

Near Medora
Building the first railroad in McKenzie County, *c.*1913

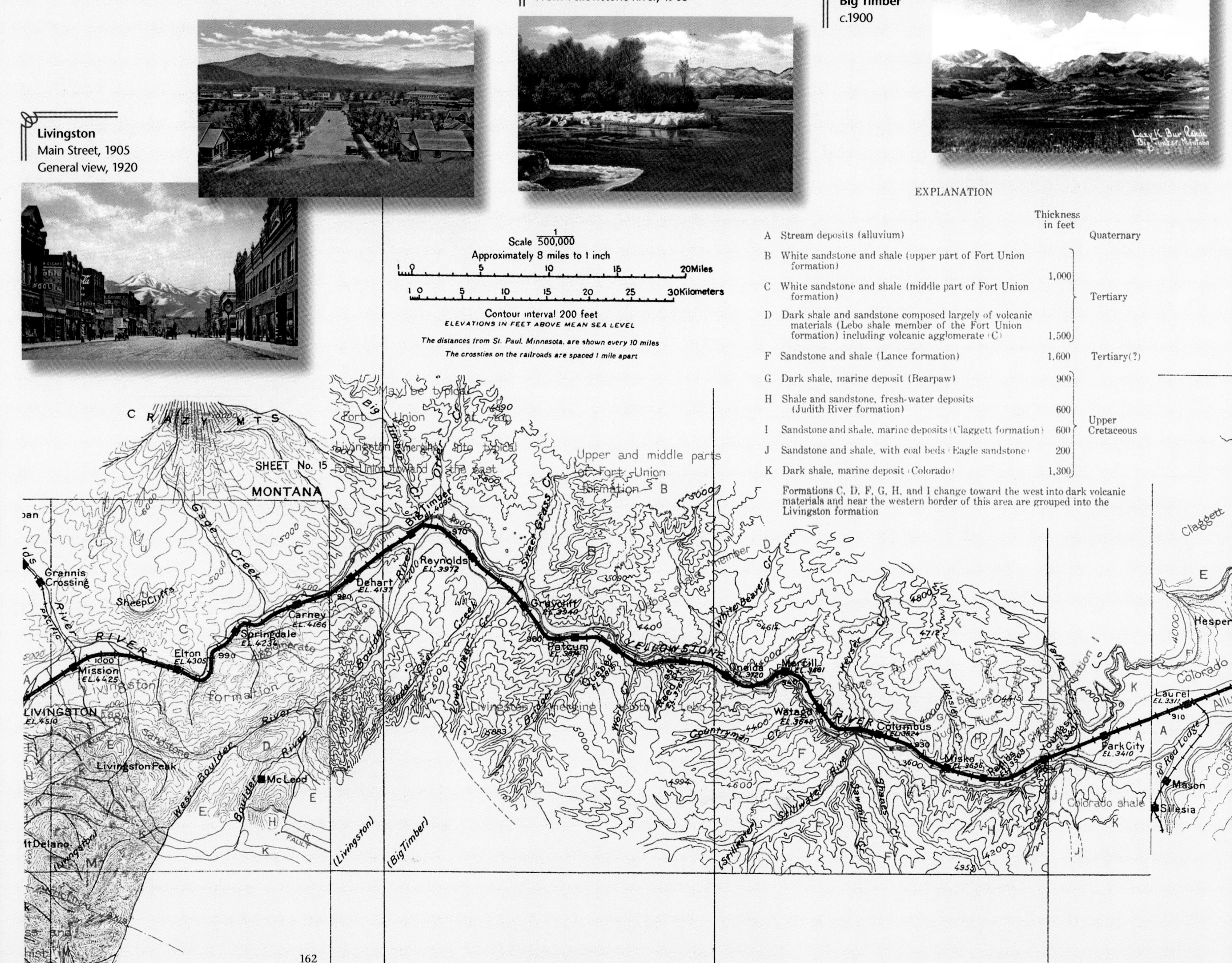
Lazy K Bar Ranch
Big Timber, Montana
Scale 1/500,000
Approximately 8 miles to 1 inch
0 5 10 15 20 Miles
0 5 10 15 20 25 30 Kilometers
Contour interval 200 feet
ELEVATIONS IN FEET ABOVE MEAN SEA LEVEL
The distances from St. Paul, Minnesota, are shown every 10 miles
The crossties on the railroads are spaced 1 mile apart
EXPLANATION
Thickness in feet
A Stream deposits (alluvium) — Quaternary
B White sandstone and shale (upper part of Fort Union formation)
C White sandstone and shale (middle part of Fort Union formation) — 1,000 — Tertiary
D Dark shale and sandstone composed largely of volcanic materials (Lebo shale member of the Fort Union formation) including volcanic agglomerate (C) — 1,500
F Sandstone and shale (Lance formation) — 1,600 — Tertiary(?)
G Dark shale, marine deposit (Bearpaw) — 900
H Shale and sandstone, fresh-water deposits (Judith River formation) — 600
I Sandstone and shale, marine deposits (Claggett formation) — 600 — Upper Cretaceous
J Sandstone and shale, with coal beds (Eagle sandstone) — 200
K Dark shale, marine deposit (Colorado) — 1,300
Formations C, D, F, G, H, and I change toward the west into dark volcanic materials and near the western border of this area are grouped into the Livingston formation
CRAZY MTS
SHEET No. 15
MONTANA
Upper and middle parts of Fort Union formation
Grannis Crossing
Sheep Cliffs
Mission EL. 4425
LIVINGSTON EL. 4510
Livingston Peak
Elton EL. 4305
Springdale EL. 4236
Carney EL. 4166
Dehart EL. 4137
Big Timber EL. 4095
Reynolds EL. 3972
Greycliff EL. 3940
Pelcum
Oneida EL. 3720
Merrill EL. 3681
Wstago EL. 3649
Columbus EL. 3624
Misko EL. 3565
Park City EL. 3410
Laurel EL. 3311
Hesper
Mason
Silesia
McLeod
Mt Delano
YELLOWSTONE RIVER
Livingston formation
Colorado shale
Claggett
(Livingston)
(Big Timber)

Crazy Mountains
From Yellowstone River, 1905

Big Timber
c.1900

Livingston
Main Street, 1905
General view, 1920

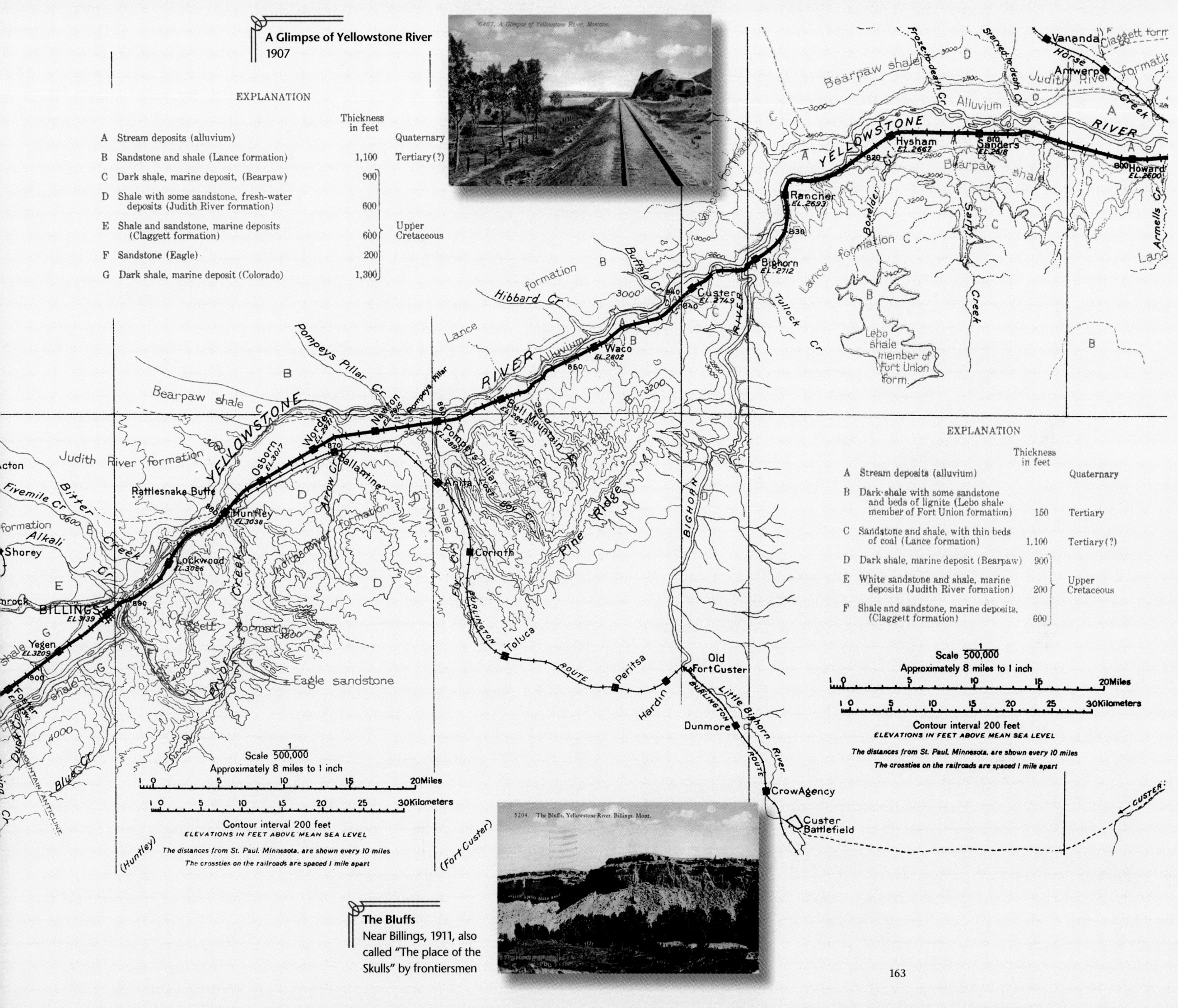
6467. A Glimpse of Yellowstone River, Montana.
EXPLANATION
Thickness in feet
A Stream deposits (alluvium) Quaternary
B Sandstone and shale (Lance formation) 1,100 Tertiary (?)
C Dark shale, marine deposit, (Bearpaw) 900
D Shale with some sandstone, fresh-water deposits (Judith River formation) 600
E Shale and sandstone, marine deposits (Claggett formation) 600 Upper Cretaceous
F Sandstone (Eagle) 200
G Dark shale, marine deposit (Colorado) 1,300
YELLOWSTONE RIVER
Vananda
Antwerp
Hysham EL.2667
Sanders EL.2618
Howard EL.2600
Rancher EL.2693
Bighorn EL.2712
Custer EL.2749
Waco EL.2802
Bull Mountain
Pompeys Pillar
Newton
Worden
Osborn EL.3017
Ballantine
Anita
Huntley EL.3038
Rattlesnake Butte
Lockwood EL.3086
BILLINGS EL.3139
Yegen EL.3209
Shorey
Corinth
Toluca
Peritsa
Hardin
Old Fort Custer
Dunmore
Crow Agency
Custer Battlefield
BIGHORN RIVER
Little Bighorn River
Pine Ridge
Eagle sandstone
Bearpaw shale
Judith River formation
Claggett formation
Lance formation
Lebo shale member of Fort Union form.
Pompeys Pillar Cr
Hibbard Cr
Buffalo Cr
Tullock Cr
Sarpy Creek
Armells Cr
Alkali Creek
Fivemile Cr
Bitter Creek
Blue Cr
BURLINGTON ROUTE
(Huntley)
(Fort Custer)
EXPLANATION
Thickness in feet
A Stream deposits (alluvium) Quaternary
B Dark shale with some sandstone and beds of lignite (Lebo shale member of Fort Union formation) 150 Tertiary
C Sandstone and shale, with thin beds of coal (Lance formation) 1,100 Tertiary (?)
D Dark shale, marine deposit (Bearpaw) 900
E White sandstone and shale, marine deposits (Judith River formation) 200 Upper Cretaceous
F Shale and sandstone, marine deposits, (Claggett formation) 600
Scale 1/500,000
Approximately 8 miles to 1 inch
0 5 10 15 20 Miles
0 5 10 15 20 25 30 Kilometers
Contour interval 200 feet
ELEVATIONS IN FEET ABOVE MEAN SEA LEVEL
The distances from St. Paul, Minnesota, are shown every 10 miles
The crossties on the railroads are spaced 1 mile apart
5204. The Bluffs, Yellowstone River, Billings, Mont.

A Glimpse of Yellowstone River
1907

The Bluffs
Near Billings, 1911, also called "The place of the Skulls" by frontiersmen

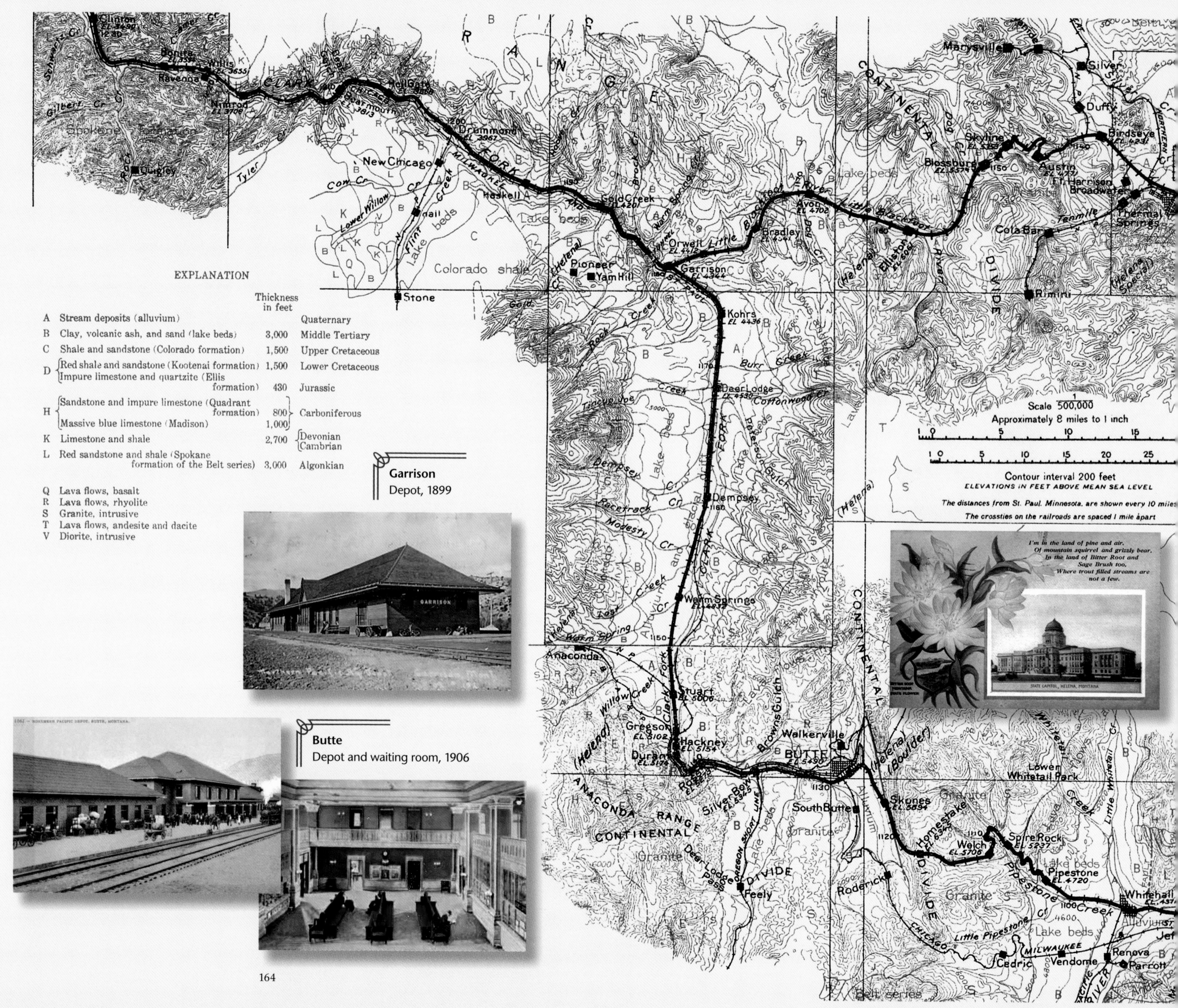
EXPLANATION
Thickness in feet
A Stream deposits (alluvium) — Quaternary
B Clay, volcanic ash, and sand (lake beds) 3,000 Middle Tertiary
C Shale and sandstone (Colorado formation) 1,500 Upper Cretaceous
D Red shale and sandstone (Kootenai formation) 1,500 Lower Cretaceous
Impure limestone and quartzite (Ellis formation) 430 Jurassic
H Sandstone and impure limestone (Quadrant formation) 800 Carboniferous
Massive blue limestone (Madison) 1,000
K Limestone and shale 2,700 Devonian Cambrian
L Red sandstone and shale (Spokane formation of the Belt series) 3,000 Algonkian
Q Lava flows, basalt
R Lava flows, rhyolite
S Granite, intrusive
T Lava flows, andesite and dacite
V Diorite, intrusive
Scale 1/500,000
Approximately 8 miles to 1 inch
Contour interval 200 feet
ELEVATIONS IN FEET ABOVE MEAN SEA LEVEL
The distances from St. Paul, Minnesota, are shown every 10 miles
The crossties on the railroads are spaced 1 mile apart
I'm in the land of pine and air,
Of mountain squirrel and grizzly bear,
In the land of Bitter Root and
Sage Brush too,
Where trout filled streams are
not a few.
STATE CAPITOL, HELENA, MONTANA
NORTHERN PACIFIC DEPOT, BUTTE, MONTANA.
GARRISON
Clinton
Bonita
Ravenna
Nimrod
Bearmouth
Drummond
New Chicago
Stone
Haskell
Gold Creek
Pioneer
Yam Hill
Garrison
Orwell
Bradley
Avon
Elliston
Kohrs
Deer Lodge
Dempsey
Warm Springs
Anaconda
Stuart
Gregson
Hackney
Durant
Walkerville
BUTTE
Silver Bow
South Butte
Feely
Roderick
Skones
Homestake
Welch
Spire Rock
Pipestone
Whitehall
Cedric
Vendome
Renova
Parrott
Marysville
Silver
Duffy
Skyline
Blossburg
Austin
Birdseye
Ft. Harrison
Broadwater
Thermal Springs
Colabar
Rimini
Lower Whitetail Park
CONTINENTAL DIVIDE
ANACONDA RANGE
Colorado shale
Lake beds
Granite
Belt series

Garrison
Depot, 1899

Butte
Depot and waiting room, 1906

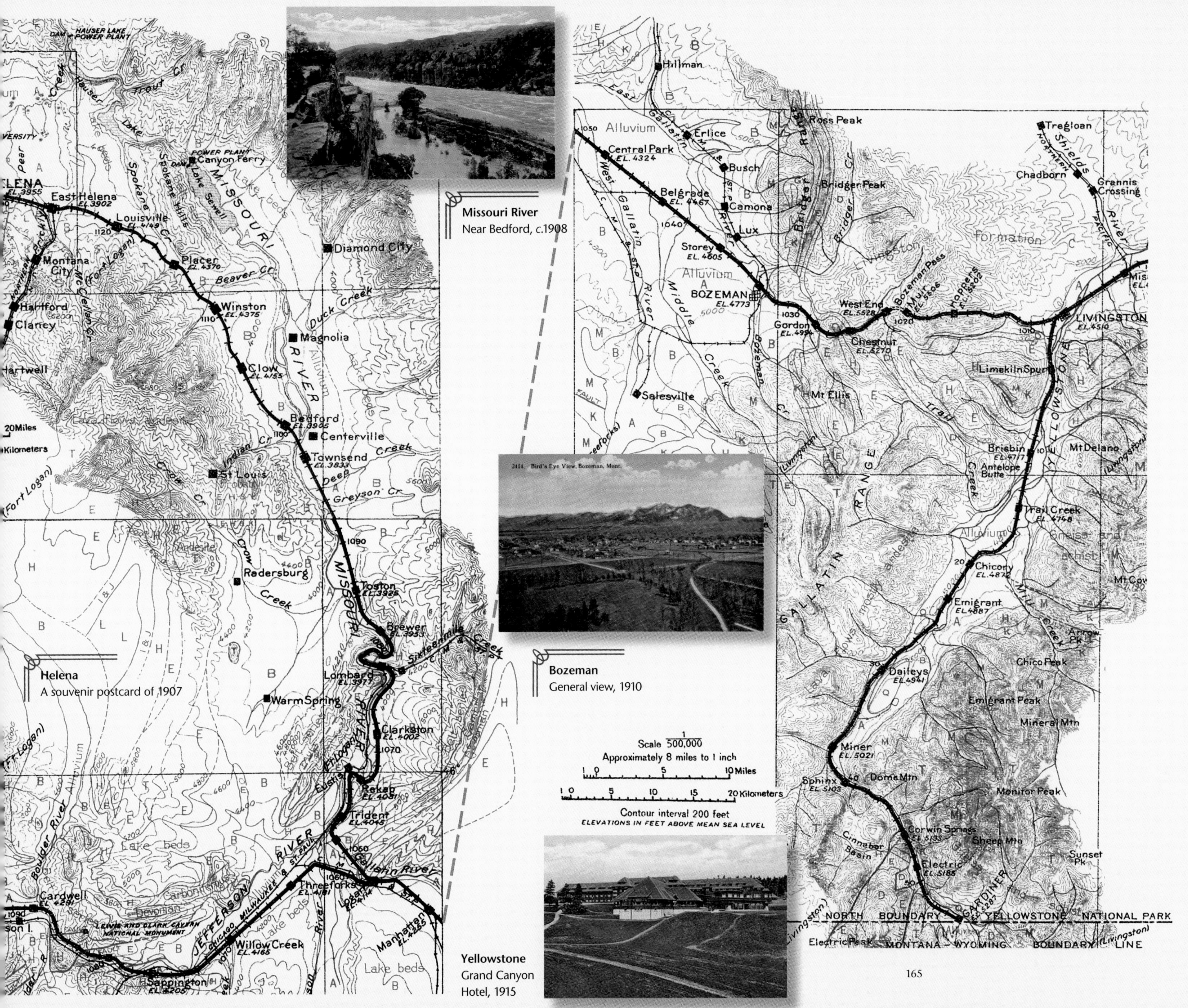

Missouri River
Near Bedford, c.1908

Helena
A souvenir postcard of 1907

Bozeman
General view, 1910

Yellowstone
Grand Canyon Hotel, 1915

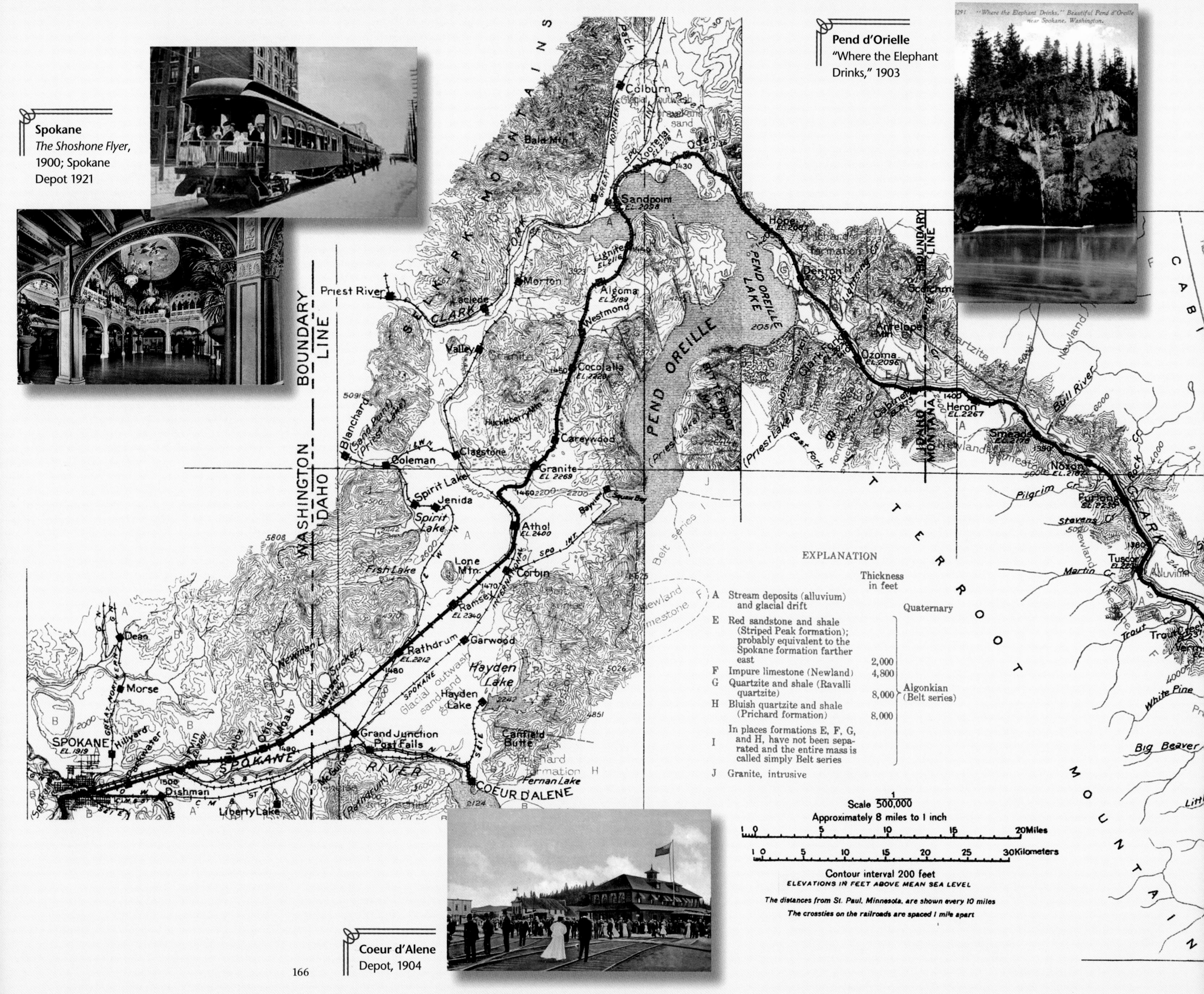

Spokane
The Shoshone Flyer, 1900; Spokane Depot 1921

Pend d'Orielle
"Where the Elephant Drinks," 1903

Coeur d'Alene
Depot, 1904

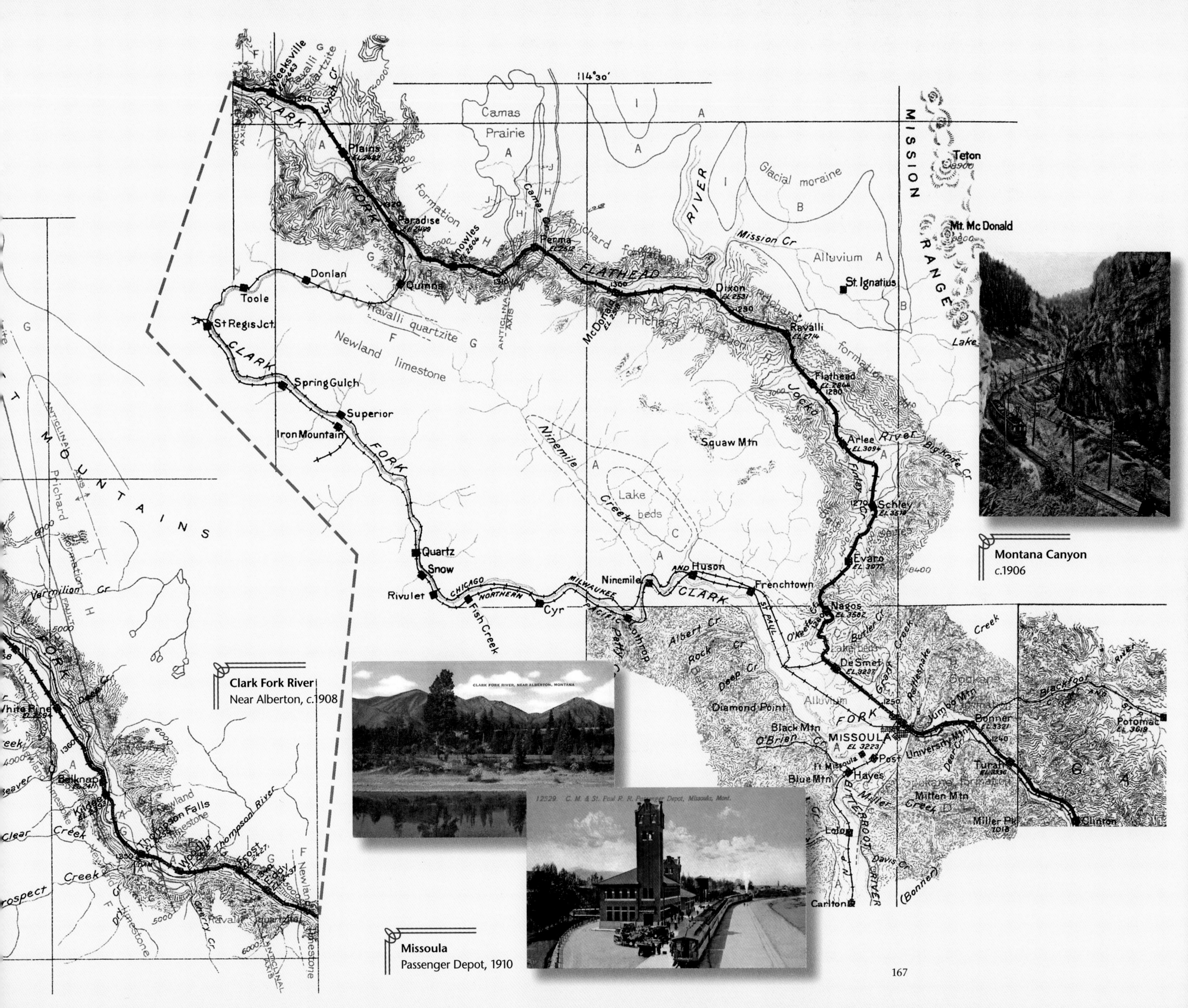

Clark Fork River
Near Alberton, *c.*1908

Missoula
Passenger Depot, 1910

Montana Canyon
*c.*1906

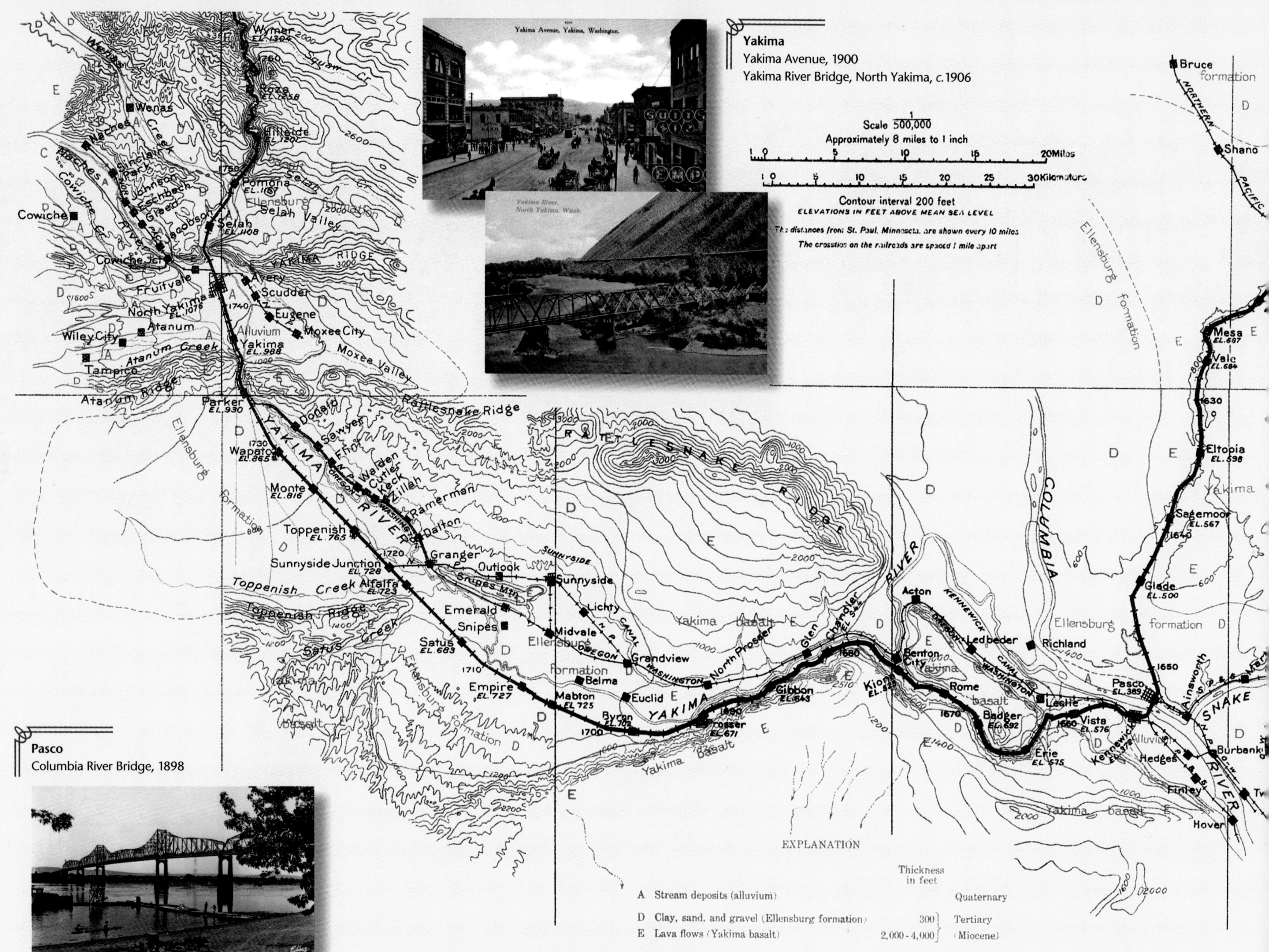

Yakima
Yakima Avenue, 1900
Yakima River Bridge, North Yakima, *c.*1906

Pasco
Columbia River Bridge, 1898

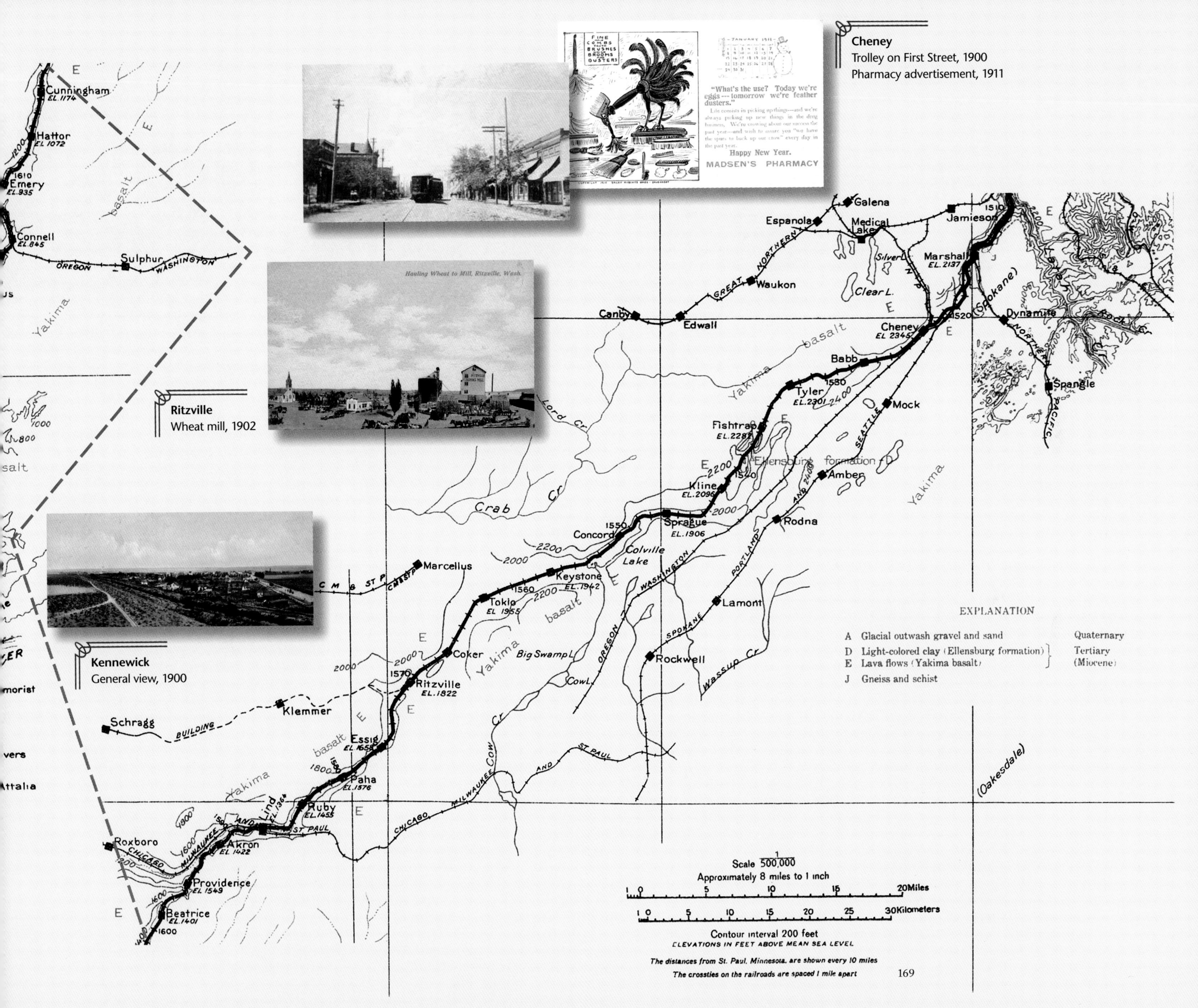

Cheney
Trolley on First Street, 1900
Pharmacy advertisement, 1911

Ritzville
Wheat mill, 1902

Kennewick
General view, 1900

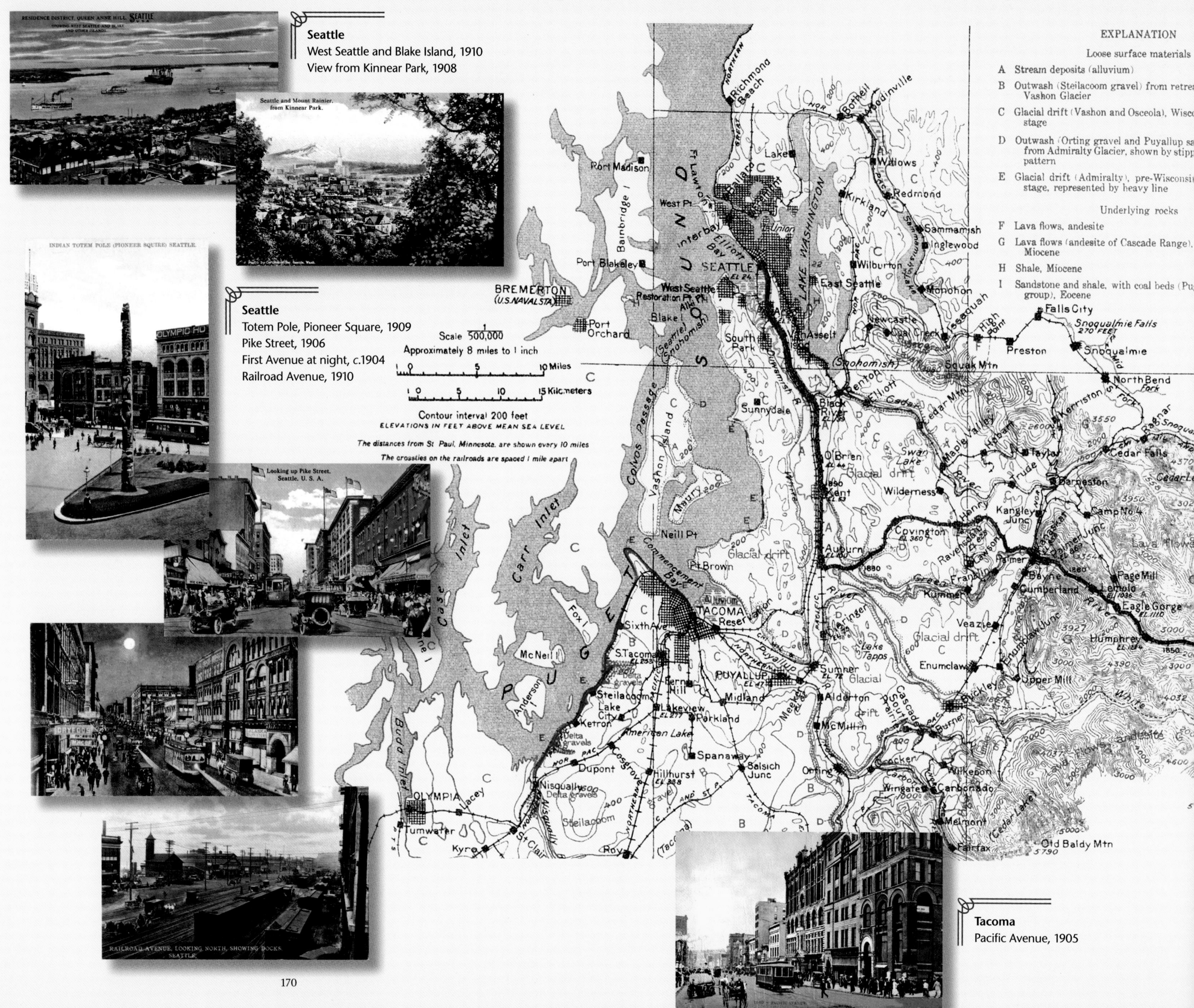

Seattle
West Seattle and Blake Island, 1910
View from Kinnear Park, 1908

Seattle
Totem Pole, Pioneer Square, 1909
Pike Street, 1906
First Avenue at night, *c.*1904
Railroad Avenue, 1910

Tacoma
Pacific Avenue, 1905

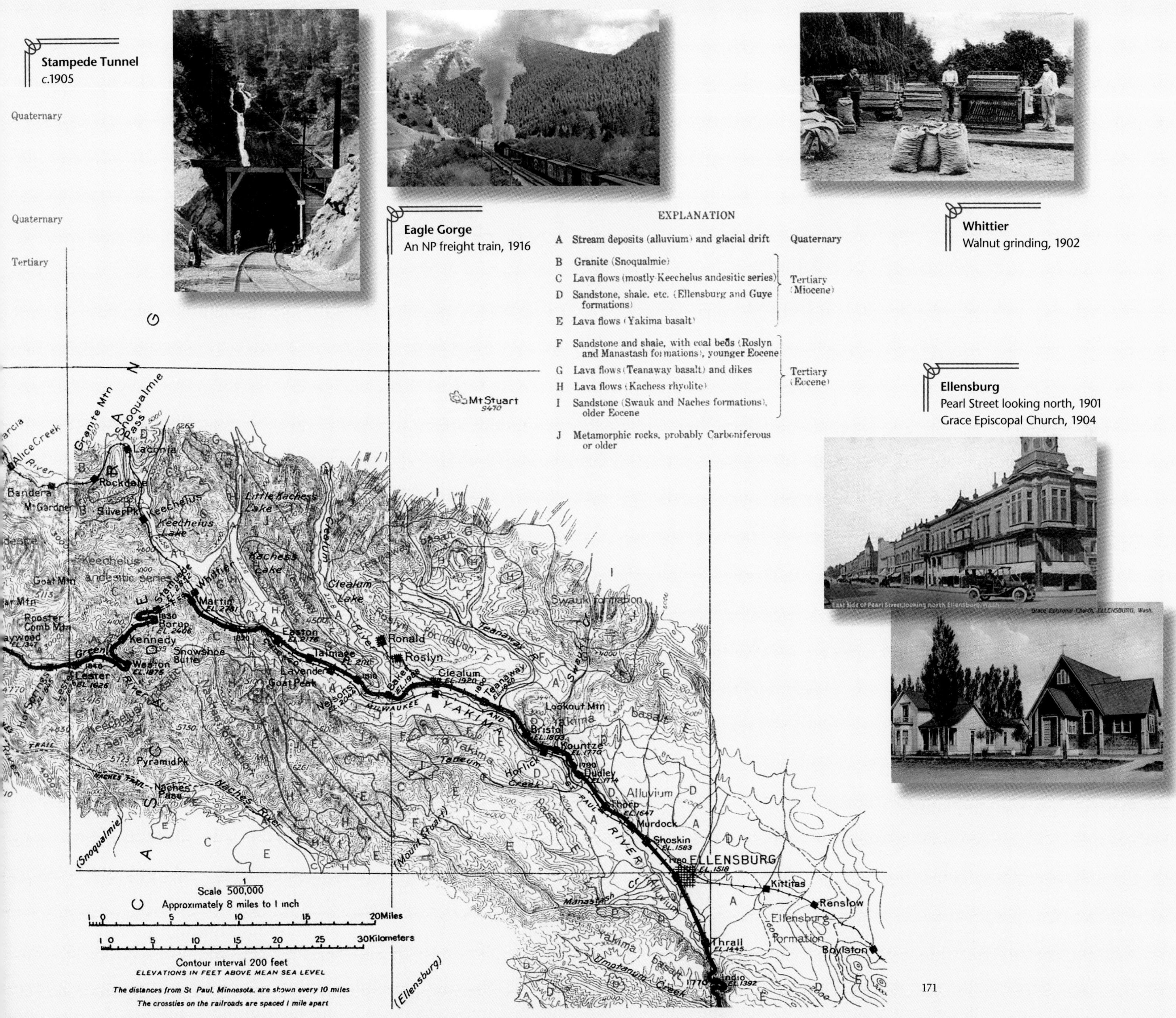

Stampede Tunnel
c.1905

Eagle Gorge
An NP freight train, 1916

Whittier
Walnut grinding, 1902

Ellensburg
Pearl Street looking north, 1901
Grace Episcopal Church, 1904

THE SANTA FE ROUTE

KANSAS CITY TO LOS ANGELES, WITH A SIDE TRIP TO THE GRAND CANYON

Pennsylvania-born Cyrus Kurtz Holliday (1826–1900) was the leading proponent of the line that evolved into the Santa Fe Railway. Having worked for a railroad contractor in Meadville, Pennsylvania, he was knowledgeable in railroad matters, but his primary skills were those of a promoter and a skilled orator. In 1854, prior to his railway ambitions, Holliday helped establish the town of Topeka, Kansas. Authorized by the Kansas Territorial legislature in 1859, and first known as the Atchison & Topeka Railroad, Holliday founded his line in 1860.

The famed Santa Fe Trail was among routes favored by westward-moving pioneers. This trail ran west from the Missouri River near Kansas City, meandering across the plains and deserts to the southwestern trading center at Santa Fe. By American standards, this city was an ancient settlement, having been established in 1598 as "La Ciudad Real de la Santa Fé de San Francisco" ("The True City of the Holy Faith of St. Francis"). Eventually it became the capital of the state of New Mexico. The Santa Fe Trail embodied the spirit of the American Southwest, invoking visions of wagon-trains slowly traversing wide open spaces under a blazing sun in a bright azure sky and with ruby-red sunsets silhouetting the distant mountains. Caravans consisting of as many as 26 ox-drawn wagons would make a seventeen-day overland journey to Santa Fe, where travelers to the West Coast would continue on the old Spanish Trail. During the California Gold Rush of 1849, thousands traversed this route to seek their fortune; at its peak, the trail hosted 50,000 wagons annually.

In 1863, capitalizing on the historic intrigue (and before the line had laid its first mile), Holliday renamed his railroad the Atchison, Topeka & Santa Fe. Yet romantic visions alone couldn't build the line. A decade of delays stemming from

Cyrus Kurtz Holliday (above); an advertisement for land for sale by the Atchison, Topeka and Santa Fe Railroad Company (right).

NOW IS THE TIME TO BUY.
"THE BEST THING IN THE WEST."
LEAVE YOUR STUMPS AND GRUBS
PRAIRIE
WOODLAND
A START ON THE PRAIRIE.
A START IN THE WOODS.
THE RICH VALLEY
LANDS
OF THE
Atchison, Topeka and Santa Fe R. R. Co.
SITUATED ON THE BEAUTIFUL
COTTONWOOD AND ARKANSAS RIVERS,
IN SOUTH-WESTERN KANSAS.
3,000,000 ACRES
FOR SALE ON ELEVEN YEARS' CREDIT.
Send for a large circular, giving full information about PRICES OF LAND, TERMS OF SALE, DISCOUNTS FOR IMPROVEMENTS, Exploring Tickets, and Rebate of Fares to Land Buyers. Address,
A. S. JOHNSON, Acting Land Commissioner, Topeka, Kansas.
PLENTY OF RICH GOVERNMENT LANDS FOR HOMESTEADS.

The *California Limited* in Apache Canyon, from *The Great Southwest*, Fred Harvey, Kansas City, c.1914 (left).

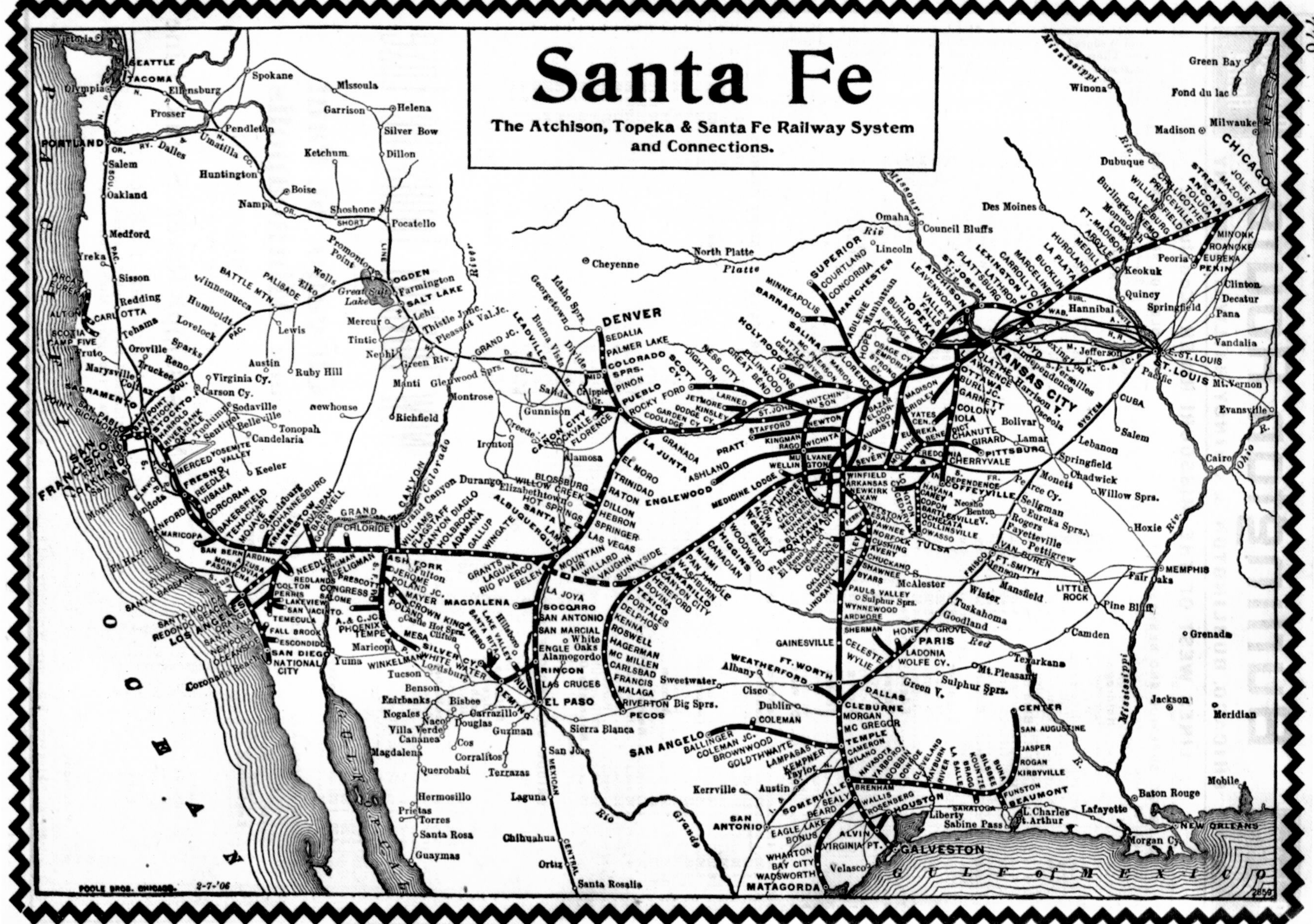

Santa Fe network map, 1906.

the American Civil War, and a dearth of working capital, saw Holliday's line lag behind other western schemes. Finally, with the help of generous Federal land-grants, the railroad got underway in 1868, and in April the following year the Santa Fe operated its first scheduled revenue-earning train between Topeka and nearby Wakarusa.

In the 1870s the Santa Fe blazed its iron road across the plains, reaching the Kansas–Colorado border by 1872. The Santa Fe didn't just build a railroad, however; it was also instrumental in settling the plains and colonizing communities along its lines, although this irrevocable force of change reduced the West's once magnificent buffalo herds to hides and bone. Doing so brought an end to the way of life enjoyed by Native Americans in the region who for centuries had coexisted with the buffalo. Open range cattle herds—and later wheat fields—came in their stead and the Santa Fe enjoyed the fruits of this change; first profiting from the transport of settlers, and later from transport of their harvests.

While Holliday had been the early vision behind the Santa Fe, William Barstow Strong, who became president of the line in 1881, directed the Santa Fe during its crucial expansionist period.

Although the Santa Fe had its sights further west, its first serious quest was for Colorado traffic. Unlike the boomtowns that grew up along the railway, Denver offered a prize as it was keen to have an iron path eastward and was already an established source of traffic. Even more enticing was the prospect of mineral traffic high in the Rockies at Leadville, Colorado. The Santa Fe wasn't the only show in town, and its westward expansion soon found conflict with the region's other great railroad scheme, the Denver & Rio Grande (D&RG). Among the most colorful episodes in western railroad history were gun battles between workers of the Santa Fe and those of General William Jackson Palmer's three-foot gauge D&RG.

In 1878, Strong's Santa Fe and Palmer's D&RG vied for control of Raton Pass—the low mountain crossing used by the Santa Fe Trail—on the border between Colorado and New Mexico. While the Santa Fe soon prevailed, a year later the lines were to clash again, and with more serious repercussions as they scrambled for control of the Royal Gorge. In this squabble, shots were fired on more than one occasion, and various degrees of law were employed before a settlement was reached. The Santa Fe's westward visions were incompatible with the Rio Grande's aspirations, but peace was finally mediated, and the Santa Fe accepted access to the Leadville Mines via jointly used trackage with the Rio Grande (which required dual gauge tracks through the Royal Gorge), while it relinquished Denver to the D&RG (although a decade later, when the peace was broken, the Santa Fe built its own line to Denver parallel to the D&RG's north of Pueblo).

With the Santa Fe's Colorado ambitions largely squelched, the railroad pushed westward via Raton Pass and then over New Mexico's Glorieta Pass, reaching Albuquerque in 1880. Much to the disillusionment of Holliday, however, in following this path the line avoided a direct route through its namesake. Although historic Santa Fe had represented a romantic goal, the region's rugged geography precluded a direct line there from the east. Instead, the railroad built an eighteen-mile branch from its mainline at Lamy to Santa Fe. The year 1880 also proved crucial, as the Santa Fe reached an agreement with the St. Louis & San Francisco Railroad to jointly take up the Atlantic & Pacific's charter authorizing construction along the 35th parallel to California. The Santa Fe got the better of this deal as the latter line built near its westward goal.

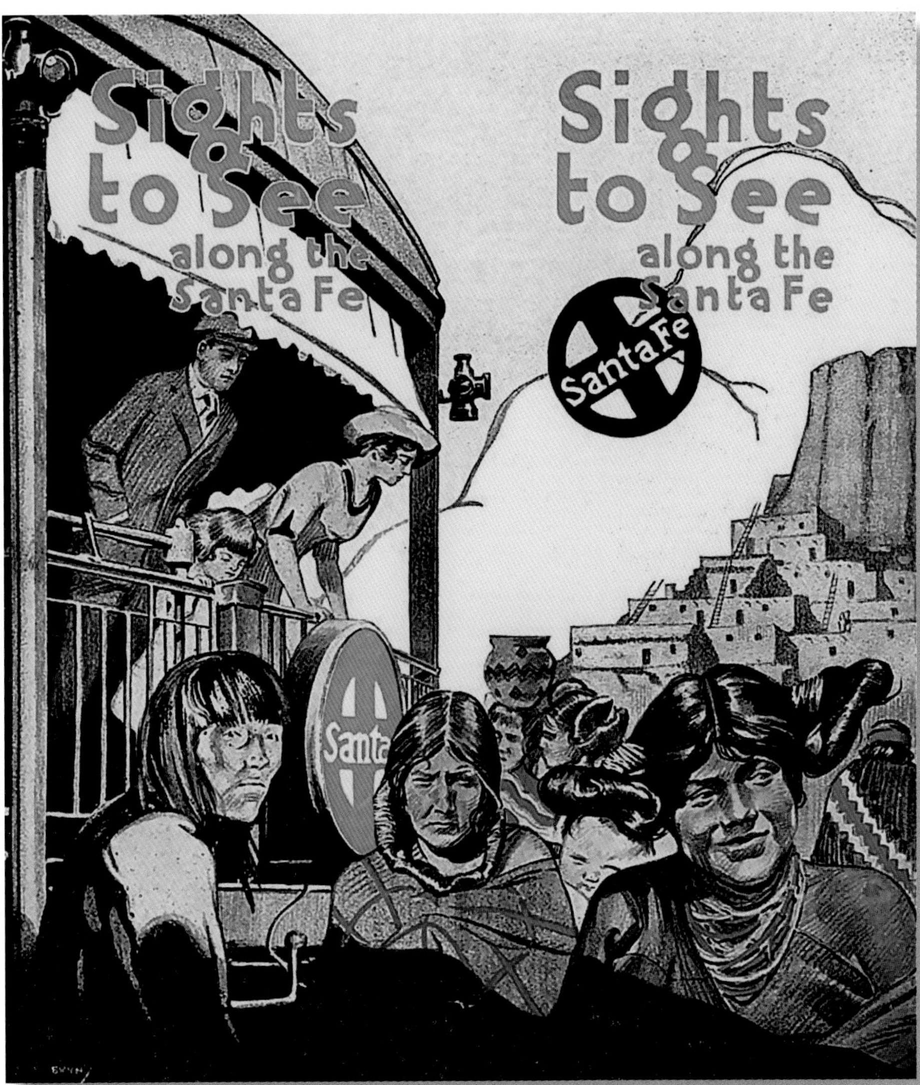

Sights to See along The Santa Fe, advertising booklet, 1910 (above).

Holliday's dreams envisioned a railroad empire reaching southward to Mexico City as well as west to California. So, as the Santa Fe built west, it also arranged with Mexico for construction of another line to the Pacific port of Guaymas. On the way southwest, this line connected with the Southern Pacific's Sunset Route at Deming, New Mexico. This served little advantage to the SP except initially to block the Santa Fe's expansion, and it remained an insignificant route despite the historic precedent of technically forming America's second transcontinental railroad link. As it turned out, the SP would try to block the Santa Fe repeatedly as the two companies vied for territory and traffic. In 1883, when the Santa Fe reached the Arizona–California border near Needles, it met with the SP's recently constructed line across the Mojave Desert–built specifically to keep the Santa Fe out of California in order to preserve the SP's fragile statewide transport monopoly. Strong proved the master of this game, however, and ultimately the Santa Fe assumed control of this crucial line in California.

California's Cajon Pass follows a natural cleft between the San Bernardino and San Gabriel Mountains northeast of the Los Angeles Basin. This was the foremost natural obstacle to the Santa Fe's engineers in building a line to the California coast (right).

Ascending Cajon Pass (below). Both from *The Great Southwest*.

Simultaneous with its westward Atlantic–Pacific construction, the Santa Fe encouraged connections in southern California. In order to obtain eastward connections, the railroad worked with the city of San Diego, which presented itself as a logical Pacific terminal, and together they built the California Southern Railroad in a north-easterly direction to connect with the Atlantic & Pacific route. This line followed a coastal route to Del Mar, then struck off inland via Temecula Canyon to San Bernardino, where it was temporarily blocked by the SP.

When the Santa Fe completed its line over California's Cajon Pass in 1885, it finally could boast of its own through transcontinental route from the Missouri River to the Pacific Ocean at San Diego. Yet its Temecula Canyon line was susceptible to violent flooding and proved too expensive to maintain. In the meantime, the Santa Fe's intentions evolved, and in 1887 it connected to Los Angeles. Then, in 1888, the company constructed a superior route to San Diego following the Pacific Coast southward from

Santa Fe 0–4–0 Switcher by San Diego Harbor, 1880s.

the Los Angeles Basin. This benefited the railroad, but instead of being its primary Pacific terminus San Diego was now served by what was effectively a branch from Los Angeles.

After 1887, the Santa Fe organized its own direct route between Kansas City and Chicago. By 1888 the road not only had the most direct route between these two crucial gateways, but operated the only through route from Chicago to California under the control of one railroad. Yet rapid expansion left the Santa Fe in a precarious financial position. Following the great financial Panic of 1893, the Atchison, Topeka & Santa Fe Railroad was reorganized as the Atchison, Topeka & Santa Fe Railway, and during the next few decades it was led by Ed

Ripley (1845–1920), a powerful man of vision who honed the railroad into one of the great western lines.

Among the crucial segments put in place during Ripley's early years was the Santa Fe's connection to California's Bay Area, which stabbed right at the heart of its rival's empire. In the mid-1890s, the Santa Fe's affiliate San Francisco & San Joaquin Valley Railroad built through its namesake valley. Separating the two lines was the barrier of the Tehachapis, a difficult terrain traversed by the SP's sinuous main line opened in 1876, made famous by the Tehachapi Loop. While the Santa Fe weighed the costs of a parallel route crossing the equally rugged Tejon Pass, it ultimately convinced the SP to grant it trackage rights over the Tehachapis between Mojave and Bakersfield. In this way the two railroads shared one of California's most difficult crossings.

Dearborn Station in Chicago before the fire in 1922 that destroyed the weathervane on top of the tower (right).

An advertisement from 1911 for the Santa Fe's *California Limited*, the railroad's deluxe service (below).

"SANTA FE ALL THE WAY!"

The Atchison, Topeka & Santa Fe not only offered through service from Chicago to California, it did so on its own rails and own trains. The company's unified control was represented in its famous slogan, "Santa Fe All the Way!"

Westward-bound passengers boarded Santa Fe trains at Chicago's Dearborn Street Station, where a great iron shed covered tracks that were also served by the Erie Railroad, the Monon, and other lines providing connections to and from the East. In 1909, the Santa Fe's first class fare from Chicago to San Francisco was $62.50 with an additional fee of $14 for a sleeping compartment. Second class was offered at $52.50, and money could be further saved by booking overnight accommodation in a tourist car, priced at half that of a sleeper. The scheduled running time was 75 hours, but many passengers chose to break the journey at midway points to enjoy spectacular scenic highlights, take in a cultural interlude, and refresh themselves from the stresses and confines of steam railway travel.

The Santa Fe's twelve-hour run to Kansas City was an unremarkable sprint across the rolling prairies of Illinois and Missouri. Its route between the two Midwestern gateways was built for the shortest distance, and as a result there were few noteworthy towns along the way. Among the largest was Galesburg, Illinois, where the Santa Fe crossed the main lines of its midwestern rival, the Chicago, Burlington & Quincy. The most impressive structures on the line were the 2,963-foot-long Mississippi River span at Fort Madison, Iowa, and the Missouri River crossing at Sibley, Missouri, 25 miles east of Kansas City.

Located near the confluence of the Missouri and Kansas Rivers, Kansas City—really two cities of the same name on opposite banks of the Missouri—was the most significant population center and railway junction between the end points of the Santa Fe route. Its main line was one of twelve primary railroad lines serving the city, and as a result Kansas City developed as one of the most important railroad gateways in the United States. Its Union Station, built at great expense in the early twentieth century, was in 1915 the largest passenger station west of New York City.

Like the old trail, the Santa Fe route was not just one line, but a collection of many. West of Kansas City, its lines split, offering travelers two ways to reach Emporia. The old main line ran via Topeka and the village of Holliday—named for the Santa Fe's founder. The "cutoff" was a short cut built in later years that missed the route's birthplace but saved fifteen miles of grade. West of Emporia is Newton, Kansas—named for the Boston suburb of Newton, Massachusetts—which served as the Harvey County seat as well as the location of railyards and a crew exchange point. The town was the focus of extensive Mennonite settlement beginning in 1874, and was said to have had a population of 100,000 by the twentieth century's second decade. Mennonites were ethnic Germans emigrating from Russia, where they had settled during Catherine the Great's reign to escape religious persecution. They brought with them a strain of winter wheat from the steppes of Central Asia which developed as one of Kansas's principal crops, becoming an important source of traffic for the Santa Fe. As the focal point of their community, Newton was the site of the first Mennonite college.

West of Newton, the Santa Fe's routes diverged again, with lines to Texas and Oklahoma to the southwest, and the old main line to Colorado continuing west. Its older, and more northerly, main line was the preferred passenger route. However, the completion of the Santa Fe's Belen cutoff in 1908, connecting west Texas lines to a low-grade line across eastern New Mexico, provided an alternative routing for most transcontinental freight and some California-bound passenger trains. Longer, and less dramatically scenic than the northerly main line, the cutoff's highlight is at Abo Canyon, a narrow defile in the mountains west of the summit at Mountainair.

"The First Santa Fe Train," from the cover of *The Great Southwest* (above).

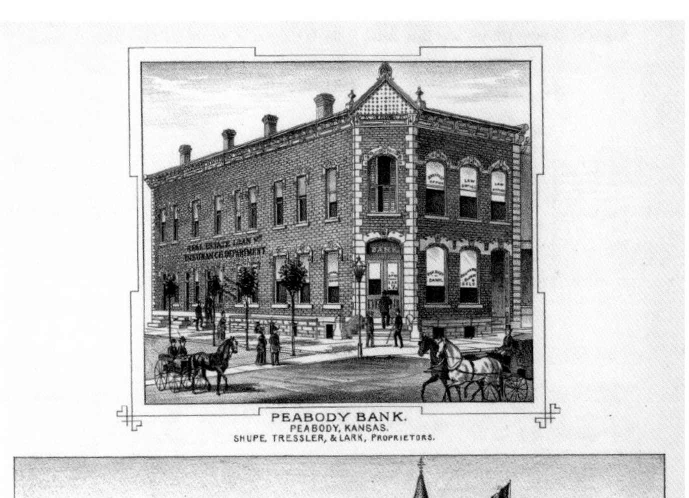

PEABODY BANK.
PEABODY, KANSAS.
SHUPE, TRESSLER, & LARK, PROPRIETORS.

CLARK'S HOTEL AND RESTAURANT.
OPPOSITE SANTA FE' DEPOT. $1.50 TO $2.50 PER DAY, FIRST CLASS IN EVERY RESPECT, WITH ALL MODERN IMPROVEMENTS,
BARBER-SHOP, BATH, BILLIARD, SAMPLE AND LUNCH ROOMS ALL IN CONNECTION. GEO. E. CLARK, PROPR. NEWTON, KANSAS.

Newton, Kansas, showing the Peabody Bank and Clark's Hotel and Restaurant opposite the Santa Fe Depot (left).

The Alvaro Hotel, Albuquerque, named after Captain Harnando de Alvarado, a Spanish Captain in the 1500s, from *The Great Southwest* (above).

A Zuni Indian settlement, a 1910 postcard (below right).

Most passenger trains continued due west via Dodge City (formerly Fort Dodge, named after General Henry Dodge, one-time governor of Wisconsin Territory). Although seemingly flat to the eye, the Santa Fe's line gradually rises as it spans the Kansas plains. Topeka is at 868 feet above sea level, while Dodge City, 368 miles from Kansas City, is at 2,478 feet as the line continues to gently climb until reaching the Rockies.

In the valley of the Arkansas River, where the Santa Fe crosses from Kansas into Colorado west of Coolidge, the line reaches 3,341 feet, but there is little visible change in terrain, although the sky above is often the rich azure associated with the West as opposed to the hazy white more common in the heavily agricultural plains. In the summer season, great storms sweep across the plains, bringing lightning, hail, and sometimes the greatly feared funnel clouds. At La Junta, Colorado, elevation 4,045 feet, the Santa Fe has another significant junction, where its Denver route divides from the transcontinental line. A branch of the old Santa Fe trail crossed the railroad 400 feet east of the station, and although more than 75 miles distant, on clear days the first hints of the Rockies can be viewed in the west. On its way west, the railroad avoids the steepest and highest peaks, instead finding the low saddle in the mountains at Raton Pass.

GLORIETA PASS AND WEST

Beyond Raton, the Santa Fe crosses a broad, arid valley. At Las Vegas, New Mexico, elevation 6,392 feet, westward trains paused to take on helpers for the climb over Glorieta Pass. The summit at Glorieta is 7,421 feet, two hundred feet lower than Raton but every bit as steep. To the west, tracks drop down through the New Mexico desert, through Lamy, to Albuquerque, where for the first time since Trinidad the population greatly exceeded the elevation. Beyond Albuquerque the line begins its gradual ascent of the high desert, passing through a landscape punctuated by colorful rock formations.

As the trains snaked through the deserts and canyons, passengers took in the constantly evolving panorama with appreciative awe. Distinctive lava-capped mesas are seen to the north, while between Horace and Grant and beyond rise dome-shaped mountains. Visitors from the East accustomed to lush green fields or Appalachian forests found little familiar in the dry, barren scenery of New Mexico, yet were fascinated by the ever-changing cliffs and mountains that rolled by beyond the windows of their coaches.

At Gonzales, more than 1,050 miles from Kansas City, is the summit of the Zuni Mountains, where the Santa Fe crosses the Continental Divide at an elevation of 7,250 feet. Although a less dramatic mountain crossing than Raton and Glorieta, this represents a far more significant separation of watersheds. To the east, water flows toward the Atlantic; to the west it empties into the Colorado River basin and flows toward the Pacific. Beyond Gonzales, the Santa Fe's line temporarily divides, allowing east- and westward trains different alignments that favor the grade.

Gallup, New Mexico, at 6,503 feet, had been an important stop, traditionally serving as a meal break, and it was one

Arizona's Diablo Canyon, from *The Great Southwest.*

of many places where locomotives were serviced and crews exchanged. It was also an important trading post for native Navajo and Zuni. Their reservations to the south and north of the railroad were significant attractions to travelers taking the time to explore western New Mexico. Zuni Pueblos had been built hundreds of years earlier, and by 1900 these ruins fascinated visitors.

Compared with New Mexico, eastern Arizona was less spectacular, much of the land characterized by broad open desert. The line passed Holbrook, named for Atlantic & Pacific's chief engineer, H. R. Holbrook, who built much of the line. West of Winslow, 4,843 feet above sea level, passengers were treated to Canyon Diablo—the Devil's Canyon—where the Santa Fe spanned a cleft in the earth 222 feet deep and 560 feet across. This required an immense bridge, the earliest version dating to 1882, and involved a multitude of construction, an iron-tower-bent viaduct with Pratt-style deck-truss spans that seemed remarkably light considering its height. Later, the Santa Fe replaced this viaduct with a magnificent steel arch.

From here the railway climbs to the 6,902-foot summit at Flagstaff, where the line passes through the tall pines of Coconino National Forest, then begins its long descent to the Colorado River, crossing at Topock near Needles after the longest unbroken grade in the United States. The massive bridge at Topock marks Santa Fe's entrance to the Golden State. West of the desert oasis at Needles, the line rises across the great barren sweep of California's Mojave Desert, cresting at Ash Hill. In the desert at Barstow, named for Santa Fe president William Barstow Strong, Santa Fe had substantial facilities, including freight yards, locomotive shops, and a Harvey House hotel. West of the town its two principal California routes divide, the original line continuing west toward Los Angeles by way of Cajon Pass and San Bernardino, and the route toward San Francisco Bay heading toward the junction with Southern Pacific at Mojave, and thence across the Tehachapis. California was the destination for most passengers; some were casual visitors, others stayed for a lifetime.

The Santa Fe's route is more than an American icon; it has developed as one of the premier East–West freight corridors. In 1995, the Santa Fe merged with Burlington Northern (itself a 1970 merger of Burlington, Northern Pacific, Great Northern) to form one of America's most extensive railroad networks. Today, the old Santa Fe hosts long container trains originating at west coast ports for destinations all over the United States, while Amtrak's *Southwest Chief* provides a daily long-distance service between Chicago and Los Angeles.

RATON PASS

Hitting the Santa Fe Trail

The first, and perhaps best known, of Santa Fe's mountain crossings is at Raton Pass in the Sangre de Christo Mountains. This was home to Richens L. Wootton–"Uncle Dick Wootton"–one of the West's most famous pioneers, who by the 1860s was operating a toll road over Raton Pass, where he assisted wagon trains in their passage west.

The Santa Fe's survey crews enlisted Uncle Dick to help them in their battle with General William Palmer's Rio Grande railroad for control of this crucial natural divide. The Santa Fe's claims to Raton stood on soft ground, since the Rio Grande had received an earlier charter for Raton, but Palmer was slow to develop his line, and only rushed into action when he learned of Santa Fe chief engineer William Barstow Strong's plans to build west by way of Raton. With Wootton's help the Santa Fe had grading forces on Raton before Palmer's team arrived, and won the day. If Palmer had prevailed, the old Rio Grande main line over Raton may have stretched from Denver to Mexico, creating a completely different railroad history.

Raton Pass was a difficult part of the Santa Fe's transcontinental line. To the east the line was lightly graded, but here it climbed steeply. At Trinidad, Colorado, 5,971 feet high and near the foot of the grade, trains arriving from the east had additional locomotives added to serve as "helpers" over the mountain. In many cases a leading helper would be added at the front while another locomotive would be attached to the back as a "pusher." As trains crawled toward Raton Pass, from where the railroad closely followed the old Santa Fe Trail, passengers were offered glimpses of the vast expanse of the plains they had just crossed while being awed by views of Colorado's famed Spanish Peaks. At the summit, just shy of the New Mexico state line, the Santa Fe built two parallel tunnels, the older of which featured a bore of 2,041 feet. Although at 7,622 feet above sea level this was the highest point on the Santa Fe, it was only the first of several mountain summits on the way west.

On the west slope of the pass is the town of Raton, 6,666 feet above sea level. Once a crucial oasis for travelers along the Santa Fe Trail, with the coming of the railroad Raton became for a while merely a servicing stop where trains dropped their helpers and took on coal and water, and passengers were afforded a few minutes to stretch their legs or take a photograph. Raton was gateway to the Taos Valley, however, and later developed as a popular layover point.

Richens L. Wootton (top).

The Spanish Peaks from between La Junta and Trinidad, from *The Great Southwest* (right).

The Raton Tunnel at the summit of Raton Pass, 7,548 feet above sea level, from *The Great Southwest* (far right).

GRAND CANYON BRANCH

Greatest of Gorges

Grand Canyon from Yavapai Point, from *The Great Southwest* (opposite).

El Tovar, on the rim of the Grand Canyon, a Harvey House Hotel at 6,866 feet above sea level, provided accommodation for 250 guests, and the Bright Angel Camp Hotel nearby was even larger (below).

Most famous and perhaps most awe inspiring of all the scenic wonders of the American West is the Grand Canyon. Here, over millions of years the rushing waters of the Colorado River have carved the greatest of all gorges in the desert plateau of southern Arizona. The canyon varies from four to eighteen miles across, is more than a mile deep, and extends for some 217 miles, although the most dramatic section that draws the most visitors is 56 miles long.

European discovery of this geological wonder has been credited to García López de Cárdenas of Coronado's sixteenth-century exploratory mission from Spain. Little notice was paid to this enormous gash in the earth, however, until the mid-nineteenth century, and then it was thought of not as a natural wonder, but simply as an impediment to travel; when the Santa Fe's survey teams laid out their grade in the 1870s and 1880s they made sure to do so well south of the gorge.

The Grand Canyon did attract occasional curiosity seekers, but it was too remote for most travelers until the coming of the Santa Fe. Although the main line ran far to the south of the canyon, stage coaches running north from Flagstaff, Williams, and Ashfork brought intrepid tourists to gaze in awe over the south rim. The layers of sandstone and limestone radiating reddish-orange hues that complement the shades of the setting sun against a seemingly infinite horizon soon became an iconic image of the Southwest, and developed ever-greater public interest in the canyon.

In 1899, a group of eastern capitalists started a branch railroad from a junction with the Santa Fe at Williams. This railroad town was named for the legendary Arizona pioneer Bill Williams who, having been jilted by his muse, wandered west in the early nineteenth century with visions of converting the natives. Yet it was he, not they, who was converted, and Williams spent years living among the Utes until, as European settlement encroached on Arizona, the Utes came to believe that Williams had betrayed them and killed him. But this was decades before the railroad arrived, and half a century before the junction was established that was to bear his name.

The original branch was called the Santa Fe & Grand Canyon, and was built northward toward copper mines near Anita, where its promoters hoped to generate freight revenue from mining produce as well as taking advantage of growing tourist interest in the canyon. However, in common with many other builders of small railways, vision outstripped capital and the line failed nearly twenty miles from the gorge. Ever opportunistic, the Santa Fe, which was then under the progressive administration of Ed Ripley, took control of the branch and by 1901 had completed the 64-mile line from Williams to the south rim. The Santa Fe immediately capitalized on the tourist potential and through the Fred Harvey Company established fine hotels near the railway terminus—the Bright Angel Lodge and El Tovar. Although Harvey died prior to the opening of these institutions, Keith L. Bryant wrote in his *History of*

the Atchison, Topeka, and Santa Fe Railway that Harvey had asked well-known artist Thomas Moran to paint panoramas for the hotels of the Grand Canyon to convey its grandeur.

The opening of the Santa Fe's branch to the canyon greatly improved access and tourists began to arrive in droves. Many traveled to Williams on one of the Santa Fe's famed transcontinental limiteds before changing to the branch line. Later, the railroad's *Grand Canyon Limited* provided through sleeping cars directly to the south rim terminus. So valued was this traffic that in 1929 the Santa Fe speeded the train's schedule.

Visitor numbers to the Grand Canyon by rail remained steady into the late 1940s, although in general Santa Fe's tourist traffic had begun its decline. Today, a tourist railway provides a popular excursion service over the line, which until 2007 boasted a regular steam-powered service. Sadly, however, this nostalgic operation was deemed uneconomic, and the classic old locomotives were retired from service in favor of less-romantic internal combustion power.

The branch itself is comparatively unremarkable. While at its end the line reaches nearly to the canyon's precipitous edge, most of the 64 miles cross relatively barren plateau and passengers cannot view the grandest vistas until after disembarking at Grand Canyon Station. Yet the line has some interesting views. In its first few miles north of Williams it crosses a basalt plateau where black lava cinder cones rise in the distance. To the east, passengers are treated to views of Mount Sitgraves, and, beyond, the peaks of the San Francisco Mountains. Some forty miles north of Williams is the lava-capped red sandstone Red Butte, rising like the ruins of an ancient pyramid from the limestone plateau.

The Grand Canyon, painted by Thomas Moran in 1904 (below).

The San Francisco Mountains, from *The Great Southwest* (right).

NEEDLES, CALIFORNIA

Pinnacles in the Desert

After a long descent of the Arizona Divide from the summit at Yampai, the Santa Fe bottomed out at the crossing of the Colorado River at Topock, Arizona (the name, translated from a local dialect, means "bridge"). Here, in 1909, the Santa Fe maintained an impressive 1,100-foot-long iron cantilever bridge to span the river that at this point forms the boundary between Arizona and California. In 1945, this was replaced with a massive double track bridge consisting of three heavy deck-truss spans. At just 496 feet above sea level, this bridge was the lowest point on the Santa Fe since leaving Chicago and Kansas City, both of which are at greater elevations.

Located along the Colorado River floodplain west of Topock, the town of Needles, California is a desert oasis named for three unusual rock formations along the Colorado River which are aptly described in *Baedeker's Guide* as "curious pinnacles of purple porphyry and trachytic granite." At the bottom of the grade in both directions and with a good source of water, Needles was the logical spot to service engines, and the Santa Fe established a division point here where locomotives and crews were exchanged. The railroad also maintained here the largest icing facilities in the desert for replenishing ice in refrigerated boxcars that were taking Californian fruit and vegetables eastward. In the days before mechanical refrigeration, insulated freight cars cooled with ice were crucial in the development of California agriculture ,and allowed Americans nationwide to enjoy fresh produce all year.

Beyond Needles the railroad climbed into the desert, cresting at Goffs Summit (2,585 feet above sea level) before dropping into the broad, barren plain characterized by dry salt lakes and alkali flats. Here the air is remarkably clear, allowing for incredible visibility, with mountain peaks more than seventy miles distant seeming as if they are just hills a few miles away.

The line passed through a variety of tiny communities where the population rarely exceeded a hundred souls. The largest was Amboy, California, where the Amboy crater, a volcanic cinder cone five miles in diameter and rising two hundred feet above the desert floor, can be seen to the south of the route. West of Amboy, the railroad builders assigned exotic-sounding names such as Bagdad, Trojan, Siberia, and Klondike to points along the line, although most of them never enjoyed substantial population. All the while the railroad ascended the plateau, a dry and forlorn desert crossing that contrasted with some of its spectacular mountain traverses.

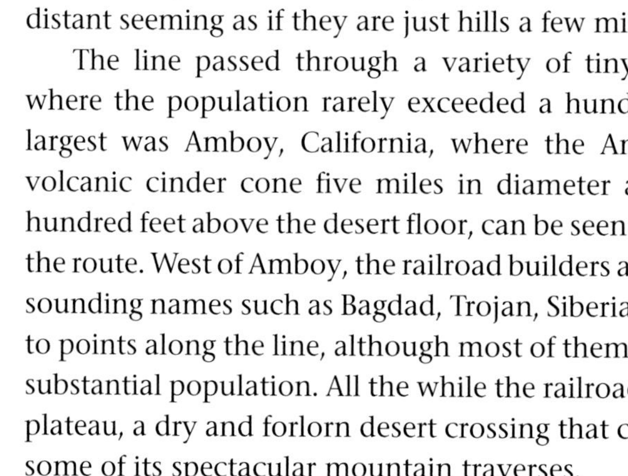

Needles Station in the 1920s (above).

Native Americans selling beadwork on the station in front of El Garces Hotel at Needles (right).

The Needles Mountains and the Colorado River, from *The Great Southwest* (far right).

HARVEY HOUSES

Feeding Southwestern Tourists

Formative western railroad travel was as legendary for its Wild West characters and atmosphere as it was for abysmal culinary experiences. Before the days of the dining car, primitive trackside railroad eateries provided just the bare essentials. Train schedules did include eating stops, but these were rarely much longer than it took to change locomotives while passengers tried to wolf down the nineteenth-century version of fast food. Travelers had a very limited time to disembark, elbow their way to the lunch counter, order, and eat. When the whistle blew to reboard the train, the meal was finished, regardless of how far along they were with dinner!

British-born Fred Harvey (1835–1901) changed this unhappy state of affairs by blending his two fields of expertise—railroading and restauranting. While serving as a western freight agent for Santa Fe competitor the Chicago, Burlington & Quincy, Harvey saw a golden opportunity to provide superior railroad dining. To his astonishment, the Burlington declined his proposal to improve the railroad's trackside eateries, but undaunted, in 1876 Harvey approached the Santa Fe's Charles F. Morse who embraced his ideas. The "Harvey House" soon emerged as both a western icon and a symbol of Santa Fe's superior transcontinental service.

Harvey's unusually high culinary standards, combined with a practice of hiring attractive, unmarried women as waitresses —popularly known as "Harvey Girls"—endeared his restaurant to travelers and railroaders alike. Not to be confused with disreputable establishments in the West that were also known for their employment of unmarried women, Harvey expected his waitresses to uphold high moral standards. They were paid $17.50 a month and were provided with free dormitories where they lived under the strict chaperonage of a matron. Girls were required to be in bed by 10 p.m., and were not permitted any appearance of impropriety such as receiving male visitors.

Harvey's menu was vastly superior to the beans and fried beefsteak of questionable origin served at conventional trackside beaneries. Although he charged a stiff price (meals cost 75 cents in 1888), the selection and quality was worth an extra few cents. In addition to traditional items such as stuffed turkey or roast beef topped off with a slice of apple pie, Harvey offered exotic foods including lobster salad *au mayonnaise*, pickled lamb's tongue, baked veal pie, English peas *au gratin*, salami of duck, and bananas.

The first Harvey House was located at Topeka, Kansas, but the winning formula soon led to expansion all along Santa Fe's lines between Chicago and Los Angeles. Among the best known were the Harvey Houses at Gallup and Lamy, New Mexico, and Barstow, California, as well as institutions such as the Casteñada hotel and restaurant at Las Vegas, New Mexico.

Fred Harvey (above).

The Harvey House at Gallup (right).

Two Harvey girls at the Hutchinson Harvey House in 1910 (top right).

The Indian Building at Albuquerque Station and Harvey House complex, both of which no longer exist, from *The Great Southwest* (far right).

INDIAN BUILDING.
FRED HARVEY.

The Harvey House remained synonymous with Santa Fe's high standards of quality and civility.

Harvey began to operate Santa Fe's dining cars after 1893 as these rolling restaurants rapidly took the place of traditional meal stops. By 1901 he had more than thirty cars, yet for many years wayside Harvey House restaurants survived, continuing to offer good meals to passengers waiting for trains as well as train crews and local residents. Harvey gave the Santa Fe's trains a distinction afforded no other line; no wonder travelers preferred "Santa Fe all the way!"

There was no better conveyance for tourism than the railroad as the twentieth century dawned, and the Santa Fe and Harvey aimed to capitalize on growing interest in the American Southwest. The Fred Harvey Company began to promote hotels as more than mere conveniences, but as destinations unto themselves. One of the first was the deluxe Montezuma Hotel at the Montezuma Hot Springs six miles from Las Vegas, where the Santa Fe had extended a branch as early as the 1880s. Guests were encouraged not just to stay for a night, but to make this retreat their holiday destination. It was a success, and Harvey went on to build a variety of luxurious, Southwestern-themed hotels at choice locations along the Santa Fe.

In the early twentieth century, the Santa Fe and the Fred Harvey Company hired well-known interior decorator Mary E. J. Colter to style their hotels with a distinctive blend of Spanish and Native American art and motifs, and by promoting colorful, original Native American styles they provoked a widespread interest in Navajo and Hopi art and culture that further encouraged tourism. Later the Santa Fe blended Native American motifs into its passenger train styling and advertising, which culminated with its deluxe *Super Chief* of the late 1930s that combined Native Motif and Art Deco style with Hollywood flair. More than any other, this train captured America's imagination and became another Santa Fe icon.

By 1945, when Judy Garland preserved the essence of the Harvey experience in the Metro-Goldwyn-Mayer movie, "The Harvey Girls," the glory days of the Harvey House eateries were in the past, although Harvey's name remains a part of the Santa Fe legacy.

Harvey Houses (below, from left to right) at Barstow, Fray Marcos, and Dodge City.

The El Ortiz Harvey House at Lamy, built with adobe, from *The Great Southwest* (far right).

El Ortiz

THE OFFICIAL GUIDE OF THE RAILWAYS

Santa Fe

Grand Canyon Line

CHICAGO, ST. LOUIS AND CALIFORNIA—GRAND CANYON LINE.

WEST. June 17, 1906.	Mls	No. 3 California Limited. Daily.	Example. Daily Service.	No. 1 California Express. Daily.	No. 1-7 Cal. & Mex. Express. Daily.	No. 9-7 California Fast Mail. Daily.
Lv. Chicago (Santa Fe)	0	8 00 P M	Sunday.	10 00 P M	10 00 P M	9 00 A M
Ar. Kansas City ..	458	8 35 A M	Monday.	10 30 A M	10 30 A M	8 50 P M
Lv. St. Louis (Burlington)	....	11 28 P M	Sunday.	11 28 P M	11 28 P M	9 06 A M
Lv. St. Louis....(C. & A.)	....	11 28 P M	Sunday.	11 28 P M	11 28 P M	9 06 A M
Lv. St. Louis...(Mo. Pac.)	....	10 10 P M	Sunday.	10 10 P M	10 10 P M	9 00 A M
Lv. St. Louis....(Frisco.)	....	....	....	8 41 P M	8 41 P M	....
Lv. St. Louis...(Wabash)	....	10 15 P M	Sunday.	10 15 P M	10 15 P M	9 10 A M
Lv. Kansas City (Santa Fe)	458	8 45 A M	Monday.	11 00 A M	2 35 P M	9 00 P M
Lv. St. Joseph ..(Santa Fe)	....	7 35 A M	Monday.	7 35 A M	....	7 00 P M
.. Atchison	....	8 20 A M	..	8 20 A M	....	7 45 P M
.. Leavenworth. ..	....	....	....	7 25 A M	....	....
.. Topeka........ ..	525	10 25 A M	..	1 15 P M	....	10 35 P M
.. Newton........ ..	659	2 00 P M	..	5 25 P M	8 30 P M	2 05 A M
.. Hutchinson.. ..	693	2 45 P M	..	6 50 P M	9 40 P M	2 50 A M
.. Dodge City.. ..	827	4 50 P M	..	10 00 P M	1 00 A M	4 55 A M
Ar. La Junta...... ..	1029	9 55 P M	..	4 40 A M	7 45 A M	10 20 A M
Lv. Denver..(Santa Fe)	0	4 00 P M	Monday.	8 00 P M	8 00 P M	3 50 A M
.. Colorado Spgs.. ..	74	6 45 P M	..	10 30 P M	10 30 P M	6 40 A M
.. Pueblo........ ..	117	8 05 P M	..	11 45 P M	11 45 P M	8 05 A M
Ar. La Junta...... ..	181	10 00 P M	..	1 30 A M	1 30 A M	10 00 A M
Lv. La Junta..(Santa Fe)	1029	10 10 P M	Monday.	4 55 A M	10 40 A M	10 40 A M
.. Trinidad....... ..	1111	1 00 A M	Tuesday.	8 05 A M	1 45 P M	1 45 P M
Lv. Las Vegas..... ..	1245	6 10 A M	..	2 00 P M	7 05 P M	7 05 P M
Ar. Santa Fe..(Santa Fe)	1328	12 01 Noon	Tuesday.	6 15 P M	9 40 P M	....
Lv. Albuquerque.(Santa Fe)	1377	11 25 A M	Tuesday.	8 15 P M	12 45 Night	12 45 Night
Ar. Gallup.......... ..	1535	4 10 P M	..	2 40 A M	5 15 A M	5 15 A M
.. Winslow	1665	7 05 P M	..	7 05 A M	8 25 A M	8 25 A M
Ar. Williams...... ..	1737	10 50 P M	..	11 25 A M	12 35 Noon	12 35 Noon
Ar. Grand Canyon (G.C.Ry.)	....	7 00 A M	Wednesday	4 30 P M	4 30 P M	4 30 P M
Lv. Grand Canyon.. ..	....	3 00 P M	Tuesday.	8 30 A M	8 30 A M	8 30 A M
Ar. Ash Fork..(Santa Fe)	1780	11 52 P M	Tuesday.	12 37 Noon	1 56 P M	1 56 P M
Lv. Ash Fork..(Santa Fe)	1780	7 05 A M	Wednesday	6 00 P M	6 00 P M	6 00 P M
Ar. Prescott	1840	9 22 A M	..	8 25 P M	8 25 P M	8 25 P M
Ar. Phœnix........ ..	1976	3 45 P M	..	2 50 A M	2 50 A M	2 50 A M
Ar. Jerome....(U.V. & P.)	1848	12 25 Noon	Wednesday	9 25 A M	9 25 A M	9 25 A M
Ar. Seligman (Santa Fe)	1808	1 05 A M	Wednesday	2 05 P M	3 20 P M	3 20 P M
.. Kingman..... ..	1895	2 33 A M	..	4 20 P M	5 02 P M	5 02 P M
.. Needles....... ..	1957	4 20 A M	..	6 25 P M	7 20 P M	7 20 P M
.. Barstow....... ..	2126	9 25 A M	..	2 25 A M	12 55 Night	12 55 Night
.. San Bernardino... ..	2207	1 00 P M	..	5 45 A M	4 25 A M	4 25 A M
.. Riverside..... ..	2215	2 10 P M	..	6 21 A M	6 21 A M	6 21 A M
.. Orange	2254	6 05 P M	..	9 36 A M	9 36 A M	9 36 A M
.. Pasadena..... ..	2258	2 50 P M	..	7 55 A M	6 19 A M	6 19 A M
.. Los Angeles. ..	2267	3 15 P M	..	8 25 A M	6 45 A M	6 45 A M
Ar. San Diego	2393	6 20 P M	..	12 45 Noon	12 45 Noon	12 45 Noon
Ar. Santa Barbara..(S.P.)	2422	8 00 P M	Wednesday	12 05 Noon	11 10 A M	11 10 A M
Lv. Barstow (Santa Fe)	2126	9 40 A M	Wednesday	1 50 P M	1 45 A M	1 45 A M
Ar. Kramer	2159	....	....	3 15 P M	2 32 A M	2 32 A M
Ar. Johannesburg.(Santa Fe)	2187	....	....	5 20 P M	....	....
Lv. Mojave.(Santa Fe)	2197	11 15 A M	Wednesday	For Local Time-Tables, see other pages of Santa Fe.	3 35 A M	3 35 A M
Ar. Bakersfield.. ..	2267	2 00 P M	..		6 50 A M	6 50 A M
.. Fresno........ ..	2377	4 37 P M	..		10 45 A M	10 45 A M
.. Merced....... ..	2433	5 55 P M	..		12 15 Noon	12 15 Noon
.. Stockton	2500	7 20 P M	..		2 30 P M	2 30 P M
.. Oakland...... ..	2571	10 20 P M	..		5 45 P M	5 45 P M
.. Point Richmond ..	2571	10 05 P M	..		5 25 P M	5 25 P M
Ar. San Francisco.. ..	2578	10 55 P M	..		6 20 P M	6 20 P M

EAST.	No. 4 California Limited. Daily.	Example. Daily Service.	No. 2 Atlantic Express. Daily.	No. 8 Chicago Express Daily.
Lv. San Francisco..(Santa Fe)	9 30 A M	Sunday.	....	8 00 P M
.. Point Richmond. ..	10 10 A M	..	....	8 50 P M
.. Oakland...... ..	9 30 A M	..	....	7 50 P M
.. Stockton	12 10 Noon	..	....	11 25 P M
.. Merced....... ..	1 40 P M	..	....	1 30 A M
.. Fresno........ ..	3 18 P M	..	....	3 25 A M
.. Bakersfield.. ..	6 00 P M	..	....	8 00 A M
Lv. Mojave....... ..	9 02 P M	..	....	11 25 A M
Lv. Johannesburg.(Santa Fe)	....	....	9 00 P M	....
Lv. Kramer (Santa Fe)	....	....	10 20 P M	12 23 Noon
Ar. Barstow	10 40 P M	Sunday.	11 45 P M	1 15 P M
Lv. San Diego (Santa Fe)	1 45 P M	Sunday.	1 45 P M	11 30 P M
.. Los Angeles. ..	6 00 P M	..	8 00 P M	7 30 A M
.. Pasadena.... ..	6 25 P M	..	8 32 P M	7 55 A M
.. Orange........ ..	6 10 P M	..	6 10 P M	....
.. Riverside	7 25 P M	..	7 25 P M	....
.. San Bernardino ..	7 45 P M	..	10 25 P M	9 50 A M
.. Barstow	10 55 P M	..	1 45 A M	1 40 P M
.. Needles...... ..	3 45 A M	Monday.	8 15 A M	8 05 P M
.. Kingman	6 03 A M	..	11 10 A M	10 45 P M
Lv. Seligman..... ..	10 15 A M	..	4 27 P M	3 05 A M
Lv. Jerome...(U. V. & P.)	6 00 A M	Monday.	10 50 A M	10 50 A M
Lv. Phœnix ...(Santa Fe)	1 15 A M	Monday.	8 50 A M	8 50 A M
Lv. Prescott..... ..	7 55 A M	..	2 57 P M	2 57 P M
Ar. Ash Fork...... ..	10 25 A M	..	5 10 P M	5 10 P M
Lv. Ash Fork..(Santa Fe)	11 15 A M	Monday.	5 57 P M	4 06 A M
Ar. Grand Canyon.(G.C.Ry.)	4 30 P M	Monday.	7 00 A M	....
Lv. Grand Canyon.. ..	8 30 A M	..	3 00 P M	....
Lv. Williams..(Santa Fe)	12 25 Noon	Monday.	6 54 P M	5 27 A M
.. Winslow...... ..	3 30 P M	..	10 25 P M	8 51 A M
.. Holbrook..... ..	....	....	11 20 P M	9 46 A M
.. Gallup........ ..	7 20 P M	..	2 40 A M	1 50 P M
Lv. Albuquerque.... ..	12 09 Night	..	8 25 A M	7 45 P M
Lv. Santa Fe..(Santa Fe)	....	....	9 00 A M	7 30 P M
Lv. Las Vegas.(Santa Fe)	4 50 A M	Tuesday.	2 00 P M	1 25 A M
.. Trinidad	9 40 A M	..	7 45 P M	7 15 A M
Ar. La Junta..... ..	11 47 A M	..	10 30 P M	10 15 A M
Lv. La Junta..(Santa Fe)	12 10 Noon	Tuesday.	3 10 A M	10 25 A M
Ar. Pueblo....... ..	1 55 P M	..	5 00 A M	12 15 Noon
.. Colorado Spgs.. ..	3 20 P M	..	6 35 A M	1 30 P M
Ar. Denver	6 00 P M	..	9 30 A M	4 10 P M
Lv. La Junta..(Santa Fe)	11 57 A M	Tuesday.	10 45 P M	10 30 A M
.. Dodge City.. ..	5 31 P M	..	5 20 A M	6 32 P M
.. Hutchinson . ..	8 25 P M	..	9 05 A M	10 35 P M
.. Newton...... ..	9 30 P M	..	10 10 A M	12 15 Night
Lv. Topeka....... ..	12 55 Night	..	2 35 P M	4 30 A M
Ar. Leavenworth ..	....	....	7 35 P M	11 55 A M
.. Atchison..... ..	9 15 A M	Wednesday	6 50 P M	9 15 A M
.. St. Joseph... ..	9 55 A M	..	7 45 P M	9 55 A M
Ar. Kansas City. ..	2 35 A M	..	4 30 P M	6 40 A M
Ar. St. Louis (Burlington)	5 50 P M	Wednesday	6 59 A M	5 50 P M
Ar. St. Louis...(C. & A.)	5 50 P M	Wednesday	6 59 A M	5 50 P M
Ar. St. Louis..(Mo. Pac.)	6 01 P M	Wednesday	7 10 A M	6 01 P M
Ar. St. Louis..(Wabash)	6 10 P M	Wednesday	6 50 A M	6 10 P M
Ar. St. Louis...(Frisco.)	....	....	7 15 A M	....
Lv. Kansas City (Santa Fe)	2 40 A M	Wednesday	5 00 P M	7 30 A M
Ar. Fort Madison ..	8 17 A M	..	12 17 Night	2 06 P M
Ar. Chicago...... ..	2 15 P M	..	7 35 A M	8 47 P M

Grand Canyon Line

Santa Fe

Equipment—Chicago, St. Louis and California—Grand Canyon Line.

For Schedule and Map, see preceding page.

Nos. 3 and 4—California Limited. Daily. Pullman Drawing-room Sleepers Chicago, Los Angeles and San Francisco; Winslow to Grand Canyon (on No. 3); Phœnix to Los Angeles (on No. 3) Tuesday and Saturday; San Francisco to Bakersfield (on No. 4). Buffet Smoking Car Chicago, Los Angeles and San Francisco. Pullman Observation Sleeping Car Chicago and Los Angeles. Parlor Car Los Angeles and San Diego. Dining Car Chicago, Los Angeles and San Francisco. Chair Car Barstow and San Francisco. Chair Cars St. Louis and Kansas City; Williams and Grand Canyon; La Junta and Denver (on connecting trains). Pullman Drawing room Sleepers St. Louis and Kansas City; Ash Fork and Phœnix (on connecting trains). Wide-vestibuled and electric lighted throughout. Only regular first-class one way or round trip tickets will be honored.

No. 1—California Express. Daily. Pullman Drawing-room Sleepers Chicago to Kansas City, Chicago to Los Angeles, Ash Fork to Phœnix, Kansas City to Albuquerque (for El Paso), Denver to Trinidad. Tourist Sleepers Chicago and Kansas City to Los Angeles; Denver to Los Angeles; Kansas City to Los Angeles Friday (from Minneapolis, via C. G. W. Ry.) Tourist Sleepers daily St. Louis to Los Angeles, alternating via Alton, Burlington, Missouri Pacific and Wabash east of Kansas City. Chair Cars Chicago to Los Angeles; Williams to Grand Canyon. Dining Car Marceline to Kansas City. Parlor Car Los Angeles to San Diego. Pullman Drawing-room Sleepers and Chair Cars St. Louis to Kansas City and Burrton. Personally conducted Tourist Sleeper excursions Chicago to Los Angeles Tuesday, Thursday and Saturday.

No. 2—Atlantic Express. Daily. Pullman Drawing-room Sleepers Los Angeles to Chicago; Phœnix to Ash Fork; Trinidad to Denver; Albuquerque to Kansas City (from El Paso). Tourist Sleepers Los Angeles to Denver and Chicago. Tourist Sleeper daily Los Angeles to St. Louis, alternating via Alton, Burlington, Mo. Pac. and Wabash east of Kansas City. Tourist Sleeper Los Angeles to Minneapolis every Thursday, via C. G. W. Ry. north of Kansas City. Chair Cars Los Angeles to Chicago. Dining Car Kansas City to Marceline. Pullmans and Chair Cars Burrton and Kansas City to St. Louis. Personally conducted Tourist Sleeper excursions Los Angeles to Chicago Monday, Thursday and Saturday.

No. 1-7—California and Mexico Express. Daily. Equipment of No. 1 Chicago to Kansas City. Pullman Drawing-room Sleepers Kansas City to Los Angeles, Needles to San Francisco, St. Louis to Kansas City, Ash Fork to Phœnix. Tourist Sleepers Kansas City to San Francisco; La Junta to Los Angeles. Chair Cars and Coaches Kansas City to San Francisco. Chair Cars St. Louis to Kansas City; Williams to Grand Canyon. Parlor Cars Los Angeles to San Diego. Personally conducted Tourist Sleeper excursions Chicago to San Francisco Tuesday, Thursday and Saturday.

No. 8—Chicago Express. Daily. Pullman Drawing-room Sleepers San Francisco to Chicago; San Francisco to Fresno; San Diego to Los Angeles; Los Angeles to Needles; Kansas City to St. Louis; Los Angeles to Phœnix (Sunday and Thursday). Tourist Sleeper San Francisco and Los Angeles to Chicago. Chair Car San Francisco to Chicago; Los Angeles to Barstow; Kansas City to St. Louis. Observation-Cafe Car Kansas City to Chicago. Personally conducted Tourist Sleeper excursions San Francisco to Chicago Monday, Thursday and Saturday.

No. 9-7—California Fast Mail. Daily. Pullman D. R. Sleepers Chicago and Kansas City to La Junta; La Junta to Los Angeles; Needles to San Francisco. Tourist Sleepers Chicago to Los Angeles; La Junta to San Francisco. Chair Cars Chicago to La Junta; La Junta to San Francisco; Barstow to Los Angeles. Parlor Car Los Angeles to San Diego. Cafe-Observation Car Chicago to Kansas City.

CHICAGO, COLORADO, UTAH AND PACIFIC COAST LINE.

STANDARD OF TIME.—*Central time*, east of Dodge City. *Mountain time*, west of Dodge City.

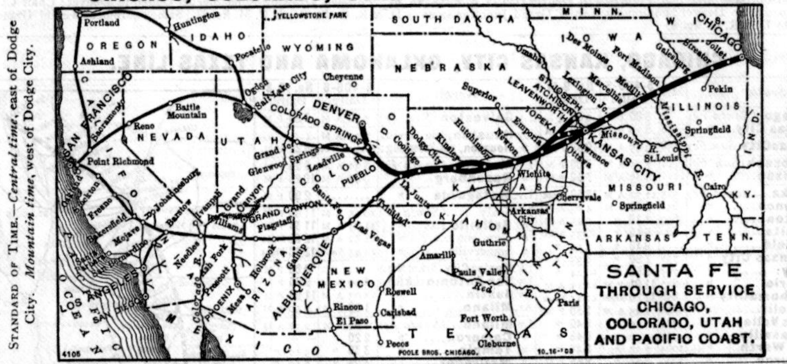

For Time and Equipment west of Denver, see next page.

No. 9 Daily.	1-7-607 Exp. Daily.	No. 5 Exp. Daily.	Mls	STATIONS.		No. 6 Exp. Daily.	No. 10-8 Exp. Daily.	602-2 Daily.
9 00 A M	10 00 P M	6 00 P M	0	lve. Chicago ....(Santa Fe)	arr.	9 15 A M	8 47 P M	7 35 A M
1 08 P M	2 45 A M	11 35 P M	182	lve. Galesburg	arr.	4 07 A M	3 36 P M	2 03 A M
2 25 P M	4 05 A M	1 05 A M	237	lve. Ft. Madison	arr.	2 35 A M	2 06 P M	12 17 Night
5 35 P M	7 15 A M	4 30 A M	352	lve. Marceline.......... ..	arr.	11 02 P M	10 40 A M	8 45 P M
8 50 P M	10 30 A M	8 30 A M	458	arr. Kansas City	lve.	7 30 P M	7 10 A M	5 00 P M
9 06 A M	11 28 P M	11 28 P M	....	lve. St. Louis.......(Burl. Route)	arr.	6 59 A M	5 50 P M	6 59 A M
9 06 A M	11 28 P M	11 28 P M	....	lve. St. Louis..........(C. & A.)	arr.	6 59 A M	5 50 P M	6 59 A M
9 00 A M	10 10 P M	10 10 P M	....	lve. St. Louis....(Missouri Pac.)	arr.	7 10 A M	6 01 P M	7 10 A M
....	8 41 P M	8 41 P M	....	lve. St. Louis.......(Frisco Sys.)	arr.	7 15 A M	....	7 15 A M
9 10 A M	10 15 P M	10 15 P M	....	lve. St. Louis ....(Wabash)	arr.	6 50 A M	6 10 P M	6 50 A M
9 00 P M	2 35 P M	9 45 A M	458	lve. Kansas City......(Santa Fe)	arr.	8 55 P M	6 40 A M	4 30 P M
10 00 P M	Via	10 50 A M	499	lve. Lawrence........... ..	arr.	5 37 P M	6 00 A M	3 15 P M
10 40 P M	Emporia Br.	11 55 A M	525	lve. Topeka.............. ..	arr.	4 55 P M	4 20 A M	2 10 P M
12 10 Night	6 05 P M	1 45 P M	586	lve. Emporia	arr.	3 05 P M	2 25 A M	12 15 Noon
2 05 A M	8 30 P M	4 10 P M	659	lve. Newton	arr.	12 25 Noon	1 30 A M	10 00 A M
2 50 A M	9 40 P M	5 35 P M	693	lve. Hutchinson	arr.	11 25 A M	12 35 Night	8 40 A M
4 55 A M	1 00 A M	8 50 P M	827	lve. Dodge City	arr.	6 40 A M	7 50 P M	4 10 A M
7 50 A M	4 33 A M	11 40 P M	928	arr. Syracuse	lve.	4 10 A M	5 18 P M	1 28 A M
9 00 A M	6 05 A M	1 12 A M	977	arr. Lamar.............. ..	lve.	2 58 A M	3 58 P M	12 15 Night
10 20 A M	7 45 A M	3 00 A M	1029	arr. La Junta............ ..	lve.	1 40 A M	2 35 P M	10 45 P M
12 15 Noon	9 50 A M	5 00 A M	1093	arr. Pueblo.............. ..	lve.	11 45 P M	12 45 Noon	8 05 P M
1 30 P M	11 10 A M	6 35 A M	1136	arr. Colorado Springs.. ..	lve.	10 30 P M	11 20 A M	6 45 P M
2 36 P M	12 02 Noon	7 50 A M	1158	arr. Palmer Lake	lve.	9 45 P M	10 35 A M	5 40 P M
4 10 P M	1 35 P M	9 30 A M	1210	arr. Denver............ ..	lve.	8 00 P M	9 00 A M	4 00 P M

No. 9—Daily. Pullman D. R. Sleepers Chicago and Kansas City to Denver; Newton to Denver (from Galveston). Tourist Sleeper Chicago to La Junta (for Los Angeles). Chair Car Chicago to Denver. Cafe-Observation Car Chicago to Kansas City.

No. 5—Daily Pullman Drawing-room Sleeper Chicago to Kansas City; Chicago to Denver; La Junta to Denver (from Trinidad); Kansas City to Colorado Springs (from St. Louis, via Wabash). Chair Cars Chicago to Ft. Madison; Chicago to Denver. Dining Car Chicago to Kansas City.

No. 1-7-607—Daily. Pullman Drawing-room Sleepers Chicago to Kansas City and La Junta. Tourist Sleepers Chicago to Kansas City and La Junta. Chair Cars Chicago to La Junta. Coach La Junta to Denver. Dining Car Marceline to Kansas City.

No. 602-2—Daily. Pullman Drawing-room Sleepers La Junta to Kansas City and Chicago. Chair Car and Coach Denver to La Junta. Tourist Sleepers La Junta to Chicago. Chair Car Denver to La Junta; La Junta to Chicago. Dining Car Kansas City to Marceline.

No. 6—Daily. Pullman Drawing-room Sleepers Denver to La Junta (for Trinidad); Denver to Chicago; Kansas City to Chicago; Colorado Springs to Kansas City (for St. Louis). Chair Cars Denver and Kansas City to Chicago. Dining Car Kansas City to Chicago.

No. 10-8—Daily. Pullman Drawing room Sleepers Denver to Kansas City; Kansas City to Chicago; Denver to Newton (for Galveston). Tourist Sleepers Kansas City to Chicago. Chair Cars Denver to Kansas City; Kansas City to Chicago. Cafe-Observation Car Kansas City to Chicago.

Santa Fe — Grand Canyon Line

ATCHISON, TOPEKA & SANTA FE RAILWAY.

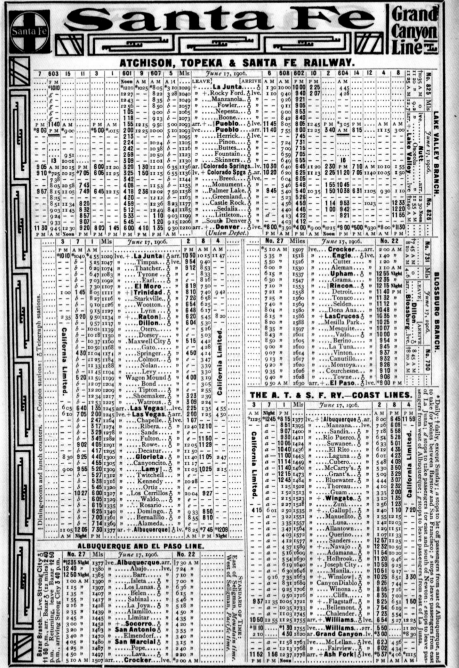

7	603	15	11	3	1	601	9	607	5	Mls	June 17, 1906.	6	608	602	10	2	604	14	12	4	8
....	P M	....	....	....	....	Noon	A M	A M	A M	....	LEAVE] [ARRIVE	A M	A M	P M	P M	....	A M	....	....	....	....
....	*1010	....	....	....	....	*1210	*1025	*805	*310	1029	+ ....**La Junta**.....♁	130	1000	1000	225	....	445	....	....	....	....
....	g –	....	....	....	....	1227	– –	822	328	1040	" +.Rocky Ford. ♁ lve.	110	940	940	207	....	426	....	....	....	....
....	g –	....	....	....	....	1243	– –	835	b –	1049	" ....Manzanola..♁ "	– –	926	921	– –	....	– –	....	....	....	....
....	g –	....	....	....	....	1256	– –	850	b –	1057	" ......Fowler....♁ "	– –	911	905	– –	....	– –	....	....	....	....
....	g –	....	....	....	....	105	– –	900	b –	1065	" .....Nepesta....♁ "	– –	900	853	– –	....	– –	....	....	....	....
....	g –	....	....	....	....	118	– –	913	b –	1073	" ......Boone...... "	– –	842	840	– –	....	– –	....	....	....	....
P M	1140	A M	....	P M	A M	155	1215	950	500	1093	arr. + ..‖**Pueblo**...♁lve.	1145	805	805	1245	P M	*305	P M	....	A M	A M
*800	P M	*900	....	*500	*1015	200	1225	1000	510	1093	lve......**Pueblo**....arr.	1140	755	800	1225	340	A M	815	....	1115	300
– –	....	– –	– –	– –	– –	213	– –	– –	b –	1095	" ......Herrick...♁lve.	– –	– –	745	– –	– –	– –	– –	– –	– –	– –
– –	....	– –	– –	– –	– –	224	– –	1024	b –	1105	" ......Pinon....♁ "	– –	724	731	– –	– –	....	– –	– –	– –	– –
– –	....	– –	– –	– –	– –	242	– –	1038	b –	1116	" ......Buttes....♁ "	– –	709	715	– –	– –	....	– –	– –	– –	– –
– –	....	951	– –	– –	– –	259	– –	1050	b –	1123	" .....Fountain..♁ "	– –	659	705	– –	– –	....	– –	– –	– –	– –
– –	13	1001	....	– –	– –	309	– –	1101	b –	1130	" .....Skinners..♁ "	– –	649	655	– –	– –	16	– –	– –	– –	– –
905	A M	1015	P M	600	1120	320	130	1110	635	1136	ar.‖**Colorado Springs**..lv.	1030	640	645	1120	230	P M	710	A M	1010	155
910	*725	1025	*705	605	1125	325	150	1115	655	1136	lv. + **Colorado Spgs** ♁.ar.	1020	620	625	1113	225	1120	705	1140	1005	150
– –	738	– –	– –	– –	– –	342	– –	– –	b –	1144	" ......Breed....♁lve.	– –	604	605	– –	– –	– –	– –	– –	– –	– –
– –	805	1058	743	– –	– –	408	– –	1153	b –	1155	" ....Monument.♁ "	– –	546	546	– –	155	1045	– –	– –	– –	– –
957	815	1105	749	645	1215	418	236	1202	750	1158	" ...Palmer Lake.♁ "	945	540	540	1035	150	1038	631	1105	930	110
– –	825	– –	– –	– –	– –	430	– –	1212	b –	1163	" ....Greenland..♁ "	– –	523	526	– –	– –	– –	– –	– –	– –	– –
– –	851	1134	820	– –	– –	459	– –	1236	823	1177	" ...Castle Rock.♁ "	– –	456	459	– –	114	953	– –	1023	– –	1233
– –	903	1145	832	– –	– –	512	– –	1249	841	1185	" .....Sedalia...♁ "	– –	440	445	– –	100	942	– –	– –	– –	1220
– –	924	– –	857	– –	– –	533	– –	110	903	1199	" .....Littleton...♁ "	d –	413	422	– –	– –	921	– –	– –	– –	1155
– –	933	– –	907	– –	– –	545	– –	120	915	1206	" ..South Denver♁ "	– –	403	412	– –	– –	– –	– –	– –	– –	– –
1130	945	1230	920	800	145	600	410	135	930	1210	arr. + ..**Denver**..♁lve.	*800	*350	*400	*900	*1215	*900	*500	*930	*800	*1130
											(Union Depot.)										
P M	A M	Noon	P M	P M	P M	P M	P M	P M	A M	....		P M	A M	P M	A M	Noon	P M	P M	A M	A M	P M

LAKE VALLEY BRANCH.

No. 825	Mls	June 17, 1906.	No. 826
†1035 A M	0	lve......**Nutt**......arr.	1230 Noon
1110 "	9.2	" ....Osceola.... "	1155 A M
1125 A M	12.7	arr. + .**Lake Valley**...lve	†1140 A M

BLOSSBURG BRANCH.

No. 731	Mls	June 17, 1906.	No. 730
†745 A M	0	lve.....**Dillon**.....arr.	845 A M
810 A M	4.6	arr..**Blossburg**..lve.	†820 A M

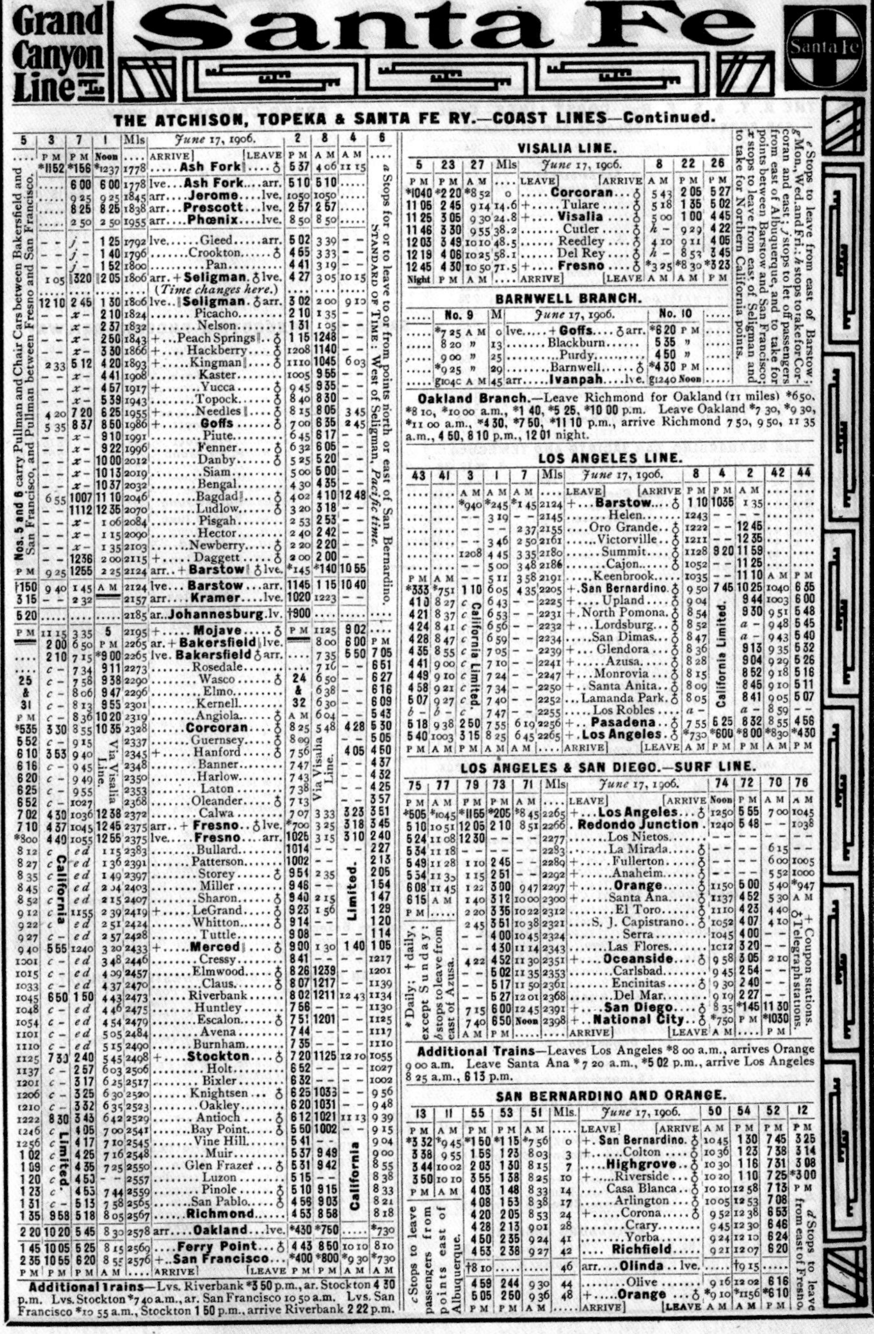

THE ATCHISON, TOPEKA & SANTA FE RY.—COAST LINES—Continued.

5	3	7	1	Mls	June 17, 1906.	2	8	4	6
....	P M	P M	Noon	....	ARRIVE] [LEAVE	P M	A M	A M	....
....	*1152	*156	*1237	1778	.....**Ash Fork**‖....♁	537	406	1115	....
....	....	600	600	1778	lve...**Ash Fork**....arr.	510	510	....	
....	....	925	925	1845	arr....**Jerome**....lve.	1050	1050	....	
....	....	825	825	1838	arr...**Prescott**...lve.	257	257	....	
....	....	250	250	1955	arr....**Phœnix**....lve.	850	850	....	
	– –	j –	125	1792	lve......Gleed.....arr.	502	339	– –	
	– –	j –	140	1796	.......Crookton......♁	455	333	– –	
	– –	j –	152	1800	..........Pan..........	441	319	– –	
	105	‖320	‖205	1806	arr. + **Seligman**.♁lve.	427	305	1015	
					(Time changes here.)				
	1210	245	130	1806	lve..‖**Seligman**.♁arr.	302	200	910	
	– –	x –	210	1824	.......Picacho........	210	135	– –	
	– –	x –	237	1832	........Nelson........	131	105	– –	
	– –	x –	250	1843	+...Peach Springs‖..♁	115	1248	– –	
	– –	x –	330	1866	+....Hackberry....♁	1208	1140	– –	
	233	512	420	1893	+.....Kingman‖....♁	1110	1045	603	
	– –	x –	441	1908	........Kaster........	1005	955	– –	
	– –	x –	457	1917	+.......Yucca......♁	945	935	– –	
	– –	x –	539	1943	........Topock......♁	840	830	– –	
	420	720	625	1955	+......Needles‖....♁	815	805	345	
	535	837	850	1986	+......**Goffs**......♁	700	635	245	
	– –	x –	910	1991	..........Piute........	645	617	– –	
	– –	x –	922	1996	.........Fenner......♁	632	605	– –	
	– –	x –	1000	2012	.........Danby......♁	525	520	– –	
	– –	x –	1013	2019	..........Siam.........	500	500	– –	
	– –	x –	1037	2032	.........Bengal........	430	435	– –	
	655	1007	1110	2046	.........Bagdad‖......♁	402	410	1248	
	– –	1112	1235	2070	.........Ludlow......♁	320	318	– –	
	– –	x –	106	2084	.........Pisgah........	253	253	– –	
	– –	x –	115	2090	.........Hector........	240	242	– –	
	– –	x –	135	2103	........Newberry.....♁	220	220	– –	
	– –	1236	200	2115	+.....Daggett......♁	200	200	– –	
P M	925	1255	225	2124	arr..+ **Barstow**‖♁lve.	*145	*140	1055	
†150	940	145	A M	2124	lve...**Barstow**...arr.	1145	115	1040	
315	– –	232		2157	arr....**Kramer**....lve.	1020	1223	– –	
520	....	....	....	2185	ar..**Johannesburg**.lv.	†900	....	....	....
P M	1115	335	5	2195	+.....**Mojave**.....♁	P M	1125	902	....
	200	650	P M	2265	ar. + **Bakersfield**‖lve.		800	600	P M
....	210	715	*900	2265	lve. **Bakersfield** ♁arr.	....	735	550	705
....	c –	734	911	2273	........Rosedale........	....	716	– –	651
25	c –	758	938	2290	.........Wasco......♁	24	650	– –	627
&	c –	806	947	2296	..........Elmo..........	&	638	– –	616
31	c –	813	955	2301	.........Kernell........	32	630	– –	609
P M	c –	836	1020	2319	.........Angiola......♁	A M	604	– –	543
*535	330	855	1035	2328	.......**Corcoran**....♁	825	548	428	530
552	c –	915	Via Visalia Line.	2337	........Guernsey.....♁	809	Via Visalia Line.	– –	505
610	353	940		2345	+.....Hanford.....♁	756		405	450
616	c –	945		2348	.........Banner.........	747		– –	437
620	c –	949		2350	.........Harlow.........	743		– –	432
625	c –	955		2353	.........Laton..........	738		– –	425
652	c –	1027		2368	........Oleander.....♁	713		– –	357
702	430	1036	1238	2372	.........Calwa.........	707	333	323	351
710	437	1045	1245	2375	arr.. + **Fresno**..♁lve.	*700	325	318	345
*800	440	1055	1255	2375	lve.....**Fresno**....arr.	1025	315	310	240
812	c	ed	115	2383	........Bullard.........	1014	– –	– –	227
827	c	ed	136	2391	........Patterson.......	1002	– –		213
835	c	ed	149	2397	.........Storey......♁	951	235		205
845	c	ed	204	2403	.........Miller.........	946	– –		154
852	c	ed	215	2407	.........Sharon......♁	940	215		147
912	c	1155	239	2419	+.....LeGrand.......♁	923	156		129
922	c	ed	251	2424	........Whitton......♁	914	– –		120
927	c –	ed	257	2428	.........Tuttle.........	908	– –	– –	114
940	555	1240	320	2433	+.....**Merced**‖....♁	900	130	140	105
1001	c –	ed	348	2446	.........Cressy.........	841	– –	– –	1217
1015	c –	ed	409	2457	........Elmwood.....♁	826	1239	– –	1201
1033	c –	ed	437	2470	.........Claus.......♁	807	1217	– –	1139
1045	650	150	443	2473	.......Riverbank.......	802	1211	1243	1134
1048	c –	ed	446	2475	........Huntley........	756	– –	– –	1130
1054	c –	ed	454	2479	........Escalon......♁	751	1201	– –	1125
1101	c –	ed	505	2484	.........Avena.........	744	– –	– –	1117
1110	c –	ed	515	2490	........Burnham........	735	– –	– –	1110
1125	730	240	545	2498	+....**Stockton**....♁	720	1125	1210	1055
1137	c –	257	603	2506	..........Holt..........	652	– –	– –	1027
1201	c –	317	625	2517	.........Bixler.........	632	– –	– –	1002
1206	c –	325	630	2520	......Knightsen ... ♁	625	1033	– –	956
1210	c –	332	635	2523	........Oakley.........	620	1031	– –	948
1222	830	343	642	2529	........Antioch .....♁	612	1021	1113	939
1246	c	405	700	2541	.......Bay Point.....♁	550	1002	– –	915
1256	c	417	710	2545	........Vine Hill.......	541	– –		904
102	c	425	716	2548	..........Muir..........	537	949		900
109	c	435	725	2550	..... Glen Frazer ...♁	531	942		855
120	c	450	– –	2557	.........Luzon.........	515	– –		838
123	c	453	744	2559	.........Pinole ......♁	510	915		833
131	c –	513	758	2565	.......San Pablo.....♁	456	903		821
135	958	518	805	2567	......**Richmond**......	453	858		818
220	1020	545	830	2578	arr....**Oakland**...lve.	*430	*750	....	*730
145	1005	525	815	2569	....**Ferry Point**...♁	443	850	1010	810
235	1055	620	855	2576	+ ..**San Francisco**...	*400	*800	*930	*730
P M	P M	P M	A M	....	ARRIVE] [LEAVE	P M	P M	A M	A M

(California Limited.)

Nos. 5 and 6 carry Pullman and Chair Cars between Bakersfield and San Francisco, and Pullman between Fresno and San Francisco.

a Stops for or to leave to or from points north or east of San Bernardino. STANDARD OF TIME: West of Seligman, Pacific time.

Additional Trains—Lvs. Riverbank *3 50 p.m., ar. Stockton 4 30 p.m. Lvs. Stockton *7 40 a.m., ar. San Francisco 10 50 a.m. Lvs. San Francisco *10 55 a.m., Stockton 1 50 p.m., arrive Riverbank 2 22 p.m.

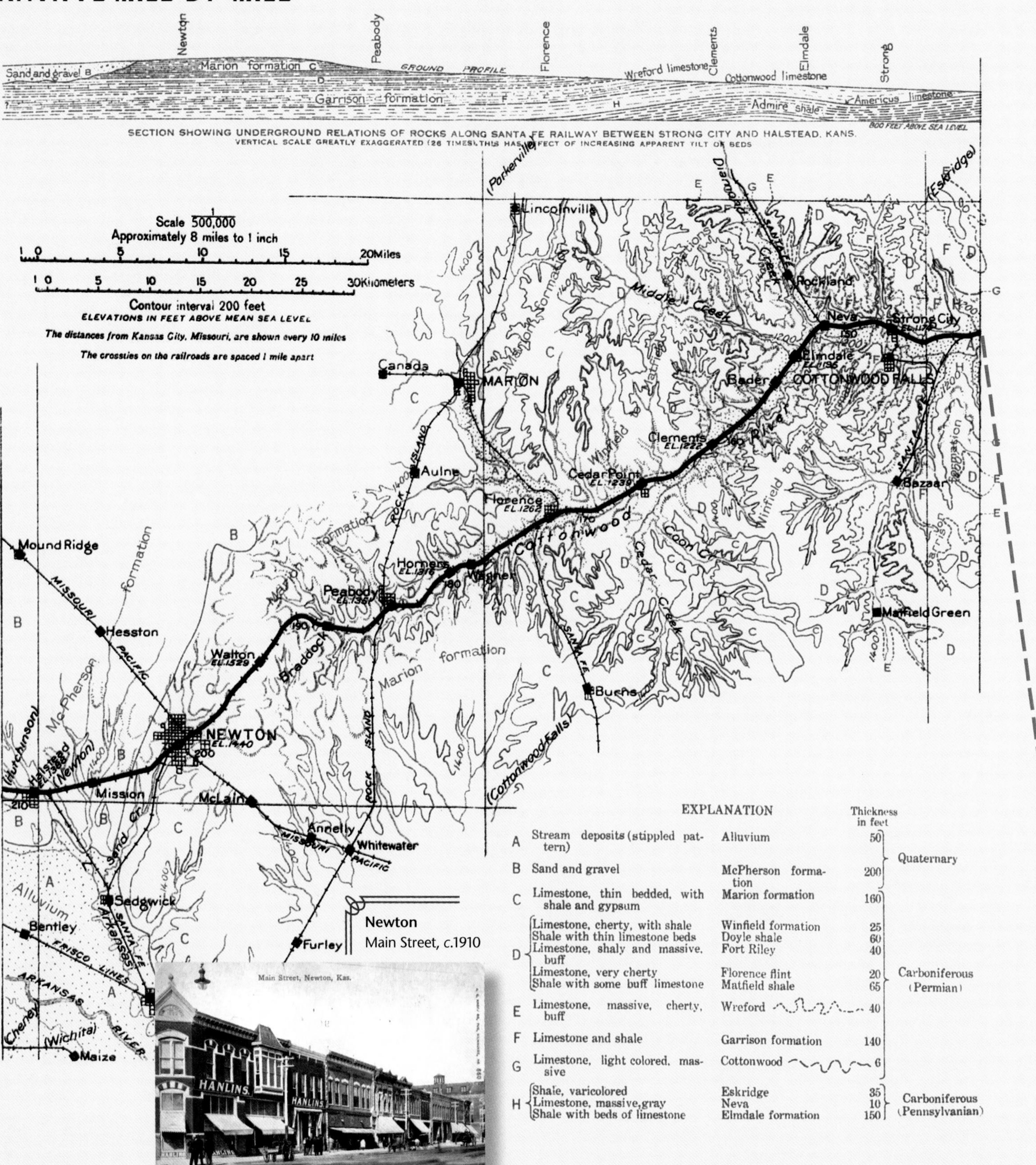

Newton
Main Street, *c*.1910

EXPLANATION

A	River deposits (stippled pattern)	Alluvium
B	Limestone	Wreford
C	Shale and limestone	Garrison
D	Limestone	Cottonwood
E	Shale Limestone Shale	Eskridge Neva Elmdale
F	Limestone	Americus
G	Shale with limestone layers	Admire
H	Limestones separated by shale	Emporia
I	Shale with thin limestone	Willard
J	Limestone	Burlingame
K	Shale Limestone and shale Shale with coal near top	Scranton Howard Severy
L	Limestones separated by shale	Topeka
M	Shale and sandstone Limestone and shale Shale	Calhoun Deer Creek Tecumseh
N	Limestones separated by shale	Lecompton
O	Shale	Kanwaka
P	Limestones separated by shale	Oread
Q	Shale	Lawrence

Approximate southern limit of Kansan ice sheet of glacial e[...]
The lines show the eastern limit of each belt of limestone, n[...] outcrop.

Scale 1/500,000
Approximately 8 miles to 1 inch
Contour interval 200 feet
ELEVATIONS IN FEET ABOVE MEAN SEA LEVEL
The distances from Kansas City, Missouri, are shown every 10 miles
The crossties on the railroads are spaced 1 mile apart

Allen
Admire
Dunlap
AMERICUS
Neosho
EMPORIA
Plymouth
Toledo
Cottonwood River

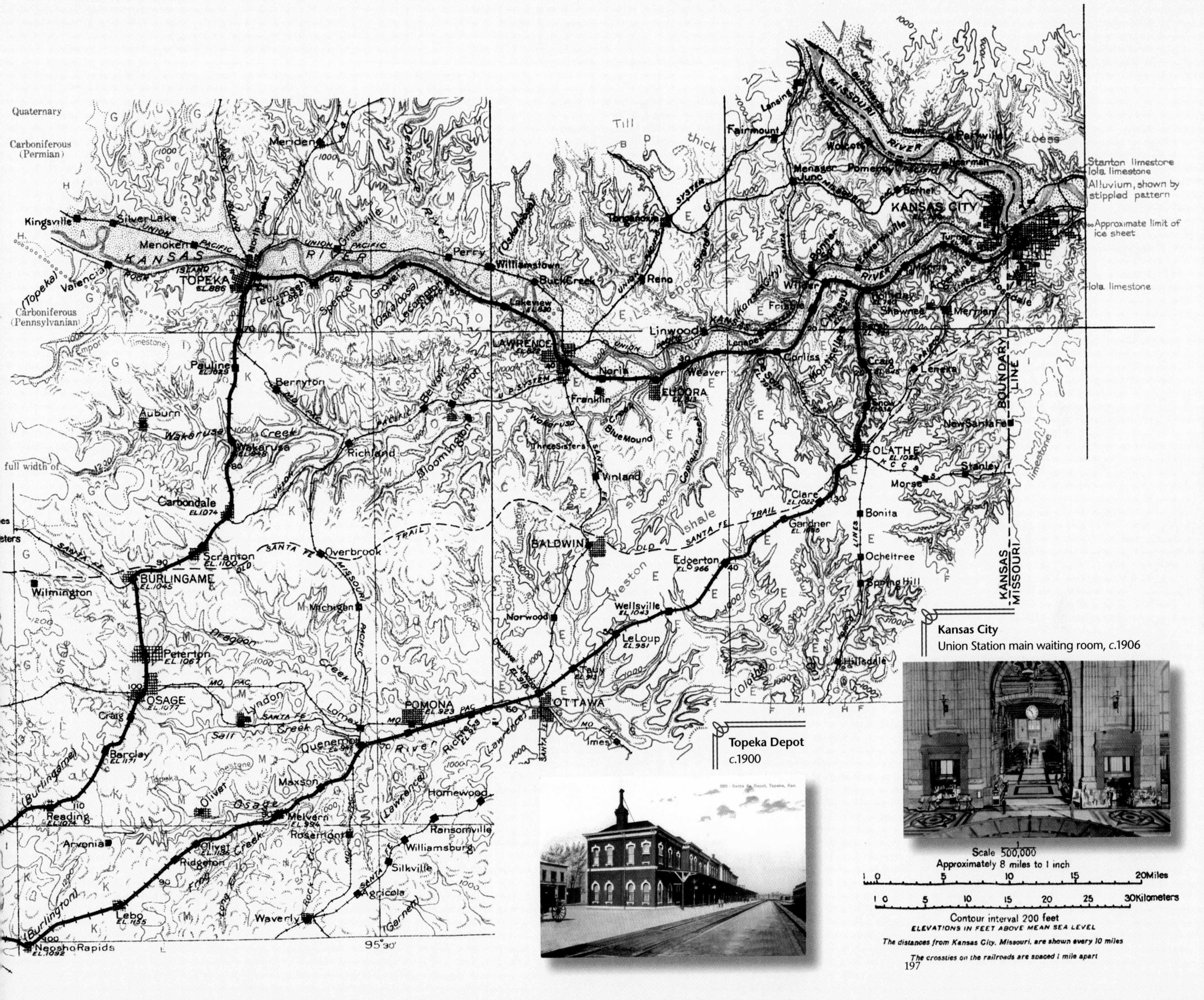

Topeka Depot
c.1900

Kansas City
Union Station main waiting room, *c.*1906

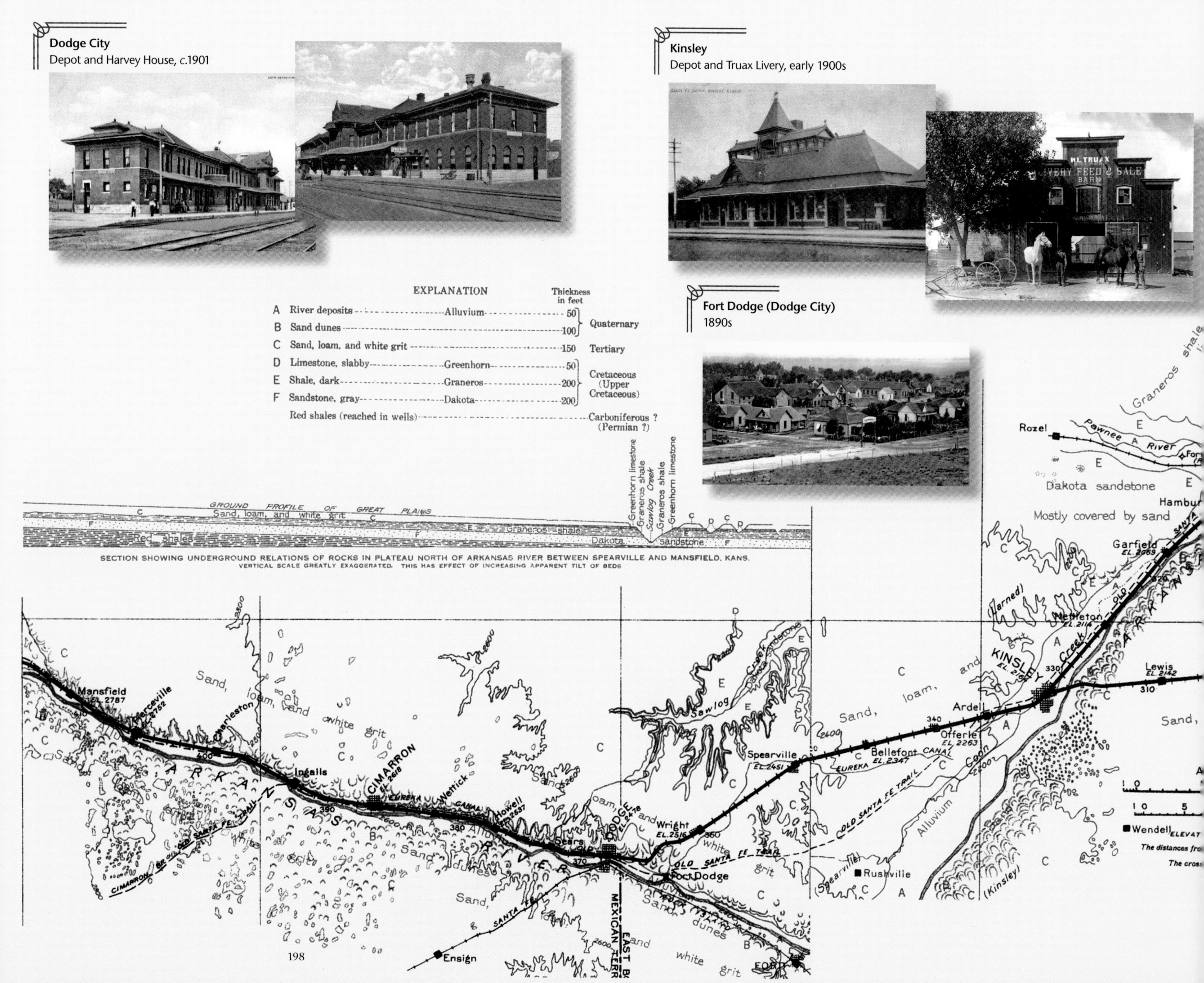

Dodge City
Depot and Harvey House, *c.*1901

Kinsley
Depot and Truax Livery, early 1900s

Fort Dodge (Dodge City)
1890s

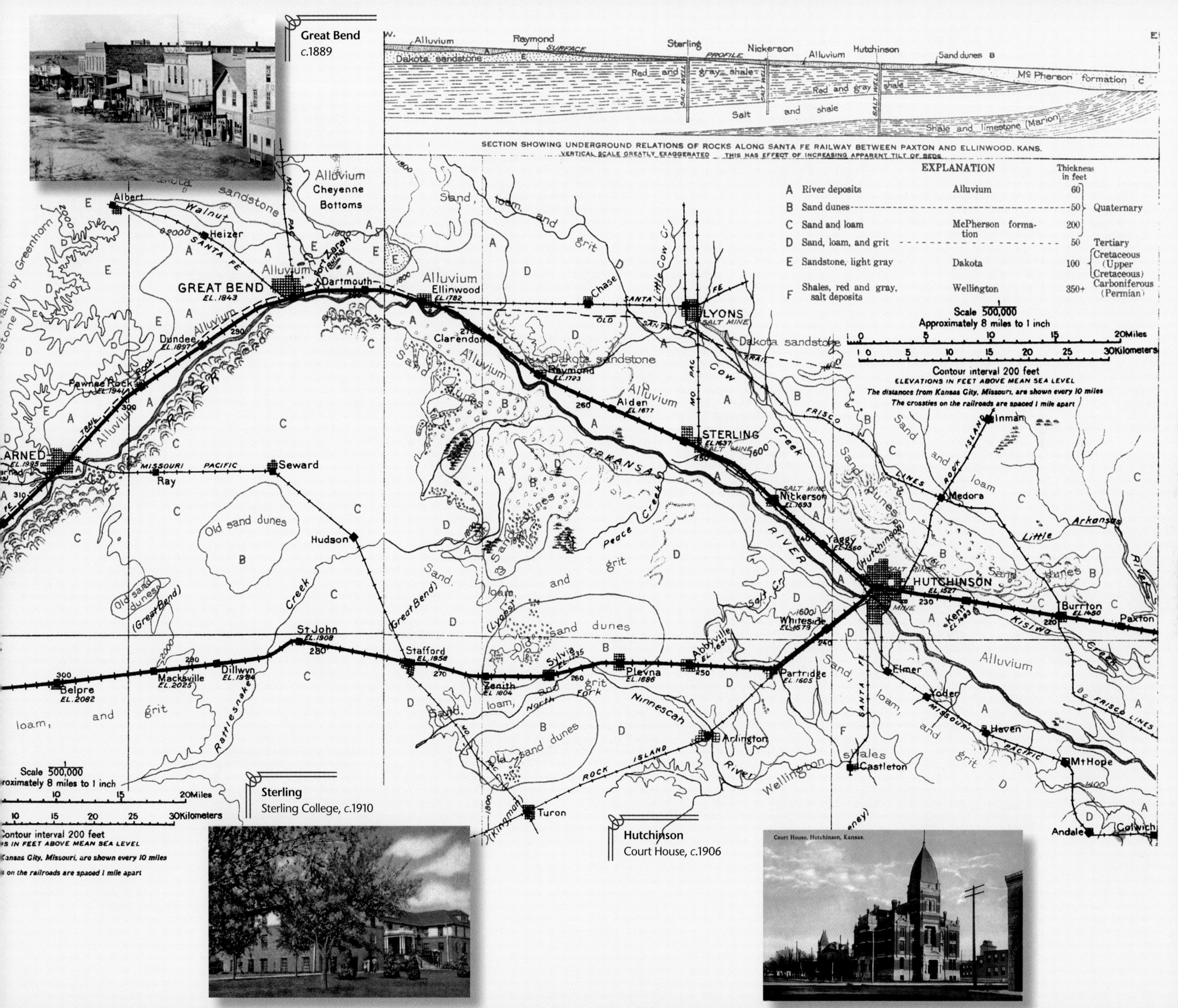
SECTION SHOWING UNDERGROUND RELATIONS OF ROCKS ALONG SANTA FE RAILWAY BETWEEN PAXTON AND ELLINWOOD, KANS.
VERTICAL SCALE GREATLY EXAGGERATED THIS HAS EFFECT OF INCREASING APPARENT TILT OF BEDS
Alluvium
Raymond
Sterling
Nickerson
Hutchinson
Sand dunes
Dakota sandstone
Red and gray shale
McPherson formation
Salt and shale
Shale and limestone (Marion)
SALT WELL
EXPLANATION
Thickness in feet
A River deposits Alluvium 60
B Sand dunes 50 Quaternary
C Sand and loam McPherson formation 200
D Sand, loam, and grit 50 Tertiary
E Sandstone, light gray Dakota 100 Cretaceous (Upper Cretaceous)
F Shales, red and gray, salt deposits Wellington 350+ Carboniferous (Permian)
Scale 1/500,000
Approximately 8 miles to 1 inch
Contour interval 200 feet
ELEVATIONS IN FEET ABOVE MEAN SEA LEVEL
The distances from Kansas City, Missouri, are shown every 10 miles
The crossties on the railroads are spaced 1 mile apart
GREAT BEND EL. 1843
Albert
Heizer
Dartmouth
Ellinwood EL. 1782
Chase
LYONS
Dundee EL. 1897
Pawnee Rock EL. 1941
LARNED EL. 1995
Ray
Seward
Hudson
Clarendon
Raymond EL. 1723
Alden EL. 1677
STERLING EL. 1637
Nickerson EL. 1593
Yaggy EL. 1560
HUTCHINSON EL. 1527
Inman
Medora
Burrton EL. 1450
Paxton
Belpre EL. 2082
Macksville EL. 2025
Dillwyn EL. 1984
St John EL. 1908
Stafford EL. 1858
Zenith EL. 1804
Sylvia EL. 1735
Plevna EL. 1686
Abbyville EL. 1651
Whiteside EL. 1579
Partridge EL. 1605
Kent EL. 1493
Elmer
Yoder
Haven
Mt Hope
Arlington
Castleton
Turon
Andale
Colwich
Cheyenne Bottoms
ARKANSAS RIVER
Old sand dunes
SANTA FE
MISSOURI PACIFIC
ROCK ISLAND
FRISCO LINES
Walnut
Peace Creek
Ninnescah
Little Arkansas River
Cow Creek
Rattlesnake

Great Bend c.1889

Sterling
Sterling College, c.1910

Hutchinson
Court House, c.1906

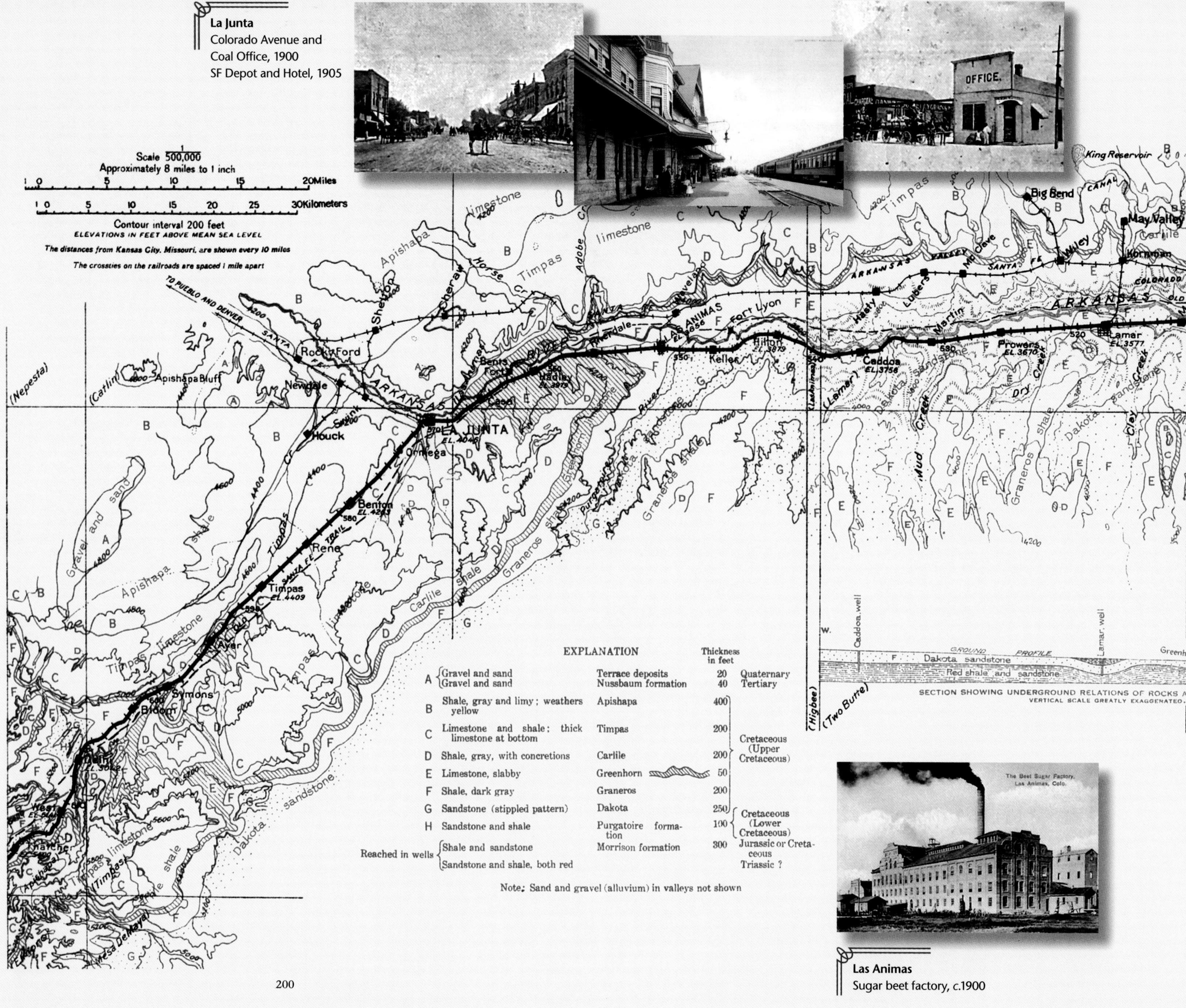
Scale 1/500,000
Approximately 8 miles to 1 inch
Contour interval 200 feet
ELEVATIONS IN FEET ABOVE MEAN SEA LEVEL
The distances from Kansas City, Missouri, are shown every 10 miles
The crossties on the railroads are spaced 1 mile apart
TO PUEBLO AND DENVER
LA JUNTA
LAS ANIMAS
Lamar
SECTION SHOWING UNDERGROUND RELATIONS OF ROCKS ALO
VERTICAL SCALE GREATLY EXAGGERATED.
EXPLANATION
A Gravel and sand — Terrace deposits — 20 — Quaternary
A Gravel and sand — Nussbaum formation — 40 — Tertiary
B Shale, gray and limy; weathers yellow — Apishapa — 400
C Limestone and shale; thick limestone at bottom — Timpas — 200
D Shale, gray, with concretions — Carlile — 200 — Cretaceous (Upper Cretaceous)
E Limestone, slabby — Greenhorn — 50
F Shale, dark gray — Graneros — 200
G Sandstone (stippled pattern) — Dakota — 250
H Sandstone and shale — Purgatoire formation — 100 — Cretaceous (Lower Cretaceous)
Reached in wells: Shale and sandstone — Morrison formation — 300 — Jurassic or Cretaceous
Reached in wells: Sandstone and shale, both red — Triassic ?
Note: Sand and gravel (alluvium) in valleys not shown
OFFICE.
The Beet Sugar Factory, Las Animas, Colo.

La Junta
Colorado Avenue and
Coal Office, 1900
SF Depot and Hotel, 1905

Las Animas
Sugar beet factory, *c.*1900

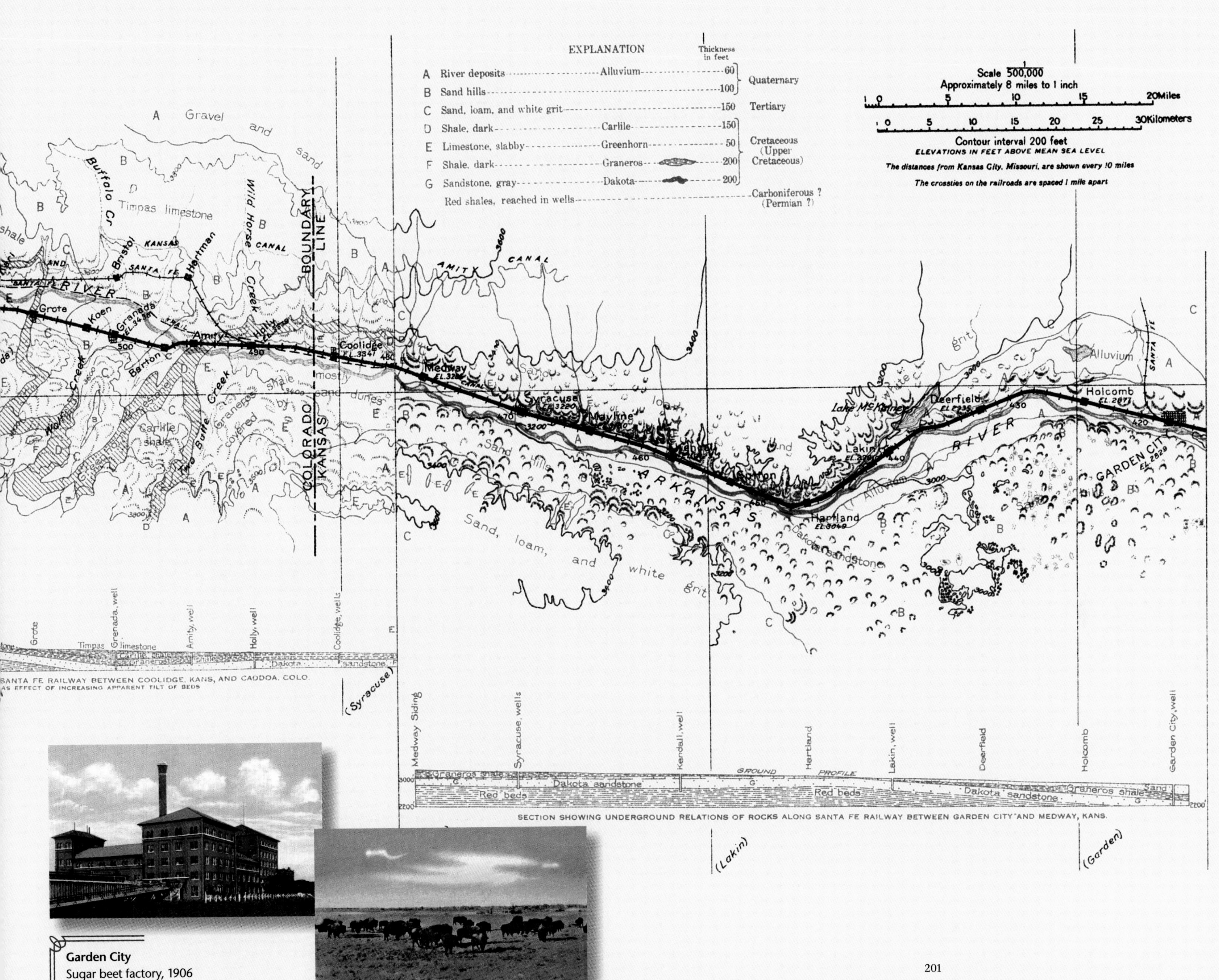
EXPLANATION
Thickness in feet
A River deposits ---- Alluvium ---- 60 } Quaternary
B Sand hills ---- 100 }
C Sand, loam, and white grit ---- 150 Tertiary
D Shale, dark ---- Carlile ---- 150 }
E Limestone, slabby ---- Greenhorn ---- 50 } Cretaceous (Upper Cretaceous)
F Shale, dark ---- Graneros ---- 200 }
G Sandstone, gray ---- Dakota ---- 200 }
Red shales, reached in wells ---- Carboniferous ? (Permian ?)
Scale 1/500,000
Approximately 8 miles to 1 inch
0 5 10 15 20 Miles
0 5 10 15 20 25 30 Kilometers
Contour interval 200 feet
ELEVATIONS IN FEET ABOVE MEAN SEA LEVEL
The distances from Kansas City, Missouri, are shown every 10 miles
The crossties on the railroads are spaced 1 mile apart
Gravel and sand
Timpas limestone
Buffalo Cr
Wild Horse Creek
KANSAS CANAL
AMITY CANAL
Bristol
Hartman
SANTA FE
RIVER
Grote
Koen
Granada
Amity
Holly
Barton
Wolf Creek
Two Butte Creek
Carlile shale
Graneros shale
COLORADO
KANSAS
BOUNDARY LINE
Coolidge
EL. 3347
Medway
Syracuse
Kendall
Hartland
Lakin
Deerfield
Holcomb
GARDEN CITY
ARKANSAS RIVER
Lake McKinney
Alluvium
Sand hills
Sand, loam, and white grit
Dakota sandstone
Grote
Grenada, well
Amity, well
Holly, well
Coolidge, wells
Timpas limestone
Carlile shale
Graneros
Dakota sandstone
SANTA FE RAILWAY BETWEEN COOLIDGE, KANS, AND CADDOA, COLO.
AS EFFECT OF INCREASING APPARENT TILT OF BEDS
(Syracuse)
Medway Siding
Syracuse, wells
Kendall, well
Hartland
Lakin, well
Deerfield
Holcomb
Garden City, well
GROUND PROFILE
Graneros shale
Dakota sandstone
Red beds
Sand
SECTION SHOWING UNDERGROUND RELATIONS OF ROCKS ALONG SANTA FE RAILWAY BETWEEN GARDEN CITY AND MEDWAY, KANS.
(Lakin)
(Garden)

Garden City
Sugar beet factory, 1906
Buffalo on the range, 1902

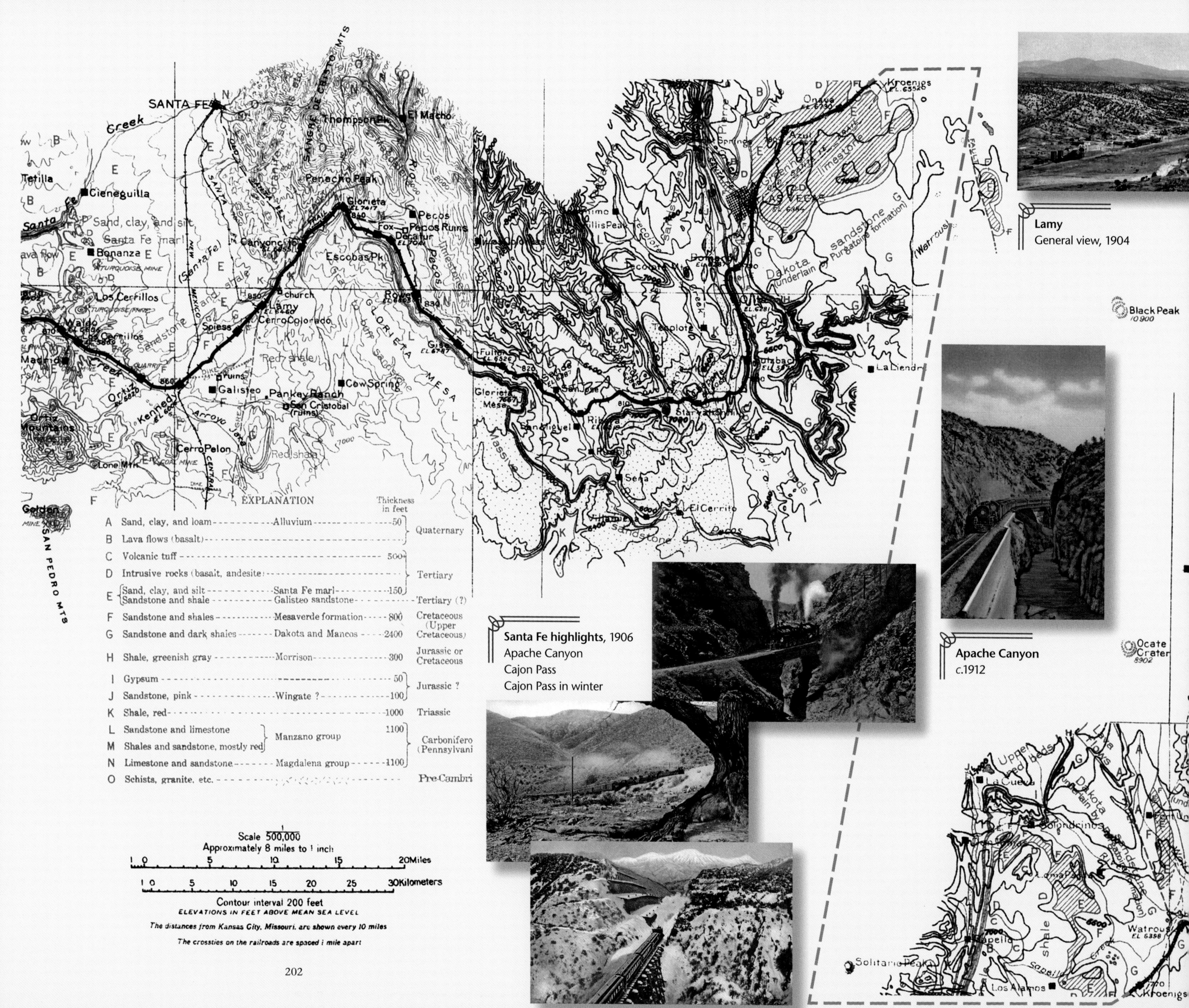
SANTA FE
SANGRE DE CRISTO MTS
Thompson Pk
El Macho
Penacho Peak
Glorieta
Pecos
Pecos Ruins
Canyoncito
Escobas Pk
Cieneguilla
Bonanza
Los Cerrillos
Waldo
Madrid
Lamy
Cerro Colorado
Galisteo
Pankey Ranch
San Cristobal (ruins)
Cow Spring
Kennedy
Cerro Pelon
Lone Mtn
Golden
SAN PEDRO MTS
Ortiz Mountains
GLORIETA MESA
Rowe
Fox
Decatur
Fulton
San Jose
Ribera
San Miguel
Sena
El Cerrito
Tecolote
Romeroville
Las Vegas
Onava
Azul
Kroenigs
Watrous
La Cueva
Golondrinos
Sapello
Los Alamos
Solitario Peak
Black Peak
Ocate Crater
La Liendre
Dakota sandstone (underlain by Purgatoire formation)
Sand, clay, and silt
Santa Fe marl
Red shale
EXPLANATION
Thickness in feet
A Sand, clay, and loam — Alluvium — 50 — Quaternary
B Lava flows (basalt)
C Volcanic tuff — 500 — Tertiary
D Intrusive rocks (basalt, andesite)
E Sand, clay, and silt — Santa Fe marl — 150
Sandstone and shale — Galisteo sandstone — Tertiary (?)
F Sandstone and shales — Mesaverde formation — 800 — Cretaceous (Upper Cretaceous)
G Sandstone and dark shales — Dakota and Mancos — 2400
H Shale, greenish gray — Morrison — 300 — Jurassic or Cretaceous
I Gypsum — 50 — Jurassic ?
J Sandstone, pink — Wingate ? — 100
K Shale, red — 1000 — Triassic
L Sandstone and limestone — Manzano group — 1100 — Carbonifero (Pennsylvani
M Shales and sandstone, mostly red
N Limestone and sandstone — Magdalena group — 1100
O Schists, granite, etc. — Pre-Cambri
Scale 1/500,000
Approximately 8 miles to 1 inch
0 5 10 15 20 Miles
0 5 10 15 20 25 30 Kilometers
Contour interval 200 feet
ELEVATIONS IN FEET ABOVE MEAN SEA LEVEL
The distances from Kansas City, Missouri, are shown every 10 miles
The crossties on the railroads are spaced 1 mile apart

Lamy
General view, 1904

Santa Fe highlights, 1906
Apache Canyon
Cajon Pass
Cajon Pass in winter

Apache Canyon
*c.*1912

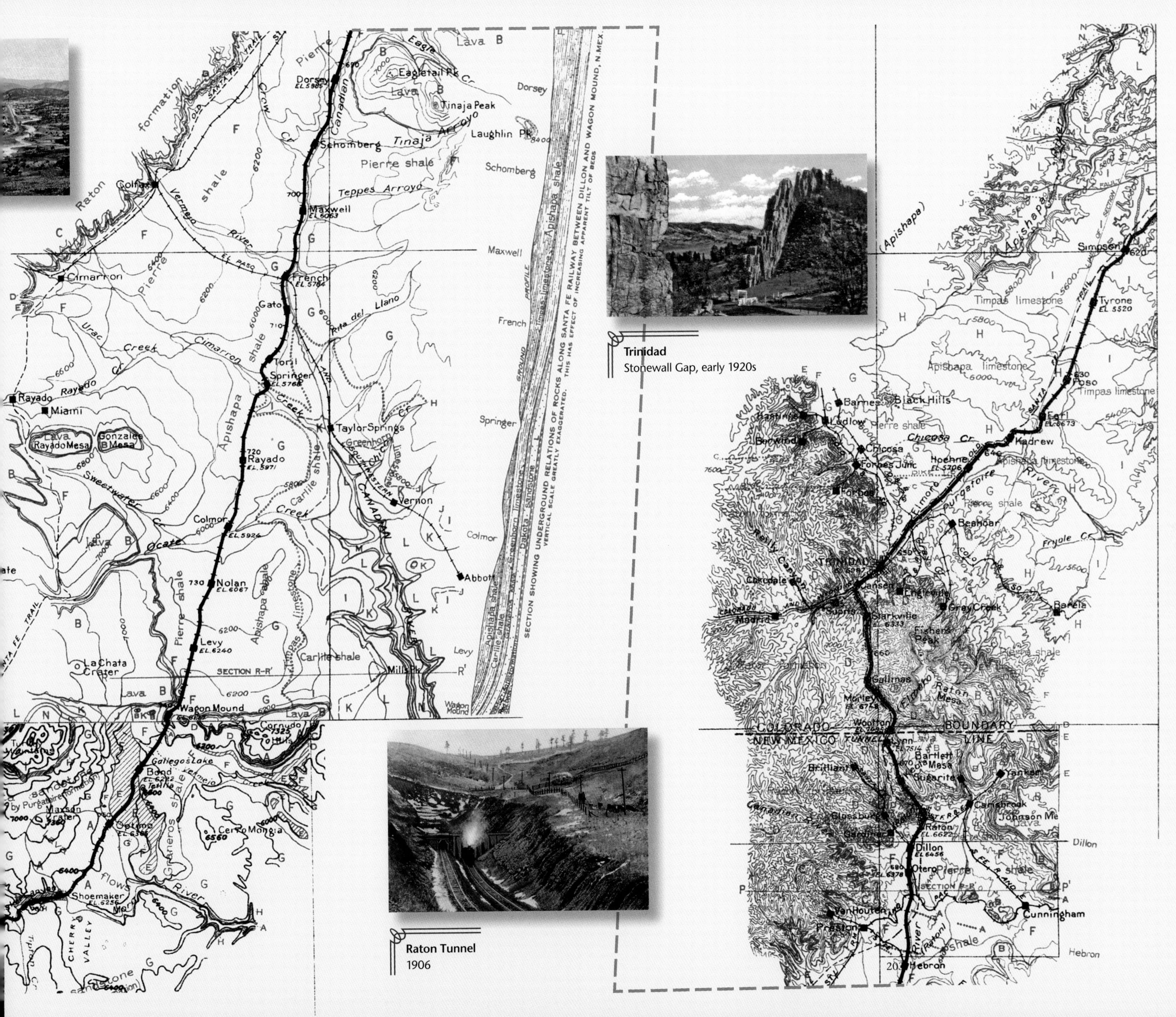

Trinidad
Stonewall Gap, early 1920s

Raton Tunnel
1906

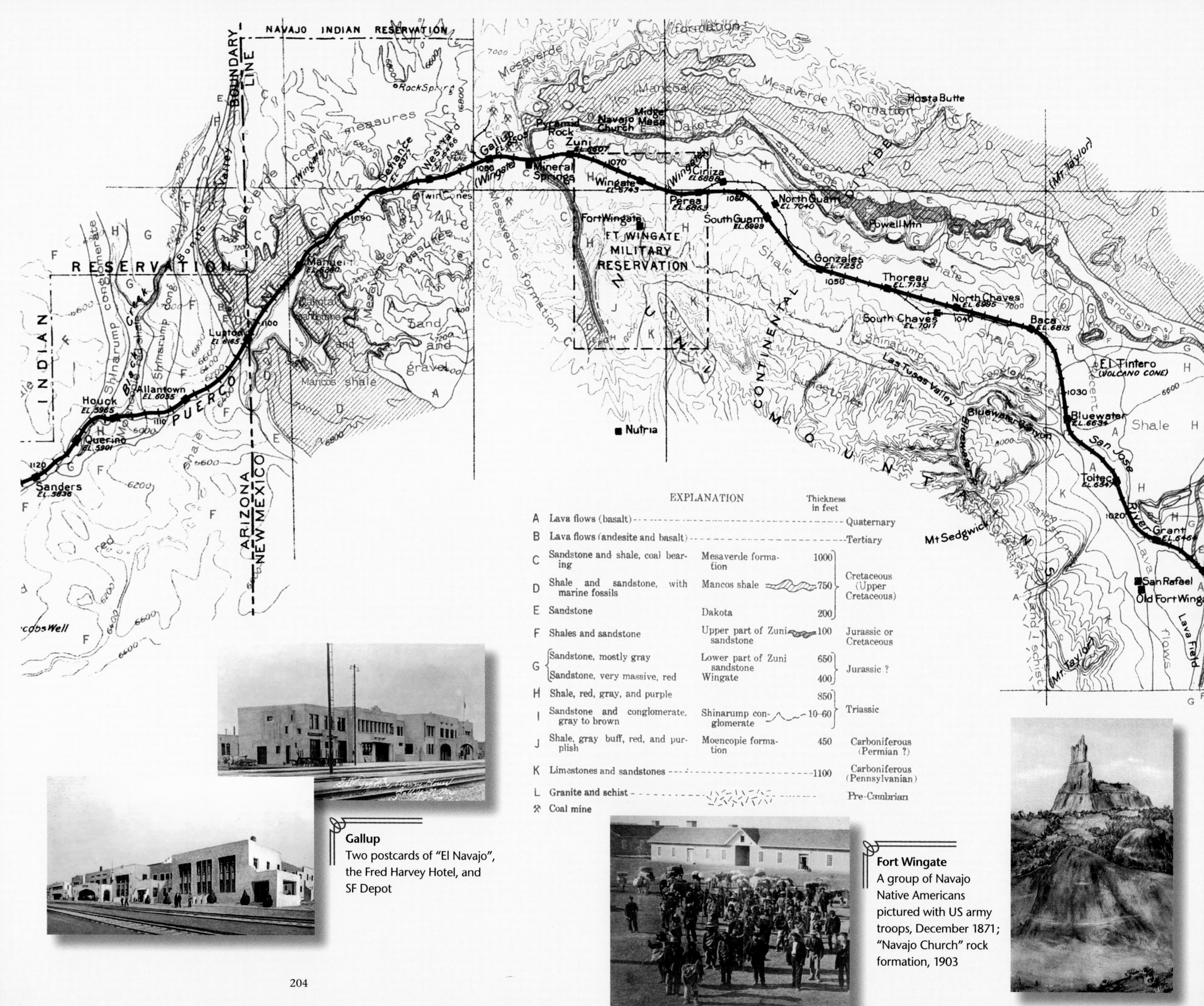

Gallup
Two postcards of "El Navajo", the Fred Harvey Hotel, and SF Depot

Fort Wingate
A group of Navajo Native Americans pictured with US army troops, December 1871; "Navajo Church" rock formation, 1903

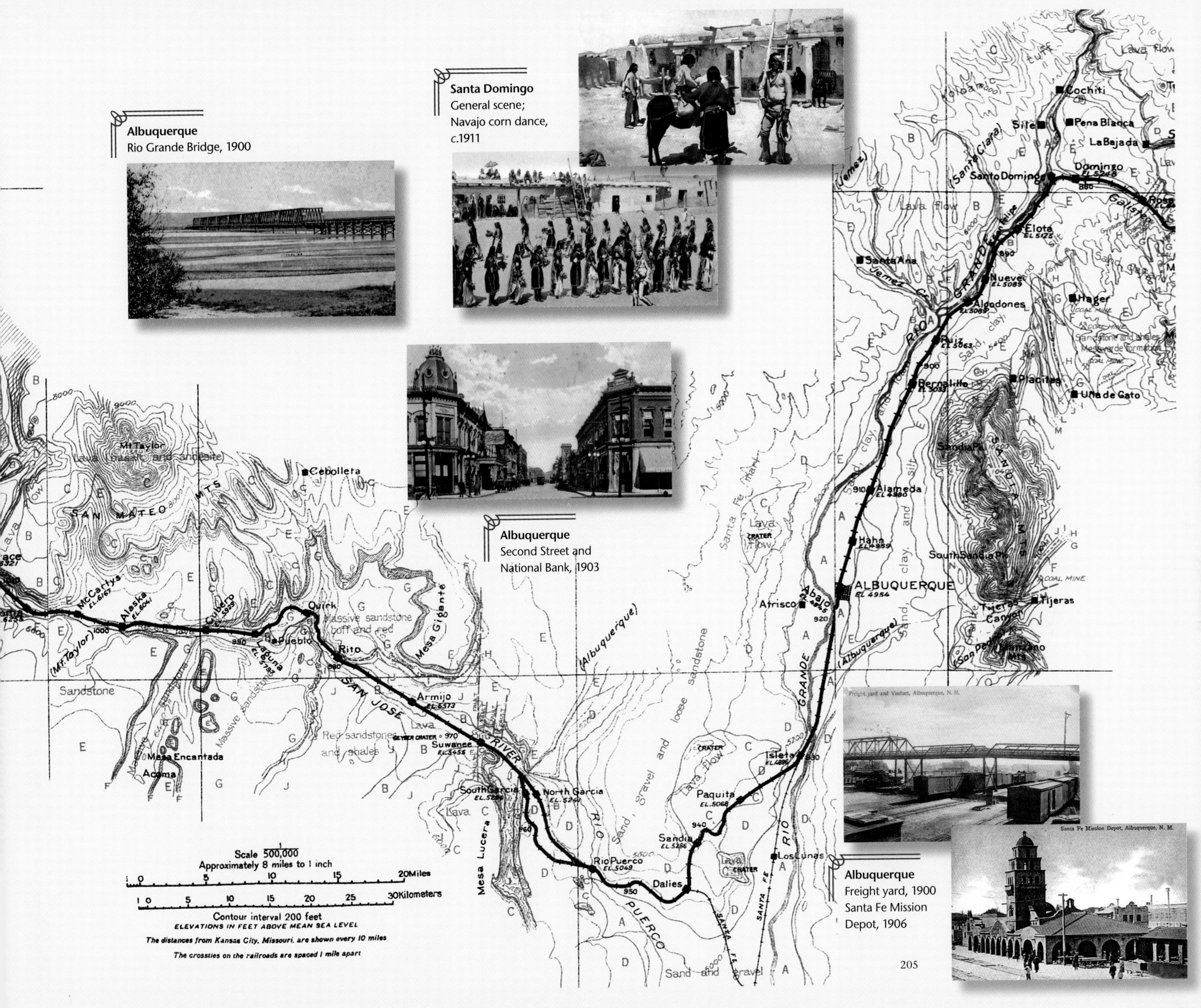

Albuquerque
Rio Grande Bridge, 1900

Santa Domingo
General scene;
Navajo corn dance,
*c.*1911

Albuquerque
Second Street and
National Bank, 1903

Albuquerque
Freight yard, 1900
Santa Fe Mission
Depot, 1906

to Grand Canyon (see opposite)

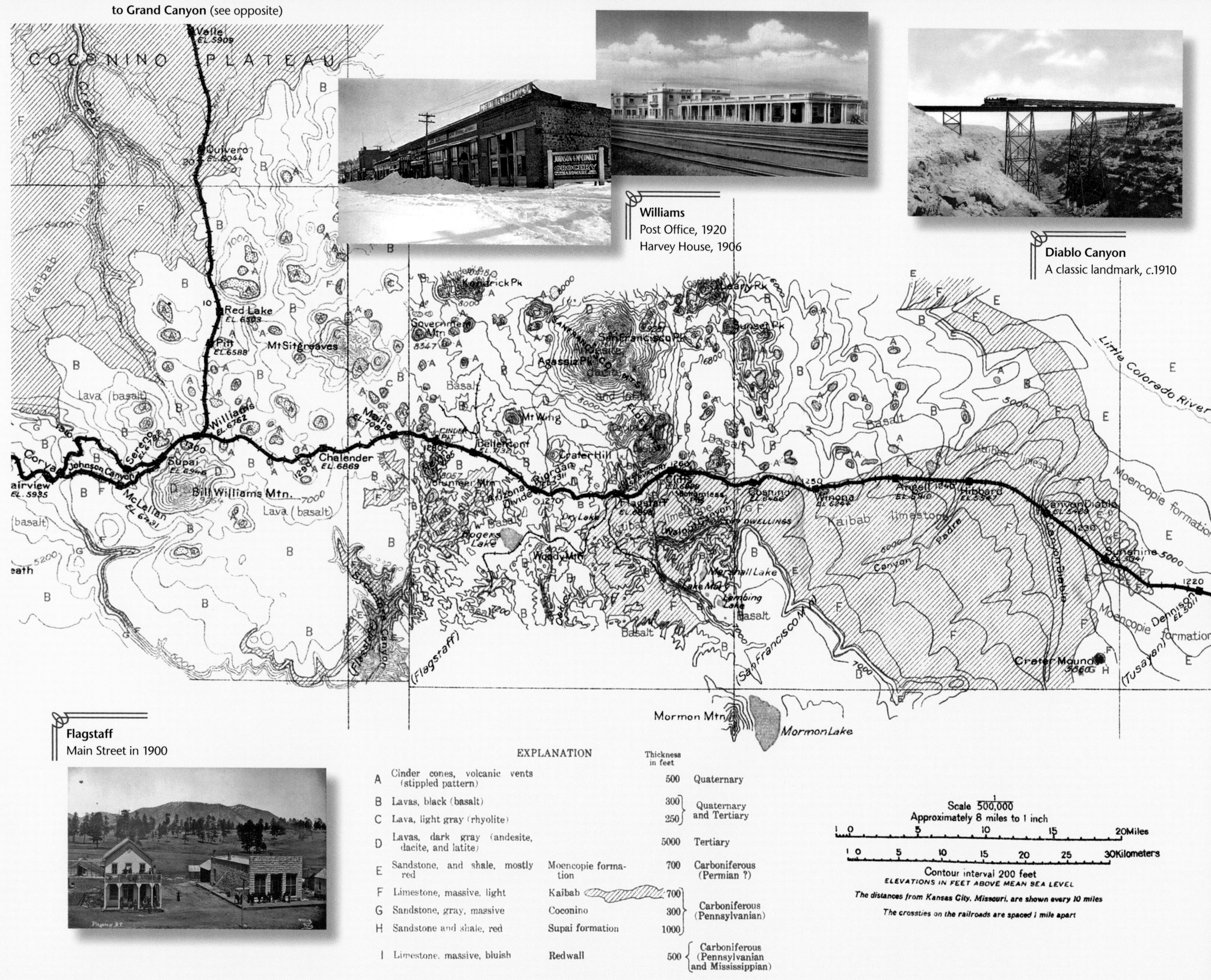
COCONINO PLATEAU
Valle EL. 5909
Quivero EL. 6044
Red Lake EL. 6503
Pitt EL. 6588
Mt Sitgreaves
Lava (basalt)
Williams EL. 6762
Supai EL. 6946
Bill Williams Mtn.
McLellan EL. 6431
Fairview EL. 5935
Johnson Canyon
Chalender EL. 6869
Maine
Kendrick Pk
Government Mtn
San Francisco Pk
Agassiz Pk
Mt Wing
Bellemont
Crater Hill
Volunteer Mtn
Riordan
Arizona Divide
Flagstaff
Rogers Lake
Woody Mtn
Dry Lake
Sunset Pk
O'Leary Pk
Cliffs
Cosnino
Winona EL. 6244
Walnut Canyon
Cliff Dwellings
Marshall Lake
Lake Mary
Lumbing Lake
Basalt
Angell EL. 5910
Hibbard EL. 5557
Canyon Diablo
Sunshine EL. 5341
Little Colorado River
Moencopie formation
Kaibab limestone
Padre Canyon
Crater Mound
Dennison EL. 5017
Mormon Mtn
Mormon Lake
EXPLANATION
Thickness in feet
A Cinder cones, volcanic vents (stippled pattern) 500 Quaternary
B Lavas, black (basalt) 300 Quaternary and Tertiary
C Lava, light gray (rhyolite) 250
D Lavas, dark gray (andesite, dacite, and latite) 5000 Tertiary
E Sandstone, and shale, mostly red Moencopie formation 700 Carboniferous (Permian ?)
F Limestone, massive, light Kaibab 700 Carboniferous (Pennsylvanian)
G Sandstone, gray, massive Coconino 300
H Sandstone and shale, red Supai formation 1000
I Limestone, massive, bluish Redwall 500 Carboniferous (Pennsylvanian and Mississippian)
Scale 1/500,000
Approximately 8 miles to 1 inch
0 5 10 15 20 Miles
0 5 10 15 20 25 30 Kilometers
Contour interval 200 feet
ELEVATIONS IN FEET ABOVE MEAN SEA LEVEL
The distances from Kansas City, Missouri, are shown every 10 miles
The crossties on the railroads are spaced 1 mile apart

Williams
Post Office, 1920
Harvey House, 1906

Diablo Canyon
A classic landmark, *c.*1910

Flagstaff
Main Street in 1900

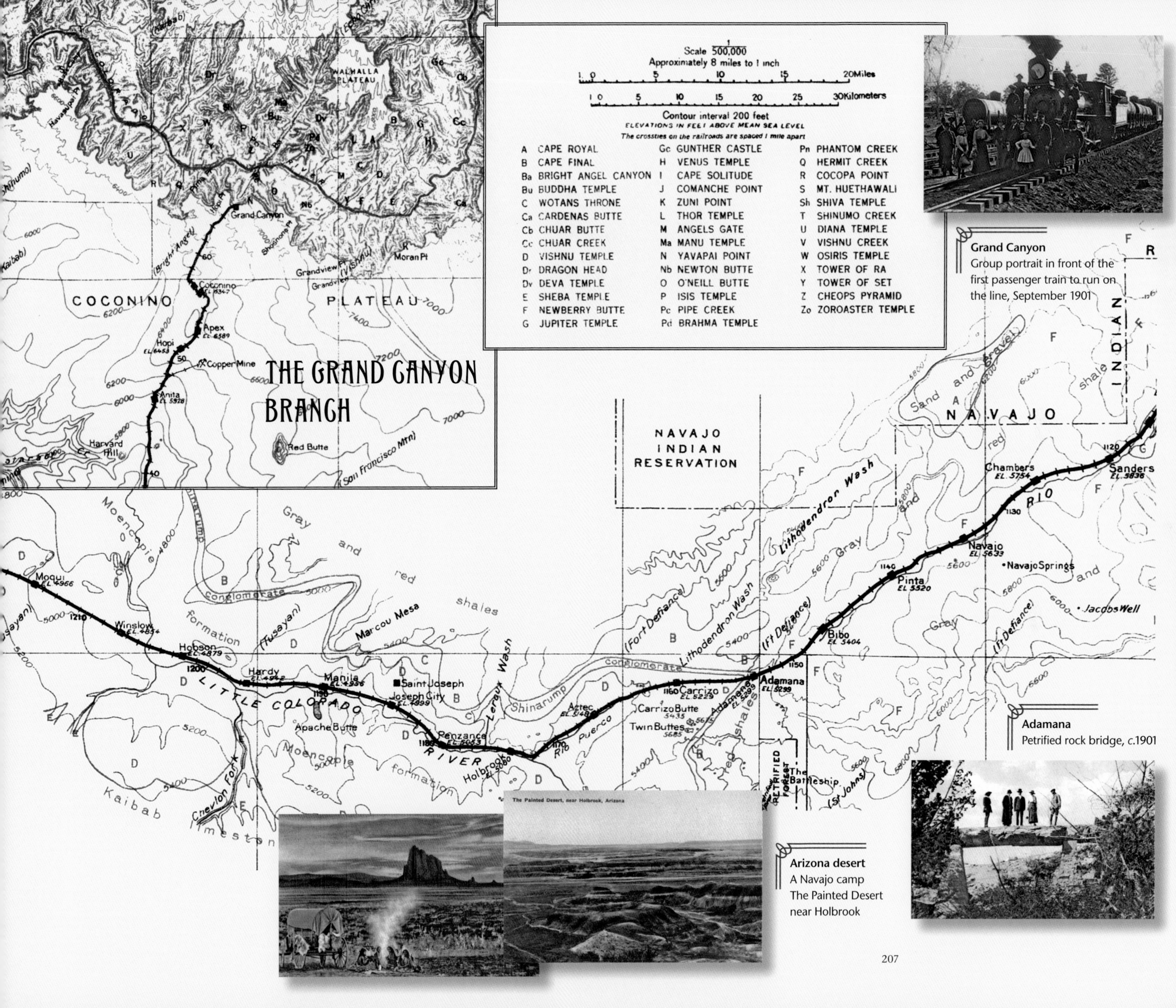

Grand Canyon
Group portrait in front of the first passenger train to run on the line, September 1901

Adamana
Petrified rock bridge, *c.*1901

Arizona desert
A Navajo camp
The Painted Desert near Holbrook

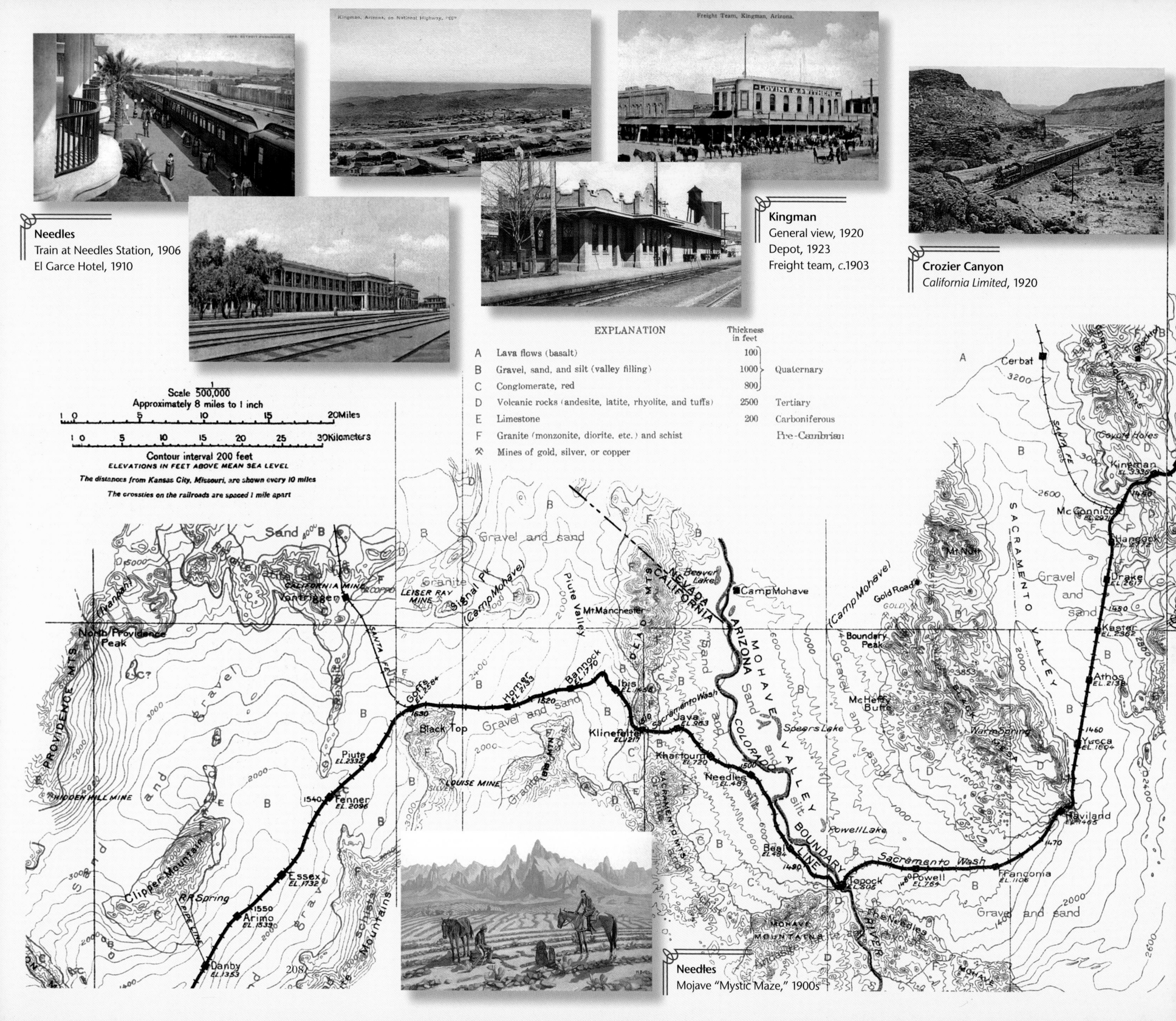

Needles
Train at Needles Station, 1906
El Garce Hotel, 1910

Kingman
General view, 1920
Depot, 1923
Freight team, c.1903

Crozier Canyon
California Limited, 1920

Needles
Mojave "Mystic Maze," 1900s

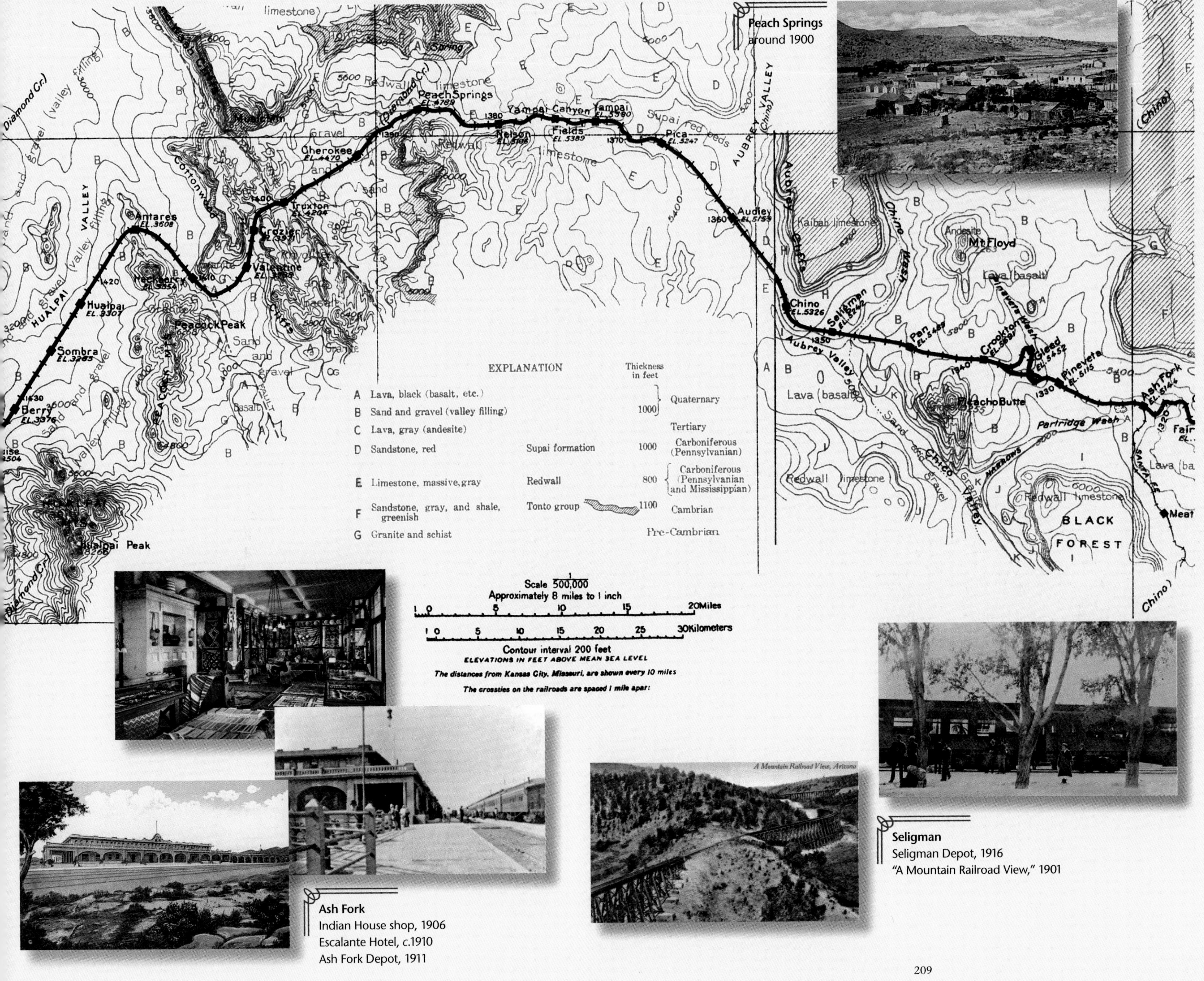

Peach Springs
around 1900

Ash Fork
Indian House shop, 1906
Escalante Hotel, *c.*1910
Ash Fork Depot, 1911

Seligman
Seligman Depot, 1916
"A Mountain Railroad View," 1901

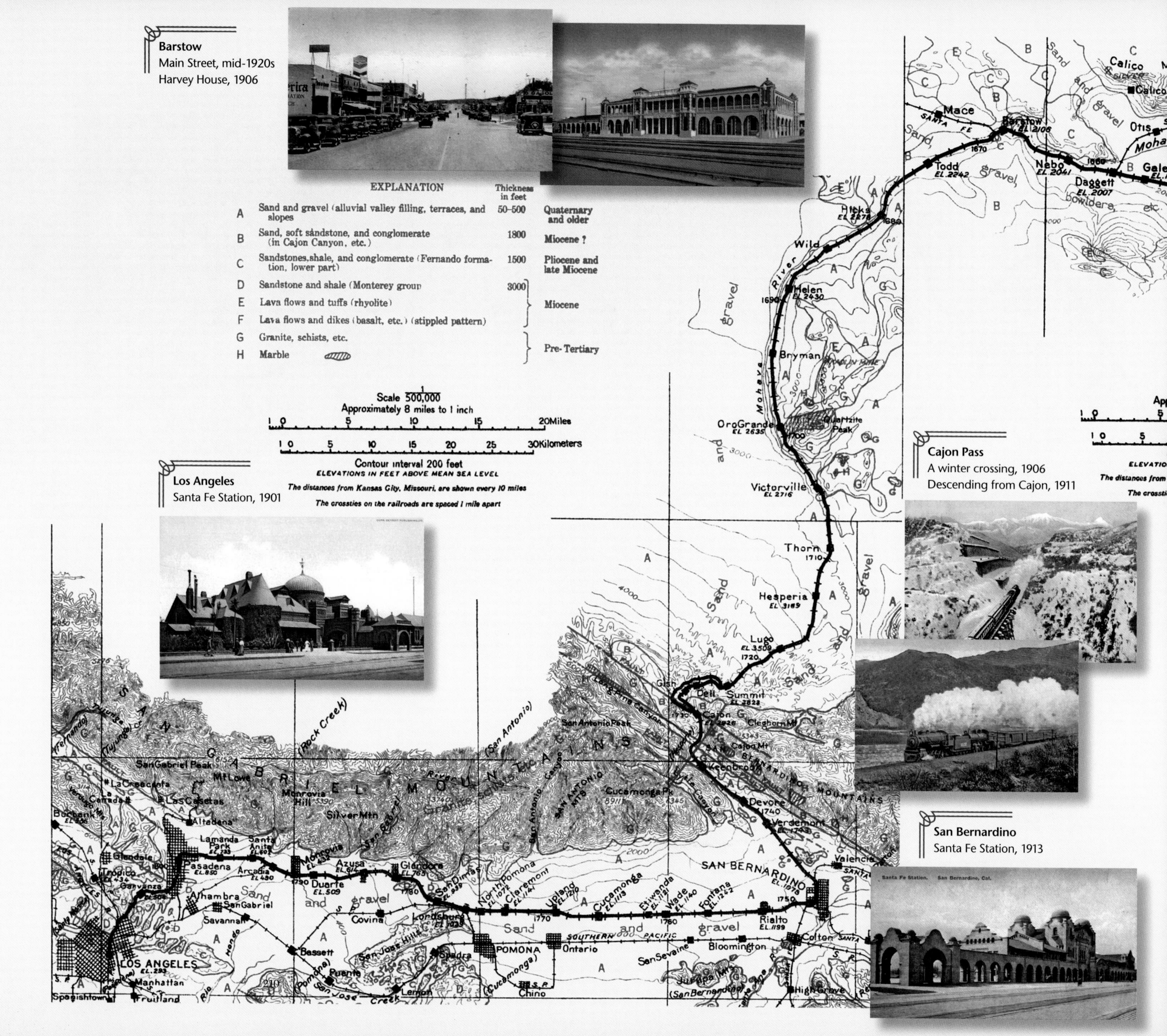

Barstow
Main Street, mid-1920s
Harvey House, 1906

Los Angeles
Santa Fe Station, 1901

Cajon Pass
A winter crossing, 1906
Descending from Cajon, 1911

San Bernardino
Santa Fe Station, 1913

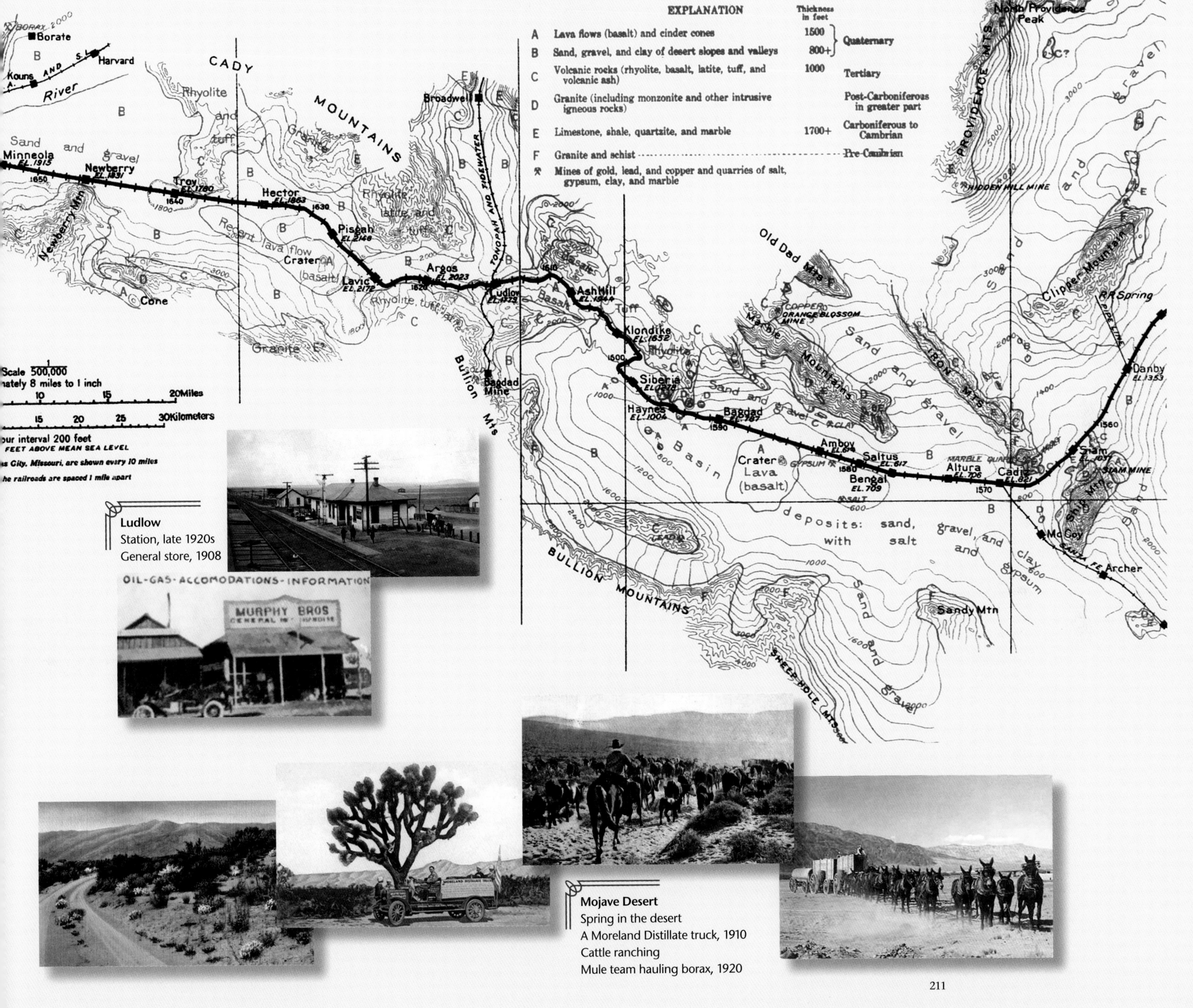

Ludlow
Station, late 1920s
General store, 1908

Mojave Desert
Spring in the desert
A Moreland Distillate truck, 1910
Cattle ranching
Mule team hauling borax, 1920

THE DENVER AND RIO GRANDE ROUTE

DENVER TO SALT LAKE CITY VIA THE ROYAL GORGE

In the early 1860s, the frontier city of Denver, which had been founded in 1858 as a mining town during the Pikes Peak gold rush, seemed poised to benefit from a premier position on a transcontinental railroad. Nestled at the foot of the Colorado Front Range, Denver was where the plains met the Rocky Mountains and what better place for a railroad to start its climb? Yet it was not to be, and the people of Denver were dismayed by the decision to route the Union Pacific's line through the barren Wyoming high plains, 106 miles to the north of the young city.

Bypassed by the first transcontinental route, Denver continued to seek a position on a main line. The Union Pacific soon acquiesced to Denver's demands by constructing its Denver Pacific branch from Cheyenne, giving Denver a stub end service in the spring of 1870. Soon a more important line—the Kansas Pacific—arrived from the east, and with it came a dynamic engineer and skilled railroad promoter, General William Jackson Palmer (1836–1909). Awarded the Medal of Honor during the Civil War, Palmer had learnt railroad engineering from the Pennsylvania Railroad's esteemed engineer (and later president) J. Edgar Thomson. With his engineering background, well-placed connections in the realms of finance, and proven capabilities as a leader, Palmer was the right man to put Denver and Colorado on America's railroad map.

General Palmer had railroad dreams beyond those of the Kansas Pacific, envisioning a network linking Denver with Mexico City, so in 1870 he resigned from the Kansas Pacific and formed his own company, the Denver & Rio Grande (D&RG). On a business trip east, Palmer had a fortuitous meeting with William P. Mellen, an influential lawyer from New York. Palmer charmed Mellen into supporting his railroad, while courting his

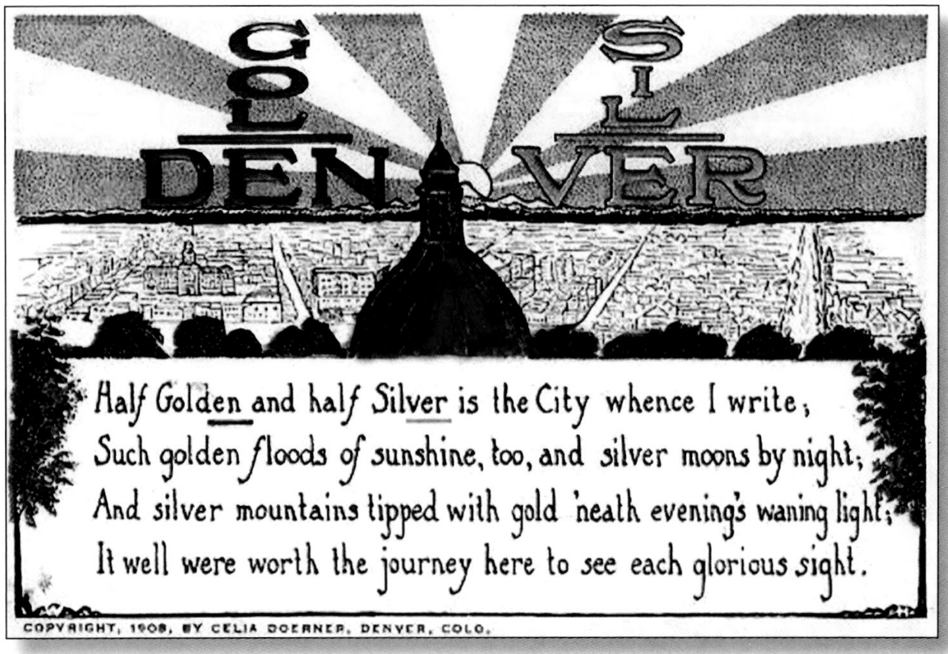
GOLD
SILVER
DEN
VER
Half Golden and half Silver is the City whence I write;
Such golden floods of sunshine, too, and silver moons by night;
And silver mountains tipped with gold 'neath evening's waning light;
It well were worth the journey here to see each glorious sight.
COPYRIGHT, 1908, BY CELIA DOERNER, DENVER, COLO.

daughter, Mary. In short order Palmer and Mary were married, and headed off to Great Britain for their honeymoon.

Not one for idle sightseeing, Palmer took the opportunity to learn about narrow gauge railroads, a popular innovation soon to spread around the world. Based on the advice of British narrow gauge proponents, Palmer adopted a three-foot track width for his D&RG line, rather than the North American standard gauge of 4 feet 8½ inches. Narrow gauge railroads offered a variety of advantages in mountain territory. Smaller locomotives and rolling stock required lower investment, with substantial cost savings in construction and operation. Also, a narrow gauge line could be built on a more sinuous path through deep canyons and over high passes by using fewer

In the early years of the twentieth century, Denver was a prime tourist destination, aggressively marketing itself and its surrounding attractions; a 1910 postcard (above).

Hell Gate, crossing the Continental Divide at 10,540 feet, from *The Rocky Mountains of Colorado*, published by The Smith-Brooks Printing Company, Denver, in 1913 (far left).

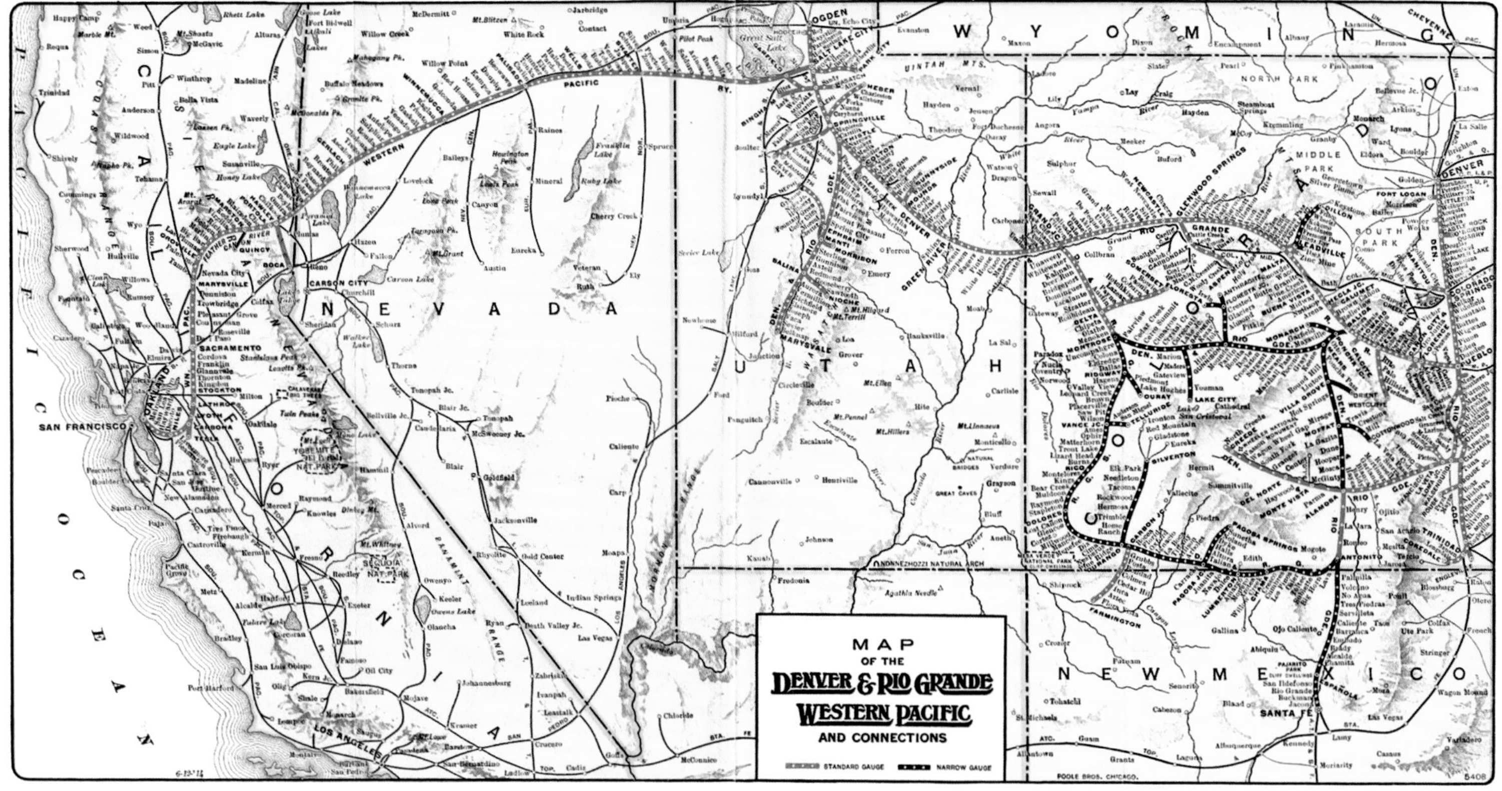

A 1910 map of the Denver and Rio Grande–Western Pacific system shortly after completion of the WP to the Pacific coast in November 1909. Red lines indicate standard gauge routes, black the D&RG's remaining narrow gauge routes. Thin black lines are competing routes.

earthworks and with little to no tunneling, whereas a standard gauge line would require substantial engineering. Thus narrow gauge could be built to places where standard gauge lines were cost-prohibitive.

On his return, Palmer wasted no time in getting the D&RG underway. Construction began southward from Denver on July 28, 1871, and the first scheduled passenger train arrived in the boomtown of Colorado Springs on October 26. Regularly scheduled passenger service began to Colorado Springs in early 1872, a remarkably short span of time by today's standards, when it takes longer to do the environmental impact studies than Palmer needed to reach his first destination.

Reaching southward across largely unsettled lands, Palmer anticipated tapping traffic moving over the Santa Fe Trail. Although Mexico was viewed as a southern terminus, the lure of Colorado mineral traffic was also an important part of Palmer's scheme. So before building across the wide expanse of desert to the south, the D&RG extended a line over Le Veta Pass to reach the fertile San Luis Valley, and pushed another branch westward from Pueblo to Cañon City, a gateway to new mining camps deep in the Colorado Rockies. From there the only practical path west was through a natural pass called the Royal Gorge of the Arkansas River. This navigated a vertical chasm that in places was just thirty feet wide and two thousand feet deep.

Palmer's progress was soon stifled, however. His arrogance had antagonized communities along his lines, so that after a few years they were less inclined to support the D&RG, which also began to suffer from inadequate financing as a result of the Panic of 1873. Furthermore, by mid-decade he faced Cyrus Holliday's Santa Fe that was pushing its way west into his territory, with many of the same goals as the D&RG.

The Santa Fe presented the most serious threat to Palmer's potential traffic, and more so to his entire railroad philosophy. He had envisioned that the southwest would be the domain of the narrow gauge, but with Santa Fe in the game, this threatened to undermine the viability of his entire slim gauge concept.

The Santa Fe was the first to occupy Raton Pass in 1878, which effectively barred Palmer's route from reaching further south. When he moved to build westward into the Royal Gorge in 1879, he again faced competing Santa Fe forces. As a result of these clashes, the D&RG refocused its efforts entirely on the Rocky Mountain region of central Colorado, Utah, and northern New Mexico.

By the 1880s the D&RG had expanded beyond the San Luis Valley to western Colorado mining communities through construction of the San Juan Extension. This ran west from Antonito, following the Toltec Gorge, over Cumbres Pass, and then crossed the Continental Divide to reach Durango, Colorado in 1881. A key branch ran northward from Durango up the Animas River to Silverton.

After settling territorial differences with the Santa Fe, the D&RG built west from Cañon City on the Royal Gorge route, reaching Salida by 1880 and Leadville by 1881. By extending a branch beyond Leadville over the 10,000-foot summit at Tennessee Pass, the D&RG tapped the mining community at Red Cliff in the west. Meanwhile it pushed another route that diverged west at Salida. This crossed Marshall Pass, ran through the Black Canyon of the Gunnison, and was extended to Montrose and Grand Junction in 1881. It was this route that was developed as the D&RG's narrow gauge main line, and by 1883 it had connections to Salt Lake City and beyond, reaching the Central Pacific/Union Pacific at Ogden where it hoped to tap into transcontinental business. Here the Rio Grande's gauge difference proved to be a serious problem, since freight and passengers were forced to change trains at both ends of its system. It also faced increasing competition as additional standard gauge lines were built into the region.

Curecanti Needle in the Black Canyon of the Gunnison, from *Rocky Mountain Views of the Rio Grande: The Scenic Line of the World*, published by The Inter-State Company of Denver in 1914.

After nearly two decades of promoting narrow gauge, the D&RG changed its tune, and in the late 1880s built its own standard gauge route between Denver and the Great Salt Lake. Instead of re-gauging the Marshall Pass crossing, it constructed a new main line on a northerly path via Tennessee Pass continuing west through Glenwood Canyon. West of Grand Junction, the Rio Grande built a new alignment to ease grades and curvature, only loosely following the route of its original narrow gauge line. So, while the railroad operated 1,861 miles of three-foot gauge trackage in 1889, by the next year roughly 600 miles of narrow gauge were abandoned or converted as it completed its own standard gauge Denver–Salt Lake main line. This was initially a concession, and not a wholesale conversion of its narrow gauge empire. For many more decades, well into the twentieth century, the road operated hundreds of miles of three-foot gauge lines and some sections were never converted. Portions of the old San Juan Extension survive today, operated as the Cumbres & Toltec Scenic and Durango & Silverton tourist lines, complete with vintage Rio Grande steam locomotives.

A stock certificate from the 1900s for the Denver & Salt Lake Railway Tunnel Company.

ALONG THE DENVER & RIO GRANDE

By the mid-1880s, Denver was a bustling railway center where several standard gauge lines from the east converged to meet the three-foot gauge Denver & Rio Grande. The change of gauge mandated a change of trains, yet few travelers complained because the quaint quality of the narrow gauge trains was as much of an attraction as the exotic destinations to which they were traveling. South from Denver trains crossed the Palmer Divide, a moderate pass, named for the railroad's founder.

Pikes Peak Avenue, Colorado Springs; open-top car at Hanging Bridge, Royal Gorge, from *Rocky Mountain Views of the Rio Grande*; a humorous 1908 postcard of Garden of the Gods.

Here passengers were afforded vistas of towering peaks to the west, but still rolled along at a moderate elevation. Serious climbing awaited further down the tracks.

Colorado Springs and its environs were the first popular destinations along the line. Known as the "Saratoga of the Far West" (after the famous spa in upper New York State), mineral springs offered refreshment and health treatments, while luxurious hotels presented a jumping-off point for forays by branch train, stage, or horseback to taller peaks. This was the gateway to both the Ute Pass and the famed Garden of the Gods which featured some of the most spectacular scenery in the American West. To the west of Colorado Springs, a branch ran to the village of Manitou–originally Villa La Font–which boasted no less than 16 springs of effervescent mineral waters. It was said that Native Americans believed the bubbling water was the result of the Great Spirit breathing. After 1891, tourists could ride the Manitou & Pikes Peak cog railway, and from 1901 the Short Line as well as connections with the Colorado Midland.

The D&RG's line continued southward to Pueblo where its lines divided, the main line heading west via Cañon City to follow the Arkansas River through the narrow confines of the Royal Gorge. Beyond the gorge, Salida was one of the largest mountain towns, owing its settlement to the coming of the railroads in 1880. Its name is the Spanish word for "outlet," and refers to this portion of the Upper Arkansas River basin. Situated at 7,050 feet above sea level and 215 miles from Denver, Salida was one of the most important junctions on the line and the location of railroad yards and locomotive shops. Visitors were impressed by the stunning views of Sangre de Cristo, Collegiate Peaks, and beyond to the Sawatch Range, best seen from a hill above the yards near the D&RG station. It was here that the old narrow gauge route diverged and meandered westward via Marshall Pass, thus giving travelers a choice of routes to the West. Although slower and requiring a change of trains, the narrow gauge Marshall Pass crossing was the preferred route of the adventurous visitor to Colorado.

DENVER & RIO GRANDE WESTERN
SCENIC LINE OF THE WORLD

Heading out of Salida on the three-foot gauge main line, visitors arrived at Poncha, 7,471 feet above sea level—location of the famed Poncha Hot Springs where water bubbled forth from the ground at temperatures between 90 and 185 degrees Fahrenheit. A branch to Monarch was an important source of mineral traffic. Further west, at Mears Junction, a secondary line wandered south toward Alamosa where it connected with the La Veta Pass route. To reach Marshall Pass, the D&RG's narrow gauge main line wound through a series of sharp reverse curves offering views of mountains on both sides of the line. Finally the line crested at the top of the pass at 10,858 feet, providing a splendid view of Mt. Ouray—nearly 14,000 feet high and covered in snow most of the year.

On the far side of the pass, the tracks descended sharply on another especially sinuous alignment to the village of Gunnison at 7,673 feet, where the railroad continued west along the river of the same name. The Black Canyon of the Gunnison was heralded as one of the greatest rail journeys in Colorado, and the D&RG was to add a special observation car on this portion of the run for passengers to better take in the views of the unusual lava formations and granite walls that in places rose a thousand feet above rail level. This deep rugged canyon, formed by the river carving its way through the rock, had remained unexplored until the Rio Grande's survey teams arrived in the early 1880s.

At the confluence of the Gunnison and Blue Creek rose a pyramid-shaped rock formation known as the Curecanti Needle, its peak more than seven hundred feet above the tracks. Beyond, the canyon walls, although less vertical, reached up to 2,500 feet above rail level. The line crossed the Gunnison many times, following its course to lower elevations, then, finally, at the edge of the desert, the Rio Grande's routes came back together at Grand Junction in western Colorado.

The standard gauge main line ran northwest from Salida, and brought travelers over Tennessee Pass by way of Malta where a connecting branch took visitors to Leadville. One of the highest towns in the United States, it was also one of the first settled in the mountains of Colorado, dating to 1859 when it was known as California Gulch. Although its name suggests that lead was first and foremost of the metals mined here, in fact gold and silver were the primary attraction to prospectors. At its height, the town claimed a population of 30,000 people, although by 1909 it had dropped to perhaps a third of that.

While the Rio Grande's original narrow gauge branch to Red Cliff climbed over Tennessee Pass on a sinuous alignment, the standard gauge main line via the Pass crossed through a 2,572-foot tunnel that saved some 250 feet in elevation. On the far side, the line dropped sharply down through the Red Cliff and Eagle River Canyons, passing mining communities and

Eagle River Canyon, from *Rocky Mountain Views of the Rio Grande*.

Glenwood Springs, from *Rocky Mountain Views of the Rio Grande* (above).

1900s postcards of the bathing pool at Glenwood Springs, and Castle Gate in Utah's Price River Canyon (top right).

villages along the way. Below Pando, as the train continued downgrade, passengers gazing up the walls of the canyon could spot mine shafts and small tramways used to extract minerals from the ground. The steep decent ended at Minturn where the railroad maintained locomotives for use in helper service eastward over the Pass, and from there the grade followed a more gentle westward profile. The most spectacular part of this journey was through winding confines of Glenwood Canyon, where for fifteen miles, on both sides of the river, towering vertical quartzite walls loomed high above the tracks.

Situated in a broad flood plain near the west end of Glenwood Canyon, at an elevation of 5,758 feet, Glenwood Springs is located where the Roaring Fork River joins the Colorado. This resort was known for its sulphur springs and pools and was a popular destination for travelers.

West of Grand Junction, the D&RG crossed the Utah state line in the midst of Ruby Canyon, named for the rich reddish rock that towered above the railroad and river. The line followed the famous Book Cliffs, hugging the desert floor that was once an ancient sea bed. At Helper, Utah, the route began to climb, passing through the towering rock formation known as Castle Gate. A snaking horseshoe curve at Kyune was punctuated by a tunnel beneath a layered rocky ridge. Further west the railroad crossed the famed Soldier Summit, a broad saddle in the mountains, which at 7,440 feet was the highest point on the D&RG in Utah. It was named for the burial place of General Albert Sidney Johnson's troops killed during the so-called Mormon War of the 1850s. On the west side of the summit the tracks descended by way of the curving Gilluly Loops—a series of horseshoe curves used to keep the gradient reasonable—into the canyon of Spanish Fork Creek.

Finally, after ascent and descent via several of America's most significant mountain crossings, the D&RG's line reached Provo, Salt Lake City, and Ogden, Utah where its line connected with the routes of the Union Pacific and the Southern Pacific (originally the Central Pacific). Because of its scenic and difficult route, the Rio Grande carried the moniker of the "Scenic Line of the World," and in later years was known as the railroad that went "Through the Rockies, not Around Them."

Veta Pass and the San Juan Extension

South of Pueblo, at the Cuchare junction, the Denver & Rio Grande's lines split again. The line originally projected toward Raton Pass reached only as far as coal mines near El Moro, and was of little interest to most travelers. However, the other route branched westward and crossed the Sangre de Cristo mountains by way of a steep, sinuous alignment over La Veta Pass, climbing at a rate of 211 feet to the mile (3.2 percent). Via this spectacular mountain line it reached into the San Juan Valley, where the railroad maintained facilities at Alamosa, then continued southward through the valley to Antonito, where it again divided. The old Chili Line carried on due south to Santa Fe, New Mexico, while the better traveled line, the D&RG's San Juan Extension, continued west across the high desert, attaining a plateau that rolled right to the edge of the Toltec Gorge, and crossing back and forth over the Colorado–New Mexico border. The tracks nimbly negotiated the rim of a precipice, where more than 1,100 feet below rushed the waters of Los Pinos Creek. Passengers were not only awed by the engineering feats of the Rio Grande's path here, but also by the foreboding south rim of the gorge with insurmountable rock walls towering some two thousand feet above the water.

After passing through the rocky confines of the Toltec Tunnel, the line continued west through the mountains. Through a series of sharp reverse curves, most famous of which was "Whiplash Curve," where the tracks doubled back upon themselves to gain elevation, the line reached a 10,000-foot crossing of the Rockies at the perilous Cumbres Pass, a crossing that completely overshadowed the later pass across the Continental Divide.

Durango at the end of the line was a popular destination, developed during 1880 in the broad lower valley of the Animas River. Famed for its trains, mines, miners, and personalities, the town was a logical layover point for travelers exploring the San Juan region. To its north, the D&RG extended a branch along the exceptionally narrow and extraordinarily deep Animas River canyon toward Silverton. Tracks were cut into a narrow shelf, and passengers could gaze out of their windows straight down at the cascading waters hundreds of feet below. This was among the most famous of all the D&RG's branch lines and in the 1950s, after the mining traffic had all but dried up, it was developed into a tourist line. It continues to operate to the present day as the Durango & Silverton, complete with steam power.

Animas Cañon, from *Rocky Mountain Views of the Rio Grande.*

THE MOFFAT ROUTE

More than a decade after the Rio Grande's standard gauge line connected Denver with Salt Lake City via Tennessee Pass, Denver-based railway promoter David H. Moffat envisioned a more direct route over the Front Range. In 1902 he founded the Denver Northwestern & Pacific Railway, which made a breathtakingly tortuous climb over Rollins Pass at 11,660 feet. Known as the Giant's Ladder, the highest main line crossing in North America, it was only intended as a temporary route since Moffat planned to tunnel under the Rockies once funds were available. In the meantime, it was perhaps the most spectacular line in the United States, and among the most difficult to operate because of heavy snowfall.

Moffat ran out of money in 1911 and died before seeing his dreams fulfilled. Others picked up where he left off, however, and, in 1922, public funds were made available for construction of the tunnel. Completed in 1928, more than six miles long with its eastern portal at an elevation of 9,198 feet above sea level, this incredible tunnel was named in Moffat's honor. Ultimately, the D&RG assumed operation of the Moffat Route, which survives as a heavily used transcontinental line.

MANITOU AND PIKE'S PEAK

The Cogwheel Road

Perhaps Colorado's best-known mountain, Pike's Peak is a tall, awe-inspiring summit, and at 14,109 feet the highest mountain in the region—roughly a mile and a half higher than nearby Colorado Springs. The peak is named for Lieutenant Zebulon M. Pike, who, on a commission from President Thomas Jefferson to explore portions of the Louisiana Purchase, "discovered" the mountain in 1806.

The spectacular views from the mountain inspired efforts to build a railway to the top in the 1880s. The first scheme—a conventional railroad with a winding 27-mile path to the top—built only eight miles of line before running out of money. In 1888, a second plan used the Abt cog system that enabled specially designed locomotives to ascend steep gradients. Instead of relying upon adhesion between wheel and rail to propel the locomotive, it had a geared wheel that interfaced with a cog track. With this system, the railway was able to ascend up to 1,320 feet per mile, reaching the summit with a line just eight and three-quarter miles long that followed a more direct path than the original adhesion plan. The Manitou & Pike's Peak Railway was completed on October 20, 1890, and ever since has been commonly known as the "Cogwheel Road," normally operated only during the summer owing to heavy snow at other times.

In 1909 the round trip fare was $5, which, at the contemporary value of the dollar, made it doubtless the most expensive trip mile-for-mile in Colorado. Yet, it was deemed worth the money for its outstanding vistas. Unlike other railways that were built to convey through passengers and carry freight, the Manitou & Pike's Peak was intended primarily to permit tourists to view the area's magnificent scenery from the summit, and to provide access to recreational trails along the way.

Travelers ascending Pike's Peak pass westward from Manitou through Engelmann Canyon, where mountain streams cascade down toward Colorado Springs, then reach a glacial terrace and lake at more than 9,000 feet. Oddly positioned only one third the way up the mountain was the "Halfway House" where passengers could disembark for a meal. Back in 1909, this cost a pricey 75 cents. As the railroad climbs it reaches above the natural tree line, revealing the bare granite that makes up the mountain. From the top, tourists took in an unparalleled view of the distant Spanish Peaks and Sangre de Cristo Range, while on clear days it was also possible to see Denver, Colorado Springs, and Manitou.

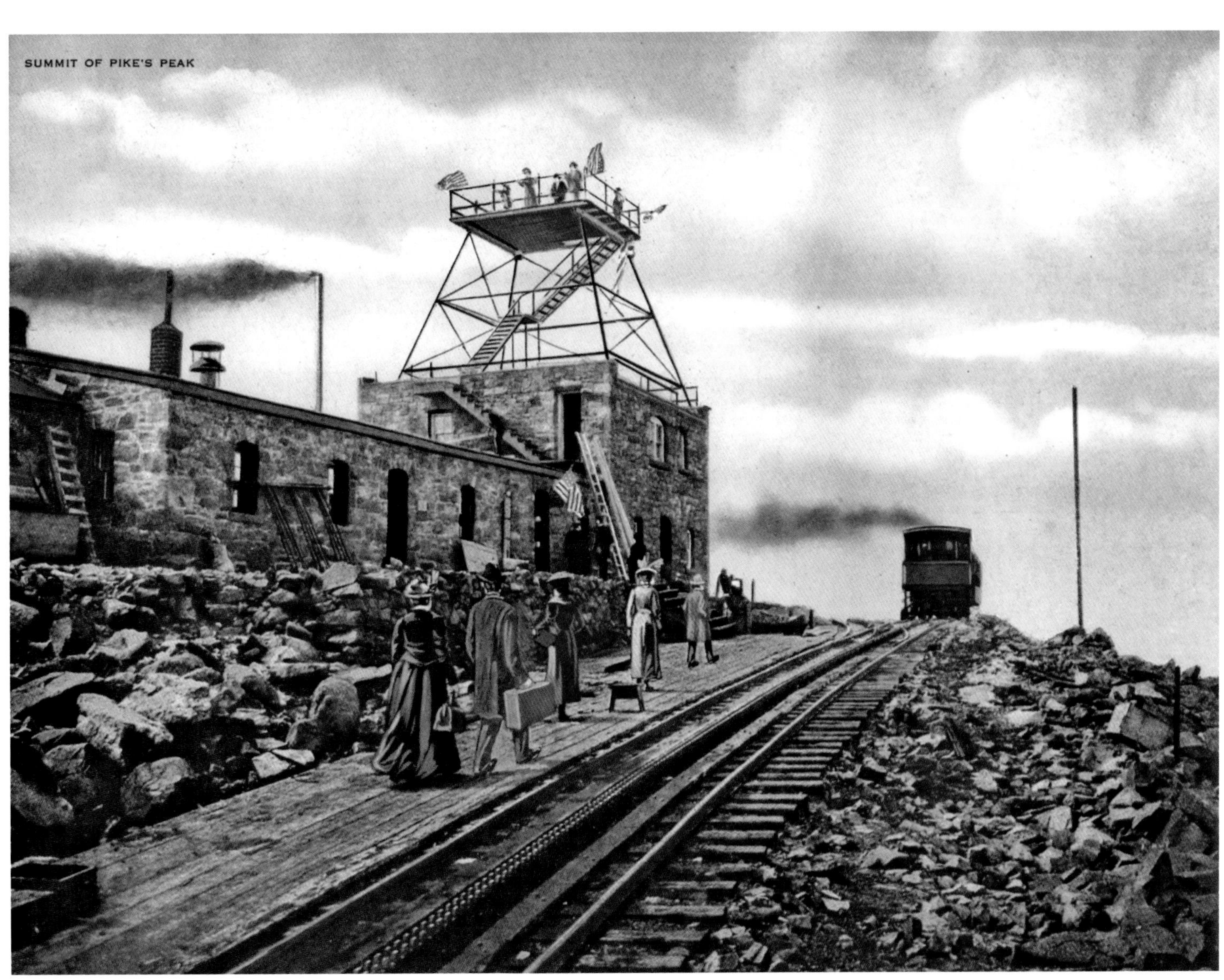

The Summit of Pikes Peak, from *Rocky Mountain Views of the Rio Grande.*

Cover of *The Pikes Peak Region*, published by The H. H. Tammen Company, Denver, in 1908 (opposite left); one of the book's illustrations, a train ascending Pikes Peak (opposite right).

THE SHORT LINE TO CRIPPLE CREEK

"The Ride that Bankrupted the English Language"

Mineral booms, popularly known as gold rushes, characterized the economy of many western communities in the latter half of the nineteenth century. In the 1890s, the region around Cripple Creek, Colorado was the latest boomtown as thousands of miners flocked in to extract mineral wealth from the mountains. This obscure town was reachable only by winding mountain roads until December 1893, when the Colorado Midland became the first railroad to reach Cripple Creek, followed six months later by the Florence & Cripple Creek. The last through railroad to reach the area was the Colorado Springs & Cripple Creek District Railway, a standard gauge railroad commonly known simply as the Short Line, completed in 1901. This 59-mile line was more famous for its spectacular Rocky Mountain crossing than its destination. Its route was characterized by an unusually tortuous profile, featuring tall wooden trestles, nine tunnels, and precarious canyon rim-running. Although mineral traffic, not passenger excursions, was the railroad's lifeblood, so unusually beautiful and breathtaking was the climb up from Colorado Springs that on a visit shortly after the line opened United States President Theodore Roosevelt declared that the Short Line was "the ride that bankrupted the English language."

15044. Grand View from Point Sublime, on Cripple Creek Short Line, Colo.

Travelers on the Short Line in 1909 were treated to a three-hour ride up the mountain for a fare of just $2.75. The line climbed steadily up to Bear Creek Canyon and its layered, sedimentary rock, then at Point Sublime the track curved through a deep rock cutting, offering views in one direction a thousand feet down into North Cheyenne Canyon, and in the other direction across the vast expanse of the plains to the east.

Further up the line, passengers would see a variety of unusual rock formations. The high point was Summit, where tracks crested 9,913 feet. This was among several notable "nose bleed" railroad crossings of the Rockies. At Victor, the Short Line ran parallel to the other lines for the last few miles into Cripple Creek.

As with most mineral booms, the glory days were intense but short-lived. Within two decades there was barely enough traffic to support one railroad, let alone three. First to go was the Florence & Cripple Creek, followed by the Short Line which shut in 1920, although as late as 1922 guidebooks were still listing the line with hopes that it might reopen. Sadly this was not the case, and one of America's most spectacular railway journeys was lost. The Colorado Midland route lasted until the 1940s.

15043. Map of Cripple Creek District, Colo.

A selection of images from a 1910 souvenir postcard booklet of the Cripple Creek Short Line.

ROYAL GORGE

Railroads at War

William Jackson Palmer's Denver & Rio Grande faced a fierce rival in the late 1870s in what became a battle for control of strategic mountain passes in southern Colorado. Although in 1878 the Santa Fe had bested D&RG in the quest for Raton Pass on the Colorado–New Mexico border, the Rio Grande looked to gain the upper hand in 1879 when the two lines vied for control of the Royal Gorge. The ensuing struggle has been described as the War of the Royal Gorge as the Santa Fe and the D&RG battled it out with lawyers in the courtrooms and guns on the ground. The prize was access to the lucrative mining districts around Leadville, where silver had been discovered a few years earlier.

For the Rio Grande it was a fight for survival. Having been shut out of Raton Pass, it needed access to the Royal Gorge to expand into southwestern Colorado and Utah. Egos were also at stake, and both companies hired gun-toting thugs to protect construction crews. When they clashed there were often bullets let loose, making it hard to differentiate grading forces from private armies. It was claimed that the clashes cost twenty lives.

Eventually peace was made, and while briefly the Santa Fe took control of Palmer's line, by 1880 he had wrested control back. Among the terms of the compromise was allowing the Santa Fe access to Leadville traffic as long as it kept out of further incursions into the D&RG's Colorado territory. To accommodate both railroads, a "dual gauge" line was built through the Royal Gorge.

The fame garnered by the so-called Royal Gorge War, combined with the spectacular scenery on the line and the fact that the Rio Grande had incorporated it into its through line from Denver to Salt Lake City, made the Royal Gorge Route popular with travelers. West of Cañon City, the Rio Grande line joined the Santa Fe's for the climb along the Arkansas through the narrow confines of the Royal Gorge. At one point the passage wasn't wide enough, so a hanging bridge was built with angled beams straddling the walls of the gorge and suspending the tracks above the violent waters of the river. This unusual feature was often shown in illustrations, and at one time the Rio Grande paused trains here for visitors to take in the awe-inspiring view. Today this is the scenic highlight of the Canyon City & Royal Gorge tourist railway that began operations after the Union Pacific closed the old D&RG route via the Royal Gorge and Tennessee Pass in the 1990s.

THROUGH THE ROYAL GORGE
COLORADO
BY DAVID M. STEELE

THIS publication is distributed for its general descriptive value. Fares, schedules, etc., may be incorrect. For current fares and service apply to ticket agents or National Parks Bureau, U. S. Railroad Administration, 226 W. Jackson Street, Chicago.

Open-Top Observation Car at the Hanging Bridge in the Royal Gorge

Through the Royal Gorge
COLORADO
from
"GOING ABROAD OVERLAND"
by
DAVID M. STEELE
Rector of the Church of St. Luke and The Epiphany, Philadelphia
Published by G. P. Putnam's Sons New York and London
Copyright, David M. Steele, 1917

IT WAS MARK HOPKINS who once said: "I never see a locomotive without wanting to take off my hat to it." I have always felt the same way. But more, in the case of these great Western railways, in view of the romance of their building and the monster size they have attained, I have tried to estimate the toil involved in their construction and the genius necessary for their operation—for the railroad as an institution is, of all things else, a thing of power. Most people do not realize this fully, just as it is customary to take every commonplace thing for granted. Railroads are so ubiquitous to-day that their absence rather than their presence is considered remarkable. But, in their knowledge of and command over the forces of nature, the men who built them put the legends of mythology to shame. They have outdone the Gods of Olympus in harnessing the elements to do their bidding; they have

THROUGH THE ROYAL GORGE

emulated Prometheus in stealing the fire from the Altar of Zeus; they have outdone Joshua in causing the very sun to stand still in the heavens while they have reduced the time of transit between points upon the schedules hour by hour. The railroads are the enemies of sectionalism and the chief agents in democracy. Especially is all this true out here where these mighty transcontinental railways, with their 57,000 miles of lines, have bridged magnificent distances, have abolished the wilderness, are sweeping the great American desert off the map, and are drawing the valleys of the Columbia and the Sacramento into the circle of the world's activities and interests.

Recalling my rides over some of these roads, I have a confused recollection of a series of perfectly clear-at-the-time impressions. I can still see in my dreams hand-cars whipped off the track to allow us to pass, and freight trains run on sidings at our swift approach. I still visualize section gangs at their work and recall their wavings in greeting as we rolled by them. I remember the sensation of crossing high bridges and the mile-long spans of trestles. I remember long, straight-away lines that seemed interminable, and far flights across ravines that gave every sensation of a ride in an aeroplane. I made notes while the engine jostled them so badly that they are almost illegible. But, in their order, they grew in ascending series of sheer admiration for the men who make these wheels go around.

Of course, I am not writing railroad folder literature, and so I must not use the language of the advertiser; but I am moved to applaud one system over which I rode all day but recently, not so much for its marvelous scenery as for the almost unbelievable engineering feats that have made its construction possible. The "scenery" is so nearly perpendicular that what one needs for observation purposes would be a glass-topped car, as in the far South Seas one requires a glass-bottomed boat. Everywhere were works of nature; but here still more there was evidence of man's triumph over nature.

What I mean is that yesterday I rode from Glenwood Springs to Colorado Springs, adown the Cañon of the Arkansas and through the Royal Gorge.

"See America"

THROUGH THE ROYAL GORGE

Each route out here has its distinctive kind of mountain scenery. One road runs around the mountains; another runs over the Rockies; the Denver & Rio Grande runs literally through them. We rode through narrow gorges with sheer precipitous sides and over brief expansive basins flat as ballroom floors, with mountain-like walls of gigantic amphitheaters a dozen miles away. We passed in review great giant cliffs, yet almost never were we out of sight or sound of tumbling, foaming water.

Which does not mean, however, we did not climb mountain grades. Here is the highest crossing, and here are the most massive mountains in the United States. It took a 317-ton Mallet type and, in addition, two huge Mogul locomotives to draw our train of fifteen cars. At many points the space is so narrow that even where there is a double-track road the two tracks have to run the one on each side of the tumbling stream.

One is amazed that such a vast amount of sightseeing is encompassed in so small a spot. But, still more, he is constantly amazed that it has been made accessible. Of the mountains, there are some gray, some white, some blue, some green; for they are bare, and snow and tree and verdure clad alternately. At point after point it is impossible to tell where the mountains stop and the clouds begin. Then, lastly, we came as by way of climax to the Royal Gorge, the place that has had its picture taken

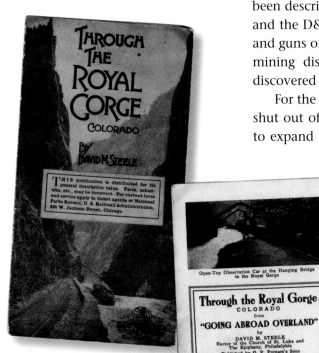

Our Train Drawn by Three Huge Engines

ON THE BRINK OF THE ROYAL GORGE
A PERPENDICULAR HALF-MILE TO THE RIVER

On the Brink of the Royal Gorge, from *Rocky Mountain Views of the Rio Grande.*

Through the Royal Gorge, a 1911 souvenir booklet (opposite).

DENVER AND RIO GRANDE MILE-BY-MILE

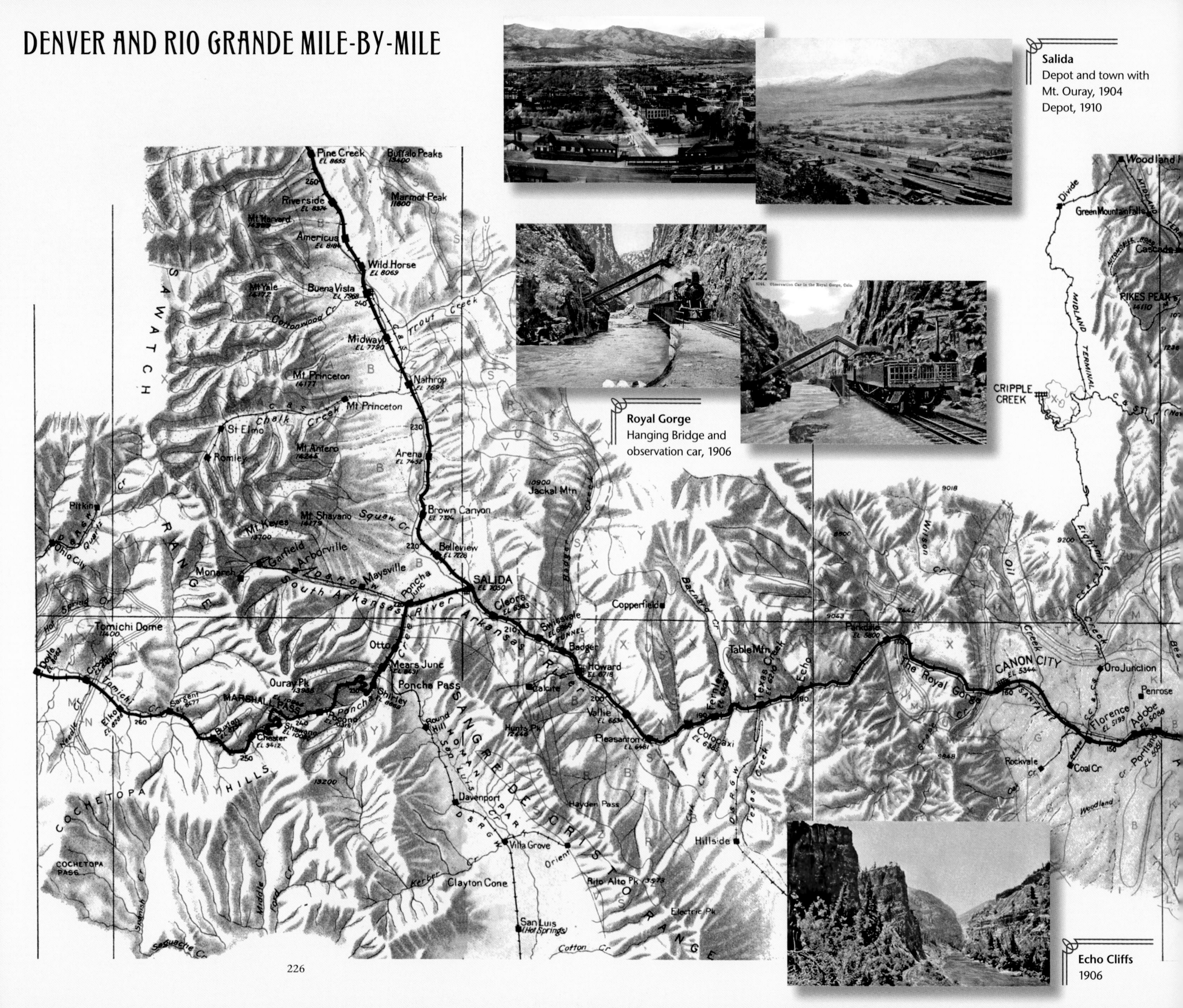

Salida
Depot and town with Mt. Ouray, 1904
Depot, 1910

Royal Gorge
Hanging Bridge and observation car, 1906

Echo Cliffs
1906

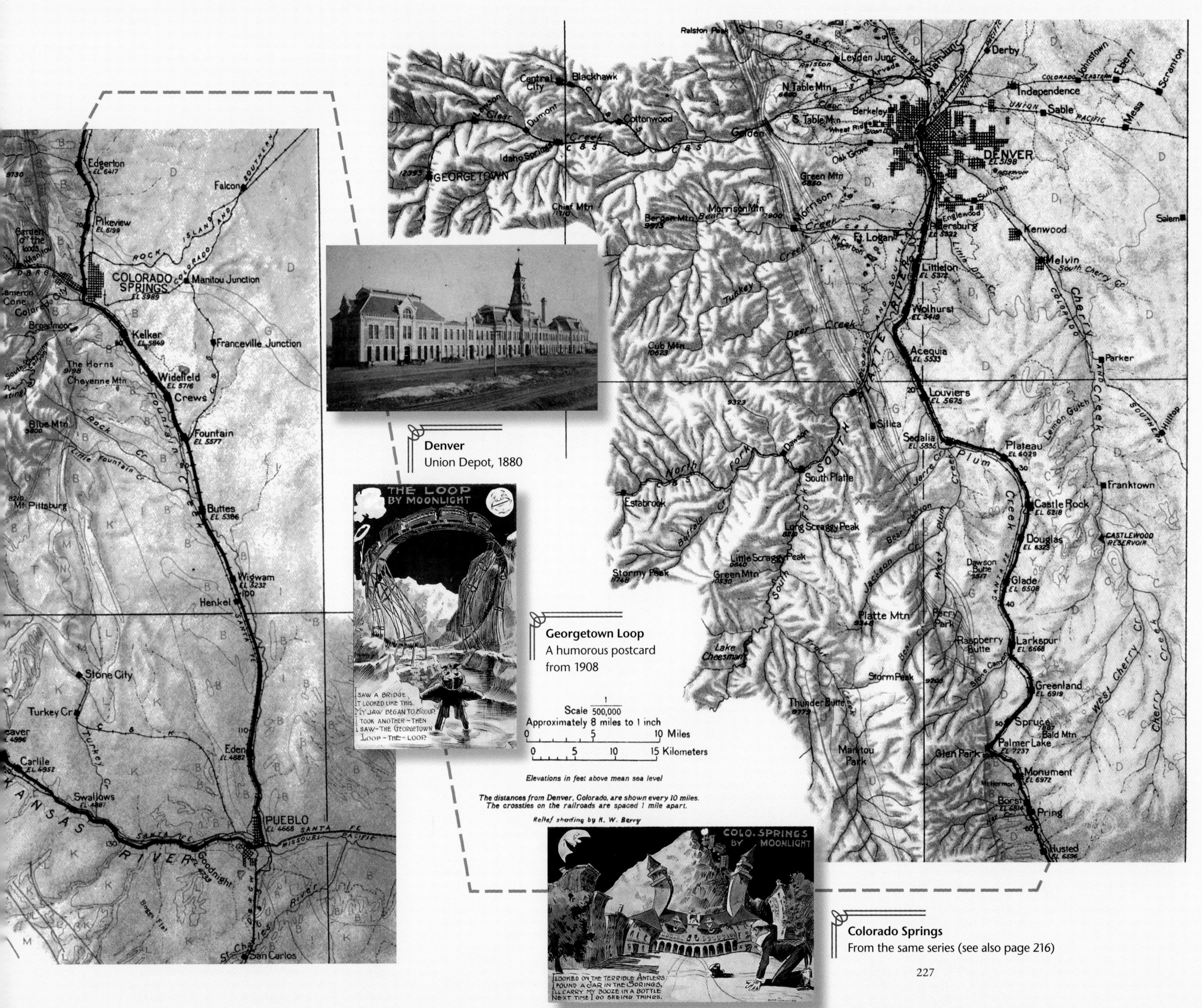

Denver
Union Depot, 1880

Georgetown Loop
A humorous postcard from 1908

Colorado Springs
From the same series (see also page 216)

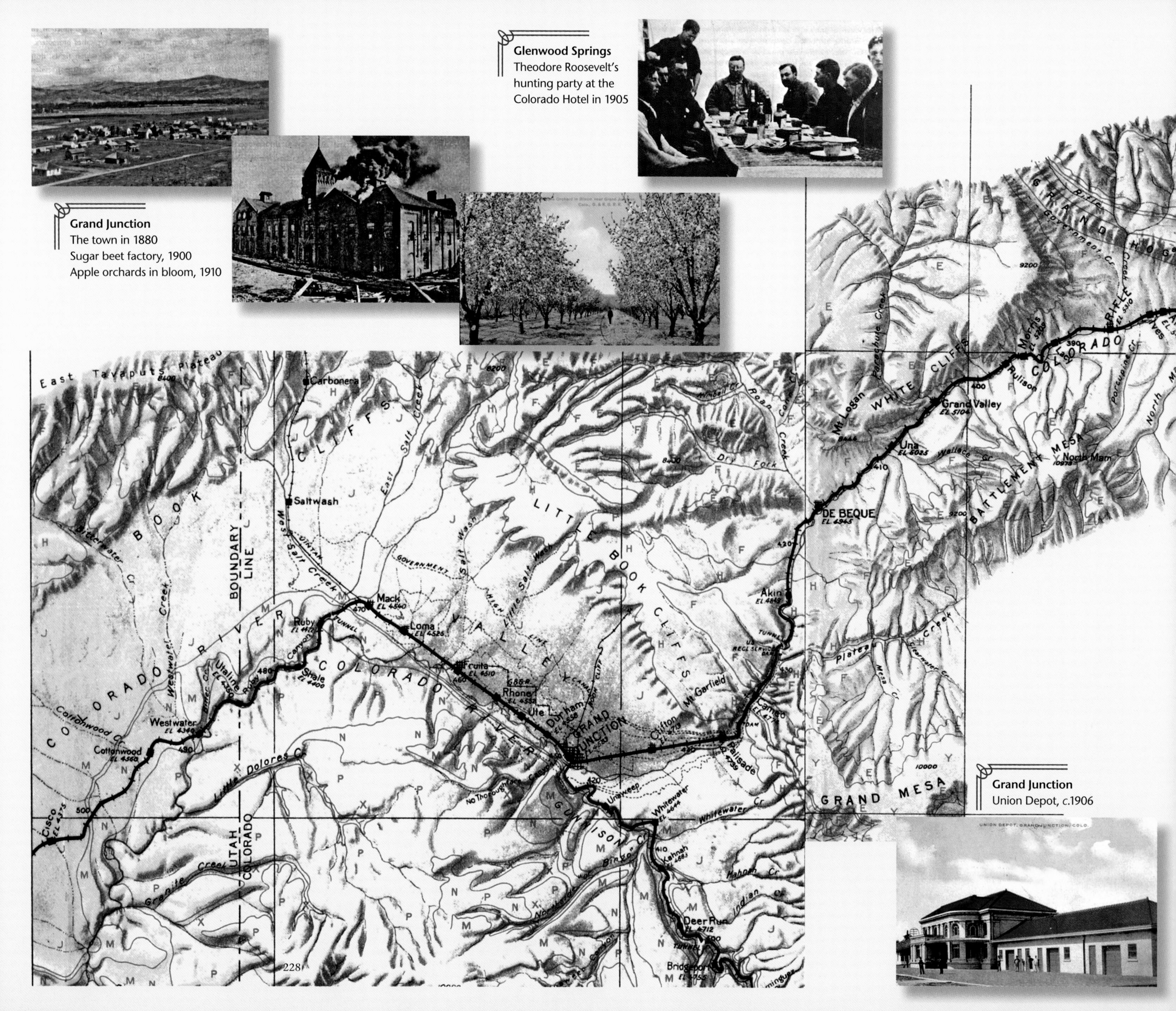

Glenwood Springs
Theodore Roosevelt's hunting party at the Colorado Hotel in 1905

Grand Junction
The town in 1880
Sugar beet factory, 1900
Apple orchards in bloom, 1910

Grand Junction
Union Depot, *c.*1906

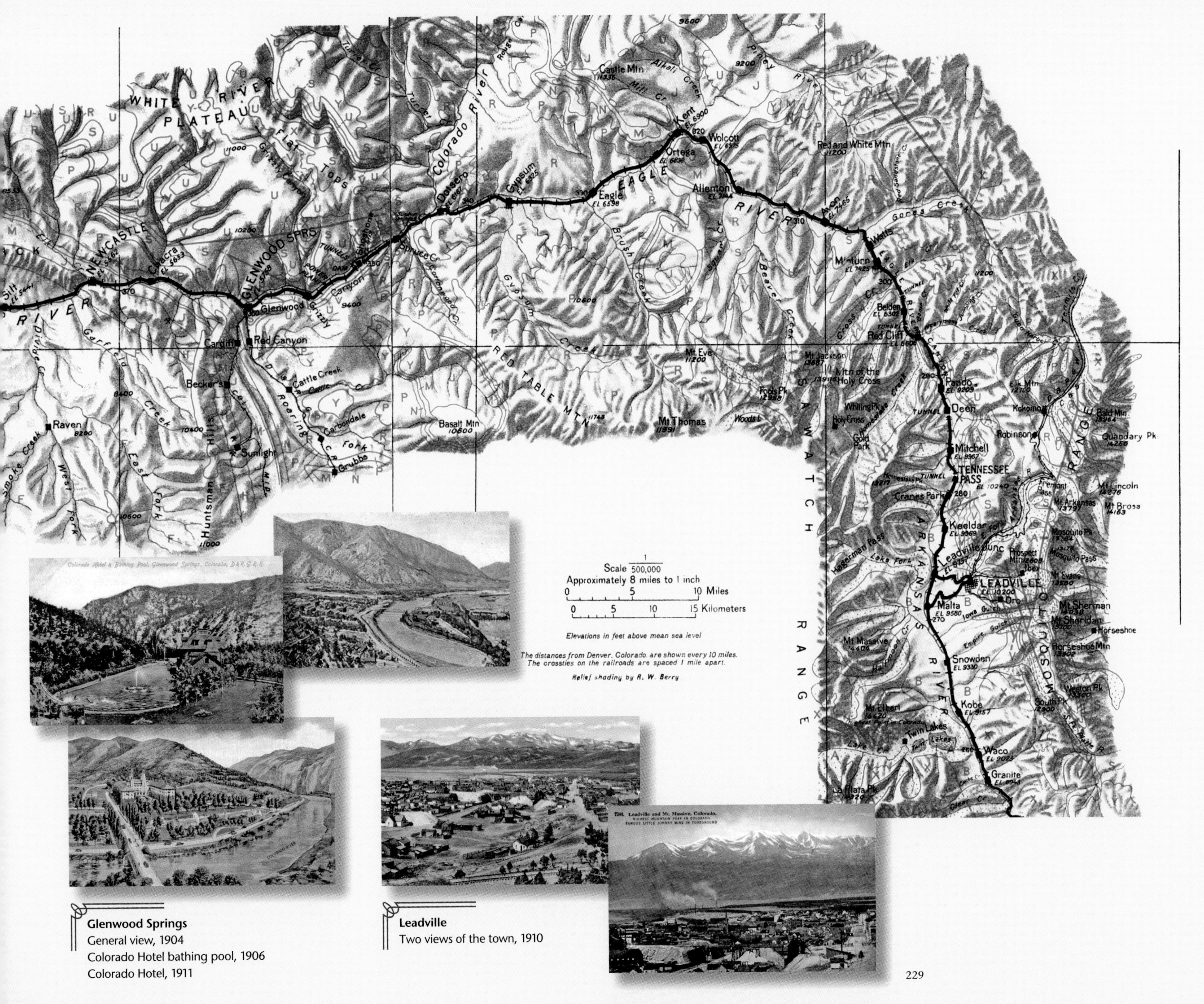

Glenwood Springs
General view, 1904
Colorado Hotel bathing pool, 1906
Colorado Hotel, 1911

Leadville
Two views of the town, 1910

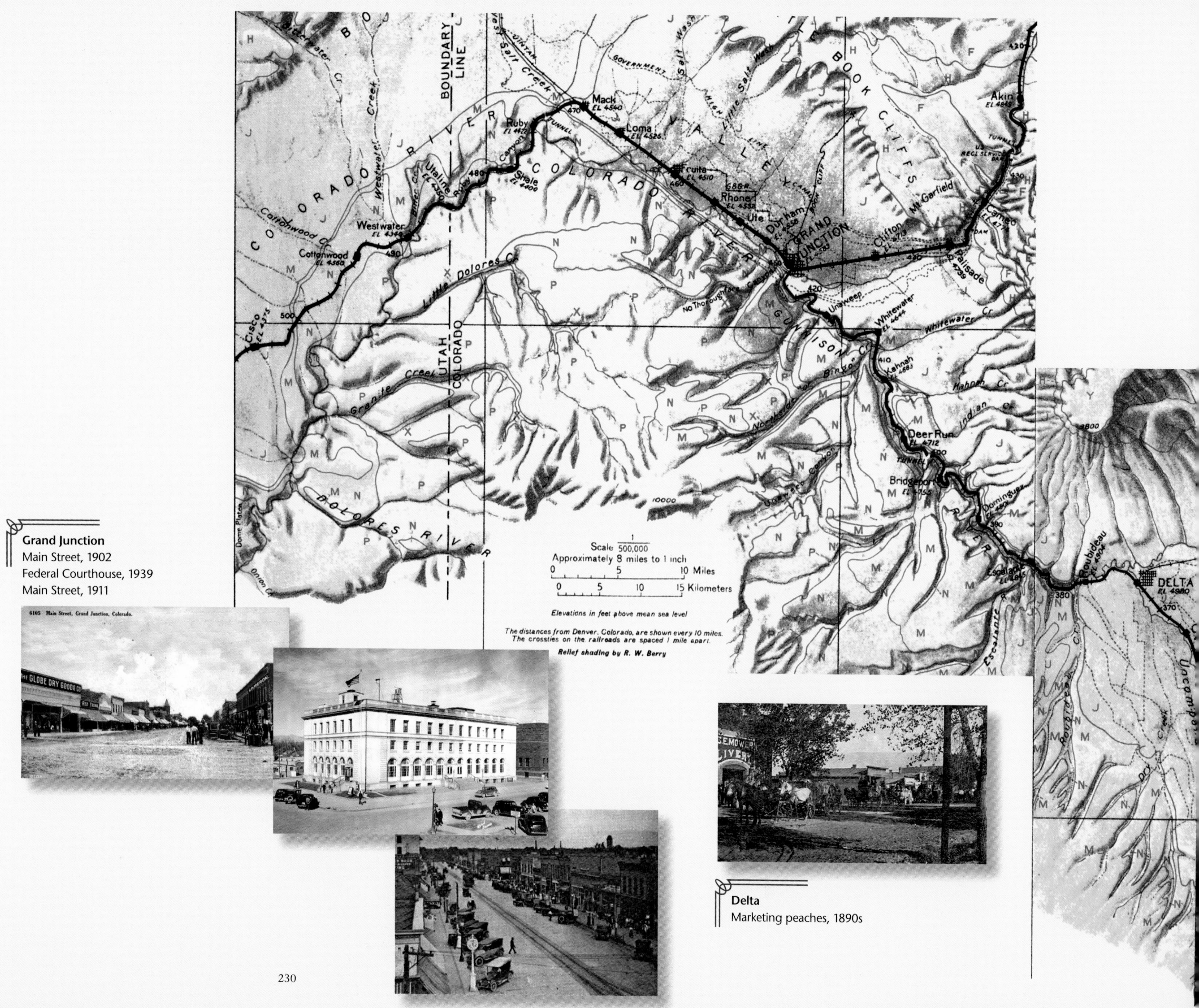

Grand Junction
Main Street, 1902
Federal Courthouse, 1939
Main Street, 1911

Delta
Marketing peaches, 1890s

Hotchkiss
Panorama from the south, 1910

Gunnison
Sapinero Bridge, Lake Fork, Gunnison River, 1911
Curecanti Needle, 1902
Black Canyon, 1910

Montrose
Montrose Depot, 1900

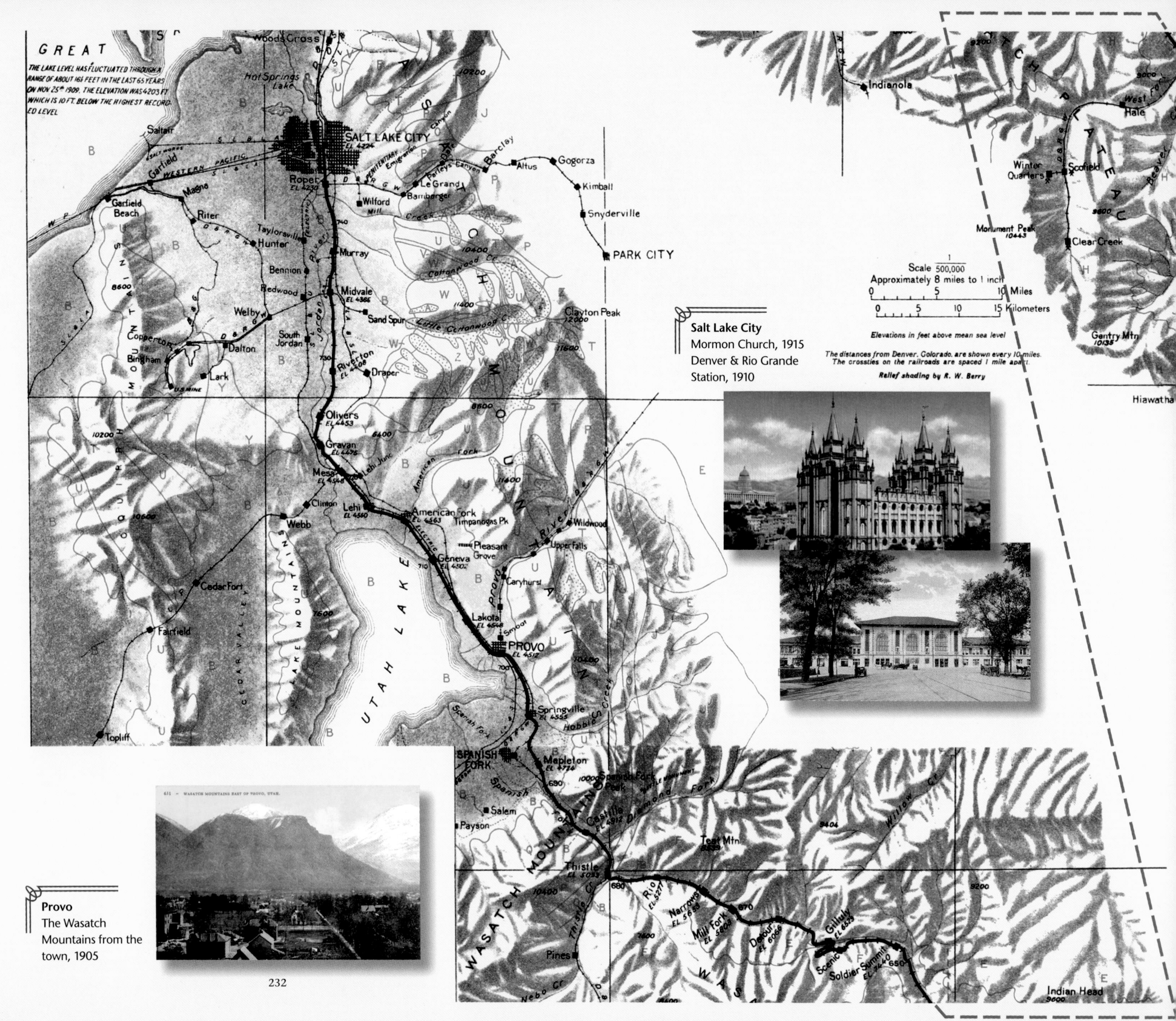

GREAT
THE LAKE LEVEL HAS FLUCTUATED THROUGH A RANGE OF ABOUT 16½ FEET IN THE LAST 65 YEARS ON NOV. 25th 1909. THE ELEVATION WAS 4203 FT WHICH IS 10 FT. BELOW THE HIGHEST RECORDED LEVEL
Woods Cross
Hot Springs Lake
Saltair
SALT LAKE CITY
EL 4224
Garfield
WESTERN PACIFIC
Magna
Garfield Beach
Riter
Roper
EL 4230
Wilford
Mill Creek
Le Grand
Bamberger
Parleys Canyon
Barclay
Altus
Gogorza
Kimball
Snyderville
PARK CITY
Taylorsville
Hunter
Murray
Bennion
Midvale
EL 4365
Redwood
Welby
Sand Spur
Little Cottonwood Cr.
Cottonwood Cr.
Clayton Peak
12000
South Jordan
Copperton
Dalton
Bingham
Lark
U.S. MINE
Riverton
EL 4508
Draper
Olivers
EL 4453
Gravan
Lehi Junc
Mesa
Clinton
Lehi
EL 4550
American Fork
EL 4563
Timpanogas Pk
Webb
Pleasant Grove
Geneva
Wildwood
Upper Falls
Provo River
Caryhurst
Cedar Fort
Fairfield
CEDAR VALLEY
LAKE MOUNTAINS
UTAH LAKE
Lakota
EL 4548
Smoot
PROVO
EL 4512
Springville
Hobble Creek
Spanish Fork
Topliff
SPANISH FORK
Mapleton
EL 4774
Spanish Fork Peak
Diamond Fork
Salem
Payson
Castilla
EL 4912
Thistle
Test Mtn.
WASATCH MOUNTAINS
Thistle Cr.
Nebo Cr.
Pines
Rio
EL 5277
Narrows
EL 5653
Mill Fork
EL 5803
Detour
EL 6066
Gilluly
EL 6523
Scenic
Soldier Summit
EL 7440
Willow Cr.
Indian Head
9600
Indianola
West Fork
Hale
Winter Quarters
Scofield
Monument Peak
10443
Clear Creek
Gentry Mtn
10135
Hiawatha
Scale 1/500,000
Approximately 8 miles to 1 inch
0 5 10 Miles
0 5 10 15 Kilometers
Elevations in feet above mean sea level
The distances from Denver, Colorado, are shown every 10 miles.
The crossties on the railroads are spaced 1 mile apart.
Relief shading by R. W. Berry
WASATCH MOUNTAINS EAST OF PROVO, UTAH.

Salt Lake City
Mormon Church, 1915
Denver & Rio Grande Station, 1910

Provo
The Wasatch Mountains from the town, 1905

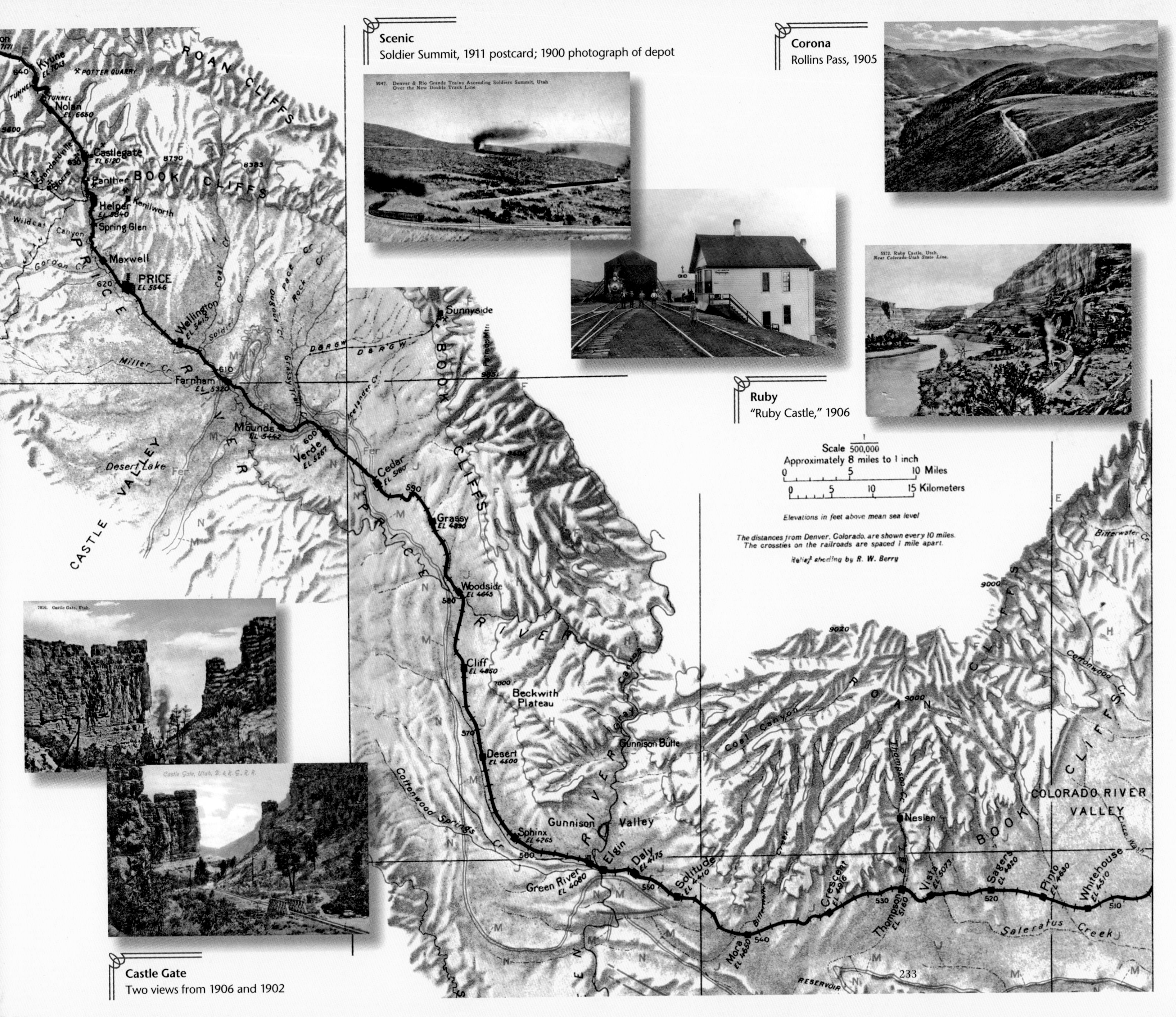

Scenic
Soldier Summit, 1911 postcard; 1900 photograph of depot

Corona
Rollins Pass, 1905

Ruby
"Ruby Castle," 1906

Castle Gate
Two views from 1906 and 1902

THE SHASTA ROUTE AND COAST LINE

SEATTLE TO LOS ANGELES VIA SAN FRANCISCO

The great transcontinental rail routes were all built east–west, tying together the older states of the east with the newly developing western states with a great network of steel roads from coast to coast. But as the transcontinental lines developed, it was evident that good north–south access was becoming increasingly important for the growing population and commerce of the West as well. While the transcontinental lines were largely built under some sort of large-scale enterprise, the north–south lines, whether locally built short routes or developed by one of the major railroads, came about in fits and starts. Much of the railroad between California and Oregon, for example, was built by groups of local entrepreneurs or with short lines, creating a road that carried them in the general direction of California–Oregon. The San Francisco–Los Angeles Coast Line had been built by the Southern Pacific almost the entire distance, but it took a period of some 37 years to finish it. In the end, all of it came under the control of the Southern Pacific, which before the end of the nineteenth century controlled the lion's share of railroads in California and much of Oregon.

The first of the lines that made up the eventual Shasta–Coast Line route between Portland and Los Angeles began building a 52-mile line north from Sacramento to Marysville in 1865 for a California and Oregon route that was intended to eventually reach Portland. By 1870 their money had run out, however, and the California Pacific came under Central Pacific control, with a line that extended some ninety miles northward from Sacramento with another six hundred miles to go to reach Portland.

Meanwhile, work had begun on another local railroad, the Oregon & California (O&C), which had similar plans. The key mover on this project was Ben Holladay (1819–87), who had started out with what became an enormous system of stagecoaches that extended all the way from the Missouri River to the Far West. But Holladay foresaw the bright future of railroads, and sold out his stagecoach empire to Wells Fargo in 1866, three years before the completion of the first transcontinental route, and moved to Oregon to get in on the new railroad boom. Holladay's first twenty miles following the Willamette Valley were completed south of Portland by the end of 1869, and the line reached onward to Salem and to Eugene by the end of 1871. But by the end of 1872 Holladay had gone broke, just as the line reached Roseburg some two hundred miles south of Portland.

The next man to try the Oregon–California route was Henry Villard (1835–1900), a German-born financier and railroad man. Villard tried first to interest the Central Pacific's Big Four in taking over the line south of California, but they were not interested. So Villard organized some money and started railroad-building himself, only to run out of funding when he had reached Ashland in 1884, a short distance before the Oregon–California line. The O&C went into receivership, and fell into the hands of the Southern Pacific in 1887. Now it was time to finish the railroad.

Now also under the control of the Southern Pacific, the California & Oregon (C&O), originally a rival of the O&C, again began building to the north after being stalled at Redding, California, since 1872.

The Dollarhide Trestle, high in the Siskiyou Mountains, northern California.

The UP's Shasta Route and Coast Line network map, 1906.

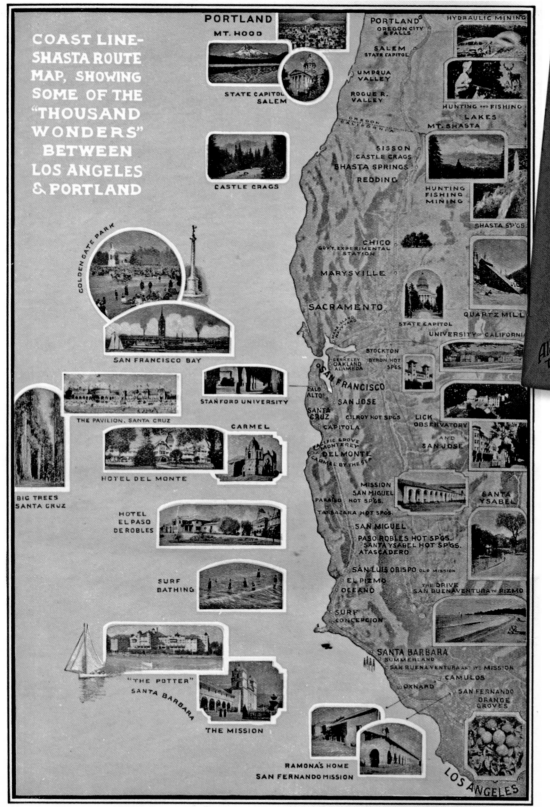

COAST LINE-SHASTA ROUTE MAP, SHOWING SOME OF THE "THOUSAND WONDERS" BETWEEN LOS ANGELES & PORTLAND

By May 1887 the C&O had reached Hornbrook, a short distance south of the California–Oregon line. There remained only the most difficult section of the entire Shasta Line, the rugged route over the Siskiyou Mountains. As the crow flies the distance between Hornbrook and Ashland was about 22 miles, but it took 36 miles to build a line that could make its way through the tumbled topography of the Siskiyou. Construction crews worked from each end of the gap, and by December 17, 1887, the line was done. Officials from both Portland and Sacramento were on hand for the occasion, and Big Four member Charles Crocker presided over the spiking down of the last connection. A journey that had taken seven days between Sacramento and Portland could now be made in a mere thirty-eight hours.

Through service began running on the same day between Portland and San Francisco on the *Oregon & California Express*. By 1901, for example, the SP operated two though trains, the *O&S* and *Shasta* expresses, over the 772-mile route between Portland and San Francisco. The trains offered drawing room sleeping cars, and buffet or dining car equipment, requiring

about a day and a half for the journey. Other popular named trains over the route at various times included the *Beaver*, *Klamath*, and *Cascade*. For many years the *Shasta* was the railroad's premier train. In 1913 it was outfitted with all new equipment and became a deluxe "extra fare" train costing passengers an additional $5.00, and for a time carried its through cars beyond Portland all the way to Seattle. The *Shasta* carried a dining car on which Southern Pacific served meals that were "equal to that of the highest-class cafes," and also offered a deluxe parlor lounge and an open observation car with an elaborate brass railed platform. The train's name was proclaimed on a large circular drumhead on the platform.

The Shasta Line provided an almost continuous variety of western scenery. The southbound *Shasta* begins its journey from a splendid station in downtown Portland. Financier Henry Villard, who had completed the Northern Pacific into Portland in 1883, wanted a suitably grand union station for the city, and had hired the notable New York architectural firm of McKim, Mead and White to design it. The work had gotten no further than starting the station's foundation when Villard had run out of money and was forced out of the NP. The work started again a decade later, with architects Van Brunt and Howe in charge, and the splendid station was completed in 1896. The three-story, red brick design of the building combined Queen Anne and Romanesque elements, while red metal tiles covered the roofs. A 150-foot-high clock tower incorporated a four-sided Seth Thomas clock.

Western Oregon's mountains are divided by the Willamette River valley into the Coast range which lies along the Pacific and the Cascade Range inland. Southbound from Portland the Shasta follows the Willamette for more than 130 miles, and the area along its way seems to encompass endless miles of trees as it traces the east bank of the river. Towns like Salem, Albany, Eugene, or Roseburg log the Douglas and ponderosa pine timber from the vast, forested area that encompasses some thirty million acres in Oregon. Branch lines or logging railroads pushed off from the Shasta main line to gather new trees for the always hungry sawmills.

Climbing upward towards the Siskiyou summit just north of the California–Oregon line, the trains paused for such stations as Grants Pass, Medford, or Ashland, which boasted

Ashland Station, 1906 (top left).

The "Old Man" of Cow Creek Canyon, between Glendale and Riddle in Oregon, from *The Shasta Route* (right).

The Shasta Route, published by H. H. Tammen, Los Angeles, in 1915 (opposite top).

Map from *The Route of a Thousand Wonders*, published by the Passenger Department of the Southern Pacific in 1908 (oppsite left).

Crater Lake, from *The Shasta Route* (top).

Sacramento River and Mount Shasta from Castella, from *The Shasta Route* (right).

Dunsmuir Station (below).

an unusually large and elegant three-story station. Fifty miles northeast of Medford lies Crater Lake National Park, created thousands of years ago from the remains of Mount Mazama. The caldera rim which surrounds the lake rises as high as two thousand feet above its surface, while the intensely blue waters reach down another two thousand. With help from the Southern Pacific, the national park was created by President Theodore Roosevelt in 1902. Another notable site was the Oregon Caves National Monument, created from limestone formations in the Siskiyou Mountains, about forty miles southwest from Grants Pass. President Howard Taft established the monument in 1909.

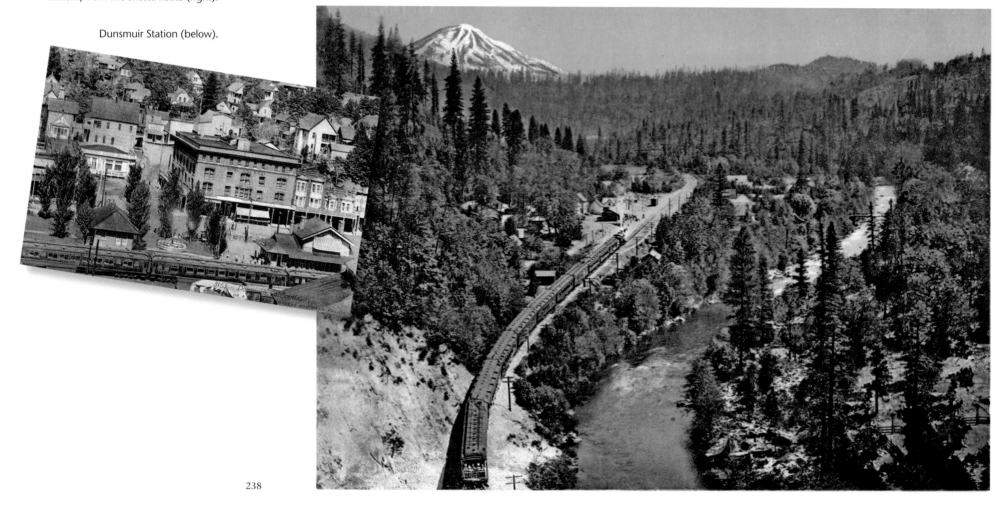

The steep grades and sharp curves of the Siskiyou section were always difficult for the SP, and they grew worse as traffic steadily increased. Some work began as early as 1909 for lines which would eventually form a bypass for the difficult crossing of the Siskiyou. Work began in earnest in 1923 and the project was completed in 1926. Originating near Eugene, the 278-mile Cascade Route would take a more easterly route through the Cascades and finally rejoin the original line at Black Butte in northern California. Difficult to build and even higher than the Siskiyou, with a summit elevation of 4,872 feet, the Cascade line nevertheless reduced the maximum grade to only 1.8 percent, cut some 51 complete circles of curvature, and was almost 24 miles shorter than the old Siskiyou Route. Passenger trains would reduce running times by about four and a half hours, and almost all passenger and freight trains shifted to the new line.

Traveling over either route, the journey across Oregon and northern California was one of spectacular scenery through the northwest's forested mountains, the wonders of the Siskiyou or Cascade grade, the great white-capped dome of Mount Shasta, or the splendors of the gorge of the Sacramento River. The Shasta Route gradually drops in elevation as it heads south through the agricultural lands of Central Valley to reach the low lands around Sacramento.

In the final stretch, a Shasta Route train shared the route between Sacramento and San Francisco with the Overland Route, facing a major barrier to through traffic in the broad and deep waters of the Carquinez Straits, which carried the waters of the Sacramento River through to San Pablo Bay, San Francisco Bay, and on to the Pacific Ocean. When the rail line was first put in service in 1879 the SP put in place the huge ferry *Solano*, the largest such vessel in the world with four tracks capable of carrying two full passenger trains, complete with locomotives, across the Straits. Later a second, even larger ferry, the *Contra Costa*, was put in service. Finally, 51 years after the ferry line had opened and freight and passenger traffic grew ever larger, the SP replaced it with an enormous bridge that was more than a mile long between Benicia and Martinez.

A second major water barrier along the line was San Francisco Bay, where a fleet of ferries completed the journey into the city. This barrier was never otherwise solved by SP or any other railroad, and likely never will be.

The Coast Line, which would complete the second half of this splendid western route, came along almost twenty years after the Shasta Line was opened. The SP had accomplished its first link between San Francisco and Los Angeles in 1876, but this was through a long and difficult route, which required a climb over the coastal hills east of the Bay Area, a long journey south through the San Joaquin Valley, and then through crossings of the Tehachapi Mountains and Soledad Canyon to reach Los Angeles.

San Francisco Bay and ferries, from *The Shasta Route*.

The earliest part of what would be the more direct and scenic Coast Route was the 49.5-mile San Francisco & San Jose, completed in 1864, which ran south through the San Francisco Bay peninsula. An extension by the SP south from San Jose would reach Tres Pinos about 1871, while a planned second route would come east from the San Joaquin Valley to link the two, but the link from the San Joaquin was never completed and Tres Pinos was as far as it would go. Another line, which would become part of the Coast Line, branched west from Carnadero towards Monterey County. Then turning south again, the line passed through Salinas and reached as far as Soledad in 1873, where it remained until 1886, when construction crews began work again towards the south, reaching Templeton by the end of the year.

The next section of line would be the most difficult anywhere on the Coast Line, passing through Cuesta Pass to reach San Luis Obispo. Work began in 1889 and took five years. Some 2,000 Chinese laborers were brought in to build the line, which required the construction of six tunnels by hand and dynamite; the longest, at the crest of the pass, measured 3,610 feet. To descend to the coastal level at San Luis Obispo the line needed grades of 2.2 percent grade on tracks that turned back and forth on the steep terrain, including a massive horseshoe curve near the bottom. With the line finally open to San Luis Obispo, through passenger trains began running between San Francisco and San Luis Obispo on May 5, 1894.

Meanwhile, work was progressing on the southern end of the Coast Line from a junction at Saugus, north of Los Angeles, with the Southern Pacific's line to San Francisco via the San Joaquin Valley. This reached the Coast Line at Santa Paula, followed the Santa Clara River to the coast, and then continued north along the coast through Ventura, reaching Santa Barbara in 1887. This left a 159-mile stage coach trip between Santa Barbara and San Luis Obispo to complete the journey for the next fifteen years. The two lines were finally brought together at Gaviota, and the first through train between San Francisco and Los Angeles ran on March 31, 1901. Further major construction was still required to complete a more direct link with Los Angeles through the Santa Susana Pass, where three tunnels had to be built to carry the line through the Chatsworth Rocks, a task which was completed in 1904.

The railroad station at Santa Barbara built in mission style, from *The Road of a Thousand Wonders* (right).

Nearing Horseshoe Curve after leaving San Luis Obispo, the train climbs to the Santa Lucia range, from *The Road of a Thousand Wonders* (below).

Shortly after the full Coast Line was opened, the SP began operating a fast limited train, the *Shore Line Limited*, over the route. This express was an all-parlor-car daytime train that covered the 470 miles between San Francisco and Los Angeles in just thirteen and a half hours, while the *Lark* provided an all-sleeping-car service over the route. In 1922 the *Shore Line* took on a new name with a faster schedule as the *Daylight*, running on a twelve-hour schedule between San Francisco and Los Angeles. In 1930 the train gained further distinction when it appeared in a new color of pearl gray and with a specially designed new Pullman observation car that was fitted with comfortable lounge cars outfitted with extra large windows to provide "an unobstructed view of mountain, valley and seacoast." On the rear of the car the builder provided a handsome open observation platform.

The second half of a journey across the Far West began at the splendid terminal built by Southern Pacific at Third and Townsend streets in downtown San Francisco. Constructed in an ornate Mission Revival style, it had been completed in time for the 1915 Panama–Pacific Exposition at San Francisco.

The splendid scenery of the Coast Line was best seen on the *Shore Line Limited* or its successor, the *Daylight*, departing around 8 or 9 a.m., and arriving at their destination in early evening. Appropriately, for its entire distance the Coast train followed the general route of the eighteenth-century Spanish road El Camino Real–"The Royal Road" –which extends from San Diego in the south to Solano, just north of San Francisco. Only a few blocks west of the Third and Townsend station, the San Francisco de Asis, Mission Dolores, still stands.

The Coast train followed the foothills on the east side of the peninsula that separates San Francisco Bay from the Pacific Ocean. Even before trains began running between San Francisco and San Jose, mining millionaire Darius Ogden Mills built a splendid estate at Millbrae, and wealthy men soon followed him to such wealthy suburban stations as Belmont, Burlingame, or Hillsborough. Further south, Big Four member Leland Stanford acquired an estate he called "Palo Alto," where he opened Leland Stanford Jr. University, later Stanford University, in 1891.

The towns south of San Francisco Bay were bounteous farmlands. San Jose grew fruits, Gilroy prided itself as the "Garlic Capital of the World," and northwest of Salinas a branch of the line to Monterey passed through tiny Castroville which liked to call itself the "Artichoke Center of the World." The area around Salinas itself grew strawberries and just about every variety of vegetable. South of Salinas the Coast Line followed the Salinas River past the Mission Nuestra Señorade de la Soledad, King City, Paso Robles, and Santa Marguerita, where the line turned west to take on the Cuesta Pass of the Santa Lucia Range, which separates the route from the Pacific coast.

After making the difficult climb over Cuesta Pass to San Luis Obispo, the Coast Line finally reached the shore line at Pismo Beach, following it closely for most of the next 140 miles on what was easily one of the most splendid railway journeys anywhere in the world. Just north of San Luis Obispo the long and steep Steiner Creek Bridge, or the Gaviota Trestle opposite the Santa Barbara Channel, were among those required to pass over the deep gorges and cliffs along the coastal grade where towns like Guadalupe, Surf, or Goleta stood along the track. In the Lompoc area, just east of the Coast Line, a large part of America's cut and seed flowers are grown, producing a colorful display in the right season.

Santa Barbara dates its earliest Spanish culture to 1782, and it continues to show a strong Spanish influence, with the city spread out over the foothills of the Santa Ynez Mountains down to the beaches. Palm trees, orchids, citrus fruit, and walnuts are plentiful in the mild climate. Ventura, established in 1782, is even older than Santa Barbara. Lying close to the Coast Line tracks are missions at San Luis Obispo, Santa Barbara, and Ventura. Finally, just beyond Ventura, the Coast Line bends away from its long coastal route. The brief passage through the Santa Susana Mountains is the last obstacle, and the *Daylight* then begins a long dash across the San Fernando Valley to its terminal in Los Angeles.

The Southern Pacific has used no fewer than three different stations at Los Angeles in the century-plus since the Coast Line opened in 1901. The first was the Arcade Depot, built in 1888. Patterned after the railroad's station at Sacramento, this was a massive brick structure with a huge, covered train shed. The Arcade lasted until 1914, when the much more expansive Central Station was completed to handle the growing traffic. This had plenty of capacity, but had the highly unpopular need to operate all of its trains down almost a mile-and-a-half of congested Alameda Street to reach or depart from the station. After twenty years of public argument, Los Angeles and the railroads completed a splendid new station in 1939 that incorporated both the city's Spanish heritage and modernity through its design and Art Deco details. Los Angeles Union Passenger Terminal remains today as one of North America's handsomest railroad stations, and serves as the southern end of Amtrak's splendid Coast Starlight route, which operates daily over the full Coast and Shasta lines and beyond all the way to Seattle.

Wonderful California, a promotional booklet from 1911 (left).

Views of the New Union Station in Los Angeles, c.1935 (below).

PORTLAND

City of Roses

Portland with Mount Hood in the distance, from *The Shasta Route* (right).

Portland Union Station, c.1913 (below).

Portland, Oregon, was founded in 1845 by two New Englanders, Boston attorney Asa Lovejoy and Portland, Maine, shopkeeper Francis W. Pettygrove, on a square mile plot located at the junction of the Columbia and Willamette rivers that they had claimed by paying a 25-cent filing fee to Oregon's then provisional government. Known originally as "The Clearing" or "Stumptown," Pettygrove won a best-of-three coin toss with Lovejoy (using a cent piece known as the "Portland Penny") to rename the 640-acre claim after the Mainer's hometown as opposed to calling it "Boston" as favored by his partner. Incorporated in 1851, Portland was the largest "city" in the Pacific northwest by 1860 with just 3,000 residents.

With so many rivers and bodies of water in Washington and Oregon, water was an important early means of transportation in the Northwest. Even when railroads began to develop in the 1850s, they were originally seen as connectors linking together bodies of water or used to go around rapids. But this soon began to shift. The completion of the Northern Pacific Railroad into Portland in 1883 linked the city with the rest of the country, and the building of other lines over the next several decades made Portland a major railroad center. The NP built a line north to Seattle, while the Southern Pacific's Shasta Route provided a link south. Another line on the south bank of the Columbia River gave the Union Pacific a connection back to the eastern part of the original transcontinental road, and the construction of a grade on the north bank of the Columbia gave both the NP and the Great Northern direct links to the east.

Early on Portland took up the cultivation of roses, which thrived in the mild and moist climate. The city calls itself the "City of Roses," and every year celebrates the Portland Rose Festival.

From almost anywhere in the city one can view the snowy peak of the 11,239-foot Mount Hood to the east, and from the top of Council Crest Park—at 1,073 feet the highest point in the city—five Cascade peaks can also be seen. Until streetcar operation ended in 1950, excursionists were treated to a spectacular trolley ride up to Council Crest on a line with a gradient of as much as 12 percent, that had to negotiate no fewer than 67 curves. The streetcars were equipped with magnetic track brakes, and several points on the line had safety "derails" to halt a runaway car.

Portland was an early leader in electric power development and electric interurban railways. What is generally regarded as the first true interurban began operating over a fifteen-mile line between Portland and Oregon City in 1893, and ultimately some 432 miles of electric interurbans were operating from Portland over half a dozen lines.

Portland's interurban and electric railways were gone by the 1950s, but recently the city has decided to revive a system of light rail vehicles and urban streetcars.

Portland homes and sidewalks lined with roses, *c.*1916.

RIDING THE SHASTA ROUTE

Mountains, Springs, and Passes

Mount Shasta, painted by Gilbert Munger, *c.*1867 (below).

The Cantara Loop with a crossing over the Sacramento River, from *The Shasta Route* (below right).

"The Scenic Line of the Pacific Coast," wrote a Southern Pacific passenger agent of the Shasta Route in 1893, and it was hard to dispute. The *Shasta Limited De Luxe*, added writer Arthur Dubin, provided "718 miles of bay, valley, canyon, forest [and] mountain."

The southbound train passed through the miles of forests and the sawmill towns along the way that made Oregon timber a major industry. In the early days the railroad was often used to carry the logs out, and rough logging railroads often transported the cut timber to sawmills. Many of these lines had such sharp curves and steep grades that they needed special locomotives, the most popular being the geared "Shay" type invented in 1880 by a Michigan logger named Ephraim Shay (1839–1916), whose design was used all over the world.

The Shasta would climb almost a mile to cross the Siskiyou Pass just north of the California–Oregon line. When Siskiyou construction began, the Southern Pacific's "Big Four" had told William Hood (1849–1926), the railroad's then chief engineer, to build as quickly and cheaply as possible and the result was one of the most difficult crossings in any main line railroad in the world. The line was almost always in curves, and eighteen tunnels had to be blasted through the mountains, the longest of which was the 3,108-foot tunnel over the summit. Curvatures were as sharp as 14 degrees, while some grades reached up to 3.5 percent.

Getting a train over Siskiyou was hard work for the train crews and their equipment, but it was a memorable experience for passengers. "The grandeur of the scenery is not to be excelled by any mountain road in the world," remarked one traveler about 1910. Postcards of the trip (see page 234) show a splendid view of a train crossing the high steel trestle on the north slope or the famous Dollarhide Trestle, where no fewer than three locomotives pulled a seven-car passenger train over the structure.

Some fifty miles to the south the Shasta passed near the splendid, white-domed peak of the 14,162-foot Mount Shasta, and at Shasta Springs trains stopped for a visit to the natural springs. Passengers could drink the clear, cold water from a fountain in a pavilion alongside the track, and could also stop over at a hotel built on top of a hill, with a cable car to carry them up.

Hardly was Shasta Spring scenery behind the train when the next memorable vista came into view. Just north of Dunsmuir the Shasta Route traversed the Cantara Loop, one of the sharpest curves on the entire railroad as it began its run down the long gorge of the Sacramento River. Eighteen tunnels were required to carry the line over the next sixty miles, and the railroad had to cross over the river no fewer than seventeen times to find room for the grade.

The drinking fountain at Shasta Springs, where the water is promoted as "A perfect table water" (top).

The train arrives at Shasta Springs, from *The Shasta Route* (left).

ARRIVING AT SAN FRANCISCO

Home of the Cable Car

San Francisco provided a memorable setting for Southern Pacific trains arriving from the east or north. After traveling down the east shore of the Bay they reached the almost two-mile-long timber structure of the Oakland Pier or Mole at Alameda, where all of the accouterments of a large railway terminal were provided in a huge, gloomy, nineteenth-century arched train shed.

San Francisco is one of the world's finest land-locked natural harbors, and it has been busy ever since the 1849 Californian "gold rush." Ships travel constantly to and from the long rows of piers that line the San Francisco waterfront, and still more dock across the way at Oakland. When the Southern Pacific reached San Francisco, the white-with-black-funnel passenger ferries that made the twenty-minute Bay crossing were double-ended, steam-powered vessels, each of them carrying such names as *Berkeley*, *Santa Clara*, or *Oakland*. The ferry provides a splendid view of the city and its hills such as Telegraph, Russian, and the exclusive Nob Hill, where all four of the Central Pacific's "Big Four"–Collis P. Huntington, Leland Stanford, Mark Hopkins, and Charles Crocker–built elaborate mansions.

San Francisco boasts the great Golden Gate Park as well as a group of splendid public buildings including the City Hall, built in 1915, whose dome is taller than that over the US Capital. Much of central San Francisco was destroyed in the great earthquake and fire of 1906, but the city was so well rebuilt that it was able to host a great international exposition in 1915. Looming over the city, rising to a peak of 900 feet and offering panoramic views, are the Twin Peaks of Mt. Davidson and Mt. Sutro.

Oakland Mole Station, *c.*1906 (above)

Market and Powell Streets, from *San Francisco: The World's Favorite City* (aboveright).

A cable car in Hyde Street, *c.*1936 (opposite).

Getting around San Francisco's notoriously steep hills has never been easy, but enterprising inventor Andrew S. Hallidie (1836–1900), a San Francisco manufacturer of wire-rope, thought his product could work for hauling street cars. Gripping a continuous wire cable that was strung in a network beneath the street, the cable cars were pulled by a central power plant strong enough to readily propel the cars up the steepest of hills. Hallidie's first cable car opened along Clay Street in the city in 1873, and soon a big boom in building similar cable car lines was underway all over the US and abroad. But it wasn't long before electric-powered streetcars were developed and proved to work even better. The cable cars soon disappeared, leaving only San Francisco where they originated still operating such a system.

CALIFORNIA MISSIONS

Along the Royal Road

An enduring reminder of early California is the remarkable chain of missions established by Spanish missionaries during the period of Spanish occupation beginning in the eighteenth century. Built over 54 years and founded by the Franciscan priest Father Junípero Serra (1713–84), the 21 missions extended northward from San Diego where the first, San Diego de Alcalá, was completed in 1760, to San Francisco where the last, San Francisco Solano at Sonoma, was finished in 1823.

The chain of missions was laid out along the California coast with each one about a day's travel apart along what was called El Camino Real, or "The Royal Road," named in honor of the Spanish monarchy that financed the expedition into California. Originally a road for horses and carts, the Camino Real's general path was later followed by the Southern Pacific's Coast Line railroad and California highway 101. Travelers from the East would have viewed the Spanish architecture with surprised delight.

The missions varied in construction with some built as simple structures of mud, adobe, or logs with thatched roofs. The missionaries at San Luis Obispo de Tolosa, however, soon had to rebuild their roof with tiles to protect against the flaming arrows fired by Indians. Others were large and imposing buildings of heavy stone with elaborate decoration.

San Luis Rey de Francia, known as the "King of Missions," was one of the largest, a cross-shaped church that could seat a thousand worshippers. Santa Barbara, the "Queen of Missions," is a splendid structure of wrought iron, terracotta, and carved wood with a spectacular ocean view from its hilltop location about 100 miles northwest of Los Angeles. San Juan Capistrano was a great stone church with seven domes and a tall bell tower that could be seen ten miles away. Much of the building was destroyed by an earthquake in 1812, but the famous swallows of Capistrano still migrate to the ruins, arriving every March on St. Joseph's Day (the 19th), and leaving in October on the Day of San Juan (the 23rd) to return to their southern hemisphere summer home in Argentina.

The missions were much more than religious institutions, as the priests engaged in agricultural production and ran workshops, looms, and granaries. Altogether, when the missions' land monopolies were broken up in 1834 they had 31,000 Indians at work and some 750,000 head of livestock. Just one mission, Nuestra Señora de la Soledad, produced more than 100,000 bushels of wheat every year.

After more than two centuries the missions have suffered earthquakes, fires, floods, and the decay of aging materials, but all 21 survive in one form or another. Some are the original structures; others have been rebuilt after extensive damage, while a few are new reconstructions. For some, only the ruin of a collapsed building now stands in its surrounding garden.

San Luis Rey Mission.

Santa Barbara Mission, established in 1782, with a view of the belfry, from *The Road of a Thousand Wonders* (right).

THE MOUNT LOWE RAILWAY

Conquering the Mountain

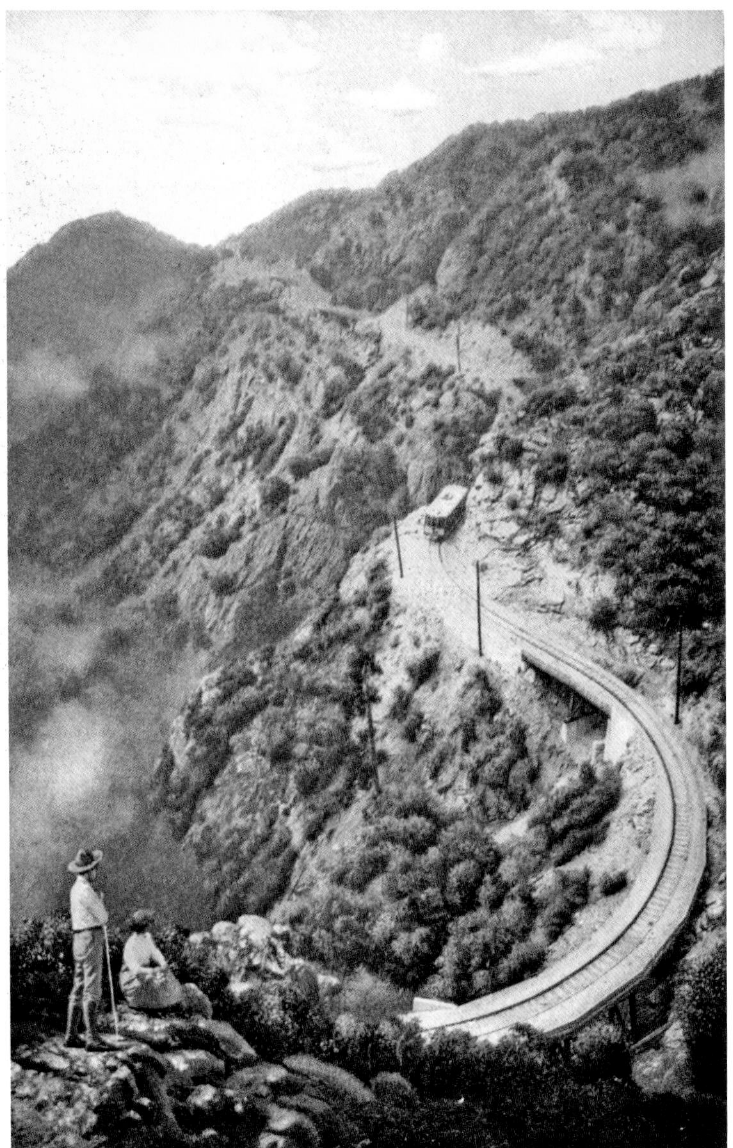

A Trip to the Sky, Mount Lowe Observatory (all the images in this section apart from the postcards are from *The World Famed Mount Lowe Trip*, published by E. C. Kropp Co. in 1917)

For many Americans, Southern California has long been a favored vacation spot. In the early twentieth century it was considerably more exotic than the cities that most came from: viewed as a land of perpetual sunshine, its attractions included mountain peaks, miles of beaches, palm trees, orange groves, and the developing movie city of Hollywood.

One of the best ways to see the attractions were the cars of the Pacific Electric Railway, an electric interurban that reached just about anywhere in Southern California and for more than thirty years operated a number of splendid excursion cars offering many popular trips.

But the most popular trip of all was on the famous Mount Lowe Railway that took visitors to the mountain's summit to look down on Los Angeles. The imaginative man who built the line was Professor Thaddeus S. C. Lowe (1832–1913), who began construction in late 1891. A trolley line carried visitors upward into Rubio Canyon for transfer to the base of the Great Cable Incline, where a large pavilion housed a dining room and a dance hall. The Incline was difficult, climbing 1,300 feet between Rubio and Echo Mountain at the top, and was traversed by two inclined cable cars, sometimes called "opera box" cars, that rose or descended at an average grade of 59 percent, counter-balanced by the cable system. A souvenir photograph of passengers seated inside the inclined cars was a *de rigueur* item on every trip.

At the top of the Incline Lowe built the Echo Mountain House, a comfortable hotel with a magnificent view of the valley below. Other attractions on Echo Mountain included a zoo, a dance hall, and an Observatory, while a 3-million-candlepower searchlight, that was said to be the largest anywhere in the world, could be seen from 150 miles at sea.

Bird's-eye view of Mount Lowe.

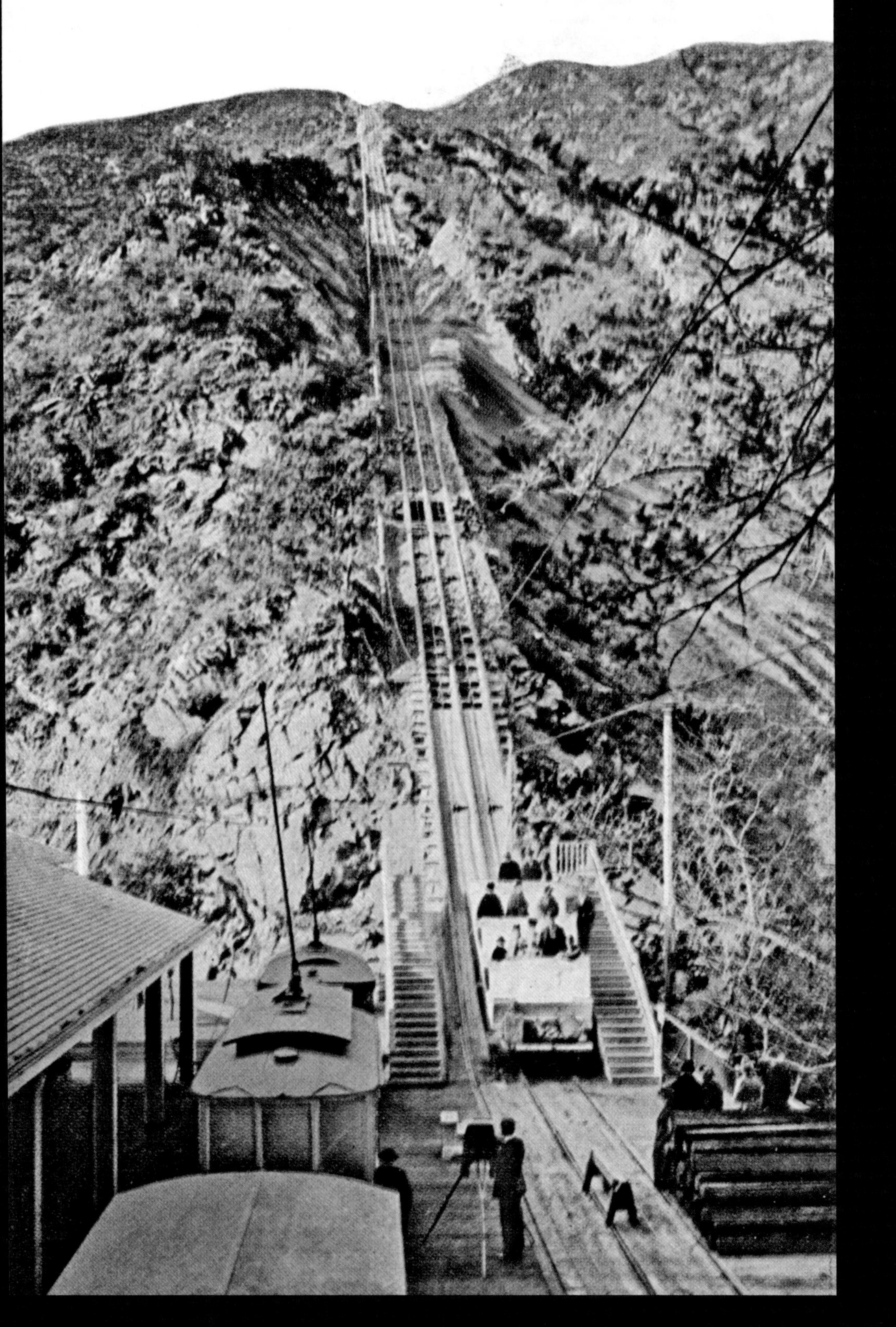

The final section of the Mount Lowe Railway was a 3.6-mile, narrow gauge (3 feet 6 inches) trolley line through spectacular scenery. Following the natural contours of the mountain, the line crossed eighteen trestles and had no fewer than 127 curves, finally reaching the summit at 5,603 feet, some 2,800 feet above Rubio Canyon. The most stunning of the many views along the trolley was the Circular Bridge: to reach a higher level the engineer had to build a circular trestle on a 75-foot radius, while climbing through 4.5 percent grades. At the summit, Lowe built Alpine Tavern, a hotel in a beautiful Swiss architecture.

The Incline Cable leading to Mount Lowe (left); the Circular Bridge (below left); at the top of the Incline (below); three cars ascending Mount Lowe (right).

At one time it was said that Mount Lowe was Southern California's most popular tourist attraction, and it lasted for more than forty years despite all of the difficulties of a mountain railway. At various times the cable house and hotels were wrecked by fires, while a landslide wiped out the Rubio Canyon Pavilion. The final blow came in 1938 when a violent rainstorm washed away large parts of the track.

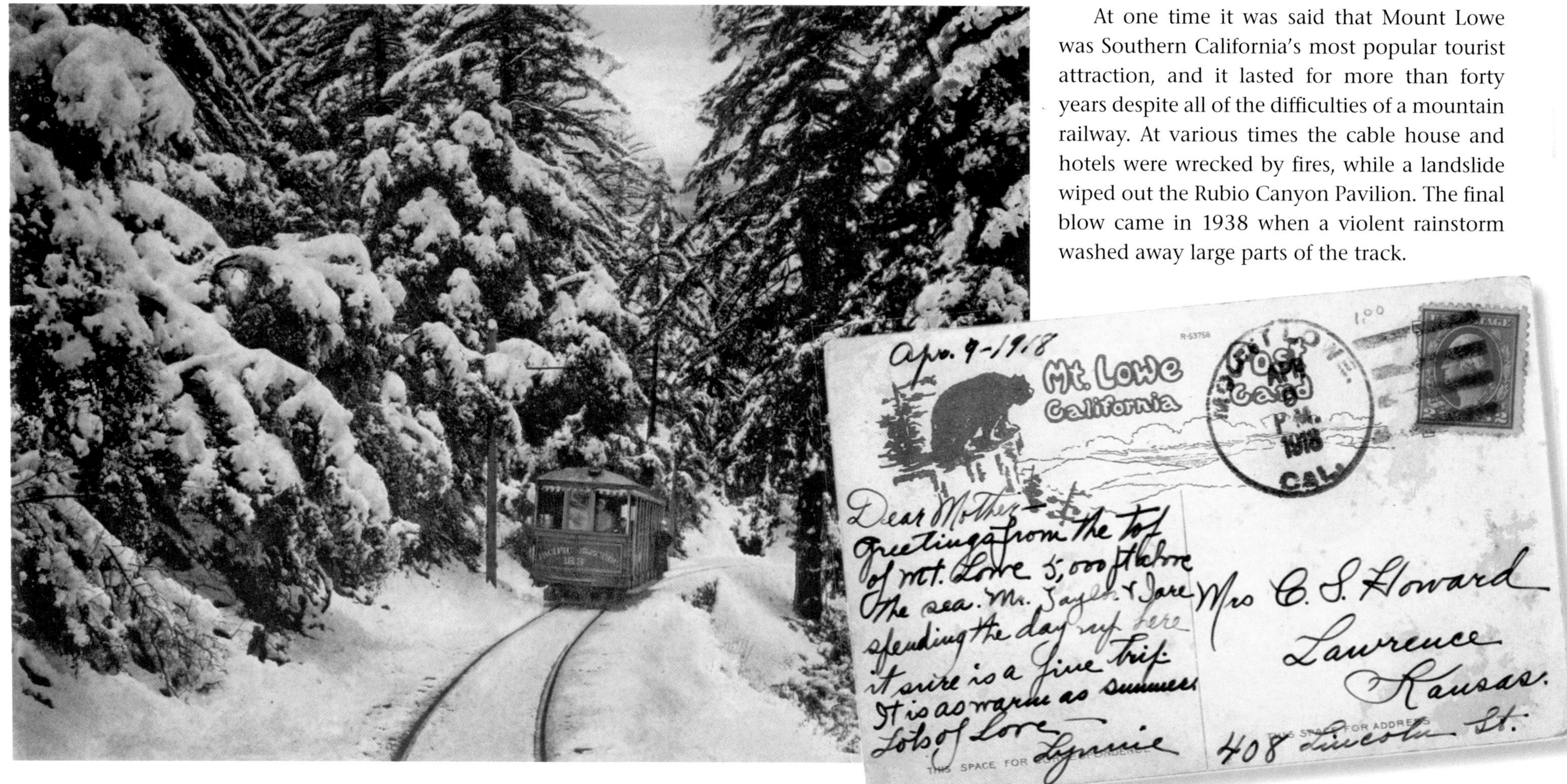

A winter scene, on the way up to Mount Lowe (above); a postcard (right) sent from Mount Lowe on April 9, 1918.

SOUTHERN PACIFIC.

CONDENSED SCHEDULE OF THROUGH PULLMAN CAR SERVICE.

OGDEN ROUTE.

....	No. 2	No. 4	No. 6
Lve. **San Francisco**....(So. Pac. Co.)	*11 00 A M	*9 00 A M	*6 00 P M
Lve. **Los Angeles**.......... "	3 50 P M	3 50 P M	11 30 P M
Lve. **Sacramento**.......... "	2 20 P M	12 50 Noon	11 35 P M
Arr.. **Ogden**................ "	2 30 P M	5 50 P M	7 10 A M
Lve. **Ogden**..........(Union Pacific)	3 00 P M	7 30 P M	8 20 A M
Arr.. **Omaha**............. "	8 18 P M	7 44 A M	5 10 P M
Arr.. **Chicago**.....(Chic. & No. West.)	9 00 A M	8 50 P M	7 30 A M
Arr.. **Chicago**........(C. M. & St. P.)	9 25 A M	9 30 P M	8 35 A M
Lve. **Ogden**....(Rio Grande Western)	2 50 P M	7 00 P M	7 45 A M
Arr.. **Pueblo**....(Den. & Rio Grande)	12 35 Noon	5 40 P M	6 50 A M
Arr.. **Denver**............... "	4 20 P M	9 45 P M	10 55 A M
Arr.. **Denver**.....(Colorado Midland)	....	9 20 P M	9 45 A M
Arr.. **St. Louis**.....(Missouri Pacific)	....	....	6 01 P M
Lve. **Denver**.....(Chic. R. I. & Pacific)	9 10 P M	....	....
Arr.. **Chicago**.............. "	7 17 A M	....	....
Lve. **Denver**.....(Burlington Route)	....	....	10 00 P M
Arr.. **Chicago**.............. "	....	....	6 55 A M

....	No. 1	No. 3	No. 5
Lve. **Chicago**.....(Chic. & No. West.)	*8 02 P M	*11 00 P M	....
Lve. **Chicago**........(C. M. & St. P.)	8 00 P M	10 25 P M	....
Lve. **Omaha**..........(Union Pacific)	9 40 A M	4 15 P M	....
Arr.. **Ogden**................ "	4 00 P M	3 45 A M	....
Lve. **Chicago**.....(Burlington Route)	11 00 P M	....	*11 00 P M
Arr.. **Denver**............... "	7 30 A M	....	7 30 A M
Lve. **Chicago**...(Chic. R. I. & Pacific)	*10 32 P M	....	....
Arr.. **Denver**............... "	9 00 A M	....	....
Lve. **St. Louis**.....(Missouri Pacific)	....	....	9 00 A M
Lve. **Denver**.....(Colorado Midland)	....	9 00 P M	9 30 A M
Lve. **Denver**....(Den. & Rio Grande)	9 30 A M	*8 00 P M	8 30 A M
Lve. **Pueblo**............... "	1 35 P M	11 55 P M	12 25 Noon
Arr.. **Ogden**....(Rio Grande Western)	2 40 P M	12 05 Night	11 30 A M
Lve. **Ogden**..........(So. Pacific Co.)	4 20 P M	4 30 A M	11 55 A M
Arr.. **Sacramento**.......... "	2 10 P M	7 40 A M	12 50 Noon
Arr.. **Los Angeles**.......... "	8 55 A M	7 05 A M	11 20 A M
Arr.. **San Francisco**........ "	5 48 P M	12 48 Noon	4 28 P M

Train No. 2—Overland Limited—Electric Lighted—Diner, Composite Observation Car San Francisco and Chicago, via U. P., C. & N. W. and C. M. & St. P. Rys. Drawing-room Sleeper San Francisco and Chicago, via D. & R. G., C. R. I. & P. Drawing-room-Stateroom Sleepers San Francisco and Chicago, via U. P., C. & N. W., and via U. P., C. M. & St. P.

Train No. 4—Standard Sleeper San Francisco to Salt Lake City, via O. S. L. Dining Car San Francisco to Ogden. Tourist Car San Francisco to Salt Lake, via O. S. L. Tourist Cars Wednesday, Thursday and Friday to Chicago and St. Louis.

Train No. 6—China and Japan Fast Mail—Standard Sleepers San Francisco to Chicago, via U. P., C. & N. W. and C. M. & St. P. Rys. Standard Sleeping Car San Francisco to Chicago, via D. & R. G. Ry. and Burl. Route. Standard Sleeping Car San Francisco to St. Louis, via D. & R. G. and Mo. Pac. Tourist Sleepers San Francisco to Chicago, via U. P., C. & N.W. and C. M. & St. P. Rys. and to Denver, via D. & R. G. Ry. Dining Car San Francisco to Ogden and Chicago.

Train No. 1—Overland Limited—Electric Lighted—Diner and Composite Observation Car Chicago and San Francisco, via C. M. & St. P., C. & N. W. and U. P. Rys. Drawing-room Sleeper San Francisco and Chicago, via C. R. I. & P., D. & R. G. Drawing-room-Stateroom Sleepers Chicago and San Francisco, via C. & N. W., U. P., and via C. M. & St. P., U. P.

Train No. 3—China and Japan Fast Mail—Sleepers Chicago to San Francisco, via C. & N. W. and U. P. Rys. and C. M. & St. P. and U. P. Rys. Tourist Sleepers Chicago to San Francisco, via C. & N. W. and U. P. Rys. and via C. M. & St. P. and U. P. Rys. from Salt Lake, via O. S. L. Diners Chicago and Ogden to San Francisco.

Train No. 5—Standard Sleeper Chicago to San Francisco, via Burlington Route and D. & R. G.; also St. Louis to San Francisco, via Missouri Pacific and D. & R. G. Tourist Sleeper Denver to San Francisco, via D. & R. G. Dining Car Chicago and Ogden to San Francisco. Tourist Cars from Chicago and St. Louis leave Ogden Friday, Saturday and Sunday.

SUNSET ROUTE.

No. 26	No. 8	No. 84	No. 10	STATIONS.	No. 9	No. 83	No. 7	No. 25
*5 00 P M	*10 20 A M	*8 20 A M	....	lve...**San Francisco**...arr.	....	4 48 P M	7 08 P M	8 48 A M
7 40 P M	1 30 P M	11 35 A M	....	lve......**Tracy**......lve.	....	2 00 P M	3 55 P M	6 02 A M
11 08 P M	6 20 P M	3 05 P M	....	lve......**Fresno**......lve.	....	10 35 A M	11 50 A M	2 40 A M
2 07 A M	10 12 P M	6 05 P M	....	lve....**Bakersfield**....lve.	....	*7 30 A M	7 55 A M	11 40 P M
5 13 A M	2 35 A M		....	lve......**Mojave**......lve.	....		4 20 A M	8 42 P M
8 55 A M	7 05 A M		....	arr....**Los Angeles**....lve.	....		*11 30 P M	*5 00 P M
No. 22	....	No. 20	....	(Via Coast Division.)	....	No. 19	....	No. 21
*8 30 A M	Trains marked * run daily. †Daily, except Sunday. ‡Daily, except Saturday.	*8 00 A M	*5 45 P M	lve...**San Francisco**...arr.	9 10 A M	9 30 P M	....	11 45 P M
9 55 A M		9 25 A M	7 30 P M	lve......**San Jose**......arr.	7 40 A M	8 05 P M	....	10 15 P M
10 41 A M		— —	8 29 P M	lve.......**Gilroy**.......arr.	6 22 A M	— —	....	9 12 P M
11 27 A M		10 55 A M	9 32 P M	lve.....**Castroville**....arr.	5 24 A M	6 22 P M	....	8 13 P M
2 54 P M		1 38 P M	1 02 A M	lve....**Paso Robles**....arr.	2 06 A M	3 36 P M	....	4 58 P M
4 25 P M		3 05 P M	2 50 A M	lve..**San Luis Obispo**.arr.	12 40 Night	2 15 P M	....	3 35 P M
8 10 P M		6 14 P M	7 10 A M	lve...**Santa Barbara**...arr.	8 10 P M	11 15 A M	....	12 10 Noon
11 45 P M		9 30 P M	11 20 A M	arr....**Los Angeles**....lve.	3 50 P M	*8 00 A M	....	*8 30 A M
....		....	12 10 Noon	lve....**Los Angeles**....arr.	12 55 Noon	....	....	....
....		....	9 30 P M	lve.......**Yuma**.......lve.	3 45 A M	....	....	....
....		....	2 42 A M	lve......**Maricopa**.....lve.	10 00 P M	....	....	....
....		....	5 40 A M	lve.......**Tucson**......lve.	7 30 P M			
....		....	7 00 P M	arr.......**El Paso**......lve.	9 45 A M			
....		....	8 00 P M	lve.......**El Paso**......arr.	8 00 A M			
....		....	8 00 P M	arr....**San Antonio**....lve.	9 00 A M			
....		....	6 00 A M	arr......**Houston**......lve.	12 30 Night			
....		....	6 45 P M	arr....**New Orleans**....lve.	*11 55 A M			

No. 50—FRESNO PASSENGER—Daily. Standard Sleepers San Francisco to Fresno and San Francisco to Raymond for Yosemite.

Nos. 9 and 10—SUNSET EXPRESS—Standard Sleepers, Chair, Composite Observation, Dining Cars, San Francisco and New Orleans. Daily Standard Sleeper Tucson and Phoenix. Tourist Sleepers San Francisco, New Orleans and East daily. Daily Standard and Semi-weekly Tourist Sleepers Los Angeles to St. Louis, via T. & P. and Iron Mountain.

Nos. 7 and 8—Drawing-room Sleeper Los Angeles and San Francisco. Drawing-room Sleeper Los Angeles and Bakersfield. Tourist Car Los Angeles and San Francisco. Diner San Francisco and Bakersfield.

Nos. 25 and 26—THE OWL LIMITED—Electric Lighted—Solid Vestibule Train between San Francisco and Los Angeles, Composite Car, Double Drawing-room Sleepers, Diner. Chair Car San Francisco to Bakersfield. Drawing-room Sleeper San Francisco to Chicago on Nos. 44 and 43 east of Los Angeles. Tri-weekly Yosemite Sleepers Los Angeles to Raymond. Sleepers Fresno and Raymond to San Francisco on No. 25.

Nos. 19 and 20—Solid Train of Composite Car, Dining Car, Drawing-room and Observation Parlor Cars between San Francisco and Los Angeles.

VIA ROCK ISLAND-EL PASO ROUTE.

26-44	10-30	STATIONS.	29-9	43-25
*5 00 P M	*5 45 P M	lve..**San Francisco**.arr.	9 10 A M	8 48 A M
7 10 A M	7 10 A M	lve..**Santa Barbara**.arr.	8 00 P M	8 00 P M
*12 01 Noon	12 10 Noon	lve..**Los Angeles**..arr.	12 55 Noon	4 15 P M
8 05 P M	9 30 P M	lve......**Yuma**......arr.	3 35 A M	8 02 A M
12 50 Noon	5 00 P M	arr.....**El Paso**.....lve.	7 45 A M	2 20 P M
2 10 P M	6 35 P M	lve.....**El Paso**.....arr.	8 00 A M	4 13 P M
11 10 P M	4 25 A M	arr..**Santa Rosa**..lve.	10 00 P M	7 07 A M
8 25 P M	6 50 A M	arr..**Kansas City**..lve.	11 00 P M	9 55 A M
7 55 A M	7 05 P M	arr.....**St. Louis**....lve.	8 59 A M	10 02 P M
10 15 A M	10 25 P M	arr....**Chicago**....lve.	8 30 A M	9 00 P M

Nos. 44 and 43—CALIFORNIA SPECIAL—Electric Lighted—Via E. P. & S. W., C. R. I. & P., C. & A., C. R. I. & P.—Diner and Buffet-Composite Library Car Los Angeles to Chicago. Observation Sleeper Los Angeles to Chicago. Drawing-room Sleeper Oakland to Chicago on Trains Nos. 26 and 25 north of Los Angeles. Tourist Sleeper and Chair Car Los Angeles to Chicago.

SHASTA ROUTE.

No. 16	No. 12	STATIONS.	No. 11	No. 15
*8 20 P M	*8 00 A M	lve. **San Francisco**.arr.	7 48 P M	8 48 A M
11 58 P M	....	arr..**Sacramento**..lve.	....	5 00 A M
8 02 P M	11 00 P M	lve....**Chicago**....arr.	7 30 A M	9 00 A M
4 20 P M	4 30 A M	lve.....**Ogden**.....arr.	7 10 A M	2 30 P M
2 10 P M	7 40 A M	arr..**Sacramento**..lve.	11 35 P M	2 20 P M
*12 15 Night	*10 55 A M	lve..**Sacramento**..arr.	4 55 P M	4 45 A M
6 25 A M	5 40 P M	lve....**Redding**....lve.	10 30 A M	10 50 P M
4 20 P M	3 30 A M	arr....**Ashland**....lve.	12 55 Night	12 35 Noon
11 35 P M	9 35 A M	arr...**Roseburg**...lve.	5 45 P M	5 05 A M
7 25 A M	5 55 P M	arr....**Portland**....lve.	*8 30 A M	*8 45 P M

Nos. 12 and 11—SHASTA EXPRESS—Drawing-room Sleeping Cars and Tourist Cars between San Francisco and Portland. Dining Car between Oakland and Dunsmuir, Glendale and Portland.

Nos. 16 and 15—OREGON AND CALIFORNIA EXPRESS—Drawing-room and Tourist Sleepers between San Francisco and Portland. Tourist Sleeper between Sacramento and Portland. Dining Cars between Sacramento and Roseburg, and Roseburg and Oakland. Drawing-room Sleeper San Francisco and Sisson. Composite Observation Car San Francisco and Roseburg. Chair Car San Francisco and Portland.

SOUTHERN PACIFIC.

SAN FRANCISCO AND OGDEN—OGDEN ROUTE.

18	14	6	4	2	20	Mls	April 1, 1906.	3	1	5	13	17	19
P M	P M	P M	A M	A M	P M		LEAVE] [ARRIVE	A M	Noon	P M			
*3 40	*7 00	*6 00	*9 00	*11 00	*7 00	0	+..**San Francisco**..♂	12 48	5 48	4 28	7 08	10 48	7 28
4 08	7 30	6 34	9 30	11 30	7 28	5	....Oakland Pier....♂	12 18	5 12	3 53	6 40	10 15	6 54
4 36	s	—	—	—	7 58	18	.......San Pablo.......♂					9 46	a
4 50	s	—	—	—	8 12	24	........Pinole........♂					9 33	6 09
5 02	s	—	—	—	8 23	29	...Vallejo Junction...♂	b	—	b	—	9 23	a
5 10	8 23	7 30	10 20	12 20	8 33	32	.....Port Costa.....♂	11 30	4 15	3 00	5 50	9 17	5 52
5 33	8 45	Via Stockton.	10 50	12 45	8 50	33	......Benicia......♂	Via Stockton.	3 50	2 35	5 25	8 55	5 33
6 12	9 19		11 22	—	9 23	50	.......**Suisun**.......♂				4 52	8 20	4 55
6 35	9 40		11 40	—	9 48	60	.......**Elmira**.......♂				4 32	7 58	4 34
6 50	9 54		—	—	10 08	69	.......Dixon.......♂				—	7 41	4 17
7 15	10 10		12 05	—	10 30	77	.......**Davis**.......♂				4 05	7 25	4 01
7 40	10 35	11 15	12 35	2 15	10 55	90	+...**Sacramento**...♂	*7 55	*2 15	*1 00	*3 40	*7 00	*3 35
P M	P M	P M	Noon	P M	P M		ARRIVE] [LEAVE	A M	P M	P M	P M	P M	A M
P M	P M	P M	Noon	P M	P M		LEAVE] [ARRIVE	A M	P M	Noon	P M		A M
*10 50	*11 35	*12 50	*2 20	*6 00		90	+..**Sacramento**..♂	7 40	2 10	12 50	3 25		9 20
11 07	—	1 08	—	5 17		98	.......Arcade.......♂	—	—	—	—		c9 01
11 19	—	1 23	—	5 32		104	......Antelope......♂				2 53		c8 52
11 27	12 15	1 38	—	5 42		108	.....**Roseville**.....♂	7 03	—	12 14	2 45		8 45
11 38	12 30	1 55	—	5 54		112	......Rocklin......♂	6 53	—	12 05	2 34		8 37
11 58	12 50	2 17	—	6 12		118	......Penryn......♂	6 38	—	11 46	2 16		8 23
12 10	1 02	2 30	—	6 22		121	.....Newcastle.....♂	6 30	—	11 38	2 07		8 15
12 40	1 22	2 50	—	6 40		126	.......Auburn.......♂	6 17	—	11 23	1 50		7 58
		3 20	—	7 00		133	.....Clipper Gap.....♂	—	—	11 07	1 30		7 42
1 45	2 35	4 03	—	7 30		144	+......**Colfax**......♂	5 37	—	10 40	12 50		*7 15
2 05	3 17	4 35	—	P M		154	......Gold Run......♂	5 07	—	10 05	12 19		A M
2 32	3 35	4 52	—			155	.....Dutch Flat.....♂	5 02	—	9 59	12 14		
2 43	3 53	5 04	—			159	.......Towle.......♂	4 55	—	9 51	12 02		
3 25	5 00	5 50	—			168	.....Blue Canon.....♂	4 25	—	9 25	11 40		
3 48	5 30	6 10	—			173	....Emigrant Gap....♂	4 05	—	9 08	11 18		
4 30	6 24	6 44	—			182	.......Cisco.......♂	3 40	—	8 42	10 53		
5 17	7 10	7 30	—			195	......Summit......♂	3 00	—	8 00	10 15		
6 15	8 10	8 12	8 25			209	......**Truckee**......♂	2 00	9 03	7 02	9 15		
						225	arr. **Lake Tahoe**. lve.						
6 47	8 35	8 47	—			218	.......Boca.......♂	1 28	—	6 32	8 37		
7 30	9 10	9 34	—			234	.......Verdi.......♂	12 49	—	5 54	7 43		
8 15	9 40	10 10	9 45			244	+......**Reno**......♂	12 25	7 40	5 25	7 10		
8 40	9 55	10 20	9 55			248	arr....**Sparks**...lve.	12 05	7 30	5 15	6 55		
							(Pacific time.)						
							(Mountain time.)						
9 45	11 15	11 30	11 05			248	lve....**Sparks**....arr.	12 55	8 20	6 05	7 25		
11 00	12 31	12 50	12 15			280	.......**Hazen**.......♂	11 07	7 08	4 25	*6 05		
A M	1 15	—				291	.......Parran.......♂	10 25			P M		
	1 46	—				313	.......Brown.......♂	9 51					
	2 16	2 27	1 42			329	+.....Lovelock.....♂	9 16	5 31	2 27			
	3 09	—				346	......Rye Patch......♂	8 29					
	3 30	3 38				368	......**Humboldt**......♂	8 04		1 26			
	3 52	—				379	......Mill City......♂	7 38					
	4 55	5 00	3 05			419	+....Winnemucca....♂	6 50	3 33	12 25			
	5 27	5 34	—			435	......Golconda......♂	6 15	—	11 51			
	6 52	6 47	5 05			471	..**Battle Mountain**..♂	4 36	1 53	10 38			
						477	.......Argenta.......♂	4 11					
	7 54	7 43	—			489	......Beowawe......♂	3 26	—	9 42			
						506	.......Cluro.......♂						
	8 30	8 20	—			514	......**Palisade**......♂	2 48	—	9 08			
	9 00	8 50	6 53			527	.......Carlin.......♂	2 30	12 10	8 50			
		9 08	—			536	.......Moleen.......♂	1 59					
	9 55	9 32	7 30			546	+.......Elko.......♂	1 35	11 27	7 47			
	10 41	10 10	—			558	......Halleck......♂	12 53	—	7 01			
	12 15	11 24	9 05			578	+......Wells......♂	11 43	9 46	6 06			
						611	......Fenelon......♂						
						631	.......Cobre.......♂	10 01		4 55			
						645	.......Loray.......♂	9 48					
	2 30	1 15	10 47			666	......**Montello**......♂	9 15	7 58	4 07			
	2 43	1 27	—			673	......Tecoma......♂	8 50	—	3 45			
						682	**Umbria Junction**.						
		1 45				684	.......Lucin.......♂	8 02					
		2 15				697	......Jackson......♂	7 45					
		2 45				710	...Newfoundland...♂	7 20					
	4 40	3 42				739	......Lakeside......♂	6 25		1 30			
		4 20				749	......Midlake......♂	5 59					
	6 05	4 57				762	.Promontory Point.♂	5 26		12 32			
	6 33	5 19				772	..Little Mountain..♂	4 58					
	7 10	5 50	2 30			786	.......**Ogden**.......♂	*4 30	*4 20	*11 55			
	A M	P M	P M				ARRIVE] [LEAVE	P M	A M	A M			

(Printed vertically in the left margin of the table:) * Daily; † daily, except Sunday; ‡ Sunday only; a stops to leave passengers from East or South of Port Costa; c stops to leave passengers from east of Roseville; f Tuesday, Thursday and Saturday; ‡ Monday, Wednesday and Friday; s stops Sunday. ♂ Stops to leave passengers from east of Sparks. † Meals.

(Printed vertically beside the table:) Sacramento Division. Salt Lake Division.

(Printed vertically beside the table:) **Salt Lake Div.—Old Line—Via Promontory**—Mixed Train leaves Ogden *8 15 a.m., arr. Montello (155 mls.) 3 50 p.m. Lvs. Montello *8 25 a.m., arr. Ogden 5 30 p.m.

(Printed vertically beside the table:) **Lebanon Branch (Oregon).**—Leave **Albany** ‡8 10 a.m., ‡3 05 p.m. for Fromm, Tallman and Irvinville, arriving Lebanon (13 miles) 9 00 a.m., 4 00 p.m. Leave Lebanon ‡9 35 a.m., ‡4 50 p.m., arriving Albany 10 25 a.m., 5 40 p.m.

Additional Trains—Leave San Francisco *5 20 p.m., arriving Sacramento 8 20 p.m. Leave Sacramento *8 20 a.m., arriving San Francisco 11 28 a.m.

LAKE TAHOE.—Fifteen miles from Truckee, on the Ogden Line of the Southern Pacific, lies Lake Tahoe, amid the Sierra Nevada Mountains, at an altitude of 6,220 feet. About 23 miles long by 13 miles wide, with a known depth of 2,000 feet, it is one of the largest mountain lakes in the world. Peaks ranging from 2,000 to 4,000 feet high surround it, their grandeur mirrored by the blue water, which is of marvelous clearness. A dozen smaller lakes are near, and all are filled with gamy fish. Tahoe is reached by the Lake Tahoe Railway and Transportation Line from Truckee, round trip fare including 70 mile steamer ride, $5.00. Stop-overs at Truckee allowed on first-class rail and Pullman tickets.

SHASTA SPRINGS.—On the Shasta Route of the Southern Pacific, between San Francisco and Portland, where all trains stop that passengers may imbibe of sparkling mineral water. A place of rare beauty and enchanting Summer resort.

PASO ROBLES HOT SPRINGS.—Midway between San Francisco and Los Angeles, famous for mineral waters. Stop-overs from two to thirty days allowed on first-class tickets between these points; round-trip tickets, good from Friday to Tuesday, including two days entertainment at the hotel, sold in San Francisco for $12.75. The most thoroughly equipped bath-house in the world; sulphur, mud and electric baths with trained nurses and masseurs in attendance.

SAN FRANCISCO AND PORTLAND—SHASTA ROUTE.

32	12	16	Mls	April 1, 1906.	15	11	31
A M	A M	P M		LEAVE] [ARRIVE	A M	P M	P M
*8 40	*8 00	*8 20	0	..**San Francisco**..♂	8 48	7 48	4 08
9 08	8 30	8 53	4	....Oakland Pier....♂	8 10	7 20	3 42
Via Willows.	9 25	9 45	32	....**Port Costa**....♂	7 15	6 23	Via Willows.
	11 15		77	........**Davis**........♂	5 25	4 30	
2 50		11 58	90	arr. } **Sacra-** { lve.	5 00		10 10
3 50	10 55	12 15	90	lve. } **mento** { arr.	4 55	4 55	9 50
4 12		12 53	108	....**Roseville**....♂	4 09		9 15
4 50		1 33	130	....Wheatland....♂	3 25		8 35
5 15		2 05	142	+..**Marysville**..♂	2 55		8 00
9 40			168	arr.. **Oroville** ..lve.			*5 50
		2 47	160	......Gridley......♂	2 23		7 28
5 50		3 45	186	.......Chico.......♂	1 30		6 25
7 31		4 22	205	.......Vina.......♂	12 57	Via Willows.	5 53
7 50	5 47	4 45	213	......**Tehama**......♂	12 57	12 18	5 33
8 15	4 20	5 20	225	+..**Red Bluff**..♂	12 35	11 55	*5 10
P M	5 00	5 58	242	....Cottonwood....♂	11 28	11 08	A M
	5 14	6 11	249	......Anderson......♂	11 15	10 55	
	5 40	6 35	260	+....**Redding**....♂	10 50	10 30	
	6 28	7 22	277	.......Kennet.......♂	10 03	9 38	
	7 28	8 30	298	.......Delta.......♂	9 08	8 40	
	8 20	10 05	324	......Dunsmuir......♂	7 45	7 20	
	8 35	10 35	327	...Shasta Springs...♂	7 15	6 55	
	10 20	11 20	338	.......Sisson.......♂	6 23	6 06	
	10 30	11 27	341	.......**Upton**.......♂	6 16	5 57	
	11 15	12 13	355	......Edgewood......♂	5 25	5 08	
	11 53	12 50	371	......Montague......♂	4 21	4 20	
	12 55	1 45	395	.....Hornbrook.....♂	3 28	3 30	
	3 00	3 52	421	......Steinman......♂	1 10	1 35	
	3 35	4 40	431	+....**Ashland**....♂	12 55	12 55	
	4 06	6 09	443	+.....Medford.....♂	11 25	11 52	
14	5 10	6 30	475	+..Grant's Pass..♂	10 05	10 40	13
A M	9 35	11 35	574	+....Roseburg....♂	5 05	5 45	P M
*6 00	12 42	2 51	649	.......Eugene.......♂	1 32	2 15	9 00
6 27	1 12	3 19	662	....Junction City....♂	1 08	1 45	8 36
6 36	1 27	—	667	.....Harrisburg.....♂	—	1 27	8 27
7 28	2 27	4 30	691	+......**Albany**......♂	11 57	12 28	7 30
8 23	3 29	5 23	720	+.......Salem.......♂	10 56	11 13	6 32
9 01	4 13	6 00	737	+....**Woodburn**....♂	10 18	10 37	5 51
9 47	5 04	6 41	757	....Oregon City....♂	9 32	9 52	5 01
10 35	5 55	7 25	772	+.....**Portland**.....♂	*8 45	*8 30	*4 15
A M	P M	A M		ARRIVE] [LEAVE	P M	A M	P M
	11 45	*8 30	772	lve. **Portland** ♂ arr.	6 50	7 00	
	3 20	2 45	917	arr.. **Tacoma** ♂ lve.	1 25	12 05	
	7 05	4 30	956	arr.. **Seattle** ♂ lve.	*11 15	*10 20	
	A M	P M					

LINES IN OREGON—West Side Division.

18	4	2	Mls	December 20, 1905.	1	3	17
P M	P M	A M		LEAVE] [ARRIVE	P M	A M	P M
†10 45	*4 50	*7 30	0	......**Portland**......♂	5 50	8 25	1 50
11 14	5 20	8 00	7	.......Bertha.......♂	5 20	8 00	1 23
11 52	6 04	8 44	21	......Hillsboro......♂	4 31	7 12	12 42
12 20	6 20	9 00	26	....Forest Grove....♂	4 15	6 57	†12 30
Night	6 53	9 33	39	...North Yamhill...♂	3 39	6 25	Noon
	7 21	10 00	50	....**McMinnville**....♂	3 10	5 59	
	7 30	10 10	54	......**Whiteson**......♂	3 00	*5 50	
	P M	10 59	76	....Independence....♂	2 10	A M	
		11 45	97	......**Corvallis**......♂	*1 20		
		A M		ARRIVE] [LEAVE	P M		

SPRINGFIELD BRANCH.

50	48	Mls	December 20, 1905.	49	47	53
P M	A M		LEAVE] [ARRIVE	P M	A M	
†6 00	†10 50	0	......**Woodburn**......♂	2 20	8 50	
6 19	11 30	6	....Mount Angel....♂	1 55	8 31	
6 30	12 10	10	......Silverton......♂	1 25	†8 20	
P M	2 02	33	......**Shelburn**......♂	10 58	A M	
	2 05	35	.......West Scio.......♂	10 55		
52	3 45	47	......**Tallman**......♂	8 55		51
A M	4 45	60	.....Brownsville.....♂	8 12		P M
†6 00	6 10	79	........Coburg........♂	7 32		4 50
9 05	6 35	83	....**Springfield**....♂	7 00		4 10
[illegible]	[illegible]	[illegible]	+**Mohawk Junction**..	[illegible]		2 15
10 40		105	arr....**Wendling**....lve.			†1 00
†2 40		88	lve....**Springfield**...arr.			3 25
2 55		93	arr.......**Natron**.......lve.			†3 10
P M			ARRIVE] [LEAVE			P M

YAMHILL DIVISION.

4	6	58	Mls	December 20, 1905.	5	57	3
	P M	A M		LEAVE] [ARRIVE			
[illegible]	*4 15	‡7 40	0	......**Portland**......♂	12 15	4 10	
	—	8 35	8	.......Oswego.......♂	9 50	3 25	
	5 04	9 55	17	......Sherwood......♂	9 23	2 10	
	5 40	11 00	26	......Newberg......♂	8 50	1 00	
	5 47	11 15	29	+**Dundee Junction**.♂	8 43	12 50	
P M	6 04	11 40	33	.....Lafayette.....♂	8 26	12 20	A M
*7 40	6 35	1 05	43	......Whiteson......♂	8 03	10 45	5 40
8 20		2 00	57	......**Sheridan**......♂	*5 05		*5 05
P M	7 00	3 00	52	......Perrydale......♂	7 30	9 35	A M
	7 30	3 50	63	........Dallas........♂	*7 00	8 40	
	P M	4 20	70	......Monmouth......♂	A M	7 50	
		5 00	79	........**Airlie**........♂		*7 00	
		P M		ARRIVE] [LEAVE		A M	

Pintsch Gas On 140,000 Cars, 6,600 Locomotives and 1,800 Buoys. || Over 150 railroads use the SAFETY systems of ..... **Steam Heat**

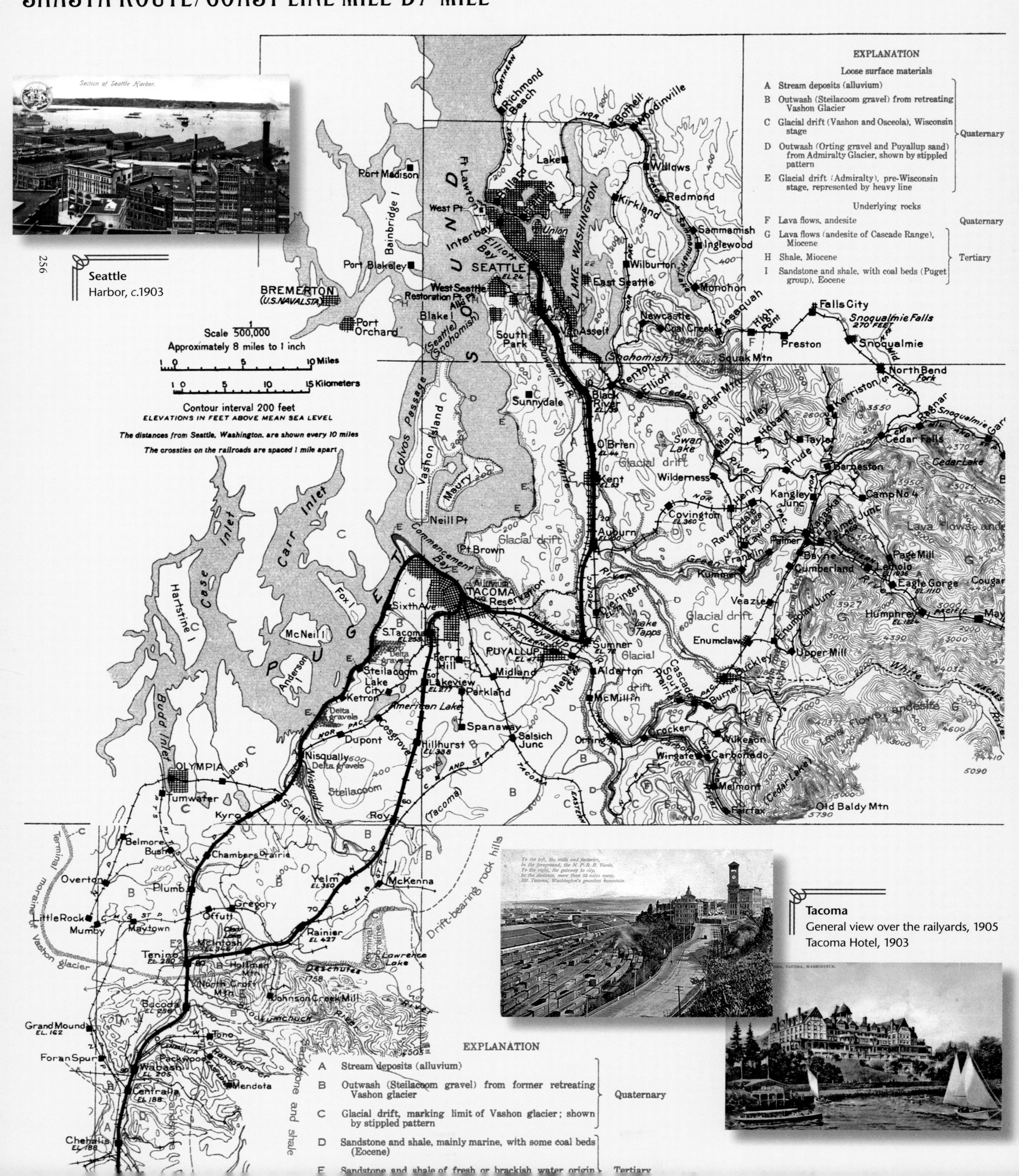
Section of Seattle Harbor.
EXPLANATION
Loose surface materials
A Stream deposits (alluvium)
B Outwash (Steilacoom gravel) from retreating Vashon Glacier
C Glacial drift (Vashon and Osceola), Wisconsin stage
D Outwash (Orting gravel and Puyallup sand) from Admiralty Glacier, shown by stippled pattern
E Glacial drift (Admiralty), pre-Wisconsin stage, represented by heavy line
Quaternary
Underlying rocks
F Lava flows, andesite
Quaternary
G Lava flows (andesite of Cascade Range), Miocene
H Shale, Miocene
I Sandstone and shale, with coal beds (Puget group), Eocene
Tertiary
Scale 1/500,000
Approximately 8 miles to 1 inch
10 Miles
15 Kilometers
Contour interval 200 feet
ELEVATIONS IN FEET ABOVE MEAN SEA LEVEL
The distances from Seattle, Washington, are shown every 10 miles
The crossties on the railroads are spaced 1 mile apart
SEATTLE
TACOMA
OLYMPIA
BREMERTON (U.S.NAVALSTA)
LAKE WASHINGTON
Commencement Bay
Carr Inlet
Case Inlet
Budd Inlet
Colvos Passage
Vashon Island
Glacial drift
Lava flows, andesite
Drift-bearing rock hills
Terminal moraine of Vashon glacier
Sandstone and shale
EXPLANATION
A Stream deposits (alluvium)
B Outwash (Steilacoom gravel) from former retreating Vashon glacier
C Glacial drift, marking limit of Vashon glacier; shown by stippled pattern
Quaternary
D Sandstone and shale, mainly marine, with some coal beds (Eocene)
E Sandstone and shale of fresh or brackish water origin
Tertiary
TACOMA, WASHINGTON.

Seattle
Harbor, c.1903

Tacoma
General view over the railyards, 1905
Tacoma Hotel, 1903

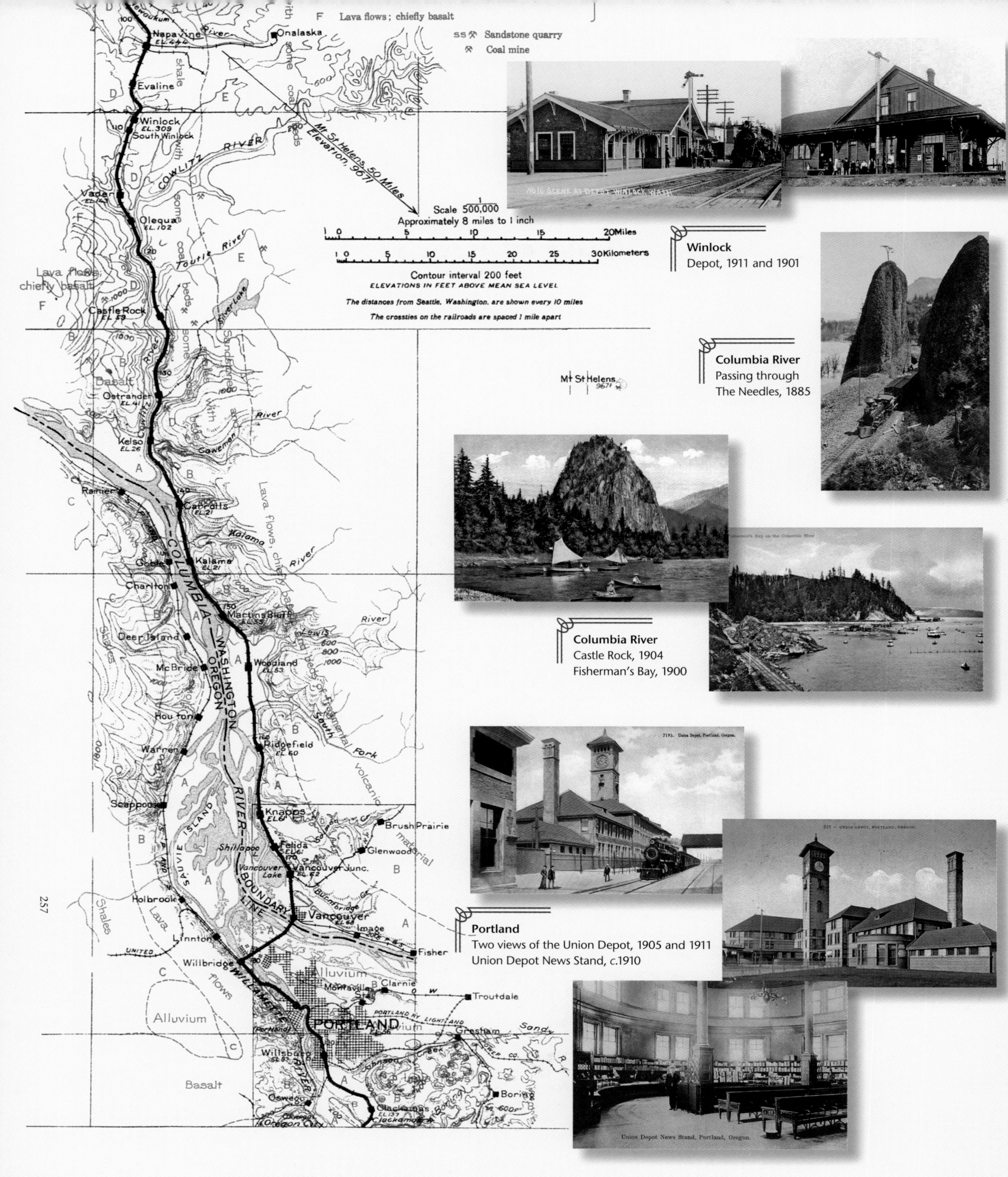

Winlock
Depot, 1911 and 1901

Columbia River
Passing through
The Needles, 1885

Columbia River
Castle Rock, 1904
Fisherman's Bay, 1900

Portland
Two views of the Union Depot, 1905 and 1911
Union Depot News Stand, *c.*1910

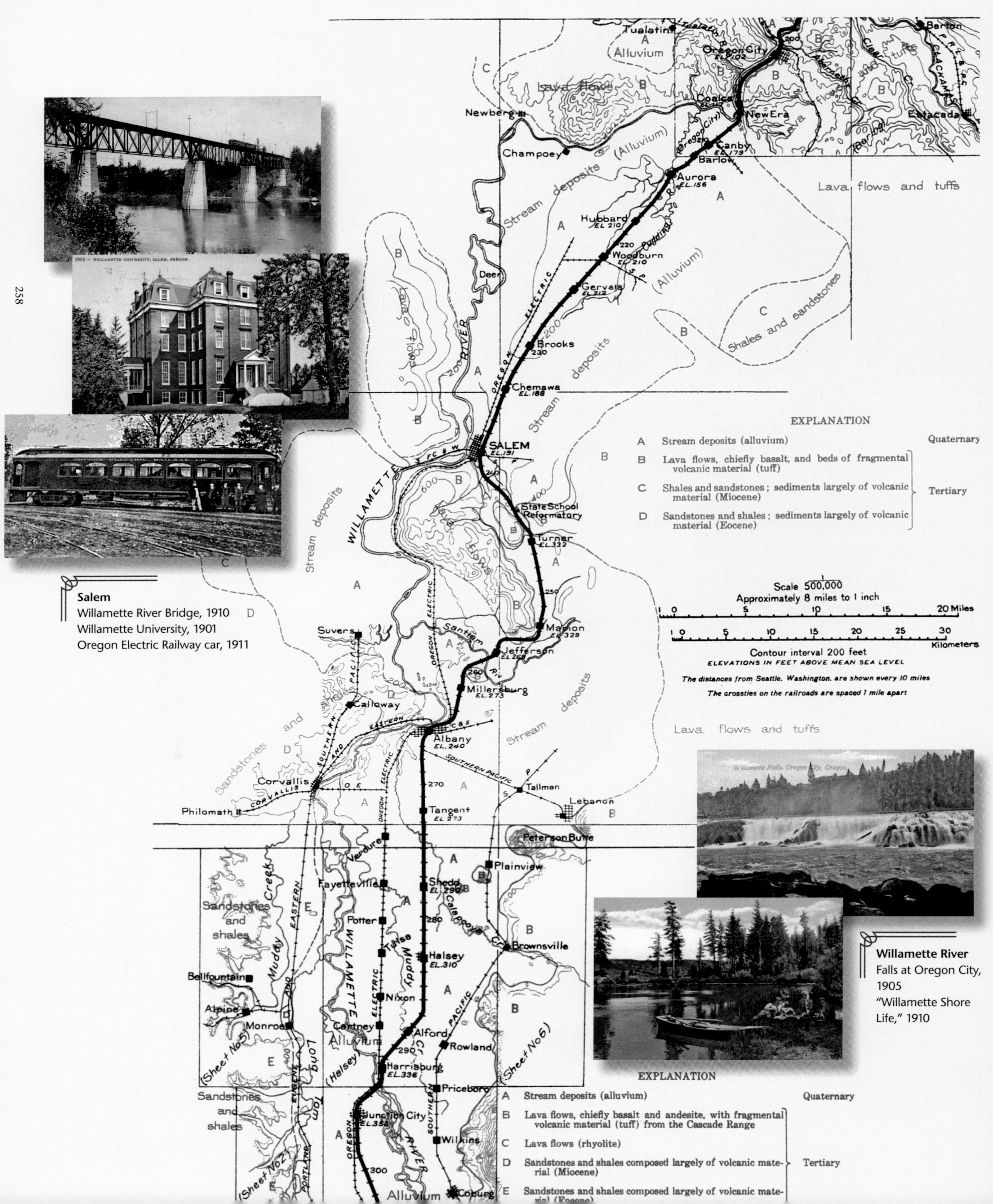
Tualatin
Alluvium
Oregon City EL.102
Barton
Clackamas
Estacada
Lava flows
Newberg
Coalca
New Era
Canby EL.179
Barlow
Champoey
Aurora EL.156
Lava flows and tuffs
Stream deposits
(Alluvium)
Hubbard EL 210
Woodburn EL 210
Gervais EL 212
Deer
Shales and sandstones
Brooks 230
Chemawa EL.188
Oregon Electric
River
Willamette
SALEM EL.191
State School Reformatory
Turner EL.332
Marion EL.329
Jefferson EL.262
Santiam Riv
Millersburg EL.273
Suvers
Calloway
Sandstones and shales
Albany EL.240
Southern Pacific
Tallman
Lebanon
Corvallis
Philomath
Tangent EL.273
Peterson Butte
Plainview
Verdure
Fayetteville
Shedd EL.290
Calapooya Cr.
Potter
Tulsa
Muddy
Halsey EL.310
Brownsville
Bellfountain
Nixon
Alpine
Monroe
Cartney
Alford
Rowland
Harrisburg EL.336
Priceboro
Junction City EL.353
Wilkins
Coburg
Long Tom
Muddy Creek
(Sheet No5)
(Sheet No6)
(Sheet No2)
(Halsey)
EXPLANATION
A Stream deposits (alluvium) — Quaternary
B Lava flows, chiefly basalt, and beds of fragmental volcanic material (tuff)
C Shales and sandstones; sediments largely of volcanic material (Miocene)
D Sandstones and shales; sediments largely of volcanic material (Eocene) — Tertiary
Scale 1/500,000
Approximately 8 miles to 1 inch
0 5 10 15 20 Miles
0 5 10 15 20 25 30 Kilometers
Contour interval 200 feet
ELEVATIONS IN FEET ABOVE MEAN SEA LEVEL
The distances from Seattle, Washington, are shown every 10 miles
The crossties on the railroads are spaced 1 mile apart
Willamette Falls, Oregon City, Oregon.
EXPLANATION
A Stream deposits (alluvium) — Quaternary
B Lava flows, chiefly basalt and andesite, with fragmental volcanic material (tuff) from the Cascade Range
C Lava flows (rhyolite)
D Sandstones and shales composed largely of volcanic material (Miocene) — Tertiary
E Sandstones and shales composed largely of volcanic material (Eocene)

Salem
Willamette River Bridge, 1910
Willamette University, 1901
Oregon Electric Railway car, 1911

Willamette River
Falls at Oregon City, 1905
"Willamette Shore Life," 1910

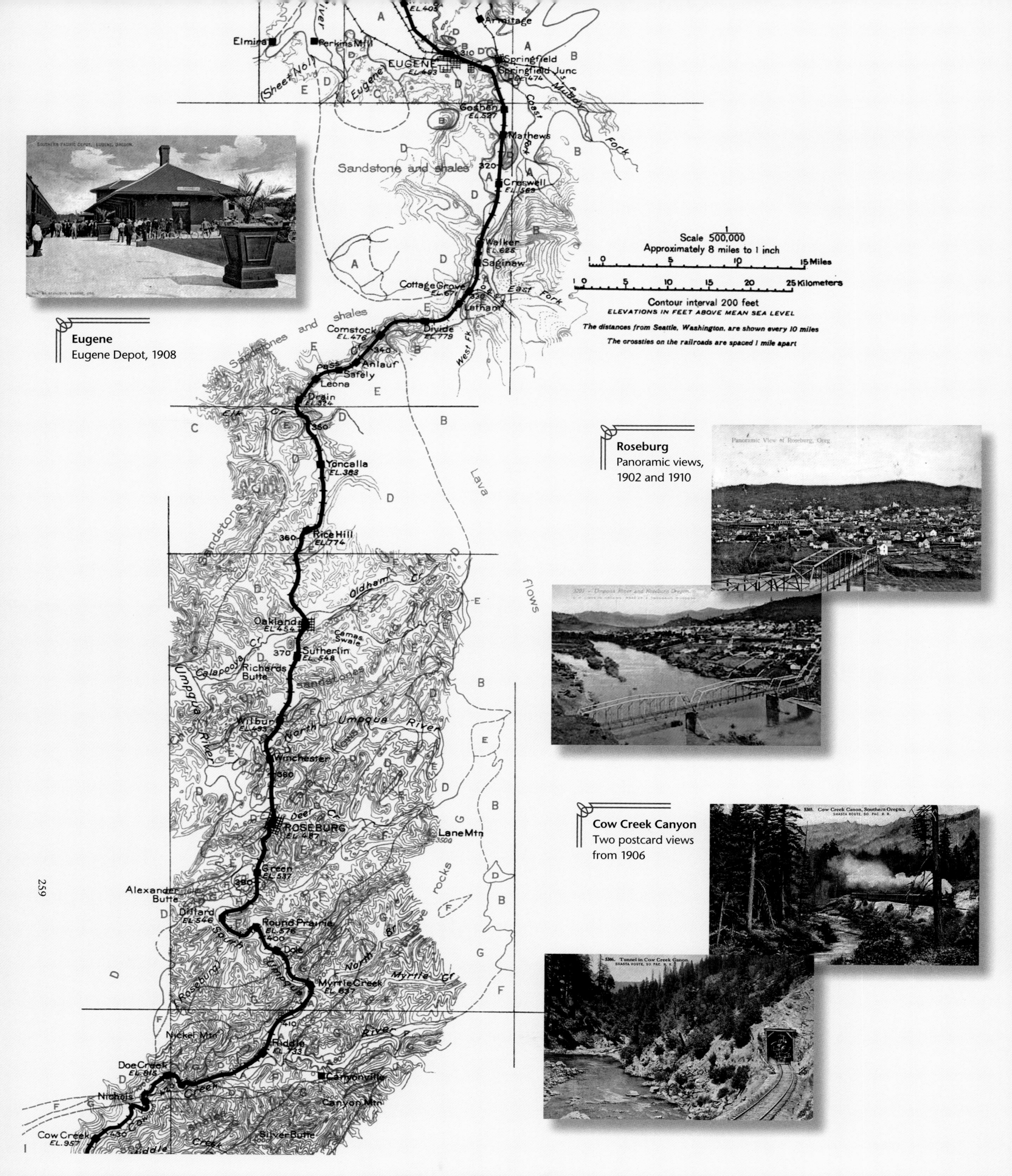

Eugene
Eugene Depot, 1908

Roseburg
Panoramic views, 1902 and 1910

Cow Creek Canyon
Two postcard views from 1906

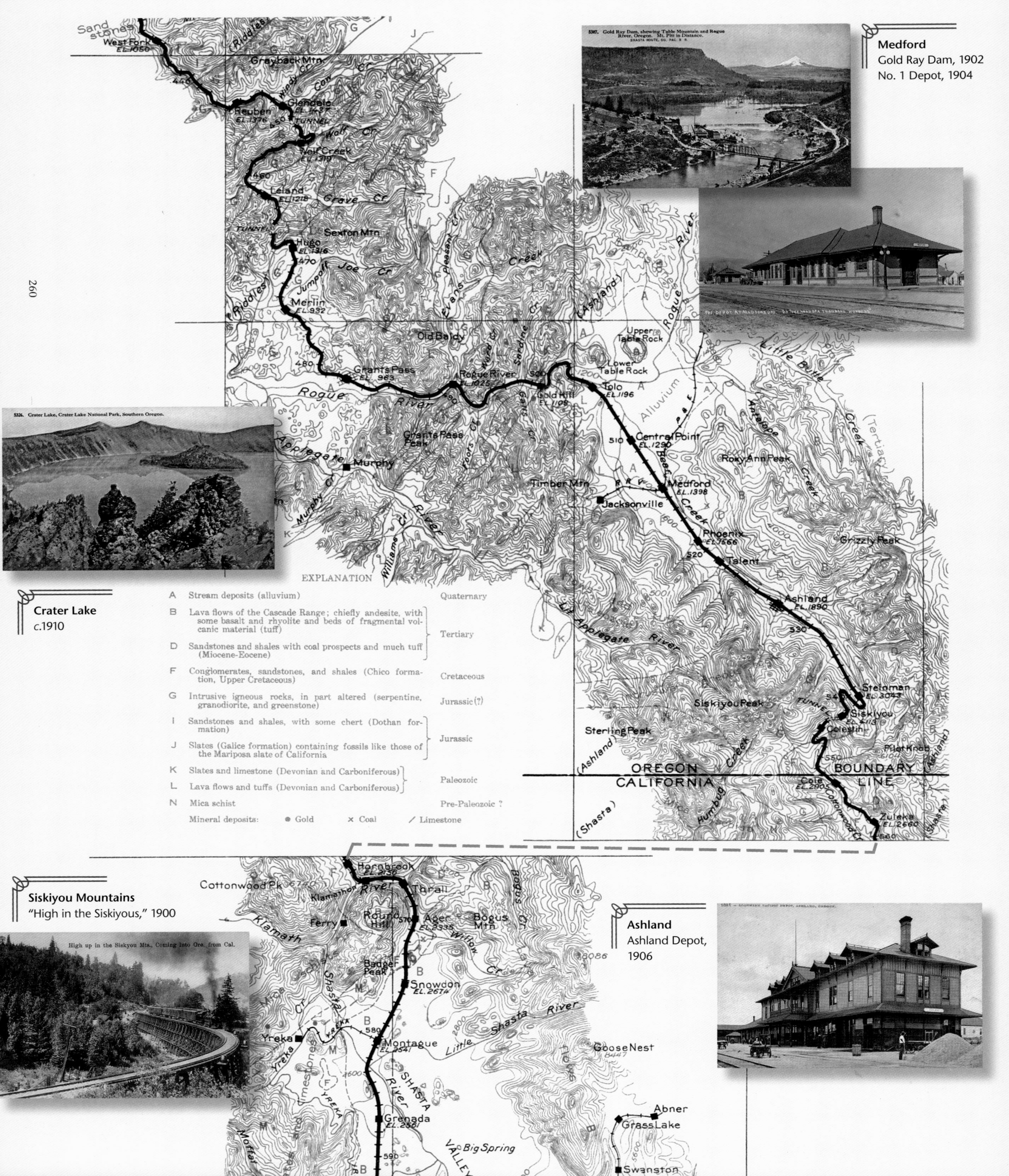

5387. Gold Ray Dam, showing Table Mountain and Rogue River, Oregon. Mt. Pitt in Distance.
SHASTA ROUTE, SO. PAC. R. R.
5326. Crater Lake, Crater Lake National Park, Southern Oregon.
High up in the Siskyou Mts., Coming Into Ore. from Cal.
West Fork EL.1050
Grayback Mtn.
Reuben EL.1376
Glendale EL.1437
TUNNEL
Wolf Creek EL.1319
Leland EL.1218
Grave Cr.
Sexton Mtn.
Hugo EL.1316
Jumpoff Joe Cr.
Merlin EL.932
Old Baldy
Grants Pass EL.963
Rogue River EL.1025
Gold Hill EL.1106
Upper Table Rock
Lower Table Rock
Tolo EL.1196
Central Point EL.1290
Medford EL.1398
Jacksonville
Timber Mtn.
Grants Pass Peak
Murphy
Applegate
Rogue River
Roxy Ann Peak
Phoenix EL.1566
Talent
Ashland EL.1890
Grizzly Peak
Lit. Applegate River
Siskiyou Peak
Sterling Peak
Steinman EL.3043
Siskiyou EL.4113
Colestin
Pilot Knob
OREGON
CALIFORNIA
BOUNDARY LINE
Cole EL.2900
Zuleka EL.2660
Hornbrook EL.2136
Cottonwood Pk.
Klamathon
Thrall
Ferry
Round Hill
Ager EL.2335
Bogus Mtn.
Badger Peak
Snowdon EL.2674
Yreka
Montague EL.2541
Shasta River
Goose Nest
Grenada EL.2581
Big Spring
Abner
Grass Lake
Swanston
EXPLANATION
A Stream deposits (alluvium) Quaternary
B Lava flows of the Cascade Range; chiefly andesite, with some basalt and rhyolite and beds of fragmental volcanic material (tuff) Tertiary
D Sandstones and shales with coal prospects and much tuff (Miocene-Eocene)
F Conglomerates, sandstones, and shales (Chico formation, Upper Cretaceous) Cretaceous
G Intrusive igneous rocks, in part altered (serpentine, granodiorite, and greenstone) Jurassic (?)
I Sandstones and shales, with some chert (Dothan formation) Jurassic
J Slates (Galice formation) containing fossils like those of the Mariposa slate of California
K Slates and limestone (Devonian and Carboniferous) Paleozoic
L Lava flows and tuffs (Devonian and Carboniferous)
N Mica schist Pre-Paleozoic ?
Mineral deposits: • Gold × Coal / Limestone

Medford
Gold Ray Dam, 1902
No. 1 Depot, 1904

Crater Lake
*c.*1910

Siskiyou Mountains
"High in the Siskiyous," 1900

Ashland
Ashland Depot, 1906

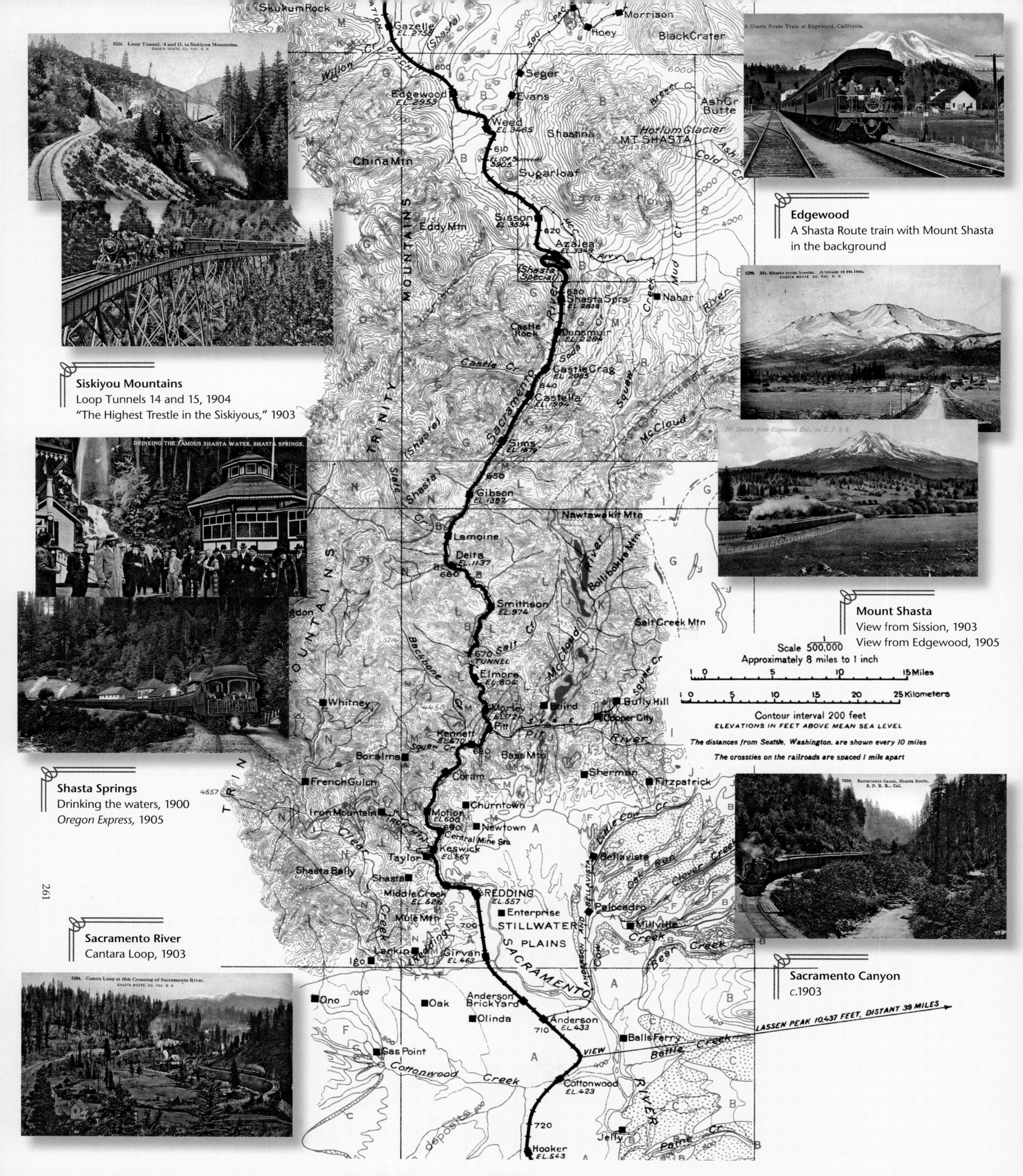

Edgewood
A Shasta Route train with Mount Shasta in the background

Siskiyou Mountains
Loop Tunnels 14 and 15, 1904
"The Highest Trestle in the Siskiyous," 1903

Mount Shasta
View from Sission, 1903
View from Edgewood, 1905

Shasta Springs
Drinking the waters, 1900
Oregon Express, 1905

Sacramento River
Cantara Loop, 1903

Sacramento Canyon
c.1903

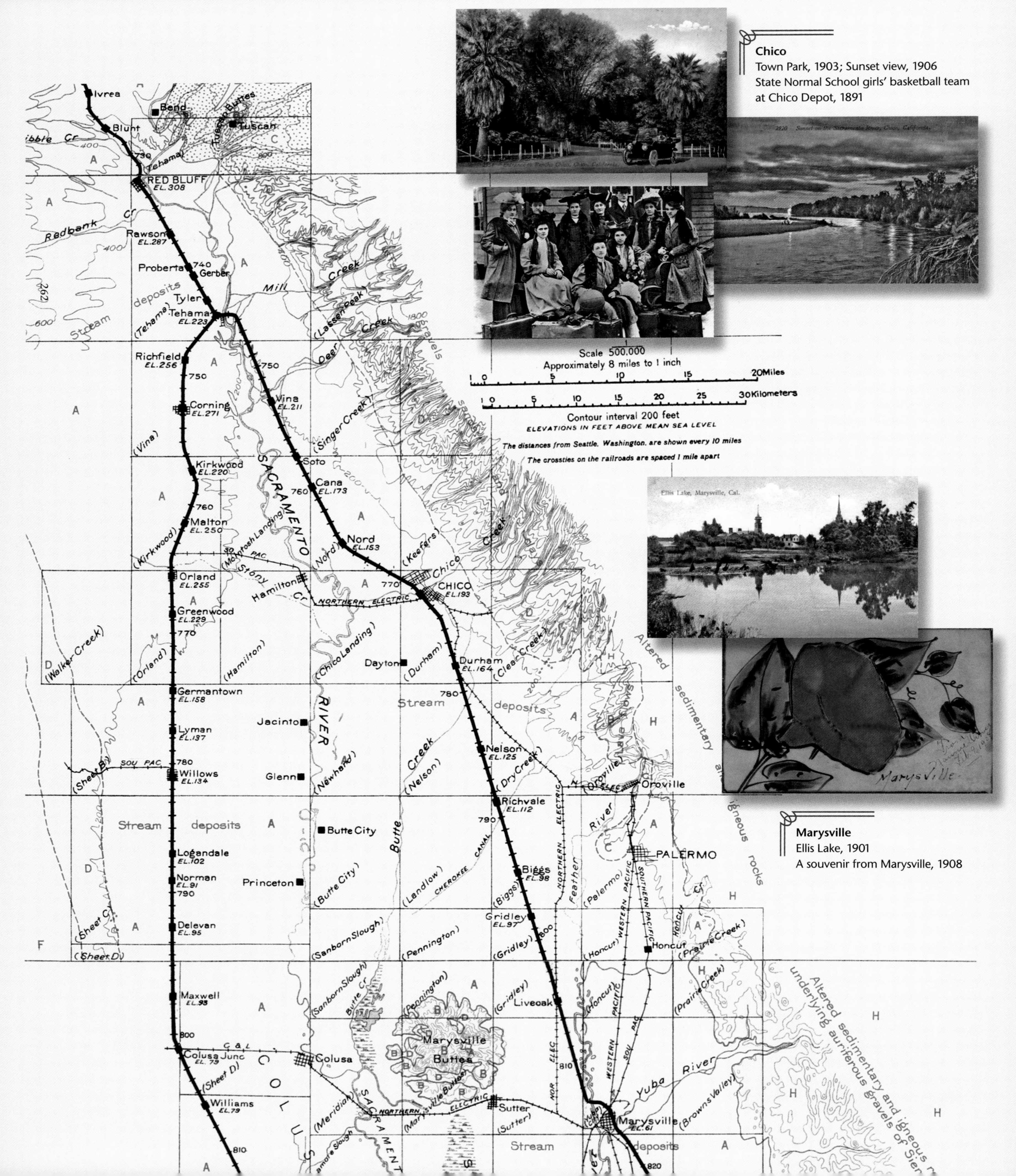

Chico
Town Park, 1903; Sunset view, 1906
State Normal School girls' basketball team at Chico Depot, 1891

Marysville
Ellis Lake, 1901
A souvenir from Marysville, 1908

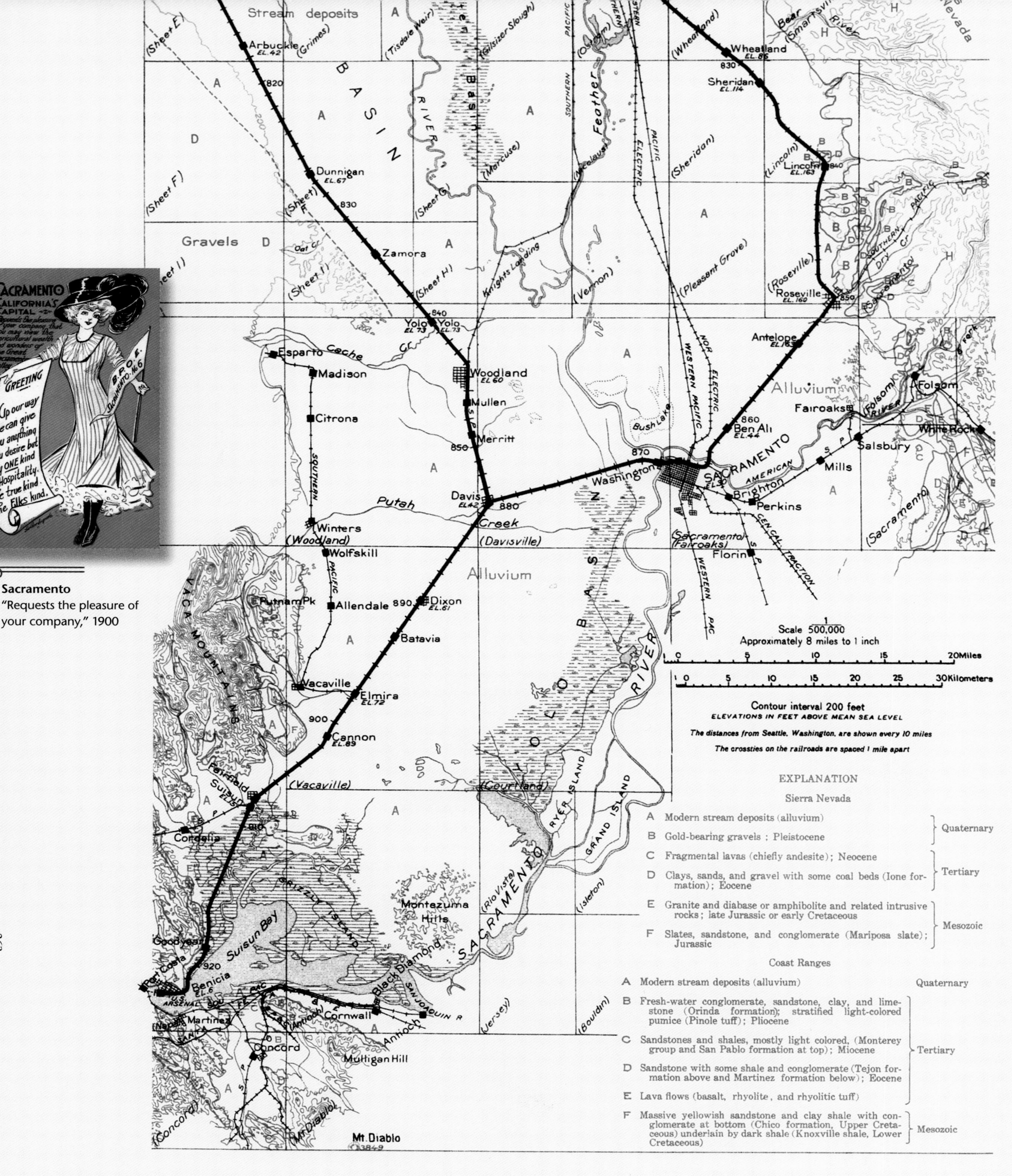
SACRAMENTO
CALIFORNIA'S CAPITAL
Requests the pleasure of your company, that you may view the agricultural wealth and wonders of the Great Sacramento Valley
GREETING
Up our way we can give you anything you desire but only ONE kind of Hospitality. The true kind. The Elks kind.
B.P.O.E. SACRAMENTO No. 6
Scale 1/500,000
Approximately 8 miles to 1 inch
0 5 10 15 20 Miles
0 5 10 15 20 25 30 Kilometers
Contour interval 200 feet
ELEVATIONS IN FEET ABOVE MEAN SEA LEVEL
The distances from Seattle, Washington, are shown every 10 miles
The crossties on the railroads are spaced 1 mile apart
EXPLANATION
Sierra Nevada
A Modern stream deposits (alluvium)
B Gold-bearing gravels ; Pleistocene
Quaternary
C Fragmental lavas (chiefly andesite); Neocene
D Clays, sands, and gravel with some coal beds (Ione formation); Eocene
Tertiary
E Granite and diabase or amphibolite and related intrusive rocks; late Jurassic or early Cretaceous
F Slates, sandstone, and conglomerate (Mariposa slate); Jurassic
Mesozoic
Coast Ranges
A Modern stream deposits (alluvium)
Quaternary
B Fresh-water conglomerate, sandstone, clay, and limestone (Orinda formation); stratified light-colored pumice (Pinole tuff); Pliocene
C Sandstones and shales, mostly light colored, (Monterey group and San Pablo formation at top); Miocene
D Sandstone with some shale and conglomerate (Tejon formation above and Martinez formation below); Eocene
E Lava flows (basalt, rhyolite, and rhyolitic tuff)
Tertiary
F Massive yellowish sandstone and clay shale with conglomerate at bottom (Chico formation, Upper Cretaceous) underlain by dark shale (Knoxville shale, Lower Cretaceous)
Mesozoic
SACRAMENTO
Stream deposits
Gravels
Alluvium
BASIN
Arbuckle
Dunnigan
Zamora
Yolo
Woodland
Mullen
Merritt
Davis
Esparto
Madison
Citrona
Winters
Wolfskill
Putnam Pk
Allendale
Dixon
Batavia
Vacaville
Elmira
Cannon
Fairfield
Suisun
Cordelia
Goodyear
Port Costa
Benicia
Martinez
Concord
Cornwall
Antioch
Mulligan Hill
Mt. Diablo
Montezuma Hills
Suisun Bay
Black Diamond
Wheatland
Sheridan
Lincoln
Roseville
Antelope
Ben Ali
Washington
Brighton
Perkins
Florin
Mills
Salsbury
Fairoaks
Folsom
White Rock
Putah Creek
Feather
VACA MOUNTAINS
GRIZZLY ISLAND
RYER ISLAND
GRAND ISLAND
SAN JOAQUIN R
AMERICAN RIVER
SOUTHERN PACIFIC
WESTERN PACIFIC
NOR ELECTRIC
CEN. CAL. TRACTION

Sacramento
"Requests the pleasure of your company," 1900

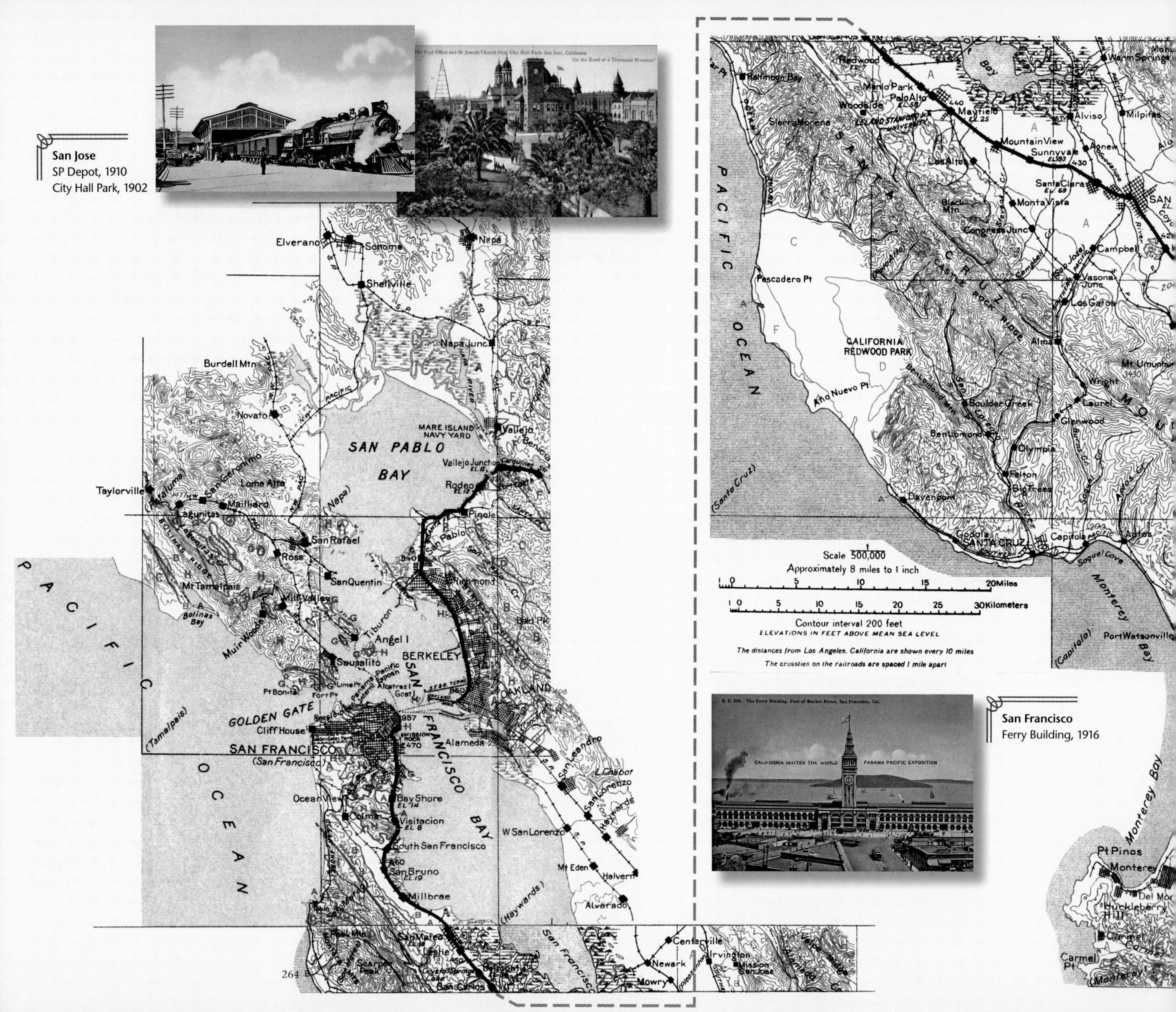

San Jose
SP Depot, 1910
City Hall Park, 1902

San Francisco
Ferry Building, 1916

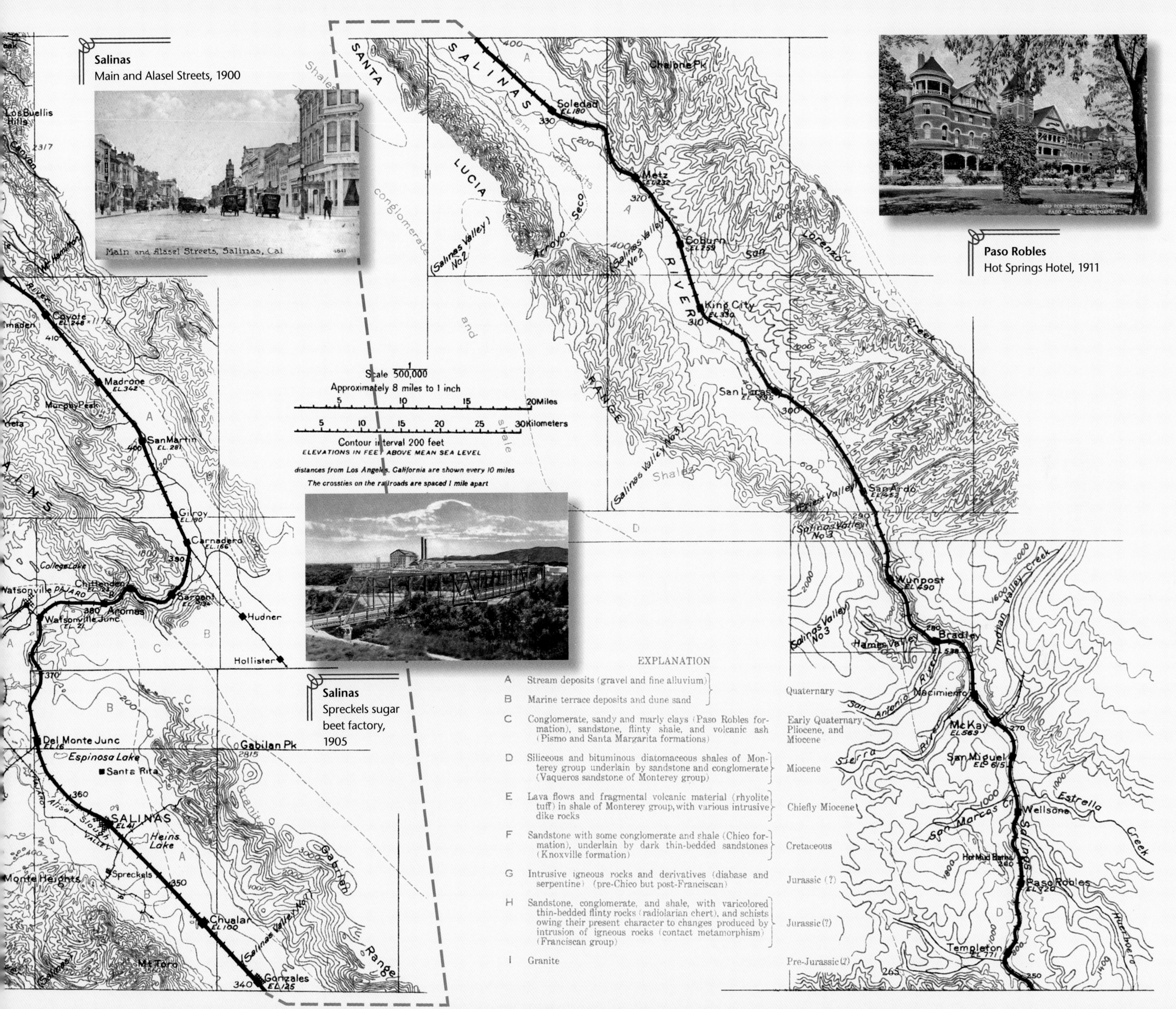
Main and Alasel Streets, Salinas, Cal
SANTA LUCIA RANGE
SALINAS RIVER
Chalone Pk
Soledad EL180
Metz EL232
Coburn EL259
King City EL330
San Lucas
San Ardo
Wunpost EL490
Bradley EL538
Nacimiento
McKay EL569
San Miguel EL615
Wellsona
Hot Mud Baths
Paso Robles EL720
Templeton EL771
Arroyo Seco
San Lorenzo Creek
Indian Valley Creek
San Antonio River
Estrella Creek
San Marcos Cr
Hames Valley
(Salinas Valley) No 2
(Salinas Valley) No 3
Salinas Valley No 1
Coyote EL248
Madrone EL342
Murphy Peak
San Martin EL281
Gilroy EL190
Carnadero EL166
College Lake
Chittenden
Sargent
Hudner
Hollister
Watsonville
Pajaro
Aromas
Watsonville Junc EL21
Del Monte Junc EL16
Espinosa Lake
Santa Rita
Gabilan Pk 2815
SALINAS EL41
Alisal Slough
Heins Lake
Spreckels
Monte Heights
Chualar EL100
Gonzales EL125
Mt Toro
Gabilan Range
Los Buellis Hills
Scale 1/500,000
Approximately 8 miles to 1 inch
5 10 15 20 Miles
5 10 15 20 25 30 Kilometers
Contour interval 200 feet
ELEVATIONS IN FEET ABOVE MEAN SEA LEVEL
distances from Los Angeles, California are shown every 10 miles
The crossties on the railroads are spaced 1 mile apart
EXPLANATION
A Stream deposits (gravel and fine alluvium)
B Marine terrace deposits and dune sand
Quaternary
C Conglomerate, sandy and marly clays (Paso Robles formation), sandstone, flinty shale, and volcanic ash (Pismo and Santa Margarita formations)
Early Quaternary, Pliocene, and Miocene
D Siliceous and bituminous diatomaceous shales of Monterey group underlain by sandstone and conglomerate (Vaqueros sandstone of Monterey group)
Miocene
E Lava flows and fragmental volcanic material (rhyolite tuff) in shale of Monterey group, with various intrusive dike rocks
Chiefly Miocene
F Sandstone with some conglomerate and shale (Chico formation), underlain by dark thin-bedded sandstones (Knoxville formation)
Cretaceous
G Intrusive igneous rocks and derivatives (diabase and serpentine) (pre-Chico but post-Franciscan)
Jurassic (?)
H Sandstone, conglomerate, and shale, with varicolored thin-bedded flinty rocks (radiolarian chert), and schists owing their present character to changes produced by intrusion of igneous rocks (contact metamorphism) (Franciscan group)
Jurassic (?)
I Granite
Pre-Jurassic (?)

Salinas
Main and Alasel Streets, 1900

Paso Robles
Hot Springs Hotel, 1911

Salinas
Spreckels sugar beet factory, 1905

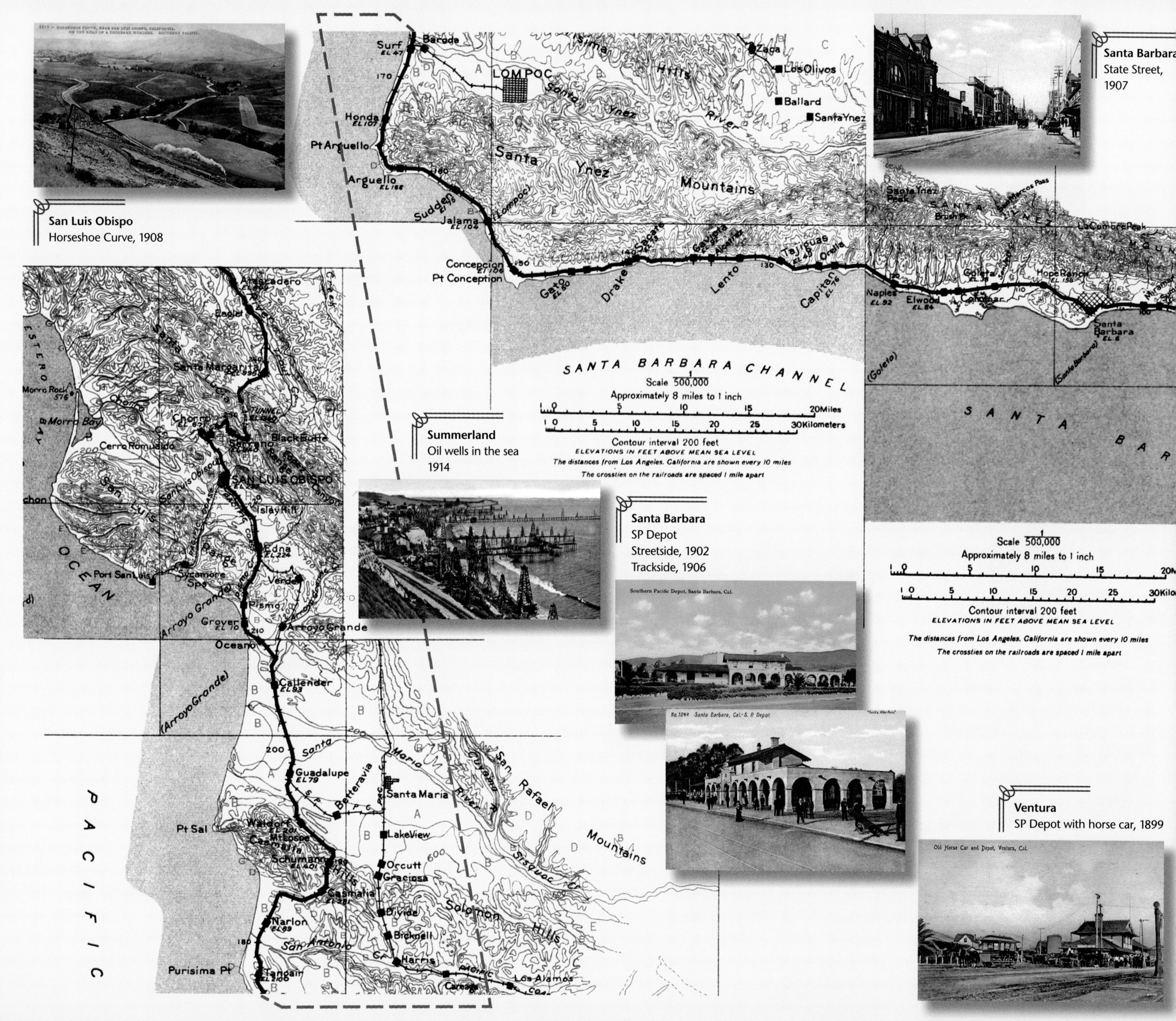

San Luis Obispo
Horseshoe Curve, 1908

Santa Barbara
State Street, 1907

Summerland
Oil wells in the sea
1914

Santa Barbara
SP Depot
Streetside, 1902
Trackside, 1906

Ventura
SP Depot with horse car, 1899

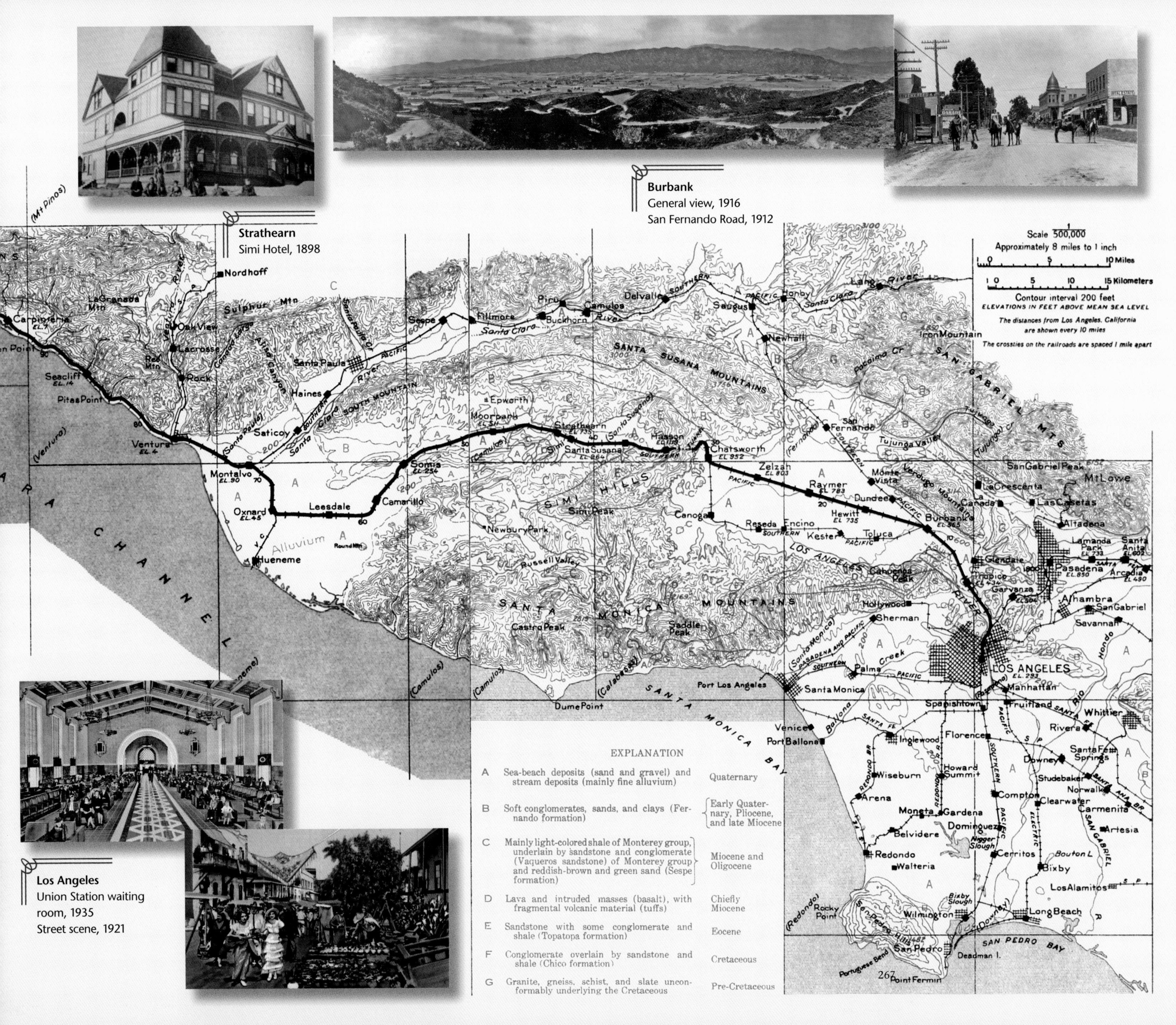

Strathearn
Simi Hotel, 1898

Burbank
General view, 1916
San Fernando Road, 1912

Los Angeles
Union Station waiting room, 1935
Street scene, 1921

THE ENTRANCE TO THE MOUNTAINS, NEAR BANFF, ALBERTA.

THE CANADIAN PACIFIC

THE MAIN LINE FROM CALGARY TO VANCOUVER

Cover of an 1893 publicity brochure (above).

"The entrance to the mountains, near Banff, Alberta," from *Rocky and Selkirk Mountains*, CPR News Service, *c.*1900 (left).

Today, Canada is connected from north to south and east to west by myriad roads, train tracks, and plane routes. While the distinct characters of individual provinces may well be more pronounced than the natures of many individual states in the United States to the south, Canada nonetheless has a strong and fairly well-integrated national character. Most contemporary Canadians (with the possible exception of Newfoundlanders) think of their Canada as a country first and a collection of provinces second.

In the mid- to late nineteenth century, however, Canada was a land divided. On one side were the developed, populated eastern provinces of Nova Scotia, New Brunswick, Quebec, and Ontario, which together formed the federal dominion of Canada in 1867. Prince Edward Island remained a colony of the United Kingdom until 1873; Newfoundland and Labrador, which together comprise a single province, was a colony of the UK until 1949.

On the other side of the continent, the fur trade and a series of gold rushes had brought rapid growth and development to the Pacific province of British Columbia (BC). Rich in natural resources and deep harbors, BC offered enormous opportunities. In between the two regions lay the vast expanses of the prairie provinces of Manitoba, Saskatchewan, and Alberta. Travel between the east and west was difficult at best, and was incredibly arduous through the mountain passes of the Rocky Mountains that extend up through southern British Columbia.

The importance of opening up the West was paramount if British Columbia and the eastern provinces were ever to be united in one country. To that end, the Canadian government established the North-West Mounted Police (now known as the Royal Canadian Mounted Police, or RCMP) to bring law and order to the western frontier lands, and sponsored the Dominion Lands Act of 1872 to encourage settlement in the Prairies. This granted 160 acres (65 hectares) of farmland to homesteaders for the price of $10 Canadian, all inclusive. For another $10 settlers had the option to double their land holdings—often a necessary measure in order to make a living farming wheat in the arid soil.

Getting to the West was still an enormous problem, however, and the government of British Columbia insisted upon the creation of a transportation link as a precondition for joining the Confederation of Canada. Although the province originally proposed a wagon road, the Conservative government of Prime Minister Sir John A. Macdonald announced the ambitious plan of building a railroad instead. Not only would a railway allow for the creation of a unified Canada, it would facilitate the movement of raw materials (largely from west to east) and manufactured goods (largely from east to west) far more quickly and in greater volume than a wagon road possibly could. Macdonald's original proposal for the creation of the rail line was a ten-year project, to be finished by July 20, 1881. There were many obstacles along the way, however, which delayed completion by several years.

Although the most geographically logical route for the train line was to dip down into the northern United States, the government of Canada was determined to keep the tracks

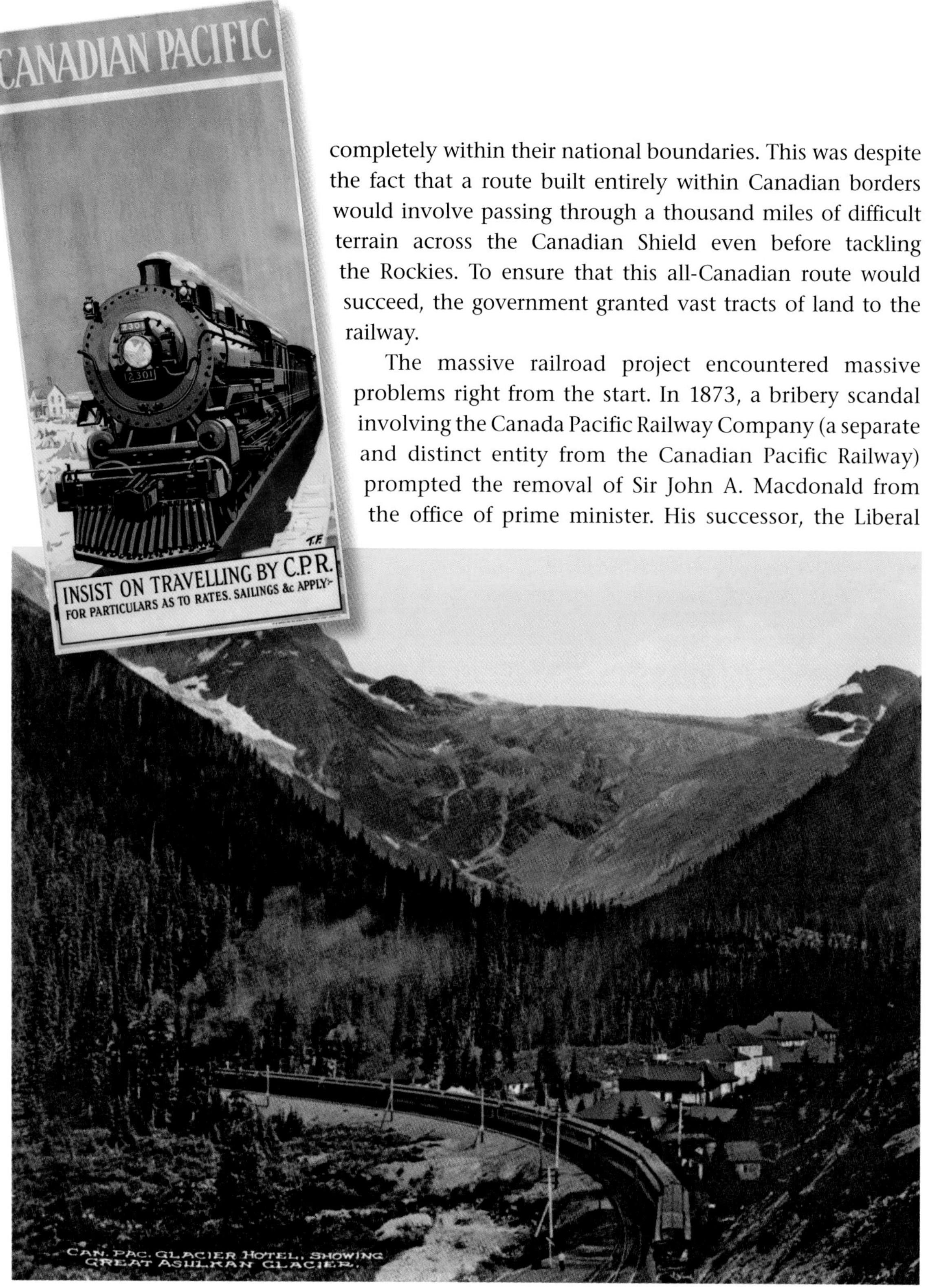

completely within their national boundaries. This was despite the fact that a route built entirely within Canadian borders would involve passing through a thousand miles of difficult terrain across the Canadian Shield even before tackling the Rockies. To ensure that this all-Canadian route would succeed, the government granted vast tracts of land to the railway.

CANADIAN PACIFIC
2301
T.F.
INSIST ON TRAVELLING BY C.P.R.
FOR PARTICULARS AS TO RATES, SAILINGS &c APPLY
CAN. PAC. GLACIER HOTEL, SHOWING
GREAT ASULKAN GLACIER.

The massive railroad project encountered massive problems right from the start. In 1873, a bribery scandal involving the Canada Pacific Railway Company (a separate and distinct entity from the Canadian Pacific Railway) prompted the removal of Sir John A. Macdonald from the office of prime minister. His successor, the Liberal Alexander Mackenzie, approved the construction of initial segments of railroad as a public project under the auspices of the Department of Public Works, although lack of public funds led to frustratingly slow progress.

In 1878 Macdonald returned to power, bringing an ambitious construction policy with him. He announced that the proposed railroad would follow the path of the Thompson and Fraser Rivers between Kamloops in south central British Columbia and the intended terminus of the line in Port Moody on the Pacific coast. The following year the federal government awarded a contract to builder Andrew Onderdonk (1848–1905) to construct the 128-mile section of track between Yale, BC, and Savona's Ferry on Kamloops Lake. Once that section had been successfully completed, more contracts were awarded to Onderdonk to build track between Savona's Ferry and Eagle Pass on one side, and between Yale and Port Moody on the other.

In 1880 the five businessmen Richard B. Angus, James J. Hill, John Stewart Kennedy, Duncan McIntyre, and George Stephen, along with two silent investors, Norman Kittson and Donald A. Smith, joined forces to form the Montreal-based Canadian Pacific Railway. This conglomerate negotiated a deal with the Canadian government to build the remaining sections of railway for the combined price of $25 million (roughly $625 million in 2009 prices) and a land grant of 25 million acres. On February 15, 1881—incidentally just around the time when Macdonald had expected to complete the line—the contract was given royal assent. On February 16, the Canadian Pacific Railway Company (CPR) was formally incorporated to begin its work.

The site of the CPR's first spike was Bonfield, Ontario (the grade to the east of Bonfield was the realm of another company, Canada Central Railway, which was later amalgamated with CPR). The route chosen by the CPR was strategic—within Canada's boundaries but close to the US border, it offered strong competition to existing American railways. One of the consequences of this strategic route, however, was that unlike the lands further north where the originally proposed route would have ran, the lands surrounding the southern tracks were too dry to support successful farms. It also crossed the territory of the Blackfoot First Nation. Their chief, Crowfoot, eventually accepted that construction was inevitable and agreed to allow the railway to cross, for which he was awarded a lifetime train pass.

Geographically, the new proposed route faced many challenges, such as Kicking Horse Pass, a mountain route across the continental divide that descended at a gradient of 4.5 percent, which was more than four times the recommended maximum gradient for rail lines at the time. Difficult terrain coupled with mounting costs made for slow progress, and in 1882 the CPR hired William Cornelius Van Horne (1843–1915), a proven talent as a railway executive, to oversee construction. Although a series of floods deterred progress, a respectable 417 miles of track were laid on the main line that year. By the end of the next year, the tracks reached through Winnipeg, Manitoba to the foothills of the Rocky Mountains,

and throughout 1884 and 1885 construction continued across that challenging range.

The work of building the rail line through the mountains was particularly difficult and dangerous, and did not hold much appeal for Canadian workers who could find employment elsewhere. As a result, the majority of the "navvies" who built the railway were emigrants, at first mostly British, Irish, and European. But when Andrew Onderdonk built the rail section through the canyons of the Fraser and Thompson rivers in British Columbia, many of the European emigrants who had worked on other sections of rail declined to risk their lives among the landslides and heavy use of explosives that characterized the mountain work.

As with the Central Pacific in the United States, Chinese labor quickly took their places. The Canadian government sanctioned the recruitment of 17,000 Chinese laborers from southern China's Guangdong province to work on the CPR. These Chinese workers were nicknamed "coolies," a term that literally means "bitterly hard use of strength" in Chinese and which quickly became a racial epithet in the West. Chinese navvies, some of them as young as twelve, earned low wages for difficult, high-risk work–sometimes as low as 75 cents a day, and although no accurate statistics were kept, it is believed that at least a thousand Chinese workers died during the construction of the railroad. The Chinese were not well-thanked for their work, either; once the last spike was driven in 1885, the Canadian government imposed a steep head tax on Chinese emigrants, a measure that was not taken with other emigrant groups.

Chinese work gang and camp on the CPR, mid-1880s (above).

1900s postcards (left)—CPR *Imperial Limited* leaving Glacier, Canadian Rockies; "Best Wishes from Canada."

CP advert, *c.*1920, featuring a train drawing by Fred Gardner (opposite top). By sponsoring artists to capture the scenery of the route, the CPR contributed to the development of the poster art genre.

Glacier Hotel showing the Great Asulkan Glacier, from *Rocky and Selkirk Mountains* (opposite bottom).

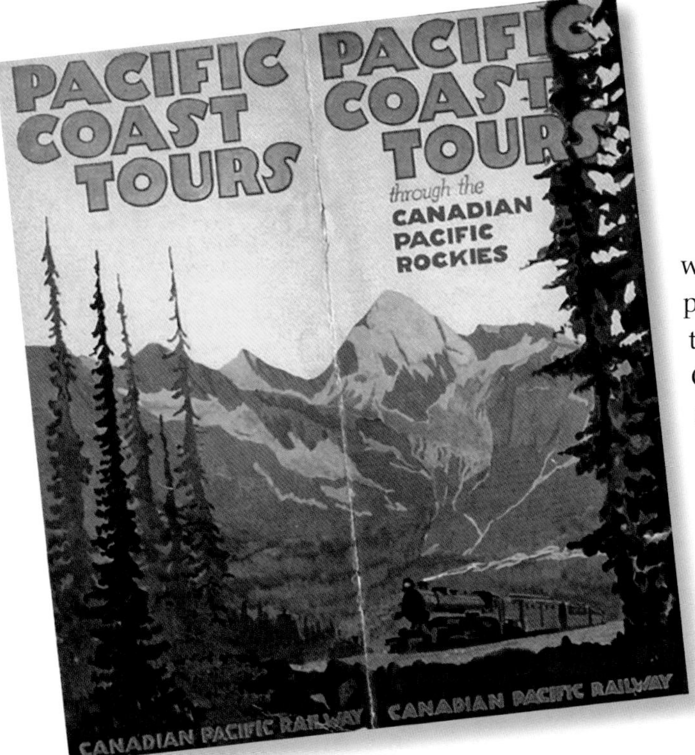

Cover of a CP "Pacific Coast Tours" brochure from the early 1920s (above).

Great Western Railway Station, Hamilton, *c.*1890 (below).

Cover of a CP "Trans-Canada Ltd" brochure, *c.*1915 (opposite top).

Illecillewaet Valley from Lookout Point, from *Rocky and Selkirk Mountains* (opposite bottom).

In fact, emigrants from other countries were warmly welcomed to Canada as part of the CPR's growth strategy. Once the western sections of rail were laid, Canadian Pacific agents worked to actively usher emigrants to Canada from many European countries. Emigrants could purchase a package from the company that included passage from Europe to Halifax on a Canadian Pacific ship, travel across the country on a CP train, and farmland waiting at the end of their journey, usually priced from $2.50 an acre. They then used that land to grow grain that was in turn shipped back east on CPR trains. Millions of agriculturalists, as well as other skilled and unskilled workers, arrived in Canada through CPR means between 1907 and 1930.

Even as the road neared completion in the 1880s, the railway was running short on funds. On January 31, 1884, the Railway Relief Bill was passed, which lent $22.5 million to the CPR. At this point, many Canadians publicly voiced doubts about the solvency of the railroad and the enormous amount of public funding sunk into the project. In early 1885, an uprising of Métis people in the District of Saskatchewan against the Dominion of Canada was bloodily quashed with the voluntary assistance of the railway, which transported troops to the region. (The Métis are a French-speaking community descended from First Nations peoples who intermarried with French Canadian settlers.) The outcome of this conflict, known as the North West Rebellion, significantly increased tensions between French Canadians and English Canadians. But as a result, public approval of the railway increased dramatically and the government loaned the CPR another much-needed $5 million to drive the road towards completion.

On November 7, 1885, Donald Smith drove the last spike at Craigellachie, BC. After the line was operational, it quickly became highly profitable, permitting the company to pay off its government debts years ahead of time. The CPR was the longest railroad in existence at the time, and had taken 5,000 horses, 12,000 men, and 300 dog sled teams to build. And yet, the road's exciting history was still in its infancy.

Even while the western crews were finishing the complicated mountain passes, crews in eastern Canada were increasing the CPR's network of lines throughout more populated areas. By 1885 they had launched a fleet of ships to transport cargo across the Great Lakes thereby linking rail lines on both sides of the Canadian–US border. The company acquired routes from other railroads, including the Ontario and Quebec Railway in 1884 and the Toronto, Hamilton and Buffalo Railway in 1895, which allowed the CPR to transport goods from all over Canada for export to the United States via New York.

On June 28, 1886, the CPR's first transcontinental passenger train left Montreal. It consisted of two first-class chair cars, two "regular" sleeper cars, two emigrant sleeper cars, one second-class chair car, a dining car, a mail car, and two baggage cars. Six days later, on July 4, it arrived at Port Moody. By the time this historic first train made its journey to the terminus, however, the CPR had already decided to extend the line to Vancouver (which then went by the quaint name of "Gastown," after loquacious local barman "Gassy Jack" Deighton). The communities of New Westminster, Victoria, and Port Moody

all held hopes of being chosen as the railroad's permanent terminus, but Vancouver was selected because of its natural deep harbor and related shipping industry potential. In 1887, the first train arrived in Vancouver.

In 1890, the company signed a 990-year lease for the New Brunswick Railway, which connected various towns and cities in Western New Brunswick, including the port city of Saint John. At the same time, the CPR built the International Railway of Maine between Saint John and Montreal, creating a transportation line for trans-Atlantic services that could operate throughout the entire year—previously sea ice blocking the port of Montreal had made cross-Atlantic travel and trade strictly a warm weather activity.

Approaching the turn of the century, the Canadian Pacific was the "King of Trade" in Canada. This coveted position attracted competition, however, especially from the Great Northern Railway, an American company which ran its lines as close to the Canadian border as it could manage. In order to both compete effectively with the GNR and access coal deposits found in the Elk River valley in the southern Canadian Rockies, the CPR built a second line across southern British Columbia. This was made possible in 1897 by $3.6 million of government aid, which was granted in exchange for "Crow Rate"—so called because the new line passed through the Rockies at Crowsnest Pass—which guaranteed a reduction in freight rates for grain products and other key commodities. The Crowsnest Pass line opened in 1899 connecting Lethbridge, Alberta to Nelson, British Columbia, and with the exception of a temporary suspension during the First World War, the Crowsnest Pass Agreement stayed in effect until 1983.

The years between 1873 and 1897 were considered by many, especially within the minority Liberal Party, to be a period of economic depression in Canada, especially compared to the spectacular economic growth that the United States enjoyed during the same period. The grain and lumber industries grew slowly but steadily, which would most likely not have been possible without the affordable, frequent, and (comparatively) rapid transport provided by the CPR. Canadian wheat was grown on the Prairies by farmers who were brought to the area and sold land by the Canadian Pacific, then it was transported by CPR trains throughout the country to industrial mills in Ontario and Quebec and finally by CP steam ships across the Great Lakes and the Atlantic ocean to reach international markets.

At the turn of the century there were two opposing views of the CPR and the Canadian West. Many Liberals, including leading politicians, tended to feel that the West did not offer great economic possibilities,

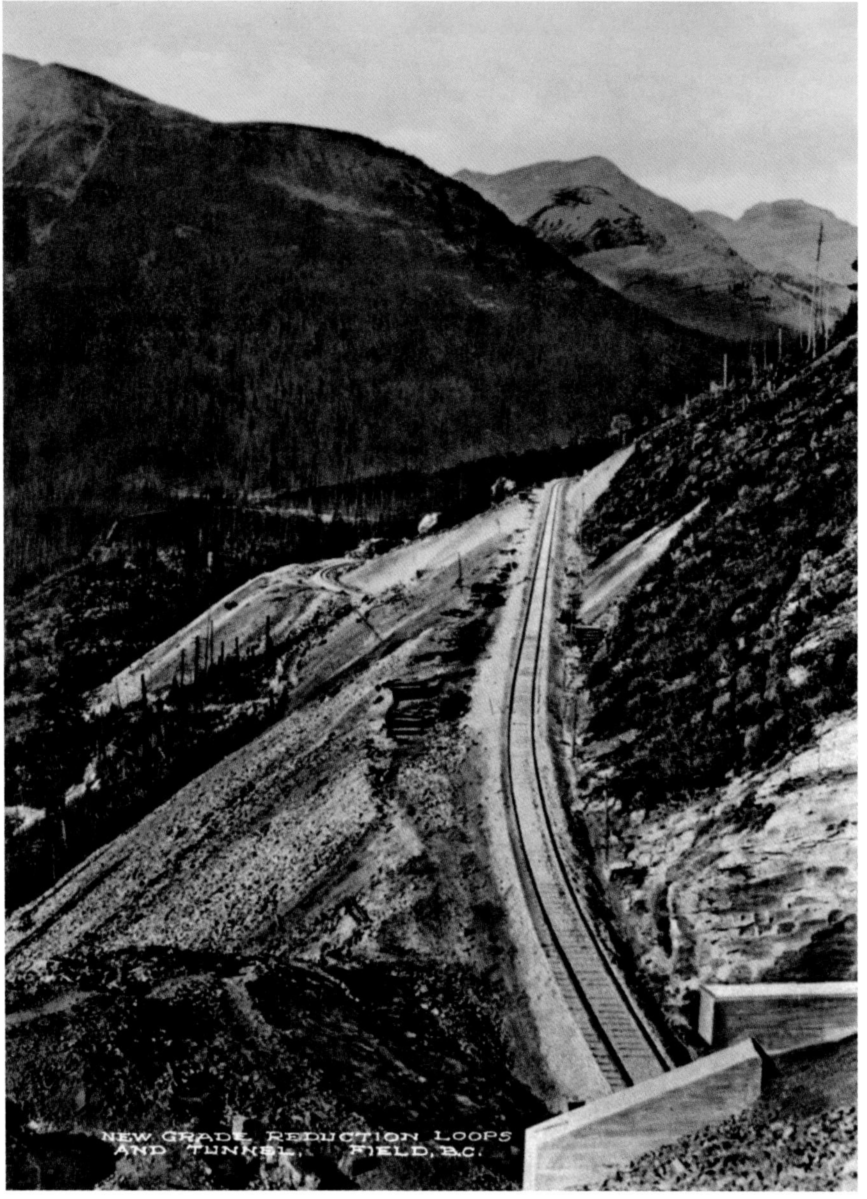

The Spiral Tunnels and loops of the newly reduced grade over Mount Stephen, Field, BC, from *Rocky and Selkirk Mountains* (above).

The Connaught Tunnel in the Rockies, from a 1920s CP brochure, artist unknown (opposite left).

CP poster advert, mid-1890s (opposite right).

whereas Conservatives pushed for commercial expansion, and some entrepreneurs thought that technological improvements in farming meant that the CPR had not developed a big enough freight shipment infrastructure.

The economic benefits related to the CPR's lines were felt most strongly in the major urban areas of the West, especially Vancouver. The other large city in Canada's ambitious western expansion was Calgary, which originated as a post of the North-West Mounted Police, and although now in the province of Alberta, was then part of the North-West Territories. It was not incorporated as a town until a year after the railway reached the area, in 1884. Ten years later the young community was enjoying a boom as an agricultural and commercial centre and had grown large enough to be incorporated as a city.

Canada is well known for long, cold winters—and nowhere in southern Canada, where the vast majority of people and developed resources are located, is this truer than in the high elevations of the Rockies. Nonetheless, the CPR went to great lengths to run trains as late in the winter and as early in the spring as possible in order to keep freight moving. The opening of the Panama Canal in 1914 had an enormous impact on shipping and trade around the world; in Canada this was particularly evident in Vancouver, as the city, which was once a shipping line terminus, became an influential point on a continuously flowing cycle of trade.

The CPR built—and bought—additional lines throughout the early twentieth century, and improved the main transcontinental line with the addition of the spiral tunnels at Kicking Horse Pass through the Continental Divide, the Connaught Tunnel in the Selkirk Mountains, and the Lethbridge viaduct over the Oldman River, Alberta. In 1912 the railroad extended the definition of "coast to coast" by purchasing the Esquimalt and Nanaimo Railway on Vancouver Island that connected to the mainland CPR line by railcar ferry. As well as dominating radio and telegraph services throughout the country, the Canadian Pacific also built, operated, and maintained several stunning hotels that became Canadian landmarks, including the Banff Springs Hotel, Chateau Lake Louise, and Hotel Vancouver. While the company had several competitors during this time, none were as profitable as the CPR. After the First World War, however, the federal government merged several bankrupt railways into Canadian National Railways, which then became the CPR's main competition.

Throughout the early decades of the twentieth century the Canadian Pacific also came to dominate steamship, lake, and river ferry service throughout British Columbia, thereby further consolidating its hold on the transportation network in the West. The company built its own steam locomotives, thus driving that industry as well. In addition to its monopoly

Montagnes Rocheuses
Le Tunnel Connaught

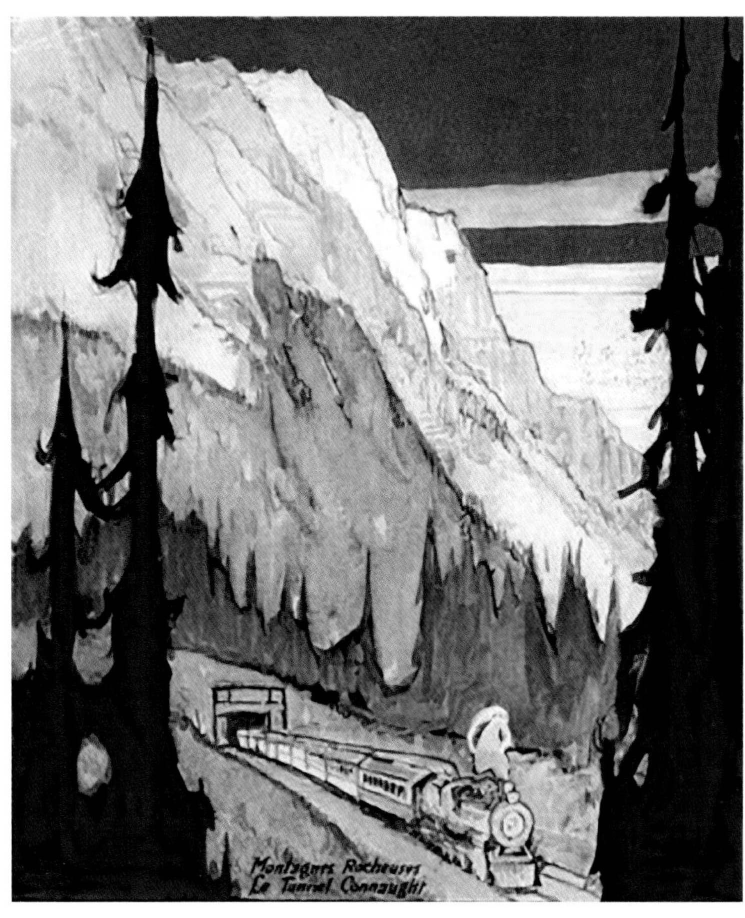

on grain transportation, the CPR also ran specialized silk trains, taking cocoons that had been shipped from the Orient to Vancouver all the way to manufacturers in New York and New Jersey. Silk trains took priority over all other trains on the line until the advent of nylon in the 1940s depressed the silk industry. At the same time, highway construction began to signal that the CPR was about to be toppled off its pedestal as the driving force behind Canadian commodities.

The legacy of the Canadian Pacific Railway is mixed. Contemporary Canada would not be what she is without it, and yet no one has the moral authority to say that progress was worth the number of lives lost in the construction of the line. For more than 120 years, the CPR has symbolized the struggles, hypocrisies, victories, and growth of Canada as a nation.

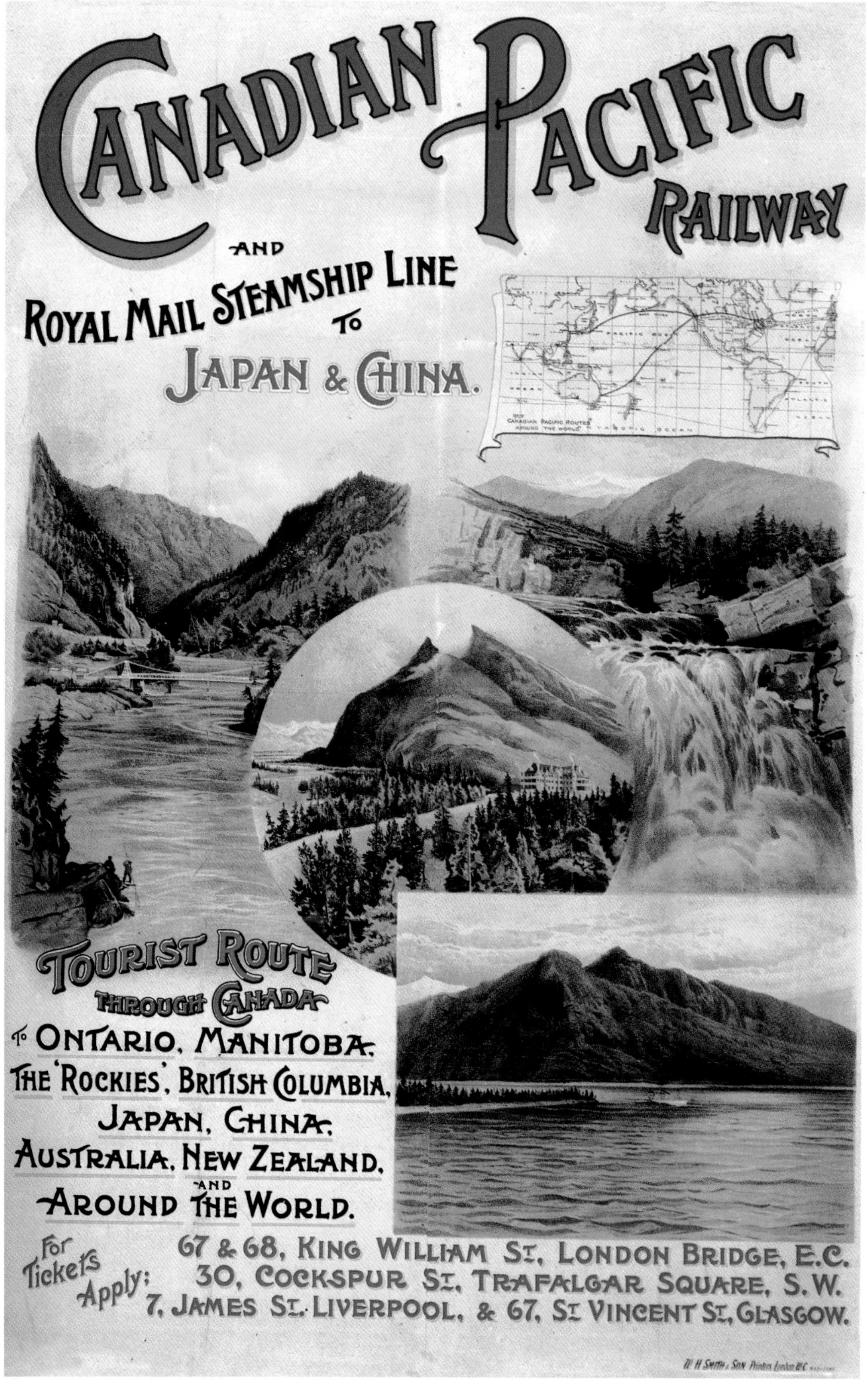

CANADIAN PACIFIC
RAILWAY
AND
ROYAL MAIL STEAMSHIP LINE
TO
JAPAN & CHINA.
TOURIST ROUTE
THROUGH CANADA
TO ONTARIO, MANITOBA.
THE 'ROCKIES'. BRITISH COLUMBIA.
JAPAN, CHINA.
AUSTRALIA, NEW ZEALAND.
AND
AROUND THE WORLD.
For Tickets Apply:
67 & 68, KING WILLIAM ST, LONDON BRIDGE, E.C.
30, COCKSPUR ST, TRAFALGAR SQUARE, S.W.
7, JAMES ST. LIVERPOOL, & 67, ST VINCENT ST, GLASGOW.

BANFF AND LAKE LOUISE

"We'll Import the Tourists"

The idea of "taking a holiday," while long a pastime of the wealthy, saw a huge rise in popularity as an activity for the middle and upper-middle classes in the second half of the nineteenth century. Initially the desire to escape the city and the workplace for the health-giving country air took the form of local excursions but later, as railroad and steamship transportation services began to improve, it became possible to visit seaside and mountain resorts. The resultant business of tourism was, by the last decades of the century, a well-developed and often lucrative enterprise.

Banff Springs Hotel, early 1900s.

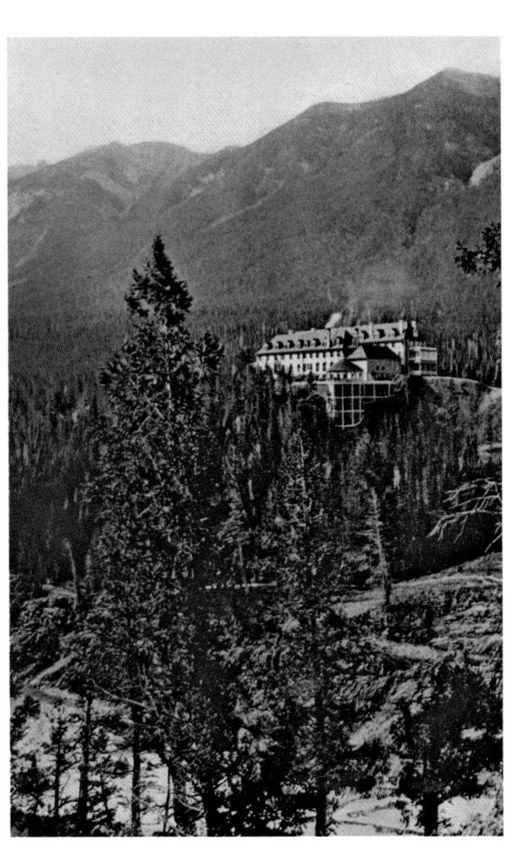

Because the cost of building the railway was so high, the Canadian Pacific immediately began examining every possible avenue to reduce its enormous debt load and to pay its heavy operating costs. So general manager William Cornelius Van Horne's response to the CPR's particularly expensive—and beautiful—mountainous section was a money-making proposition: "If we can't export the scenery, we'll import the tourists."

The CPR began its tourism venture with a look at the accommodations en route to the attractions of the Rockies. Van Horne felt that the company could best capture the tourism market by upgrading its sleeping, parlor, and dining cars. In the 1880s, the gold standard of rail tourism was the posh and elaborate Pullman parlor car, but Van Horne ordered deluxe models built to his own specifications, both longer and wider than their Pullman counterparts. He instituted ornate dining cars offering an expensive service, and the company also established its own restaurants at several train stops, especially in the mountainous regions where no other services existed.

Other measures the CPR undertook to promote tourism included opening and operating several deluxe hotels. On the route between Calgary and Vancouver, these included the Hotel Vancouver, which was built not just to lodge businessmen and tourists coming from the east and south, but also as a landing spot for wealthy travelers docking in Vancouver from the company's "Empress" ocean liners. To further attract the "right" crowd, CPR built an opera house adjacent to the hotel.

As time progressed, the CPR focused its efforts more and more on publicizing Banff in the Rockies and the surrounding area in Alberta, making it a featured stop for British tourists traveling to and from the Orient and promoting the area as a paradise for hunters and fishermen. In 1885, the Canadian government declared an area equal to ten square miles around the Banff hot springs to be reserved land, a territory that was increased in 1887 to 260 square miles. The following year, the CPR opened the Banff Springs Hotel. Designed by architect Bruce Price, it is stunningly situated just above the waterfall of Bow Falls, and the view from the hotel shows Mount Rundle, a peak renowned for its exposed, ancient seabeds. Both thermal springs and the town of Banff are within walking distance of the hotel. The architecture of the hotel itself is Scottish Baronial, creating a stunning contrast of human-built finery against magnificent, natural, mountain landscape.

As business grew, the railroad decided to open another deluxe resort in Banff, the Chateau Lake Louise. This elegant structure, situated on the eastern shore of the eponymous Lake

Lake Louise Laggan and Lake Louise Hotel, from *Rocky and Selkirk Mountains.*

"Trans-Canada Limited," a CP brochure cover from *c*.1917.

Glacier House, early 1900s (below).

The CPR hotel at Banff, Alberta, in 1903 (opposite).

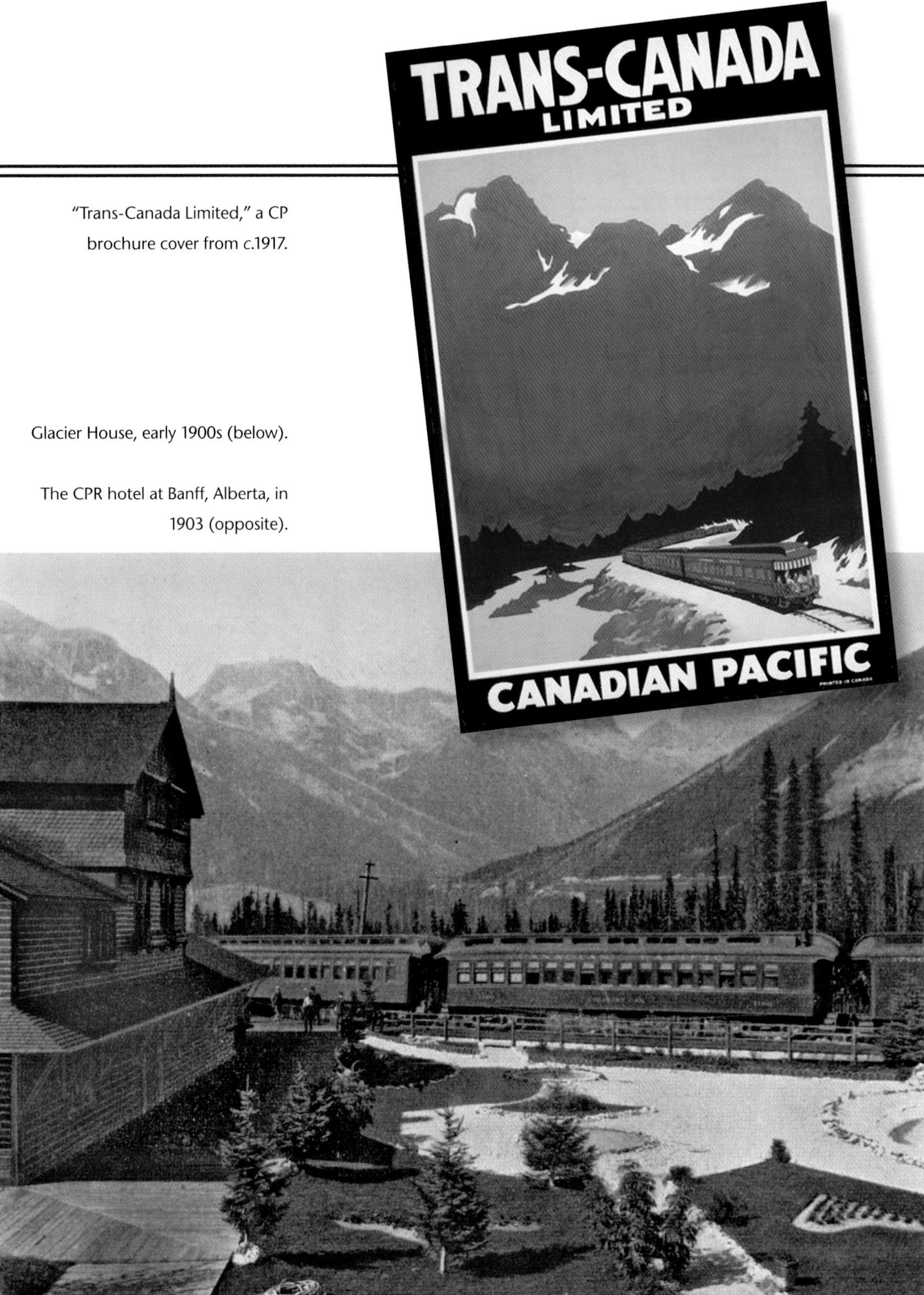

Louise, was built to take advantage of the stunning Victoria glacier rising above and the emerald green lake below.

The CPR also built less glamorous hotels that nonetheless served to support and bolster tourism as well as eliminate the need for dining cars, which were a heavy addition to the trains. These more humble offerings included the Fraser Canyon House at North Bend, BC; Glacier House near the summit of the Selkirks, and Mount Stephen House at Field on the Kicking Horse River, BC. Passenger trains stopped at these hotels to allow travelers to eat and stretch their legs before continuing the journey, making train travel an overall more pleasant experience. All three had spectacular mountain scenery and made for romantic, leisurely pit stops.

Beyond meals and accommodation, the CPR met customer interests by offering Swiss guides (genuine emigrants from Switzerland) to lead mountaineers through the Rockies for $5 a day. Ultimately, Van Horne conceived of the railway art school, a cultural venture that not only shaped and enhanced Canadian tourism but also was fundamental in developing Canadian art and artists. This scheme allowed both well-known and budding artists to take the train for free to beauty spots as long as they offered their work first to the CPR. The resultant portfolio of great advertising contributed to the development of poster art.

From this philosophy of "capitalizing the scenery" the CPR developed its overwhelming presence in Canadian tourism. By the 1920s, its tourist operations embraced Canada from coast to coast and spanned the globe. For several decades its advertising delineated the view of Canada—as a place of scenic wonders and cultural diversity—that was accepted both at home and around the world, and prevails even to this day.

BIG HILL

The Spiral Tunnels

Mount Stephen seen from the CPR line, from *Rocky and Selkirk Mountains* (opposite).

Two views of Lower Kicking Horse Canyon near Golden (below).

The "Big Hill" is the nickname given to Mount Stephen, British Columbia, in the Canadian Rockies just west of the Continental Divide. The pass over Mount Stephen is called Kicking Horse Pass, as it descends down the steep, massive slope to the Kicking Horse River, and the grade built over the Big Hill pass in 1884 constitutes one of the most ambitious, and possibly foolhardy, undertakings in the history of railroads.

The route, while seemingly unsurpassed in difficulty, was also very direct, saving several hours over the more northern Yellowhead Pass crossing. Rather than blast a 470-yard tunnel through the mountain, the CPR decided to build a temporary, eight-mile-long track over the pass. Although the standard upper limit for a track grade was 2.2 percent, in order to summit the Big Hill it was necessary to create a line twice as steep—at a gradient of 4.5 percent—to achieve the descent from Wapta Lake to the base of the mountain along the Kicking Horse River. The CPR claimed that this situation was temporary, but the steep tracks remained in operation for 25 years, until the completion of the Spiral Tunnels in 1909.

The company installed a series of three safety switches and set the speed limit for descending trains at a cautious six miles per hour for freight trains and eight miles an hour for passenger consists.—it was safer for passenger trains to go a little faster because they were, generally, far lighter than freight trains and therefore able to brake more efficiently. The safety switches led to short "runaway" spurs, each of which had a sharp reverse upgrade. A further safety precaution was to keep the switches turned to the uphill position until the switch operator was confident that the train descending toward him was in control.

The standard steam locomotives, called 4–4–0s (so named for the number and configuration of their guide and driving wheels) were ineffective against the Big Hill. In 1884 the CPR engaged the Baldwin Locomotive Works of Pennsylvania to build more powerful locomotives, called 2–8–0s, as "pusher" engines to help get the trains over the difficult grade. Then in 1887 the CPR began building its own units, eventually constructing hundreds of 2–8–0s for use over the Big Hill and for its other lines. The town of Field, BC, was created by the company as a pit stop, as a base for the switchmen, and particularly as a place to house additional locomotives for trains to summit the Big Hill.

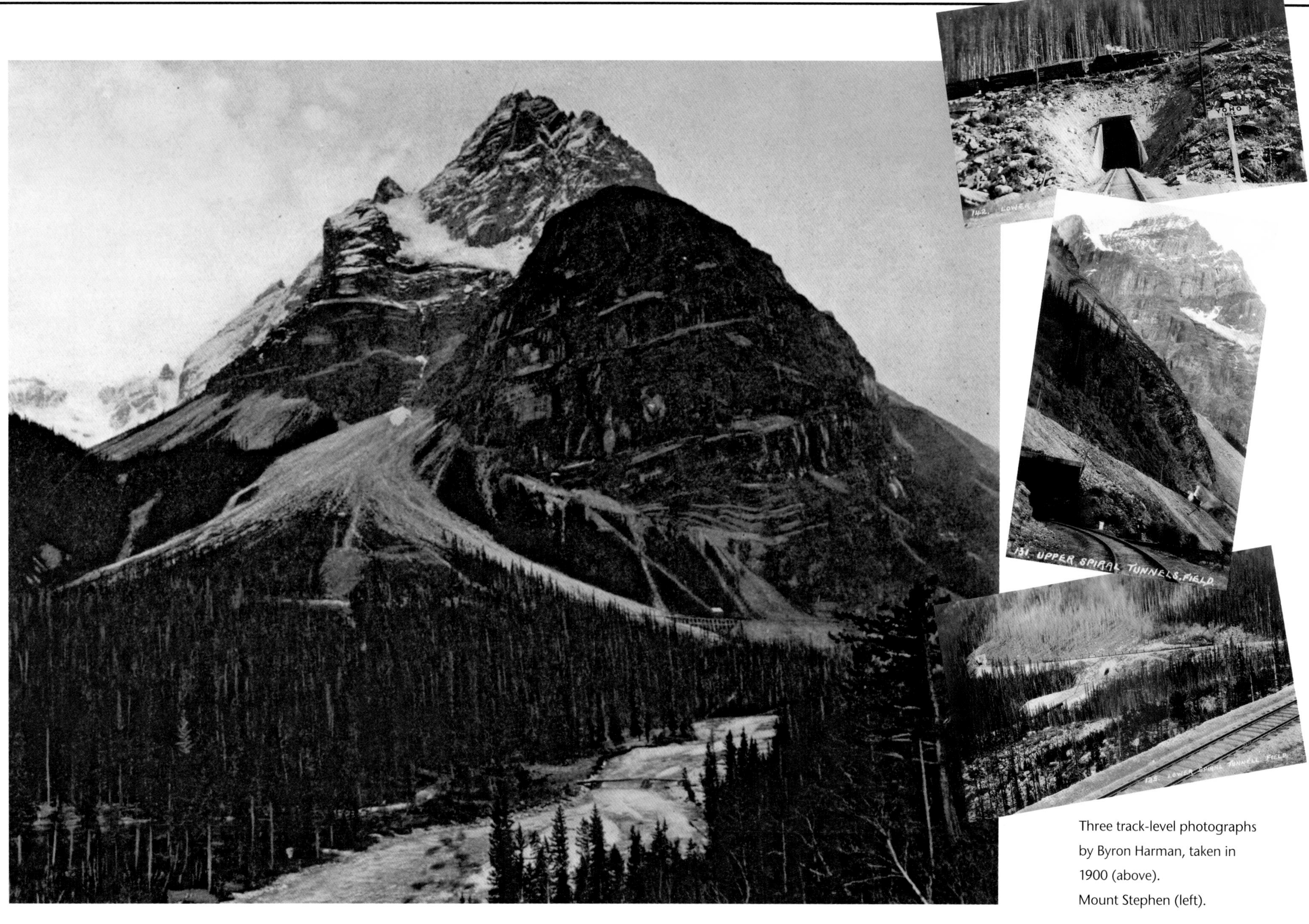

Three track-level photographs by Byron Harman, taken in 1900 (above).
Mount Stephen (left).

New grade reduction showing Mount Stephen and Kicking Horse River, from *Rocky and Selkirk Mountains* (far right).

The village of Field showing the CPR's Mount Stephen Hotel and Kicking Horse River (right).

A CP poster souvenir from 1906 of the Spiral Tunnels (below).

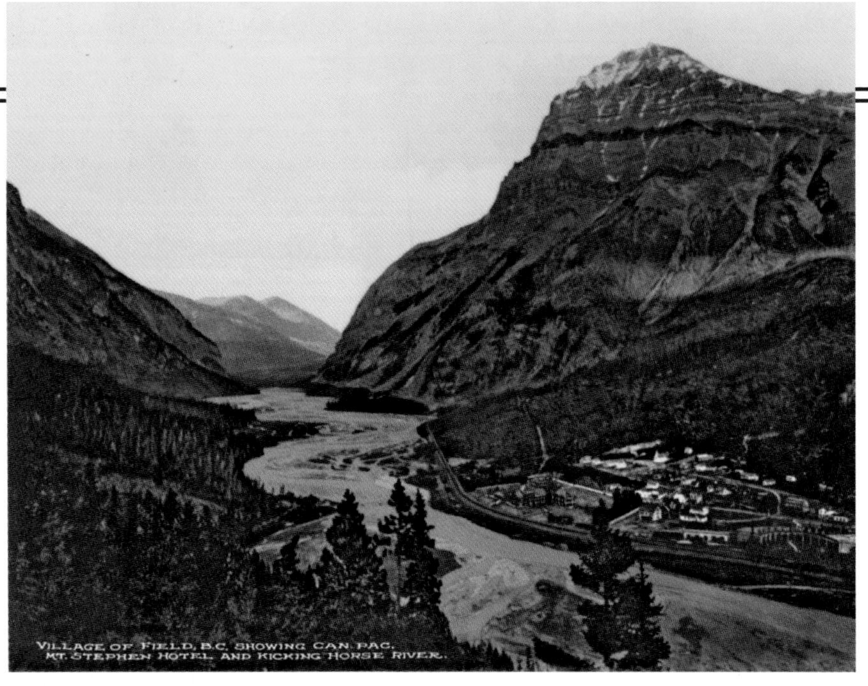

The town was named Field after Chicago businessman C. W. Field, who was being courted by the CPR as an investor.

Despite these safety measures, many disastrous incidents occurred on this heart-stopping section of line, and it became obvious that the company needed to replace the difficult "temporary" grade. In 1906, work on a new solution for the steep Big Hill section was begun under the supervision of the CPR's senior engineer, John Edward Schwitzer (1870–1911). He first considered reducing the gradient of the hill by extending the tracks to the south side of the river valley, but ultimately dismissed this approach as too risky due to frequent avalanches and landslips. Eventually, he decided that tunneling was the best solution, and employed MacDonnell, Gzowski and Company to do the work, using a labor force of 1,000 men at a cost of roughly $1.5 million (Canadian).

Mount Stephen's tunnels quickly became known as the "Spiral Tunnels." The scheme consisted of two separate tunnels, each rotating 270 degrees (three-quarters of a circle) behind the valley walls. Tunnel No. 1 was the higher of the two and descended under Cathedral Mountain for 1,000 yards to the south of the original tracks. Trains emerging from this tunnel ran in the transverse direction from the entrance point and fifty feet lower down before crossing the Kicking Horse River and entering Tunnel No. 2 under Mount Ogden to the north. This second tunnel was just a few yards shorter than the first with a similar descent. Trains exiting Tunnel No. 2 were then fully turned round to face back in the proper direction. While this solution doubled the length of the descent, it did reduce the gradient to a reasonably safe 2.2 percent, but even with this feat of engineering, the CPR found it necessary to continue using the 2–8–0 engines to ensure safe travel through the pass.

NEW GRADE REDUCTION SHOWING
MOUNT STEPHEN AND KICKING HORSE RIVER.

SELKIRK MOUNTAINS

From a Pass to a Tunnel

The Connaught Tunnel in the Selkirk Mountains, from a CPR brochure of 1920 (below).

Loop showing four tracks near Glacier, 1903 (below right).

AVOIDING THE AVALANCHES

In the heart of the Selkirk Mountains, part of what is now Glacier National Park, British Columbia, lies the historic Rogers Pass. When the CPR made the decision to route through the Selkirks, the mountains were largely unexplored. Surveying the region was a forbidding job, for which the CPR hired a forbidding man. Major Albert Bowman Rogers (1829–89) had served with the United States Cavalry before going on railroad surveys of the American prairies. In April 1881, he began his search for a mountain crossing with the promise of a $5,000 bonus and the honor of giving his name to the pass.

An 1865 expedition—led by Walter Moberly assisted by Albert Perry—had already identified the general area of Rogers Pass as a potential approach. On May 28, 1881, Rogers approached from the west, but ran out of provisions and had to turn back eighteen miles short of the pass's summit. In July 1882 he approached from the east to successfully reach the pass. Suitably proud of his accomplishment, Rogers elected to frame his payment check, rather than cash it. Only when CPR president William Van Horne gave him a souvenir gold watch as a replacement did Rogers take his compensation to the bank.

Track was laid over the pass in 1884 and the grade included some of the largest trestles and bridges anywhere on the CPR line. A series of loops on the west side of the pass were necessary to navigate the steep incline and avoid the worst avalanche areas: The pass is particularly known for its winter snowfall, which averages 32 feet a year. After the section was completed in 1885, the CPR shut it down temporarily to observe avalanche activity in the area, and as a result the next year the company built 31 snowsheds along four miles of Rogers Pass to protect the tracks from avalanches.

In 1899, eight people died in an avalanche that also destroyed a train station at the pass. In 1910, a crew working to clear a snow slide was caught in a second avalanche, killing 62 people. These tragedies spurred the building of the Connaught Tunnel, which extended for five miles beneath the mountains. Foley Bros. Welch and Stewart used compressed air equipment and more than 300 laborers to complete the task at a cost of $5.5 million. The years between 1913 and 1916 saw the successful construction of this magnificent tunnel, characterized by its mild grade of 0.95 percent and a clear sightline for the entire five miles.

The Great Glacier of the Selkirks, from *Through Mountains and Canyons*, published by Notman & Son, Montreal, in 1902.

GRAIGELLACHIE

The Last Spike

The final spike of the Canadian Pacific Railway was driven at Craigellachie, west of the Eagle Pass summit, BC, at 9.22 a.m. on November 7, 1885, joining the eastern and western sections of the line–and of the country–together. Railroad financier Donald Smith (1820–1914), the eldest of the four CPR directors present, did the honors, using a conventional iron spike. He hit the spike awkwardly, denting it, and it was quickly substituted for another, but this error did not detract from his services to the railroad; he was later knighted and then elevated to Lord Strathcona.

An ornamental silver spike had been created for the occasion, but was not available for the ceremony as the Governor General, who had it in his possession, was called back to Ottawa on business and therefore could not attend. Furthermore, the original iron spike was removed shortly after the ceremony to prevent souvenir hunters from stealing it.

"The Last Canadian Spike," painted by Geoffrey Grier in 1945 (below).

Mural at the entrance to The Last Spike memorial at Craigellachie (opposite).

While the official driving of the last spike happened four years after the original deadline for the completion of the railroad, it was a most impressive six years before the revised deadline that Macdonald had issued in 1881. The condition of the railway was rough; it was another seven months after the last spike ceremony before the tracks were usable for passenger service, and other odds and ends of construction delayed final completion until June 1886. Nonetheless, the driving of the last spike was an important symbol of national unity. Freight began shipping immediately and the rest, as they say, is history.

Early rail passengers craned out of windows to see the historic spot, but today only freight trains pass through Craigellachie, although it is still a popular tourist destination for visitors arriving by auto along the highway that follows the line of the railroad. Stones from every province and territory of the nation were used to build the monument marking the site.

Canadian poet E. J. Pratt caught the spirit of the occasion of the last spike in his 1952 narrative poem *Towards the Last Spike*:

> The east–west cousinship, a nation's rise,
> Hail of identity, a world expanding,
> If not the universe: the feel of it
> Was in the air–"Union required the Line."

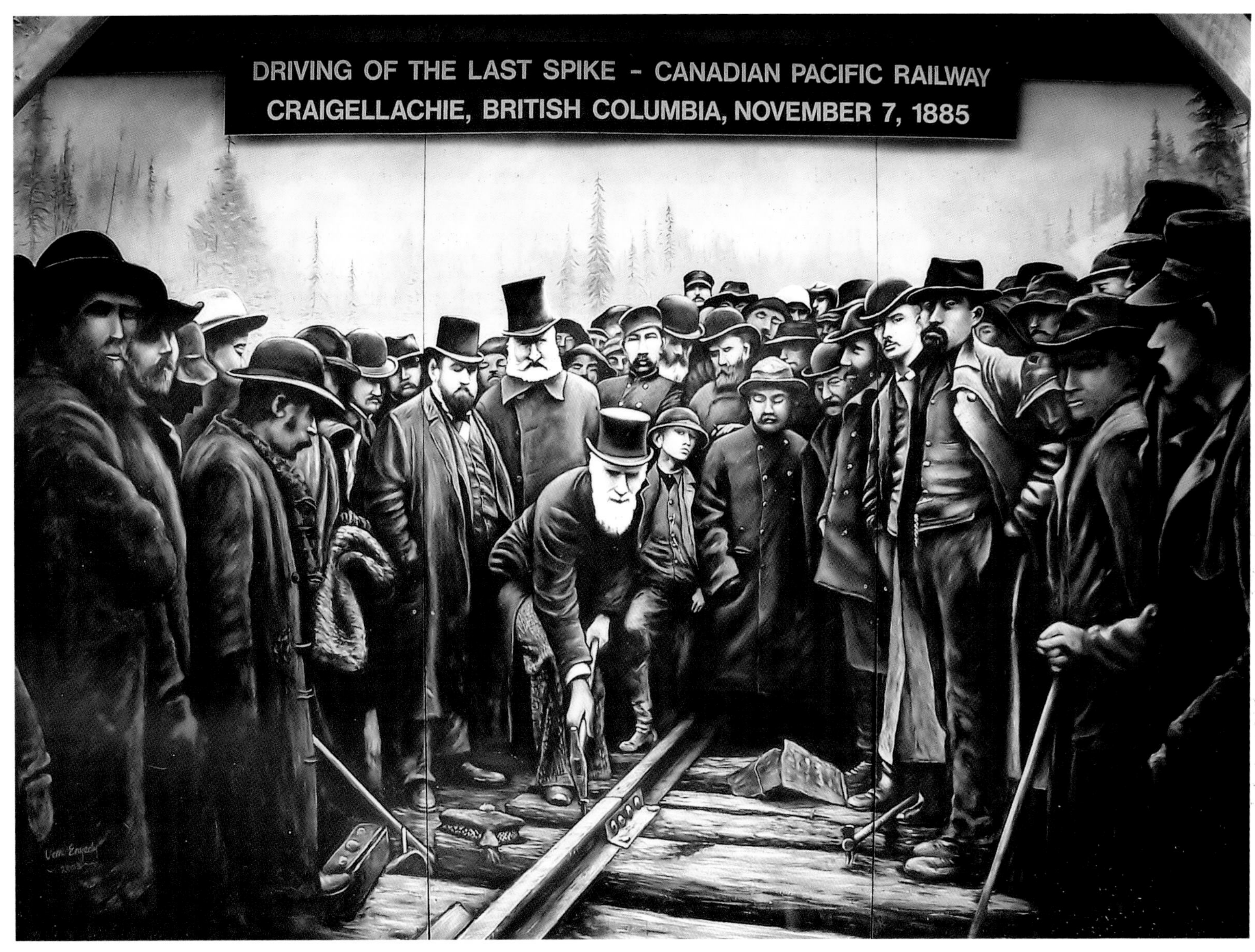
DRIVING OF THE LAST SPIKE - CANADIAN PACIFIC RAILWAY
CRAIGELLACHIE, BRITISH COLUMBIA, NOVEMBER 7, 1885

PORT MOODY AND VANCOUVER

Terminal Arrangements

Double-track steel drawbridge over the Columbia River, Vancouver, a 1906 postcard (above).

Along the water front, Vancouver, 1910 (below).

A view from Hotel Vancouver (below right).

Port Moody, British Columbia, was originally selected as the western terminus of the Canadian Pacific line in 1879. Previously a small and unremarkable town, it grew quickly through the early 1880s in anticipation of the railroad, and real estate prices soared—until CPR president William Cornelius Van Horne decided to move the terminus eleven miles west to Gastown (the early name for Vancouver), which boasted a better harbor.

To prevent land speculation the CPR purchased property in Gastown in secret before laying the extension of the road to reach the new terminus. A branch line was built in 1887, with Engine 374 pulling the first passenger train into Vancouver on May 23, 1887.

The new name "Vancouver" was chosen by Van Horne after British explorer George Vancouver, who had been the first European to enter the Burrard Inlet, the main harbor of present-day Vancouver. The city was incorporated on April 6, 1886, and soon grew in size from a thousand people in 1881 to over 20,000 in 1900, before ballooning to 100,000 by 1911, with the CPR providing much of the investment needed to build and develop the young city. Beginning with a strong base in natural resources, Vancouver's economy slowly became more and more dependent on exports moving through the seaport and onto trains. Most early settlers were hardy and prepared to carve out farms, mines, lumber mills, or logging empires, whereas soon after the CPR established its international trade links, rail passengers disembarked into a busy industrial city with the railroad company's luxury Hotel Vancouver inviting them in, its opera house offering top quality entertainment, and Stanley Park already planned as an urban amenity.

From the new terminus, the CPR was able to connect easily with Vancouver's harbor. The company immediately chartered ocean steamers to import tea from China, and the combination of steamship and CPR rail line became the shortest (and therefore highly popular) shipping route from the Orient to Britain. In 1891, the company's RMS *Empress of China* began passenger service between Vancouver and the Orient, to be soon followed by two more *Empress* liners.

The business shuttling through the Canadian Pacific's maritime services put the railroad in the black and allowed the company to rebuild some of the shoddier sections of the line in the West, such as replacing wooden trestles with steel and stone. With its plan to create a strong trading link between the eastern and western hemispheres, the CPR helped elevate the Canadian economy to world-class status.

Vancouver's second CPR station was at the foot of Granville Street. Designed by Edward Maxwell, the station and offices opened in 1898.

PACIFIC RY.—Trans-Continental Route and Soo and South Shore Lines.

For Parlor, Sleeping and Dining Car Service, and Explanation of Reference Marks, see page 592.

				1	Mls	May 6, 1906.	2	96	8	78	82
....	....	A M	A M	P M	....	LVE.] E. time. [ARR.	A M	P M	P M	....	....
....	....	*10 00	*10 00	8 30	....	....Boston....	7 30	*8 15	*8 15	....	....
....	....	†9 10	†9 10	9 00	....	.Portland (M. Cent.).	8 05	†7 45	†7 45	....	....
....	....	A M	A M	P M	....	LVE.] E. time. [ARR.	A M	P M	P M	....	....
....	....	7 50	7 50	7 30	....	.New York (N. Y. C.).	8 56	10 21	10 21	....	....
....	....	A M	A M	A M	....	LVE.] A. time. [ARR.	P M	P M	P M	....	....
....	....	†8 10	†8 10	†8 10	....	..Halifax (*I. C.*)..	8 45	8 45	8 45	....	....
....	....	P M	P M	P M	....	LVE.] [ARR.	A M	A M	A M	....	....
....	....	†5 40	†5 40	†5 40	....	+ St. John (*C. P.*)	11 20	11 20	11 20	....	....
P M	....	P M	P M	P M	....	LVE.] E. time. [ARR.	A M	P M	P M	A M	....
*11 30	....	*2 00	*2 00	*11 30	....	+..Quebec....	6 30	†2 55	†2 55	6 30	....
A M	....	P M	P M	A M	....	lv.+Montreal...ar.	P M	A M	A M	P M	....
†9 40	....	*10 15	*9 40	*9 40	0	...*Windsor St.* ♁	*6 30	7 00	*8 00	6 30	....
P M	....	P M	P M	A M	....	LVE.] [ARR.	P M	A M	A M	P M	....
†2 10	....	†2 10	†2 10	†7 30	....	+..Prescott.. ♁	†5 00	†9 50	†9 50	†5 00	....
P M	A M	A M	A M	P M	....	LVE.] [ARR.	P M	A M	A M	A M	P M
†5 00	†8 40	*1 42	*1 10	*1 15	116	+..‖Ottawa‖.. ♁	*3 00	*3 30	*4 20	†11 10	†5 57
†2 40	†7 15	†6 30	†6 30	†7 15	....	+.Brockville. ♁	*9 30	†1 00	†1 00	†2 15	†9 30
P M	A M	A M	A M	P M	....	LVE.] [ARR.	P M	A M	A M	A M	P M
†5 55	†9 34	*2 30	*1 58	*2 15	144	+Carleton Jn ♁	2 00	2 25	3 20	10 20	5 06
6 10	9 48	2 45	– –	2 30	151	....Almonte... ♁	1 42	– –	3 04	10 05	4 50
6 25	10 06	– –	– –	– –	160	....Pakenham.. ♁	– –	– –	– –	9 46	4 32
6 39	10 20	3 17	– –	3 02	168	.....Arnprior... ♁	1 11	– –	2 25	9 30	4 16
6 50	10 31	– –	– –	– –	173	....Sand Point.. ♁	– –	– –	– –	9 17	4 03
7 15	11 02	3 56	3 20	3 40	186	+.Renfrew.... ♁	12 36	1 10	1 52	8 54	3 40
7 33	11 20	– –	– –	– –	195	.....Haley's... ♁	– –	– –	– –	8 37	3 18
7 48	11 32	4 25	– –	4 09	202	.....Cobden.... ♁	12 07	– –	1 22	8 24	3 06
8 25	12 10	4 56	4 25	4 45	221	+.Pembroke. ♁	11 35	12 17	12 53	†7 50	2 30
P M	12 50	5 40	5 20	5 30	243	‖Chalk River‖ ♁	10 55	11 45	12 15	A M	†1 50
....	Noon	– –	– –	5 38	248	......Wylie......	10 38	– –	– –	....	P M
....	....	6 06	– –	– –	258	....Moorlake.. ♁	10 21	– –	– –	....	....
....	....	– –	– –	6 21	267	.....Mackey.... ♁	10 02	– –	– –	....	....
....	....	– –	– –	6 29	271	.....Rockcliffe....	9 54	– –	– –	....	....
....	....	– –	– –	6 48	281	..... Bissett ... ♁	9 35	– –	– –	....	....
....	....	7 09	– –	7 13	294	..Deux Rivieres ♁	9 10	– –	10 34	....	....
....	....	7 48	7 22	7 53	315	....Mattawa.. ♁	8 33	9 30	10 00	....	....
....	....	– –	– –	8 30	334	....Rutherglen. ♁	7 57	– –	– –	....	....
....	....	8 36	– –	8 46	341	.....Bonfield... ♁	7 38	– –	9 05	....	....
....	....	9 15	9 00	9 25	360	ar.+North Bay ♁ lv.	6 55	8 10	8 30	....	....
....	....	....	*1 30	*1 15	....	lv.+Detroit..ar.	2 55	3 10	....	....	....
....	....	....	†5 00	†8 15	....	+ St. Thomas..	8 20	11 55	....	....	....
....	....	....	P M	A M	....	LVE.] [ARR.	P M	A M	....	....	....
....	....	P M	P M	P M	....	LVE.] [ARR.	P M	A M	A M	....	....
....	....	*11 30	*11 30	*1 45	....	....Toronto....	2 55	7 00	*7 00	....	....
....	117	8 35	8 35	9 40	....	arr..North Bay.lve.	*6 45	*8 50	*8 50	....	118
....	P M	A M	A M	P M	....	LVE.] [ARR.	A M	P M	P M	....	P M
....	*2 00	9 30	9 50	10 05	360	+ North Bay‖..	6 30	7 45	8 12	....	10 00
....	2 30	↘ –	10 07	– –	370	....Beaucage....	– –	7 24	□ –	....	9 18
....	3 08	△ –	10 29	10 41	384	..Sturgeon Falls ♁	5 54	6 59	□ –	....	8 33
....	3 45	△ –	10 51	10 58	394	..... Verner ... ♁	5 34	6 34	□ –	....	8 01
73	4 41	△ –	11 28	11 31	416	.... Markstay.. ♁	4 58	5 52	□ –	74	6 38
P M	6 40	11 53	12 16	12 15	440	ar. Sudbury ♁.lv.	4 15	5 05	*5 50	A M	*4 35
†5 15	P M	11 58	....	....	440	lv..Sudbury..ar.	....	....	5 45	11 00	P M
5 48	....	– –	....	....	451	....Naughton....	....	....	– –	10 39	....
6 00	....	– –	....	....	458	...White Fish. ♁	....	....	– –	10 26	....
7 02	....	1 32	....	....	488	... Webbwood.. ♁	....	....	4 21	9 23	....
7 34	9	– –	....	....	506	.....Walford... ♁	....	....	– –	8 44	10
7 56	A M	2 22	....	....	517	......Cutler.... ♁	....	....	3 25	8 23	P M
8 35	†8 00	2 54	....	....	535	.....Algoma... ♁	....	....	2 54	†7 45	7 20
P M	8 38	– –	....	....	552	....Dean Lake.. ♁	....	....	– –	A M	6 43
....	9 19	4 02	....	....	573	....Thessalon.. ♁	....	....	1 39	....	6 04
....	9 54	4 36	....	....	591	...Desbarats.. ♁	....	....	1 04	....	5 29
....	10 21	– –	....	....	604	..... Ekoba .... ♁	....	....	– –	....	6 02
....	10 50	5 36	....	....	619	+ Sault (Can.). ♁	....	....	12 16	....	†4 30
....	11 10	5 52	....	....	622	Ste Marie (Mich.) ♁	....	....	*11 59	....	†4 00
....	A M	P M	....	....	....	(*Eastern time.*)	....	....	A M	....	P M
....	10 10	4 52	....	....	....	(*Central time.*)	....	....	*10 59	....	†3 00
....	A M	P M	....	....	....	(*Soo Line.*)	....	....	A M	....	P M
....	....	5 12	....	....	622	lv.+S.Ste.M., Mich.ar.	....	....	10 30	....	....
....	....	9 50	....	....	773	arr.Gladstone.lve.	....	....	5 55	....	....
....	....	11 35	....	....	826	arr..Pembine..lve.	....	....	4 17	....	....
....	....	P M	....	....	....	ARR.] [LVE.	....	....	A M	....	....
....	....	8 45	....	....	1106	....St. Paul....	....	....	7 20	....	....
....	....	9 30	....	....	1106	..Minneapolis.	....	....	*6 35	....	....
....	....	A M	....	....	....	ARR.] [LVE.	....	....	P M	....	....
....	....	P M	....	....	....	(*D. S. S. & A. Ry.*)	....	....	A M	....	....
....	....	10 50	....	....	787	ar. ‖Marquette.lv.	....	....	5 00	....	....
....	....	....	....	....	812	... Republic....	....	....	....	....	....
....	....	A M	....	....	....	ARR.] [LVE.	....	....	P M	....	....
....	....	5 40	....	....	874	ar. Houghton.lv.	....	....	10 20	....	....
....	75	8 55	....	....	1037	......Duluth.....	....	....	*6 20	76	....
....	Noon	A M	....	....	....	ARR.] [LVE.	....	....	P M	P M	....
....	†12 36	....	12 16	12 15	440	lve. Sudbury arr.	4 15	5 05	....	4 40	....
....	1 05	....	– –	– –	452	...Chelmsford. ♁	– –	) –	....	4 10	....
....	1 17	....	– –	– –	458	....Larchwood....	– –	) –	....	3 56	....
....	2 05	....	1 45	1 35	475	arr...Cartier ♁ lve.	3 10	3 55	....	†3 15	....
....	P M	....	1 50	1 45	475	lve..Cartier..arr.	3 05	3 50	....	P M	....
....	....	....	2 11	– –	486	..... Stralak ... ♁	– –	3 24	....	....	....
....	....	....	2 28	– –	495	....Pogamasing. ♁	– –	3 05	....	....	....
....	....	....	3 32	– –	529	.... Bisco.... ♁	– –	1 52	....	....	....
....	....	....	4 29	– –	561	. Woman River ♁	– –	12 49	....	....	....
....	....	....	5 34	– –	596	.... Nemegos .. ♁	– –	11 38	....	....	....
....	....	....	6 15	6 20	612	...‖Chapleau‖. ♁	10 55	11 05	....	....	....
....	....	....	7 34	7 43	658	..... Dalton	9 14	– –	....	....	....
....	....	....	8 03	– –	672	... Missanabie. ♁	8 48	– –	....	....	....
....	....	....	9 49	– –	724	......Amyot.... ♁	7 15	– –	....	....	....
....	....	....	10 30	10 35	744	..‖White River‖ ♁	*6 40	*6 45	....	....	....
....	....	....	P M	A M	....	ARR.] [LVE.	P M	A M	....	....	....

75	75	75	97	1	Mls	June 17, 1906.	2	96	72	76	76
....	....	....	P M	A M	....	LVE.] [ARR.	P M	A M	....	....	....
....	....	....	*10 35	*10 45	744	.‖White River‖. ♁	6 30	6 35	....	....	....
....	....	....	– –	11 14	760	.....Bremner......	6 00	– –	....	....	....
....	....	....	– –	– –	784	......Cache......	– –	– –	....	....	....
....	....	....	– –	– –	794	.....Melgund....	– –	– –	....	....	....
....	....	....	– –	12 25	800	...Heron Bay. ♁	4 45	– –	....	....	....
....	....	....	– –	1 05	819	.. Coldwell ... ♁	4 10	– –	....	....	....
....	....	....	– –	1 55	844	...Jack Fish.. ♁	3 20	– –	....	....	....
....	....	....	2 40	2 57	863	....Schreiber.. ♁	2 45	2 50	....	....	....
....	....	....	– –	3 27	877	.... Rossport .. ♁	1 58	– –	....	....	....
....	....	....	4 40	5 08	926	.....Nipigon... ♁	12 34	12 39	....	....	....
....	....	....	– –	5 41	944	......Wolf .. . ♁	12 04	– –	....	....	....
....	....	....	– –	6 14	959	......Pearl..... ♁	11 38	– –	....	....	....
....	....	....	6 48	7 28	992	+ .Port Arthur. ♁	10 35	10 40	....	....	....
....	....	....	7 00	7 40	995	+ .Ft. William.. ♁	10 25	10 30	....	....	....
....	....	....	....	....	....	ar..Eastern time..lv.	....	....	....	....	....
....	....	....	....	....	....	lv..Central time..ar.	....	....	....	....	....
....	†7 30	....	*6 20	*19 00	995	.Fort William.	9 05	21 10	....	18 00	....
....	9 35	....	7 10	– –	1019	.Kaministikwia ♁	– –	20 15	....	16 20	....
....	12 00	....	8 17	– –	1049	.....Dexter ... ♁	– –	19 19	....	14 30	....
....	13 10	....	8 50	– –	1067	....Savanne... ♁	– –	18 46	....	13 10	....
....	14 00	....	9 13	– –	1080	......Upsala.... ♁	– –	18 25	....	12 00	....
....	14 20	....	– –	– –	1085	.....Carlstadt.. ♁	– –	– –	....	11 35	....
....	15 50	....	10 04	– –	1108	.....English ... ♁	– –	17 35	....	10 04	....
....	16 15	....	– –	– –	1114	......Martin.....	– –	– –	....	9 40	....
....	17 02	....	10 37	– –	1126	.... Bonheur .. ♁	– –	17 02	....	9 00	....
....	18 00	....	11 10	23 40	1144	ar.‖Ignace‖ ♁.lv.	4 25	16 30	....	†8 00	....
....	....	....	....	....	....	LVE.] [ARR.	....	....	....	....	....
....	....	†7 30	11 20	23 50	1144	......Ignace.....	4 15	16 20	18 30	....	....
....	....	8 10	– –	– –	1159	.....Raleigh.... ♁	– –	– –	17 35	....	....
....	....	8 40	12 12	– –	1172	......Tache.... ♁	– –	15 27	16 45	....	....
....	....	12 15	13 50	– –	1224	......Eagle.... ♁	– –	13 50	12 15	....	....
....	....	13 05	14 10	– –	1234	...Vermilion.. ♁	– –	13 33	11 10	....	....
....	....	14 10	– –	– –	1248	......Parry.... ♁	– –	– –	10 10	....	....
....	....	17 10	– –	– –	1281	.....Margach... ♁	– –	– –	8 05	....	....
....	....	18 00	15 50	4 15	1289	ar...Kenora. ♁ lv.	23 50	11 55	†7 30	....	....
....	....	....	....	....	....	LVE.] [ARR.	....	....	....	....	....
†8 00	....	....	16 00	4 25	1289	...‖Kenora.....	23 40	11 45	....	....	18 30
8 15	....	....	16 08	4 33	1292	....Keewatin.. ♁	23 32	11 36	....	....	18 15
10 05	....	....	17 08	– –	1321	......Ingolf.... ♁	– –	10 40	....	....	16 30
12 15	....	....	17 52	– –	1341	......Rennie.... ♁	– –	10 00	....	....	15 00
14 00	....	....	18 30	6 42	1361	...Whitemouth. ♁	21 27	9 23	....	....	13 05
15 10	....	....	19 02	– –	1377	.....Molson..... ♁	– –	8 54	....	....	11 55
15 55	....	....	19 22	– –	1387	....Beausejour.. ♁	20 45	8 36	....	....	11 10
16 55	....	....	19 52	7 46	1401	.....Selkirk ... ♁	20 20	8 10	....	....	10 00
17 55	....	....	– –	8 14	1414	....Birds Hill.. ♁	19 51	– –	....	....	8 50
18 30	....	....	20 40	8 30	1422	ar.+ Winnipeg ♁ lv.	19 35	7 20	....	....	†8 00
....	7	5	....	....	....	LVE.] [ARR.	....	....	6	8	....
....	†8 40	†16 50	21 40	9 15	1422	+ ‖Winnipeg‖..	18 45	6 45	12 15	17 35	....
....	u –	17 06	– –	– –	1430	......Bergen	18 25	– –	11 57	u –	....
....	u –	17 20	– –	9 46	1437	......Rosser.... ♁	18 10	– –	11 42	u –	....
....	u –	17 46	– –	10 10	1451	....Marquette.. ♁	17 46	– –	11 16	u –	....
....	u –	17 58	– –	10 22	1457	.....Reaburn.... ♁	17 34	– –	11 04	u –	....
....	u –	18 09	– –	10 33	1463	...Poplar Point. ♁	17 23	– –	10 53	u –	....
....	10 25	18 40	23 14	11 10	1478	+ Portage la Prairie ♁	16 52	5 05	10 25	†15 55	....
....	....	18 54	– –	11 28	1486	.....Burnside... ♁	16 29	– –	10 03	....	....
....	....	19 06	– –	11 46	1493	......Bagot..... ♁	16 15	– –	9 49	....	....
....	....	19 18	– –	12 00	1500	..MacGregor ♁	16 03	– –	9 37	....	....
....	....	19 31	– –	12 15	1507	......Austin..... ♁	15 49	– –	9 23	....	....
....	....	19 53	– –	12 40	1515	......Sidney..... ♁	15 33	– –	9 10	....	....
....	....	20 17	24 45	13 08	1528	.....Carberry.... ♁	15 09	3 32	8 49	....	....
....	....	20 35	– –	– –	1536	......Sewell..... ♁	– –	– –	8 33	....	....
....	....	20 50	– –	13 43	1544	.....Douglas.... ♁	14 35	– –	8 20	....	....
....	....	21 02	– –	13 55	1549	......Chater..... ♁	– –	– –	8 10	....	....
3	....	21 15	1 40	14 10	1555	ar.+Brandon.lv.	14 10	2 40	†8 00	....	....
†7 30	....	....	1 50	14 25	1555	lv..Brandon ♁ ar.	13 55	2 30	....	....	[illegible]
7 50	....	....	– –	14 45	1563	.....Kemnay... ♁	– –	– –	....	....	[illegible]
8 05	....	....	– –	15 00	1571	....Alexander.. ♁	13 24	– –	....	....	[illegible]
8 23	....	....	– –	15 25	1580	....Griswold... ♁	13 05	– –	....	....	[illegible]
8 37	....	....	– –	15 37	1587	....Oak Lake.. ♁	12 50	– –	....	....	[illegible]
9 07	....	....	– –	16 10	1603	..... Virden .... ♁	12 18	– –	....	....	[illegible]
9 38	....	....	4 03	16 52	1619	.....Elkhorn.... ♁	11 45	24 37	....	....	[illegible]
9 54	....	....	4 18	17 10	1626	.....Kirkella.....	11 30	24 23	....	....	[illegible]
10 09	....	....	– –	17 25	1634	.....Fleming.... ♁	11 13	– –	....	....	[illegible]
10 24	....	....	– –	17 44	1642	....Moosomin.. ♁	10 57	– –	....	....	[illegible]
11 00	....	....	– –	18 15	1658	.....Wapella.... ♁	10 22	– –	....	....	[illegible]
11 33	....	....	– –	18 45	1672	...Whitewood. ♁	9 54	– –	....	....	[illegible]
12 05	....	....	6 20	19 15	....	ar..C. time..lv.	9 25	22 35	....	....	[illegible]
....	....	3	....	....	1687	Broadview	....	....	4	....	....
....	....	†11 15	5 30	18 25	....	lv..M. time..ar.	8 15	21 25	12 40	....	....
....	....	11 30	– –	– –	1695	.....Oakshela....	– –	– –	12 26	....	....
....	....	11 45	6 10	18 55	1703	.....Grenfell... ♁	– –	20 50	12 12	....	....
....	....	12 17	6 47	19 29	1718	.....Wolseley... ♁	– –	20 18	11 41	....	....
....	....	12 55	7 35	20 10	1738	...Indian Head. ♁	– –	19 27	11 03	....	....
....	....	13 22	8 03	20 36	1748	...Qu'Appelle.. ♁	– –	19 03	10 45	....	....
....	....	14 25	9 17	21 47	1780	+ ....Regina... ♁	– –	17 50	9 40	....	....
....	....	15 02	9 55	– –	1797	......Pense..... ♁	– –	17 10	8 56	....	....
....	....	15 45	10 35	– –	1815	.....Pasqua... ♁	4 15	16 30	8 20	....	....
....	....	....	*9 25	*20 00	0	lv...St. Paul..ar.	10 25	18 40	....	....	....
....	....	....	10 05	20 40	0	..Minneapolis..	9 45	18 00	....	....	....
....	....	....	5 20	17 20	550	+ ...Portal.....	12 30	23 30	....	....	....
....	....	....	10 20	22 20	711	.....Pasqua.....	4 30	16 45	....	....	....
....	....	....	10 35	22 35	717	ar.+‖Moose Jaw.lv.	*4 00	*16 15	....	....	....
....	....	16 00	11 25	*23 30	1821	lv.Moose Jaw‖ ♁ ar.	*3 45	15 55	†8 05	....	....
....	....	....	11 57	– –	1838	......Caron .... ♁	– –	15 23	....	....	....
....	....	....	12 38	– –	1856	ar..Parkbeg ♁..lv.	– –	*14 51	....	....	....

Varcoe Br.—Train lvs. **MacGregor** ƒ12 10, arr. at Varcoe (54.9 m.) 14 10, Rapid City (67.4 m.) 14 45. Lvs. Rapid City ƒ13 20, Varcoe ƒ13 55, arr. at MacGregor 15 55.

Continued on following page.

Teulon Br.—Train lv. **Winnipeg** †17 30, ar. Teulon (40 m.) 19 30. Lv. Teulon †6 50, ar. Winnipeg 9 00. Trains lv. Winnipeg †11 25, †17 00, ar. Stonewall 11 40, 18 15. Lv. Stonewall †8 15, †14 20, ar. Winnipeg 9 00, 15 35.

Eastern time is adopted on lines east of Fort William, Detroit and Sault Ste. Marie and west of Vanceboro, Me.

STEAM HEAT The SAFETY systems are in use on over 150 railroads in the U. S. | SAFETY CAR HEATING & LIGHTING [CO.] NEW YORK. CHICAGO. ST. LOUI[S]

CANADIAN PACIFIC RAILWAY.

For Parlor, Sleeping and Dining Car Service and Explanation of Reference Marks, see page 592.

TRANS-CONTINENTAL ROUTE.—Continued.

3	97	1	Mls	June 17, 1906.	2	96	41
....	*12 38	– –	1856	lve.....Parkbeg....arr.	– –	14 51	....
....	13 22	– –	1875	........Chaplin...... ♁	– –	14 15	....
....	14 50	– –	1912	......Rush Lake.... ♁	– –	13 00	....
....	15 25	– –	1926	........Aikins........	– –	12 28	....
....	15 50	*3 25	1932	..‖Swift Current‖ ♁	24 20	12 15	....
....	17 08	– –	1967	......Gull Lake ..... ♁	– –	10 54	....
....	19 00	5 59	2018	.....Maple Creek... ♁	21 30	9 08	....
....	19 44	– –	2037	........Forres........	– –	8 29	....
....	20 13	– –	2049	.........Walsh....... ♁	– –	8 02	....
....	20 36	7 13	2060	........Irvine....... ♁	20 14	7 40	....
....	21 06	– –	2074	.....Coleridge	– –	7 05	....
....	21 18	7 47	2076	..Dunmore Junc‖ ♁	– –	6 59	....
....	21 50	8 20	2082	..‖Medicine Hat. ♁	19 25	6 45	....
....	– –	8 40	2089	.........Stair.........	18 49	– –	....
....	– –	8 55	2096	........Bowell....... ♁	18 37	– –	....
....	– –	9 35	2117	.......Langevin...... ♁	17 56	– –	....
....	– –	10 10	2134	........Tilley.........	17 22	– –	....
....	– –	10 55	2154	.... Cassils.........	16 46	– –	....
....	– –	11 30	2171	.......Lathom.........	16 15	– –	....
....	1 50	12 47	2206	......Gleichen...... ♁	15 10	2 37	....
....	– –	13 35	2227	.......Strathmore..... ♁	14 31	– –	....
....	– –	14 05	2241	........Langdon...... ♁	14 05	– –	....
....	4 05	15 15	2262	+ .....Calgary...... ♁	13 20	24 55	....
....	– –	16 12	2284	........Cochrane...... ♁	12 13	– –	....
....	– –	16 36	2295	.........Radnor.........	11 53	– –	....
....	– –	16 57	2303	.........Morley........ ♁	11 37	– –	....
....	– –	17 27	2316	......Kananaskis........	11 15	– –	....
....	– –	17 45	2324	.......The Gap.........	11 00	– –	....
....	– –	17 58	2329	......Canmore....... ♁	10 50	– –	....
....	– –	18 28	2342	......Bankhead.........	10 26	– –	....
....	7 20	18 40	2343	+ ....Banff........ ♁	10 20	22 05	....
....	– –	19 15	2360	...Castle Mountain...	9 45	– –	....
....	8 45	19 55	....	arr...*M. time*..lve.	9 15	20 55	....
....	....	....	2378	......Laggan ♁ ...	....	....	....
....	8 00	19 05	....	lve...*P. time*...arr.	8 00	19 40	....
....	8 17	19 20	2384	........Stephen.........	– –	– –	....
....	8 30	19 35	2386	.........Hector....... ♁	– –	19 10	....
....	9 30	20 32	2394	.........‖Field‖....... ♁	6 35	18 10	....
....	10 05	– –	2409	.......Leanchoil........	– –	16 53	....
....	10 26	21 24	2417	.........Palliser....... ♁	– –	16 24	....
....	11 07	22 00	2429	.........Golden........ ♁	4 32	15 32	....
....	11 45	– –	2446	........Donald....... ♁	– –	14 55	....
....	12 18	23 07	2458	.....Beavermouth... ♁	3 32	14 23	....
....	14 08	– –	2479	.....Roger's Pass... ♁	– –	13 13	....
....	14 55	24 57	2482	.......‖Glacier‖..... ♁	2 22	12 55	....
....	15 52	– –	2497	......Illecillewaet..... ♁	– –	11 02	....
....	16 22	– –	2504	....Albert Canyon.. ♁	– –	10 31	....
....	16 49	– –	2514	..... Twin Butte	– –	9 57	....
....	17 45	3 10	2525	+...Revelstoke... ♁	23 45	9 25	....
....	20 01	5 11	2570	.‖Sicamous Junc‖ ♁	21 36	7 10	....
....	20 55	5 56	2588	.....Salmon Arm... ♁	20 55	6 23	....
....	21 48	6 50	2594	..... Notch Hill .... ♁	20 15	5 49	....
....	22 35	7 34	2620	......Shuswap...... ♁	19 30	5 06	....
....	23 09	8 06	2636	.... Ducks.........	18 56	4 32	....
....	23 55	8 55	2654	......Kamloops..... ♁	18 25	4 00	....
....	– –	10 00	2679	........Savonas........	17 09	– –	....
....	1 50	10 51	2701	......Ashcroft...... ♁	16 17	1 50	....
....	2 56	11 51	2726	....Spence's Bridge.. ♁	15 22	24 48	....
....	3 57	12 54	2748	.......‖Lytton‖...... ♁	14 25	23 43	....
....	– –	13 42	2764	........Keefers...... ♁	13 42	– –	....
....	5 35	14 22	2775	....‖North Bend‖ .. ♁	13 05	22 30	....
....	6 55	15 36	2802	.........‖Yale‖........ ♁	11 45	21 08	....
....	– –	16 05	2815	.........Hope......... ♁	11 15	– –	....
....	– –	16 22	2823	.......Ruby Creek........	10 55	– –	....
....	7 58	16 42	2834	........‖Agassiz‖...... ♁	10 33	20 00	....
....	8 16	17 02	2843	....Harrison Mills.. ♁	10 13	19 42	....
....	– –	17 22	2852	.......Nicomen.........	9 55	– –	....
....	8 55	17 42	2862	arr. Mission Junc ♁.lve.	9 35	19 03	....
....	10 05	....	2872	arr...+ Sumas....lve.	....	*17 53	....
....	11 10	....	2895	arr..‖Bellingham‖..lve.	....	16 25	....
....	13 40	....	2960	arr..Snohomish..lve.	....	14 30	....
....	15 25	....	2998	arr....Seattle....lve.	....	12 35	....
....	17 45	....	3039	arr....Tacoma....lve	....	10 55	....
....	22 55	....	3183	arr....Portland...lve.	....	*23 45	....
*19 03	9 10	17 40	2862	lve..Mission Jn..arr.	9 35	18 53	8 50
19 54	10 05	18 40	2887	ar. + Westminster Jn. ♁ lv.	8 43	17 57	7 55
20 20	10 30	19 10	2896	ar.Westminster ♁ lv.	*7 25	*17 20	*7 25
*19 25	*9 35	*17 20	2896	lve.Westminster.arr.	9 15	19 10	9 15
19 59	10 05	18 45	2887	lve.Westminster Jn.arr.	8 38	17 52	7 50
20 09	10 15	18 54	2892	arr.Port Moody ♁ lve.	8 28	17 42	7 40
20 43	10 45	19 25	2904	ar. + Vancouver ♁.lv.	*8 00	*17 15	*7 10
....	17 00	....	2988	ar. + Victoria, B.C.lv.	b1 00	*7 30	....

VANCOUVER AND PORTLAND, ORE.

			Exp.	STATIONS.	Exp.		
....	....	....	*7 10	lve..+Vancouver.arr.	20 43	....	....
....	....	....	*7 25	lve.Westminster.arr.	20 20	....	....
....	....	....	8 50	arr..Mission Jn..arr.	18 43	....	....
....	....	....	10 05	.....Sumas City.....	17 53	....	....
....	....	....	15 25	........Seattle........	12 35	....	....
....	....	....	17 40	.......Tacoma.......	10 55	....	....
....	....	....	22 55	arr... Portland...lve.	*23 45	....	....

Eganville Branch.—Trains leave Renfrew †11 07 a.m., †7 22 p.m., arrive Eganville (23 miles) 12 25 noon, 8 40 p.m. Returning, leave Eganville †7 20 a.m., †2 00 p.m., arrive Renfrew 8 33 a.m., 3 10 p.m.

Pheasant Hills Branch.—Train lvs. Kirkella ƒ11 35, arr. Strassburg ♁ (2[illegible] miles) 19 30. Ret'g, lvs. Strassburg ƒ7 15, arr. Kirkella 15 35.

ROSSLAND BRANCH.

....	64	62	Mls	May 6, 1906.	61	63	....	....
....	....	....	....	LEAVE] [ARRIVE	....	....	....	....
....	*20 50	....	0	... West Robson . ♁	....	21 00	....	....
....	20 55	†9 25	2	..Castlegar Junction..	9 15	20 55	....	....
....	21 26	10 10	12	.....China Creek.....	8 44	20 06	....	....
....	21 52	10 55	21	arr.Smelter Jn ♁ lve.	8 20	19 40	....	....
....	....	11 15	23	arr......Trail.....lve.	....	*19 20	....	....
....	19 20	†10 45	23	lve......Trail ♁...arr.	....	19 55	....	....
....	21 52	11 05	21	lve..Smelter Jn..arr.	8 20	19 40	....	....
....	22 20	11 33	28	..........Tiger.........	7 55	19 09	....	....
....	22 25	11 40	29	.....Crown Point.....	7 50	19 03	....	....
....	22 50	12 15	33	arr....Rossland ♁.lve.	†7 30	*18 40	....	....

BOUNDARY BRANCH.

41	Mls	May 6, 1906.	42
†9 30	0	lv.West Robson ♁ ar.	20 35
13 07	67	.....Grand Forks... ♁	16 54
14 00	81	..Eholt Junction ♁	16 05
15 00	91	arr....Phoenix ♁.lve.	†15 15
15 00	99	arr....Midway ♁..lve.	†15 10

MINIOTA BRANCH.

....	33	149	143	153	Ms	June 17, 1906.	154	150	144	34
....	....	j7 00	f7 00	†14 30	0	lve. + Brandon ♁ .arr.	11 15	17 10	17 10	....
....	....	7 30	7 25	14 50	6	.......Chater..... ♁	11 00	16 55	16 55	....
....	....	....	11 55	....	56	arr...Lenore....lve.	....	....	f13 00	....
....	f14 45	9 40	....	16 40	37	.....Rapid City... ♁	9 05	j14 50	....	13 20
....	16 55	....	....	19 50	77	arr... Miniota ♁ .lve.	†6 00	....	....	j11 10

WALTHAM BRANCH.

113	117	Mls.	May 6, 1906.	112	114
P M	A M	....	LEAVE] [ARRIVE	A M	P M
†5 10	†6 45	0	+ ......Ottawa (*U. D.*)..... ♁	9 35	6 15
5 20	7 05	2.0	......Hull (*C. P. Station*)... ♁	9 25	6 05
5 40	7 45	9.6	..........Aylmer.......... ♁	9 05	5 40
5 55	8 10	17.3	.... Breckenridge...........	8 51	5 10
6 05	8 25	23.1	............Eardley.............	8 41	4 55
6 09	8 37	24.9	.... Parker..............	8 37	4 50
6 17	8 49	28.8	............Mohr...............	8 28	4 40
6 26	9 05	32.7	............Quio............ ♁	8 20	4 30
6 34	9 20	35.8	...........Wyman............	8 09	4 10
6 46	9 40	39.9	..........Maryland......... ♁	7 58	3 56
6 53	9 55	42.6	.... McKee............	7 50	3 42
7 02	10 20	46.4	..........Shawville......... ♁	7 42	3 30
7 20	10 42	53.7	..........Moorehead...........	7 24	2 55
7 28	11 07	57.6	.... Campbell's Bay...... ♁	7 14	2 40
8 01	11 47	68.9	.... Fort Coulonge....... ♁	6 47	2 00
8 05	11 50	69.9	..........Davidson............	6 40	1 50
8 19	12 12	76.4	...........Mellon.............	6 28	1 30
8 30	12 30	80.4	..........Waltham........ ♁	†6 20	†1 20
P M	Noon	....	ARRIVE] [LEAVE	A M	P M

Lindsay Branch.—Trains leave Burketon Junction †10 55 a.m., †6 50 p.m., arrive Bobcaygeon (39 miles) 12 25 noon, 8 00 p.m. Returning, leave Bobcaygeon †7 40 a.m., †4 30 p.m., arrive Burketon Junction 8 50 a.m., 6 00 p.m. *May* 6, 1906.

Lac du Bonnet Branch.—Train leaves Molson x9 15, arriving Lac du Bonnet (22 miles) 11 00. Returning, leaves Lac du Bonnet x13 30, arriving Molson 15 10. *June* 17, 1906.

Lacombe Branch.—Lvs. Lacombe †13 00, arr. Stettler (51 miles) 16 30. Lvs. Stettler †7 15, arr. Lacombe 11 00.

Wetaskiwin Br.—Leaves Wetaskiwin †14 30, arr. Daysland (51 m.) 18 40. Lvs. Daysland †5 45, arr. Wetaskiwin 9 35.

MANIWAKI BRANCH.

101	103	107	Ms.	May 6, 1906.	102	108	104
P M	P M	A M	....	LEAVE] [ARRIVE	A M	P M	P M
†6 00	k1 30	a7 20	0	+ ...Ottawa (*U. D.*).. ♁	8 50	7 45	9 15
6 05	1 35	7 33	2.0	...Hull (*C. P. Station*) ♁	8 41	7 30	9 05
6 15	1 46	7 57	4.7	........Ironside..........	8 31	7 15	8 56
6 26	1 57	8 22	7.9	........Chelsea .... ♁	8 22	7 05	8 47
6 39	2 09	8 35	11.7	......Kirk's Ferry......	8 11	6 45	8 36
6 48	2 18	8 46	15.4	.......Cascades....... ♁	8 02	6 35	8 27
6 06	2 36	9 25	21.2	.......Wakefield ...... ♁	7 45	6 06	8 10
6 16	2 46	9 40	24.4	...North Wakefield.. ♁	7 35	5 50	8 02
6 26	2 56	9 55	29.5	.......Farrellton.........	7 25	5 32	7 50
6 44	3 14	10 20	34.7	.... Low......... ♁	7 13	5 10	7 40
7 00	3 25	10 40	40.8	........Venosta	6 57	4 50	7 27
7 14	3 39	11 00	46.8	.......Kazubazua..... ♁	6 45	4 30	7 14
7 20	3 46	11 07	48.5	.........Aylwin..........	6 38	4 22	7 08
7 45	4 13	11 45	59.1	.......Gracefield ...... ♁	6 15	3 50	6 40
8 05	4 38	12 07	67.0	........Blue Sea..........	5 50	3 15	6 15
8 15	4 48	12 30	71.5	........Burbidge....... ♁	5 40	3 00	6 05
8 45	5 13	1 20	82.1	.......Maniwaki ..... ♁	†5 15	a2 25	k5 40
P M	P M	P M	....	ARRIVE] [LEAVE	A M	P M	P M

Sunday Trains—Lvs. Ottawa ƒ9 00 a.m., arr. Maniwaki 12 25 noon. Lvs. Maniwaki ƒ6 00 p.m., arr. Ottawa 9 35 p.m.

Lardo Branch.—Train leaves Lardo ƒ13 00, arriving Gerrard (33 miles) 14 30. Returning, leaves Gerrard ƒ9 40, arriving Lardo 11 15.

NAKUSP AND SLOCAN BRANCH.

52	Mls	STATIONS.	51
†14 20	0	lve.....Nakusp ♁...arr.	12 15
16 48	28	........Rosebery...... ♁	9 50
17 13	32	.....Denver Canyon.....	9 14
18 20	40	arr.....Sandon ♁...lve.	†8 20

COLUMBIA AND KOOTENAY BRANCH.

....	45	43	41	Mls	STATIONS.	42	44	46	....
....	*19 15	†9 10	†8 10	0	lve.....+Nelson ♁.....arr.	22 05	16 30	10 37	....
....	20 35	....	9 25	28	....Castlegar Junction....	20 55	....	†9 22	....
....	20 40	....	9 30	30	arr....West Robson ♁ .lve.	*20 45	....	....	....
....	....	12 00	....	44	arr......Slocan City ♁...lve.	....	†13 45	....	....

22	M	ARROW LAKE BR.	23
*9 20	0	lve..+Revelstoke ♁ . arr.	17 10
10 40	28	arr....Arrowhead ♁ . lve.	*15 45

EDMONTON BRANCH.

13	Mls	May 6, 1906.	14
*7 45	0	lve...+Calgary‖ ♁. arr.	16 05
7 50	2	....Calgary Junction....	16 00
9 21	41	.........Carstairs.........	14 30
10 45	77	.........Innisfail....... ♁	13 02
11 40	95	.........Red Deer...... ♁	12 15
12 33	114	.........Lacombe...... ♁	11 20
14 00	152	...... Wetaskiwin ..... ♁	9 50
14 50	174	..........Leduc....... ♁	8 59
15 30	192	arr....Strathcona ♁..lve.	†8 20
....	....	...(*South Edmonton*)...	....

Additional Trains—Lvs. Calgary †15 15, arr. Strathcona 22 45. Lvs. Strathcona *16 00, arrives Calgary 23 30.

CROWSNEST BRANCH.

5	Ms	May 6, 1906.	6
....	....	LEAVE] [ARRIVE	....
*20 50	....	......Medicine Hat..... ♁	6 00
21 25	0	lve...Dunmore Junc ♁ arr.	5 47
23 25	55	.........Grassy Lake...... ♁	3 41
24 26	81	.........Woodpecker.........	2 46
1 25	107	arr...+ Lethbridge ♁ . lve.	1 40
3 15	143	..........Macleod......... ♁	23 40
4 25	172	..........Pincher.......... ♁	22 23
5 33	197	.... Frank .... ♁	21 18
6 23	212	.........Crowsnest .... ♁	20 30
7 48	248	..........Fernie .... ♁	18 29
10 25	311	.........Cranbrook...... ♁	15 40
11 26	333	..........Aldridge........ ♁	14 28
12 05	352	............Yahk...........	13 42
12 51	366	.........Kitchener....... ♁	12 51
14 00	394	...Kootenay Landing...	*11 20
....	....	ARRIVE] [LEAVE	....

Train leaves Lethbridge †6 45, arr. Macleod 8 50. Lvs. Macleod †14 05, arr. Lethbridge 16 30.

Okanagan Branch.—Train leaves Sicamous Junction ♁ †7 30 for Enderby ♁ (23 miles), Larkin (38 miles), arriving at Okanagan Landing ♁ (51 miles) 10 50. Returning, leaves Okanagan Landing †13 40, arriving Sicamous Junction 18 00. *May* 6, 1906.

Kimberly Branch.—Train leaves Cranbrook †7 30, arriving Kimberly (19 miles) 10 30. Returning, leaves Kimberly †11 30, arriving at Cranbrook 15 10.

THROUGH CAR SERVICE.

WESTBOUND.

No. 1—IMPERIAL LIMITED—Daily. Has Colonist and First Class Coaches and Sleeping Car Montreal to Vancouver. Sleeping Car from Toronto to Winnipeg daily, via North Bay. Tourist Car Montreal to Vancouver, Sunday, Monday and Thursday; Toronto to Vancouver, Tuesday, Wednesday, Friday and Saturday; Winnipeg to Vancouver, daily. Sleeping Car St. Paul to Banff. Sleeping Car Ft. William to Winnipeg daily. Sleeping Car St. Paul to Winnipeg, via Emerson. Dining Car Montreal to Laggan and Revelstoke to Vancouver.

No. 97—PACIFIC EXPRESS—Daily. Has First Class Coach, Sleeping Car and Colonist Car Montreal to Vancouver. Sleeping Car Winnipeg to Calgary and Strathcona. Tourist Cars for Vancouver leave Boston Wednesday, Montreal Tuesday, Wednesday, Friday and Saturday, Toronto Sunday, Monday and Thursday. Sleeping and Tourist Car St. Paul to Seattle, via Soo Pacific Route. Sleeping Car Arrowhead to Vancouver. Dining Cars Montreal to Laggan and Revelstoke to Vancouver.

No. 3—EXPRESS—Leaving Montreal week-days has First and Second Class Coaches to Detroit. First Class Coach and Sleeping Car to Chicago daily. From Toronto, has Coaches and Sleeping Car to Detroit daily. Sleeper and Coach Toronto to Chic. daily. Cafe Car Montreal to Toronto.

No. 5—CHICAGO EXPRESS—Daily. Has First and Second Class Coaches Montreal to Detroit and Sleeping Cars Montreal to Toronto and Chicago, and Ottawa to Toronto. Through Tourist Sleeper Boston to Chicago Tuesday. Cafe Car Toronto to Detroit. Dining Car west of Detroit.

No. 7—ST. PAUL, MINNEAPOLIS AND DULUTH EXPRESS—Daily. Sleeping Car Montreal to Ottawa (passengers may remain in car until 9 00 a.m.). Has First and Second Class Coaches and Sleeping Car Montreal to St. Paul and Minneapolis and to Duluth, via Marquette Route. Sleeping Car Boston to St. Paul and Minneapolis. Dining Cars en route.

No. 9—HALIFAX EXPRESS—Leaving Montreal daily, except Saturday, has First and Second Class Coaches and Sleeping Car to St. John, N.B., and Halifax, N.S. Sleeping Car Montreal to St. Andrews Tuesday, Wednesday, Thursday and Friday till July 13th, and after July 14th, Tuesday and Friday only. Dining Car Mattawamkeag to Truro.

No. 11—BOSTON EXPRESS—Leaving Montreal daily, has First and Second Class Coaches to Boston, and Sleeping Car from St. Paul and Minneapolis to Boston. Cafe Car Montreal to Boston. Parlor Car Montreal to Old Orchard and Portland. Parlor Car Boston to St. John.

No. 15—NEW ENGLAND EXPRESS—Leaving Montreal daily, has First and Second Class Coaches and Sleeping Cars to Boston. Sleeping Car Montreal to Old Orchard and Portland. Composite First Class Coach and Sleeping Car to Springfield daily, except Sunday. Tourist Sleeper leaves Chicago Friday and Toronto Saturday for Boston.

No. 12—Express from St. John, N.B., daily, except Sunday, has First and Second Class Coaches and Pullman Sleeping Car to Boston. Dining Car Truro to Vanceboro.

No. 13—Through Sleeper and Diner St. Paul to Winnipeg, via Minneapolis, St. Paul & Sault Ste. Marie Ry.

No. 30—Leaving New York (N. Y. C.) daily at 8 00 p.m., has Sleeping Car for Toronto. Parlor and Dining Car Buffalo to Toronto.

No. 40—Leaving Quebec daily, has First and Second Class Coaches and Sleeping Car for Montreal.

CAFE CARS on Nos. 7 and 8 Winnipeg and Yorkton; 17 and 18 Winnipeg and Deloraine; 55 and 56 Prince Albert Branch.

EASTBOUND.

No. 2—IMPERIAL LIMITED—Daily. Has Colonist and First Class Coaches and Sleeper Vancouver to Montreal. Sleeping Car from Strathcona to Winnipeg leaves Calgary except Monday; from Calgary to Winnipeg Mondays, and Winnipeg to Toronto daily, via North Bay. Tourist Cars from Vancouver for Montreal Mon., Wed. and Fri.; for Toronto Sun., Tues., Thur. and Sat. Dining Cars Vancouver to Revelstoke and Laggan to Montreal. Sleeper Banff to St. Paul daily, via Soo Pacific Route. Sleeper Winnipeg to Ft. William daily.

No. 96—ATLANTIC EXPRESS—Daily. Has Coach, Colonist Car and Sleeper Vancouver to Montreal. Sleeper and Tourist Car Seattle to St. Paul, via Soo Pac. Route. Sleeper Vancouver to Arrowhead and Strathcona and Calgary to Winnipeg. Tourist Sleeper Vancouver for Toronto on Mon., Wed. and Fri., for Montreal Sun., Tues., Thur. and Sat., for Boston Thur. Sleeper from Winnipeg to St. Paul, via Emerson, daily. Dining Cars Vancouver to Revelstoke and Laggan to Montreal.

No. 4—EXPRESS—Leaving Chicago (Wab. R.R.) at 3 00 p.m. has Sleeping Car and Coach to Toronto daily, to Montreal daily, except Sat. Through Tourist Sleepers Chicago to Boston Fri. From Detroit has Sleeping Car and First and Second Class Coaches daily for Toronto, running through to Montreal daily, except Sun., with Cafe Car Toronto to Montreal. Dining Car west of Detroit. Parlor Car St. John to Boston.

No. 6—MONTREAL EXPRESS—Leaving Chicago (Wabash R.R.) at 10 32 p.m. has Sleeping Cars to Montreal daily, and First Class Coach to Toronto daily. From Detroit has First and Second Class Coaches and Sleeper to Montreal daily. Sleeping Cars Toronto to Montreal and Ottawa. Cafe Car Detroit to Toronto.

No. 8—MONTREAL AND BOSTON EXPRESS—Daily. Sleeping Car Ottawa to Montreal (open at 9 00 p.m.) Has First and Second Class Coaches Minneapolis and St. Paul to Montreal. Sleeping Car to Montreal and Boston. Sleeping Car from Duluth to Montreal, via Marquette Route. Sleeping Car St. Paul and Minneapolis to Boston. Dining Cars.

No. 10—HALIFAX EXPRESS—Leaving Halifax and St. John, N.B., daily, except Sunday, has First and Second Class Coaches and Sleeping Car to Montreal. Sleeping Car St. Andrews to Montreal Wednesday, Thursday, Friday and Monday to July 13th, inclusive, and after July 14th, Monday and Wednesday only. Dining Car Truro to Mattawamkeag.

No. 12—NEW ENGLAND EXPRESS—Leaving Boston daily, has First and Second Class Coaches with Sleeping Car to Montreal. Sleeping Car Portland and Old Orchard to Montreal. Composite First Class Coach and Sleeping Car Springfield to Montreal, except Sunday.

No. 14—Through Sleeper and Diner Winnipeg to St. Paul, via Minneapolis, St. Paul & Sault Ste. Marie Ry.

No. 16—BOSTON EXPRESS—Leaving Boston daily, has First and Second Class Coaches and Cafe Car to Montreal, and Sleeping Car to Montreal, St. Paul and Minneapolis. Parlor Car Portland and Old Orchard to Montreal. Tourist Sleeper for Chicago Tuesday.

No. 9—Express from Boston daily, except Saturday, has Pullman Sleeping Car to St. Johns, N.B., First and Second Class Coaches and Dining Car Vanceboro to Truro.

No. 35—Leaving Toronto daily, has Sleeping Car for New York, via N. Y. C. Parlor and Dining Car Toronto to Buffalo.

No. 39—Leaving Montreal daily, has First and Second Class Coaches and Sleeping Car for Quebec.

PARLOR CARS are run on Trains Nos. 1, 2, 23, 24, 35, 36, 37 and 38 between Ottawa and Montreal; on Nos. 41, 54 (Cafe), 58 and 63 between Quebec and Montreal; on Nos. 77 and 80 between Ottawa and Brockville; on Nos. 27, 29, 34 and 38 between Toronto, Hamilton and Buffalo; on Nos. 3 and 4 between Vancouver and Seattle; on Nos. 41 and 42 between Nelson and Midway, B.C.; on Nos. 9 and 10 between Calgary and Edmonton.

PACIFIC COAST STEAMSHIP CONNECTIONS.

Leave **VANCOUVER**—**C. P. Ry. Co.'s B. C. Coast Service Steamers for Skagway**, connecting with W. P. & Y. Ry. for points in Alaska and Yukon Territory. S.S. *Princess Beatrice* or *May* 11 00 p.m., July 1st, 7th, 13th, 17th, 25th and 31st. **For Nanaimo**—Week-days only, on arrival of Transcontinental Trains. **From Nanaimo** 7 00 a.m. daily, except Sat. and Sun., Sat. only 8 00 a.m., connecting with Transcontinental Trains.

Leave **VICTORIA**—**C.P.Ry.Co.'s B.C. Coast Service Steamers for Seattle**—S.S. *Victoria* 1 00 p.m., except Thursday. From Seattle, 12 00 night, except Thursday.

C. P. Ry. Co.'s B. C. Coast Service Steamers for Skagway, connecting there with the White Pass & Yukon Ry., for all points in Alaska and the Yukon Territory. S.S. *Princess Beatrice* or *May* 11 00 p.m., July 6th, 12th, 16th, 24th and 30th.

C. P. Ry. Co.'s B. C. Coast Service Steamers for Port Simpson, Naas, etc.—S.S. *Tees* 11 00 p.m., 1st and 15th of each month (Vancouver 2 00 p.m. 2d and 16th of each month) for Surf Inlet, Skeena River, Port Simpson, Naas and intermediate points. Calls at Skidegate trip of 1st and at Bella Coola trip of 15th.

C. P. Ry. Co.'s B. C. Coast Service Steamers for Ahouset, Quatsino, Cape Scott, etc.—S.S. *Queen City* 11 00 p.m., 1st, 7th, 14th and 20th of each month for Ahouset and way ports, 7th and 20th of each month for Quatsino, 20th of each month for Cape Scott and way ports.

BRITISH COLUMBIA LAKE AND RIVER SERVICE.

COLUMBIA AND KOOTENAY STEAMER LINES.

ARROW LAKE AND COLUMBIA RIVER ROUTE.

Steamers "Rossland," "Kootenay" and "Minto."

*9 20 A M	Miles 0	lve. **Revelstoke**...(*C. P. Ry.*) arr.	5 10 P M	....
10 55 A M	" 28	lve. **Arrowhead**....(*Steamer*) arr.	3 25 P M	....
1 45 P M	" 64	arr.......... **Nakusp**.......... lve.	12 25 Noon	....
8 35 P M	" 152	arr.......... **Robson**.......... lve.	*11 00 P M	....

SLOCAN LAKE ROUTE.—Steamer "Slocan."—Steamer leaves Rosebery †10 15 a.m., †4 50 p.m. for New Denver, Silverton and Enterprise, arriving Slocan City 1 00, 7 40 p.m. Returning, leaves Slocan City †6 30 a.m., †2 00 p.m. for Enterprise, Silverton and New Denver, arriving Rosebery 9 30 a.m., 4 00 p.m.

KOOTENAY LAKE—Kaslo Route.—Steamer "Kokanee."

....	†8 00 A M	lve.......... **Nelson**.......... arr.	3 15 P M	6 25 P M
....	11 20 A M	arr.......... **Kaslo**.......... lve.	j12 15 Noon	f3 00 P M

OKANAGAN LAKE.—Steamer "Aberdeen."—Steamer leaves Okanagan Landing *f* 11 00 a.m., arriving Kelowna 2 30 p.m., Penticton 6 10 p.m. Returning, leaves Penticton *j* 6 00 a.m., calling at Kelowna 9 30 a.m., arriving Okanagan Landing 1 00 p.m.

KOOTENAY LAKE—Lardo Route.—Steamer "Kokanee."—Leaves Kaslo *f* 11 30 a.m., arriving Lardo 12 50 noon. Leaves Lardo *f* 1 30 p.m., arrives Kaslo 2 50 p.m.

CROWSNEST ROUTE.—Steamer "Moyie."—Leaves Nelson *4 30 a.m., arriving Kootenay Landing 10 00 a.m. Returning, leaves Kootenay Landing *1 00 p.m., arriving Nelson 6 10 p.m.

TROUT LAKE ROUTE.—Steamer "Procter."—Leaves Trout Lake City *f* 7 30 a.m., arrives Gerrard 9 30 a.m. Leaves Gerrard *f* 2 45 p.m., arrives Trout Lake City 4 45 p.m.

Connections.—At Kootenay Landing and Arrowhead with Canadian Pacific Ry. steamers to Kootenay points.

STANDARD TIME—*Atlantic time.*—East of Vanceboro, Me. *Eastern time.*—Vanceboro, Me., to Fort William, Sault Ste. Marie and Detroit. *Central time.*—Fort William to Broadview, including Manitoba branches. *Mountain time.*—Broadview to Laggan and branches. *Pacific time.*—Laggan to Vancouver and branches. ● Daily, except Friday. ‖ Meal stations. + Coupon stations; ♁ Telegraph stations.

Explanation of Reference Marks.—* Daily; † daily, except Sunday; ‡ daily, except Saturday; ¶ daily, except Monday; § Sunday only; *a* daily, except Saturday and Sunday; *b* Friday only; *c* Tuesday and Friday; *d* stops to take on for Detroit and west; *e* stops to let off from Montreal or beyond; *f* Monday, Wednesday and Friday; *g* stops to take on for Toronto or beyond; *h* stops to let off from Toronto or beyond; *i* Monday only; *j* Tuesday, Thursday and Saturday; *k* Saturday only; *l* stops to let off from Detroit and west; *m* daily, except Sunday and Monday; *n* stops to let off from Toronto and points east only; *o* Tuesday and Thursday; *p* stops to let off from west of Chatham and to take on for Toronto and points east only; *q* Saturday and Sunday only; *r* stops to let off from west of Streetsville Junction; *s* stops Sunday only; *t* stops to take for points beyond Mattawamkeag; *u* stops for passengers to and from points north of Portage la Prairie; *v* stops to take passengers for west of Fredericton Junction; *w* Sunday, Tuesday and Thursday; *x* Monday, Wednesday and Saturday; *y* stops Saturday only; ◻ Stops to leave passengers from points on Soo Branch and points west. △ Stops to take passengers on Soo Branch and points west of Sault Ste. Marie only. ◗ Stops to leave passengers from points beyond Cartier. ■ Will commence running Monday, July 2d, and be discontinued after Saturday, September 15th.

For Parlor, Sleeping and Dining Car Service and Explanation of Reference Marks, see page 592.

Commencing May 6, 1906.

No. 97 Pacific Express.	No. 1 Imperial Limited.	STATIONS	No. 2 Imperial Limited.	No. 96 Atlantic Express.
9 40 P M	9 40 A M	lve....**Montreal**...arr.	6 50 P M	7 00 A M
1 10 A M	1 15 P M	........**Ottawa**........	3 10 P M	3 40 A M
3 20 A M	3 40 P M	........**Renfrew**........	12 36 Noon	1 10 A M
9 00 A M	9 25 P M	arr....**North Bay**...lve.	6 55 A M	8 10 P M
11 50 P M	1 45 P M	lve.....**Toronto**.....arr.	2 55 P M	7 00 A M
8 35 A M	9 40 P M	arr....**North Bay**...lve.	6 45 A M	8 50 P M
9 50 A M	10 05 P M	lve....**North Bay**...arr.	6 30 A M	7 45 P M
12 16 Noon	12 15 Night	lve.....**Sudbury**.....lve.	4 15 A M	5 05 P M
7 00 A M	7 40 P M	arr. (Eastern time.) **Ft. William.** lve.	10 25 A M	10 50 P M
6 20	19 00	lve. (Central time.) arr.	9 05	21 10
16 00	4 25	........**Kenora**........	23 50	11 55
20 40	8 30	arr. **Winnipeg** lve.	19 35	7 20
21 40	9 15	lve. arr.	18 45	6 45
1 40	14 10	arr. **Brandon** lve.	14 10	2 40
1 50	14 25	lve. arr.	13 55	2 30
9 17	21 47	.**Regina** (Mountain time.).	5 22	17 50
11 25	23 30	lve...**Moose Jaw**..lve.	4 00	16 15
21 50	8 20	lve...**Medicine Hat**.lve.	19 25	6 45
4 05	15 15	........**Calgary**........	13 20	24 55
7 20	18 40	........**Banff**........	10 20	22 05
8 00	19 05	........**Laggan**........	9 15	20 55
9 30	20 32	........**Field**........	6 35	18 10
14 55	24 57	........**Glacier**........	2 22	12 55
17 45	3 10	........**Revelstoke**........	23 45	9 25
5 25	14 12	arr. **North Bend** lve.	13 05	22 30
5 35	14 22	lve. arr.	12 55	22 20
10 45	19 25	arr...**Vancouver**..lve.	8 00	17 15

TWO THROUGH EXPRESS TRAINS

EVERY DAY, EACH WAY, BETWEEN

Montreal, Ottawa, Toronto and Vancouver

COMMENCING MAY 6, 1906.

WESTBOUND—The "Imperial Limited"—The Pacific Express.

EASTBOUND—The "Imperial Limited"—The Atlantic Express.

† Daily, except Sunday; ‡ daily, except Saturday; ¶ daily, except Monday.

CANADIAN PACIFIC RAILWAY CO'S ROYAL MAIL STEAMSHIP LINES.

ATLANTIC SERVICE.—Montreal and Liverpool, via Quebec.

NAME OF STEAMSHIP.	Intended Sailings from Montreal.	NAME OF STEAMSHIP.	Intended Sailings from Liverpool.
Lake Manitoba	Thursday........June 14, 1906.	Empress of Britain	Saturday........June 9, 1906.
Empress of Britain	Saturday........June 23, 1906.	Lake Champlain	Tuesday........June 12, 1906.
Lake Champlain	Saturday........June 30, 1906.	Empress of Ireland	Saturday........June 23, 1906.
Empress of Ireland	Saturday........July 7, 1906.	Lake Erie	Tuesday........June 26, 1906.
Lake Erie	Thursday........July 12, 1906.	Empress of Britain	Saturday........July 7, 1906.
Empress of Britain	Saturday........July 21, 1906.	Lake Manitoba	Tuesday........July 10, 1906.

ROYAL MAIL STEAMSHIP SERVICE.—JAPAN AND CHINA.

INTENDED SAILINGS—EASTBOUND.						NAME OF STEAMSHIP.	INTENDED SAILINGS—WESTBOUND.					
Hong Kong. Wednesday.	Shanghai (Woosung).	Nagasaki.	Kobe.	Yokohama.	Vancouver.		Vancouver. Monday.	Yokohama	Kobe.	Nagasaki.	Shanghai (Woosung).	Hong Kong.
Dep.	Arr.	Arr.	Arr.	Arr.	Arr.		Dep. 12 45	Arr.	Arr.	Arr.	Arr.	Arr.
1906	1906	1906	1906	1906	1906		1906	1906	1906	1906	1906	1906
May 2	May 5	May 7	May 9	May 12	May 26	....Monteagle....	June 4	June 20	June 22	June 24	June 26	June 30
May 9	May 11	May 14	May 15	May 18	May 30	Empress of Japan	June 11	June 25	June 26	June 28	June 30	July 3
May 23	May 26	May 28	May 30	June 2	June 16	......Tartar......	June 25	July 14	July 16	July 18	July 20	July 24
May 30	June 1	June 4	June 5	June 8	June 20	Empress of China	July 2	July 16	July 17	July 19	July 21	July 24
June 20	June 22	June 25	June 26	June 29	July 11	Empress of India	July 23	Aug. 6	Aug. 7	Aug. 9	Aug. 11	Aug. 14
June 27	June 30	July 2	July 4	July 7	July 19	....Athenian....	July 30	Aug. 18	Aug. 20	Aug. 22	Aug. 24	Aug. 28
July 11	July 13	July 16	July 17	July 20	Aug. 1	Empress of Japan	Aug. 13	Aug. 27	Aug. 28	Aug. 30	Sept. 1	Sept. 4
July 18	July 21	July 23	July 25	July 28	Aug. 10	....Monteagle....	Aug. 20	Sept. 5	Sept. 7	Sept. 9	Sept. 11	Sept. 15
Aug. 1	Aug. 3	Aug. 6	Aug. 7	Aug. 10	Aug. 22	Empress of China	Sept. 3	Sept. 17	Sept. 18	Sept. 20	Sept. 22	Sept. 25
Aug. 8	Aug. 13	Aug. 13	Aug. 15	Aug. 18	Sept. 1	......Tartar......	Sept. 17	Oct. 6	Oct. 8	Oct. 10	Oct. 12	Oct. 16

Steamships for Japan leave Vancouver on arrival of Canadian Pacific Ry. "Pacific Limited" and (except Athenian and Tartar), call at Victoria, B.C., to embark passengers, and returning to land passengers. Athenian and Tartar do not carry first-class passengers. Steamers sail frequently from **Hong Kong** to **Manila, Philippine Islands**, and passengers by this line, transfer at **Hong Kong** to **Manila** steamers. Steamships may leave intermediate ports (Yokohama, Kobe, Nagasaki and Shanghai) in advance of the dates given in the time-table. The usual stay at intermediate ports is: Yokohama, 24 hours; Kobe, 12 hours; Nagasaki, 10 hours; Shanghai, 12 to 24 hours, according to tide. These periods may be reduced or increased according to circumstances. Passengers should ascertain from company's agents at those ports the exact hours of departure.

CANADIAN-AUSTRALIAN ROYAL MAIL STEAMSHIP SERVICE.

Intended Sailings, Southbound.	Vancouver.	Honolulu, H.I.	Suva, Fiji.	Brisbane.		Sydney, N.S.W.	Intended Sailings, Northbound.	Sydney, N.S.W.	Brisbane.		Suva, Fiji.	Honolulu, H.I.	Vancouver.
	▲	Dep.	Dep.	Arr.	Dep.	Arr.		Dep.	Arr.	Dep.	Dep.	Dep.	Arr.
Name of Steamship.	1906	1906	1906	1906	1906	1906	Name of Steamship.	1906	1906	1906	1906	1906	1906
Maheno......	May 25	June 2	June 12	June 17	June 18	June 19	Miowera......	May 14	May 16	May 17	May 22	May 30	June 7
Miowera......	June 22	June 30	July 10	July 15	July 16	July 17	Aorangi......	June 11	June 13	June 14	June 19	June 27	July 5
Aorangi......	July 20	July 28	Aug. 7	Aug. 12	Aug. 13	Aug. 14	Maheno......	July 9	July 11	July 12	July 17	July 25	Aug. 2

▲ Steamships leave Vancouver on arrival of C. P. Pacific Limited.

Steamships call at Victoria, B.C., both ways. Passengers can ascertain from commanders of ships the time allowed at intermediate ports. Passengers for New Zealand points will be forwarded via Sydney.

From points west of Chicago, Sault Ste. Marie and Port Arthur berths can be secured from Assistant General Passenger Agent, Vancouver; east of those points from the General Passenger Agent, Montreal, through any Canadian Pacific Ry. Agent.

UPPER LAKES SERVICE.—Lakes Huron and Superior.

EXPRESS STEAMSHIPS "ALBERTA," "ATHABASCA" AND "MANITOBA."

Intended Sailings—Westbound. (STANDARD—*Eastern time.*) Intended Sailings—Eastbound.

Ports of Call.	Mls	Time.	Days.			Ports of Call.	Mls	Time.	Days.		
Toronto (via C. P. Express Train)..lve.	0	1 50 P M	Tues.	Thu.	Sat.	Fort William......................lve.	0	10 30 A M	Fri.	Sun.	Tues.
Owen Sound " "........arr.	122	5 40 P M	Tues.	Thu.	Sat.	Port Arthur......................lve.	5	11 00 A M	Fri.	Sun.	Tues.
Owen Sound......................lve.	122	5 50 P M	Tues.	Thu.	Sat.	Sault Ste. Marie..................arr.	280	12 30 Noon	Sat.	Mon.	Wed.
Sault Ste. Marie..................arr.	397	1 00 P M	Wed.	Fri.	Sun.	Owen Sound......................arr.	555	8 30 A M	Sun.	Tues.	Thu.
Port Arthur......................arr.	672	11 00 A M	Thu.	Sat.	Mon.	Owen Sound (via C.P. Exp. Train)..lve.	555	9 00 A M	Sun.	Tues.	Thu.
Fort William......................arr.	677	12 00 Noon	Thu.	Sat.	Mon.	Toronto " "........arr.	677	12 55 Noon	Sun.	Tues.	Thu.

THE TYLER TUBE & PIPE CO. BOILER TUBES Guaranteed to Pass A. R. M. M. Specification. WASHINGTON, PA. 26 Cortlandt St., New York. Old Colony Bldg, Chicago. GEO. E. MOLLESON, Manager R.R. Dept., NEW YORK.

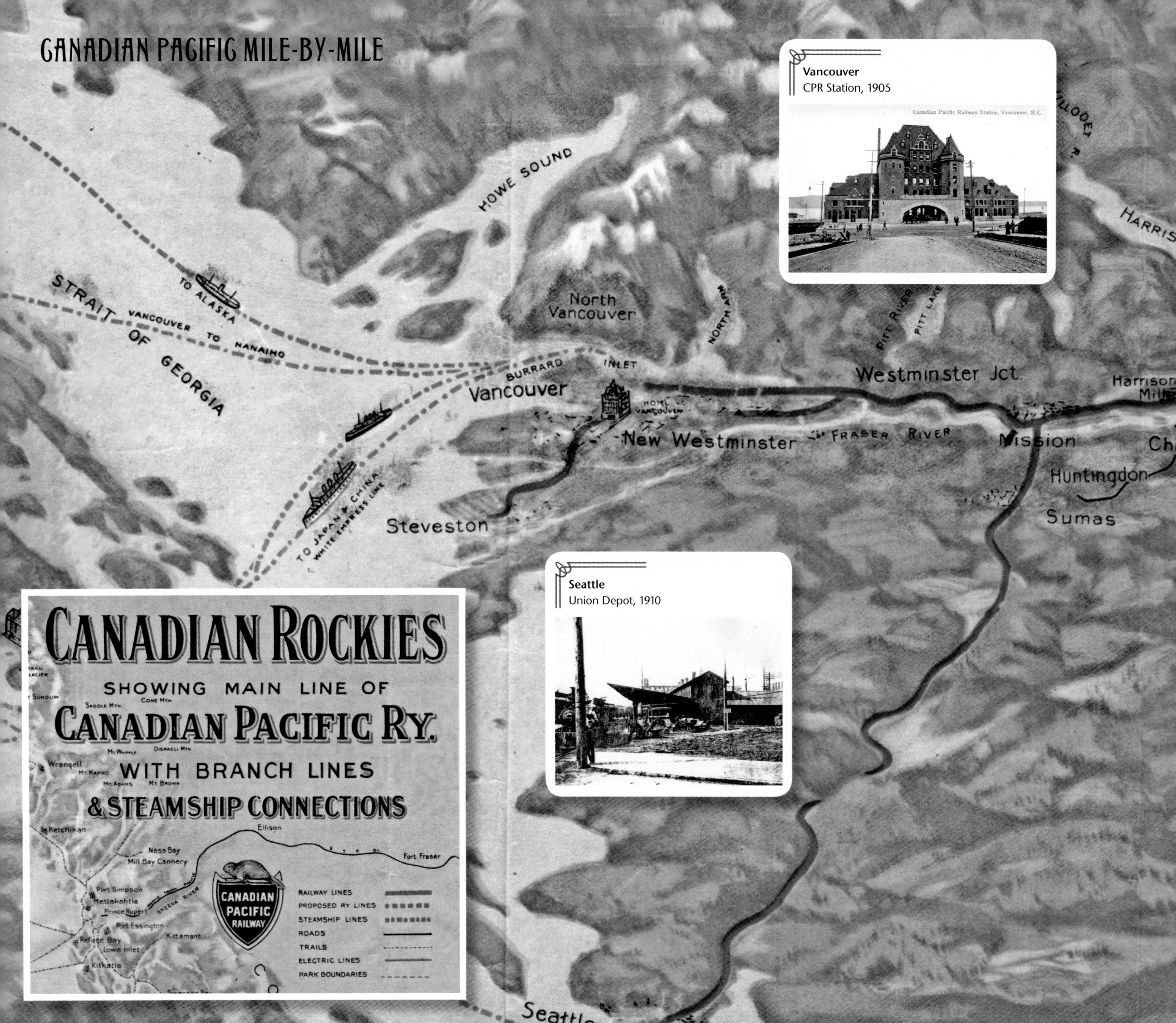
HOWE SOUND
STRAIT OF GEORGIA
TO ALASKA
VANCOUVER TO NANAIMO
TO JAPAN & CHINA
WHITE EMPRESS LINE
North Vancouver
NORTH ARM
PITT RIVER
PITT LAKE
BURRARD INLET
Vancouver
HOTEL VANCOUVER
Westminster Jct.
Harrison Mills
New Westminster
FRASER RIVER
Mission
Huntingdon
Sumas
Steveston
HARRIS
Seattle
CANADIAN ROCKIES
SHOWING MAIN LINE OF
CANADIAN PACIFIC RY.
WITH BRANCH LINES
& STEAMSHIP CONNECTIONS
Wrangell
Ketchikan
Nass Bay
Mill Bay Cannery
Ellison
Fort Fraser
Port Simpson
Metlakahtla
Prince Rupert
Port Essington
Refuge Bay
Lowe Inlet
Kittamant
Kitkatla
SKEENA RIVER
CANADIAN PACIFIC RAILWAY
RAILWAY LINES
PROPOSED RY. LINES
STEAMSHIP LINES
ROADS
TRAILS
ELECTRIC LINES
PARK BOUNDARIES
Canadian Pacific Railway Station, Vancouver, B.C.

Vancouver
CPR Station, 1905

Seattle
Union Depot, 1910

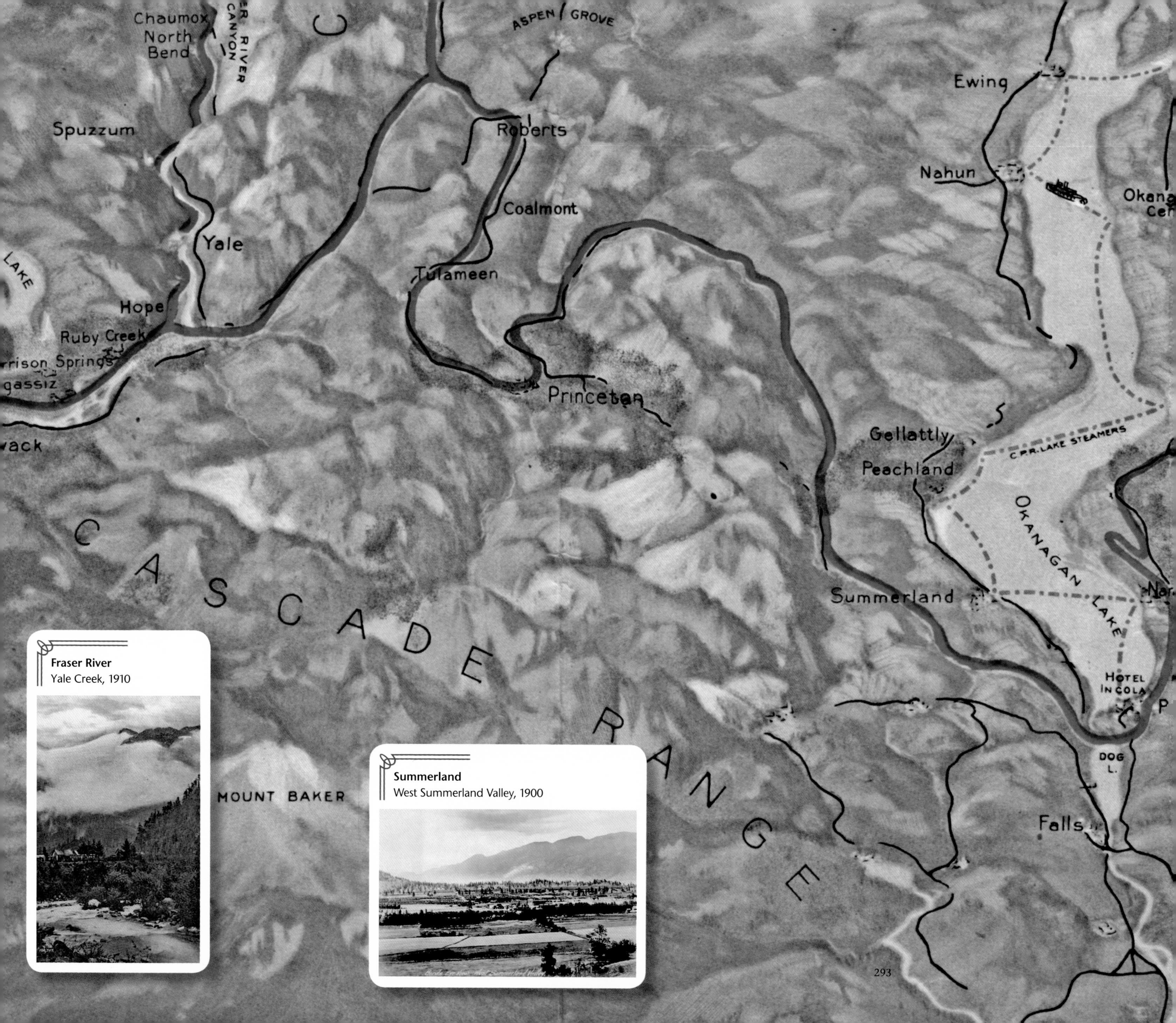

Fraser River
Yale Creek, 1910

Summerland
West Summerland Valley, 1900

Fraser River Canyon
*c.*1900

Kamloops Lake,
A 1900 photograph
by Byron Harman

Revelstoke
First Street, 1900

Sicamous
The original settlement at Eagle Pass Landing, 1886

Arrow Lake
Sinixt fishermen in a sturgeon-nosed canoe, 1900

Glacier
Imperial Limited near Glacier, 1910

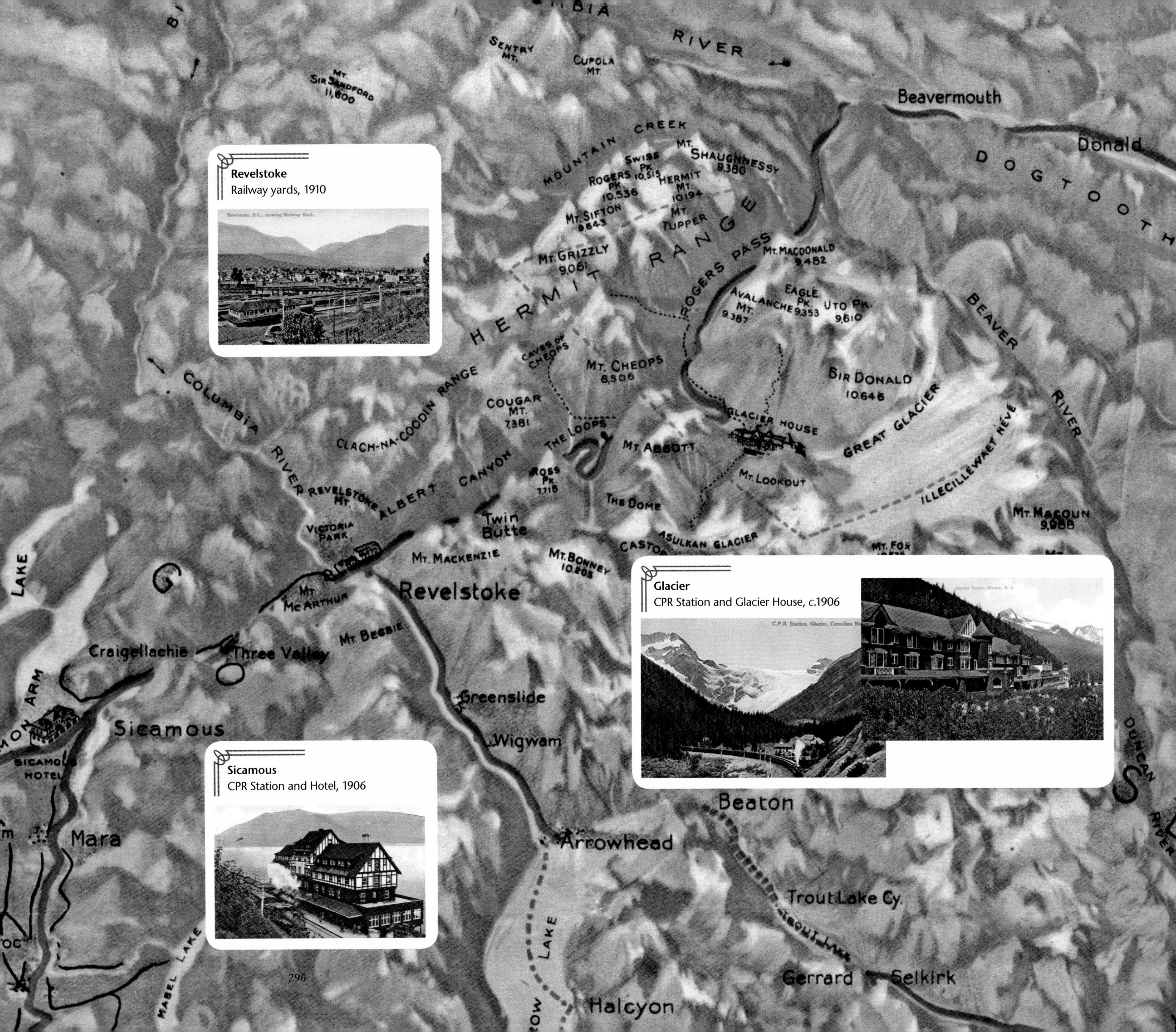

Revelstoke
Railway yards, 1910

Glacier
CPR Station and Glacier House, *c.*1906

Sicamous
CPR Station and Hotel, 1906

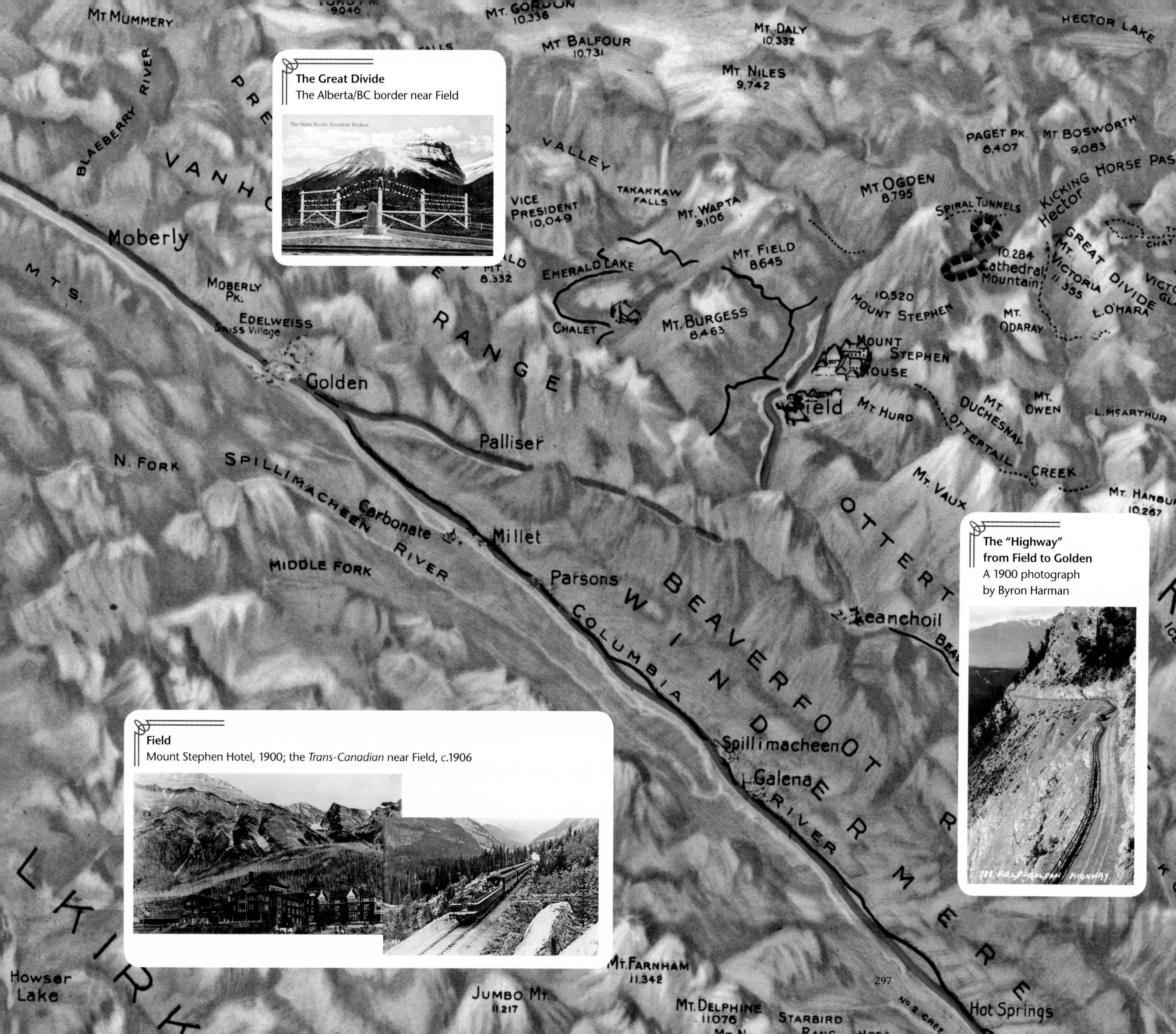

The Great Divide
The Alberta/BC border near Field
The Great Divide, Canadian Rockies.
The "Highway" from Field to Golden
A 1900 photograph by Byron Harman
788. FIELD-GOLDEN HIGHWAY.
Field
Mount Stephen Hotel, 1900; the *Trans-Canadian* near Field, *c.*1906
Mt. Mummery
Mt. Gordon 10,336
Mt. Balfour 10,731
Mt. Daly 10,332
Hector Lake
Mt. Niles 9,742
Blaeberry River
Paget Pk. 8,407
Mt. Bosworth 9,083
Valley
Kicking Horse Pass
Hector
Mt. Ogden 8,795
Takakkaw Falls
Mt. Wapta 9,106
Vice President 10,049
Spiral Tunnels
Moberly
Mt. Field 8,645
Emerald Lake
10,284 Cathedral Mountain
Great Divide
Mt. Victoria 11,355
Moberly Pk.
10,520 Mount Stephen
Mt. Odaray
L. O'Hara
Edelweiss Swiss Village
Chalet
Mt. Burgess 8,463
Range
Mount Stephen House
Golden
Field
Mt. Hurd
Mt. Duchesnay
Mt. Owen
L. McArthur
Palliser
Ottertail Creek
N. Fork
Spillimacheen River
Mt. Vaux
Mt. Hanbury 10,267
Carbonate
Millet
Middle Fork
Parsons
Beaverfoot
Windermere
Leanchoil
Columbia River
Spillimacheen
Galena
Kirk
Howser Lake
Mt. Farnham 11,342
Jumbo Mt. 11,217
Mt. Delphine 11,076
Starbird
Hot Springs

Lake Louise
Lovers' Walk, 1910

Lake Louise
CPR Depot, a 1900 photograph by Byron Harman

Banff
Bird's-eye view, 1899; Banff Springs Hotel, 1906

Didsbury
Railway Street, early 1900s

Olds
Main Street and Station, 1902

Calgary, CPR Station
Calgary Station in 1909; the *Imperial Limited* arriving at Calgary, 1898

Canmore
The Three Sisters, *c.*1910

Penticton
First Kettle Valley train, May 1915

Kelowna
Seen across Okanagan Lake, 1909

Kootenay Landing
Train meets steamer, 1912

Sandon
Silver mine, 1900

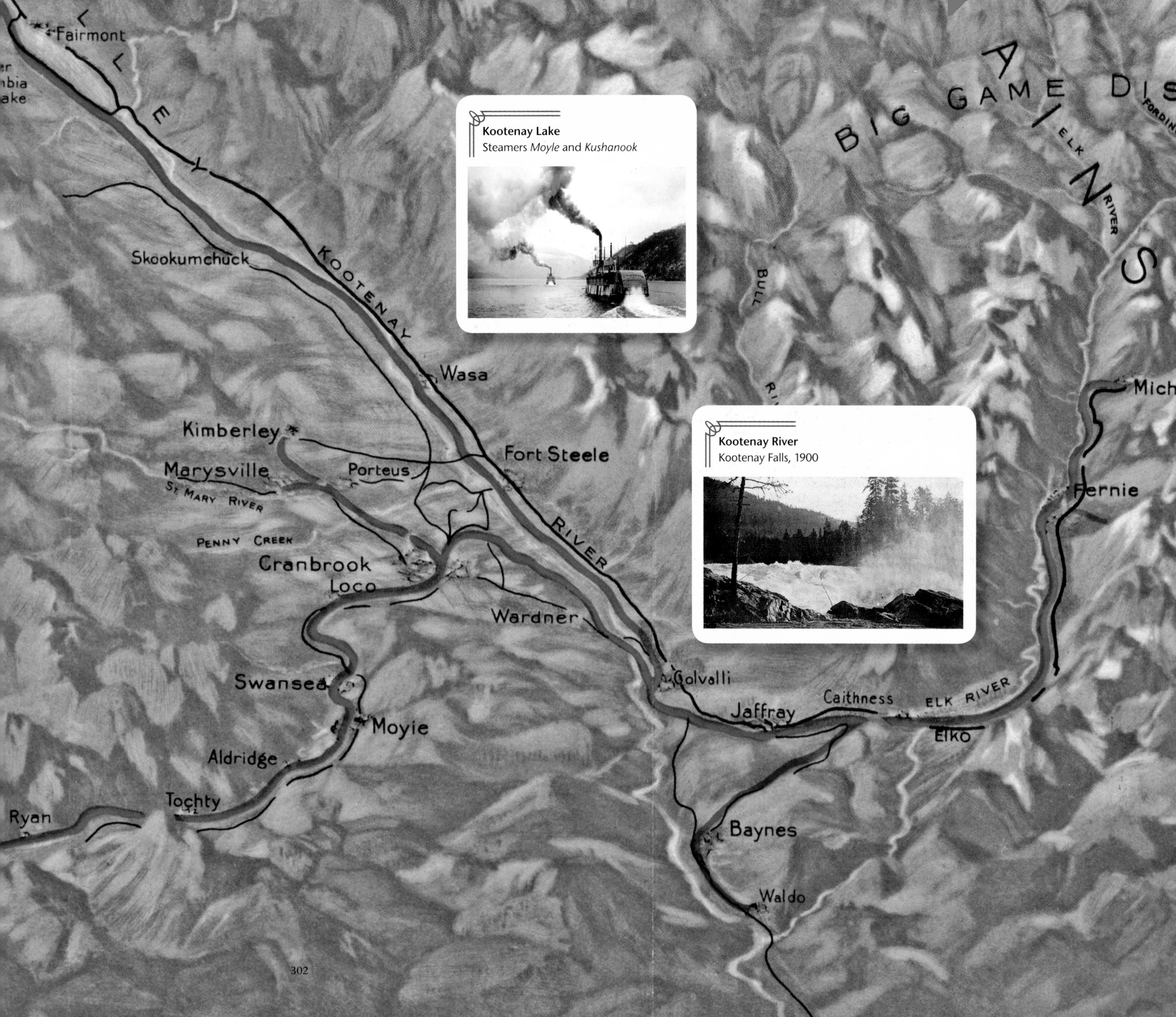
Fairmont
Skookumchuck
KOOTENAY RIVER
Wasa
Kimberley
Fort Steele
Marysville
Porteus
St Mary River
Penny Creek
Cranbrook
Loco
Wardner
Swansea
Moyie
Aldridge
Tochty
Ryan
Colvalli
Jaffray
Caithness
Elk River
Elko
Baynes
Waldo
Fernie
BIG GAME DIS
Bull
Elk River
Kootenay Lake
Steamers *Moyle* and *Kushanook*
Kootenay River
Kootenay Falls, 1900

Macleod
The town, looking east, 1910
CPR roundhouse, *c.*1903

Macleod, Alta., looking East

R. Round House, Macleod, Alta.

RICT

Claresholm

Granum

CROWS NEST MT.
9,125

CROWS NEST PASS

Crows Nest

Coleman

Frank

Hillcrest

Cowley

GOVERNMENT MOTOR ROAD

Pincher

Pincher Creek

Peigan

Macleod

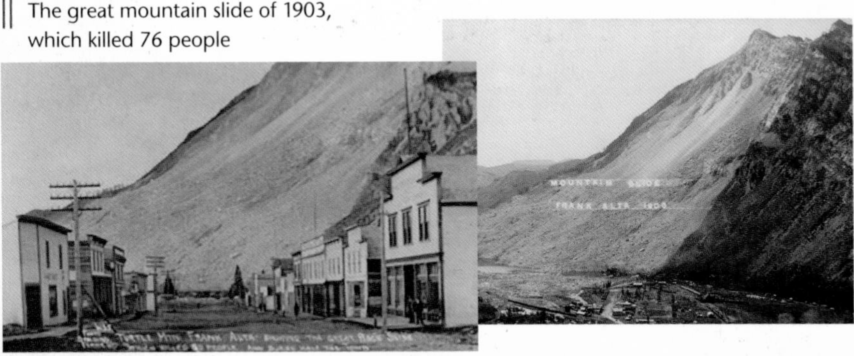

Frank
The great mountain slide of 1903, which killed 76 people

TABLE OF DISTANCES

	MILES
VANCOUVER TO CALGARY	646
REVELSTOKE TO KOOTENAY LANDING	226
SICAMOUS TO PENTICTON	139
GOVERNMENT AUTOMOBILE ROAD	
CALGARY TO BANFF AND VIA VERMILION PASS TO WINDERMERE VALLEY AND CROWS NEST BACK TO CALGARY ROUND TRIP	600

Stone Created

LOGOMOTIVES OF THE CLASSIC WESTERN RAILROAD ROUTES

"Night Trains," a Currier & Ives print.

The image of the classic wood-burning steam locomotive with its colorfully painted cab, polished brass fittings, wooden pilot (or "cow-catcher"), and enormous "balloon" smokestack, has become an intrinsic element in the romance of the West. Yet, these iconic steam engines had a relatively short lifespan and were eventually replaced by more effective, if less colorful, locomotives. The tiny locomotives of the 1860s were soon dwarfed by a series of ever-larger machines. By the 1920s, the largest locomotives in the world were working lines in the American West—some of these "iron horses" were twenty times heavier than those that helped build the railroads.

To better understand the locomotives then in everyday use, it helps to understand how they were used, where they were assigned, and the way they evolved. Locomotives of the later nineteenth century were largely defined by their wheel arrangements, numbering first the front guide wheels, then the center drive wheels, and lastly the rear or trailing wheels. Each configuration was given a type name, although, confusingly, sometimes an arrangement had more than one name. Notably the 4–8–4 had about half a dozen different names, however in the West it was generally known as a Northern. Locos were primarily built by commercial manufacturers, but their specifications were tailored individually by and for the railroad that bought them, and some lines, notably the Central Pacific, built many of their own engines to supplement those purchased commercially. "Flatland" operations—lines running across the Great Plains or along relatively level river valleys—largely used the classic American Standard type defined by its 4–4–0 wheel arrangement. Some were built with low-driving wheels (a low height from the ground meant slower speeds) for heavy freight work, and others with high-driving wheels for faster passenger service, although most featured moderate-sized wheels to be assigned as needed. In the early days, many locomotives of this type were built as wood-burners (especially in the West where coal sources were scarce), and these were often adorned with polished brass, tinted Russian boiler plate, and had colorfully painted cabs and drive wheels.

The nature of the fuel burnt in a locomotive affected the type of smokestack used. The inverted cone characterized by the balloon stack, and the famous diamond stacks often used in the West, were needed to minimize hot embers pouring forth along with exhaust gases and steam from wood-fired boilers (escaping embers tended to start trackside fires). By the 1880s many lines had switched from wood to coal, which burned more efficiently, produced fewer sparks, and did not require the complicated smokestack screens. However, since coal is a sootier fuel, it tended to coat the machinery with grime and coal dust and was therefore less conducive to colorful polished locomotives. As a result many railroads took to painting their "power" black and did away with other ornamentation that was difficult to keep clean.

In the early twentieth century railways in the far West moved towards oil-fired steam engines to overcome the relative lack of useful coal on the Pacific coast. While oil-burning engines had their own peculiarities, they did overcome many limitations associated with coal-fired engines, and oil-burners were some of the earliest large locomotive designs, vastly bigger than engines working the same rails a generation earlier.

Bigger, longer, and faster trains had been made possible as a result of improved couplers, automatic air brakes, steel rails and bridges, and steel-framed railroad cars. By the end of the nineteenth century, more powerful engines were required to accommodate ever heavier and faster trains. Furthermore, steeply graded mountain lines needed big engines with lots of tractive power. New types with more driving wheels were preferred over the old 4–4–0s and other smaller engines. In the late nineteenth century the 4–6–0 "Ten-Wheelers" with tall drivers emerged as a popular passenger engine, while light freight trains called for the use of 2–6–0 Moguls, and heavier trains required 2–8–0 Consolidations (both types introduced in the 1860s). A few railroads were partial to the 4–8–0 "Twelve-Wheeler" type, which was especially notable for its pulling ability on mountain grades.

By the turn of the century, further demands on power resulted in engines built to much larger proportions, as well as a host of innovative and new wheel arrangements. In 1900, express passenger trains in flat country were hauled by fast 4–4–2 Atlantics, and in some instances by 2–6–2 Prairies which were more powerful (but less stable) at speed; freights were moved by even larger Consolidations, and on some lines by big 2–10–0 Decapods. The Northern Pacific was among the first to use these monsters, so-named because of their ten connected driving wheels.

In the early years of the twentieth century railroad traffic had accelerated rapidly, leading to further gains in train weight and operating speed. Within a few years, the Atlantics were deemed too light and were replaced as express passenger engines by even more powerful 4–6–2 Pacifics. Freight locomotives grew to extremely impressive proportions. The Great Northern was first in the West to use massive, articulated Mallet compounds—a type that put two complete sets of running gear (cylinders, drive wheels, connecting rods, and valve gear) under a common boiler, with the rear cylinders exhausting into forward cylinders to make more efficient use of steam. Soon other railroads followed suit and a variety of Mallet types were built, including 2–6–6–2 and 2–8–8–2, typically for work in graded territory.

During the First World War era, the 4–8–2 Mountain types became popular as passenger locomotives on graded lines, and a number of railroads bought 2–10–2 Santa Fe types for freight service. Ever larger locomotives were built in the 1920s and 1930s, with the scales tipped by the Northern Pacific's 2–8–8–4 Yellowstones, and finally by the UP's massive 4–8–8–4 Big Boys built between 1941 and 1944. Diesels, which had been gaining acceptance since the mid-1930s, gradually replaced steam after the Second World War. By 1960, steam was gone from western lines except for portions of the narrow gauge Rio Grande, where it survived for a few more years.

LOCOMOTIVES OF THE SOUTHERN PACIFIC SYSTEM

The corporate entanglements of the Southern Pacific Lines were inordinately complex, with a host of subsidiaries and affiliated companies including the original Central Pacific route from San Francisco to Ogden. Although it was the Central Pacific's founders—the famed Big Four—that held corporate control, by 1885 the Southern Pacific was the dominant railroad in the West, controlling the Overland, Shasta, and Sunset Routes in addition to other lines. (The Southern Pacific Lines name appeared on most of the company's equipment after 1885. However, some locomotives continued to be sub-lettered for the Central Pacific and other affiliated lines for many years.)

Although many of the early Southern and Central Pacific engines were 4–4–0s, once bigger locomotives were available they largely relegated the old 4–4–0 to flatland service. While the 4–4–0 was not the most powerful type, it was perhaps the most versatile. Among the examples of this common American Standard were Globe Locomotive Works' products of 1868, first used as construction power at Donner, but in their later years working local passenger trains in the Bay Area.

The Central Pacific's Donner Pass crossing was without question one of the most difficult of mountain railroads, not least because of its prolonged steeply graded climbs over the Sierra Nevada, but also because of its many miles of snowsheds and tunnels. In the early years, the 2–8–0 Consolidation was prevalent in mountain service, and Southern Pacific Lines acquired more than 440 of this type. More unusual was the Central Pacific's interest in the 4–8–0 Mastodon type. Some 84 of this type were acquired between 1882 and 1898, some of which were built at the railroad's

El Gobernador, Central Pacific No. 237, built in 1884 at CP's Sacramento shop. This was the only 4–10–0 engine ever to run on an American railroad. From a painting by Richard Ward.

Sacramento, California shops. In their classic form, the CP's Mastodons featured a distinctive wooden clerestory cab contoured like a "broken bull's nose" as well as decorative scroll work on steam and sand domes. Sadly, these elegant trappings tended not to last past a locomotive's first major rebuilding. The CP's Mastodons were largely assigned to the Shasta route and also found service as helpers, both in freight and passenger service, on the various Oregon lines.

A unique expansion of the 4–8–0 was America's only 4–10–0, named *El Gobernador, "The Governor,"* of 1884, that appears to have spent more time in service as a helper on Southern Pacific's Tehachapi crossing than anywhere else. Famous for its unusual size, this locomotive was decidedly unsuccessful as it tended to run out of steam too quickly, and only remained in service until about 1892.

By the 1890s, the SP and the CP looked to 4–6–0s for express passenger work, and some 2–6–0s for freight and passenger service as well. Compounding was introduced as a way of improving efficiency through multiple use of steam and thus had two or more sets of cylinders. The SP bought a variety of the Baldwin-built four-cylinder Vauclain compounds, which were assigned to both express trains in 2–6–0 and 4–4–2 types, and as 2–8–0s for heavy freight working.

A more effective type of compound was the articulated Mallet that the Southern Pacific first bought in the 2–8–8–2 arrangement for freight service on the Central Pacific's line over Donner Pass in 1909. It soon discovered that these massive engines made so much smoke that they couldn't be operated in snowsheds in the conventional format, and so the railroad worked with Baldwin to reverse the cab and boiler arrangement, resulting in the famous "cab forward" steam locomotive design. These were perhaps the most distinctive steam locomotives in the West and unique to SP/CP routes. They were built in various arrangements for both freight and passenger work. The classic *Overland Limited* from the First World War period would have been led through Donner's snowsheds by a 4–6–6–2 Baldwin-built "cab forward" Mallet.

The Southern Pacific was famous for its Pacific types. The 4–6–2 was well suited for fast passenger work. Pacifics would have worked the *Overland* and other named passenger trains across the Nevada desert. These handsome machines were also largely Baldwin products and among the best of their type in the West. Several have been preserved, and No. 2472 has been regularly operated on excursion trains. Later, the SP moved to larger passenger types, among them the 4–8–2 Mountain, and perhaps most famously in the 1930s, to the 4–8–4. The SP's stylish, semi-streamlined 4–8–4s for service on the *Daylight* passenger trains were iconic locomotives and emblematic of California railroading of the 1930s and 1940s.

UNION PACIFIC LOCOMOTIVES

Most famous of all Union Pacific engines was No. 119, pictured prominently at Promontory Summit, Utah, at the driving of the "Last Spike" on May 10, 1869. No. 119 posed pilot to pilot with the Central Pacific's *Jupiter* to commemorate the joining of the CP and UP rails of the new Pacific Railroad. In these early days, the UP's most common type was the 4–4–0, and although 119 featured a straight stack, many of the UP's engines were famous for their elaborate diamond stacks, necessary to keep sparks from escaping and igniting the prairie grasses.

The UP was quick to investigate larger engines, and bought its first 4–6–0s in 1868. From the beginning these were deemed dual service locomotives, and were assigned as needed to heavier trains. These too were fitted with diamond stacks, broad wooden pilots, boxy headlamps, and the colorful and ornate trappings that decorated locomotives of the period. Although the UP bought its first 2–8–0 Consolidations in 1868, these were initially relegated to service on the grades in Wyoming, and it was not until the 1880s that the railroad bought them in large numbers. However, for more than a generation these engines were common as freight haulers, with the UP placing orders with Baldwin, Danforth-Cooke, and other master locomotive builders. Some were ordered as compounds, with this system offering economy through lower water and fuel consumption.

After the turn of the century, the Union Pacific's locomotives grew rapidly in size. Under the progressive regime of E. H. Harriman, who also controlled the Southern Pacific system for a period, the UP ordered 4–4–2 Atlantics for short express trains, and numerous 4–6–2 Pacifics for its longer expresses. Many of these were similar in proportion and design to those used by the SP and its affiliated lines. In the 1920s, a decade after anti-trust action separated the Harriman properties, the UP adopted big 4–8–2 mountain types for service on its long distance limiteds. By the 1930s, it had perfected the 4–8–4, and continued to order this type through the Second World War. Its final 4–8–4, No. 844, remains in service to the present day, and is among the most photographed of all American steam locomotives.

In 1909, the Union Pacific ordered its first articulated types for freight work, ponderous 2–8–8–2 Mallets. The railroad saw the benefit of big freight engines and continued to buy articulateds for the next three and a half decades. In the 1930s it pioneered the 4–6–6–4 Challenger type, designed for high-speed passenger and fast freight, then in 1941 the design was expanded to the famous 4–8–8–4 Big Boy, a type unique to the UP and among the largest steam locomotives ever built.

The Union Pacific was an early proponent of internal combustion power, and thanks to its forward-looking Motive Power Superintendent, William McKeen, the line had one of the first large fleets of gasoline-powered mechanical railcars. Known as Windsplitters, these cars featured knife-edged front ends and smooth sides to reduce wind resistance, and tended to have porthole windows that gave them a decidedly "Jules Verne" appearance. McKeen built them commercially at UP's Omaha Shops, and while the UP was his main customer, he also sold cars to many other lines, producing large numbers from 1905 into the First World War period.

NORTHERN PACIFIC LOCOMOTIVES

As with the other western lines, in its early days the Northern Pacific largely relied upon the American Standard 4–4–0. As the railroad grew in length and traffic, so did its motive needs. In 1886, the NP was the first North American line to order the massive 2–10–0 Decapod, which it used largely as a helper on Montana mountain passes. By 1900, the NP largely depended upon high-drive wheel 4–6–0 Ten Wheelers for express passenger trains, while some low-drive wheel 4–6–0s and numerous 2–8–0s did the bulk of the freight work. A number of its 2–8–0s were built as compounds, and the NP favored both the two-cylinder cross compound and the four-cylinder tandem compound arrangements. The railroad had easy access to inexpensive Rosebud lignite coal, but this had a low yield and high ash content, so the NP worked with commercial locomotive builders to develop specialized locomotives with unusually large fireboxes that would take maximum advantage of this resource. One result was the design in 1904 for 2–8–2 Mikados, among the first built in the United States for road freight service.

The NP's early-twentieth-century passenger locomotives favored the Pacific type, which it bought in large numbers for a dozen years beginning in 1905. By the First World War the length and weight of Northern Pacific passenger limiteds required bigger power, and the railroad invested in 4–8–2 Mountain types. In 1927 it aimed to expand the Mountain with an exceptionally large firebox to accommodate Rosebud lignite, which resulted in the pioneer application of the 4–8–4 wheel arrangement, a type known as the Northern in the NP's honor. Its freight locomotives reached maximum proportions with the development of the massive 2–8–8–4 Yellowstone type in 1928. The locomotive was so large, a banquet was held in its firebox! These were the world's largest steam engines until the advent of the Union Pacific Big Boy in 1941.

A typical 2–8–2 Mikado, in a 1910 photograph.

Atchison, Topeka & SF *Santa Fe* Class 2–10–2 No. 3895 crossing the Mojave Desert near Amboy, California, with 86 cars in tow.

THE SANTA FE

Typical of the western railroads, the Santa Fe began operations with 4–4–0s. These were largely sufficient for its early years, although bigger types such as 2–8–0s were assigned to graded territory. The railroad's passenger power progressed typically from 4–4–0, to 4–4–2, 4–6–2, 4–8–2, and finally by the 1920s to 4–8–4s. Among the less common passenger types were high-wheeled 2–6–2 Prairies, and some very peculiar Mallet types, including a few with articulated boilers that were notoriously unsuccessful. The railroad's freight power also progressed, but with some notable types. The Santa Fe proved to be an early proponent of the 2–10–0 Decapod, a type it advanced to the 2–10–2 Santa Fe in 1902. The application of trailing wheels was intended to aid in reverse moves, as the big engines were normally assigned to helper service on Raton Pass. After shoving a heavy freight to the summit, locomotives would reverse back down grade and trailing wheels allowed them to do this faster.

Some massive 2–10–10–2s were built for the Santa Fe in 1911. These proved too large for practical service, and were ultimately separated into more manageable 2–10–2s. In 1927 the Santa Fe adopted the 4–8–4, and in the 1930s adapted this type for freight work while also buying massive 2–10–4s. Its refinement of both these types resulted in several classes of superlative locomotives, considered among the best American steam locomotives ever built.

Since the railroad crossed some of the longest arid districts in North America, it had greater concern for water conservation than many other lines. In the 1890s and early twentieth century, the Santa Fe emerged as one of the chief proponents of compound locomotives, which promised greater efficiency and thus lower water consumption. The railroad experimented with a great variety of two- and four-cylinder non-articulated compounds, and ordered some especially large 2–10–0 and 2–10–2 Tandem compound types. Although the compound type fell out of favor and was replaced by non-articulated types after about 1910, the Santa Fe's interest translated into the odd Mallets.

Another unusual aspect of the Santa Fe's steam power was its early and extensive development of oil-burning engines. The relative dearth of coal deposits on Santa Fe's western lines, and the proliferation of oil in Southern California and Texas, made this an ideal locomotive fuel. Following the Santa Fe's successful experiments in the early twentieth century, many other lines in the far West adopted oil-burning engines.

LOCOMOTIVES OF THE DENVER AND RIO GRANDE

The Denver and Rio Grande's first train from Denver to Colorado Springs was pulled by *Montezuma*, a compact 2–4–0. In its first years, this non-standard type was the railroad's typical passenger engine and it bought four of them. At the time the railroad managed its operation with just a dozen locomotives, all Baldwin products. For freight service, the D&RG initially found the 2–6–0 Mogul was sufficient, yet as the road expanded and built higher into the mountains it needed a more powerful breed of locomotive.

On his honeymoon in Wales, Rio Grande founder General William Jackson Palmer met with narrow gauge proponent and locomotive designer Robert Fairlie, who inspired him to order one of Fairlie's unusual double-ended twin-boiler locomotives of the type preferred by Welsh narrow gauge lines. Accordingly, England's Vulcan Foundry Company built a Fairlie-type called *Mountaineer* for the D&RG in June 1873. It is best remembered as a helper locomotive on La Veta Pass but was scrapped about 1888.

During the 1870s the 2–8–0 Consolidation had become the most common heavy freight locomotive in the United States and Baldwin adapted it for D&RG narrow gauge operation beginning in 1877. Using four pairs of driving wheels, these were well suited to the D&RG's mountain grades, so during the next two and half decades the railroad bought 150 narrow gauge 2–8–0s. These worked all across the narrow gauge system—over the Palmer Divide, through the Royal Gorge, over Marshall Pass, and on the San Juan extension. Some survived for more than sixty years in service.

In the twentieth century the Rio Grande sought more powerful narrow gauge engines, and so was among the first American lines to adopt the 2–8–2 Mikado type that Baldwin had first built for Japan in 1897. The rear trailing truck allowed the Mikado to carry a large firebox, which gave it greater power. The D&RG's first fifteen three-foot gauge 2–8–2s built in 1903 were unusual among narrow gauge locomotives because they had outside frames and used outside counterweights and crankpins. These engines were reported to have stirred up the ballast and so were known as Mudhens. The success of this type led the Rio Grande to order more Mikados, with orders in the 1920s for both Alco and Baldwin. The later machines were even heavier and more powerful than the Mudhens, and many of them survived in regular service on remaining narrow gauge routes into the 1960s, with some examples still preserved.

CANADIAN PACIFIC RAILWAY

In its first two decades the Canadian Pacific Railway was a more fervent adherent to the 4–4–0 American Standard than most railways of the period, and pursued a policy of acquiring standardized 4–4–0s (based on Pennsylvania Railroad practice) virtually to the exclusion of all other types. The idea was that locomotives of identical specifications would minimize complexity in maintenance and parts supply. However, the CPR's 4–4–0 fleet was not as uniform as hoped, in part because commercial suppliers did not adhere perfectly to CPR's vision, and because as the railroad expanded a number of different locomotives were inherited through line acquisition. One of the few exceptions to its early motive power policy was the 2–8–0 built for service in the Selkirk Mountains. Although it patronized a variety of commercial locomotive manufacturers, the CPR also built hundreds of its own locomotives at its Montreal shops.

In 1889, the CPR abruptly gave up on new 4–4–0 acquisitions, instead focusing on buying 4–6–0 Ten Wheelers, a versatile type that it assigned to a variety of services. Its 4–6–0s used a straightforward, well-balanced design that gave decades of good service across the system. The CPR continued to improve upon its 4–6–0 design, and while its later Ten Wheelers were much heavier than the early machines, the railroad continued to order this arrangement for general service into the second decade of the twentieth century. In addition, by the end of the nineteenth century, the CPR had amassed a substantial fleet of 2–8–0 Consolidations (numbering more than 200) for heavy freight service.

Although the CPR took a conservative approach toward its locomotive fleet and did not rush into widespread adoption of new wheel arrangements, it occasionally experimented with unusual types. It sampled the 4–4–2 Atlantic, but did not embrace the model, and between 1909 and 1911 the company also built some highly unusual Mallets.

In 1906 the CPR adopted the 4–6–2 Pacific, which seemed like a natural progression from the 4–6–0, and bought a large number of these for passenger work. Then in 1912 the road began acquiring 2–8–2 Mikados, which it assigned to both freight and passenger services, and also sampled the 2–10–2. In the late 1920s the CPR adopted the 4–6–4 Hudson as an express passenger locomotive, while also showing an interest in the 2–10–4, which it designated as the Selkirk type. The CPR remained committed to steam for a few years longer than most railroads south of the border, and did not become fully dieselized until the 1960s.

LOCOMOTIVE BIBLIOGRAPHY

Alexander, Edwin P. *History of The Baldwin Locomotive Works 1831–1923.* Philadelphia, 1923.

— *Iron Horses.* New York: Bonanza Books, 1941.

— *American Locomotives.* New York: Bonanza Books, 1950.

Best, Gerald M. *Snowplow: Clearing Mountain Rails.* Berkeley: Howell-North Books, 1966.

Bruce, Alfred W. *The Steam Locomotive in America.* New York: Bonanza Books, 1952.

Bryant, Keith L. *History of the Atchison, Topeka and Santa Fe Railway.* New York: Macmillan, 1974.

Conrad, J. David. *The Steam Locomotive Directory of North America. Vols. I & II.* Polo: Transportation Trails, 1988.

Drury, George H. *Guide to North American Steam Locomotives.* Waukesha: Kalmbach Publishing, 1993.

Duke, Donald, and Stan Kistler. *Santa Fe–Steel Rails Through California.* San Marino: Golden West Books, 1963.

Dunscomb, Guy, L. *A Century of Southern Pacific Steam Locomotives.* Modesto: Guy L. Dunscomb and Son, 1963.

Hidy, Ralph W., and Muriel E. Hidy, Roy V. Scott, with Don L. Hofsommer. *The Great Northern Railway.* Boston: Harvard Business School Press, 1988.

Kratville, William, and Harold E. Ranks. *Motive Power of the Union Pacific.* Omaha: Barnhart Press, 1958.

Lamb, W. Kaye. *History of the Canadian Pacific Railway.* New York: Macmillan, 1977.

Morgan, David P. *Steam's Finest Hour.* Milwaukee: Kalmbach Publishing, 1959.

Signor, John R. *Donner Pass: Southern Pacific's Sierra Crossing.* San Marino: Golden West Books, 1985.

Sinclair, Angus. *Development of the Locomotive Engine.* New York: Angus Sinclair, 1907.

Solomon, Brian. *The American Steam Locomotive.* Osceola: Motorbooks International, 1998.

— *Narrow Gauge Steam Locomotives.* Osceola: Motorbooks International, 1999.

— *Super Steam Locomotives.* Osceola: Motorbooks International, 2000.

— *Locomotive.* Osceola: Motorbooks International, 2001.

— *Alco Locomotives.* St. Paul: Voyageur Press, 2009.

Steinbrenner, Richard T. *The American Locomotive Company – A Centennial Remembrance.* Warren: On Track Publishers, 2003.

Swengel, Frank M. *The American Steam Locomotive: Volume 1, Evolution.* Davenport: Midwest Rail Publications, 1967.

Westing, Frederick. *The Locomotives that Baldwin Built.* Seattle: Superior Publishing, 1966.

White, John H., Jr. *American Locomotives – an Engineering History 1830–1880.* Baltimore: Johns Hopkins Press, Toronto, 1968.

— *Early American Locomotives.* New York: Dover Publications, 1979.

RAILROAD EQUIPMENT AND ROLLING STOCK

From the 1860s to the 1930s American railway cars went through a series of evolutionary changes, resulting in radical transformations in appearance. Not only did size and weight of cars increase as a result of the installation of safety equipment and adoption of stronger materials used in construction, but the styles of design changed to suit changing aesthetic tastes. For the prospectors and pioneers who rode the passenger carriages after the Civil War, the trains of the later era would have been virtually unrecognizable.

Railroad rolling stock of the Civil War period had more in common with stagecoach construction than with railroad equipment of the twentieth century. Cars were small, largely custom-made, and were built mostly from wood, except for their running-gear and couplers, which were iron. As the railroad business grew and technology became more refined, larger freight cars with greater carrying capacity came into use, while passenger cars became larger, safer, more elegant, and more specialized. There were several reasons for this evolution—fundamental changes in railroad technology; improvements in manufacturing techniques and materials; and the traveling public's expectations of greater comfort, although most technological innovations were implemented only gradually.

Among the principal limitations of early railway cars were the primitive braking systems then in use, which restricted both size and weight of cars while limiting the maximum speeds at which they could travel. In the early days, brakes were all set manually. The locomotive engineer used an engine brake, while the brakes on the cars were tightened by hand using large, cast-iron brake wheels. Brakemen were positioned throughout the train awaiting the "down brakes" signal from the engineer. When the whistle came they would leap into action, tightening down the brake wheels and racing from car to car as fast as they could. With a squeal and a smell of brake shoe smoke, a heavy train would eventually grind to a halt. While passenger train brakemen were afforded some level of comfort, men working freight trains were required to ride precariously on the tops of cars in all weather—an uncomfortable and exceptionally hazardous practice that was eventually banned in the twentieth century.

The introduction of the Westinghouse Automatic Airbrake, using air pressure to stop the train, greatly improved train handling and railroad safety. First implemented on passenger cars in the 1870s, it took thirty years to completely equip the hundreds of thousands of freight cars in use on the North American network. Among the unintended but positive consequences of automatic airbrakes was the ability to operate much heavier trains at much higher speeds. As a result, both passenger and freight equipment could be built to much larger proportions, and trains run with greater lengths. Also contributing to improved safety, larger equipment, and longer trains was the Janney automatic coupler introduced about the same time as the airbrake. These were stronger than the old style link and pin couplers and much safer, eliminating the need to have a brakeman risk life and limbs by manually coupling cars. On some lines the use of automatic block signaling further improved safety; in the early twentieth century E. H. Harriman, who controlled both the Southern Pacific and the Union Pacific, improved safety by the installation of signals across his lines. Today the Harriman Safety Awards are given to American railroads that exhibit safety excellence.

The introduction of economically produced steel was crucial in the transformation of the North American railroad. Steel rails were stronger and less brittle than iron, allowing safe operation of heavier and faster trains, and the material also ultimately replaced both iron and wood in railcar construction. By 1900, steel-framed cars had become common, and after 1910 steel-bodied cars gradually replaced the old wooden cars. Stainless steel and aluminum were introduced in the 1930s in the construction of new streamlined passenger equipment.

The level of comfort aboard passenger cars was transformed as well. The finest and most luxurious passenger cars were strictly the domain of wealthy passengers, while ordinary travelers had to contend with less opulent accommodation, but even these cars were dramatically improved over the years.

PASSENGER CARS

Passenger cars in the post-Civil War West were scarcely larger than those used in the early days of railroading in the East and Midwest. Cars rode on pairs of iron four-wheel trucks, featured open platforms, and rarely measured more than sixty feet between coupler faces. Among the early improvements was the introduction of the clerestory roof, a raised section in the middle of the roof designed to provide better ventilation and lighting in the car. Although built on wooden frames and wooden bodies, cars were often strengthened with iron rods running beneath the body of the car. Unlike later passenger cars that were typically painted in somber tones of dark green, maroon, or gray, many early cars were brightly decorated in red, orange, yellow, or white wash.

During the 1870s and 1880s both the size of cars and the level of comfort they offered their riders grew rapidly. Sleeping cars with six-wheel trucks became common and offered a significantly smoother ride than the old eight-wheelers. The level of interior decoration improved as well. Among the finest cars available to the traveling public were Pullman Palace Cars, operated under contract with the individual railroads by the Pullman Company as part of a continent-wide sleeping car network. Pullman's patented cars were designed for both day- and night-time comfort by using convertible furnishings. Seats could be transformed into lower berths, while upper berths, suspended by chains, were folded down into place from panels in the ceiling. Lavishly decorated in high Victorian styles, these were characterized by faux-opulence and exceptionally detailed ornamentation.

The typical Pullman sleeping car of 1880 made the most of its confines of just 10 feet wide and 66 feet long, and was capable of accommodating 22 to 27 passengers in open sleeping sections. While section sleepers provided curtains for a degree of privacy, by the twentieth century passengers began to demand even greater seclusion, so section sleepers were gradually phased out in favor of cars with individual sleeping compartments.

During the late nineteenth century the Pullman Company grew to dominate North American sleeping car services and operated many fine cars on western trains. At its peak in 1915, Pullman operated cars on more than 215,000 route miles. Pullman sleepers tended to run on the railroads' scheduled passenger trains, often mixed in with day coaches, mail cars, and other passenger equipment. Most long distance trains operated "limited" schedules that made relatively few stops between major stations. The best known of these were the named trains such as Santa Fe's *California Limited* (Chicago–Los Angeles), the Southern Pacific's *Sunset Limited* (San Francisco–Los Angeles–New Orleans), and the jointly operated Chicago and North Western–Union Pacific–Southern Pacific *Overland Limited* (Chicago–Omaha–Oakland/San Francisco). These used the fanciest equipment with the most elaborate décor, operated on expedited schedules, and charged the highest fares.

In those days, passengers of means gladly paid a premium to travel in these extra-fare trains, not just to avail themselves of a higher grade of equipment and take advantage of exclusive amenities such as smoking cars, parlor observations, on-board barbers, and richly endowed rolling libraries, but also to avoid mixing with the hoi-polloi. To arrive at the coast on a posh name train implied wealth. The only better way to travel was by private railroad car, the equivalent of a private jet or a large yacht. While end-to-end running times for the speediest limiteds were much faster than ordinary trains, they were very infrequent. Deluxe rail travel was offered along the same sort of schedule as luxury ocean liners, with "sailings" across the country provided only once a week in most cases. If one could afford to travel on the finest trains, one also had the time to travel at the leisure of the railroad.

The introduction of all-steel cars after 1910 offered a greater level of safety since during collisions the wooden-bodied cars tended to "telescope" (whereby one car would slide violently over another causing great destruction) usually with terrible loss of life. Railway travel purists, however, have held that the final phase of deluxe wooden-bodied passenger cars represented the zenith in luxury transport on American rails. The safer, steel cars did not offer the exceptional elegance that the late-era heavy wooden cars provided.

NARROW GAUGE PASSENGER CARS

The Denver and Rio Grande, as America's first and premier narrow gauge line, was also the first narrow gauge railway on the continent to order specially built passenger cars. These were proportionally smaller than the standard gauge cars: 40 feet long with the interior body just 35 feet owing to open platforms at both ends. They were substantially narrower too, just seven feet wide compared with the ten-plus feet typical of standard gauge stock. Among the plush early cars were first-class coaches built by Jackson and Sharp Company of Wilmington, Delaware, which accommodated three dozen passengers. To keep aisle widths workable, narrow gauge cars often used one-by-two seating arrangements instead of the two-by-two seating typical of standard gauge cars.

While the early cars were notoriously uncomfortable, as patronage of narrow gauge lines increased, the type of equipment improved. The D&RG offered Pullman sleeping service on select narrow gauge runs between 1881 and 1902. The first cars featured ten sections (sleeping berths), but the cars were so narrow that the berths were in turn unusually cramped. Later sleeping cars also included basic dining facilities, and the D&RG had plush parlor cars on some runs. A few narrow gauge private cars also found their way on to the backs of trains.

EMIGRANT CARS

Among the legacy of the Western railroads was their role in transporting emigrants. The emigrant trains were the antithesis of the luxury palace cars of the well-known limiteds enjoyed by more affluent travelers. They offered no-frills, Spartan accommodations that provided basic transport with a minimum degree of comfort. The cars were simple and unadorned, designed to be easily cleaned inside and out at the end of the journey with a vigorous hosing down. Seats were little more than wooden benches intended to also serve as bunks for sleeping, although no cushions or blankets were provided as it was expected that emigrants would provide their own. The cars aimed to carry as many people as practical with little regard for privacy or comfort.

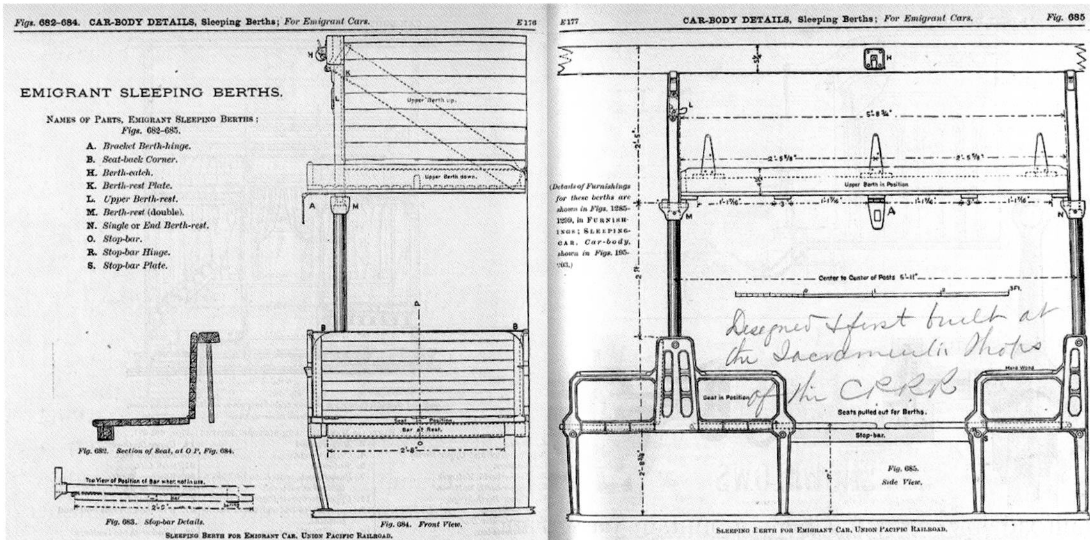

Figs. 682-684. CAR-BODY DETAILS, Sleeping Berths; *For Emigrant Cars.* E176

EMIGRANT SLEEPING BERTHS.

NAMES OF PARTS, EMIGRANT SLEEPING BERTHS:
Figs. 682-685.

A. *Bracket Berth-hinge.*
B. *Seat-back Corner.*
H. *Berth-catch.*
K. *Berth-rest Plate.*
L. *Upper Berth-rest.*
M. *Berth-rest* (double).
N. *Single* or *End Berth-rest.*
O. *Stop-bar.*
R. *Stop-bar Hinge.*
S. *Stop-bar Plate.*

Fig. 682. *Section of Seat, at O P, Fig.* 684.

Fig. 683. *Stop-bar Details.*

Fig. 684. *Front View.*

SLEEPING BERTH FOR EMIGRANT CAR, UNION PACIFIC RAILROAD.

E177 CAR-BODY DETAILS, Sleeping Berths; *For Emigrant Cars.* Fig. 685

(*Details of Furnishings for these berths are shown in Figs.* 1285-1299, in FURNISHINGS; SLEEPING-CAR. *Car-body, shown in Figs.* 195-203.)

Fig. 685.
Side View.

SLEEPING BERTH FOR EMIGRANT CAR, UNION PACIFIC RAILROAD.

CPRR Emigrant Sleeping Car designed by Lewis M. Clement, from his own copy of the 1884 *Car Builder's Dictionary* (above). An cramped and uncomfortable emigrant car, from an engraving of 1876 (left).

Whole families and all their earthly belongings—sometimes including their cats and dogs—traveled together on long journeys across the Plains on board these slow, dimly lit, crowded, and chaotic trains. Children ran up and down the aisles as women cooked on the coal stoves that heated the cars. Since the fares were very low, and often subsidized by the host railroad, progress over the line wasn't especially fast—emigrant trains were treated by the railroads as low priority "extras." Often these trains would sit in sidings for hours waiting to let the scheduled limiteds, fast freight, and other more important trains pass through. Although lacking in glamour and comfort, these trains delivered emigrants to their new homes and farms, and usually did so faster, safer, and with a far greater level of speed and comfort than had been afforded their earlier counterparts who had traveled overland by stage, horseback, or foot in prior years.

FREIGHT CARS

Although their personal comfort occupied the minds of most western travelers, it was revenues from the freight trains that most concerned railroad accountants. Freight business contributed far more to a railroad's bottom line than fares from long-distance passenger limiteds. When arriving at a major terminal such as Omaha, Denver, Sacramento, or Barstow, passengers would see long strings of freight cars, particularly the common wooden boxcar. In the classic era these were 34 feet long, painted rust-brown, and adorned with the railroad's logo or slogan on the side. The most versatile of equipment, a boxcar could be loaded with just about any type of cargo imaginable from merchandise to grain. These cars had roof-mounted "catwalks" to allow brakemen to run from car to car in order to wind down iron brake wheels. Specialized insulated boxcars, known as "reefers" (short for "refrigerator cars") were used to transport Californian produce east on special freights with expedited schedules. Reefers were cooled with large blocks of salted ice installed from hatches at the ends of the cars. Since ice melted as reefers made their way east, it required replenishment at regular intervals where railroads maintained icing stations. These cars were easily distinguished by their bright yellow and orange paint, and in their heyday tens of thousands of reefers were on the move across America's transcontinental lines.

When running empty, railroads would routinely leave boxcar doors open. Traveling vagrants, known as hobos, might be seen taking a free ride in these cars. While technically frowned upon, the hobo played a vital role in supplying railroads with a mobile, temporary labor force. If track workers were needed in Arizona in August, or men required to shovel snow on the Sierra's Donner Pass in January, the word would go out and within days unshaven men in bowler hats and tatty overalls would arrive looking to earn a few bits and a hot meal for their labors. When they arrived by open boxcar instead of as paying passengers, superintendents and other officials conveniently found the time to look at the scenery, or perhaps attend to paperwork. Other railroad employees, however, were more opportunistic and might shake down transients for a few cents as "payment" for their transport. Few of these coins ever made their way into the railroad's coffers.

Also common among freight rolling stock was the basic flatcar which could be used for moving heavy loads, work equipment, or other shipments ill-suited to the confines of a boxcar. Open-top gondolas and hopper cars were used for the transport of mineral ores, coal, and other bulk cargo. Tank cars were used to move oil—and often water—for railroad use; in remote arid locations where it was difficult to procure mineral-free water for locomotive boilers, let alone for drinking, railroads would haul tank cars great distances to ensure a steady supply of boiler water.

On light branch lines railroads operated "mixed" trains where both freight and passenger cars ran together. Although not the fastest way to travel, mixed trains were dearly loved by railway enthusiasts since these offered a leisurely, colorful way to see the countryside and experience railroading. When trains stopped to pick up or set off freight cars along the way, it was possible to leave the train and wander around, perhaps take a few photographs, or step into the local saloon for refreshment.

SNOWPLOWS

Railroad lines crossing high mountain passes and broad stretches of open plains often encountered deep snow in season. In the early days the most common type of railroad snowplow was the classic "wedge plow" that was shoved forward by one or more locomotives and used its shape and inertia to push snow off the grade. These were heavily weighted to prevent them being driven up and off the tracks by drifting snow or layers of ice on the track, and operation of plow trains was a perilous affair to those who worked them. The Central Pacific's Donner Pass crossing was famous for its exceptionally deep snow, and during the nineteenth century as many as eight steam locomotives shoved "Bucker-type" wedge plows up grade under enormous plumes of snow and smoke to clear the line.

The nineteenth century's most significant snow-clearing innovation, however, was the rotary snowplow which first appeared in the early 1880s. This tool was better suited for moving exceptionally deep snow that accumulated in high western passes. An on-board steam engine powered a large rotating fan that drew snow into the plow using self-adjusting bladed cones, and threw it from a roof-mounted chute. With one or more locomotives pushing from behind, this plow made for an awesome sight as a great, continuous, arched plume tossed snow from the line, and most of the big western railroads bought them including the Canadian Pacific, Central Pacific, Northern Pacific, and Union Pacific. The Rio Grande also had a fleet of three-foot gauge rotaries for service in the Colorado Rockies.

ROLLING STOCK BIBLIOGRAPHY

Beebe, Lucius. *The Overland Limited.* Berkeley: Howell-North Books, 1963.

— *The Central Pacific and the Southern Pacific Railroads.* Berkeley: Howell-North Books, 1963.

Beebe, Lucius, and Charles Clegg. *Narrow Gauge in the Rockies.* Berkeley: Howell-North Books, 1958.

Best, Gerald M. *Snowplow: Clearing Mountain Rails.* Berkeley: Howell-North Books, 1966.

Crump, Spencer. *Riding the Cumbres & Toltec Scenic Railroad.* Corona del Mar: Zeta Publishers, 1992.

Dethier, Jean. *All Stations: A Journey Through 150 Years of Railway History.* London: Thames & Hudson, 1981.

Droege, John A. *Passenger Terminals and Trains.* New York: McGraw-Hill, 1916.

Dubin, Arthur D. *Some Classic Trains.* Milwaukee: Kalmbach Publishing, 1964.

— *More Classic Trains.* Milwaukee: Kalmbach Publishing, 1974.

Hilton, George W. *American Narrow Gauge Railroads.* Stanford: Stanford University Press, 1990.

Hofsommer, Don. L. *The Southern Pacific 1901–1985.* College Station: Texas A&M University Press, 1986.

Hornung, Clarence P. *Wheels Across America.* New York: A. S. Barnes, 1959.

Klein, Maury. *Union Pacific, Vols. I & II.* New York: Doubleday, 1989.

Lamb, W. Kaye. *History of the Canadian Pacific Railway.* New York: Macmillan, 1977.

Le Massena, Robert A. *Colorado's Mountain Railroads.* Golden: The Smoking Stack Press, 1963.

— *Rio Grande to the Pacific.* Denver: Sundance Ltd, 1974.

Myrick, David F. *Life and Times of the Central Pacific Railroad.* San Francisco: Book Club of California, 1969.

Ryan, Dennis and Joseph Shine. *Southern Pacific Passenger Trains. Vols. 1 & 2.* La Mirada: Four Ways West Publications, 1986, 2000.

Shearer, Frederick. E. *The Pacific Tourist.* New York: Bounty Books, 1970.

Signor, John R. *Beaumont Hill.* San Marino: Golden West Books, 1990.

— *Donner Pass: Southern Pacific's Sierra Crossing.* San Marino: Golden West Books, 1985.

— *Rails in the Shadow of Mt. Shasta.* San Diego: Howell-North Books, 1982.

— *Southern Pacific's Coast Line.* Wilton: Signature Press, 1994.

SP rotary snowplow at work on the Ogden Route, c.1910.

— *Tehachapi.* San Marino: Golden West Books, 1983.

Solomon, Brian. *Trains of the Old West.* New York: Metro Books, 1998.

— *Southern Pacific Railroad.* Osceola: Motorbooks International, 1999.

— *Burlington Northern Santa Fe Railway.* St. Paul: Motorbooks International, 2005.

— *Southern Pacific Passenger Trains.* St. Paul: Motorbooks International, 2005.

Talbot, F. A. *Railway Wonders of the World, Volumes 1 & 2.* London: Cassell, 1914.

Thompson, Gregory Lee. *The Passenger Train in the Motor Age.* Columbus: Ohio State University Press, 1993.

White, John H., Jr. *The American Passenger Car, Vols. I & II.* Baltimore: Johns Hopkins University Press, 1978.

— *The American Railroad Freight Car.* Baltimore: Johns Hopkins University Press, 1993.

Wright, Richard K. *Southern Pacific Daylight.* Thousand Oaks: MHP, 1970.

PERIODICALS

Locomotive & Railway Preservation. Waukesha, Wisconsin

Official Guide to the Railways. New York

Passenger Train Journal. Waukesha, Wisconsin

RailNews. Waukesha, Wisconsin

Railway and Locomotive Historical Society Bulletin. Boston, Massachusetts

Southern Pacific Bulletin. San Francisco, California

The Railway Gazette. London, UK

Trains. Waukesha, Wisconsin

Vintage Rails. Waukesha, Wisconsin

TIMETABLES AND BROCHURES

Southern Pacific. *Western Division Timetable 243.* 1947.

Southern Pacific. *Your Daylight Trip.* 1939.

Southern Pacific. *Your Daylight Trip. Morning Daylight,* 1949.

MUSEUMS AND PLACES TO VISIT

Anyone with a healthy interest in railroad history would find it hard to resist the temptation to visit the isolated spot in Utah where the "Last Spike" was driven on May 10, 1869. The Promontory Summit site is now part of a National Historic Site, and one and a half miles of the original railroad alignment were relaid in 1969 to allow for demonstration runs of replica steam locomotives No. 119 and *Jupiter*. These replicas of the two that met on the site on May 10, 1869 were built in the 1970s, the original machines both having been scrapped in the early 1900s. The site also permits visitors to drive along sections of the former track bed on two circuits near the summit. The famous Golden Spike itself, however, is kept on public display in the Art and History Museum of Stanford University in Palo Alto, California.

At the opposite terminus of the original Pacific Railroad route, the modern Union Pacific railroad maintains its corporate museum at Council Bluffs, Iowa. The exhibition includes artifacts, photographs, and documents that trace the history of the railroad and of the American West. The Union Pacific Collection dates back to the middle of the nineteenth century, tracking the development, construction, and operation of the railroad.

Included in the Collection are surveying instruments of the UP's chief engineer, General Grenville Dodge, and various lanterns, locks, keys, pieces of china, silver, and weapons from the late nineteenth and early twentieth centuries. The Collection also contains outlaw paraphernalia, various Plains Indian materials, as well as library resources and extensive photograph collections comprising an estimated 500,000 images from the Union Pacific,

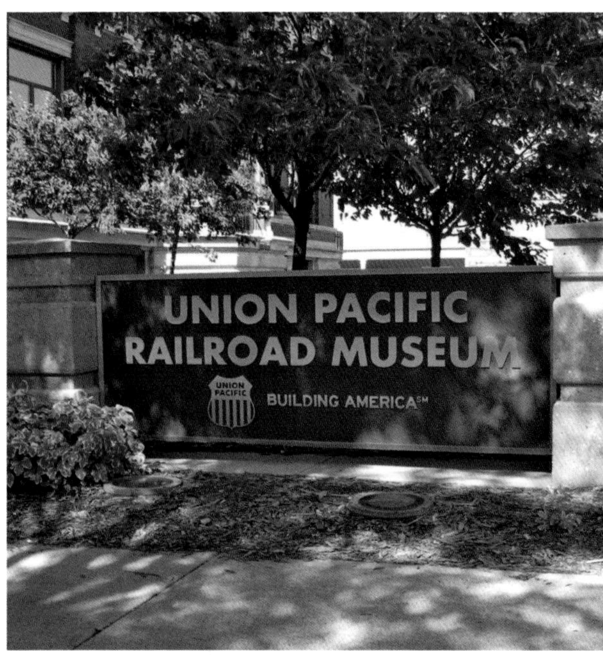

Southern Pacific, Chicago and North Western, and Missouri Pacific Railroads.

Also located in Council Bluffs is the RailsWest Museum, which is housed in the former Chicago, Rock Island and Pacific Railroad depot in the city. It includes an outdoor display of locomotives and carriages donated by the Union Pacific, as well as an assortment of railroad artifacts and exhibits: dining car silverware, a telegraph office, and memorabilia such as porters' uniforms and ticket stubs. There is also a large collection of daily newspapers chronicling the emergence and later waning of the railroad as America's prime mover. The RailsWest History Center is located in the former waiting rooms—there was a separate south waiting room for women and children, and a north waiting room for men—and the former ticket office is also part of the Museum.

However, the greatest concentration of visitor attractions is in California, which has 24 railroad-related museums and heritage railways in total. Fewer than thirty main line steam locomotives from the pre-1880 era have been preserved in the United States, and five of them are housed at the California State Railroad Museum in Sacramento. Among them are the Central Pacific Railroad's No. 1, *Gov. Stanford* and No. 3, *C. P. Huntington*, which later became the Southern Pacific's No. 1. The Museum is home to seventeen other steam locomotives dating from the mid-nineteenth century through to the 1940s, and its collection also contains a number of examples of early gasoline-powered equipment, including the Nevada Copper Belt gas-powered railcar No. 21 *Yerington*, which was built just before the First World War and foreshadowed the emergence of diesel technology

later in the century. The Museum also maintains the "Railtown 1897" site at Jamestown, where five steam locomotives built between 1891 and 1925 for use on the Sierra Railway are exhibited.

The South Coast Railroad Museum at Goleta Depot near San Diego is intended to complement the collection in Sacramento despite the 500-mile distance between the two sites. The Goleta Depot facility emphasizes the history of the Southern Pacific railroad in southern California, as well as the specific impact of the railroad depot on rural life across the country. The station itself is the center point of the Museum and the home of the collection. A Santa Barbara County historical landmark built in 1901, it has the turn-of-the-century architectural style typical of the Southern Pacific. The museum endeavors to achieve its educational and recreational goals through academic research and publications, the organization of rail trips, various community programs, and an ongoing building restoration plan.

Staying in California, the small museum in Lomita opened in 1966, making it the oldest such institution west of Denver, Colorado. Concentrating purely on the steam era, the Lomita Railroad Museum is focused around its largest exhibit, an M6 Mogul locomotive (No. 1765) complete with tender that was built by Baldwin in 1902 for the Southern Pacific. Nearby stand a 1910 Union Pacific Caboose, a 1923 Union Oil tank car, and a 1913 Southern Pacific outside-braced wooden boxcar.

The Pacific Railroad Society meanwhile has converted the former Atchison, Topeka and Santa Fe depot in San Dimas into a visitor attraction containing both a library and railroad-related artifacts. The library's collections focus on the 2nd Sub-division of the Coast Division of the Santa Fe, the Interurban operations of the Pacific Electric lines, and other railroads that served the Los Angeles basin. The Society has gathered a large collection of topographical maps, photographs, and a variety of timetables from the region. A much larger heritage railroad operation can be found at the Orange Empire Railway Museum in Perris that covers the history of the network in southern California, although the majority of the exhibits are from the modern traction era.

Rounding up the major attractions in California, those seeking a small taste of a journey on the western end of the transcontinental railroad during the steam era can find it at the Niles Canyon Railway, near Fremont. Steam-hauled trains cover a one and a half-mile section of the former Central Pacific line between Sacramento and San Francisco Bay on most Sundays throughout the year. The railroad has a collection of nine steam locomotives, among them No. 2467, a Southern Pacific Baldwin 4–6–2 dating from 1921.

Moving eastwards, steam enthusiasts can also sample heritage traction at the Nevada Northern Railway Museum. Based at Ely, the Museum runs excursion trains on two routes (weekends between April and October), although only the Keystone main line towards Ruth can be used by steam locomotives. Traction is mainly provided by an ALCO Consolidation (No. 93) built in 1908 to haul iron ore on the Northern Nevada railroad from mines around Ely. The NNRM has a second steam locomotive, No. 40, which is awaiting restoration, along with a number of coaches dating from the early part of the twentieth century.

The Nevada State Railroad Museum in Carson City has a large selection of restored nineteenth-century rolling stock, as well as a range of memorabilia and archive material. The Museum preserves the railroad heritage of Nevada, including locomotives and cars of the Virginia and Truckee Railroad and other railroads of the "Silver State." Many were bought from Hollywood studios, where they were made famous in movies and television shows. Of the 65 locomotives and cars in the collection, 40 were built before 1900, and 31 were examples that operated on the V&T.

The Museum's activities center on the operation of historic railroad equipment, including both main line and short line locomotives and rolling stock, handcars, an annual railroad history symposium, a lecture series, and a variety of themed special events. There is also an ongoing research and restoration program; five main line steam locomotives are part of the collection, including a Baldwin 4–4–0 locomotive built for the Virginia and Truckee Railroad in 1875.

Looking towards the Pacific Northwest, the Medford Railroad Park in Oregon recreates the steam era on the Southern Pacific's Siskiyou Line through a scale model railroad that offers train rides on painstakingly created seven and a half inch gauge steam locomotives. The Park is also home to a rare Willamette-class steam locomotive, which is currently being restored by the Southern Oregon chapter of the National Rail Historical Society in the hope that it could eventually be returned to use on its former stamping ground on the logging line between Medford and Butte Falls.

One gem worth seeking out is the Northern Pacific Railway Museum at Toppenish in southeastern Washington State. The Toppenish railroad depot was built by the Northern Pacific Railway in 1911 and closed in 1961. In 1989 a group of rail fans approached the city authority about leasing the depot as a museum, which led to the creation of the Yakima Valley Rail and Steam Museum Association. After restoration, the building reopened in 1992 and the following year the depot and adjacent freight house were purchased from the Burlington Northern Railroad. In 2000 the museum division was given its current name of the Northern Pacific Railway Museum.

In 1993 the museum leased 1902-built Northern Pacific engine No. 1364. A full train of heritage freight cars dating back to the 1930s is the latest restoration project to be undertaken by NPRM, while in 2006 former Northern Pacific locomotive No. 2152 moved to Toppenish having been on

An exhibit at Exporail, Delson, Quebec.

display in a municipal park in Auburn, Washington, since 1958. It is planned to restore the locomotive once the work on No. 1364 is complete.

Moving to Canada, the West Coast Railway Association has amassed the largest collection of historic rolling stock in the country outside Quebec. Located at Squamish, British Columbia, the organization has established its headquarters in a twelve-acre park that permits both indoor and external exhibits. The Association's collection consists of 65 pieces of heritage railroad rolling stock plus a significant collection of railroad-related artifacts. The oldest pieces are the business car *British Columbia* dating from 1890, and a Canadian Pacific Colonist sleeping car from 1905, although the Association also helped restore the even older CP Engine 374 that pulled the first train into Vancouver and is now on display in a special pavilion in the heart of that city. The extensive WCRA archives are dedicated to preserving material that helps tell the story of railroading in British Columbia. The collection includes over 3,000 artifacts that can be accessed for displays, live demonstrations, or documentary film production. A library also houses more than 600 books and 2,500 magazines.

ExpoRail, Canada's national railroad museum, is located in Delson, Quebec. It includes the Angus pavilion, a 90,000 square foot exhibition space that is home to a rotating roster highlighting 44 of the museum's 160 items of rolling stock, the largest single collection in the country.

In addition to "bricks and mortar" museums, there are also many railroad history websites and "online" museums on the internet about the railroads of the American West, the most extensive of which is the Central Pacific Railroad Photographic History Museum (cprr.org). This privately owned and operated free site that was founded in 1999 hosts more than 10,000 web pages and contains over 5,000 historic and contemporary photographs of the CPRR, the Union Pacific, and other related railroads. Universally regarded as the most exhaustively complete online source of photographs and primary source materials on the railroads of the American West, the Museum also contains illustrated and annotated transcriptions of many hundreds of historic documents, reports, maps, engravings, stereoviews, paintings, technical papers, articles, and other research materials instantly available for viewing by anyone in the world with an internet connection.

ONLINE SOURCES

Californian State Railroad Museum
www.csrmf.org

The Central Pacific Railroad Photographic History Museum
www.cprr.org

Colorado Railroad Museum– Golden, near Denver
www.coloradorailroadmuseum.org/museum
www.coloradorailroadmuseum.org/restoration

Exporail–the Canadian Railroad Museum
www.exporail.org

Lomita (CA) Railroad Museum
www.lomita-rr.org

Medford Railroad Park, Oregon
www.tunnel13.com/park

Nevada Northern Railway historic operating railroad museum
www.nevadanorthernrailway.net

Nevada State Railroad Museum
www.nsrm-friends.org
Gas (petrol) railcar www.nsrm-friends.org/nsrm49

Niles Canyon Preserved Railroad
www.ncry.org/history.htm
Locos www.ncry.org/roster/steam

Northern Pacific Railway Historical Association Research Library
www.nprha.org

Northern Pacific Railway Museum
www.nprymuseum.org

Ogden Union Station heritage site
www.theunionstation.org

Orange Empire Railway Museum
www.oerm.org

Pacific Railroad Museum
www.pacificrailroadsociety.org

Railroad Museum online directory
www.railmuseums.com/namerica

South Coast Railroad Museum, near San Diego, California
www.goletadepot.org

Steamlocomotive.com list
www.steamlocomotive.com/misc/museums

Union Pacific Museum
www.uprr.com/aboutup/history/museum

West Coast Railway Association
www.wcra.org

BIBLIOGRAPHY

Ambrose, Stephen E. *Nothing Like It in the World.* New York: Simon and Schuster, 2000.

Arrington, Leonard. *The Transcontinental Railroad and the Development of the West.* Salt Lake City: Utah Historical Quarterly Vol. 37, No. 1, 1969.

Baedeker, Karl. *Baedeker's The United States–Handbook for Travelers.* Leipzig: Karl Baedeker Publishing, 1909.

Bain, David H. *Empire Express: Building the First Transcontinental Railroad.* New York: Viking, 1999.

Bancroft, Hubert Howe. *History of California, Vol. VII.* San Francisco, 1890.

Barlow, John W. *Report of a Reconnaissance of the Basin of the Upper Yellowstone in 1871.* Washington, DC: US Government Printing Office, 1872.

Beebe, Lucius. *The Central Pacific & Southern Pacific Railroads.* Berkeley: Howell-North Books, 1963.

— *The Overland Limited.* Berkeley: Howell-North Books, 1963.

— *The Trains We Rode, Vol. 2,* Berkeley: Howell-North Books, 1966.

— and Charles Clegg. *Narrow Gauge in the Rockies.* Berkeley: Howell-North Books, 1958.

Berton, Pierre. *The National Dream: The Great Railway 1871–1881.* Toronto: McClelland and Stewart Limited, 1970.

— *The Last Spike: The Great Railway 1881–1885.* Toronto: McClelland and Stewart Limited, 1971.

Best, Gerald M. *Iron Horses to Promontory.* San Marino: Golden West Books, 1969.

Bowles, Samuel. *Our New West: Records of Travel Between the Mississippi River and the Pacific Ocean.* Hartford: Hartford Publishing Co., 1869.

Bryant, Keith L. *History of the Atchison, Topeka and Santa Fe Railway.* Glendale: Trans-Anglo Books, 1974.

Campbell, Marius R. *Guidebook of the Western United States: the Northern Pacific Route.* Washington DC: US Department of the Interior, 1916.

— *United States Geological Survey Bulletin 707: Guidebook of the Western United States, Part E. The Denver & Rio Grande Western Route.* Washington DC: US Department of the Interior, 1922.

Chandler, Alfred D. Jr. *The Railroads: The Nation's First Big Business.* New York and Chicago: Harcourt, Brace & World, Inc., 1965.

Chittenden, Hiram M. *The Yellowstone National Park.* Norman: University of Oklahoma Press, 1964.

Cooke, Jay. *Autobiography.* Unpublished: Minnesota and Pennsylvania Historical Society, 1894.

Cooper, Bruce C. *Lewis Metzler Clement: A Pioneer of the Central Pacific Railroad.* Ardmore: Cooper–Clement Associates, 1998.

— *Riding the Transcontinental Rails: Overland Travel on the Pacific Railroad 1865–1881.* Philadelphia: Polyglot Press, 2005.

Crofutt, George A. *The Great Trans-Continental Tourist's Guide.* New York: Geo. A. Crofutt & Co., 1870.

Crump, Spencer. *Riding the Cumbres & Toltec Scenic Railroad.* Corona del Mar: Zeta Publishers, 1992.

Custer, Lt. Col. George A. "Battling with the Sioux on the Yellowstone. " *Galaxy Magazine*: July 1876.

— "Official Report of the Tongue River and Big Horn Fights." *New York Tribune*: September 6, 1873.

Daniels, Rudolph. *Trains Across the Continent.* Bloomington and Indianapolis: Indiana University Press, 2000.

Darton, N. H. *United States Geological Survey Bulletin 613: Guidebook of the Western United States, Part C. The Santa Fe Route.* Washington DC: US Department of the Interior, 1916.

Deverell, William. *Railroad Crossing: Californians and the Railroad 1850–1910.* Berkeley and Los Angeles: University of California Press, 1994.

Drury, George H. *Guide to North American Steam Locomotives.* Waukesha: Kalmbach Publishing, 1993.

Dubin, Arthur. *Some Classic Trains.* Milwaukee: Kalmbach Publishing Co., 1964.

Duke, Donald, and Stan Kistler. *Santa Fe–Steel Rails Through California.* San Marino: Golden West Books, 1963.

Fattig, Paul. *Great American Train Robbery.* http://tunnel13.com/history/robbery.html.

Forney, M. N. *Catechism of the Locomotive.* New York: Railroad Gazette, 1876.

Frey, Robert L. ed., *Encyclopedia of American Business History and Biography: Railroads in the Nineteenth Century.* New York: Facts on File, 1988.

Frost, Lawrence A. *Custer's 7th Cav and the Campaign of 1873,* El Segundo: Upton & Sons, 1985.

Glassrud, Clarence, ed. *Roy Johnson's Red River Valley.* Moorhead: Red River Valley Historical Society, 1982.

Haines, Aubrey L. *The Yellowstone Story: A History of our First National Park,* Rev. ed., 2 vols. Niwot: University Press of Colorado, 1996.

Harnsberger, John L. *Jay Cooke and Minnesota: The Formative Years of the Northern Pacific Railroad, 1868–1873.* New York: Arno Press, 1981.

Hauck, Cornelius W. *Colorado Rail Annual No. 10: Narrow Gauge to Silver Plume.* Golden: Colorado Railroad Museum, 1972.

Hedges, James B. *Henry Villard and the Railways of the Northwest.* New Haven: Yale University Press, 1930.

Hendry, R. Powell. *Narrow Gauge Story.* Rugby: Hillside Publishing, 1979.

Hilton, George W. *American Narrow Gauge Railroads.* Stanford: Stanford University Press, 1990.

Hofsommer, Don L., *The Southern Pacific, 1901–1985.* College Station: Texas A&M University Press, 1986.

Holbrook, Steven H. *The Story of American Railroads.* New York: Crown Publishers, 1947.

Hubbard, Freeman. *Encyclopedia of North American Railroading: 150 Years of Railroading in the United States and Canada.* New York: McGraw-Hill, 1981.

The Illustrated Railroad Guide of the Union and Central Pacific Railroads. Chicago: Adams Publishing Co., 1879

Jensen, Derrick and George Draffen. *Railroads and Clearcuts: Legacy of Congress's 1864 Northern Pacific Railroad Land Grant.* Spokane: Inland Empire Public Lands Council, 1995.

Klassen, Henry C. *The Canadian West: Social Change and Economic Development.* Calgary: University of Calgary Press, 1977.

Kolko, Gabriel. *Railroads and Regulation 1877–1916.* Princeton: Princeton University Press, 1965.

Lamar, Harold, ed. *The New Encyclopedia of the American West.* New Haven: Yale University Press, 1998.

Larson, Henrietta M. *Jay Cooke: Private Banker.* Cambridge: Harvard University Press, 1936.

Lass, William E. *Navigating the Missouri: Steamboating on Nature's Highway, 1819–1935.* Norman: University of Oklahoma Press, 2007.

Lavallee, Omer. *Van Horne's Road.* Montreal: Railfare Enterprises Limited, 1977.

Le Massena, Robert A. *Colorado's Mountain Railroads.* Golden: The Smoking Stack Press, 1963.

— *Rio Grande to the Pacific.* Denver: Sundance Limited, 1974.

Lewis, Robert C. *The Handbook of American Railroads.* New York: Simmons-Boardman Publishing Corporation, 1951.

Lubetkin, M. John. *Jay Cooke's Gamble: The Northern Pacific Railroad, the Sioux, and the Panic of 1873.* Norman: University of Oklahoma Press, 2006.

Marshall, James. *Santa Fe–The Railroad That Built an Empire.* New York: Random House, 1945.

McCoy, Dell, and Russ Collman. *The Crystal River Pictorial.* Denver: Sundance Ltd, 1972.

— *The Rio Grande Pictorial: One Hundred Years of Railroading thru the Rockies.* Denver: Sundance Ltd, 1971.

Mickelson, Sig. *The Northern Pacific Railroad and the Selling of the West: A Nineteenth-Century Public Relations Venture.* Sioux Falls: Center for Western Studies, 1993.

Middleton, William D. , George M. Smerk, and Roberta L. Diehl, eds. *The Encyclopedia of North American Railroads.* Bloomington: Indiana University Press, 2006.

Mohr, Nicolaus. *Excursion Through America.* Chicago: The Lakeside Press, 1973.

Nordhoff, Charles. *California: For Health, Pleasure, and Residence. A Book for Travellers and Settlers.* New York: Harper's & Brothers, 1873.

Oberholtzer, Ellis P. *Jay Cooke: Financier of the Civil War.* New York: Augustus M. Kelley Publishers, 1968.

Orsi, Richard J. *Sunset Limited: The Southern Pacific Railroad and the Development of the American West 1850–1930.* Berkeley and Los Angeles: University of California Press, 2005.

Osterwald, Doris B. *Cinders & Smoke.* Lakewood: Western Guideways, 1995.

— *Ticket to Toltec.* Denver: Western Guideways, 1992.

Poor, Henry V. *Manual of the Railroads of the United States for 1873–74.* New York: H. V. & H. W. Poor, 1873.

Quiett, Glenn Chesney. *They Built the West.* New York: Appleton-Century, 1934.

Ransome, P. T. J. *Narrow Gauge Steam.* Yeovil: Oxford, 1996.

Ransome-Wallis, P. *World Railway Locomotives.* New York: Hawthorn Books, 1959.

Raynolds, William F. *Report on the Exploration of the Yellowstone and Missouri Rivers in 1859–60.* Washington, DC: USGPO, 1867.

Reid, Laurance S. *Narrow Gauge Locomotives: The Baldwin Catalog of 1877.* Norman: University of Oklahoma Press, 1967.

Renz, Louis T. *History of the Northern Pacific Railroad.* Fairfield: Ye Galleon Press, 1980.

Richardson, Albert D. *Beyond the Mississippi: From the Great River to the Great Ocean.* Hartford: American Publishing Co., 1869.

— "Through to the Pacific." New York: *The New York Tribune*, 1869.

Robertson, Donald B. *Encyclopedia of Western Railroad History: Vol. II, The Mountain States–Colorado, Idaho, Montana, Wyoming.* Dallas: Taylor Publishing Co., 1991.

— *Encyclopedia of Western Railroad History: Vol. III–Oregon, Washington.* Caldwell: Caxton Printers, 1995.

Robertson, R. W. W. *Stand Fast Craigellachie: The Building of the Transcontinental Railway (1867–1885).* Toronto: Burns & MacEachern Limited, 1970.

Rosser, Thomas L. *The Death of Adair.* (unpublished). Charlottesville: University of Virginia Special Collections Library.

— *Diaries.* Charlottesville: University of Virginia Special Collections Library.

Shearer, Frederick, E. *The Pacific Tourist.* New York: Adams & Bishop, 1886.

Signor, John R. *Donner Pass: Southern Pacific's Sierra Crossing.* San Marino: Golden West Books, 1983.

Sinclair, Angus. *Development of the Locomotive Engine.* New York: Angus Sinclair, 1907.

Smalley, Eugene V. *History of the Northern Pacific Railroad.* New York: Arno Press, 1975.

Solomon, Brian. *The American Steam Locomotive.* Osceola: Motorbooks International, 1998.

— *Burlington Northern Santa Fe Railway.* St. Paul: Motorbooks International, 2005.

— *Narrow Gauge Steam Locomotives.* Osceola: Motorbooks International, 1999.

— *Santa Fe Railway.* St. Paul: Motorbooks International, 2003.

— *Southern Pacific Railroad.* St. Paul: Voyageur Press, 2007.

Stanley, Colonel David S. *Journal of the [1872] N.P.R.R. Surveying Expedition from the Missouri River to the Powder River.* St. Paul: Minnesota Historical Society, 1872.

— *Personal Memoirs of Major-General David S. Stanley.* Gaithersburg: Olde Soldier Books, 1917.

— *Report of the Yellowstone Expedition of 1872.* Helena: Montana Historical Society, 1873.

Stevens, G. R. *History of the Canadian National Railways.* New York: Macmillan, 1973.

Stevenson, Robert Louis. *Across the Plains.* London: Chattus & Windus, 1892.

Sutton, John. *Building Materials on the Pacific Railway.* National Park Service, 1978. www.nps.gov/archive/gosp/research/building.htm

Taylor, Benjamin F. *Between the Gates.* Chicago: S. C. Griggs & Co., 1878.

Thode, Jackson. *Health, Wealth and Pleasure, in Colorado and New Mexico. A Centennial Edition.* Santa Fe: Museum of New Mexico Press, 1978.

Turner, Robert D. *West of the Great Divide: An Illustrated History of the Canadian Pacific Railway in British Columbia 1880–1986.* Winslaw: Sononis Press, 1987.

Villard, Henry. *Memoirs of Henry Villard: Journalist and Financier.* Boston: Houghton, Mifflin and Company, 1904.

Waters, L. L. *Steel Trails to Santa Fe.* Lawrence: University of Kansas Press, 1950.

Wilson, Keith. *Donald Smith and the Canadian Pacific Railway.* Agincourt: The Book Society of Canada Limited, 1978.

Wilson, Neill C. *Southern Pacific: The Roaring Story of a Fighting Railroad.* New York: McGraw-Hill Book Company, 1952.

Wilson, O. Meredith. *The Denver and Rio Grande Project, 1870–1901.* Salt Lake City: Howe Brothers, 1982.

Winks, Robin W. *Frederick Billings: A Life.* Berkeley: University of California Press, 1991.

Winser, Henry J. *Guide to the Northern Pacific Railroad and its Allied Lines.* New York: G. P. Putnam's Sons, 1883.

Winther, Oscar Osburn. *The Transportation Frontier: Trans-Mississippi West, 1865–1890.* New York: Holt, Rinehart and Winston, 1964.

Y. S. "The Overland Route." *The New York Times*, July 6, 1871. www.nytimes.com

Ziel, Ron. *American Locomotives in Historic Photographs.* New York: Dover Publications, 1993.

PERIODICALS, TIMETABLES, AND BROCHURES

Along the Union Pacific System: The Overland Trail and the Union Pacific Railroad. Omaha: Union Pacific Railroad Company, 1928.

Atchison, Topeka & Santa Fe R.R. Co. *Time Schedule No. 6.* 1883.

Atchison, Topeka & Santa Fe Railway Co. *Coast Lines, Valley Division Employes' Time Table No. 51.* 1921.

Atchison, Topeka & Santa Fe Railway. *Along Your Way–Facts About Stations and Scenes on the Santa Fe.* 1945.

Locomotive & Railway Preservation. Waukesha.

Official Guide to the Railways (1869–1995).

Passenger Train Journal. Waukesha.

RailNews. Waukesha.

Railroad Gazette (1870–1908).

Railway and Locomotive Historical Society Bulletin. Boston.

Trains. Waukesha.

Vintage Rails. Waukesha.

INDEX

Italics refer to illustrations

ARIZONA
NEW MEXI
MEXICO
LOWER CAL.
OCEAN
GULF OF CALIFORNIA
SANTA BARBARA CHANNEL
UNINHABITED DESERT
TIBURON ISLAND
ISLA DEL ANGEL
PRESCOTT
El Paso
Los Angeles
San Diego
Yuma
Tucson
Albuquerque
Santa Fe
Las Vegas
Mojave
Bakersfield
Santa Barbara
San Bernardino
Anaheim
Florence
Phoenix
Tombstone
Mesilla
Socorro
Fort Craig
Fort Wingate
Ft. Mohave
Hardyville
Stockton
La Paz
Ehrenberg
Camp Verde
Montezuma Well
Globe City
Gila Bend
Calabasas
Nogales
Casas Grandes
Carrizal
Ures
Hermosillo
Guaymas
Altar
Arispe
Chinapi
Magdalena
Aconchi
Opodepe
Moccasin Spring
Cottonwood Spring
Las Vegas
St. Thomas
Pioche
Hiko
Bullionville
Yampas Village
Mesa La Vaca
White Mesa
Ojo de Puenta
Peach Orchard Spring
Puebla Colorado
Zuni
Acomo
Belen
San Marcial
Fort Conrad
Ft. McRae
Ft. Selden
Dona Ana
Las Cruces
Silver City
Ft. Bayard
Ft. Bowie
Ft. Stanton
Lincoln
Trinidad
Cimarron
Taos
Silverton
Ouray
Lake City
Colorado
THE NEEDLES
RIO COLORADO
Gila
Rio Grande
Rio Salinas
Rio San Pedro
Rio Puerco
Colorado Chiquito
Owens Lake
Independence
Big Pine
Keysville
Caliente
Los Angeles
San Pedro Bay
Santa Catalina
San Clemente
San Nicolas
Cape S. Quenten
Bay Falsa
Sta. Gerirudis
San Francisco
Rosarito
San Matias
Santo Domingo

PLATEAU DU COTEAU DU MISSOURI
DAKOTA
NEBRASKA
MINNESOTA
IOWA
WISCONSIN
LAKE SUPERIOR
Fort Buford
Fort Berthold
Fort Stevenson
Fort Clarke
Bismarck
Camp Hancock
Fort A. Lincoln
Fort Rice
Fort Yates
Standing Rock Agency
Grand River Agency
Glendive
Stockade
Wolf Rapids
Miles City
Ft. Keogh
Alexander
Jamestown
Valley City
Fort Ransom
Lamoure
Fort Abercrombie
Fort Totten
Minne-Waukan or Devil's Lake
Grand Forks
Larimore
Medford
Hope
Carrington
Fargo
Moorhead
Glyndon
Crookston
Detroit City
Perham
Barnesville
Wahpeton
Fergus Falls
Lake Traverse
Brown's Valley
Big Stone L.
Aberdeen
Columbia
Ft. Sisseton
Milbank Jc.
Watertown
Redfield
Ashton
Huron
Ordway Jc.
Fort Pierre
Ft. Sully
Cheyenne Agency
Fort Thompson
Crow Creek Agency
Fort Hale
Lower Brule Agency
Red Cloud Agency
Fort Lookout
Chamberlain
Brule City
Rosebud Landing
Rosebud Agency
Bijou Hill
Rockport
Platte Creek
Mill Town
Olivet
Fort Randall
Yankton
Springfield
Flandreau
Sioux Falls
Salem
Canton
Fire Steel
Rapid City
Custer City
Black Hills
Military Station
Pine Ridge Agency
Spotted Tail Agency
Camp Sheridan
Fort Robinson
Ft. Niobrara
Niobrara
Long Pine
Plum Valley
Ft. Fetterman
Hat Creek
Lance Creek
Cheyenne
Sidney
Julesburg
Ft. Sedgwick
North Platte
Kearney
Lincoln
Omaha
Council Bluffs
Plattsmouth
Nebraska City
Tecumseh
Beatrice
Columbus
Fremont
Norfolk
Sioux City
Le Mars
Cherokee
Fort Dodge
Des Moines
Iowa City
Davenport
Dubuque
Burlington
Keokuk
Cedar Rapids
Waterloo
Marshalltown
Ottumwa
Creston
Atlantic City
Minneapolis
St. Paul
St. Cloud
Mankato
New Ulm
Winona
La Crosse
Rochester
Owatonna
Albert Lea
Duluth
Superior City
Ashland
Bayfield
Apostle Islands
Grand Portage
Red Lake
Chippewa Village
Leech Lake
Mille Lacs
Brainerd
Eau Claire
Chippewa Falls
Madison
Galena
Freeport
Rock Island
Peoria
Springfield
Quincy
Hannibal
Macon City
Kansas City
Leavenworth
Atchison
Topeka
St. Joseph
Chillicothe
St. Louis
St. Charles
Moberly
Mexico
Sedalia
Denver
Greeley
Longmont
Boulder
Golden
Ft. Collins
Sterling
Ft. Morgan
Julesburg
Concordia
Clay Centre
Junction City
Manhattan
Abilene
Salina
Beloit
Minneapolis